CHAIM WEIZMANN

STUDIES IN JEWISH HISTORY JEHUDA REINHARZ, General Editor

Chaim Weizmann, January 1926. Courtesy: UPI/Bettmann, New York

CHAIM WEIZMANN

The Making of a Statesman

JEHUDA REINHARZ

New York • Oxford
OXFORD UNIVERSITY PRESS
1993

Oxford University Press

Oxford   New York   Toronto
Delhi   Bombay   Calcutta   Madras   Karachi
Petaling Jaya   Singapore   Hong Kong   Tokyo
Nairobi   Dar es Salaam   Cape Town
Melbourne   Auckland

and associated companies in
Berlin   Ibadan

Copyright © 1993 by Oxford University Press, Inc

Published by Oxford University Press, Inc.,
200 Madison Avenue, New York, New York 10016

Oxford is a registered trademark of Oxford University Press

Library of Congress Cataloging-in-Publication Data

Reinharz, Jehuda.
Chaim Weizmann : the making of a statesman / Jehuda Reinharz.
p.   cm.—(Studies in Jewish history)
Includes bibliographical references and index.
ISBN 0-19-5072154'
1. Weizmann, Chaim, 1874–1952.
2. Zionism—History.
3. Balfour Declaration.
4. Zionist Commission.
5. Presidents—Israel—Biography.
6. Zionists—Great Britain—Biography.
7. Great Britain—Biography.
I. Title.   II. Series.
DS125.3.W45R44   1992
320.5'4'095694092—dc20
[B]   91-30376

1 3 5 7 9 8 6 4 2

Printed in the United States of America
on acid-free paper

To the Memory of
Ben Halpern

Preface

This multivolume biography of Chaim Weizmann is in many ways a history of the Zionist movement from the last quarter of the nineteenth century to the creation of the state of Israel in the mid-twentieth. The first volume, *Chaim Weizmann: The Making of a Zionist Leader*, explored factors that shaped Weizmann's personality and outlook. It analyzed Weizmann's relations with his family and other men and women, among them some of the major Jewish personalities of his day. My analysis placed Weizmann in the contexts of the World Zionist Organization and the scientific community. In brief, the first volume attempted to explain Weizmann's development as a person as well as his gradual rise in the ranks of the Zionist movement. It closed on the eve of World War I, when Weizmann turned forty years old.

In the subsequent period, 1914–22, Weizmann created the foundations of the Zionist enterprise. During these years the Zionists initiated policies, and the British reacted in accordance with their own interests. This pattern remained in force until Herbert Samuel changed it with his own initiatives in 1921–22. After that, British-Zionist relations were marked, on the whole, by British initiatives and Zionist reactions. The first chapter of Zionism's political struggle, directed by Weizmann since the fall of 1914, ended with the ratification of the Mandate for Palestine on July 24, 1922.

The present volume focuses on Weizmann as a leader and statesman of the World Zionist Organization beginning with World War I until the summer of 1922. As with the first volume, I emphasize the context as well as the man. I attempt to explain Weizmann's scientific achievements and his rise to the top of the Zionist leadership as well as to describe the political and economic milieux in which he operated. Much of the analysis focuses on the attitudes of Zionists and Arab nationalists toward their rival national movements, the contacts between Zionists and American and European Jewish communities, and the role played by various governments—particularly England—that had political stakes in Palestine. Since this volume deals with Weizmann's emergence as the undisputed leader of the World Zionist Organization, it devotes much attention to his qualities and achievements as a political strategist and statesman. Though I am also concerned with Weizmann's personal development, his relations with his wife Vera, with his children, and with other men and women, these topics occupy relatively less space than does politics. Some aspects of these relationships, already touched on here, develop only in later years and will therefore be treated fully and completely in the third volume.

The period 1914 to 1922 is a turning point in the history of Zionism and a crucial period for Weizmann, marking his emergence from leader to statesman. At the age of forty, Weizmann was a successful academic, with an honorable record as a hard-working Zionist veteran. He was trusted and respected by the leaders of the World Zionist Organization. They saw him as a potential leader in England who could shoulder increasingly heavy responsibilities in the Zionist movement as a whole. Weizmann also had a small following of dedicated young men and women in England and on the Continent who viewed him as their instructor in Zionist affairs. After 1914, Weizmann was propelled onto a different track—the statesman of a nation in the making. The British and other governments accepted him as a spokesman for a people with whom they could shape history. With this new recognition, the leadership of the World Zionist Organization quickly followed suit and accepted Weizmann as its premier representative.

Weizmann rose to power as the head of the World Zionist Organization following "external" and "internal" paths. His standing externally was not always reflected by his standing internally, though diplomatic success with the British assured him a modicum of prestige in the Zionist movement. Indeed, he was always more prone to pressures and attacks from his own constituency than from the British; this was so even in 1920–22, when he was at the apex of his political power. Thus the curious and eventually tragic circumstance developed that, even as he was seen as indispensable to Zionism, he was becoming increasingly more vulnerable. The seeds of this process can be observed in this volume.

A biography of Weizmann forces one to tackle the problem of the relationship between the individual or hero and his era. In 1898, Georgi Plekhanov, the philosophical leader of the Russian labor movement (and with whom Weizmann publicly debated in Switzerland in November 1901), published the essay entitled "The Role of the Individual in History." As an orthodox Marxist he asserted that "great men" are influential in the course of historical processes to the extent that the socioeconomic conditions of their time are conducive to their actions. Plekhanov concluded that these socioeconomic forces do not select but produce the heroes of history.[1]

In *The Hero in History*, on the other hand, Sidney Hook argues a radically different position. According to Hook, the actions of the leader are independent of his or her generation's socioeconomic conditions. Hook attributes secondary influence to these conditions and does not include them in his definition of the hero's impact.[2]

Although this is a well-worn debate,[3] it is relevant here because I deal at length with the political maneuvers that led to the Balfour Declaration. Every historian who has dealt with this process has debated Weizmann's role in its attainment.

In his essay "Weizmann and His Generation," Ben Halpern suggested—correctly, in my estimate—that it is impossible to be so clear-cut about the role of the hero in history, including the case of Weizmann. For example, those who argue that Weizmann received the Balfour Declaration on the power of his personal qualities do not necessarily contradict the theory that the contemporary economic and political conditions made such a declaration expedient for Great Britain. Halpern offers an alternative to the all-or-nothing framework in which this argument is usually cast. He divides Weizmann's public activity into an initial period in which he was primarily shaped *by* his environment and a subsequent period when he in turn exerted great influence *on* his generation.[4]

Plekhanov's and Hook's positions measure only a fraction of Weizmann's role as a leader. Neither the "ripeness" of economic and political conditions nor Weizmann's personal qualities fully explain his rise to leadership and the art of his statesmanship. A careful analysis of Weizmann in the various contexts in which he operated is likely to produce a much more nuanced and qualified interpretation. Perhaps herein lies the attraction of writing a biography. The unique quality of a life can only partially be compressed into larger historical interpretations.

Even Weizmann's bitter rivals would not have disputed that following World War I he emerged as a towering leader of the World Zionist Organization. Together with his colleagues and antagonists—such as Ben-Gurion, Brandeis, and Jabotinsky—he affected the history of the Jews in the modern world by his actions. The quarrels, attitudes, and decisions of these Zionist heroes extend beyond their own era into ours. Their policies are echoed and refracted in current debates. They dominated an important period in the building of the Jewish national home in Palestine, which became the state of Israel.

Awareness of the fact that the roots of current political problems in the Middle East and the ideological positions of Israelis and Diaspora Jews lie to some extent in the period examined here makes the study of Weizmann and his times all the more exciting. It also places great responsibility on the biographer to examine the extensive documentary material with care lest it be misused or misinterpreted. I owe a great debt of gratitude to all the archivists, librarians, and their staffs in Israel, England, and the United States who unfailingly indulged, indeed encouraged, my constant requests for documentary material in person and via mail, fax, and bitnet. The archives and libraries are listed in the bibliography, but I would like to single out the Weizmann Archives in Rehovot, Israel, whose staff and management catered to my every wish. Dr. Zalman S. Abramov, the chairman of Yad Chaim Weizmann, the authority which governs the archives, granted me special privileges to pursue my research and encouraged my work in other ways as well.

It was the good fortune of scholars throughout the world that the former curator of the Weizmann Archives was Ms. Nehama Chalom. Her outstanding knowledge of the content of the archives was matched by her unfailing enthusiasm to help those of us who came to use it. I am grateful for her friendship and interest in every phase of my work.

This volume gives me the opportunity to once again thank the late Professor Philip E. Elving of the Department of Chemistry of the University of Michigan. Phil, who began his career in one of Weizmann's labs, encouraged me to devote some months to a deeper understanding of Weizmann's chemistry and assured me that I need not be intimidated by a subject far outside my field. His perspective was an important turning point in my work, since it buttressed my conviction that one cannot understand Weizmann's Zionist accomplishments without a proper understanding of his work as a chemist. Phil was ready to explain difficult concepts and guide me through the appropriate literature whenever I called upon him.

Among the archivists whom I consulted I would like to mention in particular my friend Dr. Michael Heymann, the former director of the Central Zionist Archives, whose familiarity with the history of Zionism is reflected by his ability to recite contents of individual files. I would also like to thank his able successor, Mr. Yoram Mayork and his staff. Dr. Tuvia Friling, director of the Ben-Gurion Archives in Sde Boker, Mr. Pesach Gani of the Jabotinsky Archives, and Ofra Perlmutter of the Weizmann Archives were likewise most solicitous. Professors Eugene C. Black, Bernard Wasserstein, Dr. Yossi Goldstein, Dr. Zvi Ganin, Ambassador Shimshon Arad, Mr. Yossi Vardi, and Mr. Shimon Rubinstein drew my attention to sources I had overlooked. Dr. David Sorkin and his family were gracious hosts to me and my family during our sojourn in Oxford in the summer of 1988.

I was fortunate to be able to spend the academic year 1987–88 in Israel as a Lady Davis Visiting Professor at the Hebrew University. During that year I co-taught a graduate seminar on Weizmann with my friend Professor Evyatar Friesel. He, and the students in the seminar, constantly challenged my analysis and forced me to rethink and sometimes to change my views on various issues. My stay in Israel was made comfortable by a Senior Fellowship for Independent Study and Research, granted by the National Endowment for the Humanities. Other funds were granted during various periods by Mr. Edgar M. Bronfman and the Samuel Bronfman Foundation. I am most grateful to Mr. Moshe Rivlin, director general of the Jewish National Fund, who granted me a research stipend, and to Mr. Jacques Torczyner, a veteran Zionist leader, whose largesse and constant support are deeply appreciated.

Anyone who has worked in archives knows that some of the greatest finds result from hard detective work and others happen by coincidence. While on sabbatical in Israel in 1987–88, I was invited by the then president of the Weizmann Institute, Professor Aryeh Dvoretzky, to deliver the annual Weizmann Memorial Day lecture on "Weizmann, Acetone and the Balfour Declaration." The lecture was delivered at the Weizmann residence, which is part of the Weizmann Institute campus, to an audience that included many scientists. Four months later, Professor William Taub, one of the scientists present at the lecture, told me that after much thought he had decided to reveal to me the whereabouts of more than one hundred letters written by Weizmann to his loyal junior scientific collaborator, Harold Davies. The letters were in the possession of Davies's daughter, a friend of Professor Taub, who resides near London. When I visited her in the summer of 1988, I realized that many of these letters had never before been seen by scholars. They deal with scientific and personal issues and were subsequently sold at a public auction. I would like to thank Professor Chimen Abramsky, who confirmed the authenticity and importance of the letters for Sotheby's, and Mr. Mandy D. Moross, who donated the letters to the Weizmann Archives. He and Mr. Martin Mendoza of the Weizmann Institute Foundation in England deserve much praise for their incisive intervention in purchasing these letters and their generosity in forwarding a complete set to me.

There were many other chance encounters with people who provided me with either primary materials or with information. In this regard I want to thank Mrs. Ofra Kenan, the granddaughter of Ben-Zion Mossinson, and Mrs. Dina Ram, the granddaughter of Mordechai Ben-Hillel Hacohen, as well as Ezer Weizmann, the nephew of Chaim Weizmann. Professor Meir J. Kister of the Hebrew University drew my attention to some articles relevant to Weizmann's scientific work. I am also grateful to Mrs. Janet Ellison (née Lieberman), Weizmann's secretary beginning with the last phase of World War I, who provided some insights into his personality and work habits. Mr. R. R. Meinertzhagen gave me permission to examine the papers of his late father, Richard Meinertzhagen, which are being kept at Rhodes House Library, Oxford, for which he has my thanks.

I am very grateful to my friends Nehama Chalom, Professor Eugene C. Black, Professor Evyatar Friesel, and Dr. Michael Heymann for their willingness to read the entire manuscript. Professor Jonathan Sarna read parts of the manuscript dealing with the American scene. Their many criticisms and constructive suggestions are much appreciated. Harvey Sukenic, Stephanie Fine, and Matthew Kalman helped with various technical aspects of the manuscript. Sylvia Fuks Fried, my colleague at the Tauber Institute for the Study of European Jewry, made it possible for me to devote maximum time to this manuscript, while my secretary, Mrs. Janet Webber, was determined that this book be presented to the publisher in the most highly professional form.

I owe a special debt of gratitude to Nancy Lane, my good friend and editor at Oxford University Press, who understood why I needed to expand this biography beyond the originally projected two volumes.

My wife, Shulamit, took time out from her own writing to help in various ways, which I much appreciate.

Finally, I wish to thank Dr. Ann Hofstra Grogg, a superb copyeditor, who applies her professional skills with grace and much care. She has also prepared the index for the volume.

The book is dedicated to my teacher and friend Ben Halpern, a brilliant analyst of the history of Zionism. In the eight years before his untimely death, we collaborated on another book, while he, too, was completing a monograph on Weizmann and Brandeis.[5] Inevitably, during those years, we also discussed the present study. I miss his sage advice on every aspect of my work, his generosity of spirit, and his novel insights. More than that, I miss his warmth and friendship.

Waltham, Mass.   J. R.
April 1992

Contents

CHAIM WEIZMANN

I

War

On July 28, 1914, as Austria declared war on Serbia, Chaim Weizmann worried about the implications of this conflagration for Zionist work. At the same time he proceeded with his plans for a family vacation in Switzerland and a meeting two weeks later in Paris on the proposed Jewish university in Palestine. In the midst of the initial shock and disarray, he predicted that war would spell a "fearful catastrophe" for the Zionists, and he was hoping "that everything will yet calm down."[1] But when, on August 4, German troops crossed the Belgian border and Britain's declaration of war became effective, all immediate plans had to come to a halt. Clearly the university in Palestine would be unable in the indefinite future to command anyone's attention, and the paralyzing fear of what awaited his family and the Jewish communities in the war zones filled Weizmann's mind. With Vera and Benjy he did manage to reach Champex in the Rhone Valley, where they stayed for a few days before making arrangements to return home via Paris.[2] It was August 28 before they could return to England and try to recover their equilibrium.

By 1914, Weizmann had a recognized place among a small group of men accustomed to active responsibility for the Jewish communities dispersed across international borders. From a formal point of view, his two official positions were membership in the Greater Actions Committee (GAC) of the World Zionist Organization (WZO) and the vice-presidency of the English Zionist Federation (EZF). The war, tearing apart the connections by which Jews took counsel and extended aid to one another across national boundaries, severely handicapped coordinated action. The German Jews, including the central leadership of the World Zionist Organization in Berlin, could no longer work closely with old colleagues in the Allied countries; and their ability to respond to the distress of fellow Jews in Eastern Europe or the Ottoman Empire depended on the advance of German and Austrian armies or the influence Berlin could bring to bear in Constantinople.[3] A man like Weizmann, in England, was cut off from the legitimate authorities of the world Zionist movement, except those who chanced to find themselves on his side of the lines. Even then he could only look on helplessly as the needs and perils of Jews in the war zones and the Turkish domain were reported in frightening detail.

The neutral countries were the only locations from which the WZO could hope to keep up its international activities. Offices set up in the Hague and Copenhagen were available to Zionists on both sides,[4] but it was primarily the Copenhagen office, opened on February 1, 1915, that maintained contacts among Zionist federations, institutions, and individuals throughout the world. Initiative was also seized across the Atlantic. Just as the First World War pushed the United States into a position of power in world affairs, so it marked the emergence of American Jews into a similar position in their global community. By 1914 they had outgrown all other Jewish communities except the Russians in numbers. The old French, German, British, and Russian Jewish leaders were caught up in the wartime problems of their own countries and communities, and as enemies and belligerents they were cut off from direct cooperation with each other in Jewish matters. The war also caused the dispersal of the members of the Smaller Actions Committee (SAC) to various countries. Shmarya Levin, who had gone on a lecture tour to the United States in June 1914, stayed there throughout the war. Yehiel Tschlenow and Nahum Sokolow, both Russian subjects, left Germany during 1914, Tschlenow in early August and Sokolow in December. Victor Jacobson, also a Russian subject, left Constantinople and was allowed to come to Berlin in October 1914, where he stayed throughout the war. Thus, after December 1914, the SAC in Berlin consisted, in effect, of only Arthur Hantke, Otto Warburg, and Victor Jacobson.[5]

By contrast, the large, prospering American Jewish community lived in a powerful country that was neutral until 1917 and, as far as Palestine was concerned, remained officially neutral throughout the war because the United States did not declare war on Turkey. American Jews had access to all areas of Jewish need and until 1917 were the only major Jewry with open contacts with all the rest. It was clear to everyone that the time had come for the Americans to bear the responsibilities of leadership. The problems were, of course, substantial. Refugees had to be provided with food, clothing, and housing and protected from hostile governments, rioting soldiers, and mobs. It was necessary to make contacts and plans concerning the status of Jews in the postwar world.[6] American Jewry saw itself as being called upon to play a decisive role.[7]

Shmarya Levin, who was stranded in the United States, decided to act as quickly as possible. He joined Louis Lipsky, executive chairman of the Federation of American Zionists, in inviting the whole range of American Zionist organizations to an emergency Zionist conference in New York on August 30, 1914.[8] The conference set up a Provisional Executive Committee for General Zionist Affairs (PZC), which was entrusted with maintaining international Zionist operations during the emergency.[9] At its head was Louis Brandeis of Boston, a man who had only recently become a Zionist and a member of the marginal local Zion Association.[10] Thus, while the central Zionist office in Berlin expanded its operations in the regions under the control of the Central Powers, including Palestine, it relied on the PZC in the neutral United States to be its contact with Western, English-speaking countries.[11]

For an active spirit like Weizmann, this situation within the World Zionist Organization left a broad, if sometimes problematic, range of options for any Zionist action he might undertake. The first element he had to take into account was the Zionist situation in England, which was perhaps even more complex than in other countries because Zionist organization was not centralized.[12] The English Zionist Federation (EZF) was still nominally dominated by the Herzlian leaders Joseph Cowen,[13] its president, and S. B. Rubenstein, the London-based vice-president, with Leopold Greenberg, the editor of the *Jewish Chronicle*, operating behind the scenes. Weizmann, vice-president for the provinces,[14] represented a group that was aligned with the practical Zionists in control of the world organization, and he had close personal ties with the WZO executive, especially its Russian members. Rabbi Moses Gaster, together with Herbert Bentwich and the other leaders of the Order of Ancient Maccabeans (OAM), represented another center of Zionist influence capable of independent action through contacts with the British political and social elite. Gaster still harbored ill feelings because Weizmann had failed to join him in boycotting the English Zionist Federation and had even agreed to hold an office within it.[15] In brief, the English Zionists, whose organization was in disarray prior to the war, were unable to bridge their differences even in the face of new and momentous challenges. An American Zionist observer described affairs in England thus: "The organization is so loose over there and individuals acting so much on their own, that anything like concerted effort and organized endeavor for the single point has been very difficult for us. The disorder in Jewish life, is like all things concerning Jews, to some degree an exaggeration of the disorder in the life of their neighbors."[16]

In addition to such formally organized Zionist entities that worked more or less on their own, there were, of course, the established non-Zionist communal agencies of British Jewry. Among the most activist was the Jewish Territorial Organization (ITO), whose leader, Israel Zangwill,[17] lost no time in approaching the British authorities publicly on behalf of Jewish needs, both immediate and long range.[18] More quietly, but with greater effect, the Conjoint Foreign Committee, the recognized spokesman of the Board of Deputies of British Jewry and the Anglo-Jewish Association in all matters affecting Jewish communities abroad, could be expected to formulate Jewish policies and press them on the Allies for immediate or postwar action.[19] The executive head of this body, representing the long-recognized leaders of established English Jewry, was Lucien Wolf, an acknowledged authority on contemporary Jewish affairs and on Anglo-Jewish history.[20] Having edited an information bulletin on the persecution of Russian Jewry before the war, he soon turned to advising the government—in his role as director of the Conjoint Foreign Committee—on pro-Allied propaganda among Jews worldwide.

Even if they could unite on a policy, the Zionists could not, at this stage, hope to carry out their own plans without taking into account the views and possible actions of the non-Zionist bodies. Weizmann's official position in the EZF involved him in attempts made by this body, as well as by the members of the Smaller Actions Committee, especially Tschlenow and Sokolow, to arrive at an understanding with Zangwill and with Wolf and his circle of lay leaders.

Apart from the several organized agencies claiming to represent British Jewry and world Jewish affairs, there were a number of informal centers of influence, individuals as well as groups, who felt free to act in the Jewish interest in view of the loose organization of the community. Though he was bound by his official positions within the WZO and the EZF to adhere to the policies set by these bodies, Weizmann felt free to act within the framework of other groups as well, knowing full well that their policies diverged from the official Zionist policy. He had exceptionally good relations with many of these groups, and, by tactful maneuvering, he could work with them as well as with the organized Zionist bodies. One major center was a Manchester group that undertook to propagandize the Zionist cause. Including younger men, professionals and businessmen, as well as influential gentiles close to the liberal *Manchester Guardian*, this group was to a degree an outgrowth of Weizmann's function as EZF vice-president for the provinces. Other freelance operators were the advocates of Zionist military force cooperating with the Allies, such as Vladimir Jabotinsky, Yosef Trumpeldor, Pinhas Rutenberg, and Aaron Aaronsohn, who were active in England at various times. Neither the Manchester volunteers nor the enthusiasts who sought an Anglo-Zionist military connection were greatly inhibited by ties with the world organization, and they could more or less ignore the considerations that called for a Zionist posture of neutrality in the conflict. Weizmann, who shared their leanings and more often than not gave the direction for their work, had to conduct himself with greater public restraint in this regard.

The most important Jewish and Zionist circles that Weizmann was able to use were the young university-trained Zionists in London and Manchester who clustered around Ahad Ha'Am and, to a lesser degree, around Weizmann himself as well as around the Haham, Moses Gaster. The group included Leonard Stein, a barrister; Leon Simon, a civil servant; Harry Sacher, a journalist who at the start of the war worked for the *Daily News* before returning in the spring of 1915 to his previous post at the *Manchester Guardian*;[21] Norman Bentwich, the son of Herbert Bentwich; and the rising young Manchester entrepreneurs, Simon Marks and

Israel Sieff.[22] On the fringe of the group was Albert Hyamson, who, like Leon Simon, was a civil servant.[23] For Weizmann, and even more for Leon Simon and others of the group, Ahad Ha'Am was a moral and intellectual authority upon whose judgment they relied in matters great and small. Weizmann consulted Ahad Ha'Am on all major undertakings during this crucial period of his Zionist career.[24] If Ahad Ha'Am was the guiding spirit of this circle, controlling its ideas and movements from a distance, Weizmann can be said to have been its executive director and most enterprising member. Apart from these two transplanted Russian Jews, all other members were native English Jews with wide professional and personal ties within the Jewish and gentile communities.

When Weizmann returned to England at the end of August 1914, he was driven by a powerful urge to act but lacked a clear idea of what action was possible in his position. Even before he arrived in Manchester, he participated in conferences held by Ahad Ha'Am with Dr. Harry Friedenwald of Baltimore,[25] then president of the Federation of American Zionists, and Abraham Lubarsky, Ahad Ha'Am's close friend and, like him, an employee of the Russian Jewish tea company of Wissotsky.[26] Both Friedenwald and Lubarsky happened to be in London on their way to the United States from their respective visits to Palestine and England. As the United States was neutral, its Jews might be able to take up the task of relief and political intercession behind both the Russian and Turkish lines. But Ahad Ha'Am emerged from his talks with the Americans with his usual caution, unconvinced that American Jews could organize effective assistance to their suffering brethren.[27] Ahad Ha'Am's gloomy outlook rendered him almost unable to act, while Weizmann, who shared many of Ahad Ha'Am's assessments of the tragedy that befell Eastern European Jewry as well as the Palestinian Jewish community, was caught by the excitement of the political work at hand and the opportunities that the war offered to the Jewish people. The difference between the teacher and his disciple is best characterized by a phrase Weizmann used at a public meeting a few months before the war: "Politics is life and movement, not standstill and apathy."[28] Cautiously, but steadfastly, Weizmann was on the political move from the start of the war.

Recognizing that little could be done from London to ease the lot of Polish and, after November 1914, Ottoman Jews, Weizmann hoped that at least there could be effective preparation for a Jewish role in the ultimate peace conference. To this end it was necessary to unite Jews in the Allied and neutral countries on a common policy and agreed leadership, and American Zionists could be a critical element in such a project. Within days after returning to England from Champex, Weizmann wrote to his friends in the United States, Shmarya Levin and Judah L. Magnes, proposing a Jewish delegation of influential figures like the American ambassador in Constantinople, Henry Morgenthau; the former Italian prime minister, Luigi Luzzatti; and Baron Edmond de Rothschild of Paris. Weizmann even contemplated visiting France, Italy, and the United States to further this plan.[29]

At the same time, Weizmann was willing to encourage Pinhas Rutenberg, a mysterious and secretive figure who had been among the leaders of the Russian Social Revolutionary party until he had to flee to Italy following the collapse of the Russian Revolution of 1905. Rutenberg appeared at Weizmann's house in Manchester one night toward the end of September 1914 fired with the idea of forming a Jewish force that would fight on the Allied side. Such a force would give the Jews—assuming the Allies won—a hearing at the peace conference and might lead to the establishment of a Jewish state in Palestine. Weizmann viewed Rutenberg's plan with sympathy—as he later did Jabotinsky's similar yet independently conceived plan—and sent him on to Ahad Ha'Am, in whose house the three of them met again, joined by others.[30] Yet under Ahad Ha'Am's inhibiting influence, Weizmann was careful to avoid any open association with those headlong enthusiasts.[31] When Rutenberg made it known that Weizmann backed him in his Jewish legion project,[32] Weizmann was quick to assure Ahad Ha'Am that Rutenberg was simply "spreading rumors" and that Weizmann intended "to take radical steps to stop him."[33]

It made more sense to attempt first to enlist the local English talents for the Zionist cause. As an officer of the EZF, Weizmann was brought into the negotiations of that body with Israel Zangwill,[34] and later with Lucien Wolf, looking toward agreement on immediate and long-range policies. Without a clear conviction at the start that any of the activities offered an appropriate Jewish or Zionist strategy and a role he could effectively fill, Weizmann wrote on September 14 to Ahad Ha'Am:

> I have just received a *cable* from New York: *"Provisional Committee invites you to America at once—Levin."* I don't know, of course, why and what for, and I cannot quite imagine what use such a journey would be. But what would you advise me to do? . . . I thought of going to London to talk to you about the possibility of *"Action"* in favor of the Russian Jews, and possibly of Palestine too. Now, when the fate of Europe, and *implicite* that of Turkey too, is being decided, perhaps one ought to raise one's voice. It is difficult of course to discuss this by letter. Of course I don't like Zangwill's move [to seek a Foreign Office statement in favor of Russian Jewish emancipation] in the name of I.T.O. This is an important question however, and perhaps one should prepare for it now.[35]

Ahad Ha'Am, as might be expected, answered with a clear and unequivocal warning against precipitate action along any of the lines being considered or suggested by Weizmann:

> I received your letter of yesterday's date. I well understand your state of mind, which is much like mine and of all our comrades. But I don't share your belief that the time has *already* come for some "action." The course of

events does not yet provide any "clue" to predict the future, and there is still room for all kinds of surprises. Lately Sacher and Simon came to call and we . . . concluded that any action in the way of Z[angwill] at this time would be a sin against the Jewish people who authorized no one to act in its name. . . . As to your trip to America, I can say only this, that it seems to me utterly impossible to accomplish anything of propaganda value in such a short time. You should therefore find out first for what purpose they are asking for you.[36]

Such skeptical caution was far from foreign to Weizmann himself—certainly of his second thoughts—notwithstanding the ardor of his swift, emotional response to the challenge. He made haste to assure Ahad Ha'Am that he, too, opposed irresponsible partisan initiatives and thought only of action preparatory to eventual approaches to the powers on an official level and primarily of quiet discussions, especially of matters relating to Palestine, in such influential circles as he might reach.[37]

Notwithstanding Ahad Ha'Am's stern warning to wait for the right moment and Weizmann's own pronouncement that his mentor's advice was "most valuable,"[38] Weizmann did not hesitate to deviate from Ahad Ha'Am's chartered course. This behavior was quite in keeping with his behavior in earlier years: Weizmann listened to the revered master, almost always agreed with him on questions of policy as well as principle, but on specific issues, where he differed on tactics, he momentarily parted ways.

Weizmann's reasons for agreeing to approach Zangwill despite his professed repugnance for the latter's doings were all based on the new political situation, which required novel approaches from the Zionists. Weizmann was quite frank in articulating them to Zangwill himself. First, Weizmann was convinced that the present moment required all Jews to set aside their differences and act in concert to secure what had been built in Palestine and to save Russian Jews from the continued harsh treatment to which they were subjected.[39] Second was his firm belief, from the start, that the Allies would win the war and that England would then be instrumental in guaranteeing justice in a new world order. It was the moral obligation of Jews to seize this momentous period in human history and to lay claims for the liberation of Russian Jewry and the establishment of an organized autonomous Jewish community in Palestine. Third was Weizmann's assumption—almost two months before Turkey entered the war—that in the new world to be created after the war Palestine would fall within the sphere of influence of England. Meanwhile the Jews needed to be patient, participate in the battle between "Siegfried and Moses," and prepare for the time when important decisions would be made.[40]

Weizmann turned to Zangwill because the latter, an erstwhile member of the World Zionist Organization, was one of the most prominent English Jews of his day. He therefore offered Zangwill the opportunity to take charge: "Would you like to lead in this great and critical moment?"

he asked at the conclusion of his letter.[41] But "maître Zangwill," as
Weizmann deferentially addressed him, remained cool to the idea. Dis-
puting the certainty with which Weizmann foresaw Allied victory and
England's ability to dispense justice, he replied, "I could only lead if I
could see the way to go, otherwise it would be a case of the blind leading the blind."[42] But Weizmann did not give up. Accompanied by Joseph Cowen and Leopold Greenberg, he traveled to Brighton to meet
with Zangwill on November 7, 1914. Despite Zangwill's hostile attitude
at the meeting, and at the suggestion of the ITO official, David Jochelman, Weizmann followed with a letter to Zangwill on November 20 in
which he went so far as to dissociate himself from certain aspects of
Ahad Ha'Am's political principles and even offered concessions on the
flow of the immigration of Jews to Palestine.[43] In a brief, haughty reply,
the famed author demanded on November 23 to see Weizmann's credentials as a spokesman on behalf of the World Zionist Organization in
order to guarantee that their deliberations and agreements would not be
eventually repudiated.[44] Embarrassed and humiliated—but probably relieved—Weizmann suspended the negotiations. It was just as well; at a
meeting of the SAC in Copenhagen on December 4–5, 1914, he was
criticized by Jean Fischer of the Hague for having taken unauthorized
steps.[45] Weizmann's first attempt to cooperate with non-Zionist leaders—intended to outflank the established Anglo-Jewish oligarchy—was
a resounding failure.

Clearly, Weizmann was acting without proper authority, without a
sufficiently high office in the World Zionist Organization, and contrary
to its official policy. The WZO declared unequivocally in its December
meeting in Copenhagen that all Zionists must adopt a policy of complete
neutrality among the belligerents and demonstrate complete loyalty to
Turkey.[46] It was a policy that was affirmed many times throughout the
war by various segments of the Zionist movement.[47] Thus Weizmann's
views and actions ran counter not only to the official policy of the WZO
but also to the views of many colleagues and friends both in England
and elsewhere who had quite other hopes and expectations from the
outcome of the war.[48] Yet Weizmann was not alone in his feeling that
the Zionists could not simply sit on the fence waiting for world events
to pass them by. Ahad Ha'Am himself was not insensitive to the possible opportunities for radical improvement of Jewish prospects inherent
in the disturbed situation. He defined his views in a typically precise
and clear-sighted analysis in a letter to Weizmann that deserves to be
quoted at some length:

> I gave the [British] prime minister's speech [following Turkey's entry into
> the war as a German ally] the attention it deserves. . . . Every Jew in his
> senses must now be aware that a great historic hour has struck for Israel
> and for Palestine, and something must be done. But when you begin to
> consider what's to be done, you can only be disheartened. Here, for ex-
> ample, someone proposes in the *J[ewish] Chronicle* calling a general Jewish

meeting in London . . . with Lord Rothschild presiding. Can't we tell in advance what the results . . . would be? Those slavish souls could not even grasp what we are aiming at. It would all end in asking [Sir Edward] Grey [secretary of state for foreign affairs] to ask [Sergei] Sazonov [Russian minister of foreign affairs] to suggest in the right quarters that it would be proper to ease a little the oppression of the Jews in Russia. And if Grey should promise to do it, there would be such joy in Israel that it would bring men like us to despair in excess of shame and disgust. . . . But I do not mean to say by this that I don't recognize the possibility of great changes in favor of our national cause. Indeed, this is my obsessive daydream, and I try to keep awake in my heart all the hopes that are conceivably possible. But if those hopes are realized it will be by grace of fortune, not by anything we do to achieve it. . . . Nevertheless I well understand your state of mind (which is also mine. . .). We want to give ourselves the "illusion" that we are . . . turning the wheel of our life. It is hard at a time like this to make peace with the idea of our total helplessness. And so—let's try to "move" things. Let us try to set up various talks with influential people and prepare European public opinion (that *Europäisches Gewissen* which Nordau pictured so well at the Tenth Congress). . . . We have spoken about the content of such propaganda before, and I still hold to my view that we must not make exaggerated demands. . . .

I hope you will advise me if you get an answer from Balfour.[49]

Ahad Ha'Am, like Weizmann, was moved to cautious action by Herbert H. Asquith's Guildhall speech of November 9, 1914, following Turkey's entry into the war on the side of the Central Powers. The prime minister had declared, "It is the Ottoman government that has drawn the sword, and . . . I venture to predict, will perish by the sword. It is they and not we who have rung the death-knell of Ottoman dominion, not only in Europe, but in Asia. . . . The Turkish Empire has committed suicide."[50] Weizmann immediately drew the following conclusion from Asquith's remarks: "That should Palestine fall within the sphere of British influence and should Britain encourage a Jewish settlement there, as a British dependency, we could have in 25–30 years about a million Jews out there, perhaps more; they would develop the country, bring back civilization to it. Palestine can easily become an Asiatic Belgium in the hands of the Jews."[51] To him it was clear that the time had come for Jews to "emerge from [their] torpor and do something."[52] In early September, Weizmann had declared that the Zionists needed to prepare for the future peace conference with clear-cut demands and the assertion that the Jews are a nation.[53] By mid-November, his thinking evolved into two unshakable principles to which he clung on throughout the war: that at the end of the war the world map would be reorganized along principles of nationality and thus Jews needed to lay down their claim right away to their own national entity, and that only Great Britain could be relied upon to support Zionist demands.[54]

Both Ahad Ha'Am and Weizmann could not possibly have known that Asquith's Guildhall speech was not much more than momentary rhetoric. During the first half of the war, the British government had no intention of dismembering the Ottoman Empire. The interdepartmental de Bunsen Committee, which considered the matter in April and May 1915, came to the conclusion that Turkey-in-Asia had to be preserved intact, though decentralized. For the time being the committee followed Asquith's preferences for avoiding any new territorial commitments.[55] The committee's deliberations and final report were, of course, kept secret. Yet even those in government who were familiar with its conclusions had little doubt that once Turkey was defeated Britain would not stand aside without taking advantage of its eventual dismemberment. But the Zionists were not privy to any of these deliberations, and thus they took Asquith's speech at its face value.

Following the line agreed on with Ahad Ha'Am, Weizmann decided to secure an appointment with Arthur James Balfour, with whom he had last met just before Balfour lost his seat at East Manchester in January 1906.[56] Balfour, returned as MP for the City of London within two months, had accepted Asquith's invitation to resume his membership of the Committee of Imperial Defence at the outbreak of the war. On November 25, 1914, Balfour became a member of the War Council, which replaced the committee. Weizmann was uncertain whether Balfour would remember their previous meeting and asked their mutual good friend Samuel Alexander, professor of philosophy from Manchester University, to make the necessary arrangements.[57] On December 12, 1914, Weizmann called on Balfour at his house in Carlton Gardens. Two days later he reported to Ahad Ha'Am the highly favorable results of the meeting:

I saw Balfour . . . on Saturday. The interview lasted for an hour and a half. Balfour remembered everything we discussed eight years ago. He . . . expounded to me his view of the Jewish question, and said that in his opinion the question would remain insoluble until either the Jews here became entirely assimilated, or there was a normal Jewish community in Palestine—and he had in mind Western Jews rather than Eastern. He told me that he had once had a long talk with Cosima Wagner in Bayreuth and that he shared many of her antisemitic ideas. I pointed out to him that we too . . . believe that Germans of the Mosaic faith are an undesirable, demoralizing phenomenon, but that we totally disagree with [Richard] Wagner and [Houston Stewart] Chamberlain as to the diagnosis and prognosis, . . . after all, all these Jews have taken part in building Germany, contributing much to her greatness . . . at the expense of the whole Jewish people, whose sufferings increase in proportion to the "withdrawal" from that people of the creative elements which are absorbed into the surrounding communities—those same communities later reproaching us for this *absorption* and reacting with antisemitism. He listened for a very long time and was very moved—I assure you, to *tears*. . . . He asked me whether I wanted something practical at present. I said no . . . I'd like to call on him again, with his permission, when the roar of the guns had stopped. He saw me out into the street, holding my hand in silence, and bidding me farewell said very warmly: *"Mind you come again to see me. I am deeply moved and interested, it is not a dream, it is a great cause and I understand it."*[58]

Ahad Ha'Am hailed this success in a letter of December 16 in what for him were flattering terms and with a justified sense of having shared in the achievement: "Today I received your letter of yesterday's date and read it over and over and I am convinced that you (or more properly we) have achieved a great thing. When the time comes, B[alfour]'s aid will count more than the opposition of all our 'leaders' put together, especially since in view of the state of opinion in this country, it is very possible that the conservatives will come to power after the war, and B. will be Prime Minister. In short—more power to you!"[59]

During the war years Weizmann followed in the field the lines of action laid down by himself and particularly by Ahad Ha'Am, who looked on and received reports like a chief of staff generally conversant with the plan of campaign, fully confident of his commanding officer but not always able to know or effectively guide and control the officer's tactical maneuvers. This was the situation in moral terms, informally. In terms of official status and political realities, Weizmann's activity was to the greater degree authorized, however vague the nature of his authority; and Ahad Ha'Am exerted his influence under the mantle of deference paid to his person by his devoted disciple. What made this relationship particularly easy to maintain was the fact that it was never formal, that communication over major policy was always mixed with exchanges of information about friends and relatives as well as discussions of Weizmann's financial problems (occasionally Ahad Ha'Am lent money to his disciple). Before he moved permanently to London in September 1915, moreover, Weizmann often stayed at Ahad Ha'Am's house, and the return address on many of his letters bears the latter's Haverstock Hill residence.

Yet, despite Ahad Ha'Am's valuable support, Weizmann sensed from the start that unless he received some official accreditation as a spokesman for the WZO he would be continually challenged, perhaps even discredited, by Zionists and non-Zionists alike. He therefore sent a communication to Judah Magnes with Lubarsky when he returned to New York in early September 1914, asking for formal assurance that the American Jews, Zionist and non-Zionist, were behind him. Despite the vacuum in the leadership ranks of the WZO, Weizmann's situation was ambiguous, at best. On the one hand he was treated by the Zionist movement's leadership in the United States, Palestine, Russia, and on the Continent as the most trusted collaborator. No sooner was the PZC established, for example, than Weizmann received a cable from Shmarya Levin summoning him to the United States "at once."[60] A month later, a letter was sent by the PZC over the signature of Louis Brandeis requesting Weizmann to be its representative at the GAC meetings in Stockholm at the end of October.[61] Following Levin's example, Arthur Hantke, too, urged Weizmann to join forces with Levin in the United States, since Weizmann was deemed the most suitable and talented person for such work.[62] Finally, Magnes, without consulting his colleagues, cabled Weizmann, personally assuring him of the enthusiastic support of all classes of American Jews.[63] But the following day he added in a letter a significant qualification: "Should [Sokolow and Tschlenow] give their approval to your activities, I am of the opinion that you may regard yourself without further authority as an accredited agent of the International Zionist Organization."[64] Indeed, until Sokolow and Tschlenow arrived in England—after many delays—on December 31, 1914, and gave official sanction to his activities, Weizmann was unable to speak in the name of the WZO. Even then it was not always clear that his actions had the approval of those members of the SAC who were in contact with him.

Weizmann was acutely aware of the ambiguity of his position. He constantly reminded his friends that Ahad Ha'Am agreed with all his actions: "I have not taken a single step without his advice and consent," he assured Abraham Lubarsky.[65] Indeed, he did his best to stay in close touch with Ahad Ha'Am, even if he did not always follow the latter's guidelines. For his part, Ahad Ha'Am demanded such reports as of right,[66] and when Weizmann failed to deliver them on time he felt obliged to explain why he was remiss.[67] In addition to the moral support provided by Ahad Ha'Am,[68] Weizmann's only claim to official authority was his membership in the GAC—now splintered and unable to function—and his position as vice-president of the EZF. Although he made repeated requests to the Americans to grant him official status,[69] they were reluctant to do so. Thus, despite the lack of esteem Weizmann had for the EZF, he realized he needed it to bolster his status. Though he threatened on occasion to resign as vice-president and was even urged to do so by Tschlenow and Gaster,[70] he was too much of a realist to willingly forgo the advantages, however meager, of such a post.

Lack of status did not mean that Weizmann was content to wait for Tschlenow and Sokolow's instructions as to how to proceed. By the time they arrived, he had crystallized his thinking on the future of Zionism and taken a number of concrete steps to implement it. From the start of the war, Weizmann adopted a decisively anti-German stance, even refusing to correspond in German and advising his friends to do the same; he wished to remove from the Zionist movement the remotest appearance of a German character. "I am convinced," he wrote to Shmarya Levin, "that the outcome of this catastrophe will be a British and French victory. I cannot and do not want to envisage any other outcome. Turkey's present behavior is such that she has aroused the Allied Powers against her and she will have to pay for this. I further hope that in that case Palestine will come under English influence and England will understand the Zionists better than anyone else."[71] In one form or another, Weizmann repeated these ideas throughout the war, while careful to modulate and adjust the arguments depending on his interlocutors.

Until 1917, Weizmann was among a tiny minority in his firm attitude as to where Zionist loyalties should be directed. Almost the entire World Zionist Organization was pro-German, including many of the Americans, and only a handful of leading Zionists—among them Weizmann, Jabotinsky, and Rutenberg—were pro-British. Even Moses Gaster—a British subject who believed that immediate action needed to be taken to secure Jewish demands after the war—was not willing to place all his bets on England. In his usual frank manner he warned Weizmann: "I cannot emphasize enough the fact that the war may end in a stalemate . . . , and if the people in Germany and Turkey ever heard of what has been arranged [in negotiations and discussions with British statesmen] then I very much doubt whether—all the work which we may do will not have been done in vain. . . . I have made it here perfectly clear that this is not going to be an English question and that we are not going to play any local game; it is a Jewish question and its Jewish character must be preserved intact . . . and this is the only safe line to which we must hold."[72] Judah Magnes made similar pleas for neutrality.[73] On January 24, 1915, Magnes wrote in clear-cut terms: "The American Jews as a whole are endeavoring to be neutral. What I meant to convey was that they all sympathetically support your activities as an Englishman, just as they might support similar activities of Germans in Germany, Austrians in Austria, Russians in Russia, Frenchmen in France etc."[74]

Thus Weizmann went out on a limb not only in taking the lead in discussions with various British government officials, politicians, and Jewish leaders concerning the future of Zionism but also in deviating from the general attitude of the Zionist leadership. One of his major tasks, and ultimately one of his great successes, was to convince his fellow Zionists on three continents that his was the correct path for the movement to follow. He naturally concentrated at first on his immediate environment through personal interviews while not neglecting every opportunity to disseminate his ideas abroad through a constant flow of letters and memoranda.

From the beginning of the war, Weizmann cultivated his wide circle of influential friends for Zionist ends and made prodigious efforts to extend his contacts. As in earlier years, his Zionist allies and academic friends supported him in both his public and private capacities. Those whose aid he sought for the Jewish cause were often also his personal patrons, and he was able to make effective use of the status he achieved as an academic and a scientist to advance the Zionist interest. Throughout the war, he succeeded in interweaving his private and public careers.

The French branch of the Rothschild family, friends from the time of his campaign for a university in Palestine, became a major source of strength. Weizmann had confirmed his connections with the Baron Edmond de Rothschild when he visited in Paris on August 26, 1914. It was the baron who first urged Weizmann to contact British statesmen immediately upon returning to England,[75] a suggestion echoed by his son James.[76] Earlier that year the baron had shrewdly observed that, once stimulated, his son James would continue to interest himself in the Zionist work in Palestine.[77] Weizmann was indeed able to arouse the interest of this thirty-six-year-old monocle-wearing eccentric. James de Rothschild was a tall, erect, and strikingly dignified man who, like his father, was no conventional member of the Franco-Jewish elite.[78]

Born in France—though later naturalized as a British subject—James was called to serve in the French army soon after the start of the war. In 1913 he had married an English woman, Dorothy Pinto, who continued to reside in London while her husband was on the Continent.[79] Through her, beginning in November 1914, Weizmann carefully continued to nurture his relationship with the Rothschilds. That twenty-year-old woman was relied on to report Weizmann's plans and current developments regularly to the old baron in Paris, while keeping Weizmann in touch with the views of her husband and father-in-law.[80] She also introduced Weizmann into the circle of the London Rothschilds and their broad acquaintanceship in the governing and business elite.[81] Among the group Weizmann succeeded in tying to the cause of Zionism, and to himself as a person, were the two sons of the first Lord Rothschild. The old banker, Nathan Mayer, who died in 1915, had modified his hostile attitude toward Zionism only in the last months of his life. Walter, the second Lord Rothschild, was a zoologist and paleontologist who had little interest in banking. His younger brother, Charles, would also have preferred a career in science—he became one of the world's foremost authorities on fleas—but he reluctantly took over the reins at N. M. Rothschild until he committed suicide in 1923.[82]

With the assistance of Dorothy de Rothschild, Weizmann was also able to meet and influence the families of Walter, a bachelor, and Charles, including such remote kin and friends as the socially and politically influential marquess of Crewe, secretary of state for India until 1915 and then lord president of the council until 1916, whose late mother-in-law had been a cousin of the first Lord Rothschild. Weizmann also met Neil Primrose, parliamentary undersecretary of state for foreign affairs and likewise related to the Rothschilds by marriage. Likewise, it was Dorothy who introduced Weizmann to another remarkable relative, Rozsika, Charles's wife.[83] This Hungarian-born lady had great influence over her husband[84] and Walter, her brother-in-law. Her meeting with Weizmann was an unqualified success, and they took an immediate liking to each other. Rozsika not only served as a go-between with her tongue-tied brother-in-law but obtained for Weizmann, in 1915, interviews with the marchioness of Crewe,[85] Lord Haldane,[86] Lord Robert Cecil, Anthony de Rothschild, Walter's mother, Emma, and many others including Theo Russell,[87] who was assistant secretary to Balfour, to Sir William Tyrrell, private secretary to the foreign secretary until 1915, and later to Sir Edward Grey, secretary of state for foreign affairs until 1916.[88] One Rothschild stood out in his hostility toward Zionism, Walter's uncle Leopold, and neither the younger Rothschilds nor Weizmann could breach his intransigence.

The social contacts with the Rothschilds and their friends allowed

Weizmann, despite lack of official standing, to meet on equal terms the claims of Rabbi Moses Gaster, for example, who wished to assume for himself a privileged status of Zionist leadership. According to Gaster, a member of the government like Herbert Samuel would automatically think of Gaster as a representative Jew on any public matter concerning the Jewish community. Weizmann and his friends often used their own high-placed contacts to bolster their demands both within and without the Jewish community.[89]

In addition to the Rothschilds, the other major resource available to Weizmann initially included the academic contacts he himself possessed as well as old university friends and intellectuals who could be reached through such associates as Harry Sacher, Leon Simon, and the other members of his circle. Thus, to renew his acquaintance with Balfour, he had sought the help of Samuel Alexander. Similarly, Sacher, through his circle of university schoolmates and fellow journalists, made highly important contacts for Weizmann, especially with the group of writers, scholars, and politicians associated with the *Round Table*.[90]

The *Round Table* group coalesced around Lord Alfred Milner's famous "Kindergarten," the set of young administrators whom he recruited to the task of restoring an acceptable government in South Africa after the Boer War. One of them, Philip Henry Kerr, created the journal *Round Table* in 1909, a quarterly aiming at a solid union of the British Commonwealth. During his editorship he and other intellectuals and academics interested in the affairs of the British Empire dissected current global developments and discussed future policies. A social dimension was added through the hospitality of Kerr's good friend Nancy Astor, later Lady Astor; after the war this ardent Christian Scientist and champion of women's causes became the first woman to sit in the House of Commons. The Astors' magnificent home at Cliveden, overlooking the Thames, was open to the *Round Table* luminaries and a wide range of other persons of eminence and influence. Through his access to these circles, Weizmann became more or less well acquainted with a good part of the government of Britain, including top-ranking civil servants and several ministers.

Weizmann's anti-German bias accorded well with the *Round Table*'s frequent warnings against the danger of German aggression. Another point of mutual interest was, of course, Weizmann's notion to include Palestine within Britain's sphere of influence, an idea that appealed to the liberal-minded imperialists who were intent on maintaining and strengthening the solidarity of the empire. In a letter to Alfred Zimmern, a member of the *Round Table* group who was of German Jewish extraction and Weizmann's first direct contact with that group, Weizmann explained:

> I think that the Jewish element when included into the family of nations which constitute the British Empire, would contribute greatly towards bringing about the changes (efficiency, hard work etc.) which I mentioned. . . . Palestine with a Jewish population would be the best asset for the Empire.

England which would be instrumental in the redemption of Israel would derive an enormous benefit from it and the Imperial responsibilities which it would have to bear would be insignificant in comparison with the advantages. An imperial synthesis between England and Jewry would be the greatest thing imaginable.[91]

Weizmann had obviously made an impact on Zimmern, a scholar and authority on international institutions who later in the war joined the political intelligence department of the Foreign Office.[92] Zimmern was on friendly terms with Horace Kallen, at the time an instructor in philosophy at the University of Wisconsin and an associate member of the PZC. In May 1915 Zimmern wrote to Kallen about the attitude of some members of the Foreign Office toward Zionism: "I have had a long talk with [Lord Eustace] Percy about Palestine. . . . The upshot of our talk . . . that the Jews can count on sympathy and understanding for their national ideal from the directors of British policy . . . that the initiative in the matter lies with the Jews themselves. . . . If it is to be a practicable matter, it must be the Jews who are to make it practical and who must prepare the ways and means."[93] Alfred Zimmern may have been predisposed to favor Zionism by his own partial Jewish heritage, and he was certainly influenced by Kallen as well, who was careful to instruct him about the potential of American Jewry. But he was also greatly impressed by Weizmann's arguments and made sure to introduce him to other members of the *Round Table*.[94]

To gain entry into the powerful circles around the Rothschilds and the *Round Table* group, Weizmann sought and gained sponsors who introduced him and guided his initial steps. But his meeting with one of Britain's most influential opinion makers was fortuitous. It took place in early September 1914, at a tea party at the home of one of Manchester's well-to-do German Jewish families.[95] Here Weizmann made the acquaintance of a distinguished-looking elderly man who wore a full white beard. Weizmann did not immediately catch his full name and launched into a severe indictment of tsarist Russia's antisemitic policies, this despite the fact that Russia was a British ally. The gentleman listened attentively until Weizmann finished his tirade and then asked, "Are you a Pole?"[96] "No," replied Weizmann, "I am not a Pole, and I know nothing about Poland. I am a Jew, and if you want to talk to me about that, Mr. Scott, I am at your disposal."[97] His new acquaintance did want to speak to him about this, and it was only then that Weizmann realized that he had met C. P. Scott, the controversial and influential editor of the *Manchester Guardian*.

A few days later, Scott invited Weizmann to his home, where they had a long and far-ranging discussion on the condition of the Jews in the East and West and on the Zionists' aspirations for the future.[98] Scott listened sympathetically and offered to introduce Weizmann to his friends in the government.[99] This first meeting between Weizmann and Scott was followed by a close collaboration. The sixty-nine-year-old editor was captivated by Weizmann. In January 1915 he wrote to Harry Sacher:

I have had several conversations with Dr. Weizmann on the Jewish question and he has, I think, opened his whole mind to me. I found him extraordinarily interesting—a rare combination of the idealism and the severely practical which are the two essentials of statesmanship. What struck me in his view was first the perfectly clear conception of Jewish nationalism—an intense and burning sense of the Jew as Jew . . . and, secondly, arising out of that, necessary for its satisfaction and development, his demand for a country, a homeland, which for him, and for anyone sharing his view of Jewish nationality, could only be the ancient home of his race. To you . . . these views are familiar . . . but they . . . were not to me.[100]

Weizmann, likewise, felt from the start that Scott could be trusted with the most sensitive and even personal details. "It is the first time in my life I have spoken out to a non-Jew all the intimate thoughts and desiderata," he wrote to the editor after the second long discussion they held. "You gave me courage and please please forgive my brutal frankness. If I would have spoken to a man I value less, I would have been more diplomatic."[101]

Weizmann felt sure enough of Scott's commitment to Zionism to ask for his help soon after making his acquaintance. Using Asquith's Guildhall speech as a starting point, Weizmann assured Scott that, should Palestine fall within the British sphere of influence, the million or so Jews who would immigrate would create a strong buffer guarding the Suez Canal and preventing aggression from Turkey: "Palestine can become an Asiatic Belgium in the hands of the Jews. Would you find time and care to consider the situation from this point of view and certainly you could help us to bring comfort to a people who is now fighting on all the battlefields of Europe without the slightest hope or chance for any betterment of the position. . . . I know that you are very busy. . . . But . . . I would be exceedingly glad to hear from you."[102] Scott was not too busy when it came to requests from Weizmann. He immediately asked his new friend for a memorandum and a map of Palestine.[103]

Weizmann's relationship to Scott was never explained by either man. It is not clear what the two had in common, how often they met, and whether their conversations ranged beyond Zionism and Weizmann's contribution to the British war effort. Clearly Scott was an excellent contact for Weizmann. He seems to have been satisfied at having befriended Weizmann and aiding a movement whose goals seemed to him to be in line with Britain's international strategic requirements.[104] Throughout his career Weizmann was able to attract the interest of influential persons, both men and women, who saw in him a protégé of high promise. Once he met such persons, Weizmann had the ability to sense, almost immediately, which of them he could trust. He spoke and wrote to them with candor about Jews and Jewish aspirations, blemishes and all. This was language they were not used to; it charmed and fascinated them and drew them to the Zionist cause. Scott, too, became a patron, not merely a sympathizer willing to help achieve Zionist goals. He undertook, to a significant extent out of an impulse of chivalry, to cham-

pion the private interests of his younger friend as well as the public
cause he represented. Scott's ties with the liberal politician David Lloyd
George were of a sort that permitted him to approach the Welsh leader
with freedom whenever an appropriate occasion arose; and Scott became the intermediary most confidently solicited by Weizmann for access to the top level of government.

That Weizmann drew support from so large and varied a circle of
patrons is a tribute to his adaptability as well as a sign of the conver-
gence of British interests, as seen by his friends, with those interests he
represented. Even before British officials felt grateful to Weizmann as a
reliable ally who contributed to the British war effort, they were able to
appreciate the appeal of his exotic presence. For Weizmann did not always impress the Englishmen he met as a charming Oriental when they
lacked other grounds for sympathy. His first meetings with British officials in 1903 and 1904, which he reported to his friends with so much
enthusiasm, left at least one of his interlocutors with an impression of
an uncouth foreigner. Even after years of residence in England, Weizmann was perceived as too much the Jew by some who encountered
him in his work for the government. But he was never a leader too vain
to accept instruction. He eagerly sought the help of others and was tireless in recruiting talented assistants. In the period before the war he had
often subjected important letters and memoranda to the critical eyes of
Martin Buber and Berthold Feiwel; during the war, Harry Sacher, Leon
Simon, and later Leonard Stein performed the same service. They did
not spare Weizmann from criticism, which was sometimes brutally
frank.[105] Weizmann was equally open to the nuances of attitude among
those with whom he negotiated, and very soon he became a sensitive
connoisseur of the shades of support and opposition that the Zionist
cause encountered among Englishmen. He developed a true instinct for
the different approaches required to activate the sympathy available from
various, sometimes mutually opposed, sources of potential friends. This
instinct was sharpened and refined as the war wore on.

As Asquith pointed out, Turkey's entry into the war on November 5,
1914, on the side of the Central Powers, seemed to place in question the
integrity of the Ottoman Empire. Various proposals for its partition, along
with that of the Austrian Empire and the German colonies, soon were
floated by interested parties among the Allies and their friends. Among
the Allies, the Russians—and also the Italians, potential recruits to the
Allied Powers—were most inclined by tradition to press territorial claims
against the Turks. The French and later the British were drawn into the
bidding, not only by considerations of the power balance that might
follow the distribution of enemy possessions after the war but also under pressures from their own advocates of imperial expansion. Another
element in British policy considerations was fostered by protagonists of
the suppressed nationalities, including emigré nationalists from the
Austrian and Ottoman empires and their British sympathizers. With
everything in flux and the future open to boundless possibilities, the

Zionist idea, among many others, found its advocates in government circles even before the Zionists began their active campaign. Obviously, however, it was up to the advocates of Jewish interests to maintain the pressure needed to keep the Zionist project alive before the shapers of policy until the times were ripe for a decision.

More than anyone else, C. P. Scott was instrumental in bringing Weizmann in contact with many of the policymakers of the empire. On November 29, 1914, he wrote to Weizmann that he had spoken to Lloyd George, chancellor of the exchequer, about the Palestine question. Lloyd George had indicated that the idea was not new to him, since he had read Albert Hyamson's article on the subject in a November issue of the *New Statesman* and had been talking to Herbert Samuel, at the time president of the Local Government Board and Liberal MP. Lloyd George was interested in seeing Weizmann together with Samuel.[106] Several weeks were to elapse before Lloyd George could receive Weizmann, but, in the meantime, Scott arranged for Weizmann to meet Samuel at the latter's office on December 10, 1914.[107] Weizmann had no choice but to follow Scott's advice to meet Samuel, though he was less than enthusiastic about the prospect.[108] After all, before 1914 Herbert Samuel had no connection with the Zionist movement, nor had he shown publicly any sympathy for it.[109] It was quite natural for Weizmann to assume that, given Samuel's class and background, he would not rush to embrace the cause of Zionism.

In fact, however, this first nonbaptized Jew to hold cabinet office in England turned out to be a strong supporter of the Zionist cause. In early November 1914 he had a conversation with Sir Edward Grey, the secretary of state for foreign affairs, on Turkey's entry into the war and the possibility of its dismemberment following defeat. "Perhaps," said Samuel, "the opportunity might arise for the fulfillment of the ancient aspiration of the Jewish people and the restoration there of a Jewish State." As he outlined his ideas, Samuel did not hesitate to reveal his personal, emotional involvement in the project. This is part of the record he kept of his conversation with Grey:

> I myself had never been a Zionist, because the prospects of any practical outcome had seemed so remote that I had not been willing to take part in the movement. But now the conditions are profoundly altered. If a Jewish state were established in Palestine it might become the center of a new culture. The Jewish brain is rather a remarkable thing, and under national auspices, the state might become a fountain of enlightenment and a source of a great literature and art and development of science. . . . I thought that British influence ought to play a considerable part in the formation of such a state because the geographical situation of Palestine, and especially its proximity to Egypt, would render its goodwill to England a matter of importance to the British Empire.

Grey's response, as recorded by Samuel, is no less remarkable than Samuel's passionate appeal: "Grey said that the idea had always had a strong sentimental attraction for him. The historical appeal was very

strong. He was quite favorable to the proposal and would be prepared
to work for it if the opportunity arose. If any proposals were put forward by France or any other power with regard to Syria, it would be
important not to acquiesce in any plan which would be inconsistent with
the creation of a Jewish state in Palestine." On November 9, the day on
which Asquith gave his Guildhall speech, Samuel spoke about the same
matter to Lloyd George, who said that "he had referred in the cabinet
to this ultimate destiny of Palestine, and [he] said to me that he was
very keen to see a Jewish state established there."[110]

Weizmann had no inkling of any of these conversations when he walked
into Herbert Samuel's office at the Local Government Board on December 10, 1914. Samuel, too, knew little about Weizmann and had obviously forgotten that four years earlier, at the behest of his friend Moses
Gaster, he had acquiesced in signing Weizmann's naturalization papers
out of turn.[111] As was his wont, Weizmann began with his analysis of
the political and economic malaise of the Jews in the East and the moral
degeneration of the assimilated Jews of the West. The only corrective,
he concluded, was a place where Jews would form "the important part
of the population" and would lead a life of their own, "however small
the place might be, for example, something like Monaco, with a university instead of a gambling hall."[112]

Speaking about those English Jews who felt that they must prove they
were 100 percent English by behaving as if they were 105 percent English, Weizmann was probably aiming at those in Samuel's own social
circle. Understandably, then, Weizmann was flabbergasted when Samuel retorted that his demands were too modest, that "big things would
have to be done in Palestine" as soon as the military situation cleared
up. Samuel was not specific as to what plans he had in mind but said
he thought the Temple might be rebuilt "as a symbol of Jewish unity,
of course, in a modernized form." He then intimated to Weizmann that
similar ideas had been occupying the minds of some of his colleagues in
the cabinet. Weizmann could scarcely believe his ears. "I remember,"
he wrote in his report to the Zionist executive, "that I was pleasantly
surprised . . . that if I were a religious Jew, I should have thought the
Messianic times were near."[113] From that time until the spring of 1921,
Weizmann could count on Samuel as one of the Zionists' staunchest and
most useful allies.[114] More than others in his immediate Zionist circle,
Weizmann felt he could trust Samuel even with internal and confidential
Zionist memoranda.[115]

Weizmann had good reason to be buoyed by the unexpected results
of his meeting with Samuel. This was the second time within two weeks
that two of the most powerful and prominent notables of European Jewry
had told *him*, the veteran Zionist activist, that his proposals were too
modest. On November 25, 1914, James de Rothschild had spoken of the
formation of a Jewish state,[116] and now Samuel spoke of the rebuilding
of the Temple. Then, two days after meeting with Samuel, Weizmann

saw Balfour, with similarly encouraging results. He kept up the momentum by following Samuel's advice and contacting Gaster, who arranged for another meeting, this time at Samuel's house, on December 25, 1914. On that occasion both the Haham and Weizmann expressed their worry that all kinds of local and self-appointed bodies might flood the Foreign Office with projects and memoranda. In turn, Samuel urged them to create a representative Jewish instrument, since the British government would not look with favor on any proposal that did not emanate from, and was not backed by, international Jewry. Samuel used the opportunity to reveal that the foreign secretary was interested in a Jewish cultural center in Palestine, a "nidus," as Sir Edward called it. For their part, Weizmann and Gaster went a step further and mentioned the desirability of establishing a British protectorate over Palestine within which Jews could freely develop.[117]

The following day Weizmann was on his way to Paris to see the Baron Edmond de Rothschild, who had been kept abreast of Weizmann's activities through his son and daughter-in-law.[118] Weizmann met with the baron twice on December 28. Reflecting the situation in France, the baron admonished Weizmann to beware of the Catholics and the assimilated Jews, who would do everything in their power to prevent the settlement of Jews in Palestine. When Weizmann had presented the idea of a Jewish university prior to the war, the baron advised that he and a few of his trusted friends work quietly behind the scenes until the time was ripe to discuss their plan publicly. The baron now repeated this advice and stated that he would take action only when the diplomatic situation regarding Palestine would be cleared up between France and England.[119] Aware of Catholic sensitivities to everything relating to Palestine, the baron then arranged for Weizmann to be received by Sir Francis Bertie, a Catholic and the British ambassador to France. Bertie received Weizmann coolly, merely out of consideration for the baron. In his diary Bertie clearly indicated what he thought of the whole affair: "Edmond de Rothschild . . . sent a Russian coreligionist established in Manchester to 'talk' about what I think an absurd scheme, though they say it has the approval of Grey, Lloyd George, Samuel and Crewe: they did not mention Lord Reading. It contemplates the formation of Palestine into an Israelite State, under the protectorate of England, France or Russia, preferably of England. . . . What would the Pope and Italy and Catholic France with her hatred of Jews, say to the scheme?"[120]

If the British ambassador made it quite clear to Weizmann that he cared little for his scheme, this was of minor significance given the views of the ambassador's superiors in the Foreign Office. Moreover, though there is little evidence to support it, Weizmann came away from his visit feeling that the baron "is ready to go the whole hog. . . . He wants a *State,* nothing less."[121] Even if he did not exactly speak of a state, the baron—at least for the duration of the war—clearly supported Weizmann's desire for British rather than French control of Palestine. This fervent French patriot had a realistic view of his countrymen's attitudes toward Jews and Zionism. His promise to support Zionist efforts when the right moment arrived was another success in Weizmann's attempts to garner general support for his plans.

Upon his return to Manchester, Weizmann received a letter from Samuel inviting him to meet with him and Lloyd George for breakfast on January 15, 1915.[122] C. P. Scott was also aware of the invitation, and on the day prior to the meeting he sent Weizmann a letter suggesting the kinds of questions Lloyd George might want answered; obviously Lloyd George had raised them with the editor. *"He will,"* wrote Scott,

> I am sure, be much interested in your view of the Jews of Judea as a possible link between East and West. . . . But no doubt he will want to discuss with you much more concrete matters than those—the present strength of the Jewish element in Palestine and the possibility of its rapid expansion; its relation to the local Arab population which so greatly outnumbers it; the potential value of Palestine as a "buffer-State" and the means of evading for ourselves an undesirable extension of military responsibility; the best way of allaying Catholic and Orthodox jealousy in regard to the custody of the Holy Places—and the like.[123]

There is no contemporary record of the conversation that took place on January 15.[124] Weizmann and Samuel had similar views on the desirability of a British protectorate over Palestine, and quite possibly at their joint meeting Herbert Samuel summarized for Lloyd George the essence of a memorandum he was to distribute on January 25 to the prime minister and two or three members of the cabinet. In that memorandum Samuel suggested adopting the Zionist cause in the interest of the empire. The key paragraph reads:

> I am assured that the solution of the problem of Palestine which would be much the most welcome to the leaders and supporters of the Zionist movement throughout the world, would be the annexation of the country to the British Empire. I believe that that solution would be cordially welcome also to the greater number of Jews who have not hitherto been interested in the Zionist movement. It is hoped that under British rule facilities would be given to Jewish organizations to purchase land, to found colonies, to establish educational and religious institutions and to spend usefully the funds that would be freely contributed for promoting the economic development of the country. It is hoped also that Jewish immigration carefully regulated, would be given preference so that in course of time the Jewish people, grown into a majority and settled in the land, may be conceded such degree of self-government as the conditions of that day may justify.

Samuel then went on to explain the arguments in favor of this policy from the point of view of British imperial interests. He also listed some alternatives, which he quickly dismissed. On the whole, it was a cool and rational memorandum, but he let himself be carried away by his emotion in its two final paragraphs, in particular the last one: "The Jewish brain," Samuel assured his colleagues, as he had the foreign secretary two months earlier, "is a physiological product not to be despised. For fifteen centuries the race produced in Palestine a constant succession of great men—statesmen and prophets, judges and soldiers. If a body be again given in which its soul can lodge, it may again enrich the world. Till full scope is granted, as Macaulay said in the House of Commons, 'let us not presume to say that there is no genius among the countrymen of Isaiah, no heroism among the descendants of the Maccabees.' "[125]

Though Weizmann had similar ideas about a British protectorate in Palestine, Samuel was the first to present the idea to members of the British cabinet. Some eighteen years later Louis Brandeis wrote to his friend Julian W. Mack: "Sir Herbert Samuel called on me today. . . . Samuel says he was the first to suggest to the Govt. the Zionist project—under Britain's control. In 1914, shortly after Turkey declared war, Weizmann and Sok[olow] called on him to urge the Zionist cause. It was then assumed by the Govt. that Great Britain would win the war and Turkey lose its non-Turkish provinces. He had not, before the Weizmann Sok. call thought much of Zionism—was impressed by the project and prepared a memo which is on the files."[126] Clearly, the sequence of events as related by Brandeis is incorrect, for Samuel's interest in Zionism predated Sokolow's arrival in England and the meeting with Weizmann. Prior to writing his memorandum, however, Samuel may have consulted with Weizmann and Sokolow and, of course, with Gaster as to some of its wording.

One person who was clearly not impressed by Samuel's memorandum was the prime minister. Writing to his mistress, Venetia Stanley, Asquith remarked contemptuously:

> I have just received from H[erbert] Samuel a cabinet memorandum, headed "the future of Palestine. . . :" He goes on to argue at considerable length and with much vehemence in favour of a British annexation of Palestine. . . . He thinks we might plant in this not very promising territory about 3 or 4 million European Jews, and that this would have a good effect upon those (including I suppose himself) who were left behind. "The character of the individual Jew, wherever he might be, would be ennobled. The sordid associations wh[ich] have attached to the Jewish name would be sloughed off" etc. etc. . . . It reads almost like a new edition of *Tancred* brought up to date. I confess I am not attracted by this proposed addition to our responsibilities. But it is a curious illustration of Dizzy's favourite maxim that "race is everything" to find this almost lyrical outburst proceeding from the well-ordered and methodical brain of H.S.[127]

No doubt, some of the criticisms concerning his first memorandum were brought to Samuel's attention. Asquith's acerbic remarks were made known to him only many years later, but at a meeting with Edward Grey in late January 1915, the latter reiterated his concern about France's attitude toward the establishment of a British protectorate over Palestine and his reluctance to assume new responsibilities for the British Empire.

The foreign secretary preferred submitting the Holy Places to the supervision of a commission of representatives of the European powers.[128]

Upon reflection, Samuel composed a more moderate memorandum, titled "Palestine," which he circulated in early March 1915. It eliminated most of the rhetoric and expanded or condensed some paragraphs, but the March document did acknowledge Grey's concern that France would object to the scheme and dealt at some length with this issue. Moreover, Samuel eliminated the notion of "British Suzerainty in Palestine," or "annexation of the country to the British Empire." Instead, he advocated a British protectorate. This change constituted, of course, the most important difference between the two documents. In both memoranda he showed special sensitivity to the fate of the Arab population and the safeguarding of its rights while also highlighting the significance of winning the gratitude of world Jewry.[129]

Despite its more moderate tone, the March memorandum did not escape Asquith's sarcastic remarks: "I think," he wrote to Venetia,

> I told you that H[erbert] Samuel had written an almost dithyrambic memorandum urging that in the carving up of the Turks' Asiatic dominions, we should take Palestine into which the scattered Jews could in time swarm back from all quarters of the globe, and in due course obtain Home Rule. (What an attractive community!) Curiously enough, the only other partisan of this proposal is Lloyd George, who, I need not say, does not care a damn for the Jews or their past or their future, but who thinks it would be an outrage to let the Christian Holy Places . . . pass into the possession or under the protectorate of "Agnostic Atheistic France"! . . . Kitchener [first Earl Kitchener, of Khartoum, secretary of state for war], who surveyed Palestine when he was a young Engineer, has a very poor opinion of the place. . . . So he (K) is all for Alexandretta, and leaving the Jews and the Holy Places to look after themselves.[130]

Thus, though some cabinet members endorsed the proposal,[131] including Lloyd George, Viscount Haldane (lord chancellor), and even Grey—who was sympathetic though not in full agreement[132]—others clearly did not. Apart from the cool, even contemptuous reception by the prime minister, there came a much more detailed and vehement response from Asquith's good friend, Edwin Montagu, chancellor of the duchy of Lancaster and Herbert Samuel's cousin. In a sharply worded, confidential memorandum written to Asquith on March 16, 1915, Montagu countered his cousin's arguments one by one:

> I think it is quite clear that the position of Palestine in itself offers little or no attraction to Great Britain from a strategical or material point of view. . . . I find myself very strongly convinced that this [founding a Jewish state in Palestine under British protectorate] would be a disastrous policy. . . .
>
> 1. There is no Jewish race now as a homogeneous whole. . . . As I understand it, the whole claim of the Jews to equality of treatment with those who profess other religions in the countries in which they find themselves,

is based on the fact that they are citizens of the countries in which they have been born and lived for generations.

How would the Jews occupy themselves [in Palestine]? Agriculture is never attractive to ambitious people and the Jews in the main have long emerged into quicker, less pastoral pursuits. I cannot see any Jews I know tending olive trees or herding sheep. Literature! Are there any great or even remarkable Jewish literary men today? . . . It is hardly worthwhile transplanting one-third of the Jewish people of the world for the sake of Zangwill! Commerce! Well I should be sorry to give antisemitism an opportunity of practical expression in a prohibitive tariff against Jewish imports. . . . Hebrew to the vast majority of Jews is a language in which to pray but not a language in which to speak or write. . . . I doubt whether the president of the Local Government Board [Herbert Samuel] could translate one paragraph or phrase of his memorandum into Hebrew. . . . You would, therefore, be setting up the formation of a state out of a polyglot, many-coloured, heterogeneous collection of people of different civilizations and different ordinances and different traditions and the confusion could not be any very great improvement on that which followed the erection of the Tower of Babel.

2. But the President of the Local Government Board himself admits that Palestine could only hold *in time as a maximum* three million out of nine million people. . . . What about the six million who are left behind? . . . If Palestine became a Jewish State I am sure he [Samuel] would be asked to look after the Borough Council of Jerusalem rather than the West Riding of Yorkshire; the Lord Chief Justice [Reading] would be told to preside at the Beth Din and not at the Court of Appeal; while I should be asked to fit myself for appointing Rabbis in the Duchy of Lebanon rather than Anglican Parsons in the Duchy of Lancaster. . . . I venture to predict that in those countries where antisemitism is at its maximum, the position of Jewish citizens, when they have a country of their own to which they can be invited to clear out, would be infinitely worse than it is at present. . . .

I therefore regard the proposal of the President of the Local Government Board as a proposal trimmed with rather thin arguments of strategy and foreign policy, as a rather presumptuous and almost blasphemous attempt to forestall Divine agency in the collection of the Jews which would be punished, if not by a new captivity in Babylon, by a new and unrivalled persecution of the Jews left behind. If only our people would cease to ask for special favours and cease to cry out together at the special disadvantages which result from asking special favours, if only they would take their place as non-conformists, Zionism would obviously die and Jews might find their way to esteem.[133]

Montagu was speaking for a considerable segment of Anglo-Jewry, at least those native born and well established, if not for wider circles as well. In any case, it was apparent to all that the time was ill chosen to present Weizmann's or Samuel's ideas about a Jewish autonomous community or a Jewish state under a British protectorate. Despite Asquith's Guildhall speech of November 9, 1914, warning of the dire consequences Turkey faced by going to war, and despite Grey's expression of interest when speaking with Samuel, neither the prime minister nor the foreign secretary were firmly committed to the partition of the Ottoman

Empire.[134] Other cabinet members, more ready to accept such measures, were widely divided in their views of the particular territories that Britain needed to acquire. The time for deciding on the future of Palestine remained remote. Samuel found himself, like Weizmann, in a position in which his aims could best be immediately pursued not by presenting specific plans and proposals but by gaining broad sympathy and general familiarity with Zionist aspirations through effective propaganda. The memoranda of January and March 1915 clearly showed how committed Samuel had become to the Zionist cause. He continued to be very helpful in Weizmann's contacts with government circles and in dealing with influential Jews.

When he reached out to new people in his environment, Weizmann found a much enlarged variety of views to cope with, even among committed friends of the Zionist cause. Among both Jews and non-Jews, who were relatively new to the idea of Zionism and related issues, Weizmann sometimes found a more forthright partisanship than even he thought prudent.[135] The Zionism of such new supporters derived from their British loyalty[136] as much as, or more than, from sympathy for Jews. After Turkey entered the war, such men and women easily adopted the view that a Jewish state, independent or British protected, would serve British interests as a buffer for the Egyptian defenses on the Suez Canal. The younger Rothschilds, taking this line, thought Weizmann's Ahad Ha'Amist position—seeking only facilities for Jewish development and cultural autonomy in Palestine—was too modest, though the old baron in Paris shared the gradualist approach. Editors and staff writers of the radical liberal *Manchester Guardian*, old opponents of any extension of British imperial commitments, felt that once the collapse of the Ottoman Empire was expected, British interests in the Suez Canal (and Mesopotamia) had to be defended in Palestine. Men like the military commentator, Herbert Sidebotham, became staunch advocates of a Jewish state as a matter of British strategy. As noted earlier, there were Jews who shared this approach and drew even more immediate conclusions, advocating a Jewish military force that would fight with the Allies to stake out a claim for statehood by their own service. Weizmann, as one who placed his own bets openly on an Allied victory, had strong sympathies with this view. Nevertheless, precisely through his closer contact with British ruling circles, he learned that the more modest approach preached by Ahad Ha'Am accorded with the mood and preferences of leading Britons and was more likely to gain and hold their support.

Very early in his British contacts, Weizmann ran into the specific limits within which British imperialism, the regime of an island of free traders, had developed its tradition. He heard from Samuel of Grey's reluctance to take on added colonial burdens,[137] and he heard from Scott and an expert on Armenian affairs, James Bryce, similar doubts[138]—later overcome by these Liberal intellectuals—about assuming the responsibility of a British protectorate in Palestine. Even the staunch Conservative Balfour, who had been a Tory prime minister in his time, preferred the government of Palestine to be shared, if possible, with the United States. Alfred Zimmern reported to Horace Kallen the opinion of Lord Eustace Percy on the matter:

A British protectorate over Palestine is, it seems, highly improbable. It would create a very bad strategic frontier and would involve us in serious expenditures to defend. Our position in the Mediterranean with Russia, Serbia, and Italy as new, and much more important naval factors, will be much more difficult in any case. Palestine is not a defense of Egypt, but an exposed flank. From the purely British point of view it is not to our interests to assume responsibility for it. . . . Percy further said that as a Foreign Office official, nothing would suit him better than to secure the support of American and neutral Jews by a vague Zionist declaration, but that it would not be honest in the face of the difficulties and uncertainties of the situation. Britain's first duty now is to herself.[139]

The background of such inhibitions in men who, nevertheless, took pride in the British Empire, or Commonwealth, goes far back in British military and diplomatic tradition. The fleet, and not its land forces, served as Britain's first line of defense;[140] and throughout the nineteenth century Britain had relied on a Continental balance of power and subsidized its allies rather than supplied troops to protect its interests on land masses essential to its security and trade. The empire, governed on similar principles, was protected by British dominance on the seas, and for control on land Britain relied on local clients and native rulers more than on the predominance of its own armed forces.[141] Weizmann quickly absorbed these ideas and summed them up in exhaustive letters and discussions shared with Scott and Samuel in March 1915. But before he did so, he explained his newly adjusted tactic to his trusted collaborator Dorothy de Rothschild. Within days of Samuel's meeting with Grey and hearing the latter's reservations, Weizmann wrote:

It is obvious that we must be able to satisfy the public opinion of English liberals. The present cabinet depends upon liberal opinion greatly. How is it to be done? The only way open is to convince them that the other alternative—a Palestine under international control—presents greater disadvantages to Britain, than a Palestine under British control. . . . But also another point arises out of all of that. It is essential to enlist the support of the Conservatives as they no doubt would not raise the same objections, being imperialists. If Sir E[dward] has the support of both parties he would of course be able to face the diplomatic difficulties which may arise with France over Palestine.[142]

Weizmann had understood from Samuel that the British cabinet was not only sympathetic toward the Palestinian aspirations of the Jews but would like to see those aspirations realized. The problem arose from the fact that Britain did not wish to be involved in any new responsibilities. "In other words," Weizmann wrote to Scott, "they would leave the organization of the Jewish Commonwealth as an independent political unit entirely to the care of the Jews. At the same time there is a view prevalent that it is not desirable that Palestine should belong to any [other] great power."[143] There were then three problems Weizmann had to overcome in his attempts to convince his interlocutors: the unwillingness of Britain to get involved with a new imperial possession, the fear of antagonizing France, and the initial hesitancy of a certain school of Liberals. Since Scott belonged to that school, Weizmann's plan was to mobilize all the arguments that might appeal to such a Liberal by evoking distaste for other possible alternatives and then to suggest a Zionist program that would be as little onerous for Britain as possible.

On the first problem, Weizmann was able to present an impressive weight of considerations independently apparent to Samuel—as Samuel's memoranda indicated—and easily accepted by Scott. Weizmann demonstrated the dangers to Britain in French control or condominium administration of Palestine, and, in addition to arguments relating to imperial and strategic considerations, he mentioned a further asset for Britain: Jewish friendship, loyalty, and gratitude, "not a negligible factor." This asset had already been identified by Samuel in his memoranda and would be amplified by friends and enemies later in the war. Weizmann then hammered home a forceful conclusion: "If Great Britain does not wish anybody else to have Palestine, this means that it will have to watch it, and stop any penetration of another power. Surely, a course like that involves as much responsibility as would be involved by a British Protectorate over Palestine with the sole difference that watching is a much more costly and much less efficient preventive than an actual protectorate."[144]

Weizmann's argument was clearly effective with Scott, who had the sympathy for Jewish nationalism that Weizmann had to depend on to proceed with his positive proposal. By the time he received Weizmann's letter, Scott was already one of the most reliable and effective protagonists of Weizmann's program and therefore receptive. "I therefore thought," Weizmann went on to say, "that the middle course could be adopted; something similar to the state of affairs which existed in Egypt, viz. the Jews take over the country; the whole burden in organization falls on them, but for the next ten or fifteen years they work under temporary British protectorate."[145]

With this formulation Weizmann arrived at the position that would be his essential policy throughout his career as a leader of Zionism. It was to be the base on which he maintained a close relationship with British policy toward Palestine for nearly as long a time. That entente required much further definition of the reciprocal roles of the Zionists and the British government, an undertaking that grew increasingly problematic. But these complications did not arise at once. For the first two years of the war the vague formula Weizmann initially devised served him and his British friends more than adequately to make their close cooperation and personal friendship possible. Weizmann had no need to go much beyond his first position in relation to the British public and official circles until later.

Yet, while Weizmann's proposal was, on the face of it, vague and quite flexible to suit him and his British patrons, it clearly violated the strictures of the WZO, which had declared—for tactical reasons—strict neutrality. Moreover, there are no indications that Weizmann consulted Tschlenow and Sokolow on any part of his formula, though they were already resident in London. They knew in general terms about his negotiations, and on one occasion they met with Samuel and Weizmann, but for the most part Weizmann informed them about the results of his deliberations after the fact. Weizmann ended his report of January 7, 1915, to the members of the Smaller Actions Committee by hinting that if he acted as he did, it was "chiefly due to Ahad Ha'Am, who every day, at all times, and every moment gave us the advantage of his valuable service, and his full moral support, and submitted every step to a searching criticism and discussion. Practically nothing was undertaken without his knowledge or consent."[146] In fact, however, on at least one occasion during his negotiations with Zangwill, Weizmann withheld information from Ahad Ha'Am.[147] He was convinced he was on the right track and would not be deterred by either the executive of the WZO or even by his mentor.

Over the next eighteen months Weizmann divided much of his time between his chemistry and lobbying for his Zionist goals over teas, at dinner parties, and in parlor meetings. He had only one formal conversation—in August 1915—with an official of the Foreign Office, Lord Robert Cecil, the parliamentary undersecretary for foreign affairs. The arguments Weizmann used with Cecil were similar to those he presented to Scott. The impression he made on the undersecretary, who was at first repelled by Weizmann's physical appearance, was not unlike the impression Weizmann made on the editor of the *Manchester Guardian* and is best recorded in Cecil's own words: "It is impossible to reproduce in writing the subdued enthusiasm with which Dr. Weizmann spoke or the extraordinary impressiveness of his attitude, which made one forget his rather repellant and even sordid exterior. Perhaps a phrase he used may convey something of the impression which he made. He said, 'I am not romantic except that Jews must always be romantic, for to them the reality is too terrible.' "[148] In time, Cecil would join the group of government officials who supported Weizmann's plans, but this was not until 1917.

At first Weizmann had to negotiate and maneuver for position much less with the general British public than with the Jewish community. This was not his own preference. His early enthusiasm for organizing world Jewry in a united front soon cooled as he realized the implications of his own position as a committed British partisan. The friendly contacts with Judah Magnes and Shmarya Levin—one a vocal pacifist and the other a firm believer in Zionist neutrality in the war (though he leaned toward support for Germany and Austria)—came to an abrupt end when they began to accuse him of exacerbating the persecution by the Turks of the Jewish community in Palestine through his strong pro-British stance. They also suspected him of supporting the plans of Yosef Trumpeldor, Jabotinsky, and the other advocates of a Jewish legion in active service with the Allies. Magnes's telegrams and letters [149] were in reference to the activities of the Alexandria-Palestine Committee for the protection of Jewish colonization work, set up, with headquarters in Alexandria, by Palestinian Jewish refugees, and the formation, at the beginning of January 1915, of a Jewish fighting force. [150] Weizmann had nothing to do with these groups [151] though he was not unsympathetic to the idea of a Jewish fighting force that would aid the British war effort. Nevertheless, he resented Levin's and Magnes's accusations, though subsequently Magnes tried to soften the impact of his harsh cables and letters [152] and continued to treat Weizmann as a valued confidant. [153] Ahad Ha'Am himself felt impelled to protect Weizmann's reputation and protested in strong language the unwarranted charges, [154] as did Yehiel Tschlenow. [155] For his part, Weizmann concluded that his position of confidence in England, especially after he undertook official war-connected duties as a scientific adviser to the Admiralty, made it necessary for him to cease all communication with World Zionist Organization headquarters. He severed contacts with Zionists in enemy countries, even through liaison offices in neutral countries, like Denmark. Only by such detachment could he be effective in the role he had chosen to play in England.

Yet in England, too, Weizmann was continuously confronted with difficulties placed in his way by his fellow English Zionists. His problems with the EZF leadership were to be expected. As early as September 1914, Weizmann suspected that Leopold Greenberg was trying to undermine his standing with Zionists and non-Zionists alike. Joseph Cowen did not feel he needed to consult with a provincial leader who had been a thorn in his side for a long time. [156] And then there was, of course, the Haham, Moses Gaster, who, as usual, was dissatisfied with the way he was treated. Weizmann could not very well ignore the Haham, much as he would have loved to do so. After all, Gaster claimed he was Herbert Samuel's mentor in Jewish and Zionist affairs and that Samuel expected Weizmann to coordinate Zionist policy with his friend. Weizmann did not have sufficient information to prove or disprove the Haham's claim and decided to be cautious. The relationship between Weizmann and Gaster, which had soured well before the outbreak of the war, was therefore artifically revived, but it remained stormy and unpleasant. The Haham made no secret of how he felt about Weizmann. Gaster, who wanted to replace the EZF with his own group, [157] felt that Weizmann had betrayed the cause by continuing to serve as that organization's vice-president. In early 1915 he wrote to his friend Jacob Moser of Bradford: "I am afraid he [Weizmann] is always trying to hunt with the hunters and to run with the hounds. He tries to keep [a] foot in both camps."[158]

In January 1915 the annual conference of the EZF narrowly defeated a resolution (an amended version of one proposed by its president, Joseph Cowen) demanding a drastic reconstitution of the Smaller Actions Committee and the removal of the central office to the Hague.[159] The conference had also reappointed Weizmann to the vice-presidency. Never tired of complaining, and frank in his approach, Gaster wrote to Weizmann:

> I have just been told that you are back from Paris. It appears to me passing strange that you could not find five minutes time to stop in London and report. . . . It is rather a queer way of co-operation. I see moreover that you have been again elected, of course with your consent, to be vice-president of the E.Z.F. I would like to know now exactly where we stand. . . . I wonder where loyalty has gone and where discipline is. This [the proposal brought before the EZF] is rank anarchy. . . . Kindly explain to me the whole situation.[160]

Weizmann's reply came by return mail. "The tone of your letter, which has reached me today surprised me a little." After explaining why, for objective reasons, like schedules and sickness, he could not see the Haham, Weizmann continued:

> I beg to say that for the last 2-½ months I have been working under the greatest possible strain and with all energy. . . . I may say, that a considerable share of all the work done has fallen to me. I claim no credit for it, but I certainly much desire one elementary thing—harmony and confidence. Your last letter raises grave doubts in me and as my health could not possibly stand the additional strain of friction I don't desire to stand in anybody's way. . . . I can work only as a free man, enjoying the confidence of his colleagues and I don't care to entangle myself or anybody else into quarrels.[161]

Gaster was, of course, not satisfied with the answer and in a second letter demanded to know why Weizmann continued to hold an official position within the EZF.[162] Weizmann replied that he wished to avoid friction and that he desired to give the appearance of unity in order to strengthen the Zionist cause, a demand that had been made by their now mutual friend, Herbert Samuel.[163] In fact, in March 1915 Weizmann succeeded in forming a joint negotiating team between the EZF and the Order of Ancient Maccabeans and to shape the function of this new entity in relation to the Smaller Actions Committee.[164]

The source of the conflict, however, remained Gaster's increasing awareness of and resentment over the fact that Weizmann failed to consult him and Weizmann's insistence that he could function only as "a free man" with the backing and confidence of his colleagues. This confidence was never provided by the cantankerous and self-aggrandizing rabbi, who felt that he deserved to be the key person in all discussions.[165] Once Weizmann moved to London in September 1915, he relied almost completely on Ahad Ha'Am and his own circle of assistants, none of whom took much note of Gaster. For the time being, Weizmann could not afford to break with the Haham, whom he described in a letter to Ahad Ha'Am as a "nasty individual!"[166] Gaster, too, was content—for the time being—to maintain an uneasy truce.[167] Only in the spring of 1917 did Weizmann feel confident enough to cut all ties to his erstwhile mentor.

The British Jewish community was another matter. Weizmann was compelled to concern himself with its diverse views and possible actions, if only to protect his own flanks. But it was a task he faced with little spontaneous interest. He shared the misgivings of Ahad Ha'Am about the utility of involving the British Jewish notables, the vested establishment, in shaping policies for the postwar solution of the Jewish problem. In this he initially had the concurring advice of Baron Edmond de Rothschild, who thought that he himself, and his personal connections, were sufficient to represent world Jewry in cooperating with the Zionists. However, younger Rothschilds—James in particular—and Herbert Samuel, urged Weizmann to come to terms with Lucien Wolf, Claude Montefiore, and the other pillars of the organized Anglo-Jewish community.[168] Given his own tenuous position as a self-appointed representative of the WZO, if not of world Jewry, Weizmann had no choice but to seek the widest possible consensus. This was a conclusion he had come to even before he met with Herbert Samuel on December 10, 1914,[169] and which he continued to uphold even after the initial negotiations with the representatives of Anglo-Jewry's establishment had collapsed.[170]

Weizmann's fellow officers in the English Zionist Federation had themselves some share in the public agitation to call a general conference of British Jews, in effect superseding the Conjoint Foreign Committee.[171] This activist outburst had aroused Ahad Ha'Am's sour disapproval. Finally, working on quite other lines, Weizmann's entourage of recruits, particularly Harry Sacher and Leon Simon, approached Lucien Wolf in private conversations. Circumstances required Weizmann to keep Zionist policy within the tactical guidelines he had adopted for himself, preventing deviations to any side.

Weizmann was engaged in those months in what he called a "dance on eggs," a phrase he borrowed from Theodor Herzl.[172] One among many Jewish and Zionist spokesmen, all seeking like himself to control events and keep others in line, he moved to counteract pressures from different sides and maintain a balance of movement in the direction he chose. While pressing Pinhas Rutenberg and his friends to subordinate their efforts to his as they pursued their goal of a Jewish legion, he kept an eye on Sacher's talks with Lucien Wolf. Moreover, though Tschlenow and Sokolow were clearly his superiors in the Zionist hierarchy, he did not quite trust the "the 'ows'," as he and his circle of confidants called them in private correspondence, to make the right move. For example, he made a concerted and ultimately successful effort to prevent the two

Russians from meeting with Herbert Samuel except in his presence.[173] On the other hand, Weizmann met with Samuel whenever he felt the need to report or discuss new developments.[174]

On November 17, 1914, prior to the proddings by James de Rothschild and Herbert Samuel to deal with the Anglo-Jewish establishment, Harry Sacher met with Lucien Wolf.[175] The initiative came from Sacher, who wished to sound out Wolf, recently appointed to guide the Conjoint Foreign Committee's work on the problems pertinent to the war. Since Wolf's anti-Zionist views were well known,[176] Sacher proceeded cautiously. As he reported to Weizmann: "I said that I was not a political Zionist and that what I was concerned about was that we should have full liberty to colonize in Palestine and to develop Jewish culture, that we should have the active sympathy of the rulers in Palestine in doing so, and the financial assistance of Western Jewry. Political demands or a Jewish State I should not press for or raise if we could get Jewish unanimity on such a basis as this."[177] Sacher had made it clear that the Zionists he represented were anxious to find a common ground on which to unite with the "leading" Jews. Though he was skeptical whether these views represented official Zionist policy, Wolf was naturally delighted to hear such views and assured Sacher that there was much sympathy for such work.[178] He freely admitted that those he represented were frightened of the bogey of political Zionism, of a Jewish state that would raise awkward questions of allegiance: "They were apprehensive that the Powers might give them the terrible gift of Palestine to rule for the Jews."[179]

Sacher's description of his group's program was less than frank, as had been Weizmann's own description when he had first approached Zangwill. After all, by mid-November 1914 Weizmann had already spoken and written about a politically autonomous Jewish community in Palestine, not simply a cultural center. But he realized that in talking with someone like Wolf, who himself was a less-than-frank negotiator, the Zionists had to tread gingerly. Thus his reminder to Sacher not to adopt too accommodating an attitude was more for the record than a stern reprimand; indeed, here they reversed roles, since it was Harry Sacher and Leon Simon who had reprimanded Weizmann for his negotiating stance with Zangwill. Yet, whereas in the case of Zangwill, Weizmann had minimized the teachings of Ahad Ha'Am, the reverse was true during the negotiations with Wolf. Sacher's initial approaches to Wolf had been couched in Ahad Ha'Amist terms, virtually renouncing political Zionist aims, but they were articulated in a conversation and not in writing.

It was a different matter when it came to the similarly biased memorandum Sacher and Simon prepared to aid in Weizmann's talks with influential Englishmen. Weizmann asked for revisions on the tactful grounds that the strictly cultural approach, while suitable for a Jewish public, had to be supplemented with more material arguments, of pressing Jewish need and British interest, if one wished to appeal to non-Jews in terms they readily understood.[180] The memorandum is no longer extant, but clearly Weizmann got what he wanted, perhaps even more than he bargained for, since it spoke about a Jewish state. Simon, using Weizmann's own reasoning, wrote at the end of 1914: "If we don't want a 'State' we had better say so clearly, because that is what the Goyim think of when they think of our claims at all."[181]

After speaking to his principals, Wolf continued to remain favorable to Sacher's overtures, which, the executive members of the Conjoint judged, were limited to proposals of humanitarian cultural and practical projects that would not alarm their members. But he proceeded leisurely, sensing that Weizmann had no real authority to cut deals on behalf of anyone but his own group. "Who are the persons and organizations," he asked Sacher, "representing your views and in what measure do they represent the great body of Zionists?"[182]

Wolf had obviously hit a raw nerve, and Weizmann's response, albeit to Sacher, came back by return mail:

> The gentlemen of the type of L[ucien] W[olf] have to be told the candid truth at present and made to realize that *we* and not *they* are the masters of the situation, that if we come to them it is only and solely because we desire to show to the world a *united Jewry* and we don't want to expose them as "self-appointed leaders." . . . Starting with nothing I, Chaim Weizmann, a *yied* from Pinsk and only *almost* a Professor at a provincial university, have organized the *flower* of Jewry in favor of a project which probably by Rothschild (Lord) and his satellites is considered as mad. . . . My success is due to one fact and you must impress it upon the porter of Mr. Rothschild— I represented the opinion of thinking Jews and that opened all doors to me.
>
> Further! If people speak at present of Palestine, if *goyische* statesmen take us seriously it is because we have worked there for the last thirty years. . . .
>
> I, Chaim Weizmann and you Harry and you Leon—say nothing of A[had] H[a'Am]—are the accredited representatives of the Jewish people. . . .
>
> I am exceedingly sorry to write in the Gasterian style but you must point out to those "Johnnies" that we do the real work and we shall carry it further, with or without them. If they don't go with us they will find themselves in a position of generals without an army. . . .
>
> . . . We have a programme and shall have the support of a great majority of Jews. They stand alone. They can do no harm, but we shall cut the grass from under their feet. I have kept quiet all these years, but now I am going to fight openly and *sans trêve,* but before opening the fight we shall attempt everything to rope in those Jews and work with them harmoniously. If they don't come they will be removed from their pedestal.[183]

Having unburdened himself, Weizmann was now ready to meet the "Wolves," as he called his adversaries. For his part, Wolf demanded a written formulation of the Zionist proposals.[184] If these requirements were met, he held out the prospect that the Conjoint Foreign Committee would invite Sacher and his friends to a conference—thus, of course, asserting the prerogative of his group to act with authority for British Jewry and so control the access of Jews to the government.[185] Moreover, Wolf was adamant in his belief that the Conjoint Foreign Committee was the only body authorized to deal with the government. "Dr. Weitzmann [*sic*] would be very ill-advised to pursue his negotiations with politicians," he told Sacher, if the Zionists wished true cooperation.[186]

For his part, Weizmann was at that time resisting strenuously—to the point of threatening to resign his vice-presidency—the independent maneuvers of his EZF colleagues Cowen and Greenberg.[187] He used the authority of Tschlenow and Sokolow against them, too, demanding restraint in deference to their authority until they arrived to take charge of the negotiations. Even after the arrival of the two Russians, he had to continue to warn the EZF leadership in London to refrain from any independent action. Throughout the last two months of 1914 and early 1915, Weizmann's tactic was to continue to interest Wolf in negotiating with the Zionists while restraining the EZF from charging ahead with its own plans. Wolf, who was very well informed of the Zionists' internal problems as well as their real political aims, was content to move slowly, though he was under considerable pressure to come to an understanding with the Zionists on a "Jewish agenda." He must have calculated that all the cards were in his possession in any case. Weizmann then was able to use Wolf's demands to delay a response until the arrival of Tschlenow and Sokolow, members of the WZO Smaller Actions Committee, who were awaited in England and who alone could authorize him to speak officially. His counterproposal, to meet with the other side in preliminary discussions without submitting a written proposal,[188] was parried in turn by Wolf, who rejected it on behalf of his principals, but said he would be ready to confer personally.[189] Weizmann and Wolf did meet on December 22, 1914, and apparently had a pleasant conversation.[190] Yet while the two sides were jockeying for position, Wolf sought to discredit the impression that Weizmann spoke for the Anglo-Jewish community at large. That privilege, Wolf pointed out, to Sir William Tyrrell, private secretary to the foreign secretary, was the exclusive prerogative of the Conjoint Foreign Committee.[191]

Tschlenow and Sokolow, who arrived on December 31, 1914, were active in London, with side trips to Paris during the early months of 1915. Among the first issues they dealt with were the proposed talks with the Conjoint Foreign Committee. Like Weizmann, the two Russians refused to submit to Wolf's demand to present their proposals in writing.[192] Finally, the joint presidents of the Conjoint agreed to discuss the Palestine question informally. In the meantime, Wolf had seen Herbert Samuel on February 28, 1915, and expounded his view that the cultural policy, including perhaps a Jewish university, free immigration, and facilities for colonization, together with equal political rights for the rest of the population, should be "the limit of our striving."[193] Not content with lobbying with Samuel, Wolf wrote two weeks prior to the meeting with the Zionists to ask for an interview with Lloyd George to be able to counter the Zionist arguments: "I understand that he [Lloyd George] has seen one of the Zionist leaders [Weizmann] and some of my colleagues on the Conjoint Committee think that he ought to know what we think."[194] Clearly the Conjoint Foreign Committee was laying the groundwork for a policy that would have the backing of leading Anglo-Jews and high-ranking government officials—precisely Weizmann's own strategy.

The "informal" conference took place on April 14, 1915, and included, on the Zionist side, Tschlenow and Sokolow representing the Smaller Actions Committee, Gaster, Joseph Cowen and Herbert Bentwich, president of the Order of Ancient Maccabeans. Weizmann was absent due to his commitments at the Admiralty, where he had just begun his scientific work. The Conjoint was represented by its joint presidents, D. L. Alexander and Claude Montefiore, H. S. Henriques and Lucien Wolf. The Zionists were given the floor, and they got straight to the point. Sacher's apolitical presentation to Wolf of November 1914 was not even mentioned. The Zionist aims were clear. They asked if the Conjoint Foreign Committee would help them secure facilities in Palestine for the creation of a Jewish commonwealth. Such facilities would include the granting of preferential political and economic rights to a Jewish chartered company in order to enable the Jewish settlers to increase at a quicker pace than other minorities.[195] After the Zionists presented their views, the meeting adjourned.

On April 27, 1915, the Conjoint Foreign Committee sent a written statement of its response, which said, among other things:

> The Conjoint Committee regret to be compelled to give a negative answer . . . on the following grounds. . . . That they are of opinion that the most hopeful solution of the Jewish problem still lies in the direction of civil and political emancipation in lands in which the Jews are persecuted and oppressed. . . .
>
> That they regard the nationalist postulate of the Zionists and their scheme of special rights for the Jews in Palestine as calculated to stimulate Anti-Semitism, and to imperil the rights enjoyed by Jews in countries where their political emancipation has already been won.[196]

In their rejoinder the Zionists expressed the view that:

> while civil and political emancipation is a demand of elementary justice in all civilized countries, it cannot be regarded as a solution of Jewish difficulties. . . . Only when the Jewish people is itself emancipated will Jews attain to that status which is necessary to secure for them immunity from persecution. . . . This required the creation of a Jewish center—a home for Jews as well as Judaism in the old Jewish land. . . . There is abundant evidence that Jewish attempts at assimilation have often been a strong stimulus for anti-semitic agitations. The Conjoint Committee ignored the question of its own attitude towards an English Protectorate or other scheme of control of Palestine by the British Government.[197]

On this last point the Conjoint Foreign Committee once again "noted with regret," in the reply of June 11, 1915, that:

Apart from the fact that the Zionists have already been made aware orally of the views of the representatives of the Committee on this question, it should be obvious that at this juncture it would be highly inappropriate, and even tactless, from the point of view of the harmonious cooperation of the Allies, to raise this question in any formal shape. Moreover, the Committee, as an exclusively British body, cannot well discuss, and still less concert, measures in regard to a question of British Imperial policy with other bodies largely composed of foreign, and to some extent even of enemy alien, elements.[198]

The non-Zionists, correctly seeing in the Zionist formula a challenge and a proposed alternative to their faith in emancipation as a solution—everywhere—of the Jewish problem, also saw in it an implied claim that the Jews—everywhere—belonged to a distinct political entity. This implication, they felt, threatened to sustain antisemitic charges that the Jews were disloyal to their citizenship in the countries that had emancipated them, and they feared in the Zionist claim to a special, favored status as immigrants to Palestine a similar effect, detrimental to Jewish demands for equal rights in the Diaspora. While the Zionists were ready to deny such implications, arguing that they were false interpretations of Zionist principles, they were adamantly opposed to the non-Zionist formulas that omitted to call for national status for Jews in Palestine and a legal framework to facilitate the large-scale resettlement of Jews there as a national right. On these disputed issues, the negotiations came to an end, as was inevitable. Neither Weizmann in his negotiations with Zangwill, nor Sacher in his with Wolf, could hope to get very far once the issue of the "national postulate" came up and was seriously discussed.

For his part, Weizmann was not unhappy to see the negotiations collapse. A compromise with the Conjoint Foreign Committee would have tied his hands to prescribed guidelines and rules of conduct. He was now more or less free to pursue his lobbying and agitation—as were Wolf and his colleagues—with British sympathizers in all walks of life. Yet the time was not yet ripe for "action," as he had hoped in September 1914. At the end of the year he wrote in a gloomy mood to Vera: "Another year comes to an end. . . . Who can say whether the destiny of a free Israel is being forged amidst the guns? Has it fallen to our lot, my dearest, to share in the great story of Jewry's restoration?"[199] By the spring of 1915, Weizmann had begun to forge the destiny of Israel by laying the groundwork for the political formula that—though not yet articulated by either the British or the WZO—would eventually be acceptable to both.

II

Acetone

During the few months following the outbreak of the war, Chaim Weizmann was immersed in political activity, outlining to his friends in the United States, England, and elsewhere one plan after another that would help prepare the Zionist movement for pressing its demands before the postwar peace conference. But he was also busy at Manchester University. Many of the younger members of the staff had enlisted, and those who remained had to take on extra chores. In addition, he felt it was his duty to enlist in a training corps.[1] With frequent and exhausting seven-hour round trips to London,[2] conferences with British politicians and Jewish notables, and a heavy correspondence, he had little time to rest or even to devote to his experiments. Yet by 1914 he had made some important advances in his fermentation process that went beyond those discoveries made in 1910–12 by himself and others working for the Synthetic Products Company, Ltd., owned by E. Halford Strange.[3] In February 1910, William Perkin, the senior professor of organic chemistry at Manchester University, employed Weizmann in research on the production of synthetic rubber for which Perkin had a contract with Strange, whose firm attempted to find a good method of making isoprene, which presumably would enable its scientists to convert it into synthetic rubber.[4]

Once Weizmann was hired by his senior colleague, he suggested in turn that Professor Auguste Fernbach, director of the Fermentation Laboratory at the Pasteur Institute, also be asked to join the research team. Fernbach agreed, and by the autumn of 1910 an Anglo-French research syndicate was formed to investigate the question of synthetic rubber simultaneously in Manchester and in Paris.[5] Early in 1911 both Fernbach and Weizmann had found a mixture of bacteria that would ferment the starch in potatoes, yielding amyl alcohol, among other products. Thereupon they concentrated their efforts on the amyl alcohol route to isoprene and synthetic rubber. By the end of March 1911 the experiments in Paris and Manchester were found to produce butyl alcohol, and from that time the energies of the researchers were diverted toward ascertain-

Weizmann on the eve of World War I. Courtesy: Central Zionist Archives

ing the means by which this material could best be obtained. The first task was to discover or select the particular bacillus that would give the best results. This bacillus was discovered in June 1911 by Fernbach— hence referred to as BF (Bacillus Fernbach, later changed to FB)—and a culture of that bacillus was sent to Weizmann that same month together with cultures of other bacteria. Among these was one Fernbach referred to as the butylic bacillus of Fitz, which came from a seed R. H. Fitz, one of the pioneers of bacteriology, had placed in a tube twenty-five years earlier. Fitz had published various papers beginning in 1878, from which it appeared he had succeeded in isolating a bacillus that would ferment some of the carbohydrates to produce butyl alcohol. Whether or not the culture sent by Fernbach was, in fact, the bacillus of Fitz, it proved to be a very inert and degenerate fermenter and could not ferment maize at all. It may very well have been a degenerate member of the species FB.[6]

While Weizmann and Fernbach were struggling to make headway on the question of fermentation with a view to converting starch into sugar and then into alcohol,[7] an important discovery was made in March 1912 by one Mr. Kane, the works manager of Strange's company in its factory at Rainham. Using FB and working with some crude methods of distillation, Kane realized that, in addition to other products of the fermentation of starch, there was a considerable quantity of acetone.[8] Kane's work appears to have been the first simultaneous production of acetone and butyl alcohol by fermentation of carbohydrates.[9] The discovery of acetone was, of course, made known to Weizmann, who did not immediately grasp its industrial implications.[10] Strange, on the other hand, realized at once that this discovery could have momentous implications for his business.[11] Acetone, used at the time largely as a solvent, was made by dry distillation of wood. One of its most important uses was to reduce the temperature of the explosion and thus slow the erosion of gun barrels, allowing for the firing of more rounds per barrel. But of even greater importance was acetone's ability to make propellants "smokeless." When treated with acetone, cordite burns with a minimum of smoke—a discovery that became very important when World War I broke out.[12]

In the weeks that followed Kane's discovery there were sharp disagreements between Weizmann and Perkin over the financial terms of their contract, and on June 23, 1912, Perkin dismissed Weizmann from the Anglo-French team.[13] After his dismissal, Weizmann took a brief holiday and then continued his research in bacteriology with a much more thorough study of the butyl alcohol and acetone-producing organisms than had previously been made. His research was partially supported by funds provided by his friend Julius Simon. Moreover, after he was appointed reader at Manchester University in 1913, Weizmann had at his disposal excellent laboratory facilities specifically equipped for research in biochemistry.[14] From July to November 1912, he devoted himself to a careful study of the literature on this subject.[15] Weizmann was a master in the art of combing scientific literature, and his excellent memory, command of languages, untiring energy, and patience in experimental work all served him well. He studied the literature from about 1878, when Fitz had first produced butyl alcohol through the fermentation of glycerol. One particularly interesting paper, written by Gustav Bredemann in 1909, described the morphological and biochemical properties of a large number of closely allied bacteria that had been isolated by various workers from time to time and had the common property of fermenting nutrient media containing starch or other carbohydrates. But Bredemann had dealt with the subject more from a botanical than a biochemical viewpoint, and contradictory statements or experiments by various authors left the matter far from clear. Weizmann then began to investigate many bacteria—Bredemann had mentioned twenty-nine—some of which Weizmann isolated from various samples of soil, others of which he had acquired in November 1913 from Kraal's museum in Vienna.[16]

During the rest of 1912 and throughout most of 1913, Weizmann continued to attempt to isolate a bacillus that would give him consistently good results. It was a slow and often frustrating process, and on November 4, 1913, he wrote to his erstwhile collaborator and Fernbach's assistant, Moses Schoen, asking him for two favors: "To send me cultures of FB. Mine are old and I fear that they are no longer able to work well," and "Write me once more exactly how you perform your maize fermentation. I did it according to your instructions, but without being able to obtain a correct and good fermentation. . . . It is probable that I am doing everything right, but there must be some trick somewhere."[17] Three weeks later, Schoen replied with obvious discomfort:

> Your question as to the maize fermentation puts me, I may say quite frankly to you, in a very difficult position. The state of affairs is namely that according to the experiments at Rainham, the manufacture has assumed now quite a different form from that in which we have carried it on here up to the present. I must take advice as to whether I have the right to communicate this method of manufacture. What we have done up to the present would have no interest for you. . . . I do not know whether I have a right without first enquiring of the interested parties, to make any communication in a matter which no longer belongs to me. I cannot ask "straight out." On the other hand I run the risk that you would take my refusal in bad form and would be angry with me. Please do not do that. I trust you will understand my position. . . . It has always been my endeavour to discover ways in which we could work together. Unfortunately I am in too subordinate a position to take any independent steps.[18]

Having made up his mind to discover the right bacillus, Weizmann was undaunted by the refusal of the Pasteur people to share information. Some time in 1914 he had an insight that put him on the right track. His idea was that the most likely source of organism that would ferment a cereal mash such as maize was the cereal itself or parts of the growing plant. So obsessed was he by this notion that the failure of numerous experiments conducted along these lines did not deter him. His method was as follows: He inoculated a large number of test tubes, containing hot sterilized maize mash with small quantities of maize meal, then he cooled the tubes and inoculated them at 37°C.[19] After two or three days of inoculation, he examined each tube. He discarded those showing no signs of gas formation, and among the others he searched for a tube having an odor of butyl alcohol.[20] After many failures he at last succeeded in finding a tube with the odor of butyl alcohol, and from this tube he finally obtained a pure culture of a bacillus to which he gave the name Bacillus Y. For many years thereafter Weizmann and his collaborators called this bacillus, simply, BY.[21] Later on, because the bacillus in its sporing form assumes the shape of a clostridium and the characteristic products of the fermentation are acetone and butyl alcohol, it was given the systematic name Clostridium aceto-butylicum Weizmann.[22]

In his university laboratory Weizmann had the assistance of a student named Jacob Holker who, while working under Weizmann and with his apparatus, isolated a bacterium from maize that had the desired effect of fermenting maize to butylic alcohol and to acetone. Weizmann and the others working in the laboratory called this bacterium HB (Holker's Bacterium). A thesis describing it was submitted to Manchester University in 1915 in the joint names of Weizmann and Holker.

There was apparently no sufficient evidence to prove that the bacter-

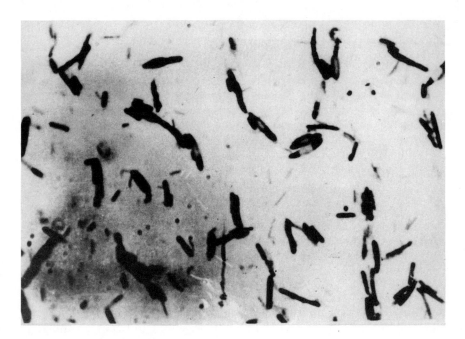

Bacillus BY. Courtesy: Weizmann Archives

ium isolated by Jacob Holker was identical with the one isolated by Weizmann or that they came from the same source. Rather, it seems that they were working on parallel lines and that Holker's later claim that he had provided the basis for Weizmann's large-scale production of acetone was without foundation.[23] Curiously, a copy of an agreement between Holker and Weizmann, probably from early January 1916 and drawn by Harold Addleshaw, Weizmann's solicitor in Manchester, specifies payments to Holker by Weizmann based on any royalties the latter might receive from their joint discovery. It is interesting to note that the terms Weizmann offered to Holker were almost identical to those Perkin had offered Weizmann some six years earlier.[24] There is no evidence extant that the contract between Weizmann and Holker was ever consummated, but the fact that it was drawn by Weizmann's solicitor would seem to indicate that Weizmann did believe—at least initially—that Holker had a claim.[25] Weizmann's patents for the war years do not list Holker as a co-inventor.

Weizmann found that his newly discovered bacillus had the ability to ferment starch directly, without prior treatment, since it contained maltase, which can split starch to "fermentable" sugars. Thus Weizmann's bacillus (BY) had the ability to ferment maize directly without the aid of a stimulant, whereas Fernbach's bacillus (FB) could not ferment unhydrolized maize appreciably, with or without a stimulant. Moreover, BY could liquify gelatin, which FB could not do. BY was not sensitive to oxygen as was FB, and BY could ferment potatoes more completely than did FB.[26] At the end of the fermentation process Weizmann discovered that the solution he obtained contained butanol, acetone, and a little ethyl alcohol. There were three times as much acetone as alcohol and twice as much butanol as acetone. These three solvents could then be separated from one another in pure form by fairly simple distilling operations. In finding a vigorous organism tolerant to acid conditions and enabling a superior yield of butyl alcohol plus acetone, Weizmann proved his skill as a biochemist. He had isolated and improved a bacillus that was far more active than that used by Fernbach, one capable of fermenting carbohydrates such as rice, maize, and horse chestnuts.[27] Weizmann did not immediately realize the potential significance of acetone; his interest was only in butanol as a necessary raw material for his synthetic rubber experiments.[28] Thus he did not at first intend to patent his invention. His original purpose was to publish the result of his research as a contribution to scientific literature.[29]

Halford Strange, on the other hand, who had realized some two years before World War I the potential importance of acetone for the British government and as a source for enriching himself,[30] had in the meantime expanded his company by raising subscriptions for shares.[31] Thus, while Weizmann's attention after his dismissal continued to be focused on the possibilities inherent in synthetic rubber, Fernbach, Schoen, Kane, and others working for Strange concentrated their energies on the production of acetone.[32] In the course of their researches, Fernbach and Schoen discovered a variant of FB, a bacillus they named FBBB and that was intended to be used in the fermentation of sawdust. In the meantime, Kane continued his work of installing a plant at Rainham. The plant was put into operation in the middle of 1913 using potatoes as its raw material. Fermentation work closed at Rainham in about June 1914, because in the meantime Strange had established a fermentation plant at King's Lynn[33] where, between September 28 and November 4, 1914, a series of demonstrations was conducted by the staff of the Synthetic Products Company in the presence of William Rintoul, head of the research department of Nobel's Explosives Company.[34] The material used in these demonstrations was potatoes, and the bacteria employed were FB and possibly FBBB.[35] The demonstrations were not very successful. More than 25 percent of the starch in the potatoes remained unconverted, and the total production of acetone and butyl alcohol from the starch that was converted amounted to only 4 percent of the potatoes. Rintoul calculated that the amount of starch in the potatoes averaged 16 percent. Nevertheless, the British government was in desperate need of acetone, and on April 19, 1915, Strange entered into a contract with the government for the supply of acetone. To carry out this contract, the government made an advance of £15,000 to the Synthetic Products Company to be applied to the expansion of its King's Lynn plant, which had been temporarily closed since November 1914.[36] Thus, in April 1915 the

King's Lynn plant was reopened, and work under the government contract began. Difficulties arose from the very beginning,[37] however, and Strange was never able to supply the minimum quantity of acetone—7 tons per week—stipulated in the contract. The plant was averaging instead less than 1 ton per week. Moreover, the acetone produced did not reach the specification standard and needed redistillation.[38] At the same time the managers of the plant were constantly worried that the supply of potatoes would not be adequate.[39]

During the same period in which Strange and his staff were demonstrating their fermentation process to Rintoul and negotiating a new contract with the government, Rintoul received a letter from Weizmann. One of Weizmann's colleagues at Manchester, Professor Harold B. Dixon, suggested that Weizmann inform Nobel's of his research and process for producing acetone.[40] Rintoul lost no time. Without notice, he appeared at Weizmann's university laboratory on February 9, 1915, to examine his laboratory and notebooks.[41] Rintoul was sufficiently intrigued with what he saw that within a fortnight he returned with a team of experts from the Nobel factory at Ardeer in Scotland. Weizmann had in the meantime checked with Charles Cook, the engineer at the university who had built for him the apparatus at the laboratory on a two-kilogram scale, to make sure that all would be ready for Rintoul's visit.[42] The visitors watched Weizmann demonstrating his process over a number of days.[43] The dour and canny Rintoul was now convinced that Weizmann had exactly what he desperately sought on behalf of Nobel's.[44] He immediately advised Weizmann, who had merely intended to publish his invention, to apply for a patent, and Weizmann did so the following month.[45] Rintoul also agreed to a contract very favorable from Weizmann's point of view.[46] A few months later—in August 1915—several hundred tons of TNT exploded at Ardeer and destroyed the Nobel plant. Rintoul, who thought it would take a long time to rebuild the plant, asked Weizmann to release Nobel from the contract, and Weizmann immediately agreed to do so.[47] But even before the disaster at Ardeer, Rintoul had informed his former works manager at Nobel's, Colonel Sir Frederick Nathan, of Weizmann's process. Sir Frederick—who besides being an explosives expert was also for many years the commander of the Jewish Lads Brigade—had early in 1915 been appointed adviser to the Admiralty on cordite supply. He was immediately convinced by Rintoul that the Manchester scientist was the man they were looking for and invited Weizmann to come down to London to discuss his process and its adaptability to government factories.[48]

Sir Frederick also realized at once what the men at Nobel's had recognized—that Weizmann's acetone process was the only source of acetone that could be produced in England on a scale large enough to ensure self-sufficiency in the supply of a material that was critical to the Royal Navy.[49] As has been pointed out, one of the important uses of acetone was in the preparation of smokeless powder or cordite, a pro-

pellant used in heavy artillery. Cordite is a mixture of 64 parts nitrocel-
lulose and 30.2 parts nitroglycerol stabilized with 5 parts petroleum jelly.
If this mixture is gelatinized with 0.8 percent acetone before being formed
into the desired shape, it burns with a minimum of smoke—of great
importance, since it means that the location of guns, especially the big
naval guns, could be concealed.[50] As a scholar of military explosives has
pointed out, "Cordite could not be manufactured without acetone, and
without cordite the guns would need to be extensively rebuilt to accommodate hotter propellants that would otherwise quickly erode their barrels."[51] In short, acetone was an irreplaceable ingredient in the manufacture of cordite, the major propellant employed in all projectile
manufacture in Britain—from bullets for the smallest handgun to shells
for the greatest howitzer.[52]

To understand why men such as Rintoul and Nathan were so excited
over Weizmann's process, it is necessary briefly to survey the condition
of Britain's munitions industry at the beginning of the war.[53] The solvent then used in cordite manufacture, acetone, was produced almost
entirely by the destructive distillation of wood (about 1 ton of acetone
was obtained from about 80–100 tons of birch, beech, or maple)[54] and
was imported from the great timber-growing countries—Germany, the
United States, Canada, and Austria. Under normal conditions, the price
for this material was low, and British firms could not compete for the
market. In 1913 the Office of Forests and Woods erected a factory at
Coleford, in the Forest of Dean, where a plant for carbonizing waste
hardwood was laid out along modern German lines.[55] Nevertheless, in
terms of the national need, the output of acetone in this factory (100–
400 tons yearly) was insignificant. In fact, all the forests of Great Britain
would probably have been insufficient for the production of acetone by
the accepted method.[56] Thus Great Britain was dependent upon imported acetone and by 1914 had accumulated only 3,200 tons at the Royal
Gunpowder Factory.

By the spring of 1915, the position in the American acetone market
had become extremely delicate. British cordite firms were competing with
one another and with the agents for the Allies. Prices were driven up,
and some American contractors threatened to default on their orders.
Even if all the overseas supplies had been available at the start of the
war, they would still have fallen considerably below the national requirements.[57] As has been seen, the British government was disappointed by Strange's Synthetic Products Company. The government had
also turned for help to Perkin, who proposed a catalytic process for the
production of acetone from ethanol (ethyl alcohol) worked out by J.
Crosfield and Sons. Ethanol was converted into acetaldehyde, acetaldehyde into acetic acid, and acetic acid into acetone. Under agreement
with the government, the firm erected a plant for an estimated output
of 100 tons monthly. It was complete in March 1917, but considerable
difficulty arose in bringing the acetone up to government standards. The

output never passed beyond the experimental stage of some 4 tons weekly, and after August 1917 the Perkin process was used only for the production of acetic acid.[58] Thus, of the three scientists in whom the government placed its hopes—Fernbach, Perkin, and Weizmann—only Weizmann was able to meet the requirements of the British cordite industry. He was able for the first time to apply successfully a biotechnological process on an industrial scale, a process in which bacteria were used instead of chemical reagents.[59] Moreover, Weizmann's process was probably the first to produce synthetic aliphatic organic compounds (in contrast to aromatic organics) on a large scale.

On April 21, 1915, Weizmann met Nathan in London and immediately agreed to carry out large-scale trials for the Admiralty.[60] He was so honored by the recognition he received for his work from the highest quarters that, without consulting his solicitor—as he had done when negotiating with Rintoul—he proposed postponing remuneration or royalties during the period of crisis. Should the Admiralty manufacture acetone by this process after the war, he would leave the question of remuneration in its hands. Apparently Weizmann and Nathan agreed that after the war Weizmann could patent and exploit his invention in any country he wished for commercial purposes.[61] For the duration, Weizmann's patent (no. 4845) could not be published and was to be kept secret.[62] For the time being, Weizmann requested only £500, which would enable him to continue his research and hire Harold Davies, his faithful collaborator since 1910, as an assistant. What seemed to be an inordinately hasty action, in complete contrast with Weizmann's long-term wish to consolidate his financial situation, accorded in fact with his aristocratic predilection—his wish to be seen as an independent person, not beholden to British officials for financial favors. Possibly he did not want to seem to be taking personal advantage of the military situation; his desire to appear genteel and English led him to mimic what he had come to see in English elite circles as the proper way to behave.

Nathan was only too happy with this arrangement, which he authorized on May 12, 1915.[63] In his autobiography, Weizmann asserted that Nathan then took him to meet Winston Churchill, first lord of the admiralty, who bellowed: "Well Dr. Weizmann, we need thirty thousand tons of acetone. Can you make it?" Churchill, claims Weizmann, was satisfied with the answer and gave him carte blanche.[64] In fact, there is no evidence that Weizmann met Churchill at that time. It is unlikely that Weizmann—who had a strong need to inflate his importance—would have met the scion of the duke of Marlborough without at least mentioning such an encounter in his letters or noting it in his appointment book.[65] Nathan alone, it seems, had authorized Weizmann's appointment and large-scale experiments. In any case, soon after Weizmann began working for the Admiralty, Churchill was dismissed from office as the man responsible for the Dardanelles debacle and shunted aside to the duchy of Lancaster, and Arthur James Balfour was named first lord of the admiralty. Though there is no evidence from written sources, quite possibly Balfour's strong interest in the promotion of scientific research and his awareness of Weizmann's work for the government created an additional bond between the two.[66]

Weizmann started by building a pilot plant. The Admiralty selected the Nicholson gin factory in Bromley-by-Bow, which was ready by July 1915.[67] The first large trials were successfully conducted at the end of July 1915 on a 60-gallon scale and afterward on a 2,000-gallon scale.[68] The results were even better than Weizmann had expected: "We obtained a yield of about 7½% and I committed myself only to 7% in all my negotiations with the Admiralty. Sir Frederick Nathan was at the works yesterday, saw the experiment and was very satisfied indeed."[69] A few weeks later Weizmann was already experimenting on an even larger scale, and, despite some minor problems, work also went well.[70] The Admiralty decided in September 1915 to set up a 15,000-gallon iron tank on the premises of the Royal Naval Cordite Factory at Holton Heath, near Wareham, Dorset. The trials there were completed in mid-January 1916, with satisfactory results. The Admiralty then decided to build its own plant for the annual production of 2,000 tons of acetone and 4,000 tons of butyl alcohol by the Weizmann process. It was completed in 1916 at Poole, near Wareham (the site of the Royal Naval Cordite Factory), placed under the direction of Captain Arthur Desborough, RN, and made a successful start in 1917.

In the meantime a number of key administrators in the Ministry of Munitions were also watching with interest Weizmann's preparations for and successful conduct of his first large-scale experiments. To Ahad Ha'Am, Weizmann mentioned that the Admiralty officials and Lord Moulton "are very pleased."[71] Moulton, a lawyer and a scientist, had been concerned with the question of munition supplies since early on in the war. In November 1914 the responsibility for maintaining an adequate supply of high explosives and of the raw materials for their manufacture was assumed by the newly established Committee on High Explosives under Moulton's chairmanship. In January 1915 this committee was merged in the Explosive Supplies Branch of the War Department, and in May 1915 this organization was taken over by the newly created Ministry of Munitions and was henceforth known as the Department of Explosive Supplies. Moulton was appointed director general of explosive supplies.[72] The first minister of munitions in Asquith's coalition cabinet was Lloyd George.[73] A year of war on a scale never foreseen, the creation of armies larger than ever contemplated, and the demand for unprecedented quantities of matériel showed the necessity of providing centralized direction of war production. Lloyd George's forceful personality made him an ideal candidate for providing that direction. His year of office at the Ministry of Munitions transformed the British economy as well as his own national standing.

C. P. Scott, an old supporter and friend of Lloyd George, had already

introduced Weizmann to Lloyd George, then chancellor of the exchequer, in January 1915.[74] No sooner was Lloyd George installed in his
office at the Ministry of Munitions than Scott brought Weizmann's valuable process to his attention.[75] Lloyd George received Weizmann on
Monday, June 7, 1915. The entire interview lasted only a few minutes,
and Weizmann did not even have a chance properly to discuss the acetone process. All he could manage to squeeze into the conversation was
the need to mobilize French and Swiss scientists to help British scientists
in the manufacture of explosives. He offered to go to the Continent and
hire the best men for the job. Lloyd George nodded in approval and
hurried on to the next appointment.[76] To make certain that the points
he had made would indeed register with the minister, Weizmann sent a
memorandum on the subject a few days later.[77] Lloyd George was not
at all concerned by the fact that Weizmann had already handed over his
process to the Admiralty. He immediately instructed Moulton to be in
touch with Weizmann and work out the necessary arrangements that
would tie Weizmann to the Ministry of Munitions as well. At the end of
August 1915, the Ministry of Munitions conducted its own trials of
Weizmann's process and was satisfied with the results.

As soon as the first round of experiments at the Nicholson gin factory
were over, Weizmann wanted official recognition for his work. He reported to Scott: "I took the liberty to mention to [Sir Frederick Nathan]
that I would have very much liked that the Admiralty should in some
form recognize it [the successful experiments] by giving me a certain
status; this should not involve necessarily any payments; that I would
leave it entirely to them to find the form. He agreed with it and said
that the matter will be considered in a few days." Weizmann wanted
similar recognition from the Ministry of Munitions:

> I see that Mr. Lloyd George is announcing the formation of a scientific com-
> mittee for the Ministry of Munitions and I would not like to be again left
> out in the cold; but it is quite likely that I shall be "forgotten" if Dr. Addison
> has charge of the matter, as he would not like to see me. But I owe it to my
> position and to my future to make a stand now and I hope you will not
> think me petty or mean if I speak of it. I gave and am ready to give all I can
> unreservedly, but would like to be placed on the same footing with other
> chemists or scientists who have all the credit although they did less. Of
> course I cannot speak to Mr. L.G. about it, much less to Mr. Addison and I
> am craving for your kind advice.[78]

Sir Frederick, grateful for Weizmann's invaluable service, was as good
as his word. In September 1915, Weizmann was made "Temporary Honorary Technical Adviser to the Admiralty on Acetone Supplies," an appointment that carried with it a grant of £2,000 a year for two years for
scientific research. At the same time, Scott seems to have intervened on
Weizmann's behalf directly with Lloyd George. Thus, despite the combined opposition of Christopher Addison and Moulton—the two key

officials in the Ministry of Munitions—Weizmann was that same month given a one-year appointment as "Chemical Adviser to the Ministry of Munitions on Acetone Supplies," with a salary of £1,500 and an allowance of £500 for removal expenses from Manchester to London.[79] His research was henceforth conducted at the Lister Institute in London at the joint expense of the Admiralty and the Ministry of Munitions.[80] Until the autumn of 1915, Weizmann spent numerous hours on the train between Manchester and London; the physical and emotional strain was difficult to bear. With the appointment letters in his possession, he moved to London by mid-September 1915.[81] At the request of the Ministry of Munitions, Weizmann was given leave of absence from Manchester University.[82]

All that remained to do, Weizmann thought, was to work hard and fulfill the expectations placed in him for the production of acetone. He began an exhausting schedule shuttling between the Lister Institute, Bromley, and the Ministry of Munitions office in Storey's Gate.[83] It was grueling but satisfying work, which he slowly and consciously began to combine with Zionist politics.[84]

Weizmann sought to perform yet another valuable scientific service for Great Britain. Picric acid and trinitrotoluene, the two most important high explosives employed by the British services, were manufactured respectively from the raw material phenol and toluene, two of the many chemical substances obtained by distillation of coal tar. In times of peace these products were used in the manufacture of dyestuffs, an industry that had its birth in England but then largely passed into the hands of German chemists. In August 1914, therefore, the Germans were able to turn with ease the vast resources of a flourishing coal tar industry to the production of high explosives. In England, although large quantities of coal were carbonized every year, a general lack of interest in the synthetic dye industry meant that the tar distillers had never considered it worth their while to utilize to the utmost the chemical resources of the coal. With the outbreak of the war, the supply of coal tar products assumed a new and unexpected significance. Benzene, another of the distillation products of coal tar, also became very important in explosives supply because the commercial product usually contained a high percentage of toluene and also because the benzene itself offered a starting point for the preparation of supplies of synthetic phenol when the natural supplies ceased to be adequate.[85]

Weizmann, whose early researches had focused on the dyestuff industry, was once again one of the few scientists in England ready and able to tackle the problems created by the shortages of toluene and phenol. He may have heard details of these shortages from Moulton[86] and at once offered his assistance.[87] Again it was Scott who made Lloyd George aware of Weizmann's expertise in this respect,[88] and on October 26, 1915, Weizmann was able to explain to the minister in person how he would go about alleviating the shortages through synthetic production. By February 1916 he had largely solved the problem of converting butyl alcohol into benzene and toluene and had received assurances from the Ministry of Munitions that production would begin on a large scale in the near future.[89] But by the end of 1916 or early in 1917 there was no longer need for these products since new, more efficient methods were discovered.[90] On the other hand, the Admiralty utilized another derivative of the Weizmann process, namely the conversion of butyl alcohol into methyl ethyl ketone, as a solvent in cordite manufacture, which was also used for the manufacture of aeroplane dope,[91] a product the French government was also eager to purchase.[92] This process had been fully developed by 1917 and was carried out at the cordite factory of the Canadian Explosives Company, Ltd.[93]

Weizmann's contributions and resourcefulness surely deserved the highest commendations. Instead, he found himself from the outset faced with difficulties placed in his way by the bureaucracy. From the moment he came in contact with the Ministry of Munitions, he encountered the intense and unexplained hostility of Christopher Addison and Lord Moulton.[94] Possibly they disliked the fact that this relatively obscure provincial chemist, a foreigner and Jew to boot, could gain access to Lloyd George without having to curry favor with them but simply by mobilizing C. P. Scott. Whatever the reason, Weizmann found that although he had received written permission from Moulton to travel to France and Switzerland to hire chemists for the British war industry, the officials at the Ministry of Munitions were opposed to his trip. Their opposition was stiffened, it seems, when they found out that the French government was seriously interested in Weizmann's process.[95] Scott, who in any case had a low opinion of Moulton,[96] was aware of the difficulties the director general of explosive supplies was causing Weizmann and spoke to Lloyd George about it on a number of occasions.[97] Lloyd George himself had no liking for the independent Moulton, but since he could not easily dismiss him, he borrowed Nathan from the Admiralty as a consultant to the Ministry of Munitions, where he could act as a check on Moulton.[98] But Nathan was powerless against Moulton, who seems to have succeeded in planting the seed of suspicion against Weizmann in Lloyd George himself. When Scott met the minister for lunch on November 14, 1915, and mentioned that Weizmann wanted to accept the French government's invitation, Lloyd George exclaimed: "Don't let him settle anything about that till he has seen me." Later that day Scott recorded in his diary: "It is quite plain they don't really trust Weizmann and that there is a settled resolution not to let him go outside this country if they can help it—I fancy Ld. Moulton is at the bottom of this. Shall take first opportunity of challenging."[99]

The opportunity came within a fortnight. On November 26, Scott arrived with Weizmann and Herbert Samuel for lunch with Lloyd George. Before joining the others, Scott had a few minutes alone with Lloyd George in which to ask whether the persistent and unaccountable opposition to Weizmann's being allowed to leave the country for important scientific work originated with Moulton or whether there was any mistrust of Weizmann on the ground that he might give valuable information to Germany. Lloyd George absolutely repudiated any mistrust on his part: "When I trust a man I trust him altogether—It's no use trusting by halves." At lunch all four spoke quite freely about Moulton's "incompetence, vanity and obstructiveness." After Samuel left, they agreed that in the afternoon Lloyd George would meet Scott, Weizmann, and Nathan to discuss the matter further. When Scott arrived, Nathan was waiting outside the minister's office. "He expressed, in a short conversation, before W[eizmann] arrived, a high opinion of him, but seemed to think he was a little difficult to work with." When they all gathered in Lloyd George's office, they continued to disparage Moulton's work. "In the course of the conversation," remarked Scott in his diary, "it appeared that Ll[oyd] G[eorge] has absolutely no competent scientific chemical adviser on the problems of synthetic or bio-chemistry on which everything depends . . . so it all comes back to Weizmann." Having spent the better part of the day discussing Weizmann's role in the Ministry of Munitions, Lloyd George was now convinced that Weizmann had been treated unfairly and advised him to go to Paris; if challenged he was to say that he had Lloyd George's authority.[100] However, Major Walter Bagot, an official in the Ministry of Munitions acting on Moulton's authority, would not release Weizmann's English passport. Once again Weizmann turned to Scott,[101] who immediately forwarded Weizmann's letter to Lloyd George with his own note:

It seems pretty plain that Weizmann's position in relation to Lord Moulton is untenable and it is also pretty plain that unless the conditions are altered and the whole acetone process on the great scale placed under different control, you will not get your supply of acetone. Under a man like Sir F. Nathan who understands how to carry out such an undertaking and how to treat the men who, on the scientific side, are responsible for it, everything would go like clock-work, as everything does at the Admiralty. I don't know whether it would be possible to isolate this part of the munitions work, but I am afraid that unless a change can be made Weizmann will say it is useless for him to try to carry on. Perhaps you will see him on the matter.[102]

Apparently Lloyd George acted at once to have Weizmann's passport returned. But the affair did not end there. Scott's unfavorable comparison of Lloyd George's ministry with the Admiralty and the clear threat that Weizmann might withdraw from any further work under the Ministry of Munitions forced Lloyd George to a showdown with Moulton and his subordinates. Two weeks later, while having breakfast with Scott and Weizmann, Lloyd George gave a vivid account of the scene. He had been furious with them over the withholding of Weizmann's passport and had told them "that it was monstrous to treat a distinguished scientist who had given the best service to the country in that way. The

Minister even told them he'd be glad to accept their resignation—which they did not offer." Scott concluded his entry that day by observing: "What evidently had enraged him particularly was that they should treat Weizmann as a Jew and a foreigner in a way they would not venture to treat a man in a different position."[103]

On December 5, 1915, Weizmann left for France; he returned on December 10. Not much is known about his trip except that he saw Baron Edmond de Rothschild as well as Sir Francis Bertie, the British ambassador to France, and had discussions with French officials and scientists on the acetone process.[104] Upon his return, Weizmann concentrated all his energies on the large-scale tests that were to be conducted at the Royal Naval Cordite Factory in Holton Heath in mid-January 1916. They were a great success this time, as they had been when conducted for the Admiralty in July 1915. "The result," wrote Weizmann to his relative and collaborator Joseph Blumenfeld, "was simply brilliant. Instead of the expected 7% of acetone we got an output of 7½%; instead of 48 hours, fermentation took only 24 hours, exactly twice as fast. The whole operation was carried out in iron equipment. The matter has now progressed considerably and all the acetone required will be made here by this method. The method has passed all the tests and experiments much better than we all expected."[105] Again it was Scott who traveled especially from Manchester to London to inform Lloyd George in person of Weizmann's brilliant success.[106] A month later he repeated the journey, this time arriving at the Ministry of Munitions with Weizmann, who explained to Lloyd George yet another accomplishment—his conversion of butyl alcohol into toluene, promising to do the same for picric acid.[107] Less than a year earlier, Weizmann could not have dreamed that he would be working for the government, successfully conducting large chemical experiments in the service of his adopted country. War clearly afforded opportunities to those with useful skills and expertise, even if they came from the provinces and had no natural entry to government circles. Writing to Harold Davies, Weizmann could not contain his glee and sense of triumph: "In thinking of the progress we made in our fermentation, I cannot help wondering how neglectful Fernbach has been. He had years of time and experience, he had a splendid lab, money and help and just did nothing. I come to the conclusion that Strange has been badly had [by Perkin and Fernbach]."[108]

Following the successful experiments at the Admiralty site, the Ministry of Munitions decided in February 1916 to manufacture acetone by the Weizmann process on a very large scale, relying at the same time on the sale of the butyl alcohol by-product to make the manufacture a commercial success. Since it was estimated that there would be insufficient freight to import maize both for the acetone process and for the manufacture of potable spirit, it was decided to adapt the plants of some distilleries for making acetone.[109] Six distilleries were chosen, and in March 1916 work began to convert them for the manufacture of acetone, which they undertook to produce for the duration of the war. It was difficult to convert even those six distilleries initially found suitable; eventually only two produced acetone[110] and their consumption of grain was inefficient. Still, by February 1917 the two distilleries were capable of producing 228 tons of acetone a month.[111]

At the end of February 1916, Weizmann composed a long memorandum to Nathan, who had in the meantime been appointed by Lloyd George as director of propellant supplies at the Ministry of Munitions and thus Weizmann's direct superior. Recounting the evolution of his service to the government, Weizmann went on to highlight his many discoveries and achievements over the past year. The duties imposed upon him with the conversion of distilleries and the training of new staff all over the country had not been part of the original contracts with either the Admiralty or the Ministry of Munitions, but he was willing to undertake them. The new goal that had just been announced by the government was for 30,000 tons of acetone. Weizmann estimated that the government would save in its production some £2 million through the various processes he had handed over free of charge.[112] What it all meant was that once again Weizmann felt that his own status was not commensurate with his substantial accomplishments. "Somehow," he complained to Nathan, "I remain a temporary and anonymous worker and it is in the interest of the important work I have to perform that this state of things should be altered and my authority strengthened."[113] It is not clear whether by "important work" he was referring to the production of acetone or Zionist activity. Possibly he meant both, and apparently Scott did not need any more explanations. The tireless editor intervened with Nathan and Addison and persuaded them to change Weizmann's official status.[114]

As he did when working for the Admiralty, Sir Frederick found it easy—and cheap—to satisfy Weizmann with yet another high-sounding title. On April 5, 1916, Nathan wrote that now that it had been decided to make acetone on a large scale in the distilleries, their conversion and the actual routine of manufacture would become the responsibility of a separate branch of the Department of Explosive Supplies in the Ministry of Munitions.[115] Weizmann was to be named "Superintendent of the Lister Institute Government Laboratories," in charge of the research work and the preparation of bacteria; he was also charged with the training of bacteriologists and would have the status of technical adviser on all scientific and experimental work in connection with the production of acetone.[116] Though pleased with his new title, Weizmann was far from happy that he had been, in effect, excluded from the very distilleries that were using his process. His removal from direct supervision of the work in the distilleries created problems of communication and execution of the work from the very start. Often the managers of the distilleries received their instructions from officials in the Ministry of Munitions who did not consult Weizmann first. The inevitable consequences were that proper methods were not always used and the results of acetone fermentation were below what was expected. "Under the circumstances," Weizmann complained to Scott, "I can do no good. The acetone will never become a success."[117] Moreover, Nathan, his erstwhile ally against Moulton, seemed to be switching sides and began to deal harshly with Weizmann on a number of occasions.[118] Perhaps this was due to the fact that, as Sir Frederick had confided to Scott a few months earlier, Weizmann "was a little difficult to work with." Weizmann would have most likely tried to reverse some of Nathan's decisions, but he was then faced with new problems that preoccupied him for the next few months.

On December 2, 1915, Professor Harold B. Dixon,[119] who had followed Weizmann's career since his early days in Manchester, wrote to his junior colleague about a visit he had had that morning from Halford Strange of the Synthetic Products Company. Having heard that Weizmann was working on acetone for the government, Strange made the journey to Manchester to ascertain details about Weizmann's process. Dixon wrote that he did not divulge any unnecessary information except to say that Weizmann was working for the government on acetone and that his process was original. Dixon also informed Weizmann that Perkin, too, had had disagreements with Strange and had severed relations with the Synthetic Products Company. With Perkin out of the picture, would Weizmann not consider collaborating with Strange again? After all, Fernbach was earning large royalties under the old (FB) fermentation process, some of which should rightly belong to Weizmann. "To the best of my knowledge," concluded Dixon, "Strange is both generous and straight in his business dealings. . . . I should think that a meeting might be advantageous."[120]

Weizmann's negative response came by return mail, just before his trip to Paris: "What you say about Strange is rather interesting, but I am afraid I can do very little at present as the process is the property of the Admiralty and any negotiations can only be done through the Admiralty. The process, as you know, does not fall at all within the range of things patented by Strange so that certainly there can be no question of any infringement."[121] Upon his return from France, Weizmann found a letter from Strange that tried to entice him to a meeting with Strange and Fernbach by dangling before him substantial royalties on the basis of their old agreement.[122] Strange's attempted rapprochement with his erstwhile employee reflected the poor state of affairs at his company. A year earlier—while he was prospering—he had rebuffed Fernbach's suggestion that he mend relations with Weizmann: "With regard to Weizmann I cannot see what advantage is to be gained by endeavouring to purchase his friendship. I think any concession to him at the present time would merely excite his further cupidity."[123] Though he had no knowledge of what had transpired behind his back, Weizmann had had enough experience with Strange to know the man could not be trusted. In a curt reply, written on the stationery of the Lister Institute, Weizmann reminded Strange of the abortive negotiations in 1912–13 and concluded that he could not see that anything could be gained from a meeting but he would be willing to entertain any proposal that Strange and Fernbach would place before him in writing.[124]

In the meantime, while writing to Weizmann for an interview, Strange had also decided to force the issue by turning directly to the Ministry of Munitions, with which he had close contacts by virtue of his own government contract. Early in December 1915 his solicitors—Clapham, Fraser, Cook and Co.—wrote to Moulton. In that letter and others written over the next couple of months they submitted documents that in their opinion proved that Weizmann had been using a process that belonged to their client. Moreover, they expressed Strange's and Fernbach's apprehensions that Weizmann was about to sell this process to the French government. On March 1, 1916, they reiterated: "We would particularly call your Lordship's attention to the statement that the alleged Weizmann process is stated to produce one part of acetone and two parts of butyl alcohol, which is exactly the same proportion made by the Fernbach process, which was communicated by our client [Strange] and Professor Perkin under his employment agreements binding him to secrecy."[125]

These allegations only confirmed the suspicions Moulton had nursed since Weizmann had been appointed to the Ministry of Munitions. Moulton informed Nathan, who, late in April 1916, called Weizmann to his office for an explanation.[126] Nathan, who had the scientific background to pass judgment, was apparently satisfied that Weizmann was the discoverer of the BY bacillus. But this time it was Fernbach himself, probably coaxed by Strange and represented by the latter's solicitors, who turned to Nathan requesting an interview.[127] On May 26, 1916, Nathan and Moulton met Fernbach, Strange, and their lawyers. Moulton explained to them that the Department of Explosive Supplies had no authority to adjudicate claims. He also informed Weizmann of Strange's and Fernbach's consent to decide the matter by arbitration.[128] Weizmann was adamant about the originality of his own process and would not budge.[129] To be on the safe side, he sought the advice of Atkinson Adam, the patent agent to whom Rintoul had referred him for the patenting of his process. Adam confirmed that Fernbach and the Synthetic Products Company had no case. He and Weizmann's solicitors in London—Brestows, Cooke and Carpmael—agreed that since it was the government that used Weizmann's process, the only legal avenue for Strange and Fernbach was to sue the government—an unlikely possibility.[130] This assumption was subsequently borne out, though for some months afterward Strange's solicitors continued to threaten Weizmann with court proceedings unless he agreed to arbitration.[131] Weizmann had in the meantime taken the precaution of assembling all materials relevant to his process and his period of employment by the Synthetic Products Company to prepare for any legal proceedings against him.[132] The solicitors for both sides continued to exchange letters until the end of August 1916, but then Strange, recognizing that the government was fully ready to back Weizmann on the issue, allowed the brewing scandal to simmer down. It came to a boil once again only after the war.

What must have been particularly grating for Strange and Fernbach was the fact that their process, employing the FB bacillus at the King's Lynn plant, had done quite poorly. In view of the unsatisfactory results and the financial position of the Synthetic Products Company,[133] the factory was taken over by the government on March 14, 1916, under the Defence of the Realm Act, and turned over to the direct control of the Propellant Branch of the Department of Explosive Supplies.[134] No sooner was the contract with the Synthetic Products Company terminated and its staff dismissed from the plant than the government informed the factory's managers that Weizmann's process for making acetone from maize, rather than from potatoes, would henceforth be employed. This was rubbing salt into the wounds of Strange and Fernbach, and their irate reaction is understandable.[135] Weizmann himself was asked—and agreed—to oversee the work at the King's Lynn factory.[136] Yet, acting on the advice of Atkinson Adam and his lawyer in London, Weizmann tried to back out of his commitment.[137] To Lloyd George, Weizmann expressed his hesitation "to go to King's Lynn and in the presence of their work people put my process into practice, unless I can feel sure that they have failed entirely to produce acetone from maize. . . . I am sure you will appreciate that I cannot go into their works . . . unless I feel quite satisfied that there is already a record of the fact of such failure which will prevent them from alleging, after I have worked my process at their factory and attained satisfactory results that my process is in any way identical with theirs."[138]

Lloyd George, who was soon to leave the Ministry of Munitions to become secretary for war, passed on the correspondence to Christopher Addison. The latter wrote imperiously that he had heard from King's Lynn that Weizmann was refusing to send his cultures on various grounds:

> As you are aware, the arrangement with yourself includes the supply of your culture to the Ministry for the purposes of the State to be used in the conduct of your process in the production of acetone in the distilleries and other places which we take over or adapt for that purpose. This is one of them. I shall be glad, if you will immediately in accordance with our arrangement give . . . whoever may be appointed by the Department for that purpose, the necessary cultures to be used in the King's Lynn Factory. . . . In view of the present acetone position you will agree, I am sure, that no avoidable delay should be incurred. . . . You may be sure we will take every precaution that no advantage is taken of your culture being sent to this particular factory.[139]

Weizmann had no choice but to comply with Addison's "request."[140] He did have the satisfaction of decisively proving in Strange's own backyard that the BY bacillus was superior in every way to the FB bacillus. By March 16, 1916, the average production of acetone at King's Lynn employing the FB bacillus in potatoes was approximately half a ton per week. Once the government took over—still using FB and potatoes—the average improved to more than 1 ton a week. On June 19, Weizmann's bacillus began to be employed using maize as the raw material. From that date until December 13, 1916, the average weekly production of acetone was well over 4 tons a week. Weizmann was able to surmount initial difficulties at King's Lynn using his by then extensive knowledge.[141] Thus, from January 1, 1917, until the end of that year he was able to produce more than 5 tons a week,[142] more than ten times the average produced through Fernbach's process.[143] In July 1916, it was estimated that with Weizmann's bacilli the total output of acetone from all existing sources could reach 18,000 tons a year,[144] a factor that could be multiplied by the number of distilleries employed.[145]

However, the production of acetone by the Weizmann process using 500 tons of maize a month as raw material[146] ceased in February 1917 when the Ministry of Food prohibited the further use of imported grain as raw material for acetone production. This step almost—but not quite—put an end to the Weizmann process in England.[147] Some of Sir Frederick Nathan's collaborators in the Ministry of Munitions suggested that horse chestnuts be used instead of maize.[148] Weizmann immediately developed a scheme for making acetone from horse chestnuts and acorns, which have a high carbohydrate content.[149] Experiments were carried out at King's Lynn. During the autumn of 1917 some 3,000 tons of chestnuts were collected throughout England through voluntary efforts, mainly on the part of schoolchildren.[150] The quantity was restricted by transport difficulties, and initially the output that began at King's Lynn in April 1917 was hampered by the poor quality of the material.[151] Weizmann overcame this difficulty shortly before the factory closed in July 1918.[152]

By the beginning of 1917, demand for the production of acetone in England had declined in any case. The British government had taken over factories in Toronto (early in 1916) and Terre Haute, Indiana (early in 1917), which produced acetone by the Weizmann method, so the cessation of English production had a beneficial effect on the war effort.[153] Buying 7 tons of acetone from the American distilleries situated in the maize belt required less space than shipping 100 tons of maize. Moreover, a new kind of cordite, RDB, had been developed in the meantime in England, which used ethyl alcohol rather than acetone.[154]

While acetone was slowly losing its importance by the end of the war, butyl alcohol, which had once been called "futile alcohol" by William Perkin, would soon be recognized for the commercial possibilities that made Weizmann a wealthy man after the war. During the war, the most important concern of those working with butyl alcohol was how to dispose of it. With the coming of peace the process executed a kind of somersault, for while the price of acetone fell rapidly, the use of butyl alcohol, in the form of butyl acetate as a constituent of varnishes and spraying lacquers, was recognized. With the increase in the manufacture of cars in the United States, there was demand for quick-drying lacquers, which butyl acetate supplied. Thus it came about that the Commercial Solvents Corporation of America acquired the Weizmann patents, bought the distillery in Terre Haute, and continued employing the Weizmann process but this time with butyl alcohol as the main objective and acetone as a by-product. Later the company erected another plant in Peoria, Illinois, which in the peak years produced 30,000 tons a year. This large production of butyl alcohol in the United States at an average price of well under $100 per ton gives some idea of the boost the Weizmann process had given to industry. In 1912 the rare solvent had sold for some £19,000 per ton![155]

But in mid-1916 Weizmann was still deeply worried about his financial security. He had hoped to sell his acetone process to the French and Italian governments, and in the autumn of 1916, after all parties were convinced that Weizmann's process was superior to Fernbach's, he was confident that a contract with these governments was imminent.[156] This time it was Fernbach who—if he could not win a contract for his own invention—could at least rejoice in spoiling Weizmann's success. The French manufacturer to whom Weizmann was about to sell his process,[157] apparently in collusion with Fernbach, suddenly declared that Fernbach, too, had a sound method for the making of acetone. The manufacturer apparently wanted to squeeze better terms from Weizmann and in the process withheld information from the French government, which finally withdrew from the transaction. The Italian government, expecting to benefit from the production of acetone in France, was thus also no longer interested. Weizmann's dreams for large profits were decisively crushed by December 1916, almost exactly one year after the French naval attaché had urged him to go to Paris.[158] As his hopes for profits on the Continent were withering away, Weizmann must have often reflected on the rather hasty offer he had made at the beginning of his negotiations with the Admiralty and the Ministry of Munitions to renounce all remuneration for his process until after the war. On September 30, 1916, his contract with the Ministry of Munitions had just terminated, and prospects for making large sums of money in France and Italy had vanished. Though he had not yet resigned from Manchester University, he seems to have decided to remain in London. After living for a while with his family in rented quarters at 41 Campden House Road, the Weizmanns finally moved to their new house at 67 Addison Road in October 1916.[159] In the meantime they also held onto their house in Manchester, which added to their expenses. Finally, Vera Weizmann, who had to give up her position as medical officer at the Manchester clinic for expectant mothers, was expecting their second son, Michael, born on November 16, 1916. The loss of a second salary, the burden of maintaining two houses, and the new family responsibilities weighed heavily on Weizmann. A few days before Michael's birth, he wrote to Dorothy de Rothschild: "My own position is not secure. I cannot help thinking that I am living in *false prosperity*, which may come down like a pack of cards at any time. All the hopes were built on the pledge given to me by the Government. I don't suggest that the pledge won't be redeemed, but the way things go nowadays the redemption of promises are put off *ad infinitum* and the form which this redemption may take is a matter beyond my control."[160]

Yet, matters were not quite as bleak as Weizmann portrayed them. As his appointment with the Ministry of Munitions drew to an end, the Admiralty offered him a one-year appointment that carried a salary of £1,500, exactly what he had been earning at the Ministry of Munitions. During this period he was to continue his work at the Poole factory and at the Lister Institute in the development of the production of acetone as well as various by-products. He was also asked to make himself available, free of charge, to the Ministry of Munitions. The letter of appointment also stipulated "that this period [of employment with the Admiralty] will enable an opinion to be formed as to the actual success to be achieved in connection with the production of Acetone and the by-products from the point of view of assessing the amount of the award which you should be paid for your services as an inventor in the matter. My Lords have in view ultimately the payment of a lump sum down in full recognition of your services."[161]

In fact, discussions concerning remuneration were already well advanced. On March 23, 1916, a short while after the successful large-scale experiments with Weizmann's bacillus, Scott made a special journey to London to see Reginald McKenna, chancellor of the exchequer, to discuss the remuneration for Weizmann's process. Scott recorded in his diary that McKenna was fully sympathetic and "resolved that [Weizmann] should have his reward."[162] Five days later Weizmann, too, met McKenna and came away satisfied that he would be suitably rewarded.[163] Having given the matter some thought, McKenna once more discussed it with Scott, and they agreed on a capital sum of £50,000—a figure that Balfour, the first lord of the admiralty, also agreed to. The figure was suggested by Scott in accordance with Weizmann's wish to have a capital sum that would yield £2,000 a year in interest.[164] Despite the fact that Moulton and Nathan had advised delaying the matter,[165] once again Scott outmaneuvered them by getting Lloyd George to agree that it would be settled directly between the Admiralty and the Treasury without reference to the Ministry of Munitions. Balfour, however, unwilling to take decisive action without the full endorsement of his officials, vacillated and delayed the necessary authorization.[166] McKenna himself seemed to be inclined for a while to give Weizmann the award for his work on butyl alcohol, since the acetone process was given to the government free of charge.[167] The matter dragged on for months. In the meantime there were cabinet changes in December 1916: Lloyd George became prime minister (after six months as war secretary), Balfour became foreign secretary, and McKenna resigned. Their replacements— Christopher Addison, Edward Carson, and Andrew Bonar Law—had to be introduced to the subject of Weizmann's contributions and claims all over again, a task that Scott took upon himself with zeal and dedication.[168]

On March 9, 1917, no doubt after prior discussions with Weizmann, Scott informed his protégé that he was about to see the first lord of the admiralty, Sir Edward Carson, and he asked Weizmann to describe in some detail the services he had rendered to the government that "can be regarded as worth a reward of £50,000."[169] In reply, Weizmann recounted his various services in the production of acetone, butyl alcohol, benzene, and toluene. He summed up his memorandum with the estimate that at the present time the government was producing about 40 tons of acetone per week by his process and that he expected this figure to rise soon to 70 tons. He also reminded Scott that he had been prevented by the government from utilizing his process in the United States, thus incurring great financial loss. Weizmann also claimed that the Italian government was offering him a royalty of £6 per ton for use of his process.[170]

As usual, Scott performed his mission for Weizmann expeditiously and competently and apparently instructed Weizmann to write directly to the Admiralty, which Weizmann did on March 21, 1917. In his letter Weizmann pressed the Admiralty to make a decision on the question of his award. He claimed that the use of his process had met a national need and was also a success financially, both directly and indirectly, since it had prevented a great increase in the price of American acetone. He submitted the following proposals: (1) that the amount to be awarded him for his work in connection with his patents and the utilization by the government be taken up immediately; (2) that the amount so awarded should cover the use by the government during the war of his products for all naval and military purposes; (3) that after the war the government retain the right to use his inventions in all government factories for the manufacture of war materials without any further payments; (4) that he be at liberty to make arrangements with any of the Allied governments or their contractors with a view to their utilizing his processes for the manufacture of war materials both during and after the war; (5) that he retain the exclusive benefit of all his inventions both in England and abroad for all purposes outside government factories, but subject to the rights reserved to the government.[171]

The internal memoranda and minutes written by officials of the Admiralty in response to Weizmann's letter display a clear note of impatience. The officials reminded each other of the extent to which the Admiralty had assisted in developing Weizmann's inventions; he could not have proceeded with his work without the large sums of money invested in it by the government. They also pointed out that the restrictions imposed on the publication and foreign patenting of his inventions had the object of keeping the knowledge of the inventions from the enemy as long as possible. Some of the officials, moreover, remarked in their minutes that certain of Weizmann's inventions—such as his proposal to convert butyl alcohol into coal tar derivative products, including toluol, benzol, and anthracine—were not quite as useful to the war effort as Weizmann claimed. As to methyl ethyl ketone, they claimed he had simply perfected an already published process by reworking the details of sulphuration, which he had hoped to render more economical by the adoption of a different catalyst not hitherto proposed. It appears that Weizmann had offered this process to Nobel's, which did not regard the matter as a commercial proposition.[172]

These less than complimentary assessments on the part of some of the officials in the Admiralty could not, however, stop the process of granting Weizmann his due reward.[173] Writing to a colleague at the Treasury, Sir Graham Greene, the permanent secretary at the Admiralty, pointed out, "Dr. Weizmann has apparently some influential friends and they have now approached the present First Lord and pressed that the question of award should not be longer delayed." Yet, pointed out Sir Graham, "up to now the full commercial manufacture of acetone by Dr. Weizmann's process is not yet in complete working order, and it may not be possible for some little time yet to assess the complete success of the process, and therefore, presumably the amount of the award which should be paid to Dr. Weizmann."[174] Weizmann himself admitted in his letter of March 21, 1917, that "the question whether my processes will prove to be useful for commercial and industrial purposes has yet to be ascertained."[175] Since Weizmann was "anxious that some steps should be taken to consider his services," the first lord nevertheless decided to appoint an *ad hoc* committee to consider the matter.[176] But in addition to the pressure exerted by Scott and Weizmann, the Admiralty was also intent on honoring its pledge to Weizmann, made in the fall of 1916, that during his term of service for the Admiralty, which was to end in August 1917, he would be notified of the lump sum to be awarded to him.[177] Robert Chalmers of the Treasury, who was notified of this pledge by Sir Graham Greene, replied that he had no objection to constituting a committee provided Weizmann would promise not to appeal its decision. Moreover, he was concerned by a rumor he had heard from the Ministry of Munitions that there was a company which asserted "that Dr. Weizmann has 'lifted' their patent." To protect the government from paying twice, it was necessary to ensure that Weizmann would not actually get his money until after the war, when all claims had been settled.[178]

These objections did not prevent Weizmann's "influential friends"— Scott, McKenna, and others—from seeing to it that a committee was finally constituted in June 1917. Despite Greene's and Chalmer's objections that it would be improper for Reginald McKenna to head the committee because of his close personal interest in Weizmann,[179] McKenna did chair the committee. It included Sir Robert Chalmers representing the Treasury, Vice-Admiral Sir Archibald G. H. W. Moore representing the Admiralty, Professor W. J. Pope for the Ministry of Munitions, and Mr. J. Swinburne, an engineer and patent expert.[180] The committee met for the first time on June 15, 1917, and devoted the entire one-hour session to questioning Weizmann. On the whole, the attitude of the members toward him was friendly. The questions revolved around the economic side of his process and the difference between it and that using potatoes.[181] Weizmann assured the committee that his process was quite different from Fernbach's. At the same time he expressed worry over the fact that his process and cultures were dispersed in many factories and laboratories working for the government, thus being vulnerable to misuse by others.[182] On the matter of expense, Weizmann came armed with a report prepared by the superintendent of research at King's Lynn which showed that during a given week when the factory produced 4 tons and 3 pounds of acetone and approximately 8¾ tons of butyl alcohol, there was a net profit to the factory of £911.5.6½.[183]

The only other witness to appear before the committee during its second and final meeting on June 29, 1917, was P. G. Henriques, deputy director general of the Finance Department of the Ministry of Munitions; one of Henriques's duties was to supervise the explosives and propellant branches of that department. On the whole, Henriques was quite uninformed about the actual significance and methods of working of Weizmann's process except in the most general terms. He was much more knowledgeable on the financial side. He estimated that the government spent £102,708 to prepare six distilleries to use the Weizmann process and another £160,828 for working expenses. Henriques's evidence makes quite clear that the expense and efficiency with which the Weizmann process was used in each one of the distilleries depended a great deal on the suitability of the equipment and working staff. Thus the expense at Nicholson's distillery at Bromley was prohibitive, whereas at Poole it was much more reasonable.[184]

It took another three weeks for the committee to reach a resolution. In a terse, two-paragraph statement it announced its findings on July 19, 1917:

> We have reached the conclusion that the Weizmann process for producing acetone can only be regarded as a war emergency measure at the present time. In our opinion the payment of royalty of four pounds per ton on all acetone already produced and that may be produced in this country by this process until the end of the war would be a fair payment for the British government to make. Should the use of this process be continued after the war, the question of any further payment to Dr. Weizmann should then be considered afresh.[185]

McKenna informed Scott of this decision on August 9, 1917,[186] and the indefatigable editor wrote on August 14 to the Treasury asking for formal announcement of the award. In response, Robert Chalmers, who had represented the Treasury on the award committee, authorized the Admiralty on September 4, 1917, to proceed with payment in accordance with the committee's recommendations.[187] Complying with this request, the Admiralty informed Weizmann of his award on September 14, 1917.[188] Weizmann could finally sigh with relief. "For the time being the worries are over and that is something," he wrote to Scott, the man most responsible for securing him the award. "I take this opportunity to thank you most heartily for the brotherly interest you took in that affair which would have dragged for ever so long if not for you."[189]

Weizmann had committed himself in advance to accept the decisions of the award committee,[190] but that pertained only to the award on acetone production in England. Under the terms of this award Weizmann was to receive £3,232 up to October 31, 1918.[191] Nothing prevented him from asking for payment for the production of acetone and other products outside of England. Thus, on December 1, 1917, after further consultation with his patent lawyer, Weizmann wrote to the secretary of the admiralty that there were further issues to consider regarding his award:

> I do not wish to comment in any way on the amount of the Award, as I agreed to accept whatever decision the Committee might arrive at on this question. I feel, however, that it is only right that I should point out that the Committee did not take into consideration the question of any benefit which may result to the country from the production of Butyl Alcohol by my process as they considered that such product was of no value. I therefore ask that, if and when the Butyl Alcohol produced by means of my invention can be disposed of at a profit (and I understand that this has already proved to be the case) a proper arrangement should be made for granting me a royalty on such product, based on the benefit according to the country, in addition to the royalty on Acetone covered by the Committee's Award. . . . As the Award deals only with the production of Acetone and further with such production in this country only, I assume that separate arrangements will have to be made as regards the payment of a royalty in respect of (a) Acetone manufactured and to be manufactured according to my invention in Toronto, (b) Acetone to be manufactured in India as soon as the latter factory commences production, and (c) Butyl Alcohol produced by means of my invention at both such factories if such last mentioned product is already or shall hereafter result in a benefit to the country.[192]

A few months later, in March 1918—just prior to the official termination of his appointment with the Admiralty on June 1, 1918—Weizmann went to Palestine at the head of the Zionist Commission. The preparations leading to this event and the hectic months that followed upon arrival in Palestine prevented him from personally pursuing his case for an award. In January 1919, however, his patent lawyer, Atkinson Adam, wrote again, this time to the Ministry of Munitions, reiterating Weizmann's demands of December 1917. It is possible that one reason for the long delay in pressing Weizmann's case with the government was not only the latter's absence from England but the claim of one of his collaborators, David Alliston Legg, who wished to share in Weizmann's award as a co-patentee in respect to at least one of Weizmann's patents. Clearly Legg had a good case because in his letter of January 1919, Adam assured the Ministry of Munitions that arrangements had been made to satisfy Legg's demands.[193] In its reply of February 13, 1919, the Ministry of Munitions agreed to the award in the United States, limiting it to production up to December 31, 1918. The award was to be calculated on the basis of the production of acetone at the rate of 4 pounds per ton with no additional allowance for butyl alcohol or methyl ethyl ketone. With the abstention of one member, the award committee, which was convened once again in March 1919, stated that with regard to the use of the Weizmann processes after December 31, 1918, it recommended that a royalty be paid of 4 percent calculated on the price at which each product "is taken on charge or disposed of."[194]

Once again the wheels of the bureaucracy ground slowly. In January 1920, Sir Graham Greene wrote to the secretary of the treasury that it was estimated that the total quantity of acetone produced by the Weizmann process up to October 30, 1918, was 3,852 tons plus 7,769 tons of butyl alcohol.[195] In May 1920, Sir Graham wrote again with a breakdown of production and sums earned by Weizmann as follows: 2,494 tons of acetone were produced in Canada, earning Weizmann £9,976; 550 tons were produced in the United States, earning him £2,200. In addition, the Weizmann process had produced 239 tons of acetone for the Admiralty, earning £955, and 566 tons for the Ministry of Munitions, earning £2,264. Thus the total production of acetone by the Weizmann process until December 1918 was 3,849 tons (three tons less than estimated by the Ministry of Munitions in January 1920), and the total award granted on the basis of this production was £15,396.[196]

The case seemed to be resolved, yet once again some of the officials began to ask questions. On the one hand it was decided to inquire of the India Office whether it had produced any acetone with the Weizmann process.[197] On the other hand, some questioned whether the figures of production in the United States were accurate.[198] Once again McKenna interceded at Weizmann's request and protested to Sir Warren Fisher, secretary of the treasury: "The refusal to act upon the award of the arbitrators in his case is apparently being made a ground for giving the unfortunate man nothing at all."[199] Sir Warren replied by return mail, explaining to McKenna that it was the Ministry of Munitions which was holding everything up and promising to act immediately.[200] On June 15, 1920, Sir Warren informed McKenna that he had been notified that further information was being sought from the Admiralty and the India Office before a complete settlement could be made. Nevertheless, he was authorizing an immediate payment of £10,000 to Weizmann, without prejudice to his case and pending final results of findings.[201]

The extant evidence indicates that for his various inventions Weizmann was paid £10,000 in the spring of 1920, but no record shows whether any further sums were paid. Even if Weizmann did receive further sums—not an impossibility given Greene's report of January 1920—it is likely that he had to pay taxes as well as share some of the award with Legg. In his memoirs Weizmann remarked with a note of bitterness that he had received a "token award" for his work—a total of "ten shillings for every ton of acetone produced during the war."[202] If he did receive only £10,000 instead of the promised £15,396, then his award, based on the tons of acetone produced during the war, amounted to some £2.6 per ton, not ten shillings.

In retrospect it is clear that, from a financial point of view, Weizmann had not been generously rewarded by the government for his wartime services.[203] By the time the government discontinued his process in February 1917, it had been tested on a scale of 90,000 gallons in England and 150,000 gallons in Toronto and Indiana—the largest scale on which a fermentation had ever been carried out.[204] Such an enormous expansion proved unique among microbiological processes in industry, and Weizmann had good reason to be proud of it. If one detects in his letters and memoirs a note of bitterness or disappointment concerning remuneration, these feelings do not seem to have affected his attitude to England in the period immediately after the war. For one thing, he knew well that, if the government exploited him financially, it had also afforded him the opportunity for the testing and research of his process on a scale hitherto unknown. The chemical knowledge he gained during his work for the Admiralty and Ministry of Munitions served him well in exploiting his process commercially during the interwar years.[205]

Much has been made of Lloyd George's statement in his *War Memoirs* that when Weizmann solved the problem of acetone shortage, the minister of munitions turned to him and said: "You have rendered great service to the State and I should like to ask the Prime Minister to recommend you to his Majesty for some honor." According to Lloyd George, Weizmann replied: "There is nothing I want for myself." "But is there nothing we can do as a recognition of your valuable assistance to the country?" responded Lloyd George, who reported Weizmann as replying, "Yes, I would like you to do something for my people." Whereupon Weizmann proceeded to describe the aspirations of the Jewish people for repatriation in their sacred land. "That," concluded Lloyd George,

was the fount and origin of the famous declaration about the National Home for the Jews in Palestine. As soon as I became Prime Minister I talked the whole matter over with Mr. Balfour, who was then Foreign Secretary. . . . We were anxious at the time to gather Jewish support in neutral countries. Dr Weizmann was brought into direct contact with the Foreign Secretary. This was the beginning of an association the outcome of which, after long examination, was the famous Balfour Declaration. . . . So that Dr Weizmann with his discovery not only helped us to win the War, but made a permanent mark upon the map of the world.[206]

This apocryphal story has been repeated often by others.[207] But in his own memoirs Weizmann ironically commented on Lloyd George's story "that history does not deal with Aladdin's lamps."[208] He had good reason to be irked. At Lloyd George's request, he had written a detailed, factual memorandum on his wartime services that the former prime minister intended to use—but obviously did not—in his *War Memoirs*. The story spread by Lloyd George, and repeated so often later, is nowhere to be found in Weizmann's own account.[209] Yet it became popular legend and even inspired George Bernard Shaw to write in June 1936 a short, satirical three-act play entitled *Arthur and the Acetone*. In the second act, Shaw parodies the episode as follows:

> Arthur: Doctor Weizmann, we must have that microbe at your own price. Name it. We shall not hesitate at six figures.
> Dr. Weizmann: I do not ask for money.
> Arthur: There must be some misunderstanding. I was informed that you are a Jew.
> Weizmann: You were informed correctly. I am a Jew.
> Arthur: But, pardon me, you said you did not ask for money.
> Weizmann: Precisely. I do not want money.
> Arthur: A title, perhaps? Baron? Viscount? Do not hesitate.
> Weizmann: Nothing would induce me to accept a title. I would have to pay more for everything.
> Arthur: Then may I ask, without offence, since you want none of the things that everybody wants, what the devil do you want?
> Weizmann: I want Jerusalem.
> Arthur: It's yours. I only regret that we cannot throw in Madagascar as well. Unfortunately, it belongs to the French government. The Holy Land, on the other hand, belongs naturally to the Church of England, and to it you are most welcome. And now will you be so good as to hand over the microbe.[210]

Regardless of the factual status of Lloyd George's account and its popular dissemination by playwrights and scholars alike, it faithfully reflects the awareness of men in the war cabinet that the man negotiating for the Zionists had rendered a tremendous service to the country at a time when it was in dire need of acetone. Probably no other scientist in the British dominions could make a similar claim. Suffice it to quote the opinion of Michael J. Walsh, who in late 1915 became William Rintoul's assistant at Nobel's and was in a position to know something about the importance of Weizmann's work: "Weizmann found himself with a free hand and the resources of the British Empire behind him to manufacture the acetone on which the survival of the British Empire depended. Those of us who knew the details of the strategic importance of Weizmann's acetone process, which was the only source of acetone outside the German Empire, knew that it was the most crucial single factor of the many factors which ensured the survival of England at this critical period in her history." [211]

Walsh's statement is, to say the least, exaggerated. A detailed statement prepared by the Ministry of Munitions in November 1918 shows that Weizmann's process accounted for some 9.6 percent of all acetone produced for the war effort between 1916 and 1918. Nevertheless, given the constraints of time, equipment, manpower, and other factors, this was a magnificent achievement. The following table provides a comparative illustration of Weizmann's success. [212]

British Production of Acetone during World War I

Process	1915 (tons)	1916 (tons)	1917 (tons)	1918 (tons)	Total (tons)	Percent
Wood distillation	2,126.1	10,895.7	12,104.7	9,910.0	35,036.5	87.1
Weizmann	—	268.3	1,244.0	2,339.7	3,852.0	9.6
Other processes	11.2	7.0	1,317.6	—	1,335.8	3.3
	2,137.3	11,171.0	14,666.3	12,249.7	40,224.3	100.0

Thus, whatever the merit of the Zionist case, the man who presented it, deserved—and received—recognition and respect not easily elicited from the bureaucrats of the British Empire. One could amend his proposals time and again, but one could not easily disregard this man who had done so much for Britain. Whether or not the conversation between Lloyd George and Weizmann actually took place, [213] Lloyd George and his closest colleagues in the cabinet placed full confidence in Weizmann precisely because of his contribution to the war effort. One needs only to recall the desperate position in which Lloyd George and Balfour found the Ministry of Munitions and the Admiralty when they took office in mid-1915. As soon as he realized the importance of Weizmann's contributions to the British war effort, Lloyd George made it clear he had full confidence in the naturalized scientist. This attitude on the part of Britain's most powerful politician was no doubt transmitted to and quickly registered by other ministers and their assistants. This attitude received added force after Lloyd George became prime minister in December 1916. The trust in Weizmann could hardly be divided between the scientist and the Zionist statesman.

The men at Whitehall and in Downing Street who had placed their faith in Weizmann the scientist to solve a problem of national magnitude were easily persuaded to extend the same support to Weizmann the Zionist leader. Weizmann understood from the beginning of his work for the government that his success with the acetone process would open many doors when the time came. As he put it to Dorothy de Rothschild in July 1915: "If all that succeeds, it would help our Palestinian work very considerably and perhaps the Jewish star will bring some luck this time." [214] At the beginning of 1917, when the negotiations that finally

Staff of British Acetones, Toronto. From left: McLachlin (Mr. Hayward's assistant), A. E. Gooderham, Jr. (assistant manager), L. Gooderham (Mr. Legg's assistant), Mr. Shaw (expert on heating and cooling), Horace B. Speakman, A. E. Gooderham, Mr. Hayward (constructing engineer), David Alliston Legg. Courtesy: Weizmann Archives

led to the Balfour Declaration reached a critical stage, Weizmann's intuition was borne out. Fifteen years earlier, while on holiday in Leysin, Weizmann had been torn between chemistry and Zionist politics. By 1917 science was fully harnessed in the service of Zionist diplomacy. Weizmann's acetone work had a major impact on the British policymakers, even though Lloyd George's view that the Balfour Declaration was a *quid pro quo* for acetone is a fanciful exaggeration. As demonstrated here, Weizmann's actual scientific products—not merely the standing and credibility they gave him—were of prime importance. This assertion is based on two factors. First are his spectacular discoveries. The second is a more subtle phenomenon that has been underestimated thus far: the personal relations that Weizmann developed within the British government and bureaucracy by virtue of his work for the Ministry of Munitions and the Admiralty. During these years Weizmann not only got to know the bureaucrats at all levels of government, but he became part of that bureaucratic machine and therefore an insider. To be sure, he was an insider in a strange way—a naturalized foreigner with foreign interests, but also with a favorable view of British interests.[215] That he was a representative of the Zionist cause did not harm his standing, since the British government was in any case favorably disposed toward

Stock room, British Acetones, Toronto. Courtesy: Weizmann Archives

Zionism for its own reasons. The fact the Weizmann had become an insider, a person with whom British leaders had worked well and on whom they could count, made him a reasonable representative of the Zionist movement in British eyes. As an insider, he could negotiate with British politicians as an ally rather than as an adversary.

As noted before, in 1914 men such as Leopold Greenberg, Joseph Cowen, and Moses Gaster—not to speak of Yehiel Tschlenow and Nahum Sokolow—were perceived by the Zionists and the British government as the proper Zionist representatives with whom to negotiate. Weizmann did not even possess the Zionist credentials to be seen as the movement's spokesman. Moreover, though naturalized, he was regarded as a foreigner and, in a country so status conscious as England, had not attained the standing that a fellowship of the Royal Society or a professorship would automatically have granted him. His major personal resources were his contacts with the Rothschild family, with the academic community (including the *Round Table* group), and, of course, his scientific role, which reached its peak in 1915–16. By the end of 1916, however, no one doubted that Weizmann had attained the status of *primus inter pares*. That accomplishment was due to his war work, to the administrative, social, and scientific achievements that provided vital links with powerful British politicians. But it was also due to his enormous dedication to the Zionist cause and his belief that it ought to be tied to Great Britain's destiny.[216] Weizmann's connections with British politicians and civil servants were to a large extent the result of the government's coincidental need for his discoveries. Although these ties were begun fortuitously, Weizmann's political genius was in linking these scientific achievements to his conception of Zionism's aims almost as soon as the Great War began.[217]

III

Generating Support for Zionism

Toward the end of 1916, Chaim Weizmann wrote to Dorothy de Rothschild one of those frank, soul-searching letters he was wont to write when he was angry or depressed. Two years into the war he felt he had not made sufficient progress in his professional and public endeavors. He was "a Schlimassel," a loser whose financial and professional prospects seemed gloomy. The letter was written during a period when the question of the reward for his patents had not yet been decided and the hoped-for lucrative contract with the French government had fallen through. What fueled Weizmann's frustration was his sense that he was treading water in the realm of Zionist politics:

> This upheaval in the world has roused everybody except the Jews. It has not brought a single man, who would be capable to guide the people to a great destiny. All the Zionists I know are in their line nice, well-meaning, good and able people. But they have to give 95% of their energies to other purposes and only after they have satisfied those demands they can devote the sad remainder to Jewish work. No wonder therefore, that all we do now is disjointed, haphazard, looks more like an adventure, than like an organized conscious effort of a people struggling for better days. Add to that the disruption in Russian Jewry, the mainstay of the people, *la grande misère*, swallowing up every ounce of energy there. . . .
>
> In face of all that one is sometimes driven to despair and one's own efforts appear almost like an irony, like the attempt of the fool who tried to empty the sea with a bucket. . . .
>
> It is difficult to do any useful work in such a state of mind.[1]

Weizmann's malaise was not temporary. Four weeks after writing this letter, Dorothy de Rothschild wrote a concerned letter to Vera Weizmann: "Lately, no doubt under the strain of worry and overwork, his [Weizmann's] nerves, and possibly with them, his patience, seem to have given out."[2] Two weeks later she wrote to Vera again: "We saw Dr. Weizmann for a few moments yesterday; I am afraid he seemed very downhearted which I fear is only natural with this accumulation of worries. . . . I hope he does not make any rash decisions."[3]

Yet, even as he wrote his letter to his young patron, Weizmann was perceived by neutral observers as having achieved a great deal and as one of the few people in England who could be relied upon to advance the cause of Zionism. Isaac Leon Kandel, an international authority on comparative education who was visiting England in late 1915, wrote to his colleague and friend, Horace Kallen, the following report extolling Weizmann's virtues:

> You probably know that nothing of a tangible nature has been done in England. From the account that I received Weitzman [sic] shouldered the whole burden of developing a sentiment for Zionism among the leaders of English politics. Through C. P. Scott of the Manchester Guardian he won the ear of Lloyd George, was then passed on to Herbert Samuel [postmaster general] who gave him a favorable hearing. Mr. Balfour was next reached and was much impressed. Lord Bryce and members of the Round Table were approached and interested through Zimmern. From another side, also through Weitzman, an entree was obtained to the Rothschild family. Weitzman has been in close touch with Baron Edmund [sic] Rothschild and has found an ardent supporter in his daughter-in-law, who is now in England. Through her he has interested a few members of the English Rothschild[s] including Lady Crewe. . . . All these are in favor of supporting the Jewish claim in Palestine and of establishing a Jewish State under the English flag. The Foreign Office alone remained impervious to attack of any kind. Lord Percy (I think) turns out to be a Zionist but will not hasten Providence. But during the whole time that Weitzman was conducting the negotiations the political and military situation was changing. Things appeared brightest during the early days in March when the Dardanelles were being fixed by the fleet. Times have changed since then.[4]

Kandel's sources for this report are not known. Clearly, he had spoken to Weizmann, but he no doubt also heard from others, who confirmed the veracity of the details. In the small circle of active Zionists, Weizmann's stock was very high. Indeed, even as the political and military fortunes of England ebbed and flowed, Weizmann's personal stature both in England and abroad continued to grow. Writing to Louis Brandeis in the spring of 1916, Lord Eustace Percy, who had just returned from service in Washington, asked: "Do you know Weizmann here, who I am told is the best representative here of your views and politics? I have only met him once, but was greatly struck by him."[5] He did not know Weizmann personally, replied Brandeis, "but I have heard much about him, and my friends here consider him absolutely trustworthy, and one of the best informed of all the Zionists. I am very glad that you are getting into touch with him."[6] The American Zionists realized quite early into the war that Weizmann was their best and most reliable contact in England. Until he had resigned, in June 1915, from the Provisional Executive Committee for General Zionist Affairs (PZC) over the issue of the American Jewish Congress,[7] Judah Magnes had been the main American contact with Weizmann. Within a month after his resignation, the PZC tried through its administrative secretary, Benjamin Perlstein, as well as Horace Kallen, to reestablish contact with Weizmann,[8] who did not respond. He was irked by Kallen's demand that he account for $250 the PZC had sent him for travel expenses. Moreover, given Shmarya Levin's anti-Russian sentiments, Weizmann was not sure where the sympathies of the other members of the PZC lay and felt it would be better not to communicate with them.[9] Assuring Weizmann of his high regard for Weizmann's work, Kallen wrote a conciliatory letter in which he also pointed out that although the official stance of American Zionists had to be neutral, the individual members of the PZC were in sympathy with the forces of democracy and would welcome Weizmann's cooperation.[10]

Clearly Weizmann had managed to acquire the kind of status in international Zionist circles that he had craved for the better part of his career. While in August 1914 he had been just another dedicated and active member of the WZO, by the end of 1915 he was generally recognized as one of the front-rank Zionist leaders whose counsel had to be sought and heeded before action could be taken in England.[11] He had good reason to be pleased with the way events had propelled him to a position of prominence. Yet by the end of 1916 he was frustrated and impatient. His friend Harry Sacher gave perhaps the best explanation for this state of mind. "You are a man of action with a natural gift for diplomacy and politics," he wrote to Weizmann in the summer of 1915 to explain the difference between Weizmann and his co-workers.[12] Weizmann worked furiously hard and expected immediate results. The fact of the matter was that throughout the latter part of 1915 and 1916 the time had not yet come for "action." In the meantime, the Zionists, as well as all other interested parties, had no choice but to jockey for position until the right opportunities presented themselves.[13]

Yet Weizmann and his colleagues in the EZF and WZO were not content to simply sit idle. Weizmann continued to cultivate his social and political contacts.[14] Moreover, he was involved in an attempt to consolidate the Zionist forces in England. At the invitation of Joseph Cowen and Weizmann,[15] fourteen Zionist leaders met at the Hotel Great Central on January 23, 1916. Among those present, in addition to Weizmann and Cowen, were Ahad Ha'Am, Herbert Bentwich, Leopold Greenberg, Vladimir Jabotinsky, Leon Simon, and Nahum Sokolow.[16] Gaster, invited by Weizmann to attend, declined in his usual disdainful and haughty manner.[17] At the meeting Weizmann expounded on his assessment of future Zionist work, and the group resolved to set up a committee to direct political activities. Despite his absence, Gaster was named to the committee, as was Yehiel Tschlenow, who had left England to return to Russia the previous summer. The other members were Bentwich, Cowen, Sokolow, and Weizmann. It was subsequently decided that this committee should be called "The Zionist Executive for England."[18] Extant minutes reveal that the composition of the committee, often referred to, simply, as "The Political Committee," varied.[19]

The committee set itself three tasks: to maintain contact with scattered Zionist organizations abroad, to deal with the anti-Zionists, and to create pro-Zionist sympathies among influential non-Jewish groups. By October 1916 the committee had also drafted an "Outline of Programme for a New Administration of Palestine and for a Jewish Resettlement of Palestine in Accordance with the Aspirations of the Zionist Movement," a title that was changed to, simply, "Scheme for a New Administration of Palestine and Its Resettlement by Jews." This document, which incorporated Theodor Herzl's idea of a Jewish company with a charter for the Jewish colonization of Palestine, was repeatedly revised by the Political Committee and formed the basis of ideas underlying the subsequent British Mandate for Palestine. The Political Committee held its last meeting on January 27, 1917.[20] On the whole, it served to give an appearance of Zionist harmony in dealings with other Zionist and non-Zionist bodies, in England as well as abroad.[21] Given its composition, it left Weizmann much leeway to negotiate as he saw fit with only minimal consultations with Cowen and Sokolow.

Thus, though dissatisfied with the pace at which he could direct events, Weizmann and his colleagues were far from idle. Moreover, in spite of his constant worry concerning the award from the government, Weizmann's personal fortunes had been dramatically improved by the end of 1916. For about a year after the start of the war, Weizmann had led a nomadic and exhausting life. In addition to the frequent—sometimes weekly—seven-hour round trips he was making from Manchester to London on Zionist or professional affairs,[22] he also often journeyed to the Continent. During his sojourns in London he often lodged with Ahad Ha'Am; after Sokolow and Tschlenow arrived in London at the end of December 1914, he also stayed in the apartment they shared on 118 Sutherland Avenue in Maida Vale.[23] Following Tschlenow's return to Russia during the summer of 1915, Sokolow moved to the Regent Palace Hotel, while Weizmann sometimes stayed at the Waldorf Hotel. His journeys lasted from an overnight trip to London to two-week stretches during which he traveled to the Continent. This constant travel put pressures on his family. Vera was now holding a job and taking care of Benjy and frequently had to cope alone with his and her own frequent illnesses. Both mother and child needed medical care and long periods of recuperation, often taken at the sea or with relatives on the Continent.[24] Weizmann's own health was far from perfect and a constant source of worry.[25] With so many pressures, there were tensions between Chaim and Vera. He constantly needed to reassure her of his love, blaming all the unpleasantness he had caused on his physical and emotional state.[26]

Things began to improve after Weizmann received his official appointment at the Ministry of Munitions in September 1915, which carried with it an annual salary of £1,500 and £500 for expenses to relocate from Manchester to London. This new salary exceeded the combined salaries he and Vera had in Manchester and covered the increased cost of living in London as well; it also allowed Weizmann to repay some of his debts.[27] It was high time—and financially feasible—to end the shuttling between Manchester and London, and on September 29, 1915, Weizmann moved into a rented flat at 3 Justice Walk, Chelsea,[28] which he shared for a while with Vladimir Jabotinsky. The flat was in a small house in an ancient alley behind a church on the shores of the Thames.[29]

At the beginning of January 1916, Vera and Benjy arrived in London and for a few days lived together with Weizmann and Jabotinsky.[30] By mid-January 1916 the Weizmanns had moved to more spacious rooms at 41 Campden House Road in Kensington.[31] By mid-October 1916, about a month after the Admiralty had decided to employ Weizmann on terms identical to those he had at the Ministry of Munitions, the Weizmanns moved to an elegant house on 67 Addison Road in Kensington.[32] This fifteen-room mansion was the kind of home the Weizmanns had always aspired to live in; it equaled in grandeur and style those homes of their friends they had long admired—the Simons in Germany and the Schusters in Manchester.

Situated on a wide, tree-lined street, this was a three-story structure built in a neoclassical style with a semicircular gravel driveway. Ten brick steps led to an impressive entrance, which led to an even more impressive interior. There were wooden parquet floors, marble baseboards, and stained glass borders on the windows at the landing between the first and second floors. The large living room was gracefully separated by an arch from the sunny and flower-filled conservatory. The other side of the first floor had a large dining room with a dumbwaiter for transporting food from the kitchen below. There were two bedrooms on the second floor for the family and two smaller rooms for the maids on the third. Each of the top floors had its own bathroom. Both the first floor and second floor had fireplaces, a marble one on the second floor. Matching the scale of the house were the gardens in the back. They were twice as large as those of the adjoining houses and much more beautiful. Since 1601 these had been public gardens, and the mulberry trees in it had been planted during the reign of King James I.[33] In this house Chaim and Vera's second son, Michael, was born on November 16, 1916; as in the case of Benjy, it was again the Haham Moses Gaster who was accorded the honor of being the *sandak*, holding Michael during the circumcision ceremony.[34] In 1919, when their lease expired, the Weizmanns moved to a nearby and even larger house on 16 Addison Crescent.

Weizmann must have often reflected on the fact that twelve years earlier he had arrived in England without any means, without even a secure academic position, and with little but dreams that one day he would be able to make a fortune off his chemical patents. In 1916 he had not

yet made his fortune, but promises from government officials led him to
believe he would soon be compensated. At last he could entertain, without embarrassment, the members of the social elite whose homes he had
been frequenting since the fall of 1914. Vera fully shared in these dreams
and expectations. She seems to have given up her job as medical officer
in Manchester for a new career as a political hostess without much regret.[35]

As the Weizmanns' social life became increasingly active, Vera combined tea and Zionist politics with her natural elegance. Her beauty,
impeccable intuition, and accumulated knowledge of the mores and
manners of upper-class British society were a great asset, and she was a
willing partner in the world of the salons within which she and Chaim
moved.[36] She became friendly with some of Weizmann's female patrons.
On one occasion, just prior to moving into their large home on Addison
Road, she seems to have discussed financial worries with Rozsika Rothschild. A few days later there arrived a reassuring letter from Rozsika
saying that she and Charles were quite confident that Weizmann's
"marvellous work must be recognized. Meantime," she added "I hate
the idea of your worrying about furnishings in your future home and I
venture to suppose that you will let me help you—I send you a cheque
for £500. . . . You will pay it back to me, but should the impossible
happen . . . I hope you won't mind accepting it from me as a present,
which would only cement our friendship."[37] No doubt Vera consulted
with Chaim before returning the check with thanks to Rozsika. As in
the case of the remuneration for his patents during the war, Weizmann
refused to accept a gift that would have placed him in the position of a
dependent client; Rozsika Rothschild well understood the motivations
for the decline of her offer.[38] Dorothy de Rothschild was also ready to
help financially. At the end of 1916, when Weizmann told her of his
financial worries and even intimated that he was ready to drop everything and return to his post at Manchester University, the worried young
woman wrote to Vera that she was sure things would eventually work
out and did not doubt the Admiralty would honor its commitments. In
the meantime, "I do wish I could help you, and would indeed be pleased
if you would accept enclosed cheque."[39] Interestingly, both Rozsika and
Dorothy sent their letters and checks to Vera, not Chaim; was it because
they felt Vera would be more ready to accept their gifts? There is no
response extant to the offer of help from Dorothy, but one may assume
that this check, too, was returned with thanks. Both incidents serve to
illustrate the fact that the line between Weizmann's personal and public
affairs was often—and intentionally—quite blurred.[40]

With the Rothschild ladies managing appointments and schedules for
him and being kept informed of his progress, Weizmann expended considerable energy in acquiring for the Zionist cause the marchioness of
Crewe and Nancy Astor. Within days of meeting Lady Crewe, he wrote
her one of his "sad and sordid" letters as he called them, the kind he

used to introduce—with such great effect—his non-Jewish prospective supporters to the cause of Zionism. Answering the question of what made him take up Zionism, he wrote:

> We who come from Russia are born and bred in an aspiration towards a new and better Jewish life. It must not only be a comfortable life but a *Jewish* one, a normal Jewish life, just as the Englishman leads a normal English life. . . . We who come from Russia, where a most modern and perfect machinery is set up to crush the Jewish body and soul are least frightened of the so-called antisemitism. . . . We equally hate antisemitism and philosemitism. Both are degrading. We are conscious of the fact that we have contributed our share towards progress and shall continue to do so in a higher degree, when we can live as free men in our free country. . . . There are of course Jews who have thrown in their lot with the countries they have adopted. They desire genuinely to "disappear" as Jews. We are sorry that this process is going on, but we cannot stop it and make no attempt to do so. The few will go, the majority will survive.[41]

This kind of talk by a Jew—bold and self-assured—was not the stuff of daily experience for British high society. Members of the social elite were intrigued and fascinated by Weizmann's tenor, and it rarely failed to leave its mark. In late March 1916, Dorothy de Rothschild telephoned Weizmann to report that at a dinner party in the Crewe home she had overheard a conversation between Lord Robert Cecil and the lady of the house. The marchioness declared that "we all in this house are 'Weizmannites.' "[42] Nancy Astor was similarly impressed. At a lunch in her elegant home specifically arranged so that she and others of her circle could listen to what Weizmann had to say, he held forth on the history and present state of Zionism. Vera recorded in her personal diary, which she began keeping that day, "Mrs. Astor was very interested and confessed, that she had been rather prejudiced against Jews, as she has never met before the Jews with such views and attitudes; her Jewish acquaintances were people like Rothschild and Montagu."[43] Despite Nancy Astor's ambivalence toward Jews—an attitude shared by many of her friends—she joined the ranks of the men and women in the upper echelons of British society who supported Weizmann personally. It was because of the particular manner in which he presented it that they were willing to accept the Zionist cause. A few months after the dinner party in her house and following some further talks with Weizmann, Nancy Astor was sufficiently interested in Weizmann to invite him to spend the night in her country estate, offering to come to London if he could not make it.[44]

The strong impact Weizmann had on these circles can be gauged by the fact that ten days after she admitted her prejudices against Jews, Nancy Astor gave another dinner party to which she invited Arthur James Balfour, who had been unable to come to the earlier dinner but had expressed the wish to see Weizmann. Also invited were a few American journalists and Philip Henry Kerr, the editor of the *Round Table*, who by the end of the year would become a member of Lloyd George's personal secretariat, exerting a great deal of influence behind the scenes until his resignation in 1921. Throughout the evening, Nancy Astor tried to turn the conversation to the subject of Zionism. "You must speak Zionism to Dr. Weizmann," she interjected apropos of nothing, making for an awkward situation.[45] On that particular occasion those present preferred to gossip about the government, but Weizmann's presence at the table was a sufficient indication of the status he had acquired as an insider. He no longer needed to schedule as many appointments to discuss Zionism in the offices of statesmen and politicians. He could get his points across much more effectively in a leisurely manner to men such as Kerr, Balfour, and Reginald McKenna, knowing that at least one or more of the hosts or guests would interject to support his point of view. This was the kind of setting within which Weizmann thrived and for which he was well groomed by Dorothy de Rothschild—"Dotty," as she was known to her close friends. Dotty had set up what amounted to an informal advisory group—over which she and James presided—composed of Charles and Rozsika Rothschild and the marchioness of Crewe. They provided Weizmann with important intelligence and advice on how to behave at dinner parties, what to say or not to say, and of whom to be wary.[46] It was information vital to his political campaign.

All along Weizmann kept a watchful eye on developments among the Jewish and Zionist groups. Somewhat in the style of Herzl, Weizmann tried to keep the several active forces in play, so that they would not undermine, but if possible advance, a policy he was projecting to address the varied pressures of his non-Jewish contacts. Those approaches in which he took little interest, he watched with a cautiously passive tolerance. Other approaches, with which he could be identified himself, needed his personal control lest they be recklessly indulged in a spirit of dangerous "maximalism." This danger applied to the agitation for declaring Palestine a Jewish state within the British Commonwealth and to the several campaigns for establishing a Jewish military unit to fight in Palestine as part of the Allied forces. Both implied alignment with the Allies and so matched Weizmann's sympathies but ran counter to the explicit neutrality of the WZO. There were also side effects that made agitation for a Jewish fighting unit especially unpopular among the great majority of British Jewry. Since Weizmann's hopes for success in the larger issues he was pressing on his government contacts would be shattered if he were repudiated by the Jewish public, as Jabotinsky was by the end of 1916, Weizmann had a narrow path to tread.

From the very first the idea of a Jewish legion to fight with the Allies evoked fears that the Turks might respond with reprisals similar to their ruthless attacks on the Armenians;[47] and Weizmann, among others suspected of being dangerously pro-Allied, was considered a threat to the safety of Palestinian Jews for irresponsibly advocating such projects. The first tangible expression of the legion idea was the Zion Mule Corps

(ZMC), organized in Egypt by Palestinian refugees and local Jewish recruits and sent to transport supplies to the front lines in the ill-fated
Gallipoli campaign. The leader of the enterprise was the Russian reserve
officer Captain Yosef Trumpeldor. Jabotinsky had initiated the proposal
for a military unit among the refugees in Alexandria but refused to join
the Mule Corps since he considered a mere labor corps demeaning to
the Jews and inadequate for the political purposes he had in mind.[48]

Despite Jabotinsky's withdrawal from the scheme, some four hundred
volunteers had enlisted in the ZMC under the command of Colonel John
Henry Patterson.[49] The ZMC went ashore on the Gallipoli peninsula,
where it served with distinction under trying conditions.[50] General Ian
Hamilton, the commander in chief of the British Mediterranean force,
expressed his admiration for the ZMC in a letter to Jabotinsky: "From
the outset I have been much interested in the Zion Mule Corps. . . .
The men have done extremely well, working their mules calmly under
heavy shell and rifle fire, and thus showing a more difficult type of
bravery than the men in the front line who had the excitement of the
combat to keep them going."[51] The Zion Mule Corps was disbanded on
May 26, 1916, four months after it had been returned to Egypt. During
that same period Trumpeldor renewed his contacts with Jabotinsky, who
for the past year had been working hard to promote his military and
political schemes. As the Zion Mule Corps was preparing to join the
Gallipoli campaign, Jabotinsky went to Italy and France, where he carried on a vigorous campaign to create a Jewish combat unit, hoping to
serve in the eventual conquest of Palestine by the Allies and to provide
a trained Jewish militia for Palestine after the war. He coordinated his
activities with Pinhas Rutenberg, who went to the United States with
the same goals in mind.[52] By the end of April 1915, Jabotinsky arrived
in London to lobby for the creation of a Jewish legion. Though he received some encouragement, particularly from Wickham Steed, the senior editor for foreign affairs of the *Times,* he met with a generally cool
reception from the person who counted most, Earl Kitchener, the secretary of state for war.

By mid-May 1915 Jabotinsky was on the road again—to Stockholm,
Copenhagen, Petrograd, Moscow, Odessa, and Kiev. Everywhere his
idea of a Jewish fighting force met with hostility. The official and unofficial Zionist leadership—with few exceptions—was solidly stacked against
him. At its meeting in Copenhagen in June 1915, the GAC took Jabotinsky to task and condemned his political and military projects in no uncertain terms.[53] Leon Simon rejected the idea as Jabotinsky's "wildest
scheme . . . a scheme quite impossible of realization and fraught with
great danger to our people."[54] Gaster thought Jabotinsky's scheme the
work of an adventurous journalist.[55] Menahem Ussishkin, who had been
Jabotinsky's opponent since the early congresses, felt confirmed in his
dislike of the man.[56] It was only natural that the pro-German Shmarya
Levin belittled Jabotinsky's "unfortunate Legion,"[57] but so did Jabotin-

sky's good friend Victor Jacobson, who was firmly opposed.[58] The Poalei Zion in the United States also chimed in, warning against any action that would place the Jewish nation firmly in the camp of one of the belligerents.[59]

This kind of firm opposition would have daunted most men; but Jabotinsky was made of different stuff. In mid-August 1915 he returned to London and continued with his campaign. The situation seemed hopeless, but he had some support: Joseph Cowen and Dr. David Eder, a psychoanalyst who had strong sympathies for Israel Zangwill's ITO but was slowly coming under Weizmann's influence. And then there was Weizmann himself. In his memoirs of the period Jabotinsky gratefully recalled Weizmann's support, though he noted the decisive differences between their temperaments:

> Dr. Weizmann was in favor of my plans, but he admitted to me honestly that he could not and did not care to make his own political work more complicated and difficult by openly supporting a project formally condemned by the Zionist "Actions Committee" and extremely unpopular with the Jewish population of London.
>
> Once he told me, and it was very typical of him: "I cannot work like you, in an atmosphere where everybody is angry with me and can hardly stand me. This everyday friction would poison my life and kill in me all desire to work. Better let me act in my own way; a time will come when I shall find the means to help you as best I can."[60]

But the opportune time for such help—that is, publicly acknowledged help[61]—had not yet come, and for Weizmann, who in the fall of 1915 had made Jabotinsky his roommate in his new quarters in Chelsea, a delicate problem arose requiring tact and skillful maneuver. Though they both agreed on the necessity for a Jewish legion, Jabotinsky's approach was quite different from that of Weizmann. Whereas the latter was careful not to cross swords openly with either the Zionist establishment or its informal leadership, all of whom were opposed to the idea, Jabotinsky threw himself heart and soul into the battle. He elicited and received letters of recommendation from C. P. Scott;[62] Count Alexander Benckendorff, the Russian ambassador to London;[63] General Sir Ian Hamilton;[64] and Colonel John Henry Patterson.[65] Moreover, with the aid of Leopold Amery, who had seen service in Gallipoli and was then on the military staff of Lord Robert Cecil,[66] and Charles Masterman, assistant director of the Department of Information at the Foreign Office,[67] Jabotinsky seemed to have sufficient support to make considerable headway. Indeed, the Foreign Office seemed well disposed and understood the propaganda value such a Jewish fighting force would have, particularly among American Jews,[68] but the War Office persisted in its negative attitude, and, for the moment, the matter had to be dropped.[69]

In February 1916, the same month in which Lord Robert Cecil informed Jabotinsky that not much could be done until the "Military Authorities . . . changed their minds,"[70] compulsory military service was introduced in England.[71] Married men were excluded until a further stipulation that became effective on May 25, 1916. This state of affairs focused public attention on the Eastern European Jewish immigrants, who constituted a large percentage of the total Jewish population in England of 250,000–300,000.[72] By 1914 estimates of the Jewish population of London alone ranged from 150,000 to 180,000. Of those, about 100,000 lived in the East End, particularly in Whitechapel, St. George, and Mile End Old Town.[73] Many of the recent arrivals had not been naturalized, with the result that some 30,000 of them, of military age, were eluding conscription.[74] As a whole, the immigrants did not consider the war to be their affair.[75]

The repugnance of immigrant Jews for service in a war for the defense of tsarist Russia became a source of special irritation in England.[76] The hostility aroused against alien Jews, who were exempt, was punctuated by violent outbursts on the East End and in Leeds, among other places. It led Herbert Samuel, who since January 1916 was once again in the cabinet as home secretary and therefore the minister primarily concerned with the question of military service of unnaturalized Russians of military age, to take action. On June 29, 1916, Samuel told the House of Commons that these Russians would be expected "either to offer their services to the British Army or to return to Russia to fulfill their military obligations there."[77] Amid the turmoil and protest that ensued within the immigrant community[78] the native-born Zionist leaders, Joseph Cowen and Leopold Greenberg, added coals to the fires by strongly endorsing Samuel's stand and castigating the recalcitrants.[79] In light of this stormy debate, Samuel softened his stand and on July 24, 1916, informed the House of Commons that he would consider sympathetically the proposal that the government should facilitate the early naturalization of Russians electing to join the British army.[80] A few days earlier, on July 19, the home secretary had been visited by Weizmann, who tried to persuade him to use methods other than coercion to induce enlistment in the British army.[81] It is possible that Weizmann's arguments contributed to the change in Samuel's approach to the matter and perhaps to the decision to give the Russian Jews until September 30, 1916, to enlist voluntarily.[82] The grace period was extended a second time, to October 25, 1916.[83]

Weizmann felt he could no longer remain on the sidelines. Early in August 1916, about a week after Samuel's conciliatory speech, he joined other leading Russian Jews, including Sokolow and Jabotinsky—and, of all people, Lucien Wolf—in a committee chaired by Gregory Benenson, the managing director of the Russian and English Bank. Ironically, it was probably Wolf who was responsible for adding Weizmann and Sokolow to the committee since, as Wolf argued in a memorandum to Samuel, their silence on the matter of enlistment gave the wrong impression that they were opposed to it.[84] This so-called Russian Committee established "propaganda committees" in Manchester, Liverpool, Leeds, and Glasgow and contacted the Yiddish press in an effort to secure support.[85] Its purpose was to encourage enlistment on a voluntary basis. Weizmann, Sokolow, and Benenson, who met with Samuel at the end of August 1916, were told time was of the essence and urged to act as expeditiously as possible.[86] Throughout his tenure on the committee Weizmann tried to mediate between the government and the Russian Jews of the East End. He and his colleagues were able to persuade Samuel to postpone the deadline for conscription twice, but at the same time they also labored hard to extract some concessions from potential recruits. Indeed, the special police branch that monitored the activities of the committee reported of a large meeting, presided over by Weizmann, on September 14, 1916, in which Weizmann appealed to the two hundred persons present to enlist voluntarily, while others called for a compromise formula.[87] The compromise suggested by the Russian Committee was the enlistment of the Russian Jews into Home Defence and Labor Battalion units—a proposal also favored by Wolf—which would be more palatable to the Russian Jews since they could remain in England instead of serving on the front.[88]

It became clear that the home secretary and others involved in efforts of enlistment were not willing to offer any further exceptions for the Russian Jews. A visit, on September 19, by Benenson and Weizmann to Arthur Henderson, the cabinet's paymaster general, failed to alter this stance.[89] An official in the War Office commented on the memorandum that Henderson wrote following the visit to his office: "Special terms for the Russians would be very hard to justify to the public." The Russian Jews, as Weizmann pointed out to Henderson in their meeting, preferred to take the chance that they would not be deported even if they refused to serve in the British army. Moreover, the committee had to face the strong opposition to its work being mounted by the Foreign Jews Protection Committee formed by Jewish organizations in the East End of London to campaign against the government's proposals. The result was that only some three hundred men had enlisted by the latter part of September 1916.[90]

For Weizmann himself there was an embarrassing, though brief, personal aspect to this whole affair. On August 31, 1916, he received a summons to report for military service two weeks hence. At the age of forty-one he still qualified for service under the further stipulation effective May 25, 1916. He replied by return mail that he was working for the government and in any case would turn forty-two within three months.[91] While writing this letter Weizmann must have remembered how once before he had narrowly escaped serving in the cause of Russia. This time the task of extricating himself from an unpleasant duty was much easier; nothing more was heard from the military authorities.

In the meantime Jabotinsky was conducting his own campaign with the aid of his trusted lieutenant Meir Grossman, who arrived from Copenhagen in London in September 1916 to edit *Unsere Tribune*,[92] and Yosef Trumpeldor, who arrived in October.[93] Despite his carefully crafted plans[94] and widely distributed broadsheets,[95] Jabotinsky was even less successful than the more moderate Russian Committee. His harsh and uncompromising language on the duties of the Russian immigrants to their national pride and their adoptive country failed to arouse sympathy for his ideas. In the eyes of Whitechapel Jews, in fact, he became obnoxious. Unlike Weizmann and his colleagues who attempted to encourage voluntary, rather than coerced enlistment—an approach urged simultaneously by radicals and liberals for citizens as well—Jabotinsky retained the option of pursuing his own line, of recruiting for a Jewish legion still to be approved by the government. But in the fall of 1916, unlike his strategy a year earlier, he presented the Jewish legion as a suitable means for overcoming the distressing reluctance of alien Jews to serve in any existing military organization. In September 1916 he was able, with aid from public funds secured by Samuel, in addition to the regular contributions supplied by Cowen, to widen and intensify his campaign.

The response was far from what Jabotinsky had hoped and prophesied. He was reviled as a "warmonger" and "capitalist lackey"[96] and made the butt for all the fear and resentment the immigrant community could not well vent against the government. A police report of a meeting chaired by Jabotinsky on October 16, 1916, illustrates the sentiment against him in the East End:

> The meeting commenced soon after 8 p.m. and between 200 and 300 persons were present, mostly men of military age. As soon as the chairman rose to open the meeting, a deafening noise was made by the moving of chairs, stamping of feet, whistling and hideous yells, making it impossible to hear anything that was being said. . . . They then surged towards the platform, where Mr. Jabotinsky was sitting with two other gentlemen. Several of the men mounted the platform and cries [of] "Traitors" could be heard from among the crowd. It could clearly be noticed that most of those present were determined to prevent any speeches being made. Soon after 9 p.m. the uniformed police . . . were called in . . . and persuaded the people to leave the building.[97]

Ten days after this meeting Jabotinsky wrote to Samuel admitting failure.[98] Cowen, who had sacrificed his prestige by his vocal support of both conscription and the idea of a Jewish legion, was repudiated by his own Zionist constituents, and in February 1917 he withdrew as president of the EZF, to be replaced by Weizmann.

The controversy around the enlistment of the Russian Jews had minor military significance but important symbolic and psychological implications. The war, which had spread rapidly from a Balkan quarrel to a clash between Great Power coalitions that was justly named a world war, had made the adherence of even the smallest strategic force a matter of consequence for the contestants. If either side was known to be wooing a minor political or military element, or seemed to enjoy an advantage through the sympathy of such a group, it aroused a competitive concern and activity on the other side. Those who could not be drawn into active participation—particularly the large neutral nations but also significant minor factions—were plied with propaganda to ensure their benevolence, or at least fend off any bias in their practice of neutrality.[99] The Jews, a widely scattered people whose interests were affected both in the immediate ravages and in the uncertain outcome of the war in Europe and the Middle East and who represented an appreciable force in the most important neutral country, the United States, were among those focused for special attention from the start.[100] Whether they could hope to influence policy to their advantage in regard to their future status in Russia or in Palestine largely depended on the shifting fortunes of war.

Turkey's fortuitous entry into the war stirred the imaginations of many, who began to think of new possibilities in Palestine. Weizmann later noted that religious sentiments and romantic idealism brought him more converts to Zionism among British leaders than did strategic calculations.[101] Sympathy for Jews was not the only sentiment that inspired in British minds visions of a bright new future for the collapsed Ottoman realm. Lloyd George was emotionally committed to the division of the Ottoman Empire among ethnic successor states more on account of Turkish atrocities against the Armenians and Greeks than from his early biblical schooling and idealization of the Hebrew race. The British proconsuls stationed in Egypt and the Sudan at once saw glad prospects of a postwar British-ruled realm of Arab principalities from Egypt to Mesopotamia, rivaling in extent and riches the viceroyalty of India, with a new Arab caliphate making it the center of the whole Muslim world.[102] But making such realms a reality required military successes that did not seem feasible.

The deadlock on the Western front made some "Easterners" among the strategists urge bold thrusts to break the stalemate by attacking Turkey and gaining the adherence of the Balkan countries. One such plan, favored by Lord Kitchener, envisaged an assault from the sea upon Alexandretta, the northernmost port of access to Syria.[103] The calculation was that this assault might set off an uprising of Arabs against Ottoman rule, with multiple advantageous effects: it would undercut the Turkish call for a *jihad*, a holy war of all Muslims, against the Allies; it would support the faltering attack on Mesopotamia, launched from India by way of the Persian Gulf; and it would give Britain a secure connection from the Mediterranean to the Persian Gulf oil fields after the war.[104] But another venture—the assault on the Dardanelles, which the Russians requested to relieve Turkish pressures in the Caucasus—absorbed whatever manpower could be spared from the Western front. Moreover, further consideration led to severe doubts about the tenability of a position at Alexandretta and renewed awareness of the postwar frictions among the Allied powers that a partition of the Ottoman realm would produce.[105] The interdepartmental de Bunsen Committee recommended maintaining the Ottoman realm intact, with autonomy for its ethnic provinces. If partition could not be avoided, it favored British retention of the southern Syrian areas, including Palestine and Sinai, rather than Alexandretta, in order to provide a bastion for the Suez Canal.[106]

As for the immediate issue of a military posture in the area during the war, the British doctrine remained essentially defensive. It sought to preserve, in Egypt and Mesopotamia, the positions Britain had established before the war while avoiding commitments that would unnecessarily disturb the *status quo* in the rest of the region until it became clear what changes the war might bring. Thus the British in Egypt initially used the Suez Canal as their line of defense rather than attempting an advance into the Sinai beyond. But even this limited strategy did not preclude seeking support from interested parties in the area; in fact, it required this support. By the beginning of 1915 the Turks had proved that, under German supervision, they could send a force across the Sinai desert and, by attacking at the canal, threaten to block its traffic. Simply beating back the attack, in the fighting on February 3–4, 1915, did not remove the threat;[107] and the commanders in Egypt became more interested in the overtures made earlier by the sharif of Mecca, Hussein, and his sons.[108] Such allies could, at the very least, impede a new Turkish attack by denying camel transport; and their mere abstention from the *jihad* the sultan had proclaimed against the Allies would undermine a subversive appeal—rated as very dangerous—to the Muslims in India and elsewhere in the British Empire. Moreover, as the Gallipoli campaign began to run into difficulties, the commander there applied to Egypt for a diversion among the Arabs that could, he hoped, reduce the commitment of Arab troops serving with the Turks on his front.[109] The British may well have supposed that such limited military involvement might be obtained from disaffected Arabs with no great political compensation. Syrian nationalists in Cairo had been able to place spies for Britain behind the Turkish lines without specific political promises from the Allies; and when such promises came later, in the Declaration to the Seven of June 16, 1918, the pledge of self-determination to the Syrians was counterposed to earlier commitments to other parties, including Arabs, which had become known to the public and might affect the future of Syria.[110] Among these were promises made to the sharif of Mecca who, by December 1916, had proclaimed himself grandly as "King of the Arabs."[111] In his case, political considerations of the widest scope, framed after the Hedjazi potentate had joined hands with the Arab nationalists of Damascus, were raised from the beginning as the precondition for Arab military commitment.[112] Viewed as ludicrously exaggerated by the surprised Britons when they were first broached in July 1915, the considerations were accepted in principle, subject to vaguely defined reservations by Sir Henry McMahon, the high commissioner in Egypt, in October, when conditions had changed.[113] He was under pressure at that time to find some relief for the hard-pressed Gallipoli expedition by

subverting Turkey's Arab troops; the Arab nationalist agent, Mu-
hammed Sharif al-Faruki, had made the matter seem urgent with (evidently baseless) reports that the underground Arab societies were about
to succumb to German inducements to identify themselves with the
Turkish *jihad*.[114] Acting on his own—and much to the dismay of
the India Office, which was violently opposed to stirring up revolt in
the Arabian peninsula[115]—McMahon offered sufficient support for postwar "independence" of the Arabs from Turkish sovereignty to secure a
vague assurance from the sharif that the Arabs "remain firm to our resolution . . . for which we await the opportunity suitable to our situation."[116]

McMahon's negotiations with the Sharif Hussein implied, at the least,
a postwar partition of the Ottoman Empire, a policy the long-range strategic plans of the de Bunsen Committee had not favored. Military needs
of immediate urgency, which produced such political deviations in the
case of a relatively minor military factor like the incalculable Arabs, also
applied to Britain's major allies as well as the undecided Balkan and
Adriatic countries. Agreements were suggested, and some concluded,
to win allies or keep them or forestall their joining the foe. These agreements contemplated dividing the Ottoman possessions in Europe and
Asia among Russia, Italy, and Greece; and, of course, the two Western
powers, France and Britain, felt bound to secure their own future interests in the same way. The conservative British policy, wedded to the
status quo ante, was worn down not only by the diplomacy dictated by
its alliances but by changing military perceptions of its position in Egypt,
which also fostered a more aggressive approach on the Turkish front.

In November 1915, Lord Kitchener visited Egypt and ordered that the
line of defense be moved forward to points ten kilometers east of the
Suez Canal so that the recurrent Turkish threats of its blockage might
be ended. Soon after, Sir Archibald Murray, the chief of staff in London,
took charge of evacuating the force bogged down in Gallipoli and then
assumed command in Egypt. He began a slow, methodical advance into
the Sinai peninsula, building a railroad and water pipeline to supply his
forward troops as he moved in. This change in the plan for Egypt's
defense implied the intention to hold a substantial British buffer zone to
the east of the canal.[117] It also reactivated the need for the long-mooted
Arab revolt. Previous efforts to induce the sharif to raise a revolt in Syria
or an attack on the Baghdad rail lines in support of the hard-pressed
British contingent in Mesopotamia had met with little response and were
postponed by the sharif on the grounds of his own precarious position.[118] Now, however, the Arab revolt was begun on June 5, 1916, with
an attack on the garrison in Mecca by the sharifian tribal force.[119] Initial
successes were not followed by further Arab victories, and the sharif,
fearful of Turkish reprisals, was compelled to invite his new allies, the
infidel British and French, to dispatch soldiers to help him even if it
meant breaching traditional bans on unbelievers in the Islamic holy land.[120]

At that time, too, the Turks were again threatening the Suez Canal, only to be beaten back on July 19.

Under the circumstances, the Arab revolt, while stalled, was not effectively repressed. The Allied commanders, about to venture further in the Sinai to the border of Palestine, undertook to reorganize and bolster the revolt.[121] By November, Murray was ready to move. Following his victory at El-Arish, on December 21, 1916, the attack on Palestine could begin,[122] bringing to a head the question of its position in the future peace settlement.

These military contingencies of 1915–16 had raised the issue of dismantling the Ottoman Empire and had produced inter-Allied agreements affecting Palestine before the Lloyd George government was installed in early December 1916. The attack on the Dardanelles, undertaken at Russia's request, led to a Russian demand for control of Constantinople and the Straits. British acceptance of this claim, on March 12, 1915, "subject to the war being carried on and brought to a successful conclusion, and to the desiderata of Great Britain and France in the Ottoman Empire and elsewhere being realised," also stipulated "that the Mussulman Holy Places and Arabia shall under all circumstances remain under independent Mussulman dominion." In acknowledging these terms, the Russians noted the need "to elucidate at once" whether the "independent Mussulman dominion" proposed meant retaining Turkish suzerainty and a Turkish caliphate, "or it is contemplated to create new independent states." The meaning of "independence" was obviously quite indefinite in these discussions. In positive terms, the Russians stated their support, until further clarification, for an "independent Muslim government" of the Muslim Holy Places and desired "that the Caliphate should be separated from Turkey."[123]

The French, meanwhile, had asked for Russia's approval of the annexation of Syria (and Cilicia) by France, and the French ambassador in Moscow, Georges Maurice Paléologue, stated that, in his opinion the reference to Syria was meant to include Palestine. Paléologue was reminded that "there is in Jerusalem an independent governor" under current Ottoman practice, and the Russian ambassador in Paris was instructed to elucidate whether Paléologue's view was the official French position, since it would be "indispensable to study the question with closer attention, if the Holy Places are involved."[124] With this reminder of the cause from which the Crimean War had sprung, the future of Palestine in Allied postwar planning remained undecided.

The secret agreement between the Entente powers and Italy concluded in London on April 26, 1915, simply confirmed the previous Allied understanding regarding "Arabia and the Moslem Holy Places in Arabia" and provided for a "just share" for Italy if Turkey were partitioned. It also promised "consideration" for Italian interests if altered zones of interest were agreed on "in the event of the territorial integrity of the Turkish Empire being maintained."[125]

The correspondence between Sir Henry McMahon and King Hussein was not considered by the British to affect Palestine, though Arab spokesmen and King Hussein himself—who did not raise the point at the time—in later years claimed otherwise.[126] Specific agreements regarding the Holy Land were negotiated by France and Britain in the Sykes-Picot talks, to which Russia concurred. The Anglo-French discussions began in October 1915, when the British advised the French ambassador in London of British correspondence with the Arabs. That exchange had culminated in McMahon's acceptance of Arab claims, under reservation of French and British requirements in specific areas falling within the range of the original Arab demands. On January 3, 1916, the two negotiators, Charles François Georges Picot and Sir Mark Sykes, had agreed on a draft, which they took to Petrograd for Russian concurrence in March. Concurrence was granted, on condition that the Western Allies approved Russian territorial claims in northern Anatolia. The agreement was sealed in an exchange of notes between the several governments on May 16, 1916, with a final Russian reservation regarding rights in the Black Sea being acknowledged in October 1916.[127]

The Anglo-French exchange of notes, sealing the Sykes-Picot Agreement in May 1916, was concerned with the future status of those Ottoman areas where the Arabs were to be independent or British or French regimes were to be set up. If the Arabs did indeed "cooperate" and were able to occupy the towns they claimed—"Homs, Hama, Damascus and Aleppo"—France and Britain were to "recognize and protect [later revised to "uphold"] . . . an independent Arab State or Confederation of Arab States . . . under the suzerainty of an Arab chief." The area of "independence" (which still might amount to no more than autonomy or as much as full sovereignty) would include the Arabian peninsula— or the Muslim Holy Places—and the interior to the north of it as far as the region of Aleppo. In the northern part of this area France, and in the south Britain, would have special rights and supply advisers to the Arab government. Both powers were allocated additional areas where they could "establish such direct or indirect administration or control as they desire and they may think fit to arrange with the Arab State or Confederation."[128] In this way, the British interest in the oil fields and seaports of Mesopotamia and traditional French interests in the Levant coast were secured. To the south of the French-held Levant, the ports of Acre and Haifa were to be British and serve as a road terminal and railhead in the future, connecting the Mediterranean with the Persian Gulf as a British right-of-way. The rest of Palestine—roughly the Ottoman-independent *sanjak* of Jerusalem—was designated by the signatories to be governed by "an international administration, the form of which is to be decided upon after consultation with Russia, and subsequently . . . the other Allies, and the representatives of the Shereef of Mecca."[129] These, then, were war commitments that did not dwell on absolutely precise frontiers but were directed toward strategic conceptions.

With these agreements, the British, together with other Allied nations, had taken a decisive step toward scrapping old strategic conceptions of the Ottoman regime as a buffer between the rival ambitions of greater powers that might clash disastrously in its absence. A dangerous road was opened for new rivalries and contentions, however, involving many of the same nations presently allied in the war. This circumstance led many to favor a separate peace with Turkey that might preserve its territorial integrity.[130] Another alternative would be to divide the Ottoman realm among its subject nationalities, and this idea began to find support among the advocates of self-determination. Mark Sykes, the recognized British expert on the Middle East, was one such convert to this approach, and his vision of a postwar future for the lands detached from Turkey was built on Armenian and Jewish, as well as Arab, nationalism. His understanding of Zionism, in particular, was a new perspective acquired during negotiations with Picot, when the forces of Jewish opinion and Zionist nationalism were called to his attention by the ministries concerned in London.[131] Then, when in his new capacity as assistant secretary to the war cabinet Sykes was asked to prepare a new policy for the Ottoman area in the recently formed Lloyd George government, he was already committed to the principle of partitioning the region, and he began a more thorough study of Zionism and the Jewish public.[132]

British officers brought to the appraisal of the Jews as an element in their wartime and postwar strategies not only their immediate experience in the field in sectors where Jewish opinion was a factor but traditional perceptions common to the childhood training of all but differently developed by each. Weizmann, as noted earlier, was impressed with the greater efficacy, in gaining British friends for Zionism, of biblical and romantic traditions over Zionist arguments concerning the military value of the Jews as allies, immediately and in the future.[133] He also found that, like Herzl, he could negotiate more effectively by being neutral about such antisemitic attitudes as his British counterparts might harbor, accepting them as the basis for reasonable discussion and for mutually agreeable rational solutions of common problems. In addition, Jews—as well as the Arabs whose cause was taken up with such ardor by romantic cynics like St. John Philby and T. E. Lawrence—found some of their most forthright and committed supporters by tapping the common tendency of officers involved with them, especially as troop commanders, to identify with the cause of the often inept and hapless but humanly appealing men they led or sponsored. Among the Zionist advocates gained in this way were Colonel John Henry Patterson, the Irish commander of the Zion Mule Corps, and the Tory MP and War Office official Leopold Amery.

One common British stereotype, especially prevalent among men concerned with Russian and Ottoman affairs, attributed to the Jews a powerful, malign influence in those regions. This widely shared antisemitic bias was sharpened by the salient involvement of Jews in major political concerns of the time. The sympathy Jews aroused in England as victims of Russian pogroms in the 1880s was even at that time mixed with hostility among those who suspected that the victims must have done something to deserve such widespread violence. The flood of immigrants to England that followed generated an anti-Jewish animus that led the philosophical Balfour, among others, to regard the increase of those unassimilable Asians with misgiving and to view with some understanding the racist speculations of Houston Stewart Chamberlain and Cosima Wagner in Germany—a perspective Balfour frankly admitted to Weizmann in the fall of 1914. When tsarist Russia became a British ally, those who had previously been skeptical of Jewish allegations of Russian atrocities not only listened sympathetically to counterpropaganda on this point but found persuasive the Russian-sponsored antisemitic conspiracy theories linking Jewish capitalists and revolutionaries in a plot to seize power throughout the world and overthrow legitimate governments and social orders everywhere.

Similar, more or less antisemitic themes began to be spun out about the Jewish role in Turkey, especially in the wake of the Young Turk revolution of 1908. Salonica, a heavily Jewish port town, was the main center from which the revolution arose, and its Masonic lodge, to which the leading Young Turks belonged, had a strong Jewish contingent. Counted among Jews, in the view of Britons and others who wove the myth of a Jewish conspiracy behind the Young Turk uprising, were members of a Judeo-Muslim sect, the Doenmeh, one of whom, David Bey,[134] managed the finances of the new regime. Added to this influence was the prominent role of German Jewish bankers, who had a strong financial stake in the Turco-German military alliance.[135] The idea of an international Jewish conspiracy seemed particularly ominous when even French Jews were thought to be involved with German Jewish financial interests and the leading American Jewish notables were men like the Schiffs, Warburgs, and others with German Jewish banking connections.

A mood of suspicion prevailed in the response of Sir Cecil Spring-Rice, British ambassador to Washington, to proposals for counteracting anti-Allied sentiment among German and Russian Jews in the United States. His letter to Robert Cecil reflects widespread views among the British:

> The influence of the Jews [in the United States] is very great. They are well organized and especially in the press in finance and politics their influence is considerable. Most people would tell you that as a whole their sympathies are with the Germans. . . . The official head of the Jewish party here, Jacob Schiff, is strongly pro-German. The great Jewish bank has German affiliations. . . . The principal Jewish paper the "Tag" is strongly pro-German. The great mass of the Jewish voters are actuated by a strong hatred of Russia. This really is the governing motive. . . . Thus in spite of the friendly attitude towards England and France taken by the prominent members of

the Jewish community the net result is that Jewish influence here is pro-German. . . . Our weak point is of course the hatred of the Jew for Russia. This will last as long as the Jewish disabilities in Russia last and I presume that is a matter of which Russia alone can be the judge. The disabilities are mainly the result of the superior business intelligence of the Jews and appear to be likely to last as long as the ordinary Russian cannot compete with the ordinary Jew. These are the brutal facts.

Spring-Rice concluded his long letter: "The heads of the Jewish communities in France and England should be warned of the general impression which exists here of the anti-ally sympathies of the great mass of the Jews in the United States. . . . There is a danger threatening the Jew in England and France of which they should be warned." [136]

The opinion of the United States, and of American Jews, became a matter of growing concern in London as the war wore on. Weizmann, Jabotinsky, and others brought up the topic in their discussions with the British officials. [137] Bogged down in trench warfare and compelled to endure dreadful carnage, the British also experienced a rapid decline of their financial resources. To carry on, and to sustain their hard-pressed allies, they had to seek credit from their American suppliers. [138] At the same time, their blockading of enemy trade with neutrals clashed directly with American interests. This major tenet of British strategy wore thin the initial sympathy of many Americans for their Anglo-Saxon kin, who were believed to have valiantly aided the violated Belgians. It caused a groundswell of resentment already fed by the Anglophobia of Irish Americans, German Americans, and others. The British could ill afford to ignore any chance to conciliate any American group, including the Jews, and Spring-Rice gained little credit by his outburst.

The fact of the matter was that, with antisemitic, despotic Russia on the side of the Allies, the choice for American Jews was clear. American Jews of German descent had close ties to other German Americans and shared with them a strong attachment to their old home and culture. Initial Jewish sympathies were carefully cultivated by the Central Powers through a friendly attitude to the Jews in the war zone and active propaganda in the United States. [139] Thus the Yiddish daily *Di Varheit* suffered a crippling loss in circulation when it adopted a pro-Allied editorial position at the beginning of the war. The Jewish workers' basic hostility to the tsarist regime was stiffened by ideology, for American Jewish radicals leaned toward an antiwar position. Other Jewish progressives, including leading Zionists like Judah Magnes and Henrietta Szold, joined in the pacifist activity of the socialist preacher Norman Thomas.

The general American public, on the other hand, had traditional sympathies for Britain and France and was aroused by reported German atrocities in Belgium. A major humanitarian relief campaign resulted, in which pro-Allied sentiment colored official neutrality. Such Anglophile leanings were shared in the early war years primarily by those Jews who were most fully accepted by their non-Jewish peers. Among Zionists, professors like Richard Gottheil[140] and Horace Kallen, or persons close to the Wilson administration like Brandeis and Felix Frankfurter, or even the initially pacifist Stephen Wise, were the most susceptible to the pro-British sympathies prevalent in the gentile milieu where these men occupied positions of prominence and trust.[141] But a policy of neutrality was enforced upon members of the PZC, whatever their personal sympathies.

A neutral attitude not only conformed to American official policy; it seemed imperative under the circumstances. Only a carefully guarded neutrality made possible whatever connection the PZC could maintain with Zionist activities in Berlin and London as well as Copenhagen and Constantinople. Particular caution was necessary to avoid offending Turkey if the relief work in Palestine was to continue unimpeded and the Jewish community to be protected against repression by a Turkish military regime already deeply suspicious of Jewish nationalism. Fear of reckless and partisan statements by delegates made a number of leading Zionists share the apprehensions of Jacob Schiff and Louis Marshall about the proposed wartime convening of the American Jewish Congress.

The Allies, who organized propaganda councils for a wide variety of subject nationalities in the Austro-Hungarian and Ottoman empires and for related ethnic groups in neutral countries, took note of their problem in regard to the Jews, especially those in the United States. On the basis of observed facts and associated fancies, Jews became the objects of a certain concern among British officials in which hostility was mixed with cautious—indeed, overestimated—appreciation of the strategic weight of Jewish opinion. The attitudes of American Jews were particularly worrisome in view of the potentially decisive weight of the great neutral republic. The sufferings of Jews in border zones controlled by Russia amid the shifting tides of battle[142] aroused American Jews, long committed to antitsarist lobbying in American politics; and the mass of Eastern European Jewish immigrants lent their own passion to the anti-Russian policy of their old-line communal leaders, pro-German by inheritance and personal background.[143]

Clearly, the alliance with Russia in the Triple Entente was a handicap of major proportions for Britain and France in any approach to American Jews, whose long-standing antipathy to the country of pogroms and anti-Jewish laws was raised to fever pitch by the mass removal of Jews from the Russian borders, carried out with unusual brutality when the war broke out. German policies stood in sharp contrast, and German victories in the East were seen by Jews everywhere as a veritable godsend. German Zionists were prominent in founding in the fall of 1914 the Komitee für den Osten, a Jewish agency organized to cooperate with the authorities in occupied Eastern Europe in aiding the stricken Jewish communities.[144] The Komitee took on as part of its duty the conduct of pro-German propaganda among Jewish communities, and on their behalf Dr. Isaac Straus, a German industrialist and Zionist who had become a friend of Weizmann through Julius Simon and been a major supporter of the campaign for a Palestine chemical institute within the planned Jewish university, went to the United States to work among Jews in aid of Ambassador Count Johann-Heinrich Bernstorff.[145] His success there was soon noticed, producing heightened concern in Allied circles.[146]

The French were the first to respond actively to German propaganda among American Jews. Dr. Naoum Slousch, professor of Hebrew at the Sorbonne and a Zionist who traveled in the United States throughout November 1915, believed that one way to counter the effects of Russian violence against Jews and promote American Jewish sympathies for the Allied cause was to issue a declaration favoring an independent Jewish colony in the south of Palestine; he repeated his suggestion in May and August 1916.[147] In November 1915, Professor Victor Guillaume Basch, an eminent historian at the Sorbonne, was sent to the United States for work in the Jewish community. Basch, a socialist, was sympathetic to Zionism, having been among Weizmann's group of scholars who enlisted in the campaign for the Jewish university before the war. Basch directed his attention in the United States to the working-class leadership in particular, and he had invited Weizmann and Sokolow to meet him in Paris in October, before his departure.[148] A committee of eminent Jews, the Comité de Propagande Française auprès des Juifs des Pays Neutres, was set up to influence Jewish opinion in the neutral countries, acting in concert with Basch's mission.

The Conjoint Foreign Committee was informed of the new venture and asked to work on parallel lines. Lucien Wolf, who adopted the suggestion with alacrity, was supplied with the reports and conclusions that began to come from Basch. Basch's reports were far from encouraging. Russian and German Jews in the United States were as cool to the Allies as had been feared. Whatever modifications in Russian policy could be wrought by Allied pressure—under war conditions probably very little—would still be insufficient to change minds. But Allied support for Jewish aspirations in Palestine might cause a shift in sympathy, for, despite rumors of German gestures toward the same end, Allied support would be more meaningful as the Allies were not burdened by an alliance with Turkey. These circumstances were implicit in Basch's recommendations that very general expressions of sympathy might suffice; and he noted the current ascendancy of the Zionists in the American Jewish community and the excellent political connections they enjoyed under the leadership of Brandeis.[149]

At the very time that Basch was in the United States, the British naval blockade against munitions shipments and other American trade with Germany was a source of irritation thoroughly exploited by anti-British circles of American opinion. In the Ottoman war zone, at the same time, the British military command was adopting a more aggressive strategy

toward advancing into the Sinai and to Palestine.[150] The general concern
with Jewish opinion, rather academic until then, was made more urgent
by such developments.

From the beginning of the war, the Western Allies were pressed by
advisers on Jewish affairs to induce the Russians to ease their repression
of Jews in their domains, but the Allies were unable to do more than
make a few apologetic, ineffective suggestions to an ally on matters of
its domestic policy. Horace Kallen, professor at the University of Wisconsin, suggested a different approach to Alfred Zimmern, a member of
the *Round Table* group who was at the time a visiting professor at Kallen's university. Kallen's letter, forwarded to Lord Eustace Percy in the
Foreign Office in November 1915, proposed that Britain could counter
German pronouncements about the rights of Eastern European Jews by
analogous statements favoring "Jewish rights in every country, and a
very veiled suggestion concerning nationalization in Palestine."[151] By the
end of 1915 similar proposals were being considered as a result of Victor
Basch's report to the Comité de Propagande Française, and these were
conveyed to Wolf, Britain's expert on Jewish affairs.

When Kallen's proposal was considered by the Foreign Office, and
there was talk of sending an agent to the United States to work with the
Jewish press, Wolf was not thought the man for the job, evidently because of his tensions with the Zionists. But his observations after reading Basch's recommendations were thought all the more impressive as
coming from a non-Zionist expert on Jewish opinion. When Wolf launched
his effort in late 1915 to parallel the French initiative, he began with
Basch's findings, to which he supplied his concurring analysis.[152] The
main issue was the constant refrain of his appeals to the government:
Russia's anti-Jewish policy had to stop.

The British, however, proved even less inclined to raise this issue with
their slightly uncertain ally than were the French. Wolf had not enhanced his popularity in official quarters with his insistence that the
British push the Russians about the treatment of Russian Jews, and when
his arguments were disregarded, he pressed forward on the other front.
While declaring himself opposed to Zionism, he concurred with Basch's
judgment that the Zionist influence was rising among American Jews
and agreed that an appropriate statement in favor of Jewish interests in
Palestine would be effective in gaining sympathy among them.[153] He
then went a step further and on March 3, 1916, in a letter to Lancelot
Oliphant of the Foreign Office, offered his own formula for an Allied
statement of sympathy with Jewish aims in Palestine. Wolf set forth the
position offered—and rejected—by the non-Zionists to the Zionists in
their discussions of the previous year.[154] In March 1916 this draft was
proposed for Allied consideration by Sir Edward Grey, the secretary of
state for foreign affairs, during the negotiations in Petrograd regarding
the Sykes-Picot Agreement. As the other Allies showed no great interest
in the proposed statement, the matter was dropped. Grey concluded

that if such a statement were to serve its purpose, it would, in any case, have to be written in a spirit more acceptable to the Zionists.[155] He undoubtedly had the American Zionists in mind.

The immediate need to conciliate Jewish opinion in the United States was paralleled by the rise in the level of British activity on the Egyptian Sinai front in early 1916 and the concurrent Sykes-Picot negotiations. The attention of the Western Allies was centered mainly on the adjustment of their mutual claims and on the role of the Arabs in an anti-Ottoman coalition. The prospective Arab rebels of the Hedjaz had to be taken into account in the strategy, and thus also in the diplomacy, of Allied plans for defeating and partitioning Turkey. But both the French and the British also worked with Syrian and Armenian émigrés and espionage agents;[156] and the French encouraged these dissidents to recruit military units among their fellowship.[157] Offers of Jewish military assistance now became more attractive; but of course the military and political officers on the scene sought to avoid any commitments that could prejudice British freedom of action after the war. Thus Jabotinsky's campaign in England enjoyed British favor but no real success in 1916. At the end of the year, the Nili espionage ring, centered around the Aaronsohn family in the Palestine village of Zichron Yaakov, was finally accepted and activated by the British strategists and commanders.[158]

In March 1916 the British entertained another proposal that coincided with Wolf's initiative. It was forwarded by a non-Zionist Jewish leader, the influential Alexandrian banker Edgar Suarès, and was meant to counter a suggested German protectorate over Palestine that he said was favored by pro-German Jews.[159] This was a kind of pressure to which Foreign Office personnel responded more readily than to Wolf's urgent pleading. Sir Henry McMahon, the high commissioner in Egypt, reported Suarès as proposing, as a way to win over Jewish sympathy, a British protectorate in Palestine that would open the country to Jewish immigrants and leave "the management of its internal affairs . . . in the hands of Jews . . . under British Protection."[160]

This communication, with its suggestion of German moves to win Jewish opinion, produced advisory opinions by responsible officials that were woven into the emerging British policy. At the same time, the reports of Jewish attitudes in the United States, the new approach to the defense of Egypt, and the rapidly maturing Sykes-Picot negotiations were demanding staff decisions. Sir Arthur Nicolson, the permanent undersecretary of state for foreign affairs, was not convinced that the Zionists dominated Jewish opinion; he "was under the impression the Zionists were in a considerable minority." Also, since the Sykes-Picot terms about to be presented to Russia for concurrence provided for an international administration of Palestine, he felt Britain could not suggest another arrangement.[161]

Other opinions in the Foreign Office held that "an arrangement completely satisfactory to Jewish aspirations in regard to Palestine might . . .

have immense attractions for the great body of Jews." More particularly, since this adviser, Hugh O'Beirne, shared the prevailing assumption of men in the field regarding the powerful influence of Jews in the Young Turk movement, he suggested that Britain might "conceivably be able to strike a bargain with them as to withdrawing their support from the Young Turk Government which would then automatically collapse." Recognizing the objective difficulties of a Zionist project in a predominantly Arab Palestine, O'Beirne proposed the following: "While there would necessarily be an international administration of some kind in Jerusalem itself it is conceivable that in the rest of Palestine the Jews could be given special colonising facilities which in time would make them strong enough to cope with the Arab element, when the management of internal affairs might be placed in their hands under America's protection."[162] Concurring with O'Beirne's assumptions and resultant conclusions, Lord Robert Cecil minuted a few days later: "I do not think it is easy to exaggerate the international power of the Jews."[163]

Acting on this advice, the secretary of state for foreign affairs overruled objections and instructed that the French ambassador be informed of the suggestions that "Jewish opinion is now hostile and favours a German Protectorate over Palestine, [but] might be entirely changed if an American Protectorate was formed with the object of restoring Jews to Palestine."[164] Paul Cambon, the French ambassador, doubted whether his own or the Russian government would welcome this new British idea; and accordingly, on March 11, 1916, a cable was drafted in the foreign secretary's name by Lord Crewe, Weizmann's acquaintance and a member of the Rothschild circle, for submission to the respective governments by the British ambassador in Paris, Sir Francis Bertie, and the British ambassador in Petrograd, Sir George Buchanan. The cabled instructions, in terms taken largely from O'Beirne's memoranda on the subject, conveyed the formula recently proposed to the British by Lucien Wolf for a statement of sympathy with Jewish interests in Palestine as being "unobjectionable" and receiving sympathetic consideration. But, the instructions continued, "The scheme might be made far more attractive to the majority of the Jews if it held out to them the prospect that when in the course of time the Jewish colonists in Palestine grow strong enough to cope with the Arab population they may be allowed to take the management of the internal affairs of Palestine (with the exception of Jerusalem and the Holy Places) into their own hands."[165]

Contrary to Cambon's anticipation, the Russian response was favorable. On March 15, 1916, Buchanan was able to cable back to the Foreign Office that the Russian foreign minister, Sergei Sazonov, viewed the settlement of Jews in Palestine with sympathy, provided that the Holy Places be under an international regime and that all Christian churches be ensured equality of rights.[166] The Russians had shown themselves open to similar suggestions made to them earlier by the Zionist leader Yehiel Tschlenow. France, however, proved cool to a last-minute change in their agreement with the British. On March 22, 1916, Ambassador Bertie cabled to the Foreign Office that Aristide Briand, the French minister for foreign affairs, objected to the British proposal since it would arouse the "susceptibilities of Arabs whom it is advisable to treat with caution. . . . Consideration of scheme could not be usefully taken up until after question of creation of Arab Empire has been solved." The French, moreover, did not think that the Zionist demands had anything to do with world Jewish opinion.[167] This chilly response put an end to the British initiative, and the Sykes-Picot negotiations were drawn up in final form with no supplementary provision in favor of Jewish aims in Palestine.

This negotiation also marked the end of Wolf's claim to primacy as the representative of Jewish interests before the government. After waiting more than three months for an answer from the Foreign Office, he was finally told that the French government had rejected his proposals because of lack of unity among Jews.[168] At the beginning of July 1916 he received a polite but brief note in effect telling him that his suggested formula had been put on hold until further notice.[169] This news impelled him to visit France in July to meet with Baron Edmond.[170] The latter favored Wolf's "formula" of March 1916, which was similar in spirit to that of Basch, and he felt that Weizmann would not object to it. He urged his son James, then recuperating from a war wound in London, to bring the two parties together and effect some understanding between them.[171]

In March 1916 a majority of the Political Committee had, in fact, voted to try to resume the discussions with the Conjoint Foreign Committee, and Herbert Samuel had given Wolf to understand that the Zionists might very well accept the Conjoint's formula for Palestine.[172] Moreover, both sides were told on different occasions by senior members of the Foreign Office, as well as by Samuel, that they needed to demonstrate Jewish unity before their demands could be taken seriously. It is doubtful that they entered the discussions with any real hope that a joint agreement would result. Wolf and his associates were particularly angered at the very moment of their impending meeting by the publication in July of 1916 of *Zionism and the Jewish Future*, a volume edited by Harry Sacher and partly funded by Baron Edmond de Rothschild. In general, this volume, which had a respectable sale of three thousand copies, did not contribute anything new in terms of factual knowledge about the history of Zionism or its prospects for the future, but Moses Gaster's essay, "Judaism as a National Religion," and Weizmann's "Zionism and the Jewish Problem," must have been particularly grating to Wolf and his circle. Two paragraphs in Weizmann's short essay seemed specifically aimed at them:

> The conditions under which Jews live in the Western World make it impossible for their communities to render to Jewry at large the particular service which has been performed hitherto by the Jewish settlement in Eastern Europe, despite their marked superiority in political freedom, in economic stability, in adjustment to the demands of modern culture. For one effect of political and social emancipation on the Jews of the West has been to break

up their solidarity. They have gained the right to participate in the lives of modern nations, not as a national or sub-national group, but as individuals. True, the different Jewish communities are still grouped around their synagogues and other institutions, chiefly of a philanthropic character. "Judaism," conceived as a religious system, takes the place of the sense of attachment to the Jewish people and its traditions and ideals. But from the point of view of Jewish solidarity the substitute is woefully inadequate, and its inadequacy becomes more glaring from generation to generation. On the one hand, the culture and aspirations of the State in which he lives play an ever-growing part in the inner life of the individual Jew, and restrict more and more the sphere of activities in which his Jewishness expresses itself; and, on the other hand, the conception of what it means to be a Jew becomes more and more vague and uncertain for lack of a concrete embodiment of Jewish life which could serve as a guiding norm. Hence the natural progress of the emancipated Jew is through assimilation to absorption in his environment.

This process would proceed to its logical end even more rapidly were it not checked by anti-Semitism. For the efforts of the emancipated Jew to assimilate himself to his surroundings, quite honestly meant and largely successful though they are, deceive nobody but himself. The record of the emancipated Jew in loyalty to his country, in devotion to its ideals and service to its interests, is unimpeachable. None the less, he is felt by the outside world to be still something different, still an alien, and the measure of his success and prominence in the various walks of life which are thrown open to him is, broadly speaking, the measure of the dislike and distrust which he earns. Thus the phenomena of assimilation and of anti-Semitism go on side by side, and the position of the emancipated Jew, though he does not realize it himself, is even more tragic than that of his oppressed brother.[173]

No doubt, both Weizmann and Wolf agreed to meet primarily out of deference to James de Rothschild and his father. The meeting took place at James de Rothschild's house on August 17, 1916, and, as could have been predicted, the discussions were a total failure. Wolf did not inform Weizmann that he had submitted his "formula" to the Foreign Office on March 3, 1916. In a memorandum written the day of the meeting he set forth his version of what took place. He had told Weizmann, he recorded, that the Conjoint Foreign Committee would be prepared to cooperate with the Zionists on the basis of the formula he had suggested earlier "and with such amplifications of it as might be mutually agreed upon . . . but we stipulated that that work should not be based on any overt or official assumption of the existence of a Jewish nationality, and that it should not compromise any demand for privileges and preferences in Palestine in which the non-Jewish population would not equally share." Weizmann clearly did not agree to Wolf's demands, as the latter put it: "Dr. Weizmann showed no disposition to come to terms with us, either on the subject of nationality or special right."[174] Wolf showed James de Rothschild and Weizmann this memorandum, and as they disagreed with Wolf's interpretation of parts of the conversation, Wolf promised to incorporate their changes.[175]

But even before Wolf had received the corrections to his memorandum of August 17, he wrote a personal letter to James de Rothschild outlining his reasons for thinking that the meeting with Weizmann had proved "that there are vital and irreconcilable differences of principle and method between us." Wolf pointed to "Dr. Weizmann's assertion of a Jewish nationality" considered in light of his essay "Zionism and the Jewish Problem" as well as in light of Gaster's claim that it is "an absolute self-delusion" to believe that any Jew can be at once "English by nationality and Jewish by faith." These statements, wrote Wolf, "constitute a capitulation to our enemies."[176]

Wolf had another reason for protesting against an assertion of a separate Jewish nationality. It was

> an act of bad faith, inasmuch as it is a repudiation of the solemn pledges by which the Jewish communities of the Western world obtained their emancipation. . . . If the Jews of Western Europe and America to-day were to adopt Dr. Weizmann's principle, they would have either to renounce the rights they enjoy as citizens of the countries in which they live, or to incur the reproach of having obtained them by false pretences. The worst of it is that all these dangers are incurred without any corresponding advantage on the other side. Some Zionists pretend . . . that the establishment of a Jewish state in Palestine would solve the Jewish Question, inasmuch as it would provide a home for a large proportion of the Jews now crowded in the ghettos of Eastern Europe, and, by its political and moral influence, would secure better treatment for the remainder. This is a complete delusion. . . .
> On the other hand, the plan of political and social assimilation, as accepted by the Jewish people over a hundred years ago, has a record of splendid achievement to its credit.[177]

Finally, Wolf complained that the Zionists had changed their methods in midcourse. Without naming him, Wolf was referring to Harry Sacher's initial approach to him in November 1914 on the basis of "a cultural scheme . . . by which a settlement in Palestine on a religious basis, without any aggressive accentuation of nationality or other political aims, was contemplated." Wolf was opposed to any special rights for Jews in Palestine and warned that the Conjoint Foreign Committee "can have nothing to do with Zionism, as expounded by Dr. Weizmann. . . . I believe that . . . their reply to Dr. Weizmann's question, as to what they would do in the event of the Zionists applying to the Suzerain Power for a Charter, will be that they would oppose it tooth and nail." In the last sentence of this long, "personal" letter, Wolf mentioned, almost in passing, that the "formula" of the Conjoint had already been submitted to the government. This, in effect, made a mockery out of his conclusion in which he stated that he hoped "that a loyal understanding, based upon the compromise the Committee have already proposed, will still be arranged."[178]

Indeed, the revelation that the Conjoint Foreign Committee had already acted on its own became embarrassing for Wolf and his two principals, Claude Montefiore and D. L. Alexander. At a meeting of the

Board of Deputies on October 22, 1916, Alexander communicated the text of the formula but did not state that it had already been submitted to the government.[179] Leopold Greenberg, the editor of both the *Jewish World* and *Jewish Chronicle*, was not about to let such a scandal go unnoticed;[180] he had received from James de Rothschild a copy of Wolf's letter of August 31 and on November 1 published the information in the *Jewish World*.[181] In a letter to James de Rothschild, Weizmann pointed out that "while the gentlemen of the Conjoint Committee are posing before you and before the general public as being extremely anxious to make peace with the Zionists . . . while they are suggesting that it would be a breach of faith if we should take independent action . . . they have submitted this formula to His Majesty's Government no doubt as representing the wishes of the Jews."[182]

It was only on October 11, 1916, that James de Rothschild passed to Wolf the Zionist reply to the latter's memorandum of August 31. It centered on a definition of terms, particularly "nationality," and firmly rejected Wolf's formula as being composed of "vague and undefined phrases."[183] The Zionists' lengthy memorandum was countered by an even longer reply by Wolf on November 20 in which he dealt with the matters raised by his opponents on both theoretical and practical grounds.[184] In addition to these "official" memoranda, there was a concurrent exchange of "private" letters and notes interpreting and refuting various points raised in the larger documents; a virtual avalanche of paper was expended in the mutual recriminations and mounting animosity that resulted from these exchanges.[185] Throughout this period James de Rothschild and his father attempted to mediate between the two sides. On November 10 the baron wrote to Weizmann from Paris, strongly urging the Zionists, in their own best interests, to reach an agreement with the Conjoint Foreign Committee.[186]

But by then the controversy had already taken on a life of its own, and though Sokolow and Wolf had attempted to reach an agreement on a nonideological, practical basis and, in fact, were close to doing so by the end of 1916,[187] Weizmann was not interested in such a compromise. Though wary of the Conjoint's power both within the Jewish community and through its government contacts, he felt that the Zionists were strong enough in the fall of 1916 to declare their impatience with the Conjoint's sparring maneuvers.[188] In truth, Weizmann was worried that the Conjoint Foreign Committee would be in a position to emerge as the body formulating a policy of settlement in Palestine.[189] What Weizmann wanted was for the Conjoint to leave Palestinian issues strictly in the hands of the Zionists, and he was pleased to leave to them, in return, the task of caring for the welfare of Russian Jewry. Thus, the conflict with the Conjoint Foreign Committee was, from Weizmann's and his friends' point of view, functional and quite welcome.

The Zionists were thus annoyed—and puzzled—by Baron Edmond de Rothschild's insistence that they forge a compromise with the Conjoint.

After all, was he not the one who had constantly disparaged the "assim-ilationists" of Wolf's type? And hadn't he contributed funds to *Zionism and the Jewish Future,* which had so upset Wolf and his friends? In fact, prior to contributing his essay to the volume, Weizmann had sent it to Dorothy de Rothschild and apparently received her approval.[190] Weiz-mann must have wondered whether her husband was aware of her role. It is not clear to what degree James was simply complying with his fa-ther's wishes to be the mediator between the Zionists and the Conjoint and to what degree he truly believed that a compromise was possible. In any case, Weizmann's anger at being dragged into discussions he knew would be fruitless was directed at James de Rothschild, and only indirectly at the old baron, through Dorothy de Rothschild. In the midst of the accusations and counteraccusations, Weizmann felt he had to bring matters to a head and thus force the Rothschilds to choose sides. Writ-ing to James in mid-October 1916, he was willing for this to be his last letter to his patrons though he must have felt that, despite its harsh tone, it would have the desired effect; righteous and well-timed anger had worked well in the past with certain types of Jews and non-Jews alike, as it had with the Schuster women in 1912–13, upon whom he wanted to impress his own more committed Jewishness. Weizmann's letter began by recalling past offenses before it moved to its climax:

> It is my absolute conviction that, whatever we do, whatever we concede, however much we water down our Zionist principles, they [the Conjoint and their affiliates] won't work with us, they will and must work against us. Our interests *clash* and no paper formula can bridge over a gulf which is widening every day. We did not desire this fight; they brought it about, they started it 25 years ago, when we first began our activities, they relent-lessly continued it through these years, in season and out of season and they will certainly not allow us to gain an advance now. If we desire to succeed we must assume that we shall have these people as our bitterest enemies. . . .
>
> At present they may perhaps have enough power to undo the work which has been done here for the past 2½ years, but they won't stop our progress in Palestine and after all, that is the only thing that matters. Success here may be a very great help to the movement and to the Jews in general, a failure here caused by the interference of the "Jews" is tantamount to a moral pogrom. We shall face it!
>
> It is therefore impossible for us to yield on points of principle. I deeply appreciate your desire to bring about a peaceful solution. I have considered it as a very great privilege always that we could talk over and discuss these matters together. I was looking forward to the glorious time, when we would *work* together there in Palestine, where your Father began so gloriously. . . . We are both children of the *Galuth* if not of the Ghetto, but your chains are golden ones and mine are iron; your *Galuth* is a beautiful one, mine was sordid and hard. This is perhaps the reason why I am less generous, less tolerant, less broadminded. Please forgive and forget! That is all I can say in justification of my attitude. I must leave it to you to decide whether it is

still worth your while bothering about us at all at present. You know and
we know that you have done your best.[191]

Clearly James had done his best to bring an accord between Wolf and
the Zionists, but he was sufficiently well acquainted with the *dramatis
personae* to know that no peaceful resolution was possible. His heart,
moreover, was really with the Zionists; had he not been the one to advocate a Jewish state a year earlier? Feeling deceived by Wolf, on the
one hand, and pushed by Weizmann to choose sides, he threw his lot
with the Zionists. Even as his father continued to pressure Weizmann—
as late as November 10—to come to terms with the Conjoint, James arranged for a luncheon with members of the English Rothschilds that was
to mark a reconciliation between him and Weizmann.

Significantly, this luncheon took place on November 15, 1916, at the
home of Lady [Emma Louisa] Rothschild, widow of the first Lord Rothschild, who had a change of heart on the matter of Zionism just prior to
his death in March 1915. Present were also her sons, Charles and Walter, the second Lord Rothschild. In addition to James de Rothschild,
Herbert Samuel also joined the family.[192] There is no record of the conversation that took place, but it can be safely assumed that the Zionist
"Demands," soon to be presented to the government, were discussed.
Two weeks later, after both Charles and James read—and approved—
the document with only minor stylistic suggestions, Rozsika insisted that
it be her husband, Charles, and not James de Rothschild, who should
submit it to the appropriate ministry on behalf of the Zionists.[193] Weizmann could only reflect silently to himself on how successful he had
been in converting the Rothschilds into such ardent Zionists. This was
one clear victory for the Zionist cause.

By January 1917, Wolf, too, realized that the Conjoint and the Zionists
were on an irreversible collision course.[194] In the meantime Wolf was
careful to keep the Foreign Office informed of the internal squabbles
between his committee and the Zionists, and on December 1, 1916, he
sent Lancelot Oliphant, Cecil's senior adviser, a copy of all the official
memoranda.[195] Two weeks later Oliphant politely thanked Wolf for the
materials, but in a minute a few days earlier, he had commented in
obvious exasperation: "When Jews fall out, it is none too easy for Christians to decide whether the Zionists or anti-Zionists are in the wrong."[196]
But Wolf had not yet given up on the Foreign Office, and, after Balfour
was in office a month and a half, he went to see him to argue the representative nature of the Conjoint and the validity of its point of view.
Always a gentleman, and certainly interested in what was going on within
the Jewish community, Balfour showed a lively interest in Wolf's presentation but no more.[197]

The failure of the talks prepared the way for a decisive confrontation
between the Conjoint and the Zionists over the balance of opinion in
the Anglo-Jewish community. James de Rothschild was already re-

aligned with the Zionists,[198] and this was not the only significant accession of strength that the Zionists, and Weizmann in particular, enjoyed as the situation developed.

In their rivalry, the Conjoint Foreign Committee and the Zionists contended for recognition by the Allied governments as the authorized representative of Jewish interests. On the non-Zionist side, spokesmen in England and France, drawn from the wealthiest and most prominent local community leaders, could argue that they were citizens of unquestioned loyalty with whom the government traditionally dealt on Jewish matters; and they did not fail to point out that Zionist leaders like Sokolow and Tschlenow had until recently worked out of the WZO headquarters in the enemy capital, Berlin. The Zionists, on the other hand, could argue—at least in England, where the Conjoint Foreign Committee (unlike its counterpart, the Alliance Israélite Universelle) was a strictly British body—that only they represented the Jewish people on an international scale. Their claim was bound to grow stronger as the war made international pressures increasingly important in the considerations of the warring nations.

The non-Zionists recognized their eroding position from the beginning of the war. The Alliance Israélite Universelle and the Conjoint Foreign Committee had met as early as November 12, 1914, to consider postwar issues, including the possibility that the Allies might give the Jews, in Sacher's version of Wolf's report, "the terrible gift of Palestine to rule."[199] The growing international involvement in the stalemated war made this speculation increasingly realistic as time went on; and it also lent more weight to a body like the WZO precisely because of its international reach and its strength in strategically important countries like the United States and Russia.

Aware of the quickly changing international climate—with the British forces clearing Egypt of the Turks and the prospect of a British offensive northward toward Palestine—and no doubt jolted by the realization that Wolf and the Conjoint Foreign Committee had months before presented the Foreign Office with a Palestine formula of their own, the Zionists knew it was high time for them to present their own formula for Palestine lest they be left out of the political equation altogether. In fact, as early as mid-March 1916, without any inkling as to what the Conjoint was contemplating at that very moment, the Political Committee discussed a proposal for eventual presentation to the British government[200] but did not seem to follow through on that suggestion. Now such a memorandum became an urgent necessity. At a meeting on September 30, 1916, the executive of the EZF charged Sokolow with preparing a draft statement for eventual presentation to the government. Sokolow had apparently been at work on such a document for some time, and on October 9, 1916, he presented the committee with a draft.[201]

Sokolow's first draft was called "Outline of Programme for the Jewish Resettlement of Palestine in Accordance with the Aspirations of the Zionist Movement." It went through two revisions. The third draft was finalized at the end of November by a committee consisting of Sokolow, Weizmann, Gaster, and Herbert Bentwich. This was a short document known as "The Demands" and concluded with the following summary: "Palestine is to be recognised as the Jewish National Home. Jews of all countries to be accorded full liberty of immigration. Jews to enjoy full national, political and civic rights according to their place of residence in Palestine. A Charter to be granted to a Jewish Company for the development of Palestine. The Hebrew language to be recognised as the official language of the Jewish Province."[202]

This document was apparently shown to Herbert Samuel on January 19, 1917, and Gaster sent it to Sir Mark Sykes on January 31, 1917, just prior to the meeting on February 7 at Gaster's house. This was apparently also the document taken by Sokolow to Paris when he went to negotiate with the French government in March 1917. Weizmann sent it to Philip Kerr on April 23, 1917, and it was later given to William Ormsby-Gore, the political officer who accompanied the Zionist Commission to Palestine in February 1918. In a letter to Louis Brandeis on April 7, 1917, Sokolow explained why the draft of this document had involved so many revisions: "Perhaps for the first time in the history of our movement we felt the necessity of clothing Zionism in the garment of political reality."[203] Though it was circulated, this document was never officially presented to the British government, perhaps because the official approval of Brandeis and Tschlenow, as the representatives of the United States and Russia respectively, was never received, and because in July 1917 the drafting of the Balfour Declaration began.

The twenty-seven-page memorandum that accompanied "The Demands" was probably written by December 1916 and covered much the same ground, though it also expounded on the nature and origins of the Jewish problem and those solutions that had been tried in the past and had failed—assimilation, emigration, and emancipation. Although he did not consider the memorandum final, Weizmann sent it to Kerr with "The Demands" on April 23. The memorandum can be seen as the outgrowth of attempts made in 1915 to prepare a document on "The Zionist Solution of the Jewish Question." Weizmann had first asked Sacher to prepare such a document in December 1914 so that he could present it to Lloyd George, whom he was about to meet for the first time. Sacher and Leon Simon prepared a draft, but Weizmann considered it unsatisfactory because, with its concentration on spiritual matters, it seemed to have been written "more for the Jews" than for the gentiles.[204] In January 1915, at a meeting with Tschlenow, Sokolow, and Gaster, Herbert Samuel also requested that the Zionists prepare a memorandum on Zionist desiderata, but this request does not seem to have been fulfilled until December 1916. Though both "The Demands" and the memorandum were never officially submitted to the British government, they helped crystallize the ideas and goals of the London Zionist leadership, giving its various members a common starting point from which to deal with British officials.[205]

Quite independently from the English Zionist executive, another group, composed mostly of Weizmann's Manchester friends, founded the British Palestine Committee (BPC) toward the end of 1916. The aim of the BPC, according to an undated memorandum, was "to interest English people, English men and women in the idea of a Jewish Palestine under the British Crown. . . . The formation of such a State would be a noble ideal worthy of the British nation, and of the sacrifices that it has made in this war."[206] The moving spirits of the BPC were Harry Sacher, Simon Marks, and Israel Sieff with the encouragement of Herbert Sidebotham, at that time military correspondent of the *Manchester Guardian*. Closely allied with the Manchester group was a London group consisting of Albert Hyamson, Leon Simon, and Shmuel Tolkowsky, an agronomist who came to London from Palestine in 1915. The BPC's publication, *Palestine*, began to appear on January 26, 1917. Most of the articles were written by Sidebotham and by its editor, Sacher. All issues carried right below their masthead the group's motto: "The British Palestine Committee seeks to reset the ancient glories of the Jewish Nation in the freedom of a new British Dominion in Palestine."

The editorial policies of *Palestine* were not under the direct control of the Zionist leaders. Despite the close personal relations between the leaders of the BPC and Weizmann and despite the fact that they often consulted him and sought his help,[207] they did not always follow his advice. This lack of coordination caused occasional frictions and embarrassed the London Zionist leadership, which was identified by others with the BPC. In fact, with the exception of Sidebotham, all members of the BPC were Jews and Zionists. Efforts to recruit Wickham Steed, who was sympathetic to a British Palestine, were rejected by the latter on the grounds that a Jewish Palestine "would be an offence to Holy Russia."[208] Another potential recruit was Sir Mark Sykes, whom the BPC wanted to enlist as a patron. "We are encouraged in this hope," wrote the Manchester group, "by the foremost place that you have given to British and Imperial interests in the East, in your writing and speaking of the war."[209]

Sir Mark explained in his reply that his employment at the Committee of Imperial Defence made it impossible for him to accept the role of patron of the BPC. However, he continued, "I may say that I have always considered that Jewish Nationalism is inevitably destined to play a great part in the future. I trust and believe that it will prove a factor in the cause of peace, and I am sure that nothing but good can come of familiarising the public with those Jewish aspirations and hopes which if realised will do so much to raise . . . the Jewish people to a higher plane as a whole."[210]

In fact, since returning from Petrograd in early April 1916, after concluding the agreement with Russia and France, Sykes took up the task of rewriting British policy regarding the Ottoman area, including Palestine, and began to explore its Jewish angles.[211] At that point he was already utterly convinced of the worldwide importance of Jews and Zionists.[212] Through his contacts with Herbert Samuel, Sykes must have become aware of the controversy between the Zionists and the Conjoint Foreign Committee. This tension, and other events, forced him to decide for himself, as others in the British government were doing, where the government must turn to woo Jewish sympathy through a Palestine policy. If a pro-Zionist statement was required, as the Foreign Office had made clear in the March 1916 cables to Paris and Petrograd, one should consider Zionist, not non-Zionist, formulations in framing it. Thus, in addition to studying the files of the Foreign Office and the war cabinet containing the early Samuel memoranda and other materials in which the Jewish factor was considered, Sykes expanded his contacts with Jewish spokesmen, especially those with access to Zionist circles.

After December 7, 1916, when the new government under Lloyd George took office with Balfour given almost total control over the Foreign Office, Sykes and others concerned with Middle Eastern matters acted on behalf of a new government coalition considerably more interested in the subject. The long-delayed Arab revolt that had begun in June, and a British offensive from Egypt sometime after, came under review by the war cabinet. Sykes had matured his conception of a reorganized succession to the Ottoman Empire built upon Arab, Armenian, and Jewish nationalist states. Now, under new leadership, he made a conscious effort to get to know the key personalities in the Zionist movement.

Some Zionist contacts were available to Sykes through his work with British military and political officers who dealt with local agents in the Ottoman front. Among these was Aaron Aaronsohn, the Palestinian botanist and agronomist who arrived in London late in October 1916 and offered the services of the espionage organization he had set up in Palestine.[213] Sykes, one of the first officers to meet this odd character who burst unannounced on the scene, interviewed him to establish his *bona fides*.[214] The memoranda Aaronsohn prepared in London and later in Cairo, where he was attached to the staff as commander of his own espionage ring behind the Turkish lines,[215] were not only impressive in their detailed knowledge of the local situation but also based on the concept of an Arab-Armenian-Jewish strategic alliance with the British, covering present military collaboration and future political ties, that was highly congenial to the views Sykes increasingly favored.[216]

Sykes's initial contacts with Jews in London also reflected his new overall strategic approach. He used the good offices of James Malcolm, an Armenian ally active in pro-Allied propaganda and recruitment in his own community, to meet Jews, especially Zionists, capable of playing a similar role, or already doing so, in London and Paris. Sykes first consulted with Moses Gaster, who initially greatly impressed him.[217] Throughout the spring and fall of 1916, Sykes met with the Haham, who

provided him with background information about the Zionist movement.[218] Sykes was just as enamored by Aaronsohn, whose frank Jewish
patriotism was so different from the views of other Jews he had met.
After the latter's departure for Egypt in late November, Sykes continued
his contacts with Gaster, but he began to realize that the rabbi's boastful
promises about managing all Zionist affairs single-handedly were just
the empty words of a self-centered man.[219]

Given Sykes's interest in meeting the Zionist leadership, he certainly
would have met Weizmann sooner or later. Curiously, it was not Gaster
who introduced them. In his autobiography Weizmann ascribed this fact
to Gaster's "tendency to keep his 'finds' to himself and to play a lone
hand."[220] Such behavior was characteristic of the Haham, but one must
also keep in mind that throughout this period the relationship between
Weizmann and Gaster was shaky. Gaster's diary reveals the anger and
even contempt he felt for Weizmann because of the latter's conduct in a
variety of contexts. Referring to Weizmann's work with Cowen, Gaster
described him as "doublefaced and treacherous."[221] In September 1916,
referring to Weizmann's speech at a meeting to recruit Jews from the
East End, Gaster recorded: "Weizmann must have spoken as usual—
loosely and committed himself to what he could not do."[222] On January
28, 1917, Gaster recorded a phone conversation with Weizmann: "He
rings up and I felt he was embarrassed like one caught at thieving. . . .
He started whining about home troubles, otherwise he would have called.
I know this is not true. Is he not intriguing [with the] EZF behind my
back and thinks I do [not] know? He had met Sir Mark Sykes and found
out that he was an old friend of mine. . . . Of course this must have
embarrassed him very much for he knew that Sir Mark would tell me
all about it. . . . So he found himself in rather a tight fix."[223]

Though he may have been taken aback by the fact that Gaster had
been in communication with Sykes for some nine months without informing his Zionist colleagues, Weizmann was not the one who had
initiated the meeting with the new assistant secretary in the war cabinet.
According to James Malcolm's unpublished account,[224] it was Malcolm
who first contacted Leopold Greenberg in late January 1917, having remembered some previous conversations with the veteran editor.[225] Malcolm asked Greenberg to arrange a meeting for him with Zionist leaders;
the meeting took place—probably on January 26, 1917—in Weizmann's
house on Addison Road with Sokolow and a few others also in attendance. Malcolm told of his conversations with Sykes, and after Weizmann expressed his interest, called Sykes to make an appointment;
Weizmann could not see Sykes the following day, and Sokolow went
instead. Malcolm was impressed by Weizmann: "My impression of Dr.
Weizmann at this first meeting was of a man careful and yet quick to
grasp the possibilities of a situation. . . . His tall figure, his whole
bearing, his pale face and keen eyes and his natural geniality, made a
great impression on me."[226] Accompanied by Greenberg, Weizmann was

introduced to Sykes by Malcolm on January 28, 1917. Like Malcolm, Sykes, too, was impressed by the Zionist leader.[227] Two days later they met again, and Sykes asked Weizmann to arrange for a larger meeting with Zionist leaders together with Herbert Samuel. It was arranged for February 7, 1917.

Sykes must have known quite a bit about Weizmann long before he met him, for it is unlikely that Weizmann's many high-level contacts in the various ministries—possibly even Lloyd George and Balfour—would not have mentioned his name to the assistant secretary known to have a special interest in Zionism. The favorable impression Weizmann made on Sykes confirmed his reputation as a Zionist leader.

Sykes may also have been aware that Weizmann's leadership was about to receive formal sanction. At the very moment Weizmann was meeting with Sykes, he was being pressed to allow himself to be nominated at the forthcoming annual conference of the EZF as president, in succession to Joseph Cowen, whose position had been greatly weakened by his role in the enlistment affair. Somewhat in the style of Gaster, Weizmann set conditions that had to be met before he would agree to be nominated: he insisted on running unopposed by Cowen, and he wished to bring in with him his friends as members of the executive council, among them Sieff, Marks, Sacher, Simon, Tolkowsky, and Bertram Benas of Liverpool and Selig Brodetsky of Bristol University.[228] Cowen realized that his effectiveness as president had waned, and he retreated gracefully in favor of Weizmann.[229] At the annual conference of the EZF, on February 11, 1917, Weizmann was duly elected president. He was unable, however, to bring all his allies into the London executive; only Benas, Brodetsky, Sacher, and Sieff were elected as representatives from the provinces.[230] Nevertheless, this was an occasion for rejoicing, since those who were elected to the executive were, on the whole, a group friendly to Weizmann. Significantly, Weizmann felt for the first time strong enough in his position not to request—even for appearance' sake—that Gaster be included in the executive; indeed, this time around no one made any special effort to enlist the support of the Haham. That evening Weizmann and his friends celebrated over dinner at the Savoy. With Weizmann at the helm of the EZF, James de Rothschild pledged £500 to help improve the finances of the organization.[231]

Weizmann's new official status as president of the EZF had little effect on his influence on government circles, which was, if anything, a consequence of the acceptance he had attained among British political and academic leaders at a time when their interest in Zionism had risen sharply.[232] Weizmann remained, in effect, the chosen instrument of the British for conducting their relations with the Zionists. Though a position of strength for a Jewish leader, it nonetheless created problems for Weizmann in achieving full acceptance for himself and his policies in the constituency he supposedly represented and was presumed to be able to control. Thus, though in itself a meaningless title, the presidency of the EZF did add at least a cloak of legitimacy to Weizmann's diplomatic activities. In fact, some two weeks prior to his official elevation to this post, the Political Committee, fully cognizant of the status Weizmann had achieved during the first two years of the war, declared in its penultimate meeting on January 21, 1917, that it had full confidence in "Dr. Weizmann and Mr. Sokolow to carry on negotiations with the Government."[233]

In the days before the February 7 meeting the various Zionist groups and individuals refined their collective demands even as they jockeyed for position. Sykes was "the man on whom the Zionist hopes hung," Gaster confessed in his diary,[234] and both he and Weizmann wanted to be the one to present Sykes with "The Demands." Sokolow had presented this document to the EZF executive on October 9, 1916, yet it was not in final form until the very end of January 1917. After further alterations by Leon Simon[235] and having passed the scrutiny of Ahad Ha'Am,[236] Herbert Samuel, and Alfred Zimmern,[237] an improved draft was submitted by Moses Gaster to Mark Sykes on January 31, 1917.[238]

The memorandum Gaster submitted to Sykes did not specifically mention the desire of the Zionists to establish a Jewish settlement in Palestine under the aegis of Great Britain. As Gaster explained to the assistant secretary in his cover letter:

> Of course we are only too anxious to be under British protectorate, as you know, but the Zionist movement is not an English movement; it has to a certain extent an international character, and the Zionists in the enemy countries may take strong umbrage at our putting all our eggs into one basket, and placing ourselves, as it were, unreservedly in the hands of the British Government . . . and if such a Memorandum falls into the hands of the enemy I need not point out to you the danger that may accrue from the publication of it to the Jews in Turkey. For this reason we preferred not to mention explicitly the British Government in the Memorandum.[239]

In his discussions with Gaster, Sykes had mentioned the possibility of an Anglo-French condominium without revealing the existence of the Sykes-Picot Agreement. Early in July 1916, in fact, Sykes introduced Gaster to Picot, and the two had a long conversation. According to his diary entries, the Haham seemed to indicate to Picot that the Zionists would favor French and English involvement in Palestine.[240] Since Gaster did not inform any of his Zionist colleagues of these discussions, they did not have an inkling of Sykes's plans and ideas concerning Palestine.[241] It was not until James de Rothschild met Sykes for the first time on January 24, 1917, and the latter met Weizmann a few days later, that they could infer from their conversations that Sykes was contemplating an Anglo-French condominium.

The members of the BPC whose *raison d'être* was a British Palestine were up in arms. Sacher and Sieff immediately wrote to Weizmann to protest this arrangement. Sacher set out all the arguments against a condominium,[242] while Sieff insisted that the BPC needed to continue to press publicly for a solely British Palestine and, if need be, fight the Foreign Office to attain this goal.[243] C. P. Scott, who had become a patron of the BPC,[244] was likewise alarmed and tried to set an appointment for Weizmann with Lloyd George so that any notion of dual control with France could be put to rest.[245] In his reply to Sieff, Weizmann suggested patience and moderation; any further action could wait another week or two, until after the conference. This time the members of the BPC heeded his advice.[246]

Weizmann clearly did not wish any further unnecessary friction. He had his hands full trying to maneuver among James de Rothschild, Cowen, and Gaster. The latter became particularly troublesome as the date of the conference approached. "Gaster thinks that he has got the monopoly now," Weizmann wrote to Sieff. "He was laying down the law last Thursday night, and I had to tell him off once or twice. On the other hand I feel that just at present one must keep everybody and not let people drift; I am trying my best in that direction at a very great expenditure of energy and nerves. . . . We are carrying such an amount of dead weight with us in all this work."[247]

Weizmann was referring to an unpleasant meeting he and Sokolow had at Gaster's house two days earlier, at which there was a great deal of wrangling. When the meeting was over Gaster recorded: "Grossly disappointed with these men . . . taking [such] liberties!"[248] Sokolow and Weizmann had brought Sacher with them to the strategy session on the eve of the conference, and Gaster had not expected to see Sacher and did not want him there. "It was a most disgraceful exhibition of bad faith and of low intrigue on the part of these people," fumed the Haham; he promised to set the record straight after the conference.[249] He did not realize that Weizmann—who in the past had almost always deferred to him—kept his peace solely in order to give Sykes the impression of a united Zionist front. In fact, the conference, which took place at Gaster's house at his insistence,[250] was to be the last time he would be allowed to assume a leadership role among the Zionists. Sykes had already seen enough to realize "that Weizmann should take the leading part in the negotiations."[251]

"The most important Meeting ever held concerning Zionism was held *here* under my Chairmanship," recorded Gaster in characteristic immodesty.[252] This time he was not much off the mark. The meeting, which brought together the Zionist leadership with the authorized representative of the British government, was indeed a watershed in Zionist history. In view of the deadlock in negotiations by the end of 1916, Sykes's initiative seemed a godsend to the Zionists. Weizmann and his colleagues realized how crucial the meeting was for their future plans. As Sieff had put it in his letter to Weizmann three days before the meeting: "It is our duty to insist upon a British Palestine in every conversation the Zionists have with Sir Mark. I do not think one ought to underestimate the weight of Sir Mark's opinion on the . . . Foreign Office; and I believe that the . . . Foreign Office will lean on the advice of Sir Mark to a greater degree than we perhaps imagine. . . . So that our duty is to attack the danger at the source, i.e. to demonstrate to Sir Mark the evil and dangerous results which would follow a joint [British-French] administration of Palestine."[253]

Clearly, all who understood the internal dynamics of the Zionist leadership realized that Weizmann had emerged as the paramount Zionist leader who would negotiate with Sykes. In good part Weizmann's position was a direct consequence of the changes in the British government in December 1916. David Lloyd George, who as minister of munitions had been one of the sponsors of Weizmann's acetone project, became prime minister. Balfour, who as first lord of the admiralty had been Weizmann's other ministerial chief, was named foreign secretary. The Zionists did, of course, lose Herbert Samuel and the marquess of Crewe, who, faithful to Asquith, left the government when Lloyd George succeeded as prime minister. Worse yet, Samuel's anti-Zionist cousin, Edwin Montagu, accepted the post of secretary of state for India despite his friendship with Asquith. Still, staunch Zionist supporters in the cabinet now included Alfred Milner, the mentor of the *Round Table* group, and a new friend, Jan Christiaan Smuts of South Africa. Moreover, the war cabinet secretariat now included two firm supporters—Leopold Amery and William Ormsby-Gore. Together with Mark Sykes, these younger men formed a powerful and influential group who felt free to take the initiative and submit ideas of their own. Sir Mark's involvement in the negotiations with the Zionists deserves to be highlighted since it involved a personal and radical transformation of his part in formulating British policies. After all, the signatures on the Sykes-Picot Agreement had hardly dried, and he was already engaged in a contradictory political orientation. Clearly he was not reflecting merely his own change of heart but Lloyd George's new strategy for the Middle East.

The changes in personnel, so favorable to Zionist prospects, coincided with a new interest in winning Jewish support that had been manifested in the last months of the Asquith government and came to a head in the meeting between Sir Mark Sykes and the Zionist leaders on February 7, 1917. During the first two months of the Lloyd George government, Sykes had refined his ideas of a succession to the Ottoman Empire built upon Arab, Armenian, and Jewish nationalist states. Now, at the meeting at Gaster's house, he explored Jewish politics. There the last door was opened that led, through a long and tortuous path, to the Balfour Declaration and the Mandate for Palestine and all that followed in the subsequent history of Britain and the Jews.

IV

Toward a British Declaration

On February 11, 1917, a few hours after his official installation as president of the English Zionist Federation, Chaim Weizmann declared at a meeting that Jews were now standing at the parting of the ways between *galut* and their redemption. At this turning point in Jewish history they had to prepare themselves. The Jewish problem and the Jewish claim now had the attention of the highest quarters.[1] Weizmann chose his words carefully and gave no indication as to what political changes were taking place. Nor could his audience have guessed that he had by that time undergone a profound change in his own strategic orientation.

By 1917 Weizmann was giving relatively little attention to his responsibilities as leader of the local Zionist organization. The focus of his activity had shifted radically since his service as the workhorse of the student Zionist organization in Berlin or the executive head of the Democratic Faction. It was even markedly altered from his perspective at the outbreak of the war. Then he had thought in terms of helping organize a united Jewish front for the eventual peace conference and had envisaged his job as exploiting the openings to influential non-Zionist Jewish circles that his Rothschild connection, acquired through his work for the Jewish university project, had recently given him. But the London Rothschilds had opened doors to even more promising connections with the non-Jewish elite of Britain, and his academic friendships, together with those of his younger Zionist associates, gave him unrivaled access to this vital sector of opinion. A further advantage, of no less critical importance, accrued from his service as a scientist in the government employ, which allowed him to meet the staff at all levels of the various ministries concerned with the issues that might arise in any serious consideration of Zionist aspirations. With such exceptional opportunities for advancing Zionism in the quarters immediately responsible for policy decisions, Weizmann naturally concentrated his personal efforts where they would have the greatest impact rather than on the administrative details of the English Zionist Federation.

Unlike other Zionist leaders, Weizmann neither checked the day-today performance of the organization he headed nor took great care to place his own men in charge of operations he wished to supervise at a distance.[2] Of course Weizmann did not simply ignore the minor matters of Zionist and Jewish organization. His condition for accepting the presidency of the EZF was that some of his younger Zionist friends and co-workers be seated on the executive in sufficient numbers to back him effectively. Though he was only partially successful in forcing through this demand, it demonstrates his awareness that he still did not possess sufficient personal stature to negotiate without some official backing. Likewise he took a lively interest in Harry Sacher's successful campaign to succeed Herbert Bentwich as head of the Order of Ancient Maccabeans.

On the broader issue of gaining the support of a united Jewish community, Weizmann grew increasingly detached, seeming to accept Ahad Ha'Am's dictum that any gains the postwar settlement might bring would owe little to Jewish communal power but be granted by the victors in their own interest.[3] After some initial, random efforts to negotiate a consensus with non-Zionists, Weizmann became increasingly detached from Moses Gaster's efforts to convene British Jewry in something like the projected American Jewish Congress.[4] Instead of mobilizing the various elements in the Jewish community in support, Weizmann preferred to keep them out of his way as much as possible so he could develop his own policy in response to the varied pressures of his non-Jewish contacts. When Mark Sykes appeared on the scene, Weizmann understood he had an opportunity to implement his Zionist goals more forcefully.

Until the February 7 meeting, British responses to the pressure of Zionists for a role in the Allied coalition had been a cautious acceptance of military services whenever they seemed useful—as in the case of the Zion Mule Corps—together with careful avoidance, as far as possible, of associated political commitments. In December 1916, when Aaron Aaronsohn arrived in Cairo for service with the Egyptian Expeditionary Force, General Sir Archibald Murray was entering upon his campaign to seize El-Arish at the gateway to Palestine and in London the new Lloyd George government had just been set up. Despite these favorable circumstances, Aaronsohn had to battle hard for the minor concessions for prestige he required.[5] He never thought of asking for explicit political commitments for Zionism, although he hoped, of course, that they might be implied. For this reason, he—like Weizmann—rejected compensation of a sort that would stamp him as an ordinary mercenary.[6] He also succeeded in maintaining his prerogative as the commander of a unit, not an individual operative, in the face of British attempts to assume direct command of his espionage ring's contacts.[7] Nevertheless, the main political advantage gained from his effort lay in the personal ties and confidence he established by his authoritative and reliable advice on current tactical and long-range strategic problems involved in the British advance into Palestine.

Similar considerations apply even more clearly to Vladimir Jabotinsky's campaign for a Jewish legion, with its much more explicit political
implications. What enabled Zionism to achieve a concrete beginning of
this project in late 1916, as Murray's attack on El-Arish was under way,
was the fact that remnants of the Zion Mule Corps, evacuated to Egypt,
reenlisted. Some 120 of them transferred to London and were accepted
as a unit for combat duty in the Twentieth Battalion, London Regiment,
then training in Hazeley Down, near Winchester.[8] But their acceptance
as a unit required the combined efforts of Colonel John Henry Patterson,
Leopold Amery, and other friends. In his parallel efforts, Jabotinsky not
only had to accept Amery's advice and severely water down the political
aspects of the memorandum he prepared for the British,[9] but eventually
he enlisted, in sheer frustration, as a private soldier in the newly formed
unit.[10] It took much of 1917 and the successful politicking of Weizmann,
Sokolow, and others[11] to win for the Jewish military units the symbolic
recognition of their national identity—their special emblem—that under-
scored their political significance, at least in an understated British manner.

The conference at Rabbi Moses Gaster's house on February 7, 1917,
afforded the Zionists the opportunity to present their desiderata before
Mark Sykes, whose official title as assistant secretary to the war cabinet
was enhanced by the trust Lloyd George placed in him as a major voice
in Middle Eastern affairs. Those assembled at Gaster's house were as
representative a group of Zionists as any during the war: Moses Gaster
chaired the meeting; also in attendance were Lord Walter Rothschild
and his kinsman James de Rothschild, Nahum Sokolow, Herbert Samuel, Joseph Cowen, Herbert Bentwich, Harry Sacher, and Chaim Weizmann. The Zionists made it clear that they opposed any condominium
arrangement or other form of international control over Palestine, while
they stressed the strategic importance of the country for Britain. On the
other hand, they proposed that Britain be granted suzerainty over Palestine while recognizing the claim of a Jewish nation within its boundaries. The development of the country would be entrusted to a chartered
company that would deal with questions of religion and culture and
regulate immigration to Palestine.

Sykes, who claimed he attended the conference in a private capacity—
a claim neither he, nor the others present, took seriously—pointed out
that the proposed suggestions would, no doubt, encounter opposition
from Russia, Italy, the newly emerging Arab nationalist movement, and
in particular from France, which had claims over Palestine. In response
to the question by James de Rothschild as to whether there was any
British commitment to France regarding Palestine, Sykes at first stated
that Britain had made no such pledge. Later in the discussion—without
hinting at the agreements reached with Georges Picot and Sergei Sazonov—Sykes claimed that "with great difficulty the British Government
had managed to keep the question of Palestine open." Herbert Samuel

declined Sykes's invitation to elaborate on that point. As the more than two-hour session came to a close, Sykes proposed that someone be appointed to represent the Zionist views to Picot. At the suggestion of James de Rothschild,[12] who most likely was briefed by Weizmann in advance of the meeting, Sokolow was chosen to conduct the negotiations.[13]

Weizmann was thus able to terminate Gaster's career as a Zionist diplomat. Weizmann knew he had a much better chance to influence and direct Sokolow's movements than those of the headstrong rabbi. Sending Sokolow to the Continent had, for Weizmann, the added advantage of his remaining the sole master of all diplomatic maneuvers in England. The Haham never forgot, nor forgave, the fact that he had been shunted aside. In a long and bitter letter to James de Rothschild, written two days after the meeting, Gaster commented: "You also are certainly not aware that such a suggestion [to appoint Sokolow as spokesman] had come from Dr. Weizmann on the evening previous to our meeting, and that I then hotly resented it."[14] In the following months Gaster never missed an opportunity to indicate that he was much better suited for diplomatic missions than Sokolow, who had been nominated for his post through "improper procedures."[15] He added this grievance to the long list of resentments he held against Weizmann and impatiently waited for the opportunity to place a spoke in the latter's diplomatic and political wheels.[16]

Yet despite his hurt feelings, Gaster confessed to his diary that what transpired between Sir Mark and the Zionists on February 7 was of great importance.[17] The following day Weizmann wrote to Private Jabotinsky, who was training in Hazeley Down: "In our Palestinian affairs an important step, I hope, was taken yesterday. . . . I regard this conference as an historic one. . . . It's the first time in the history of our movement that we have come so close to the heart of the matter."[18] The days and weeks that followed were, in Ahad Ha'Am's words, "critical."[19]

On February 8, 1917, Sokolow met Georges Picot at the residence of Mark Sykes, who took but a small part in the discussion. In response to Picot's question as to how the Jews proposed to organize themselves as a nation in Palestine, Sokolow replied that they would establish themselves in the same way as the French and English had established themselves in Canada or the Boers in South Africa—by settling on the land. When the Frenchman inquired as to which government Mr. Sokolow had in mind when he spoke of the organization of Jews in Palestine under a new government, Sokolow replied forthrightly that the Jews long had in mind the suzerainty of the British government. In response Picot simply reminded Sokolow that this was a matter for the Entente to decide. For a moment it seemed that the conversation was about to take an unfavorable turn. Sir Mark intervened and put forward the idea he had mentioned the day before of an English chartered company for the development of Palestine on Zionist lines, but this, too, did not please

Picot. Clearly he was unwilling to give ground on this subject, having made it clear earlier in the conversation that there was no possibility of France's renouncing its aspirations in Palestine in favor of Great Britain. "Ninety-five percent of the French people were strongly in favor of the annexation of Palestine by France," Picot declared. Nevertheless, he promised to do his best to explain the Zionist program to his superiors. After some further clarifications, the discussion was terminated.[20]

At Sykes's suggestion, Sokolow called on Picot the next day at the French Embassy. In reply to Sokolow's suggestion that much was to be done in France to clear away misunderstandings and prejudices in regard to Zionism, Picot replied that no immediate moves were necessary. In fact they might backfire and provoke a violent counteragitation. He personally would see to it that the facts about Zionism were communicated to the proper quarters and would do his best to win French sympathies for the movement. Once again he expressed his strong opposition to the idea of a chartered company with special privileges, as it would lead other nationalities in Palestine to ask for the same. Picot, who described himself as "a friend of the Jews," assured Sokolow "of the great and sympathetic interest which France took in their work," but he also advised that making their devotion to the Entente more evident and public would be even more useful to the Jews. As on the previous day, the conversation became general and aimless toward the end of the meeting, but Picot's assurance that France was not hostile to the Zionist cause was certainly good news for Sokolow.[21]

Following these three successive meetings, Sykes, Sokolow, and Weizmann met on February 10, 1917, at Sykes's residence to review the situation. On the whole, Sir Mark was pleased with Sokolow's success in educating Picot as to the Zionist demands. At the same time, he wished to proceed carefully. Since Picot had placed so much emphasis on Jewish-sponsored propaganda—albeit in the United States and other neutral countries—Sokolow inquired whether such activity in favor of Zionism ought to be promoted among non-Jews in England. Mindful of the secret agreements to which he was party, and particularly France's strong stand on the matter of Palestine, Sykes countered that he could see no objection to a purely pro-Zionist propaganda as long as the idea of British suzerainty was kept in the background for the time being, as it was likely to intensify the French opposition. In this connection he repeated his anxiety over the journal *Palestine*, which he considered so insistent on championing British interests that it made their goals harder to achieve.[22]

Sir Mark may have been referring to *Palestine*'s lead article on February 1, 1917. Arguing for British political control over the country, it stated at the outset that "Even if Palestine were not the ancient home of the Jewish state, its military importance to the British Empire is so great that its possession would be a disagreeable military necessity; and the fact that modern Jews are sighing after their ancient home has this very practical bearing on the matter that it changes what would otherwise be merely a disagreeable necessity into an attractive duty, or at the lowest, into a valuable opportunity."[23] This was the kind of blunt political discussion of British interests in Palestine that Sykes wanted eliminated from public view. On February 18 he asked Weizmann to voice strong displeasure about an article apparently written by Tolkowsky and revised by Sacher.[24] The article, which dealt with the boundaries of Palestine, had appeared in *Palestine* on February 15. It proposed borders starting just north of Sidon; running eastward far enough to include Damascus and, if that was not possible, to the southern extremity of Mount Hermon; then southward, on a line giving Palestine the Hauran as well as territory east of Maan, so as to include the Hedjaz Railway; then southwest to a point slightly south of Akaba and from there reaching the Mediterranean at Rafah.[25]

Weizmann responded to Sykes's urging and tried to curb the enthusiasm of his Manchester Zionist friends, Harry Sacher and Israel Sieff.[26] But the usually agreeable and disciplined Sieff made it clear that the British Palestine Committee was not going to budge:

> There is no doubt in my mind that Sir M. has come to an agreement with the Arabs and his interest in Jewish political aspirations in Palestine is only secondary. The very fact that he claims part of the Hauran and the Hedjaz Railway for the Arabs is proof positive that he has agreed to hand these over to the Arabs, without in any way taking into consideration the harm he is doing to Jewish hopes and Jewish rights in Palestine. It is evident to me that he has, in short, "sold us" to the Arabs, whose support is of much greater importance to him than that of the Zionists. He is but, after all, carrying on the English tradition of foreign policy, which is opportunism. . . .
>
> Now, then, I ask you, must we sit down and say nothing? Is it not our duty to ourselves, as well as to the future Israel . . . to fight this Arab agreement? . . .
>
> You may diplomatically hint that you are not responsible for the "hotheaded youths" of the British Palestine Committee. . . . Of course I know you agree with us.[27]

Though the BPC had been formed with Weizmann's full knowledge and consent[28] and although he agreed with its ideas, Weizmann differed in his tactics and was primarily concerned to please Sykes. Sacher and Sieff, as well as Simon Marks and the other Manchester and London members of the BPC, were torn between their loyalty to Weizmann, who had been their mentor in Zionist affairs, and their strongly held belief that "we've got to keep our own end up."[29] They therefore tried to accommodate Weizmann's demand for moderation as much as they could without compromising their own belief that certain boundaries and British suzerainty must be demanded publicly.[30] But despite their personal admiration and respect for Weizmann,[31] tensions inevitably erupted into open conflict from time to time. Weizmann and his London group threatened to withhold the £500 subsidy they promised in order to keep *Palestine* afloat on account of the editorial board's breach of discipline. Moreover, no doubt because of Weizmann's direct influence and daily contact with them, some key members of the London BPC, such as Shmuel Tolkowsky, began to withdraw their support from their Manchester friends.[32] By the spring of 1917 two very distinct approaches had been developed to achieve the same aims. Leon Simon put it thus:

> I think the London group far too much the victim of its emotions. . . . I *know* I am a better politician than the whole lot of them in London. . . . Where you and I agree and where we differ from the London folk is that they are determined to tie Zionism with the F[oreign] O[ffice] and to take anything the F.O. is graciously pleased to grant. I don't trust the F.O. and I am convinced that we shall never do anything with them except by convincing them that we are a *power*. That, Chaim and his tactics will never achieve.[33]

That same day Harry Sacher wrote to Weizmann: "A clear distinction should be drawn between your method of work and that of the BPC. Both pursue the same end but by different roads. You are the diplomatists and must walk warily. We work with coarser material and in the cruder fashion it necessitates. It is not the business of the BPC to be at all times and under all circumstances agreeable to the Foreign Office."[34]

Two days later Sacher again wrote to Weizmann, this time emphasizing not the differences in tactics but the way both groups viewed the Foreign Office. The root of the differences which have arisen between the London group and "ourselves in Manchester," wrote Sacher,

> is firstly the difference of attitude towards the Foreign Office. You believe that the Foreign Office intends to do its best for us, I am convinced that it will do as little as it is compelled to do and that it will sacrifice our interests lightly to evade trouble for itself. Secondly, it follows that, whereas you think it right to make consideration for the feelings of the Foreign Office a very important guide in our tactics, I am convinced that every kind of pressure we can mobilise must be brought to bear against the Foreign Office.[35]

These disagreements strained to the limit—but did not break up—the personal relations of Weizmann and his Manchester followers. Weizmann was, as usual, unable to comprehend how a loyal friend and disciple could disagree with him on substantive issues. He demanded "discipline" as one of the personal ties he maintained with his inner circle, and when denied, he could turn with great anger against his most trusted supporters. In a letter now lost and in conversation with Simon Marks, he apparently stated in no uncertain terms what he thought of Sieff's "disloyalty." Deeply wounded by Weizmann's sharp criticism, Sieff wrote a letter to Weizmann that probably best illustrates the emotional toll the controversy had taken on some of its participants:

I intend to send in my resignation to the B.P.C. It almost breaks my heart.
. . . It is not because I disagree with you. On the contrary. Your political
instinct has always been true. It is because I dare not imperil the cause as
you say, by giving way to my instinctive ideas. I am desolated that it should
have meant an addition to your burden of activities and worries. . . . I
heard with sorrow that you are disappointed with me and my work, and
that you had expected better results. I am deeply pained that you consider
my Zionism as "hobby Zionism." . . . Zionism has become the greater part
of my life, and God knows what more I could have done, short of total
neglect of my business and family, which would benefit neither the cause
nor those whom I love. . . . Compared with the giants of Zionism I am
but a dwarf in experience and activity. But I beg of you not to impugn my
sincerity and earnestness. . . . I owe my Zionism to you; what I have learnt
is from your lips; I have continually striven to please you, to satisfy you,
and to gain your good opinion. My failure in all this is a heavy burden to
carry. Your friendship which I hope I shall never forfeit has been a source
of pride to me.

I cannot write more, for your letter and your words . . . hurt me beyond
conception. As for me I send you my love, and trust that you will try to
retain pleasant memories of our cooperation in Zionist work.[36]

Sieff did not resign. Within two weeks of his emotional appeal for
Weizmann's grace he recovered sufficiently to write to his mentor that
he so strongly believed in the cause which the BPC espoused to put
up his own money to support *Palestine*.[37] Nor did the disagreement
between Weizmann and his Manchester followers permanently impair
their relationship. In fact, even as he chastised the Manchester "hot
heads," Weizmann was having some doubts of his own. At just that
time Sacher wrote, "The danger was here in England—the F[oreign]
O[ffice] and M[ark] S[ykes]. . . . That is the last thing W[eizmann] will
believe."[38]

Some two months earlier, no doubt because of Sykes's plans to set up
an Arab suzerain over the Jewish national entity in Palestine, Weizmann
complained privately to C. P. Scott about Sykes's tendency to subordinate the Jewish interest to his Arab plans.[39] As the diaries of Scott indicate, he tended to agree with Weizmann's assessment and, of course,
with the BPC's more vocal assertions. After meeting the assistant secretary, Scott recorded: "an interesting person and one of the best of the
progressive Tories . . . an immense believer in the future of the Arab
race. . . . As to Palestine he was rather inclined to compromise."[40]
Herbert Sidebotham had the same impression of Sykes after meeting
with him in early March.[41] Writing from Paris in early April, Sokolow,
too, felt that the work of the Manchester group was important and urged
that it be pursued with even greater zeal.[42]

Sykes had met with the Zionist leadership in February to enlist them
for political service. Unlike the military concessions in connection with
the idea of a Jewish legion, the political concessions made to Zionist
aims had to be far more evident from the start. Of course, the British

here, too, made every effort to retain their freedom of action. Thus neither during the various meetings in February nor later did Sykes—in spite of pointed questions—do anything to inform the Zionists of his agreements with the French regarding Palestine. His main object at the time was to enlist the Zionists, under his guidance, in a far-reaching diplomatic campaign to influence the other Allies to accept the kind of supplementary pro-Zionist modification of the Sykes-Picot terms that the French had vetoed earlier. For this purpose, Sokolow was assigned to work with Sykes—accompanied by the Armenian, James Malcolm—in Paris and later in Rome; and Weizmann looked forward to a similar role in Egypt, and later in Palestine and in the United States.

The British offensive into Palestine proceeded during the winter months but ended in two failures to take the town of Gaza in March and April 1917.[43] In the uncertainty about the continuation of an "Eastern" strategy in the moment of defeat, Sykes felt the need to warn his superiors that they must abandon the Zionist line they had taken up if there were no British advance into Palestine to justify it.[44] The British, of course, did not abandon their Palestine offensive. They dismissed the bumbling Murray and sent Edmund H. Allenby to reorganize and renew the attack late in 1917.

In addition to the need to bolster British chances to retain Palestine after their troops should have occupied it, the Zionists now gained importance from a new quarter. In March 1917 the Russian Revolution and in April the American entry into the war against Germany radically altered all military and political calculations. To Allied advisers the Jews now seemed especially important as a factor in keeping Russia in the war, or taking it out, and in stimulating or impeding the active participation of the United States.[45] In this psychological warfare for Jewish support, the British saw themselves pitted against what seemed to them a dangerously successful German policy. They also appreciated the difficulty they faced in gaining their own ends without alienating American opinion or one or another sector of the Jewish public or, particularly, disturbing the delicate balance of their relationship with the French and other Allies. The French had many of the same concerns.[46]

Against this background and in view of the impending departure of Sir Mark Sykes and Georges Picot for Egypt, on March 30, 1917, Sir Mark called a meeting at his residence with Sokolow, Malcolm, and Weizmann. They decided that Sokolow and Malcolm would proceed to Paris as soon as possible. The two left the following day with a letter of introduction from the French Embassy in London. A letter from Georges Picot to Alexandre Felix Joseph Ribot, the premier,[47] and a note from Jules Cambon, the secretary general of the Foreign Ministry, to Picot, make it clear that French officials were notified and briefed well in advance about the London talks and were waiting to meet Sokolow.[48] Toward the end of April 1917, Vera Weizmann summed up Sokolow's activities in Paris:

Mr. Sokoloff [sic] went to Paris at the beginning of the month. His first report was most pessimistic: French will not hear of British Protectorate; they want Palestine for themselves. They will give Jews the "rights", but not an autonomy or a charter. Then followed a shower of most enthusiastic telegrams, that everything is successful. . . . At last a long letter came which explains the change of attitude. Frenches [sic] suddenly understood Zionist aims, very sympathetic and agree to adopt our programme, as British are willing to do. And Sokoloff thinks that in three weeks in Paris he has achieved more than it was achieved in England in three years.[49]

Vera Weizmann's cynical undertone in describing Sokolow's activities in Paris was less than generous, and it probably reflected her husband's attitude. No doubt it also reflected the gloomy mood among the Zionists and their friends who had just then discovered that Britain had made commitments to the French which could severely handicap Zionist plans in Palestine. C. P. Scott himself stated that very week, "Sokolow's visit to France was a blunder."[50] In Vera's case there may have also been a tinge of jealousy as she recorded Sokolow's doings in her diary. As her memoirs and Chaim's clearly reveal, the Weizmanns were not impressed by Sokolow's abilities. Yet Sokolow was the ideal person to carry on the negotiations with the French and later with the Vatican and the Italians. He was patient, urbane, multilingual, and highly sophisticated. And he brought to the art of diplomacy his gentle, understated, and nonthreatening personality. Throughout his sojourn in Paris, Sokolow consulted frequently with Baron Edmond de Rothschild, sometimes two or three times a day.[51] The baron was most supportive, though his position as a French patriot was delicate. Sokolow's negotiations were difficult, and he had to tread carefully through the minefield of French national and religious feelings regarding Palestine. He reported to Weizmann from the start that though the negotiations were difficult, they were not impossible and he was confident that at least some of the Zionist demands would be accepted.[52]

Mark Sykes, however, who within a few days had followed Sokolow and Malcolm to Paris, was pessimistic as to the outcome of the discussions between Sokolow and the French Foreign Ministry officials[53] and wrote in this mood to Balfour on April 8, 1917.[54] A day later, Sykes's assessment changed completely. That morning Sokolow had been received at the Quai d'Orsay by a group of high-ranking French officials: Jules Cambon, his brother Paul Cambon, Georges Picot, and Pierre de Margerie, chef de cabinet at the Quai d'Orsay.[55] It is not exactly clear what the French promised to do to advance the Zionist cause, and clearly the issue of suzerainty was allowed to lie dormant for the moment. Yet both sides assessed the meeting as highly successful, and Sokolow was allowed to use official French channels to send cables to Brandeis and Tschlenow that asserted, "After favourable results in London and Paris . . . I have full confidence Allied victory will realise our Palestine Zionists [sic] aspirations."[56]

Though the French were careful not to commit themselves to the Zionists before the Italian government was sounded out, the result of the meeting was a Zionist victory that could largely be attributed to Sokolow. In his brief report to Balfour, Sykes summarized the matter as follows: "The situation now is therefore that Zionist aspirations are recognized as legitimate by the French." Moreover, continued Sykes with great satisfaction, "M. Sokolow also assures me that the bulk of the Zionists desire British Suzerainty only . . . provided things go well the situation should be the more favourable to British Suzerainty with a recognised Jewish voice in favour of it."[57] While Sokolow turned his attention to garnering support among French Jews, Sykes proceeded to Italy for meetings with the Italian government and the Vatican.[58] From there he reiterated the French officials' strong encouragement for Sokolow to come to Italy, where he had paved the way for the Zionist diplomat.[59]

Sokolow's diplomatic mission in Italy was as successful as had been his negotiations in France.[60] His meetings with Monsignor Eugenio Pacelli, the assistant secretary for extraordinary ecclesiastical affairs in the Secretariat of State, two days later, were difficult but by no means unfriendly.[61] On May 4, Sokolow was received in private audience by Pope Benedict XV.[62] It was a warm and friendly interview, with His Holiness expressing himself in favorable terms concerning the return of the Jews to Palestine and alluding to his sympathy for the suffering of the Jews in Eastern Europe.[63] Similarly, Sokolow's meetings with the officials of the Italian government, including Prime Minister Paolo Boselli on May 12, were pleasant though noncommittal.[64]

Armed with these friendly gestures from the Vatican and the Italian government, Sokolow returned to Paris toward the end of May and was warmly received by Premier Ribot and Jules Cambon.[65] On May 25, Sokolow approached Cambon with a request for a written declaration, a request he reiterated on June 2, 1917. The official reason he gave for this request was that it would be handy to have it at the All-Russian Zionist Conference, which was to open in Petrograd at the beginning of June.[66] In fact, Sokolow also wanted a written statement because he feared that the pro-Zionist resolve of the French government might weaken under renewed pressure from French Jewish anti-Zionists, particularly the Alliance Israélite Universelle.

Cambon obliged Sokolow with a letter on June 4, 1917. In it he assured Sokolow that the French government was in sympathy with his cause, the triumph of which was bound up with that of the Allies.[67] The Cambon letter, which was never officially published by the French, was in fact the first instance of a government committing itself to a statement admitting to the existence of a Jewish nationality and recognizing its historical connection with the Holy Land.[68] Sokolow immediately brought the letter to the attention of the British Foreign Office, and it was later read by Balfour at the war cabinet on October 4, 1917, while the Balfour Declaration was being hammered out. Sokolow's intuition that a written statement was essential was confirmed by events, and, as it turned out, Cambon's letter was written in the nick of time. Soon after, the French, who were disappointed in not having received anything tangible in return for the Cambon letter, cooled considerably toward Zionist aspirations in Palestine.

Clearly then, Sokolow was entitled to feel proud of his accomplishments in France and Italy. By all accounts it was a *tour de force* for a representative of a scattered and amorphous organization to be received respectfully and sympathetically by the heads of two important states and by the pope whose predecessor, Pius X, had thirteen years earlier turned a deaf ear to all of Theodor Herzl's arguments.

But, as Vera Weizmann's diary reveals, her husband—Sokolow's junior partner in the World Zionist Organization's hierarchy—was less than pleased and rather worried by his colleague's activities, especially after he received Sokolow's long-awaited letter of April 19. Not only did Weizmann distrust the motives of the French government; he also underestimated Sokolow's skills as a diplomat. Moreover, he was afraid the French would use the negotiations "as an argument *vis-à-vis* the English in telling the English that they also agree with the Zionists and would do for the Zionists all the English are prepared to do."[69] While waiting for Sokolow's full report on his high-level meetings at the Quai d'Orsay on April 9,[70] Weizmann and his friends could only speculate as to what was actually going on in Paris. In a letter to Leon Simon, Harry Sacher summed up the views of his colleagues at the BPC:

> I don't like Sok[olow]'s trip to Italy just as I disliked his trip to Paris. C.P.S[cott] and Sider [Sidebotham] are very emphatically of the same opinion. They say that it is not our Zionist business to negotiate with French and Italian Governments. There is no parity. It is for the British Government to do that negotiating. They also fear that while Sok. can do no good *he may compromise us Zionists.* This whole enterprise is as unfortunate as [it is] mysterious, and I say that in spite of Sok's reassuring telegrams. In any case why doesn't Sok. send long letters with a full detailed account of what he has been doing? Israel [Sieff] and I sent last night a telegram to Chaim urging him to recall Sok. to London by telegraph.[71]

Scott and Sidebotham also counseled that Sokolow be "recalled,"[72] and Weizmann did his best to comply, for the suggestion accorded with his own inclination. But he had to tread carefully; Sokolow, after all, was the authorized representative of the WZO, not the London and Manchester leadership. Weizmann objected to the fact that Sokolow's cables to Tschlenow and Brandeis announcing the satisfactory interview on April 9 contained the phrase, "After favourable results in London and Paris," thus coupling, as if of equal weight, the negotiations with the British and the French, though he realized that it was the French officials who suggested the addition of the word "Paris."

In fact, Sokolow, who used French official channels to communicate his message to Petrograd and Washington—much as Weizmann communicated his through official British channels—had little choice in the matter but to comply. Weizmann's telegram of April 27—"Your work in France may be interpreted as negotiations on behalf of our movement in favour of French alternative. On no account [is] such an impression admissible"[73]—was therefore gratuitous and possibly sent to allay the worries of British officials as well as the BPC group. On May 1, Weizmann sent a detailed letter to Sokolow stating that he was "speaking on behalf of all our friends and collaborators here in asking you to shorten your stay on the Continent and proceed to London if possible at once."[74] No doubt hurt by the suggestion that he was deviating from the agreed strategy, Sokolow could only reply by cable that he was "astonished" at the fallacious reports on his work in France.[75]

It was only on May 12, after his audience with Pope Benedict XV, that Sokolow replied at length to Weizmann's urgent demands to call off his diplomatic mission. Referring to Weizmann's insulting remark that the French *volte-face* toward Zionism was owing not to Sokolow's skills but to the fact that they wanted to establish a condominium in Palestine, Sokolow replied that the French were simply aware now of the fact that Zionism had become a power to be reckoned with. Sokolow also made it clear that he told the French straightforwardly of the Zionist aims and had left the question of suzerainty open. Moreover, he could not refuse the request of the French government to insert the word "Paris" in the telegrams to Brandeis and Tschlenow, nor their insistent urging—and Sykes's—that he go to Rome. Now that he had, he was sure that it was a useful step in building support for the Zionist cause.[76]

Weizmann was forced to admit that Sokolow's meeting with the pope had produced a "brilliant result"[77] and later in May sent him, on behalf of the English Zionist Federation, an official message commending his "indefatigable and successful labours."[78] These congratulations did not mean that Weizmann ceased his requests for Sokolow's return, but he no longer sought to curtail the latter's diplomatic rovings. Indeed he wanted to extend them and hoped Sokolow would attend the All-Russian Zionist Conference in Petrograd scheduled for the beginning of June 1917. Weizmann felt that Sokolow could counteract anti-British trends in Russia, a plan the Foreign Office supported[79] but did not originate, as Weizmann intimated to his friends.[80] But Sokolow was unwilling to alter his schedule of appointments in Rome and Paris.[81] He finally returned to London on June 17, 1917, where he was impatiently awaited by the English Zionists.[82] During his two and one-half months' absence from London, much had happened. The ideological cauldron that had been bubbling within the Jewish community for the previous six weeks came to its final boiling point the day Sokolow arrived in England.

As early as the summer of 1916 the Zionists and the Conjoint Foreign Committee realized that a compromise between them was no longer possible. A decisive battle was only a question of time. Meanwhile they skirmished, each side weighing the opportune moment for attack. What was different about the controversy in 1917 was that it had become public, beginning with Lucien Wolf's article on "Zionism," which appeared in the *Fortnightly Review* on November 1, 1916, and called Jewish nationalism a dangerous movement that must be checked.[83] The Zionists, naturally, responded in the *Jewish Chronicle* and elsewhere and published pamphlets by Leon Simon and Harry Sacher.[84] Contacts were still not broken off. Wolf, in fact, initiated the next round of correspondence with a letter to Sokolow on March 8, 1917. But in a radical switch from his approach a year earlier, Sokolow now demanded from Wolf unconditional recognition of the Basle Program,[85] whereas Wolf demanded the retraction of this precondition.[86] By that time both Sokolow and Wolf knew, of course, that the Zionists were in a much stronger position to make demands, though Sokolow still advised his colleagues both in England and abroad that contacts not be broken off altogether as long as there was some chance for a *modus vivendi*.[87]

Sokolow's call for a careful step-by-step assessment of the relationship between the Zionists and the Conjoint was dictated by his own moderate temper but possibly also by the well-heeded admonition of Baron Edmond de Rothschild that the Zionists must come to terms with the anti-Zionists. Yet, when he arrived in Paris in early April 1917, Sokolow found that the baron was no longer interested in this affair; he was fully consumed by his close watch of political negotiations between Sokolow and the Quai d'Orsay. In England, meanwhile, the ideological temperature began to rise. Even the sedate Lord Rothschild declared in a letter to Weizmann—who now once again resumed command of all Zionist affairs—his willingness to do battle with the Conjoint.[88]

Wolf and his colleagues were made suspicious by what they heard from their friends in Paris about high-level Zionist negotiations with the French government carried on, so it seemed, with the connivance of the Foreign Office.[89] In a conversation with Lord Milner on May 16, Claude Montefiore could not help but observe the hardly veiled pro-Zionist attitude of one of Lloyd George's closest advisers.[90] So shaken was he by the interview that Montefiore decided to reveal its contents to only a few members of the Conjoint. In a letter to Milner, written on the following day, Montefiore wrote: "I beg of you to trust your own fellow citizens, who, at all events, are Englishmen through and through, and whose sons are serving in England's armies, rather than foreigners who have no love for England, and who, if the fortunes of the war went wrong, would throw her over in a trice, and hurry to Berlin to join the majority of their colleagues."[91] Montefiore would have been even more alarmed had he read the confidential letter from Mark Sykes to Sir Ronald Graham some three weeks earlier in which Sir Mark warned that "His Majesty's Government should beware of activities of Monsieur Lucien Wolff [sic] and those who think with him or are inspired by him. He is [an] anti-Zionist who desires to focus Jewish power at some point

Nahum Sokolow at the Twelfth Zionist Congress, 1921. Courtesy: Central Zionist Archives

outside Palestine though he has on more than one occasion masqueraded as a Zionist; he has done this in order to stave off Zionist aims."[92]

Whatever bits and pieces of information the leaders of the Conjoint were able to glean was enough to propel them into action. On May 17, Montefiore summoned a meeting of the Conjoint Foreign Committee to ask for approval of a statement on Palestine; the majority approved it.[93] Three days later, even before the statement was published, Weizmann addressed an extraordinary meeting of the English Zionist Federation. In the central passage of his speech, Weizmann stated:

> One reads constantly in the Press and one hears from friends, both Jewish and non-Jewish, that it is the endeavour of the Zionist movement immediately to create a Jewish state in Palestine. . . . While heartily welcoming all these demonstrations as a genuine manifestation of the Jewish national will, we cannot consider them as safe statesmanship. . . . It must be obvious to everybody who stands in the midst of the work of the Zionist Organization . . . that the conditions are not yet ripe for the setting up of a

state *ad hoc*. States must be built up slowly, gradually, systematically and patiently. We, therefore, say that while the creation of a Jewish Commonwealth in Palestine is our final ideal—an ideal for which the whole of the Zionist Organization is working—the way to achieve it lies through a series of intermediary stages. And one of these intermediary stages, which I hope is going to come about as a result of this war, is that the fair country of Palestine will be protected by such a mighty and just power as Great Britain. Under the wing of this Power Jews will be able to develop, and to set up the administrative machinery which, while not interfering with the legitimate interests of the non-Jewish population, would enable us to carry out the Zionist scheme. I am entitled to state in this assembly that His Majesty's Government is ready to support our plans.[94]

Though Weizmann's speech was not printed in full in the *Jewish Chronicle* until May 25, its gist must have been communicated to Wolf and his colleagues. Even had they known that, in fact, Weizmann's speech had not been approved by anyone in the Foreign Office, his willingness to proclaim publicly the British government's support for Zionist plans meant that he was sufficiently confident that such a statement would not be disputed by official sources. In any case, his speech only confirmed Wolf's and his colleagues' conviction that they did the right thing when they published in the *Times* of May 24 a statement on the Zionist question signed by the Conjoint's joint presidents, D. L. Alexander and Claude Montefiore. This statement decisively rejected the Zionist national ideology. It also took strong exception to what was described as the intention of the Zionists to give their settlers special rights in reference to those enjoyed by the rest of the population.[95] On May 28, 1917, the *Times* published responses from Lord Rothschild, whose letter was edited by Weizmann; Chief Rabbi Dr. Joseph H. Hertz; and Weizmann. In his letter Weizmann addressed the two points raised by the Conjoint:

It may possibly be inconvenient to certain individual Jews that the Jews constitute a nationality. Whether the Jews do constitute a nationality is, however, not a matter to be decided by the convenience of this or that individual. It is strictly a question of fact. . . . The Zionists are not demanding in Palestine monopolies or exclusive privileges. . . . It always was and remains a cardinal principle of Zionism as a democratic movement that all races and sects in Palestine should enjoy full justice and liberty.[96]

The controversy that ensued privately as well as in synagogue assemblies and over the pages of the general press split Anglo-Jewry as never before. Both the Zionists and the anti-Zionists marshaled their forces to buttress their ideological arguments with shows of mass support. An offer by the Conjoint to resume negotiations[97] was brushed off by Weizmann.[98] As the controversy continued to mount, the matter finally came before the Board of Deputies, which on June 17, by a vote of 56–51, condemned the statement on Zionism published in the name of the Conjoint Foreign Committee in the *Times* of May 24. It also declared that the committee had lost the confidence of the board, impelling Alexander to resign.[99] A confidential letter from Ronald Graham to Lord Hardinge, the permanent head of the Foreign Office, summed up the result of the June 17 meeting: "This vote means the dissolution of the Conjoint Committee and it will no longer be necessary to consult that body."[100]

It seems that the Foreign Office was as pleased as the Zionists to be rid of a thorny internal dispute that hampered its use of the Zionists for propaganda purposes. A letter from Harry Sacher to Leon Simon indicates that a certain unnamed Foreign Office official even called Weizmann to congratulate him on the victory at the board meeting,[101] the result of which was brought about, to some extent, thanks to the strong position taken by Lord Rothschild.[102]

In the final analysis, it is a moot point whether the Zionists had made gains that went beyond the dissolution of the Conjoint Foreign Committee;[103] both the Foreign Office and large segments of the Zionist and non-Zionist public interpreted this victory as having much larger significance than in fact it might have had. Harry Sacher himself had reason to celebrate; on the day the Board of Deputies cast its vote, he was elected grand commander of the Order of Ancient Maccabeans,[104] giving Weizmann yet another organizational stronghold. Clearly, local events reflected the international reality: Zionism had emerged as a force to be reckoned with.

The changing situation, shifting the focus from the local, tactical importance of Jewish support in Palestine to the worldwide significance of the Jews for the global strategy of the Allies, had a powerful impact on Weizmann's role and his personal approach. His initial dependence on Sykes's judgment declined as he intensified his contacts with other senior officials as well as leading ministers in the war cabinet, and his connections made it possible for him to take a more daring and aggressive attitude in his diplomacy. Sykes, whose attraction to Zionism was learned gradually, took a fairly modest view of the concessions Britain ought to make to the Jews to gain their support. Initially, while studying closely the new conditions created by the Lloyd George government, Weizmann responded to Sykes's call for a moderate approach. But soon, both because of Sykes's own favorable view of Arab demands and because of changing global events, Weizmann changed his tactics. As the United States and Russia, rather than the temporarily aborted Palestine campaign, became the centers of attention, Weizmann began to concern himself less with Sykes than with the changing views in higher echelons of the government at large. Naturally Sykes's long sojourn in Egypt made it easier for Weizmann to effect this shift.

In this new context, Weizmann now took a clear and decided stand for his own preferred program for the future of Palestine as a British protectorate in which a Jewish chartered company, initiated and guided by Zionists, would be empowered by public law to develop the country as the Jewish national home. In May 1917, he wrote in the lead article of the first issue of of the new EZF publication, *Zionist Review:* "We have arrived at a supreme moment in the world's history. The map of the world is to be remade. Our demand is for a small country, no bigger than Wales, where we can create a recognized collective Jewish existence."[105]

By late spring of 1917 Weizmann concluded that to promote his explicitly defined plan meant he had to defend it not only in private conversations but by fighting openly against alternatives, not yet ruled out by British policy, that might preclude it. Weizmann's strong pro-British advocacy made him suspicious of the diplomatic efforts Sokolow was conducting in France and Italy under the guidance of Sykes, whose motives Weizmann was also beginning to suspect.

Weizmann feared the possibility of an international, instead of a British, administration of Palestine. Like some of his Zionist colleagues, Weizmann realized that the political situation was sufficiently fluid to afford the chance to implement some of their dreams. He also realized that timing was important to be able to take advantage of opportunities as they presented themselves. The challenges facing him were threefold: to convince British statesmen that British and Zionist interests were identical and that the best method for penetrating and keeping a foothold in the Middle East would be to build a Jewish Palestine under British protection; to inspire the British with confidence that he and his colleagues were speaking and acting on behalf of Jewish interests and that the desire for a British protectorate was supported by a large majority of Zionists, including those residing in the United States and Russia, indeed that the Zionists, and not the anti-Zionists, were the legitimate representatives of the Jewish people; to prove that Britain's allies would not oppose a pro-Zionist stance by Britain.[106] Moreover, though in England he was now—and particularly during Sokolow's absence—the undisputed strategist of a pro-British Zionist policy, this idea had not yet been accepted by all parts of the Zionist movement. Even in England some, like Moses Gaster, felt that placing all the Zionist eggs in the British political basket was a "dangerous game."[107]

Until mid-April 1917 Weizmann, while suspicious of French designs on Palestine, continued to be unaware of the existence of the Sykes-Picot Agreement, which stood in stark contrast to his aims and strategy. In fact, from the hints Sykes dropped during the February 7 meeting and later, Weizmann may have gained the impression—certainly shared by Harry Sacher and Israel Sieff—that the real obstacle to the implementation of Zionist demands was Sykes's "Arab Scheme."[108] For this reason he agreed in principle to Sykes's suggestion that he go to Palestine to work things out with the Palestinian Arabs. Clearly, Sykes tried to negotiate the various issues with Arab delegates without giving up Palestine to a future Arab state.[109]

Weizmann feared both Arab and French designs on Palestine and decided to press the British lest anything harm Zionist prospects. On March

22, 1917, he went to see Balfour at the Foreign Office. Weizmann's report to Scott that "Mr. Balfour did not at first see the importance of the Zionist claim from the British point of view,"[110] seems surprising. That very week, possibly at the meeting of the war cabinet of March 21, Balfour had stated, totally out of the context of the general conversation: "I am a Zionist."[111] In any case, Weizmann did succeed in explaining the issues involved, though Balfour pointed out the usual difficulties that France and Italy might raise. Balfour suggested that if an agreement with France could not be reached, it might be advisable to bring in the Americans for an Anglo-American protectorate over Palestine. Weizmann pointed out that such a project was always fraught with the danger of having two masters. Balfour seemed to accept this point and then confided to Weizmann that the matter had just been discussed at the war cabinet and that it would be a good idea for Weizmann to see Lloyd George, whose views were identical to those of Weizmann, "namely that it is of great importance to Great Britain to protect Palestine." Emphasizing the importance of such an interview, Balfour suggested that Weizmann "tell the Prime Minister that I wanted you to see him."[112] It is possible that Balfour pressed for this meeting with the hope that the prime minister would reveal to Weizmann the contents of the Sykes-Picot Agreement.

Balfour's statement that Weizmann's views were identical with those of Lloyd George was important intelligence and accorded with the facts.[113] This was not totally new information for Weizmann, who had been briefed all along by Scott on Lloyd George's political views, but it was good to get confirmation from the foreign secretary himself. On March 13, both Balfour and Weizmann were dinner guests at the Astors when Lloyd George made his entrance. "No sooner came L.G. in," Vera Weizmann observed,

> as he asked Ch. in presence of everybody, if he liked the situation and the campaign in the East. Confidentially he informed Ch. that British troops were already in Gaza. He said he must see Ch. and discuss the Eastern affairs and when Ch. remarked, that he is afraid to take his time, L.G. simply said, that Ch. ought to come and inflict [himself] upon him. L.G. left early and the rest of the evening Balfour discussed Zionism with Ch. merely academical. All the private Secretariate [William Ormsby-Gore, Leopold Amery and Mark Sykes] present were thrillingly interested in it.[114]

According to Scott's notes, Lloyd George told Weizmann at the Astor dinner that "time was ripe for Government to make definite plans. . . . Once British Protectorate established they would form a great development company and get ahead."[115]

Despite Lloyd George's flippant remark that he come, Weizmann preferred the more reliable method of arranging for interviews through Scott. On April 3 the two of them breakfasted with the prime minister. Lloyd George said that for him the Palestine campaign was the only really interesting part of the war. Like Weizmann, he, too, was completely opposed to a condominium arrangement with France. He then asked Weizmann: "What about international control?" Weizmann replied that it would be a shade worse since it would not mean control but mere confusion and intrigue. The prime minister then raised the idea Balfour had floated as well: "What about joint control with America?" Weizmann said he could accept that; the two countries would pull together. "Yes," said Lloyd George, "We are both thoroughly materialist peoples"—a remark, noted Scott, "obviously dictated by the conscious superiority of the Kelt." The conversation then turned to the Russian Revolution and to the use to be made of the former members of the Zion Mule Corps.[116] All in all, Weizmann was very pleased with the discussion; unlike the circumspect Balfour, Lloyd George did not need to be convinced by Weizmann, who wrote to Sokolow the following day that Lloyd George "was very emphatic on the point of British Palestine."[117]

Still fired by his own rhetoric as well as Weizmann's and Scott's approval, Lloyd George, together with Lord Curzon, the lord president of the council and a member of the war cabinet, and Sir Maurice Hankey, the secretary of the war cabinet, met the afternoon of April 3 with Sir Mark Sykes. The latter was about to depart for the East—after a detour in France and Italy—as chief political officer on the staff of the commander in chief of the British Army, which was then operating in Palestine. According to the summary of the proceedings, the prime minister asked Sykes to explain what action he proposed to take. Sir Mark stated that he hoped to open up relations with the various tribes in that region and, if possible, to raise an Arab rebellion further north. It was then Lloyd George's and Curzon's turn to give their instructions:

> Both laid great stress on the importance of not committing the British government to any agreement with the tribes which would be prejudicial to British interests. They impressed on Sir Mark Sykes the difficulty of our relations with the French in this region and the importance of not prejudicing the Zionist movement and the possibility of its development under British auspices.
>
> The Prime Minister suggested that the Jews might be able to render us more assistance than the Arabs. . . .
>
> Sir Mark . . . said . . . that the Arabs probably realised that there was no prospect of their being allowed any control over Palestine.[118]

So confident was Sir Mark in the imminent British advance on Palestine, and so certain as to British policy *vis-à-vis* the Zionists, that the following morning he met with Weizmann several times to persuade him to follow him to Egypt within a week to ten days. Sykes felt Weizmann could be of great service as soon as Gaza was captured and "the road thus opened for an advance on Jerusalem." Though two weeks earlier Weizmann himself suggested that he accompany Sykes to Palestine, he now had second thoughts and did not rush to accept the offer.

He suggested to Sir Mark that perhaps it would be better if he came to Egypt after the British had reached Jaffa.[119] In any case, he was still deeply involved in his scientific work for the Admiralty, and, with Sokolow on the Continent, he felt he needed to keep a finger on the political pulse in England. Over the next few weeks Sykes continued to press from Cairo for Weizmann to drop everything and rush to join him. Sykes proposed "to use W. to organise the Zionist situation in Egypt easing the Judaeo-Arab situation by promoting good feeling and co-operation, assisting in the organisation of local Zionists and improving such of our intelligence service as depends on Jewish information, and making plans for political action against our advance."[120]

On May 1, 1917, Ronald Graham wrote to Weizmann that Aaron Aaronsohn advised, and Sir Mark agreed, that "your presence in Egypt is now essential in the present crisis."[121] The crisis Graham was referring to was the order given toward the end of March 1917 by Djemal Pasha, the Turkish commander in chief in Syria and Palestine, for the civilian (in fact, mostly Jewish) evacuation of Jaffa and its environs. The compulsory departure northwards of some nine thousand Jews from Jaffa–Tel Aviv took place early in April 1917 under conditions of extreme hardship.[122] These gruesome events were a convenient and timely propaganda card in the hands of the British, who throughout the war had been in the awkward position of defending Russian atrocities against the Jews.[123] William Ormsby-Gore put the matter succinctly and frankly: "I think we ought to use pogroms in Palestine as propaganda. Any spicy tales of atrocity would be eagerly welcomed by the propaganda people here—and Aaron Aaronsohn could send some lurid stories to the Jewish papers."[124] Clearly Weizmann was seen by the people in the Foreign Office as someone who could aid in this propaganda campaign. But he was unshaken in his resolve to stay in England and simply transmitted the information he received from Sykes and Graham to Jacobus Kann in the Hague, asking for the well-connected banker to use his influence and financial resources to aid the refugees.[125] At the suggestion of Jacques Mosseri, a prominent Egyptian Zionist and banker who chaired the Special Committee for Relief of Jews in Palestine, funds from England to aid the refugees were channeled through Weizmann, much to the dismay of Moses Gaster.[126] The Foreign Office, in fact, was more than happy to support the committee's appeals for financial aid among prominent British Jews and to help Weizmann in the transmittal of these funds to Palestine via Holland.[127]

The British government, in the meantime, continued to debate the Zionist question within its own councils. On April 19, 1917, a subcommittee of the war cabinet met to consider British territorial claims at the end of the war. Once again it was Lord Curzon in the chair who stated unequivocally at the start of the meeting that "in his opinion the only safe settlement was that Palestine should be included in a British Protectorate." General Jan Smuts stated that Britain "ought to secure the command of Palestine in order to protect Egypt and our communications to the East. Any other power in Palestine would be a very serious menace. . . . From the military and political point of view he considered a satisfactory settlement of this question the most important of all the questions under discussion, except perhaps that of East Africa." The subcommittee then presented its conclusions, among them: "that they hoped that it might be possible to arrange for a definite British Protectorate of Palestine" and "that they hoped that it might be possible to readjust the boundary of Palestine so as to bring it up to the river Leontes, and to include the Hauran in the British sphere."[128] Clearly, then, the idea of a British protectorate in Palestine was taken for granted by Lloyd George. His claim after the war that he had been "a very strong advocate of the conquest of Palestine"[129] was not just rhetoric. As he said to Weizmann and Scott, the Palestine campaign was the most interesting part of the war for him personally, and he wished to see a British protectorate over the Holy Land. Both the war cabinet and the Foreign Office accepted and approved this idea. After Sykes departed for Egypt, Zionist affairs became the province of the Foreign Office and particularly that of Ronald Graham, the assistant undersecretary of state. Graham assumed, as he wrote to Sir Francis Bertie, "that H.M.G. are now more or less committed to encourage Zionism, and all the hopes of the Zionists are based on a British, or failing that, an American Palestine."[130]

Graham's many years as a career diplomat sharpened his sensitivities to the complications facing the Foreign Office in its dealings with the Zionists while the Sykes-Picot Agreement was still in force. Lloyd George and other high officials had expressed their desire to change its terms, but they had not made the necessary alterations in policy. Moreover, perhaps the time had arrived to provide the Zionists with information on what the international agreements entailed:

> At the present moment we are encouraging Dr. Weizmann to leave his business here and proceed to Egypt. Further, Baron Edmond de Rothschild and Dr. Weizmann are telegraphing to Judge Brandeis . . . suggesting to him to convene a representative meeting of American Jews and to pass a resolution that Palestine should be handed over to Great Britain to administer. This may strengthen our position in the matter or it may provoke and solidify French opposition to our pretensions. But, the point I desire to raise is whether we are justified in going so far in our encouragement of the Zionist movement, which is based on a British Palestine, without giving the Zionists some intimation of the existing arrangement with France.[131]

As Ronald Graham was writing to Lord Hardinge, Weizmann was already fully aware of the British agreement with the French. On April 14, 1917, Sacher wrote to Weizmann that C. P. Scott had heard from Vicomte Robert de Caix, foreign editor of *Le Journal des Débats*, who appeared to have close connections with the Quai d'Orsay, that France *wanted* Palestine down to Acre and Lake Tiberias, the rest of Palestine to

be internationalized.[132] Two days later Scott wrote to Weizmann that he
had heard from de Caix that it had been settled that France was to have
Palestine down to a line from Acre to Tiberias, and including the Hauran,
the rest of Palestine to be internationalized.[133] De Caix's account was
substantiated on April 20 by Lord Milner, whom Scott must have approached for confirmation.[134] This was the first warning Weizmann had
of a British *commitment* in regard to Palestine, as distinct from information about the French claims as described in Sacher's letter. Contrary to
his usual tendency to act immediately, Weizmann decided to get more
information first. Scott's disparaging remark about Malcolm as "a most
doubtful sort of personage"[135] was ignored by Weizmann, for he wished
to hear firsthand what the French government's designs were in Palestine.

Malcolm returned to England on April 20, bringing with him a diary
of his and Sokolow's activities in Paris. When they met on April 23,
Malcolm informed Weizmann that de Caix's and Lord Milner's accounts
conformed to what he had heard in Paris.[136] What Weizmann was unable to determine was whether the various arrangements between France
and England were binding or there was sufficient flexibility to reopen
the discussion. He therefore turned to Herbert Samuel, who had been
home secretary during the final stages of the Sykes-Picot Agreement and
whose loyalty to the Zionist cause seemed firm. On the evening prior to
the meeting, Weizmann agreed in consultation with Tolkowsky, and with
Ahad Ha'Am's concurrence, that in his interviews with Samuel and Graham his first demand would be for Great Britain to reconsider its prior
arrangements and assume a British protectorate over Palestine. Southern
Palestine, at least, must be under British protectorate. The three ruled
out the possibility of any condominium arrangements.[137]

During their meeting on the morning of April 24, Samuel was as discreet as he had been during the February 7 meeting with Sykes. He
conceded that the arrangements with the French were not satisfactory
from the British point of view. Samuel stated that he saw no reason why
the whole question could not be reopened now that the British army
was at the gates of Palestine. He strongly advised Weizmann to go to
Egypt, but only after informing the Foreign Office that he would do so
on the basis of working for a British Palestine and mobilizing Jewish
world opinion for the same purpose.[138]

By then, Weizmann's preconditions for such a trip had become quite
clear, to no small extent due to the influence of Scott. The Manchester
editor, who, in any case, did not have a very high opinion of the Foreign
Office[139] and was suspicious of Sykes as well, repeatedly warned Weizmann against undertaking such a journey.[140] On April 24 he wrote that
he did not want Weizmann "to go on a fool's errand,"[141] repeating his
warning and reasoning for it in even greater detail the following day.[142]
The warnings by Scott and Weizmann's own sharp political instincts

militated against going to Egypt without first obtaining strong commitments from the Foreign Office.

Some ten days later, after he heard about Weizmann's interview with Samuel, Lord Rothschild, like Scott, advised Weizmann against going to Egypt since "you are the only man who can keep the Prime Minister up to the mark." Walter Rothschild, who had not yet met Lloyd George, felt strongly that Weizmann ought to see the prime minister alone and not in the company of Herbert Samuel. Rothschild was frank in his assessment of Samuel: "I saw Mr. Herbert Samuel casually one day and had a talk with him. I fear he has not quite the courage of his opinions. I mean those he expressed at our meeting, because when I suggested that matters should be pushed now because the Government had decided to defy the French, he demurred and said he hardly thought they had."[143]

Rothschild was perhaps unduly harsh. His letter to Weizmann does not indicate on what day he met the former home secretary. Samuel, quite possibly, did not wish to reveal what he knew of international agreements and was simply being polite in his answer. In any case, Samuel encouraged Weizmann to consult the Foreign Office, probably assuming that Weizmann would be able to secure the full story from the men responsible for Britain's foreign policy.

After meeting with Samuel, Weizmann had sufficient confirmation that the British had made "unfortunate commitments," as Lord Milner had put it to Scott, to warrant a direct confrontation with the Foreign Office officials. That same afternoon Weizmann went to see Graham, to whom he repeated all the information he had thus far gathered from Scott, Malcolm, and Samuel. Sir Ronald could say in good conscience that he had nothing to do with the Franco-British arrangements and that he, like Samuel, found them unsatisfactory. He suggested that Weizmann see Lord Robert Cecil, who, while Balfour was on an official visit in the United States, served as acting foreign secretary.[144] Weizmann readily agreed, and Graham set the interview with Cecil for the following day.

According to a "very confidential" letter from Ormsby-Gore to Sykes, "the Jews are fairly on the move" after they heard from de Caix about "the agreement." "Weizman [sic] came to Bob Cecil in fine rage."[145] If he did express rage, Weizmann must have done so in a manner acceptable to the acting foreign secretary since neither Weizmann's nor Cecil's official memoranda indicate that the conversation was carried in a sharp tone. The acting foreign secretary recorded that Weizmann

> began by saying that he had been told that some kind of arrangement had been made between the British and French Governments, whereby Judea should be internationalised and the northern part of Palestine, Galilea, should be given to the French Government. He objected to both provisions. . . . He said that it would take some time for the Zionists to colonise Judea, and when they had done so and desired to extend, they would have a very

strong case for "over-running" (as he put it) Galilea. With regard to the internationalisation of Judea, however, he was much more outspoken. . . .

I asked him what his attitude would be toward French Judea?

He explained that the French Government, who were atheistical at home, were Roman Catholic abroad. Catholicism was, for them, an article of exportation and, as practised in French Dominions abroad, it was in the hands of the most intolerant section of the Roman Catholic Church. Apart from that, he regarded the French as incapable of understanding the aspirations of small nations under their administration, and particularly as unsympathetic to Jewish and Zionist aspirations. . . .

He said that the Zionists in America would be unanimously against it, and in favour of a British Protectorate. . . .

As he left me, he went so far as to say that the Zionists throughout the world would regard a French administration in Palestine as a great disaster: "a third destruction of the Temple."

I was much impressed, as indeed I have been on previous occasions, by the enthusiasm and idealism of M. Weizmann.[146]

The meeting between Weizmann and Cecil can perhaps be credited with planting the seed for the Balfour Declaration, which was issued some six months later. Cecil and Weizmann reached two major conclusions. The first was that Weizmann would go to Egypt under the express understanding that he was to work for a Jewish Palestine under a British protectorate. This plan had also been the recommendation of Samuel and Graham, and on April 28, 1917, Cecil sent a telegram to Sykes informing him that Weizmann "is going out with full permission to work for a British Palestine. He and James Rothschild are instigating American and Russian Jews to agitate for this consummation."[147] The following day a cable arrived from Sykes, who had felt since February that all negotiations ought to be handled by Weizmann[148] and who had a less favorable impression of James de Rothschild: "Tell Weizman [*sic*] from me that it would be best to keep all negotiations strictly to himself and Sokolow. James R. is enthusiastic and rash."[149] In the meantime, however, the British military advance had been checked, and Weizmann decided to postpone his trip indefinitely.[150] On May 19, Sykes suggested to the Foreign Office that Weizmann be asked to appoint Aaronsohn in his place.[151] There is no record of such appointment having been made by Weizmann, but Sykes, who held Aaronsohn in high esteem, seems to have treated him as his major adviser in all Jewish affairs.[152]

The second issue on which Weizmann and Lord Robert agreed is indicated in Cecil's final sentence of his memorandum: "Of course I am not in a position to express any opinion as to how far he [Weizmann] represents Jewish feeling in this matter [a British protectorate over a Jewish Palestine]."[153] Weizmann interpreted the last portion of the hour-long interview as a hint from Cecil that, given the great political difficulties the British had to surmount to gain a protectorate over Palestine, "it would strengthen the position very considerably if the Jews of the world would express themselves in favour of a British Protectorate. Dr.

Weizmann replied that this is exactly the task which he would like to undertake to bring about such an expression of opinion."[154] Weizmann handled himself splendidly. He immediately grasped what Cecil expected of him and set the proper wheels in motion. A brief statement by the acting foreign secretary was sufficient; no further explanations were needed.

Robert Cecil and his colleagues in the Foreign Office made their own discreet inquiries; they were quite concerned about the situation in post-revolutionary Russia, where, it was reported, Jews had a strong part in the pacifist propaganda as well as among those promoting strong Anglophobia. Early in June 1917 Sykes reported to Sir Reginald Wingate, the high commissioner in Egypt, about a conversation he had with Aaronsohn, whose assessment of the situation, he suggested, ought to be shared with Weizmann:

1. Russian Jews lost faith in Great Britain because they considered Great Britain allied with Russia not out of duress, as isolated France did, but for aggressive motives.
2. This has been skillfully worked by the Bund in coalition with Poalei Zion. Both organisations consciously or unconsciously under German influence.
3. Result of 1 and 2 together have produced idea in Russian Jewish masses that Great Britain is a Tzar of Holy Russian force.[155]

The reasons for distrust of Great Britain by the Russian Jewish masses were, of course, more complicated and varied than Sir Mark could explain in a brief telegram. The fact of the matter was that Great Britain no longer commanded the respect and admiration of the Russian Jews as it had in the past.[156] Aware of these sentiments, the intelligence department consulted with Leopold Greenberg, who had a long-standing relationship with the Foreign Office. On April 16, 1917, Greenberg replied in a memorandum to the Foreign Office that the Allied cause would be greatly appreciated by Jews all over the world if their national rights were to receive due consideration.[157] Cecil, who in 1916 had supported the Grey initiative, now raised the question whether a pro-Zionist declaration would militate against the pacifist tendencies of Russian Jewry. He directed this inquiry to Sir George Buchanan, the British ambassador to Petrograd.[158] Buchanan's response was decidedly negative, and he opposed even raising this question.[159] Cecil was discouraged and ready to drop the idea of a British statement of sympathy with the Jewish national aspirations. But the issue was raised again, two weeks later, by, of all people, Buchanan himself. Buchanan reported with alarm the extent of Jewish anti-British propaganda in Russia.[160] This time Ronald Graham consulted with Weizmann, who suggested that Sokolow be sent to Russia to counteract the anti-British trend.[161] This was the advice Mark Sykes had cabled to Graham some two weeks earlier.[162] On May 14, Weizmann cabled Sokolow that his presence was absolutely essential at the All-Russian Zionist Conference, which was to begin on June 6. "Cancel your appointments and leave straight for here," cabled Weizmann imperiously.[163] As noted, Sokolow was unwilling to break his important engagements. Instead, he suggested that Weizmann ask Tschlenow to postpone the conference by a week.[164] Tschlenow declined to do so, and Sokolow returned to London a week after the conference had ended.

Sykes, who was shown by Wingate a copy of Cecil's cable of April 24 to Buchanan, sharply dissented from the views of the ambassador, claiming to Graham that it lay outside of the area of competence of the British ambassador to deal with such matters. Understanding the depth of Russian Anglophobia, Sykes advised:

> It would be quite impossible for British embassy in Petrograd to ascertain either what were the feelings of Russian Jews or what would be [the] effect on pacifists acting under Jewish influence. Any enquiries emanating from an embassy on such a question would only provoke fear and suspicion and answers quite contrary to the facts. Zionist enquiries could only be safely made through Zionists as M. Sokolow, Dr. Weizman [*sic*], Jabotinsky or some such person actually of the cause who would have their own methods of asking questions. The only channel possible would be from a Jew to a Jew.[165]

With Sokolow shuttling between Paris and Rome, Weizmann was the most qualified Zionist to make such discreet inquiries. Never one to wait for official assent—either British or Zionist—before taking action, Weizmann had already initiated his attempt to gain Russian Jewry's support for a British protectorate in Palestine on April 27, 1917. He informed Yehiel Tschlenow that after discussions with Zionist leaders and their friends in England such as Ahad Ha'Am, the Rothschilds, and Herbert Samuel, as well as with the "competent authorities," a "unanimous decision for Jewish Palestine under English Protectorate" had been reached. Most important, the Russian Jews and their organizations should approach their government in support of this program.[166] Weizmann followed his cable with a letter explaining in greater detail the reasons for his request for Russian support:

> We assume that Palestine will fall into England's hands. England is not aiming at annexing Palestine and, were she not co-operating with us, it would be doubtful whether she would have fought against internationalizing the country. On the contrary, it is feared here that with the present mood in Russia and in America it will be difficult to work for a British Protectorate except under the one condition *that the Jews themselves want it;* in other words, England is ready to take Palestine under her protection to enable the Jews there to establish themselves and live independently. . . .
>
> It is very important that Russian Jewry should voice its views and that this question in its present form and its significance should be explained to the Russian Government.[167]

Not having had any replies from Tschlenow to his cable and letter, Weizmann cabled on May 16 to Israel Rosov, a member of the GAC and president of the Russian Zionist Organization.[168] That same day a tele-gram arrived from Tschlenow stating that the Russian Zionists wel-comed the results obtained in England.[169] This was encouraging news, and on June 2, Weizmann once again pressed the case for a British pro-tectorate, assuring Rosov and Tschlenow that such an arrangement would save the Zionists from the three major lurking evils: "from Arab domi-nation, from internationalization and from French domination." Once again he assured the Russians that "England does not seek Palestine. It is of value to her only if we are to be strong there, and therefore we can obtain the maximum only through England."[170] On June 4, two days prior to the opening of the All-Russian Zionist Conference, Weizmann wired a message to the participants asking for their support for "a Jew-ish Palestine under British Trust with all necessary guarantees [for] fu-ture national development to Commonwealth."[171] That same day, Weiz-mann also wired to Sokolow, who was still in Paris, asking him to send a similar message to the conference. To avoid any possible misunder-standing, Weizmann enclosed a copy of his own cable to Tschlenow and Rosov.[172] Sokolow complied, sending a lengthy but much-qualified sup-port for Weizmann's plan. More careful and measured than Weizmann in any case, Sokolow also better sensed the Russian Zionists' mood and stated simply, "We are agreeable to consider British Protectorate as the ideal solution." He hinted that solutions and plans were proposed by other friendly powers, such as France.[173]

The result of the Petrograd conference confirmed Sokolow's assess-ment. The 552 delegates, elected by 140,000 *shekel* payers throughout Russia (except in German-occupied territories) did not pass a single res-olution in favor of British control of Palestine.[174] Moreover, even Tschle-now made only passing references to England in his address. The con-ference simply adopted a resolution declaring that the Jewish people were entitled to the restoration of "a national autonomous center in its historic home, Palestine." The conference also agreed to bring the Pal-estine question before the projected All-Russian Jewish conference.[175]

All in all, the resolutions of the conference were a bitter disappoint-ment to Weizmann. Yet the first news he had of the resolutions came from Rosov's assurance that the reference to England was "met with enthusiasm" by those attending the conference.[176] The advocates of a British protectorate over Palestine could not have known that, paradox-ically, the resolutions of the All-Russian Zionist Conference confirmed Sir Ronald Graham in his belief that Weizmann was right all along in arguing that Zionism represented the key to unlocking Russian Jewry's opposition to England. On a copy of Rosov's cable to Weizmann, Sir Ronald minuted: "The reference to England was worked by Dr. Weiz-mann, and it is certain that our best card in dealing with the Russo-Jewish proletariat is Zionism."[177]

Sir Ronald's hopes that the "Russian Jewish proletariat," or even Rus-sian Zionists, would wholeheartedly embrace the idea of a British protectorate over Palestine were to be sorely disappointed in the end. Yet British officials at all levels agreed that it was important to try. Mark Sykes, who was constantly searching for new means to win such support, suggested on the eve of the Russian Zionist conference that the badly tarnished image of Great Britain "is practically ineradicable except by American Jewish mediation."[178] This was, of course, clear to Sokolow and Weizmann as well. Concurrent with their efforts to enlist the support of Russian Zionists, both before and after the Petrograd conference, they were in communication with American Zionists and particularly with their all-powerful leader, Louis Brandeis.

American Zionists saw the war as an opportunity to pursue, more directly than before, the ultimate political goal of the movement. The hopes American Zionists pinned on Brandeis's leadership included the anticipation that his vigorous style and top-level contacts would usher in an era of political achievement. Such hopes were particularly strong among the older Zionist leaders—Jacob DeHaas, Richard Gottheil, and Stephen Wise—who had been attached to Theodor Herzl and deplored the course the Zionist movement, including its American branch, had taken in the period since Herzl's death. Brandeis shared, of course, the general assumption that the American movement had to achieve a political goal. In organizing the PZC—to which he freely co-opted his own friends and contacts regardless of their Zionist standing—he appointed a Political Committee, naming Richard Gottheil and Horace Kallen to serve on this, rather than on other, more routine divisions of the work he undertook. The two men, both highly conscious of a personal mission of political activism, took their assignments seriously, contacting visiting foreign intellectuals and diplomats in the interests of Zionism.[179]

But in the United States, as in England, it soon became evident that Zionist political work would have to be confined at first to broad, general propaganda and a building up of contacts instead of pursuing concrete political goals. In the beginning, general considerations relating to the position of the United States in regard to the conflict and the practical options for useful work open to the Zionists led many in the movement to concentrate on more immediate objectives. These were insistently defined by Brandeis as "Men! Money! Discipline!"[180] He hoped, by uniting the bulk of American Jewry in the immediate work—the membership campaign, the relief effort, and the congress struggle—to isolate the opposition and compel opponents to join in a pro-Zionist congress.[181] Active negotiation of political Zionist issues, therefore, had to wait its turn; and in the end it was precipitated in the United States by the progress made by the movement in England.

The cardinal difference between the American and British situations was, of course, the fact of American neutrality. Neutrality made it possible for—or, indeed, more or less required—the local Zionist organization to adopt a neutral official attitude as well. Thus, until 1917, the American Zionists remained well within the guidelines that enabled the

World Zionist Organization to maintain (however precariously) its international cohesion across the battlefronts; and the American contribution of material support and international connection was a major factor in that achievement. But neutrality had its significant side effects. It precluded the American movement from taking any decisive positive political positions of its own until, at least, the U.S. declaration of war on Germany—and, indeed, as the United States did not declare war on Turkey, it continued to be a restraining factor even after. Another effect was internal: official Zionist neutrality did not prevent, but in some ways exacerbated, dissent among Zionists, as in the Jewish community at large, over the major issues of sympathy for one side or the other in the world conflict.[182]

What Germany was for world Jewry in the Second World War—the arch-enemy of all Jews—tsarist Russia was in the First. The Russian oppressor was hated by all Jews, and above all by those who had fled this empire to become Americans. Ever since the Russo-Japanese War had provoked the 1905 revolution, Russian Jews in the United States had come to hope for a Russian military defeat that would bring down the tsar and usher in a new era of liberal reform. German Jews in the United States, even after a generation of Americanization, shared in good part the sympathy of other German Americans for the old country—especially in a conflict against "Slavic barbarism." This complex of attitudes tended to outweigh the leanings that Jews shared with the American majority: a tradition of esteem for both France and England and a general condemnation of the attack on little Belgium by the machine of German militarism.

The Zionist movement shared every shade of opinion that was found among other American Jews on these matters; and neither official American nor official Zionist neutrality could control the bitter differences that sometimes arose. Most Zionists, like American Jewry at large, were ardently anti-Russian. But those with more deeply rooted American associations, especially the professionals and academics who came to Zionism in Brandeis's entourage, were sensitive to the prevailing opinion in the liberal and business circles of the Protestant, Anglo-Saxon establishment.

Thus, the rank-and-file, old-line Zionists shared Downtown neutralism, strongly tinged with coolness to the Allied cause; and many, like Shmarya Levin, feared Turkish reprisals in the event of any Zionist leaning to the Allies—who, in any case, seemed to be losing the war continually. The Poalei Zion leaned to the neutralism of the Zimmerwald socialist group; and Nachman Syrkin had to leave the executive of the party at one point because of his pro-Allied position.[183] Similar attitudes prevailed among liberal American-born Zionists who were strongly involved with the immigrant community as social workers. On the other hand, among the Zionists, academics like Professors Richard Gottheil and Horace Kallen were more forthright in their pro-Allied commitment than Brandeis—mindful of his position as the head of American Zionism and his commitment to Wilsonian neutrality—allowed himself to be. The young Washington lawyer Felix Frankfurter not only shared the pro-Allied sympathies of his Harvard and official associates but became an ardent Anglophile, an attitude bolstered by close ties to British friends, like Lord Eustace Percy, in Washington.

Given the split sympathies of American Zionists, it would have been difficult for them to develop a clear political strategy based on an orientation to one or another side even had the neutral stance adopted by the WZO, as well as American neutrality, not forbidden it. Instead, partisan actions by leading Zionists were bitterly attacked by Zionists with opposing views on the war on the grounds that they violated official Zionist policy. As noted earlier, rumors of Weizmann's support for pro-British initiatives had brought down on him the wrath of Shmarya Levin and Judah Magnes and caused their correspondence to be broken off.

Louis Brandeis, Stephen Wise, and Jacob DeHaas had all taken a more or less active part in Woodrow Wilson's 1912 election campaign and had established good relations with the administration that could be useful to the Zionist cause.[184] DeHaas and Wise both claimed in their memoirs to have had talks with Wilson before the election in which he expressed sympathy for the Jews and promised support for their interests in regard to both Russia and Palestine. After the election Brandeis and Wise obtained similar general assurances from the president in private meetings.[185] All through 1915 and 1916, Wilson made occasional attempts to launch American initiatives for a negotiated peace between the belligerents.[186] Both the British blockade and the growing German submarine menace were interfering with the trade Americans were carrying on with both sides under cover of neutrality and the doctrine of the freedom of the seas. A negotiated peace would not only relieve such American grievances; it would allow Wilson to play the role he considered eminently appropriate for the emerging stature of the United States in international affairs as the impartial arbiter among selfishly contending Old World rivals. In this policy Wilson had the ready assistance of his personal political adviser, Colonel Edward M. House, who acted as his agent in conducting the necessary diplomatic maneuvers in Europe.[187]

Before the elections of 1916, Wilson's policy underwent a slow, cumulative shift that entailed changes in his foreign policy apparatus. He maintained neutrality, especially through the election campaign, and continued to seek a negotiated peace. But meanwhile the causes for irritation with Britain—at least on the part of the administration—were gradually adjusted, while the threat of unrestricted German submarine warfare grew larger. The long-standing pro-Allied bias of the established American majority and elite found expression now in pressure, at least for "preparedness" if not for outright intervention on the side of the Allies. When Colonel House proposed renewed peace negotiations to the Allies, he argued that they were a necessary final effort to solidify

American public opinion for intervention should the peace effort fail and the German submarine terror intensify. In the course of these changes, Secretary of State William Jennings Bryan, a decided pacifist, resigned and was replaced by Robert Lansing; and House was brought back from Europe to bypass the State Department as Wilson's personal director of foreign affairs at large, not merely his special agent for peace initiatives.[188]

Zionist political action was not much affected in 1916 by these changes. Like the general public, the Zionists perceived no decisive abandonment of American neutrality in official policy. The personnel shifts in the administration occasioned no Zionist change in tactics. Both Lansing and House were figures the American Zionists knew from their Democratic party work. Zionist activities, such as the relief campaign, and existing relations with the State Department simply continued. The attention of Zionists was mainly concentrated at the time—apart from membership and fund-raising campaigns—upon the battle over the American Jewish Congress. Nevertheless, interest in pursuing opportunities for political activity remained alive, if in the background.[189]

In April 1916, Brandeis reported with some enthusiasm a remarkable find that Nathan Straus had made in California on a vacation trip.[190] Straus had met William Blackstone, a Chicago businessman and leading Presbyterian layman, who in 1891 had collected an impressive number of distinguished signatories on a petition to President Benjamin Harrison to convene an international conference for the restoration of Palestine to the Jews in order to end centuries of suffering of the Chosen People.[191] Straus had this long-forgotten memorial reprinted, and Brandeis now proposed to revive it as the medium for a new approach to President Wilson.

This memorial became the main vehicle for the American Zionists' somewhat perfunctory direct political action. Sporadically over the next two years they sought an expression of explicit presidential support for the creation of a Jewish homeland in Palestine. Blackstone obtained the support of the Presbyterian General Council for his pro-Zionist proposal, and in June and July, Stephen Wise, soon to succeed Brandeis as president of the PZC, was considering the best way to present Wilson with the memorial.[192] The president, putting Wise off gently, expressed appreciation for the Zionists' not pressing the matter at that point and again declared himself in sympathy with the Zionist cause. He said that when Wise and Brandeis thought the time ripe, he would, after consultation, respond positively if they then put their request forward.[193]

Brandeis clearly understood that the president and his aide, Colonel House, intended to go into the peace conference unfettered by commitments. American Zionists, led by Brandeis, were ready to cooperate with Wilson as far as their own requests were concerned. The president was not pressed again for an explicit pro-Zionist statement until a moment during the peace conference when Zionist hopes seemed in severe jeopardy because of the opposition of Protestant circles very close to those Presbyterians who had endorsed the Blackstone memorial. In fact, the influence of Protestant clergy and lay organizations in the Wilson administration, generally very pervasive, was particularly strong in matters of foreign policy and especially Middle Eastern policy.[194] Brandeis's appreciation of their strength, and his reliance on his personal contacts among liberal and progressive Protestants in the Wilson entourage, may have contributed to the interest he took in the Blackstone petition.

Both Brandeis and Wise appreciated the value of their ties with these influential Protestant groups, so well connected with the administration and with the president himself. A special bond was available in the persons of Henry Morgenthau and Abram Elkus—both members of Wise's Free Synagogue—who succeeded one another as American ambassador to Turkey. This position had become something of a Jewish post since it had been held by Oscar Straus.[195] In Morgenthau's case, the appointment rewarded a major fund-raiser and contributor to Wilson's election campaign as well as a representative Jew presumably influential in his constituency. The Jewish concern with Palestine, moreover, made this post a suitable one; but it also raised the question whether a Jew would take proper care of the interests of the Protestant missions in Turkey and Syria, which represented the major American interest in the area. Morgenthau, following the example of Straus and emulated in turn by Elkus, was able to satisfy both the State Department and the missionary establishment on this point.[196] The Jewish ambassadors developed relations of mutual esteem and implicit confidence with the missionary leaders in the field; and indeed these ambassadors were even occasionally briefed by missionary leaders before assuming their posts. The Zionists, for their part, could count on this relationship to secure sympathetic understanding in highly influential Protestant quarters for their own needs. Prior to the Balfour Declaration, and even later, this support mattered. It helped bolster the confidence of American Zionists in their political negotiations during the final months before the Balfour Declaration.

By 1917, as we have seen, a series of critical events had sharply altered the terms under which Zionist affairs had to be conducted. Lloyd George's government brought a group into power more open to Zionist approaches and also inclined to press forward with military advances in the Middle East, including the Palestine front. Wilson's second administration had hardly begun when the Russians, in March 1917, overthrew the tsar and installed a new revolutionary regime whose future character and policies remained uncertain. Then followed the American declaration of war against Germany on April 6, 1917. Soon after, on April 22, Balfour arrived in the United States at the head of a British mission to sound out the intentions of the new ally. Among those whom he met at the reception arranged for him by Secretary Lansing in the White House was Justice Brandeis; and there followed two meetings—

on May 7 and May 10—during the weeks of Balfour's brief visit that both men rated as highly successful.[197]

In the meantime, the British and French governments permitted the Zionists to contact their colleagues in the United States and Russia through diplomatic and intelligence the channels, and Brandeis began receiving frequent reports—from Sokolow, Gaster,[198] James de Rothschild, and Weizmann—about the relationship of the London Zionists with Sir Mark Sykes and the Lloyd George government and the beginnings of Sokolow's diplomatic tour of Paris and Rome. Balfour's visit to Washington sharply heightened interest in this Zionist exchange. The London Zionists now looked to the Americans not only for material aid in political actions but for supporting political actions of their own in the suddenly vital American sector. The burst of activity initiated from the British side necessitated a new approach in the United States. While Richard Gottheil was still in close touch with Brandeis's inner circle, his insistent urging had brought about the constitution of a political subcommittee to frame policy appropriate to the changing circumstances. Until May 1917 the deliberations conducted by that group had not been brought to the PZC as a whole for discussion and decision. Now the Americans were presented with a specific program drawn up by the Zionists in England, an ally of the United States in the new situation.

The American Zionists were informed throughout the war—through a variety of informal channels and personal contacts—of the English Zionists' preference, foremost among them Weizmann, for a British protectorate over Palestine. But these plans had not been anchored to a firm British policy that would have given Weizmann and his colleagues political leverage within their own movement. This situation was, of course, radically altered with the assumption of office by Lloyd George and the round of discussions with Mark Sykes. The Zionists were now tacitly recognized—and treated—as a British ally. In exchange for being permitted to use official British communications (which gave the British full access to internal Zionist correspondence), the Zionists were expected to gain the support of their colleagues in Russia and the United States for a British Palestine. As the ranking Zionist leader in England, who, moreover, saw himself as the person who had initiated Brandeis into Zionism, Sokolow was to inform the justice of the latest Zionist negotiations with the British government. A month after the historic meeting in Gaster's home, Sokolow outlined for Brandeis the major developments that had taken place during the past two years. He gave much of the credit for Zionist accomplishments to Weizmann:

> Since Dr. Tschlenow's departure I have continued the work with our friend and colleague Dr. Weizmann. He had started it even before our arrival and since that time is most active in our work. Owing to his personal influence and untiring efforts for which I have the highest appreciation, the relations and connections between our organization and the most influential quarters in this country, have not only contributed very much to the enlargement of

the circle of our friends, but also to the deepening, the development and the strengthening of that benevolence from which we have reason to expect the best results.

Using a method similar to Weizmann's, Sokolow proceeded to outline the various political frameworks within which the Zionists could settle and develop Palestine. After ruling out all other alternatives, Sokolow stated unequivocally: "What we want in Palestine is free national development and the opening of all resources of the country by means of a Chartered Company, and this can be achieved in the best way under British suzerainty."[199]

A month later, Sokolow sent a second, detailed report on the negotiations with Sykes, the Conjoint Foreign Committee, and other internal difficulties facing the Zionist leadership in England.[200] This second letter crossed in the mail with a brief note from Brandeis stating in vague, noncommittal language that the American Zionists were "in thorough accord" with what Sokolow had reported.[201]

Weizmann picked up the correspondence with Brandeis soon after Sokolow departed for Paris. In his first letter to the justice, on April 8, 1917, Weizmann wrote of the importance of the British military campaign and the generally favorable attitude to a Jewish Palestine under a British protectorate. He had in the meantime met with Norman Hapgood, Brandeis's close friend, in the presence of Herbert Samuel; Neil Primrose, who had been a junior minister but was still joint chief whip; James de Rothschild; and Josiah Wedgwood, MP. Weizmann had impressed upon Hapgood the importance of getting the support of both the American government and American Jewry for the pro-British plan. Yet Weizmann did not immediately request a political statement. His one concrete and immediate demand was for £10,000, supplementing an additional £2,000 sent by Tschlenow, to fund the political work at hand.[202]

Weizmann's letter was written just two days after the U.S. declaration of war against Germany; he may have calculated that the American Zionists needed time to adjust to the new situation and thus did not press for immediate political action. Like Sokolow a month earlier, he simply presented the views and preferences of his group, giving Brandeis time to react. But it was only a tactical delay, observed Ronald Graham: "The latest project of the Zionists here is to mobilise the American Jews under Brandeis and get them to express in unequivocal terms their desire that Great Britain should take over Palestine."[203] Indeed, on April 21, the day before Balfour was scheduled to arrive in the United States, Weizmann and James de Rothschild wired Brandeis—who received the message only on April 25—this time stating clearly: "Only satisfactory solution Jewish Palestine under British protectorate. . . . It would greatly help [our] work if American Jews would support this scheme before their government. We also rely upon immediate expression of opinion of yourself and other American prominent Jews."[204] Two days later

Weizmann once again elaborated on this request with his standard arguments.[205]

There followed a cable to Brandeis that, though dated April 27, was transmitted only on April 30. Signed by James de Rothschild, Weizmann, and Joseph Cowen, it stated that press reports indicated that the American administration favored a "Jewish Republic in Palestine." The three signatories warned that such a republic would be unwise and again they asked for support from Brandeis and for his views.[206] Only on April 28 did Weizmann inform Brandeis of the existence of "some vague arrangements between the French and British Governments concerning Palestine. I do not think that these arrangements have a binding character, but at present they stand in the way and give rise to complications. We are trying our utmost here to clear up the matter but we would certainly need all the help from America in order to strengthen our hands. . . . America should support the plan of a British Protectorate which is the only guarantee for a future healthy Jewish development in Palestine." Weizmann enclosed Scott's letter to him of April 16 containing the information disclosed by de Caix.[207]

Except for his brief note to Sokolow, Brandeis did not, for the time being, reply to this barrage of letters and cables, though DeHaas, on behalf of the PZC, cabled Weizmann on May 1 stating that Brandeis was delaying his answer until after the interview with Balfour.[208] In the meantime the PZC cabled $10,000 on April 26, in partial response to Weizmann's request.[209] Only on May 9 did the PZC abandon its neutral stance and adopt a position in favor of a British protectorate committed to the establishment of a Jewish national home in Palestine.[210] In this the PZC followed Brandeis's decision, though he was careful to avoid anything beyond private assurances of support for Weizmann's and Rothschild's policies.[211]

Brandeis defined his stand in light of his conversations with Balfour and an extended, three-quarter-hour discussion he had with President Wilson on May 6, 1917. From Balfour he heard assurances of Lloyd George's Zionist sympathy and warm praise for Weizmann. He also learned that Balfour was inclined to the idea of a joint suzerainty, dominion, or guaranty of the United States and Great Britain in Palestine, a plan that might overcome French and Italian objections.[212] Brandeis was not disposed to favor this suggestion, since he shared the fears expressed in the correspondence from London of the pitfalls of international administration in whatever form.[213] His assumption that the United States would not involve itself in such a responsibility abroad, and certainly would not wish to tie its hands by prior agreements with the Allies, was confirmed in his long talk with the president.[214] Brandeis stated his preference for a British protectorate, advocated by Weizmann, not only to Balfour; he also forwarded the London Zionists' program to the U.S. State Department.[215]

But since he assumed that neither Balfour nor Wilson thought the time appropriate for a pro-Zionist declaration—the latter because he wanted a free hand at the war's end, the former because the French and Italians still had to be deferred to—Brandeis thought the Zionists should not now press for such statements. The Blackstone memorial, which he gave to the British for their information, should also not be urged at the moment because of its suggestion of an international regime in Palestine. American Zionists must now continue to collect members and money and maintain discipline until events built up a consensus in their favor that would allow the full measure of their hopes to be realized as a matter of inevitability.[216]

Yet while Brandeis was content to let events dictate his next political move, Weizmann continued to use political events as catalysts to elicit more decisive statements from the British themselves. On June 6, 1917, Weizmann sent Graham an English translation of an article by the right-wing German publicist Gustav von Dobeler. "A Jewish Republic in Palestine," published on May 2, 1917, made the case for support of Zionism to forestall the establishment of a Jewish republic under British aegis, a move, the writer warned his audience, that would be destructive to the political future of the Central Powers. He therefore recommended the establishment of a Jewish state under Turkish supremacy. "England in the possession of Palestine would signify the isolation of Central Europe."[217] In fact, von Dobeler's article was only the first in a series published in leading German newspapers throughout the spring and fall of 1917 reflecting a new interest in the response of German public opinion to evidence that the Zionists were being taken seriously by the Allied Powers.[218]

On June 11, Weizmann had a long interview with Sir Ronald Graham and two days later submitted to him a memorandum summarizing the conversation they had concerning German overtures toward Zionism. He provided Sir Ronald with evidence that the German government was attempting to solidify its relations with the Zionists while at the same time to undermine those between the Entente and world Zionism. At the end of his memorandum Weizmann strongly asserted that the majority of the Jewish people supported Zionism and those in the Entente countries were in favor of a British protectorate over Palestine. He concluded with a specific request:

> In view of the position described above I respectfully submit that it appears very desirable from every point of view that the British Government should give expression of its sympathy and support to the Zionist aims and should recognize the justice of the Jewish claims on Palestine, in fact it need only confirm the views which eminent representatives of the Government have many times expressed to us and which have formed the basis of our negotiations throughout the long period of almost three years.[219]

Sir Ronald had already told Weizmann during their interview that he concurred with the request that the British government issue a public statement. In his own report of the interview with Weizmann he stated that:

> It would appear that in view of the sympathy towards the Zionist move-
> ment which has already been expressed by the Prime Minister, Mr. Balfour,
> Lord Cecil, and other statesmen, we are committed to support it, although
> until Zionist policy has been more clearly defined our support must be of a
> general character. We ought therefore to secure all the political advantage
> we can out of our connection with Zionism and there is no doubt that this
> advantage will be considerable, especially in Russia, where the only means
> of reaching the Jewish proletariat is through Zionism to which the vast ma-
> jority of Jews in that country adhere. . . .
> The moment has come when we might meet the wishes of the Zionists
> and give them an assurance that His Majesty's Government are in general
> sympathy with their aspirations. This might be done by a message from the
> Prime Minister or Mr. Balfour to be read out at a meeting. . . . Such a step
> would be well justified by the international political results it would se-
> cure.[220]

Balfour, who had returned from his trip to the United States on June
9, had not been convinced by Brandeis to drop all his objections to a
sole British protectorate over Palestine. He minuted in response to Graham's proposal: "How can H.M.G. announce their intention of 'protecting' Palestine without consulting our Allies? And how can we discuss
dismembering the Turkish Empire before the Turks are beaten? Possibly
[I] should still prefer to associate the U.S.A. in the protectorate, should
we succeed in securing it."[221] Yet, by June 17 Sokolow had finally returned to England, confirming the reports he had sent all along from
Paris and Rome and in possession of the Cambon letter of June 4. Moreover, the Conjoint Foreign Committee no longer needed to be consulted
as to its views.[222] Graham could now reply to Balfour:

> I never meant to suggest that the question of "Protection" should be raised
> at all. This would be most inopportune in view of French susceptibilities
> and the Zionists here, who are well aware of the delicate nature of the
> question, although desiring a British Protectorate, do not ask for any pro-
> nouncement on this line. All they ask for is a formal repetition, if possible
> in writing, of the general assurances of sympathy which they have already
> received from members of H. [M.] Government verbally. I only suggest that
> we should give something on the lines of the French assurance—which would
> satisfy them—and it is essential we should do so if we are to secure Zionist
> political support which is so important to us in Russia at the present mo-
> ment.[223]

Lord Robert Cecil, who read Graham's response to Balfour, minuted:
"I wanted to do this several weeks ago but was deterred by the advice
of Sir G. Buchanan."[224] That same day, June 19, 1917, Balfour had an
interview with Weizmann and Lord Rothschild,[225] who put it to him that
the time had arrived for the British government to give the Zionists a
definite declaration of support and encouragement. "Mr. Balfour prom-

ised to so," reported Weizmann to Harry Sacher "and he has asked me to submit to him a declaration which would be satisfactory to us."[226] Balfour's minute that same day, written on the margins of Graham's, indicates that the invitation "to submit a formula" was made jointly "to Lord Rothschild and Professor Weizmann."[227] The skeptical foreign secretary was finally won over to the idea of a declaration by the combined force of arguments of his own office staff and the Zionists. Balfour's strong sympathies for the Zionist cause were galvanized into concrete political action only after he was convinced by Weizmann and his colleagues that they could mobilize Jews throughout the world for their cause and thus aid the British war effort.[228]

V

Gibraltar

On June 20, 1917, having seen Balfour the previous day, Chaim Weizmann triumphantly wrote to his loyal patron, C. P. Scott: "Mr. Balfour has promised to give us a document in which the British Government would express its sympathy with the Zionist Movement and its intention to support the creation of a Jewish National Home in Palestine."[1] But in the meantime developments in the United States seemed to force the pace of action in a different direction. Among them, a factor peculiar to the United States, was the rift between the Zionist Wilsonians and the supporters of the president in the Protestant establishment. Their interests began to diverge on two planes—in relation to Russia and Turkey and the American concern with both—and in the course of time, they clashed in sharp opposition. But the estrangement developed gradually, and at first there was an attempt to maintain a kind of alliance between them, especially on the part of the Zionists.

Russian affairs had always been a particular concern of American Jews, who had won the acknowledged right to press for the defense of human rights and equal justice in that country as a principle of American foreign policy.[2] Now that a democratic regime had overthrown the tsar, American Jews considered themselves especially qualified as American emissaries to the Russian ally. Louis Brandeis himself was among the names prominently discussed in forming the American mission to the new regime. Labor leaders and other spokesmen of the immigrant Russian Jewish community were thought to have privileged access to the socialist and liberal elements in Russia that might exert a vital, not easily predictable, influence over Russia's future policies on war and peace.

But other elements were equally interested in serving as the American channel to Russia.[3] In the State Department a whole corps of hastily recruited foreign area experts reexamined the stance of the United States. Charles R. Crane, a major philanthropist with close ties to the Protestant missionary circles and a special interest in foreign affairs, had supported the University of Chicago and particularly its corps of Russian experts and was the benefactor who had personally made possible the careers of significant figures in the State Department. Now his coterie of scholarly beneficiaries—especially Samuel Harper of the University of Chicago—were the dominant voices heard on Russian matters, and they were backed by investors and industrialists attracted to the potential Russian market. These professionals, who absorbed the view of Russian affairs prevalent among their Russian associates, were far from eager to see Jews represented on the proposed American mission; nor did they want labor union spokesmen and radicals included. Their views prevailed in the selection of the American delegation, which was headed by the notably conservative corporation lawyer Elihu Root. While the mission was in Russia, in June–July 1917, there began a flow of critical comments on the damaging effects of Jewish radicals—some of them Russian Jews returning from the United States—upon Russian affairs. The Zionists, nevertheless, took pains to provide the mission with Jewish contacts in Russia who, they thought, could supply reliable information on Jewish opinion and conditions.

A more complex situation arose in regard to another area of Jewish concern, the policy toward the Ottoman Empire. Protestant missionary circles, led particularly by the tireless James Barton, director of the missionary enterprise, had a direct influence in convincing Wilson not to declare war on Turkey, in spite of British urging, and to keep channels open even after the Turks broke off diplomatic relations. Popular opinion among Protestants remained hostile to the Turks, especially following atrocities committed by the Turks against the Armenians, but the Protestant leaders, anxious to safeguard their surviving client communities and also calculating the best situation for their postwar renewal of activity, wanted to preserve every bridge to the authorities in the area that remained available. They considered various options, including an American armed landing at Alexandretta on the eastern Mediterranean coast and an American trusteeship in Syria and Armenia after the war. But sentiment grew for a separate peace with Turkey that might leave the Ottoman realm intact and permit resumption of the mission enterprise on its old basis but under improved circumstances and with good chances for significant expansion.

Henry Morgenthau, who had retired from his ambassadorship in Constantinople to take part in Wilson's 1916 campaign, liked the idea of keeping the Ottoman realm intact. As ambassador he had been proud of the confidence he inspired in missionary circles, and his excellent relations with them made it easy for him to find a favorable hearing for his developing new approach. He had equal reason to rely on his Jewish connections, including the Zionists.[4] He was the one who had opened the door for the massive relief effort of the Zionists in Palestine by relaying Arthur Ruppin's initial call for aid. Morgenthau had been constantly helpful by his diplomatic interventions taken in concert with the German ambassador in Constantinople whenever the Jewish community fell under Turkish suspicion. Through the American consular and navy facilities, he recruited for Palestinian relief.[5] He now hoped to be able to induce the Turks through his personal contacts to make peace—just as, upon returning to the United States in the summer of 1916, he had incautiously, and vaingloriously, stated to the press that he could buy Palestine for the Jews through his connections.[6] Given his wide-ranging connections, Morgenthau promoted his new venture by simultaneously approaching the State Department, Colonel Edward M. House, and the Zionists.

On May 16, 1917, Morgenthau paid a call on the secretary of state, Robert Lansing, to suggest he be authorized to begin negotiating a separate peace between Turkey and the Allies through some influential Turkish friends in Switzerland. Morgenthau felt he could secure the consent of the Ottoman rulers for an Allied submarine attack on the German warships *Goeben* and *Breslau*, whose guns were trained on Constantinople. Once those ships were destroyed, the Turks would be willing to conclude a separate peace. His scheme was based on the "peculiarly cordial and intimate terms which had existed between him and Enver and Talaat when he was Ambassador."[7]

Though he did not believe "there was one chance in fifty of success," Lansing felt that "we ought not ignore any chance, however slight, of gaining so tremendous an advantage as would result from alienating Turkey from the Teutonic Alliance" and recommended the plan to President Wilson both in writing and orally.[8] When Morgenthau met with the president on May 28, the latter consented to the mission.[9] Colonel House was even stronger in his support of Morgenthau's peculiar scheme. A week before the former ambassador's departure, House wrote to Morgenthau that he had been talking about him "and of the great work you are undertaking. My thought will go with you from day to day and I shall pray for your success. . . . Those of us in the 'know' will await news of you with the deepest eagerness and concern."[10]

Arthur Balfour, who was still in the United States, was informed of the scheme by Lansing on May 22, 1917. Balfour's response, as he reported to his staff at the Foreign Office was "that speaking off hand and without consultation with my Government I could see no objection to Morgenthau cautiously feeling the ground with his Turkish friends."[11] The minutes the Foreign Office professionals appended to Balfour's cable indicate that at first they, too, saw no harm in Morgenthau's attempt to secure a separate peace with Turkey, though Lancelot Oliphant pointed out Morgenthau's "boundless desire to play a big role" and Robert Cecil cautioned that the many spies in Switzerland might make Egypt a better base of operations.[12] The latter suggestion was readily accepted by Lansing and Morgenthau during their meeting on May 28; they were pleased by the Foreign Office's approval of "Morgenthau's making the trial."[13] Lansing also suggested that to camouflage the real purpose of the mission, a very plausible excuse for Morgenthau's trip would be an attempt to alleviate the conditions of the Jews in Palestine.[14] To make the purpose of the mission more plausible to American Jews, Morgenthau suggested that Felix Frankfurter, at that time an assistant to Secretary of War Newton Baker and a known Zionist, accompany him on his trip.[15]

After the president approved the idea, Frankfurter agreed to join Morgenthau and took with him his assistant, Max Lowenthal, a young lawyer.[16] Another member of the party, added at the suggestion of DeHaas, was Eliyahu Lewin-Epstein, the treasurer of the PZC.[17] By the end of May the Americans decided that the first stop for the mission would be Gibraltar and requested that the British and French send "some one in authority . . . to discuss question thoroughly with Morgenthau."[18] At the suggestion of President Wilson, Lansing discussed the entire matter with Louis Brandeis on June 5, 1917.[19]

By the time he was asked to meet with the secretary of state, Brandeis was well aware of Morgenthau's proposed mission. Like other American Zionist leaders, he regarded Morgenthau's approach with dismay. After such a mission, officially endorsed by the State Department as well as the Zionists themselves, Morgenthau would enjoy a highly privileged position as a recognized authority on the future status of Palestine. What was known about Morgenthau's views and general disposition did not convince the Zionists that they could confidently lend themselves to promote such a prospect—certainly not without taking suitable precautions.

As the rabbi of the Free Synagogue to which Morgenthau belonged, Stephen Wise was particularly well suited to talk frankly with him. Wise apparently suggested himself as the suitable person to provide a Zionist cover to the mission, but he reported to Brandeis that Morgenthau preferred Frankfurter, who was known to the general public less as a Zionist than as a distinguished professor of law at Harvard.[20] DeHaas also worried that "Morgenthau is trying to make us pull chestnuts out of the fire for him, and at best his motives would be somewhat mixed. I should imagine that he would bring back a report that would suit the [anti-Zionists] much better than it would suit us, and the government would find it difficult to disavow its commissioner." DeHaas therefore suggested that he, or Wise, should accompany the mission.[21] In the end, since DeHaas's proposal would have tied the project too narrowly to the Zionists for the Turks' liking, it was agreed that Frankfurter would accompany Morgenthau.[22]

One objection to the Morgenthau mission not voiced by the American Zionists, but certainly on their minds, was that a separate peace with the Turks could hardly be achieved without abandoning the goal recently defined by the PZC in early May 1917 of detaching Palestine from Turkey as a British-protected Jewish homeland. The American Zionist leaders were too closely tied to the Wilson administration to oppose its concern for peace initiatives, and for a separate peace with Turkey, on such grounds. To have done so would have been to undermine the position of trust a man like Brandeis enjoyed in Wilson's circle by appearing as the agent of a special interest—and ultimately, as Brandeis often noted, to have injured Zionist prospects. The most Brandeis could do was to call attention to Morgenthau's well-known thoughtlessness, recently displayed in his ill-judged comments of the past year about inducing the Turks, for a consideration, to sell Palestine to the Jews.[23] The general awareness of Morgenthau's unguarded behavior was enough to make the State Department welcome the idea of sending along Frankfurter to keep an eye on the mission chief. "All we can do is hope for the best," noted Lansing in his diary.[24]

The Zionist cover was too thin a disguise to hide the true purpose of Morgenthau's trip. When the information reached London, the Zionists there were even more disturbed than their American counterparts and were in a position to be far more direct in opposition. The news about the Morgenthau mission was communicated to Weizmann by three reliable sources. The first was Brandeis, probably after his meeting with Lansing on June 5, who sent a cable which vaguely stated that "an American commission was traveling to the East" and recommended that Weizmann try to make contact with it "somewhere."[25] Probably on June 8, Weizmann was visited by James Malcolm, who most likely got wind of the whole affair from Arshag Shmarvonian, a former legal adviser to the American Embassy in Constantinople, now residing in Switzerland, who was asked by Morgenthau to join the mission.[26] Malcolm had also learned about other attempts at a separate peace that were put forward by a number of English Turcophils. While trying to digest and analyze the bad news with Malcolm, Weizmann received a call from Wickham Steed, the foreign editor of the *Times*, asking that he come immediately to his office. While Malcolm waited downstairs, Steed relayed the same news Weizmann had just heard from Malcolm.[27]

On this occasion, indeed, for the first time, Weizmann dared assert himself to sway an apparently impending British decision to the side that was compatible with the Zionist interest. Seeing a threat to the vision of a partitioned Ottoman Empire among Arab, Armenian, and Jewish states, Weizmann and Malcolm lodged vigorous protests at the Foreign Office. Their views were shared by Mark Sykes, who had just returned from Cairo.[28] On the morning of June 9, 1917, Weizmann saw Ronald Graham, who minuted that same day that Weizmann spoke of Morgenthau in disparaging terms and as a person with strong pro-German and pro-Turkish leanings. Later that day, Malcolm also protested to Graham against the new threat to Armenian national interests.[29]

The following day Malcolm and Weizmann arrived together at the office of William Ormsby-Gore, who reported to Mark Sykes, "Both Mr. Malcolm and Dr. Weizmann were very much excited and very angry and both stated that we were not only playing with fire in approaching the Turks at this juncture, but also imperiling the interests of the British empire." Weizmann, who was under the mistaken impression that some prominent English Turcophils were being sent to meet the Morgenthau mission, including Aubrey Herbert, MP, and Sir Adam Samuel Block, an anti-Zionist of Jewish extraction, concentrated his attack on this "renegade Jew of Galician origin" and on Morgenthau, who "was notoriously pro-German" and acted on behalf of an international ring that was "violently hostile both to Great Britain and to Zionism." Toward the end of his report Ormsby-Gore recorded that Weizmann "asked that if any Jew is to be sent to meet Mr. Morgenthau, that he, Dr. Weizmann, be sent rather than Adam Block." Weizmann then added a thinly veiled warning: "He then informed me that the Germans . . . had recently approached the Zionists with a view to coming to terms with them and that it was really a question whether the Zionists were to realise their aims through Germany and Turkey or through Great Britain. He, of course, was absolutely loyal to Great Britain."[30]

The following day, on June 11, still "in a state of some agitation," Weizmann appeared again at Graham's office, this time without Malcolm, and repeated at greater length the arguments he had presented against the Morgenthau mission, two days earlier.[31] At the same time, both in his interview with Graham on June 11 and in a letter written two days later, Weizmann continued to emphasize the specter of Germany's wooing world Jewish opinion.[32] Though he had suggested himself as the ideal person to meet with Morgenthau, he may have done so in the heat of the discussion and without prior planning. He requested of the Foreign Office that "a Zionist whom we trust" be sent to see Morgenthau. To Harry Sacher, Weizmann wrote that Sacher would be the right person for such a journey,[33] but by the time Sacher responded that he could not go before the end of June, his candidacy was no longer relevant.

On June 12, 1917, Sir Cecil Spring-Rice, the British ambassador in Washington, reported to the Foreign Office that the American ambassador in London, Walter Page, was being instructed to request that, in addition to any other emissary, the British also send Weizmann to meet the Morgenthau mission.[34] This request was made by Robert Lansing, and it may have been suggested by Brandeis, who had originally cabled Weizmann to meet the mission personally. In any case, the American suggestion that Weizmann join the mission was independent of that made by Weizmann in Ormsby-Gore's office two days earlier. Some two weeks later, on June 25, 1917, Lansing cabled to his ambassador that he hoped the latter would "leave nothing undone to secure Mr. Balfour's consent, as it is considered most important that Mr. Morgenthau see Mr. Weizmann."[35]

Apparently the lines of communication between London and Washington were less than efficient, because on June 15 Balfour minuted on a further telegram from Spring-Rice that "in so far as Morgenthau's mission concerns Palestine we presume there is no reason for sending from here anyone but Dr. Weizmann and he is leaving for Gibraltar at once. . . . I had proposed to send Sir Louis Mallet [former British ambassador to Constantinople] to meet Morgenthau but now I fear that if anyone of his status were to go it would make us look to the outside world as if we were sending an international deputation to beg the Turks to make a separate peace."[36]

Balfour's minute indicates that Weizmann was asked, on or before June 15, to meet Morgenthau. A few days later Ronald Graham noted that Weizmann agreed to go only after he heard that Frankfurter was accompanying Morgenthau.[37] By mid-June it had become clear that Weizmann's fears were exaggerated. The British government was not considering the option of leaving Turkey-in-Asia intact after the war, and the pro-Turkish British group was not involved in Morgenthau's mission. The British government had, indeed, been asked to cooperate with the American mission. Given its weak political and military situation, it could hardly refuse outright to do so. Yet soon after the initial offhanded agreement by Balfour and the apathetic reaction of his professional staff, the Foreign Office had second thoughts, as is clearly indicated from the minutes recorded from the end of May onward.[38]

After Weizmann's and Malcolm's intervention, the Foreign Office notified Washington of the opposition that had arisen and suggested dropping the plan. This the State Department declined to do,[39] no doubt considering Brandeis's cooperation to be ample assurance against Zionist objections. It is less clear why the State Department suggested that Weizmann, whose strong pro-British stance had been communicated to Washington, be sent to meet Morgenthau. As Morgenthau had made quite clear to Stephen Wise, he did not wish to have with him persons too strongly identified with Zionism. Possibly Brandeis, unable to oppose the scheme himself, insisted on Weizmann as the person most likely to be able to derail the Morgenthau mission.

When the British appointed Weizmann—sometime during the second week of June—to join the Morgenthau mission, they did so after accepting Weizmann's condition—the same condition he had made before agreeing to join Sykes in Egypt—"that it is axiomatic that no arrangement with Turkey can be arrived at unless Armenia, Syria and Arabia are detached."[40] This condition, which meant a Jewish homeland under British protection, accorded well with the Foreign Office's policy in any case. Yet until practically the last moment before his departure, Weizmann was still unaware of the fact that he had been designated as the sole British representative and suggested to C. P. Scott that Sir Mark Sykes, whose "views . . . are so dear to us," also be sent.[41] The Foreign Office offered to cover Weizmann's travel expenses, but in keeping with his policy of maintaining an independent status—as evidenced in his dealings with the Admiralty at the start of the war—Weizmann refused to accept the offer; the £400 for the journey was secured by Shmuel Tolkowsky from the Jewish Colonial Trust. On the day of his departure, June 29, 1917, Weizmann asked Simon Marks and Shmuel Tolkowsky to witness his will.[42]

Arthur James Balfour
and Weizmann in Tel
Aviv, 1925. Courtesy:
Central   Zionist   Ar-
chives

In his memoirs Weizmann wrote that on June 28, on the eve of his departure, Balfour summoned him to his office. His sole instruction to Weizmann was "to talk to Mr. Morgenthau, and keep on talking" until he had talked him out of his mission.[43] Weizmann claimed that on that occasion he was handed a letter of introduction to Sir Arthur Hardinge, the British ambassador in Madrid, requesting him "to afford Doctor Weizmann all possible facilities."[44] In view of the importance of British relations with the United States, Balfour had to keep up the pretense that the British were taking the Morgenthau mission seriously, and on June 27, 1917, he cabled to Spring-Rice that the British high commissioner in Egypt, Reginald Wingate, would afford Morgenthau all facilities to communicate any possible Turkish peace plans.[45]

But Foreign Office actions belied these diplomatic niceties. Only a week earlier, while well aware of all developments in connection with the impending Morgenthau mission, Balfour himself had discussed with Lord Rothschild and Weizmann a declaration of British sympathy for a Jewish national home—an act in direct conflict with Morgenthau's proposal that, if successful, would have kept Turkey-in-Asia intact. Balfour, like Brandeis, may have calculated that someone like Weizmann, whose considerable effectiveness he knew firsthand, was quite sufficient to obstruct

Weizmann's sisters Haya and Fruma with Fialkov. Courtesy: Central Zionist Archives

Morgenthau's mission without paying too much attention to diplomatic protocol. Colonel House, who did not know Weizmann personally but had a fair measure of Morgenthau, urged the latter, in vain, to avoid meeting the British emissaries en route to Egypt. "In my opinion," wrote House, "they should have been seen upon your return trip rather than now."[46] Had Morgenthau heeded House's advice, the outcome of his mission may well have taken a different turn.

On June 29, 1917, Weizmann traveled with a delightful but incompetent intelligence officer named Kennerley Rumford, assigned to him by the Foreign Office, through France to Spain, and at Irún they were met by another intelligence officer, who conducted them by car to San Sebastian, from whence they traveled by train to Madrid. As soon as he met his companion in Southampton, Weizmann realized that the British, though concerned, were no longer taking Morgenthau all too seriously. "Is it at all serious or just American *bluff?*" he exclaimed in a letter to Vera hours before the ship's departure.[47] His astonishment grew at the unprofessional behavior of the intelligence officer at Irún and that of his companion. It seemed that from the moment they reached Spanish territory, they were moving, as it were, with a cortege of German spies.[48]

In Madrid, where he arrived on July 2, Weizmann was well received by Ambassador Hardinge, as per Balfour's request. On the street he chanced to meet with Professor Abraham S. Yahuda, a person he did not particularly like.[49] Yahuda was on his way to see Hardinge, with whom he was on friendly terms and who apparently knew of Weizmann's destination, if not the purpose of his trip.[50] Weizmann also used his brief stopover in Madrid to visit Max Nordau, one of the venerable founding fathers of the Zionist movement, who as an Austrian citizen had to leave Paris for Madrid during the war. The two had often been at odds over Zionist policy during the past twenty years, but Nordau now seemed to support Weizmann's actions, and they parted on friendly terms.[51]

Weizmann and his motley entourage arrived in Gibraltar on July 3, while the Morgenthau party arrived the following day. Felix Frankfurter, following Weizmann's example, stayed in the fashionable Reina Cristina Hotel in Algeciras, taking the steamer to Gibraltar every morning, while Morgenthau, his wife, and the rest of their party lived in a much simpler hotel on the "neutral" Spanish side. Frankfurter, who was immediately impressed by Weizmann's personality, obviously also appreciated the latter's taste for the finer things in life.[52] The French delegation consisted of Colonel E. Weyl, a former head of the Turkish tobacco monopoly, and there seems to have been present, perhaps as an observer, the French minister of munitions, Albert Thomas. Weyl had received no instructions from his government,[53] suggesting that the French, too, were not taking the Morgenthau mission seriously. There was little time to enjoy the hotel or the scenery, since the discussions began on the day the Morgenthau party arrived.

"Our sessions were held inside of the fortress in Gibraltar with British soldiery walking up and down, guarding us while we sat inside and pursued this problem of exploring ways and means of detaching Turkey," recalled Frankfurter.[54] It was midsummer and very hot during the two days of discussion. Ironically, the only common language of the participants was German.[55] Morgenthau began with an exposition of the situation in Turkey, none of which was new to the others. Much more valuable was the contribution of his former secretary, Arshag Shmarvonian, who had left Turkey on May 29 and was able to describe the abysmal military, financial, and human conditions in the crumbling Ottoman Empire. He also described the poor relations between the Turks and the Germans and among the Turkish leadership. Weizmann wryly commented in his report: "These are the only real facts which Mr. Morgenthau was able to communicate to us." The discussion then focused on Morgenthau's immediate plans and intentions, whereupon "he became quite vague, and no amount of discussion and questioning could elucidate any definite plan or programme." What the participants could tease out of him was that he intended to utilize his friendship with Talaat Pasha, the grand vizier, and induce him to break with Enver Pasha, the minister of war, and, once that was achieved, to break with the Germans.[56]

Morgenthau was then asked two questions:

1. Does he think that the time has come for the American Government, to open up negotiations of such a nature with the Turkish authorities? In other words, whether he thinks that Turkey realises sufficiently that she is beaten or is likely to lose the war, and is therefore in a frame of mind to lend itself to negotiations of that nature?
2. Assuming that the time is ripe for such overtures, has he [Mr. Morgenthau] a clear idea about the conditions under which the Turks would be prepared to detach themselves from their present masters?[57]

In his report to Sir Ronald Graham, Weizmann recorded that "it was utterly impossible for us to obtain a definite answer." Morgenthau finally admitted that he was not justified in saying that the time had arrived to negotiate with Turkey. Weizmann also asked Morgenthau several times why he had tried to enlist the support of the Zionists in his mission. Once again, not receiving a coherent answer, Weizmann found it necessary clearly to state to Morgenthau that "on no account should the Zionist organization be in any way compromised by his negotiations . . . that on no account must the Zionist organization be in any way identified or mixed up even with the faintest attempts to secure a separate peace . . . that we Zionists feel about this point most strongly, and we would like assurances from Mr. Morgenthau that he agrees and understands this position. This assurance was given."[58]

By mid-1917 Weizmann felt sure enough of his position in the world organization to speak with authority about the wishes and plans of Zionism. He came to the conference fully backed by Nahum Sokolow and quickly won over Frankfurter, who, in any case, had a low opinion of the former ambassador. But Weizmann was also, on this particular occasion, the sole representative of Great Britain and, on the basis of the assurances given him by Ronald Graham concerning the identical aims of the British and the Zionists, felt he could make an unequivocal statement concerning them. According to a cable sent by Morgenthau and Frankfurter: "At the conference Weizmann announced that condition precedent in any negotiation with Turkey so far as Great Britain was concerned was the separation from Turkey of territory containing subject races in effect Armenia and territory south of Taurus. The disposition of such [separated] territory was a matter which he was not now competent to raise."[59]

None of the others present felt that such conditions would be accepted at the present time by the Turks. But given Morgenthau's vague ideas, Weizmann gained an advantage by making the British and Zionist point of view explicit. Though the French government was equivocating concerning a separate peace with Turkey, its representative, Colonel Weyl, was apparently less than forceful. In their cable of July 8, Morgenthau and Frankfurter clearly stated that "Weyl expressed no views of policy."[60] With Frankfurter won over to his point of view, "It was no job at all to persuade Mr. Morgenthau to drop the project. He simply persuaded himself," remarked Weizmann cynically in his autobiography.[61] All that remained was to write a joint face-saving report. It summarized the discussions that took place in Gibraltar on July 4 and 5 and concluded: "The time is not now ripe to open channels of communication with Turkish leaders. . . . Attempts at negotiation now would be construed as a sign of Allied weakness."[62]

Weizmann and his supporters, who have described the Morgenthau mission with derision, viewed its outcome as the result of Weizmann's skills as a diplomat and negotiator. No doubt the well-connected former ambassador, who could open many a door in Washington, including that of the president, had rarely in his life been spoken to with such harsh frankness. Weizmann must have realized that to derail Morgenthau's mission he had to speak plainly to the man whose mission was authorized, if not blessed, by President Wilson, Secretary of State Robert Lansing, and Colonel House. The French, too, seemed to lean toward peace negotiations with Turkey and needed to be dissuaded.[63] After the failure of the mission, all those who played a part, including government officials, found ways to extricate themselves, more or less ungracefully, from any responsibility, claiming that Morgenthau had been instructed to carry on no more than a relief mission. Lansing's diary entry for June 10, 1917, makes it evident that this was simply the official cover.[64] In any case, none of the behind-the-scenes calculations were clear at the outset of the conference—at least not to Weizmann. One can only wonder at his courage. He must have known that the Zionists had much to lose by any ambiguous result of the conference and decided to stake all his cards on a forceful opposition to Morgenthau. This was exactly the stance his British patrons had expected him to take.

Yet, in addition to Weizmann's skills, other factors made Morgenthau's trip "into a fiasco," in the words of the U.S. acting secretary of state, Frank Polk.[65] Among them was Morgenthau himself, the wrong person to carry out so complex and sensitive a mission. Given his strong need to be at center stage, he was guilty of gross indiscretions from the very start.[66] He was no match for Weizmann. Felix Frankfurter asserted that Morgenthau was "incapable of continuity of thought or effort,"[67] and Weizmann, wondering how the American government could entrust important errands to a person like Morgenthau, wrote that "the man does not know his basic facts."[68] As Shmarvonian's report made clear, moreover, the internal Turkish and international situation was not propitious for peace talks with Turkey.[69]

All of this was known to President Wilson and the professional staff at the State Department in advance of the Morgenthau mission.[70] If Morgenthau had weaknesses that militated against any possible diplomatic success, the State Department was just as guilty of sending the wrong man to fish in the murky waters of international intrigue without clear navigational instructions. To the relief of all concerned, Morgenthau never made it to Egypt or Switzerland; after a short sojourn in Madrid, he spent the next few weeks in France, eventually returning to the United States in September 1917. But his ideas about a separate peace with Turkey were not repudiated by the State Department even after his mission failed. Soon after his return Morgenthau was reported to be developing more specific plans, with friends in the missionary leadership, for keeping the Ottoman Empire in Asia intact after the war. As for a separate peace, it continued to find favor in Washington, though not with Morgenthau as the man in charge.

In his autobiography, written in 1922, Morgenthau dismissed his aborted mission with one long sentence, claiming he was not at liberty to disclose its details.[71] Neither Weizmann nor any of the other participants of the sessions in Gibraltar are mentioned. Yet, in the immediate aftermath of the conference, Morgenthau told Professor Yahuda and Nordau in Madrid "that it was not right of Dr. Weizmann to have induced the British Government to interfere with his mission." Yahuda and Nordau had several conversations with Morgenthau, who raised the subject a number of times. "I felt," wrote Yahuda, who had little reason to attribute any successes to Weizmann, "that he was very bitter about the frustration of his mission, but there was, he said, nothing more for him to do in view of Great Britain's opposition, which he attributed to Dr. Weizmann's influence."[72]

Morgenthau clearly blamed Weizmann for frustrating his efforts for a separate peace, though it is not at all clear that his subsequent anti-Zionist bias stemmed from his strong dislike of Weizmann.[73] Regardless of the other international considerations that would have probably caused his mission to collapse, it is conceivable that, particularly in light of the suffering of the Jewish evacuees of Jaffa, he could have once again played an important role as a savior of the Palestinian Jewish community.[74] There is no explanation as to why Morgenthau abandoned his relief mission to Egypt; possibly Weizmann took the wind out of his sails to such an extent that he felt too dejected to continue,[75] though he was clearly instructed by the State Department to proceed to Egypt after Gibraltar.[76]

The British, too, credited Weizmann with sidetracking the Morgenthau mission. Ronald Graham observed: "Dr. Weizmann has been eminently successful in dissuading Mr. Morgenthau from proceeding either to Egypt or Switzerland." Balfour minuted next to Sir Graham's observation an instruction to circulate Weizmann's letter to the cabinet.[77] Sykes wrote to Gilbert Clayton, Allenby's chief political officer, that "luckily Zionism held good and the plots to bring Mr. Morgenthau over and negotiate a separate peace with Turkey in Switzerland were foiled."[78]

Weizmann, who left Gibraltar on July 7 via Madrid, where he again visited Nordau, went to Paris for a holiday—and perhaps to watch Morgenthau's next move. He returned to England on July 21, 1917. The next day he reported to Ronald Graham in person all the developments of the past three weeks. In his report to Lord Hardinge, Graham noted with admiration: "Dr. Weizmann is a shrewd observer."[79] Obviously Felix Frankfurter also reported to Louis Brandeis that it was due to Weizmann that Morgenthau's mission had failed. On August 10, 1917, Brandeis cabled to Weizmann: "It was a great satisfaction to hear yesterday from Professor Frankfurter fully concerning your conference [at Gibraltar] and to have this further evidence of your admirable management of our affairs."[80] The end of the affair, whatever had brought about its inglorious demise, was to enhance Weizmann's prestige within Zionist ranks and in the eyes of those men in Britain who were at that very moment involved in devising a public pro-Zionist formula. The confidence in Weizmann is illustrated by the fact that, at Graham's request, Weizmann returned to Paris on July 23, where he met with Balfour and Lloyd George who were attending a conference dealing with the Balkan situation.[81] Weizmann reported on the Morgenthau mission and other information relating to French foreign policy.[82] He returned to London on July 29, exactly one month after he had left for Gibraltar.

From the Zionist perspective, one of the important results of the Morgenthau mission was that it occasioned a meeting between Weizmann and one of the top-flight Zionist leaders who most fully enjoyed Brandeis's confidence. Felix Frankfurter, an effervescent, gregarious man, was perhaps the best equipped of all the Brandeis entourage to respond to the touch of elegant bohemianism and the rich, folksy wit of a Weizmann, and the two men came to a quick understanding and appreciation of each other. When Frankfurter returned to the United States and Weizmann to England, the way had been smoothed for a more effective interchange and cooperation between the two Zionist centers. In the period that followed, crucial developments occurred in London. In Washington and New York, the Zionist leaders were stirred with rumors and echoes of impending events; but their independent activities continued to be reined in by Brandeis's policy of awaiting a critical moment, to be determined by the convenience of President Wilson's, rather than London's, policy. He continued to preach the doctrine of "Men! Money! Discipline!" while in New York the formal leaders of the movement were roused to restless, but somewhat undirected, activity by the pressure of events.

At Gibraltar, and later in Paris, Weizmann and Frankfurter had touched on a matter that offered an opportunity for joint action but had to be handled with discretion. As noted earlier, in February 1917 the British government had precipitated a sharp rise in the feeling about the military service of alien immigrants, largely Russian Jews, by announcing planned legislation to make them choose between serving in the British forces or in the Russian army. Meanwhile, as General Edmund Allenby was engaged in Gaza, at the door of Palestine, and the Russians rose in revolution, Vladimir Jabotinsky's scheme for a Jewish legion was raised again and given more serious attention.[83] During the breakfast meeting with Lloyd George, arranged as usual by Scott, Weizmann spoke of the great change which the Russian Revolution had produced in the feeling of the Russian Jews in England. He was sure, he told the prime minister, he could get a couple of thousand volunteers from among the thirty-thousand eligible Russian Jews in England. Scott recorded in his diary the rest of the conversation:

> G[eorge] said there could be no question now that they must either be compelled to serve in the British Army or else be sent back to Russia. Weizmann said he could not agree that the refugee who had not made England his home was under equal obligations with the native-born, but he did not dispute that the Russian Jews ought now to fight. They ought to be sent to Palestine. That would go far to reconcile them. George agreed but added that it would have the worst effect on public opinion on the Jewish claims to Palestine if they were not willing to fight for it. W[eizmann] said they will fight and fight well. He recalled the services at Gallipoli of the "Zionist Mule Corps" enlisted by Jabotinsky [*sic*] from the Palestinian Jewish refugees at Alexandria and told G. that 120 of them were at this moment serving with the 20th London Battalion at Winchester. They had implored the War Office to send them to join the army in Palestine which had so far been steadily refused and might at any moment be sent off with their battalion to France. . . . George was furious and said they [were] the very men wanted whose local knowledge would be invaluable and he would see that very day that they should go. They would be precious too in "spying out the land" as in Joshua's day.[84]

Lloyd George did not attend to the matter "that very day." Meanwhile Jabotinsky wrote to Weizmann that despite Herbert Samuel's promise to help at the right moment and Mark Sykes's encouragement to "keep the Legion idea alive," he was fearful that the idea would be buried with its bearers in France, rather than in Palestine. He implored Weizmann to use his influence and help implement the project.[85] Of course, both Jabotinsky and Weizmann knew quite well that the hurdle to implementation was not only the government bureaucracy but the lack of enthusiasm among the Jews themselves; Weizmann would have been hard pressed to produce two thousand volunteers had Lloyd George taken up his offer. As Sacher put it:

> It is we Zionists or Jews who alone are deeply interested—if we are deeply interested—in the Legion. The military folk are against it. The Foreign Office rather favours it because it thinks such a Legion might help English policy. But no drive will come from it. It is the Zionists who will have to do all the driving, because they must convince themselves the Legion is worth *their* while, worth it as a symbol of their quest for Palestine. . . .
>
> Chaim is quite right to prepare the Jewish opinion. . . . Frankly I have very little sympathy with the opponents at present. . . . All they want is to preserve their skins. . . . The sentiment is natural but I can't get enthu-

siastic about it, particularly when to save his own skin a Jew is prepared to imperil Palestine. No doubt we must be prudent, but can Chaim, if the thing is to be done at all, really wait until the foreign Jews are in [the] act of being conscribed? [*sic*] . . . No doubt it must be [drilled] into their heads that they will have to go to France if they don't choose to go to Palestine.[86]

The military authorities were not, as Sacher pointed out, in favor of Jabotinsky's plan. When his memorandum of January 24, 1917, was discussed by the War Office on April 18, Lord Derby, the secretary of state for war, was less than enthusiastic and pointed to the cool reception the idea had received among the Jews themselves.[87] Philip Kerr, who was a member of Lloyd George's personal secretariat, no doubt expressed the prime minister's view when he wrote to Graham at the Foreign Office that the creation of a Jewish legion, which "if coupled with assurances from the British Government of their sympathy with the desire of many Jews to settle in Palestine and build up a community within it, might produce a very beneficial effect in making the Jews in America and Russia much keener on helping to see the War through."[88] Clearly, then, the creation of a Jewish legion was directly related, in the minds of Lloyd George and his cabinet, to the political impact it would have. Only after they had decided that a British protectorate over Palestine was desirable, as well as some sort of a public affirmation of British support for Zionism, were they willing to move ahead with the military unit suggested by Jabotinsky.

Kerr added that Weizmann had just rung him to say that, in view of recent atrocities in Palestine, all Jewish opposition to the Jabotinsky scheme had been withdrawn.[89] Weizmann was referring to the fear held by Zionists since the idea of a Jewish fighting force was first broached in 1915: that the announcement of the establishment of a Jewish legion would induce the Turks to massacre the Jews in Palestine, much as they had done to the Armenians. Jabotinsky had disagreed all along with Weizmann on this point, and after the cruel expulsion from Jaffa–Tel Aviv, Weizmann changed his mind. He had favored the idea of a Jewish fighting force from the very beginning, but by April and May 1917 his support became public—no doubt after hearing the strong admonition of Lloyd George that the Jews must serve in the British Army.[90] Lancelot Oliphant wrote to the War Office reiterating Kerr's arguments.[91] But Lord Derby remained adamant. On May 23, 1917, he submitted a memorandum in which he repeated his contention of a month earlier that "failing some measure of compulsion it seems perfectly clear that the Army will never obtain the services of the Russian and Polish Jews in this Country."[92]

But in view of the increasing unity of Zionist aims with those of Lloyd George's cabinet, as well as the decision to complete plans for a military attack on the Palestinian front, the die had already been cast by the prime minister and his advisers in favor of the creation of a Jewish legion. On the very day Lord Derby distributed his negative report to the war cabinet, Philip Kerr distributed his own memorandum titled "Zionist Movement." The document was written, according to Kerr, after several conversations with Sergeant Jabotinsky and Dr. Weizmann, who were once again pressing for a decision with regard to the proposal to create a Jewish legion or unit for service with the Egyptian Expeditionary Force in Palestine. "The time has now arrived when this matter can be no longer delayed if this project is to be undertaken."[93]

Kerr then went on to outline the steps to be undertaken to make the scheme viable. At the end of July 1917, the War Office announced for the first time the creation of a Jewish fighting force,[94] as well as conscription of aliens, and on August 8, 1917, at a meeting organized in the offices of the War Office, and in the presence of Weizmann, Jabotinsky, Lord Rothschild, James de Rothschild, Mark Sykes, and other prominent Zionists and government officials, Colonel John Henry Patterson reiterated this announcement and explained the purpose of the newly established Jewish legion.[95] On August 23 the formation of the "Jewish Regiment" was officially announced in the *London Gazette,* and Patterson was appointed its commander.[96]

Just prior to these developments, in June 1917, Weizmann enlisted once again the aid of Scott to urge Lloyd George that, with the United States in the war against Germany and the new democratic regime installed in Russia, there was a better alternative than coercive legislation to bring Russian Jews into the armed forces. The Jewish legion, then confined to an obscure, small unit in training, could be made attractive not only to immigrant aliens in Britain but to Russian Jews in the United States if there were more recognition of the national Jewish interest it was to serve.[97] Shortly after, Weizmann had discussed with Frankfurter in Paris how the American Zionists could effectively aid in this project.[98]

The American leaders were disposed to favor this idea, even though the United States was not at war with Turkey. Brandeis, for one, added to his accustomed exhortation of "Men! Money! Discipline!" a new refrain: Young Zionists should join the armed forces.[99] The idea of recruiting young Russian Jews or British subjects in the United States to train in Canada to fight in Palestine—a battlefront of special concern for Jews, if not one where the United States was engaged—fell in with Brandeis's current mood and his long-established Zionist doctrine. By enlisting for service in Palestine, young Jews would become visibly better Americans through becoming obviously better Zionists—a clear demonstration of Brandeis's favorite debating point in argument against anti-Zionists. On the other hand, the United States was not at war with Turkey, so the American Zionist organization could not officially sponsor the project. It could help those who took the task upon themselves in unofficial ways, and did so.

The actual recruiting was done by a group of young British Jews studying in the United States, by individual Zionist enthusiasts, and above all by the Zionist socialist Poalei Zion. In addition to Pinhas Rutenberg, one of the first advocates of the Jewish legion, and the pro-Allied Nachman Syrkin, two young Palestinians, Yitzhak Ben-Zvi and David Ben-Gurion, enlisted in this project and promoted its organization with all their energy. Their initial attitude, like that of the majority of the young Palestinian Jewish labor movement, had been to urge loyalty to the Ottoman regime both out of concern for the safety of the Palestine Jewish community, exposed to Turkish reprisals, and because this was the established policy of past years. Later, however, they reconsidered and became ardent advocates of the legion. With their help the ranks of the regiment eventually recruited in the United States were filled largely by young new immigrants, in good part Poalei Zion members or sympathizers.[100]

This, then, was a project of marginal Zionist elements, to which the PZC and the Federation of American Zionists lent quiet support. Their own direct responsibilities also seemed to demand a new alertness under the changing circumstances, although the signal for decisive activity had not yet been given. During Morgenthau's trip to Gibraltar and after his return from his abortive mission, the leading Zionists began to hear disturbing rumors of his efforts to promote policies opposed to their own design for detaching Palestine from Turkey as a Jewish homeland as part of a broader partition plan for dividing the area on national lines. These rumors led Stephen Wise to bring up the matter of the Blackstone memorial again in a meeting with President Wilson on June 29, 1917. But he was still inhibited by the deference to the president's priorities and preferences, which the American Zionist leaders had decided was their own best line of policy. His report of the interview with Wilson is explicit on this point:

> I explained that Justice Brandeis and I felt that we did not wish to present the petition to him unless he felt he could accept it and make some pronouncement upon it, adding that we knew how difficult that was at this time because of our status of belligerent *vis-à-vis* Turkey. The President expressed his appreciation of the way in which we were careful not to burden him. He said: "You know of my deep interest in Zionism. . . . Whenever the time comes and you and Justice Brandeis feel that the time is ripe for me to speak and act, I shall be ready."[101]

Another matter that occupied the attention of leading Zionists in the spring and summer of 1917 was the concluding phase of the organization of the American Jewish Congress. After an agreement had been reached with the American Jewish Committee and other opponents, revisions had to be introduced and approved by the authorized delegates in a second poll before the road was clear for elections and convening of the congress, scheduled to take place at the end of the year. The elections were conducted with exemplary success both in the substantial number of votes (more than 330,000) and in the smashing success of the Zionist parties. Their control of the congress was guaranteed by an absolute majority; and as the Bund-dominated National Workmen's Committee at the last moment withdrew from the polls, the labor Zionists achieved a particularly striking victory among the Downtown immigrant community. But a disturbing note was introduced by claims that the president was opposed to convening the congress at that time.[102]

At this very time—summer and fall of 1917—Horace Kallen, who opposed postponing the congress, was assuring the Bnei Brith leaders that there was no substance in the rumors that Wilson opposed holding the congress during wartime. But shortly afterward Wise was able to confirm that the White House indeed wanted a delay. The Zionist leaders themselves felt uneasy about holding the congress before the war ended, and their apprehensions grew stronger through the summer of 1917. Antiforeign feelings were mounting in the United States, and the Yiddish press and Jewish radicals were attracting disproportionate attention. A congress would allow the Downtown ideologists to vent unbridled expressions that might, in the view of Wise and others of the leaders, boomerang and harm the Jewish community. Eventually, under heavy pressure from the leadership, the scheduled session of the American Jewish Congress was postponed until after the close of hostilities.[103] Here, too, the leaders had to observe restraints not shared by the mass of their constituents because they felt bound by the policy of the Wilson administration, upon which they pinned their hopes.

The spring and summer of 1917 were, accordingly, a time of stirring and sporadic action in the circles of American Zionist policymakers, with no clear signal for action in a defined direction. When the signal came, it was sent by the British Zionists, who were plunged into a decisive struggle at that very time.

VI

The Balfour Declaration

Chaim Weizmann came back from the Morgenthau mission and the trip to Paris at the end of July 1917 to find that in his absence the Zionist movement had entered a new and critical stage. Since the spring it had been increasingly clear to Weizmann and his close associates that they would have to mobilize all their human and organizational resources for what seemed to be an imminent public declaration by Britain committing its support for the Zionist cause. In a brief memoir of the period, Harry Sacher, Weizmann's loyal critic, described the situation in England prior to and immediately after the issue of the Balfour Declaration thus:

> The entire period of 1914–1919 was marked by two factors: the few people who were actually involved in political work and the meagre resources at their disposal. . . . We were a small group of people who rose to the occasion and assumed responsibility. . . . For a few years we did not even have an office. All the archives were contained in a box which Mr. Sokolow kept under his bed in his small room at the [hotel]. . . . It was a long process which led to the Balfour Declaration. . . . Had it not been for the work of this small group, the war might have ended without a Balfour Declaration and without a mandate. . . . I was so intimately involved with those events, that I can say with absolute certainty, that without Dr. Weizmann, we would have received neither a declaration, nor a mandate, nor international recognition in a Jewish national home in Palestine.[1]

From the earliest days of the war Weizmann worked almost as an independent agent to persuade England and his fellow Zionists that a British protectorate over Palestine was the best course of action for the empire as well as for the Jewish national cause. The support he received, when he received it, waxed and waned and came in spurts from various quarters in England and abroad. With the exception of Vladimir Jabotinsky and a small group of Manchester and London young men and women and, of course, various Rothschild family members and C. P. Scott, Weizmann had little, if any, individual or institutional support. This state of affairs changed only marginally when he became president of the weak and splintered English Zionist Federation. Indeed, the divisions within English Zionism, not to speak of English Jewry and the World Zionist Organization, as to the best political course the Zionists should follow militated against Weizmann's pursuing his goals within an organized institutional framework. Despite the hardships such independent work entailed, it was clearly most suitable to Weizmann's personality and mode of operation. For some three years—beginning in the summer of 1914—he was able to function alone, making his own contacts and most of the crucial decisions, consulting occasionally, increasingly out of a sense of obligation and collegial respect, with Nahum Sokolow, Ahad Ha'Am, and the coterie of young men and women who were devoted to him personally.

Yet by 1917 this latter group, many of whom were introduced to Zionism by Weizmann himself, became restive, demanding greater and more meaningful involvement in Zionist political affairs. The Political Committee, which, with the exception of Leon Simon, did not include any of the younger members of Weizmann's circle, lasted one year and was disbanded in January 1917. Given its heterogeneous composition, it had not played a decisive role in any case and expired almost without notice. The British Palestine Committee, which was founded in the winter of 1916–17 with Weizmann's tacit approval, developed into a marginal group often opposed to Weizmann's position. But men like Leon Simon, Israel Sieff, Simon Marks, and Shmuel Tolkowsky—not to speak of Harry Sacher—wanted to play a larger, more active role in the day-to-day negotiations conducted between Weizmann and the British government. They complained that the "Chief," as they increasingly came to call Weizmann, did not always inform them of his high-level and secret dealings; nor did he actually consult them. From time to time he dropped hints or revealed something after the fact, but only in a haphazard manner. "Chaim likes telling," commented Harry Sacher, "but without system. It's an accident whether you hear or not."[2] With time, a reservoir of resentment was building up.[3]

At the end of 1916, Shmuel Tolkowsky, spending the weekend at Sacher's home in Manchester, talked with Israel Sieff and Simon Marks about their wish to be more actively involved in Zionist negotiations. They decided to offer to establish for Weizmann a Zionist office in London that would assist him in his political efforts. They also agreed to raise the necessary funds for its operation. In return they would ask Weizmann and Sokolow to agree to the establishment of a Political Committee to serve as an advisory body.[4]

On February 8, 1917, the day after the historic conference with Mark Sykes, the group sent a letter to Nahum Sokolow, Weizmann's senior colleague, outlining their scheme. Signed by Tolkowsky, Simon, Sieff, Sacher, Marks, Samuel Landman, and Albert Hyamson, the letter sought to "draw your attention to certain defects in the machinery of the method of Zionist work in this country." After describing the work that had to be done and the need for a political "Directorate"—a secretariat and the establishment of subcommittees—the signatories went on to criticize the haphazard and disorganized fashion in which that work had been done hitherto. As a consequence, a few individuals (the first draft of the letter added, "notably Weizmann") were taxed beyond endurance. Moreover, there was no specific program of work, no sense of discipline, much work that was neglected or took too long to accomplish, no central archives or written tradition, and no general and regular discussion of the issues at hand. The remedy was apparent from the criticism. Though written to Sokolow, the letter was intended by the signatories primarily for Weizmann. No matter how capable or respected an individual might be, they stated, the responsibility of carrying the political load alone was much too heavy:

> We think that the load that must necessarily lie on your shoulders would be materially lightened if you were to appoint a small Committee of men thoroughly in sympathy with your ideals and whose confidence in you is without qualification, who moreover, as a consequence of their birth and environment, are conversant with political conditions in England. The advice and service of this Committee would be freely at your disposal, and would relieve you to some extent of the burden . . . by undertaking some of the detail work. . . . To such a Committee, members should be appointed not because of any office they hold but because of their actual personal qualifications. . . .
> A secretariat is essential to any such reconstruction.[5]

From the start it was clear to those who sent the letter to Sokolow that, were the Political Committee to be founded, it would be headed by Weizmann and be independent of the EZF. In a letter to Weizmann suggesting the reorganization of the EZF itself, Israel Sieff urged Weizmann, in office as president for only a few days, to circumvent the organization whenever political issues were at stake. Weizmann, in fact, "ought to take up an autocratic attitude" and simply nominate to that committee those men he trusts.[6] At the end of April 1917, with Sokolow on the Continent and little prospect of his returning soon, Sieff wrote a more outspoken letter as to why a Political Committee was imperative. It shows that the circle around Weizmann was keenly aware that Zionism was at a critical juncture:

> We are at a critical moment in the history of our movement. The time has arrived when the weight of Zionist opinion must be felt in the discussions which are going on as to the future of Palestine. . . . It would be idle to expect that you yourself could assume this burdensome task. Our group here have not that confidence in Sok[olow] which would allow us to give him indefinite powers. The only alternative is a committee, composed of our group, representatives from America and Russia if possible, with you or Sok. as chairman. . . . What you have done during the last two years has been Herculean, and I think the time has arrived when others must share the responsibility, which is a heavy one. . . . Should the future bring

forth disappointment, the blame will be yours. We here in Manchester have decided that this shall not be.[7]

While Sokolow was still away from London, Weizmann could delay responding, claiming he had to wait for his colleague before any action could be taken.[8] His younger colleagues, in the meantime, advised him how the committee should be constituted.[9] Like Sieff, Harry Sacher also urged that Weizmann and Sokolow dismiss the idea of a committee on a representative basis: "Just select the men you want and reject those you don't want. Among the people I suggest you reject is Dr. Gaster."[10] Weizmann, in the meantime, wrote to Sir George Macdonogh, the director of the Military Intelligence Department, and asked that Albert Hyamson, Samuel Landman, Leon Simon, Israel Sieff, Harry Sacher, and Simon Marks be exempt from military service since without their assistance "the cause of the Zionist movement in this country could not be carried on."[11] His request was granted, freeing his young disciples to work with him. Toward the end of June 1917, just prior to his departure for Gibraltar, Weizmann finally agreed that an office be opened to assist the political work. The office of the English Zionist Federation was useless for this purpose since it was located on Fulborne Street in the East End. The unofficial headquarters of all Zionist political activity in England was hitherto the Weizmann house on 67 Addison Road, with Vera Weizmann answering the telephone and helping with correspondence.[12]

Vera Weizmann was perforce involved in all the discussions taking place in Weizmann's intimate circle, at least those that took place in the Weizmann residence. Her role was much resented by Weizmann's colleagues, who felt that she unduly interfered, both influencing and inhibiting her husband.[13] Vera insisted that the proposed new office of the Political Committee be close to the Weizmann residence in Kensington, whereas Shmuel Tolkowsky and Simon Marks, who were looking for the office space, insisted that they must "escape from the constant presence and interference of Mrs. Weizmann."[14] They finally found an adequate, if inelegant, space: four small rooms with low ceilings and rather dark, at 175 Piccadilly, in mid-July 1917.[15] A young woman, Janet Lieberman, was engaged as Weizmann's personal secretary; she remained in this position until she married in 1929.[16] Leon Simon, who contemplated quitting his job at the post office in order to work at the Zionist office, was dissuaded from doing so by Harry Sacher, who (using the same language Vera Weizmann once used with Chaim, early in their relationship, when he contemplated working full time for the World Zionist Organization) stated frankly: "I don't like any of us *living* on Zionist money, because it takes from our freedom and from our influence."[17] In the event, Simon Marks, the only member of the group who had actually joined the Royal Field Artillery in May 1917, was transferred at Weizmann's request to the Reserve at the end of June 1917 and took charge of the affairs of the office, which opened in mid-August 1917.[18]

To constitute the Political Committee was more complicated. Even among Weizmann's young advisers, there was no unanimity on this question. Akiva Jacob Ettinger, an agronomist for the Jewish National Fund who came to London from the Hague at Weizmann's request, seemed to feel that such a Political Committee would limit his own influence.[19] Tolkowsky and Simon Marks, as well as Israel Sieff, were keen on seeing the committee established, whereas Harry Sacher, who had a somewhat skeptical attitude toward Weizmann's political work, thought the committee worth a try but could be done without.[20] Ahad Ha'Am refused at first to join such a committee because he felt that Sokolow did not show him enough respect and did not share sensitive documents with him.[21] Leon Simon, who was aggrieved by Weizmann because of a sharp dispute over the question of the Jewish legion, at first intended to follow Ahad Ha'Am's example.[22] Weizmann, who at various times felt that the young group around him was plotting against him, announced just prior to going to Gibraltar that they were free to set up their own Political Committee but that he would not join it.[23] After some of the disagreements were sorted out, Weizmann agreed, on June 27, to cooperate with the proposed Political Committee.[24]

The committee began its operations as the London Zionist Political Committee at the end of July 1917, when Weizmann returned to London. Its statutes named Weizmann and Sokolow as co-chairmen. It was to have an advisory role and to be informed of all political negotiations; it would meet at least once a week.[25] Its members, chosen by Weizmann and Sokolow in consultation with their close associates, were Ahad Ha'Am, Herbert Bentwich, Joseph Cowen, Akiva Ettinger, Paul Goodman, Albert Hyamson, Leopold Kessler, Simon Marks, Harry Sacher, Israel Sieff, Leon Simon, and Shmuel Tolkowsky. From time to time, when the need arose, it also co-opted into its ranks various specialists, such as Zalman David Levontin, the manager of the Anglo-Palestine Company. On August 1, 1917, it held its first meeting at the Imperial Hotel in London.[26] From Weizmann's point of view, the establishment of the Political Committee, as it was commonly called, was a mixed blessing. While it provided him with a forum before which to air his views and from which to receive advice, it had been initiated on a note of dissension and personal distrust and did not always function as a merely advisory body. Some of its members found themselves occasionally on a collision course with Weizmann. The Political Committee was clearly not Weizmann's idea, and he would have been just as happy to manage his diplomacy without it.[27] The Zionist office, on the other hand, a by-product of the Political Committee, which handled the myriad daily chores, turned out to be indispensable in the months prior to and after the issuance of the Balfour Declaration.

Due to the Morgenthau mission, ironically, Weizmann was not present at the committee's earliest discussions, which led to the first Zionist draft declaration submitted to the British government on July 18, 1917. The day after he and Lord Rothschild had gone to see Balfour, Weizmann asked Harry Sacher to draw up the draft of a declaration, adding as a guideline that it ought to say something such as: "The British Government declares its conviction, its desire or its intention to support Zionist aims for the creation of a Jewish national home in Palestine; no reference must be made I think to the question of the Suzerain Power because that would land the British into difficulties with the French; it must be a Zionist declaration."[28]

Sacher complied immediately but, characteristically, only partially followed Weizmann's guidelines. In his draft of June 22, he did not mention Britain as the potential suzerain over Palestine, although his formula stated: "The British Government declares that one of its essential war aims is the reconstitution of Palestine as a Jewish State and as the National Home of the Jewish People."[29] Sacher explained to Leon Simon why he opted for a strong statement: "On the general question—how much they [Weizmann and Sokolow] have tied themselves up with the British Government? I can give no answer. . . . When you speak of the British Government you forget it's a complex entity. I suspect Chaim is too complaisant towards Sir M[ark] S[ykes] and forgets Sir M.S.'s interest is primarily in Arabs not in Jews. . . . I don't attach much significance to L[loyd] G[eorge]'s precise phrasing because he's so loose in thought and word and morals."[30] Sacher wanted to tie England to the idea of a Jewish state—the Zionists' ultimate aim—in a way that would be unambiguously binding.

Despite Sokolow's warning that "if we want too much we shall get nothing,"[31] Sacher was adamant, and his second draft was even more forceful than the first: "I think my own draft erred in not going far enough," wrote Sacher to Sokolow.[32] With his second draft he submitted a similar draft by Herbert Sidebotham. Sidebotham's stated, "The British Government adopts as one of its essential war aims the reconstitution of an integral Palestine as a Jewish State and as the national home of the Jewish people . . . a State whose dominant national character when the hopes of its founders are realised will be Jewish in the same sense as the dominant national character of England is English."[33] Ahad Ha'Am's suggestion was, as could have been predicted, much more carefully worded: "H. M. Government after having given careful consideration . . . favourably accepts the scheme of recognising Palestine as the National Home of the Jewish People."[34] Ahad Ha'Am favored Lord Rothschild's formula, which was similar in wording to his own.[35]

In the absence of Weizmann, Sokolow was the only one among the Zionists active in London in daily contact with Sir Mark Sykes, who was assisted by a young member of the Foreign Office, Harold Nicolson. Sokolow was thus in a much better position to know how far the Zionists could go in their demands at this stage of their negotiations. Though in sympathy with Sacher's ideas, Sokolow explained to his militant colleague that it had been "suggested" that the Zionists should at first get a general approval of their aims. Sokolow's hope was "to receive from the Government a *general* short approval of the same kind as that which I have been successful in getting from the French Government."[36]

From Ahad Ha'Am's letter to Sokolow of July 11, 1917, it can be inferred that the general directions for the formulation of the Zionist draft declaration came from Balfour himself.[37] The next day, July 12, Sokolow convened at the Imperial Hotel those persons residing in London who were slated to become members of the Political Committee: Cowen, Ettinger, Simon, Marks, and Tolkowsky. The various drafts were considered and their merits exhaustively debated. At last all agreed on a formulation that came closest to the versions suggested by Sokolow and Ahad Ha'Am:

> His Majesty's Government, after considering the aims of the Zionist Organization, accepts the principle of recognising Palestine as the National Home of the Jewish People and the right of the Jewish People to build up its national life in Palestine under a protection to be established at the conclusion of peace following upon the successful issue of the War. His Majesty's Government regards as essential for the realisation of this principle the grant of internal autonomy to the Jewish nationality in Palestine, freedom of immigration for Jews, and the establishment of a Jewish National Colonising Corporation for the resettlement and economic development of the country. The conditions and forms of the internal autonomy and a Charter for the Jewish National Colonising Corporation should, in the view of His Majesty's Government, be elaborated in detail and determined with the representatives of the Zionist Organization.[38]

The following day Sokolow sent a copy of this formulation to Lord Rothschild, asking that it be shown to Mark Sykes and Ronald Graham.[39]

The Zionists, as has been noted earlier, had over the war years composed a variety of memoranda setting forth their conceptions and proposals for the future of Palestine. These were intended as aids for the interviews Weizmann and others conducted with influential Britons. The formula the Zionists arrived at on July 12, 1917, set forth a commitment Britain might make to the Jews through the Zionist organization. The basis of their proposition was essentially the old Herzlian idea of a concession under public law to a Jewish chartered company, to be constituted by the Zionists through a body, like the Zionist Congress, that would represent the democratically determined will of the Jewish people everywhere. Under the powers conceded to it, the Jewish company would build a new economic base in Palestine under the control and protection of a British administration. It would organize and train the mass of Jewish immigrants it would bring to the country, and it would provide them with the social infrastructure required to create a Hebrew-speaking community and an authentic, modern Hebrew culture.

A few days after hammering out this ambitious document, however, Sokolow informed his colleagues that it was rated (no doubt by Balfour and Sykes) too long and specific; in other words, it suggested too binding a commitment for British taste. Sokolow advised the committee to confine itself to simple restating of the brief guidelines originally given him by his British contacts. On July 17 a smaller group consisting of Sokolow, Cowen, Ettinger, and Tolkowsky met to consider a shorter version. This time they were joined by Harry Sacher, who was in London on vacation. Ironically Sacher, who earlier wanted definite commitments, now suggested the vague formula that the group accepted with minor alterations:

1. His Majesty's Government accepts the principle that Palestine should be reconstituted as the National Home of the Jewish People.
2. His Majesty's Government will use its best endeavours to secure the achievement of this object and will discuss the necessary methods and means with the Zionist Organization.[40]

The following day—July 18, 1917—Lord Rothschild forwarded this draft declaration to Balfour with a cover letter.[41]

This formula, essentially composed in Sir Mark Sykes's office, represented a considerable advance in Sykes's acceptance of Zionist requirements over his original assumption that it would be enough to offer Jews a "haven" for settlement of some emigrants or postwar refugees. In the form presented by the Zionists, the formula recognized what for Ahad Ha'Am was the central point—the historic connection of Palestine with the Jewish people—by saying it should be "reconstituted as [their] National Home." It also accepted, if only by implication, what was for Weizmann the cardinal point—the special rights accorded the Zionists, or the Jewish company they would set up, in saying that the government would discuss methods and means with them. But while the formula closely followed British suggestions framed by Sykes and Nicolson and approved in advance by Balfour, it encountered strong resistance in government quarters, and long delays ensued before it was adopted in final form.

Sykes and Balfour were notably cautious in their support of the proposed declaration. Sykes's enthusiasm for the measure, which would help effect one of the provisions of his postwar plan for the Middle East, varied with the fortunes of the campaign in Palestine. After the British setback in Gaza, he advised dropping further development of the Zionist connection since it might involve promises to them the British would find hard to keep should the military situation remain unchanged. His interest was revived when the British in June decided to reopen the Palestine campaign, and he then gave strong support both to the project of a Jewish legion and to the proposed pro-Zionist declaration.

As for Balfour, while personally committed to Zionism (only David Lloyd George was more decided in his sympathy), he shared the English (or Scottish) caution about new, explicit commitments that long held up War Office approval of a Jewish military unit and eventually permitted it to be formed only in a distinctly restricted version. Balfour was not eager to translate British sympathy for Zionism into a wartime pledge. He, too, argued in terms of Britain's possible inability to carry out pledges it might make. After the draft was submitted, he was one of the first to question its utility for the Zionists and to propose changes that would reduce the extent and specificity of English commitments. There were, nevertheless, the global concerns to consider, particularly the support of Russian Jewry and American Jewry in view of their respective governments' reluctant participation in the war. Thus Balfour prepared his own draft declaration, which differed only slightly from that of the Zionists, and sent it to Lord Rothschild on August 2, 1917.[42]

The Zionists assumed that a declaration along the lines of their proposed draft was a foregone conclusion. Weizmann, who had just returned from Paris, wrote to Sir Ronald Graham on August 1, 1917, suggesting that a speech by the prime minister three days hence would be an appropriate occasion on which to declare Britain's support for the Zionist aspirations.[43] To Harry Sacher, Weizmann wrote the same day in confident terms that "the declaration is going to be given [to] us soon."[44] In fact, however, Lloyd George did not mention Palestine in the speech he gave on August 4. By mid-August Harold Nicolson, no doubt pressed by the Zionists, wrote to the war cabinet asking for action on the Rothschild draft,[45] whereupon the appropriate official promised to act if Balfour wished to have the matter discussed at the next war cabinet meeting.[46]

In the meantime, Lord Milner took it upon himself to work up the text for a declaration. He objected to the words "reconstituted" and "secure" and proposed a cardinal change: instead of the original formulations "*the* National Home *of* the Jewish People," he suggested "*a* home *for* the Jewish People." Lord Milner's proposed draft thus read:

> His Majesty's Government accepts the principle that every opportunity should be afforded for the establishment of a home for the Jewish people in Palestine, and will use its best endeavors to facilitate the achievement of this object, and will be ready to consider any suggestions on the subject which the Zionist Organization may desire to lay before them.[47]

Milner certainly made the alterations in part with an eye toward the anti-Zionist Jews in Britain,[48] but his formula did not allay the fears of Edwin Montagu, recently appointed secretary of state for India. Montagu's appointment was announced in the papers on the day Lord Rothschild submitted his draft declaration to Balfour. Two months later Rothschild reminded Weizmann, "I said to you in London, as soon as I saw the announcement in the paper of Montagu's appointment, that I was afraid we were done."[49] Edwin Montagu's anti-Zionist views were well known, particularly to those who—like Rothschild—moved in the same social circles. While not a member of the war cabinet, Montagu was given the courtesy of a hearing throughout the deliberations about a pro-Zionist declaration as a member of the government directly concerned.

Montagu's opposition was based both on the difficulties he foresaw because of the hostility the measure could arouse among the Muslims in India and the even more personal consideration that his prestige and credibility, as the representative of Britain in Indian affairs, might be seriously damaged by the proposed measure, which would attach him, as a Jew, to a new national home in Palestine for the Jewish people. Montagu was not a recognized representative of British Jewry; he detached himself not only from Zionism but from the pressure for equal status for Jews in Russia that so much concerned other anti-Zionists like Lucien Wolf and Claude Montefiore. Montagu's impassioned arguments quite naturally raised new questions about the solidity of the Jewish consensus in favor of the Zionist program.[50]

Montagu had attacked previous suggestions that Britain support Zionism. As noted, he ridiculed his cousin Herbert Samuel when Samuel made such proposals earlier in the war and did not hesitate to launch an attack when the formula by Lucien Wolf was under consideration.[51] In August 1917, after seeing the Rothschild draft declaration, Montagu must have realized that this time around the British commitment to Zionism, which he had dreaded for so long, was about to become a reality. His reaction, in a paper called "The Anti-Semitism of the Present Government" and circulated to the members of the war cabinet, seems like the desperate and painful outcry of a man who sees his whole world crumbling before him. After outlining his anti-Zionist credo and marshaling all the arguments in his arsenal in his customary mixture of serious and sardonic language, Montagu presented the basic ingredients for a formula he could support: "I would say to Lord Rothschild that the Government will be prepared to do everything in their power to obtain for Jews in Palestine complete liberty of settlement and life on an equality with the inhabitants of that country who profess other religious beliefs. I would ask that the Government should go no further."[52]

Montagu's statement, which he gave to the members of the war cabinet, was an anti-Zionist *tour de force*. Even the authoritative and accurate reply by Ronald MacNeill, MP, also circulated to the cabinet members at the end of August, could not totally eradicate the impression made by Montagu's plea.[53]

In the penultimate paragraph of his paper Montagu made reference to what he undoubtedly perceived as an immediate and real threat—the Jewish legion. The announcement in the *Times* at the end of July 1917 that a Jewish infantry regiment was being formed, with the shield of David as its regimental badge,[54] was abhorrent to Montagu. On that particular issue he voiced the outrage of a large cross-section of Anglo-

Jewry.[55] "I can well understand," he wrote, "that when it was decided, and quite rightly, to force foreign Jews in this country to serve in the Army, it was difficult to put them in British regiments because of the language difficulty, but that was because they were foreigners, and not because they were Jews, and a Foreign Legion would seem to me to have been the right thing to establish. A Jewish Legion makes the position of Jews in other regiments more difficult and forces a nationality upon people who have nothing in common."[56]

On September 3, 1917, at the same meeting that discussed the Zionist draft declaration, Montagu scored at least a partial victory. The war cabinet decided to drop the idea of a fighting force known as a Jewish regiment; instead, Jewish units were to be formed as one or more battalions of the Royal Fusiliers, without a special Jewish emblem.[57] Though no pledge was given as to their destination, the intention was to send these battalions to Palestine.[58] It took Colonel John Henry Patterson some four months before he could raise one battalion,[59] known as the Thirty-eighth Battalion Royal Fusiliers. Later two additional battalions were added—the Thirty-ninth and Fortieth Battalion Royal Fusiliers—consisting mainly of American Jews together with locally recruited Palestinians.[60]

In his account of these events, published in 1922, Colonel Patterson seemed to understand, if not sympathize, with the non-Zionists or anti-Zionists who opposed the formation of a specifically designated Jewish unit within the British armed forces. But he could not contain his astonishment at the opposition of Weizmann's Zionist colleagues:

> It is a curious fact that, so far as I could gather, the Inner Actions Committee of the Zionist organization, with the honoured exception of Dr. Weizmann, looked at us with suspicion. The formation of Jewish Battalions did not appeal to them. How it was possible that the leaders of Zionism should not have grasped, and taken to their hearts, this gift of Jewish Battalions from the British Government, for the furtherance of their own ends, is one of the greatest examples of ineptitude that have ever come within my experience. . . .
>
> I know that Dr. Weizmann had vision enough to foresee the strength which such a legion would give to his diplomacy, but unfortunately his colleagues on the Zionist Council did not see eye to eye with him in this matter until it was too late.[61]

As an outsider, Patterson could only catch a glimpse of the heated debates that took place between Weizmann and his closest collaborators in England around the question of a Jewish legion. Despite occasional disclaimers, Weizmann had been supportive of the idea from the moment it was broached by Jabotinsky. In the early part of the war Weizmann avoided any open identification with this project, concerned as he was to build Zionist consensus in favor of his own project—a political alliance with Britain. The official Zionist policy of wartime neutrality stemmed not only from the reasons mentioned earlier—fear of Turkish reprisals[62] and the need to hold together an international body whose members were divided among the warring nations—but because it may have been thought prudent not to commit Zionist fortunes completely to one or another side in a conflict whose outcome still remained uncertain. Even Jabotinsky, who had decided that Zionism had no future under an Ottoman regime, claimed that he wished to leave open the option of possible alliance with France or Italy rather than place all his chips on England alone. When Weizmann chose to adopt the latter course, he faced a difficult task in winning the Zionist consensus in the Allied countries to his policy.

Weizmann believed—especially after the accession of Lloyd George, the reports of Balfour's visit to the United States, and Weizmann's terms for undertaking the mission to Gibraltar had been accepted—that his policy enjoyed the full support of the government. He also had reason to assume that his fellow Zionists would now come around to accept his policy on the question of the legion, and by the spring of 1917 he no longer kept his views to himself. Sokolow was supportive,[63] but, characteristically, he was too much the diplomat to assert these views in the face of strong opposition. What complicated matters further was that Jabotinsky's propaganda work for the legion required him to spend most of his time in London, and, at the Weizmanns' invitation, he came to stay with them at the beginning of May 1917. Chaim and Vera were both fond of Jabotinsky, and their ties of friendship deepened over the period of three months he was their house guest. Their association made criticism of the Jewish legion a doubly sensitive subject for those of Weizmann's collaborators who opposed the idea.

It was difficult enough to criticize Weizmann, but doubly difficult to do so knowing that the Weizmanns might pass on one's criticism to their house guest. To the extent that they disliked the idea of a Jewish unit, Weizmann's friends were distrustful of the man who conceived and promoted this project. When Weizmann broached the idea—via Simon Marks—that Jabotinsky might be added to the Political Committee, a number of its members announced that they would then resign.[64] Though they were careful not to criticize Jabotinsky in the presence of Vera, who was particularly sensitive on this issue,[65] there was a great deal of resentment among Weizmann's collaborators that Jabotinsky's presence in the "Chief's" house had identified him—and by implication, the Zionist movement—publicly and directly with the scheme for a Jewish fighting force.[66] For their part, the Weizmanns resented the interference in their private affairs, but they finally relented, and Jabotinsky relocated to the home of Simon Marks.[67]

This symbolic gesture by no means ended Weizmann's—or Vera's— support for Jabotinsky's scheme,[68] nor the opposition to it by the other members of the Political Committee. Whereas Weizmann felt that the formation of a Jewish legion would aid the diplomatic campaign he was engaged in, his colleagues, almost without exception, believed that its formation might endanger the fate of the Jewish community in Palestine;

in their view it was sufficient—indeed desirable—for Jews, Zionists included, to enlist in the regular units of the British army.

Two key members of the Political Committee—Harry Sacher and Leon Simon—were pacifists and firmly believed that, as Sacher put it, "the war is manifestly bankrupt, that peace is on the march, and that for Zionism at this stage to ally itself with militarism and imperialism would be a radical error."[69] Weizmann was exasperated with his younger circle. On August 5, during tea at his home, with Vera present, he told Tolkowsky: "Leon and Harry are for a separate peace, Simon Marks and Sieff are children, there remain only Sokolow, you and I!"[70] After an angry letter he wrote to Sacher their relations became so strained that they stopped corresponding.[71] In a letter to Nahum Sokolow, Leon Simon also protested Weizmann's policy concerning the Jewish legion, undertaken without prior consultation with other members of the Political Committee.[72]

Adding to Weizmann's problems was the fact that the members of the executive of the English Zionist Federation felt left out of all his negotiations. Samuel J. Cohen, vice-president of the EZF representing the provinces, addressed a sharply worded letter to Weizmann on August 16, 1917, demanding the consolidation of the Political Committee with the executive of the EZF.[73] That same day, at a meeting of the executive council of the EZF, a debate ensued concerning the appropriate response to the announcement by the War Office to raise a Jewish regiment. Benjamin Grad, a member of the London executive of the EZF, proposed a vote to censure Weizmann and Sokolow for lack of leadership on this issue. Weizmann, in response, announced on the spot that he was resigning his post as president. In the event Grad's motion was defeated by a vote of 14–1, and those present beseeched Weizmann to change his mind.[74]

Weizmann, it seems, welcomed this crisis, almost sought it.[75] Since the early part of 1917 he had been working intensely with almost no chance for respite. He was on edge, and his nerves were strained to a breaking point from his ceaseless political negotiations, the continuous work for the Admiralty, and his travels. After his spectacular success in Gibraltar and Paris he felt entitled to a greater measure of appreciation and respect from his colleagues, both on the EZF executive and on the Political Committee. Instead, within days of his return to London he was besieged and harassed. Enough rumors and innuendos circulated concerning his judgment as a political leader to convince him that a public test of his position was required. These thoughts must have occupied him during the days prior to the meeting on August 16, though it is quite possible that his resignation was made on an impulse. The next day he wrote to Sokolow: "My very dear Friend, I wish to inform you that after very careful consideration and after having weighed all the consequences I came to the inevitable conclusion that it is impossible for me to continue to serve either on the Executive of the E.Z.F. or on the

Political Committee. I have accordingly placed my resignation from the Presidency of the E.Z.F. in the hands of the Council and I beg leave to sever my connection with the P.C."[76]

That Sokolow was shocked and surprised by Weizmann's resignation is apparent from his reply by return mail:

My very dear Friend and Colleague,
 . . . I must tell you with all respect and consideration for your views, that I am at a loss to understand what might have inspired you suddenly with the idea of such an impossible intention. I say *suddenly*, because we had still the day before yesterday a long discussion about our work and plans for the next future and I had not the slightest idea that you were thinking of resignation. . . . Why did you not mention your intention? . . . With all my appreciation for the sentiments and undoubtedly noble motives which might have dictated your declaration [that Zionism was bankrupt], allow me, my dear friend, to protest most emphatically against your intention. We are both engaged in a work from which you cannot detach yourself without ruining it. This consideration must outweigh all other considerations, important as they may be. You are too devoted to our ideal, your responsibility is too great and your whole life is too closely bound up with Zionistic duties to undertake a step which can by no means be justified. For God's sake, give up this idea and do not destroy the work which we all were building for years and to which you have so greatly contributed. You know yourself that this work cannot be continued without you. . . .
 If there is any difficulty of opposition . . . tell me what it is and I am sure I shall find a way to remove the obstacles. But do not abandon us and myself at such a moment. I appeal to your high sense of duty, to your devotion and to our friendship![77]

This was indeed the kind of appeal Weizmann expected. There were many others as well, all written within a day or two after his resignation. They came separately from Israel Sieff and Becky Sieff; Tolkowsky, too, wrote a long letter to dissuade him from his intentions, and even Leon Simon, who had maintained a critical distance in the previous few months, wrote a personal and moving letter beseeching him to reconsider.[78] There were also direct personal appeals. Only Harry Sacher refused Simon Marks's request to write to Weizmann. Sacher increasingly distrusted Weizmann's politics and held a cynical view of Weizmann's personal motives:

I have heard from Simon [Marks]. He does not know clearly the root of the trouble but doubtless it is the Legion and the general policy of imperialism and militarism of which W[eizmann] is enamoured. Simon wanted me to write a nice letter to W. dissuading him from resigning. But I answered that if there was a serious difference of principle I could not honestly take such a course; while if Chaim merely wanted an assurance of sympathy and support we were a little beyond these irrelevancies. In my analysis the trouble has two tap-roots (I) Chaim's hankering after politics, his association with Sykes and other "politicians," his inclination towards the melodramatic (armies, diplomacy and other muck no good in themselves), all of which have tended to make him obscure the essential Jewish thing that we are after. He is too British and too C[haim] W[eizmann]. (II) Verachik [Vera] who stokes up his vanity and his passion and is in my opinion an unmitigated nuisance.

The remedy for I is close co-operation with Russia and U.S.A. . . . . There is no remedy for II, but we should mitigate the evil by refusing to discuss Zionism with V[era]. . . .

I assume that W. will not resign. . . . I should be very greatly surprised if W. did resign. He is in spite of the labour and the friction and the unpleasantness, associated with the past, far too proud of it and also at bottom far too keen on the Jewish cause to resign. If he does we must reorganise so as to get on without him. It will be a heavy loss.[79]

Sacher was correct. Weizmann had given much too much of himself to abandon the Zionist cause in midstream, on the verge of what he judged would be a successful outcome. The virtual cascade of assurances of respect and loyalty from his colleagues and disciples satisfied him—at least for the moment. On August 22, 1917, at a second meeting of the EZF executive council, after the appropriate vote of confidence was cast by those present, Weizmann seemed reconciled but did not formally retract his resignation.[80] The matter did not end there, though, since the root causes of the frustration felt by all concerned had not been dealt with. Adding to questions surrounding the Jewish legion and Weizmann's leadership was the lack of progress in the negotiations with the government.

In the meantime, the British Labour party, of its own volition, circulated in August 1917 a pro-Zionist statement calling for the creation of a state in Palestine under international guarantee to which "Jewish people may return."[81] According to Simon Marks, who saw Weizmann daily in the Zionist office, Weizmann felt frustrated that his own diplomacy had failed to win a similar declaration from the government.[82]

The simmering resentments flared up at a meeting of the Political Committee on September 4, 1917. The uncertain attitude of the war cabinet toward a pro-Zionist declaration, as expressed at its meeting the day before, contributed to the short temper of all present; the minutes of the meeting provide palpable evidence of the high tones of the discussion. That very morning Leon Simon had announced his resignation from the Political Committee in response to a disagreeable conversation he had with Weizmann.[83] Behind the scenes Harry Sacher continued to agitate against Weizmann's high-handed manner in running Zionist affairs,[84] and at the meeting itself the issue of the Jewish legion and the stance the Political Committee took toward it came up once again. Weizmann agreed to the adoption of a declaration of Zionist neutrality on the Jewish legion question, but he vehemently objected to the publication of such a declaration. As the dispute continued, Weizmann became increasingly agitated and declared that he could not work in such an atmosphere of distrust.[85]

What must have been most painful for Weizmann was the criticism of the person he had long admired and respected more than anyone else in the Zionist movement. At the meeting of the Political Committee on September 4, Ahad Ha'Am clashed openly with Weizmann. That evening, for the first time in their relationship, Ahad Ha'Am wrote Weizmann a letter taking him to task for the manner in which he behaved with the Political Committee. He reminded Weizmann that it was his duty to carefully weigh the advice given him by his colleagues and expressed severe disappointment that Weizmann did not even want to hear what they had to say. On the question of the Jewish legion, moreover, Weizmann seemed to have placed before the Zionist organization a *fait accompli* by making promises to the government not revealed to his colleagues. Was Weizmann reluctant to make public a statement about Zionist neutrality on this issue because the legion had been one of the important planks on which he had built his diplomacy?[86]

Even before he had received Ahad Ha'Am's letter, Weizmann had decided to make his resignation official. On the morning of September 5, 1917, he wrote to Nahum Sokolow "for the last time, that for compelling reasons of a personal nature it has been impossible for me to go on with the work. . . . The atmosphere surrounding me is full of suspicion, envy and certain fanaticism, in the presence of which any fruitful work is impossible for me."[87] He also wrote to Ahad Ha'Am that he could no longer endure the abuse he had suffered from those with whom he had worked for so long. He assured his old mentor "that this is not . . . a personal question." Yet in the same breath, revealing his ambivalence, he continued, "It is impossible to deny that the inevitable break affects our personal relationships, because public work has brought us all closely together."[88]

By the time Weizmann's letter reached Ahad Ha'Am, the latter already knew about Weizmann's resignation. Knowing Weizmann's sensitivity to any criticism, Ahad Ha'Am must have wanted to soften the impact of the letter he had written the night before, and he telephoned his disciple at home to discuss their differences of opinion. No sooner did they end their conversation, when Sokolow rang up Ahad Ha'Am to discuss Weizmann's resignation. Ahad Ha'Am then wrote Weizmann a second letter that illuminates their relationship as well as the position Weizmann had attained by 1917:

Dear Chaim Evzerovich,

. . . I take the liberty—for the first time in all the years of our friendship—to talk to you not simply as a friend . . . but as a *senior* colleague, who had been on the battlefield at a time when you were still a school boy, and, who most probably, either directly or indirectly had some influence on your Jewish Weltanschauung. . . .

What you intend to do is—literally—a stab in the back of the whole Zionist movement. . . . You are too wise not to understand that the consequences of your "resignation" will be a loss in the prestige of Zionist leaders in the eyes of those on whom the fate of our cause depends. . . . And not because you are the only one who can do the work. . . . There is no one who is irreplaceable. And if you left the work for some reason beyond your control, . . . it could be continued by other hands. . . . Nor, if at the very beginning you had presented yourself . . . as one elected . . . by the Zionist Organization . . . would your "resignation" cause such confusion. . . . But your situation is an exceptional one. You began your work here . . . as a private Zionist. Your personal qualities and favorable conditions brought it about that in a short time you became practically the symbol of Zionism for many men of influence. And now suddenly, one fine day, you announce you no longer concern yourself with the matter, you have resigned! To whom did you announce your resignation? Who elected you, who might be entitled to accept your resignation? You were elected by objective conditions and objective conditions will dismiss you when the time comes, when complete success or complete failure will make your further work unnecessary. But until then you cannot leave your place without evoking attitudes very damaging to the Zionists . . . and no other persons could carry on the work that you began.[89]

Ahad Ha'Am then added the text of a letter he would propose be sent to Weizmann by the Political Committee in the event he refused to retract his resignation; it would call Weizmann's proposed resignation an act of treason. He was sure Weizmann was incapable of such an act that, from the moral point of view, would be equivalent to suicide. For Ahad Ha'Am, as for Sokolow and the rest of their colleagues,[90] it was quite clear that, at this point in time, Weizmann was indeed indispensable.

The following day Weizmann informed his colleagues that he was retracting his resignation. He would remain in office until such time as the government would make its declaration.[91] C. P. Scott, Weizmann's closest and most loyal non-Jewish patron throughout the war, reiterated in his own, typically brief style, the sentiment of the Zionist activists: "A rumour reached me . . . that you were resigning your position as head of the Zionist organization in this country—that would be a real misfortune—so far as I can judge . . . you are the only statesman among them."[92] Weizmann explained that some of his colleagues had begun "to introduce Soviet tactics into the Zionist movement" for which he did not wish to be responsible; this is why he had threatened to resign, with the desired effect "of sobering them down."[93] The wily editor replied with relief and admiration: "I am glad you are keeping your people in order—a la Kerensky!—and not leaving them leaderless."[94]

Indeed, for a brief period, relations between most of the activists had been repaired. "Vera went on a two-week vacation," recorded Tolkowsky in his diary on September 7, "no doubt this will have a beneficial impact [on Weizmann]."[95] Indeed, despite their disagreements, they were all fond of Weizmann and he of them. When he felt lonely he called to invite them to visit—probably while Vera was away—and on such evenings would recount childhood stories or entertain them with Yiddish songs.[96] Even Sacher wrote Weizmann a conciliatory letter on the eve of the Jewish New Year.[97] In reply, Weizmann tried to convince the skeptical journalist that their most dangerous enemies were not the people in government he was negotiating with; these people tried their best, even if they were sometimes slow to grasp matters. Rather, it was the opposition of the Jewish anti-Zionists they now had to worry about.[98]

Weizmann was not at first fully aware of the force of the anti-Zionist opposition. At a meeting of the Political Committee on August 28, 1917, the discussion focused on what the Zionist demands would include once the British declaration had been issued, and a subcommittee was constituted to consider drafting the appropriate memorandum.[99] Both the Zionists and their supporters in the war cabinet and its secretariat were so certain of the outcome of the war cabinet meeting on September 3, 1917, that they did not adequately prepare for it. Arthur Balfour and Lloyd George were away on vacation and thus did not take part in the meeting; the prime minister contracted ptomaine poisoning and did not return to London until the last week of September. Even Ronald Graham, who had constantly played such a crucial role in promoting the Zionists' interests, was on vacation and could not advocate their cause behind the scenes.

In Lloyd George's absence, Andrew Bonar Law presided at the meeting. Though he was later charged by Scott and Wickham Steed as having opposed a pro-Zionist declaration,[100] the minutes do not reveal such an attitude. They do show that Edwin Montagu objected vehemently to any description of Palestine as the home of the Jewish people in the three drafts presented—Rothschild's, Balfour's, and Milner's. A suggestion that the matter be postponed was strongly opposed by Lord Robert Cecil, the acting secretary of state for foreign affairs. He pointed out that this was a question on which the Foreign Office had been very strongly pressed for a long time. Cecil drew attention to the importance of the Zionist organization in the United States, the support of which would substantially assist the cause of the Allies. "To do nothing," said Cecil, "was to risk a direct breach with them."[101]

In the end it was decided that the views of President Woodrow Wilson should be obtained on the desirability, in principle, without reference to the wording of any of the drafts, of a pro-Zionist declaration.[102] As instructed, Cecil cabled to Colonel Edward M. House the following day: "We are being pressed here for a declaration of sympathy with the Zionist movement and I should be very grateful if you felt able to ascertain unofficially if the President favours such a declaration."[103]

House took his time before replying. The form of the question put to him by Cecil did nothing to allay his suspicion that the British might wish to involve the United States in a joint defense of their position in Egypt, though he treated it as a matter in which the British were primarily concerned. House's advice to the president was that "there are many dangers lurking in it, and if I were the British, I would be chary about going too definitely into that business."[104]

In his cable to Cecil on September 11, 1917, House pointed out that the president had been staying with him at his summer home for two days and he had delayed his reply in order to discuss the matter thoroughly with Wilson. He could now state that in the president's opinion "the time is not opportune for any definite statement further perhaps than one of sympathy provided it can be made without conveying any real commitment. Things are in such a state of flux at [the] moment that he does not consider it advisable to go further."[105] President Wilson, backed by House's own inclination, was in effect advising the British to follow his example and hold off on further postwar commitments until the war ended or some other indefinite future time. The British, Balfour among them, understood this cable as an American veto of the proposed declaration.

These events took place without prior notice to the Zionists, or to Weizmann personally, who was then embroiled in the serious differences with his own constituency. On September 8, Weizmann met with Graham's deputy, Sir George Clerk, who—perhaps on orders from Cecil—failed to inform Weizmann on what had transpired at the cabinet meeting. Thus on the following day Weizmann suggested that the British government might want to issue a declaration on the eve of the Jewish New Year a week hence.[106] Probably only on September 9 or 10, at a meeting with Leopold Amery and William Ormsby-Gore, both members of the war cabinet secretariat, did Weizmann hear for the first time the details of what had transpired at the meeting of September 3. Alarmed, he brought the matter before the Political Committee on September 11; his suggestion to cable Louis Brandeis for help was accepted.[107] In the meantime Graham returned from his vacation, and, with his permission and assistance, Weizmann launched a series of urgent pleas to his American contacts, and to Brandeis in particular, for their aid in a situation in which the future prospects of Zionism were critically involved. So, too, was his own future as a Zionist leader.

Weizmann pinned his hopes on Brandeis as the person most capable of influencing President Wilson. In addition to "assimilationist" objections in London, Weizmann cabled, President Wilson was said to be impeding British considerations because he viewed the time inopportune. In his cable—held back by the Foreign Office and therefore received by Brandeis only on September 19, a week after it was first composed—Weizmann also included the text of the statement proposed by Lord Rothschild in July. Though the war cabinet had considered a somewhat toned-down version, successively moderated by Balfour and Milner, this was not revealed to the Zionists at that time.[108] Brandeis then telephoned for an appointment with Colonel House and, together with Stephen Wise, visited him in New York on September 24.[109]

The only available account of the discussion—a brief entry in Colonel House's journal—naturally concentrates on the author's own role, his impressions and conclusions, with little direct information about the other participants. One can imagine, however, that the president's reported veto of the suggested British statement must have seemed at odds with the assurances the Zionists had received from the same source, not only to an enthusiast like Wise but to the sober Brandeis after his May 6 interview with Wilson. They evidently compared notes with Colonel House, whose journal records that he told them that "the President was willing to go further than I thought advisable" and that he "had advised him against a more definite statement than the one . . . cabled to Cecil." On comparing that text with the text Weizmann sent to Brandeis—which, together with the entire correspondence between the Zionists, House had been supplied copies by British intelligence—House, at least, ruled that they were "practically identical."

House then approved a series of cables that Brandeis sent to London on September 24, 1917, indicating on the basis of his previous conversations with Wilson and, "from expressions of opinion given to closest advisers" (i.e., Colonel House), that the president was in entire sympathy and Brandeis himself in hearty agreement, with the formula Weizmann had sent.[110] Thus, what had been interpreted by the Foreign Office and Weizmann as an American veto was redefined as a positive suggestion for the form of a British statement of sympathy for Zionism.

If this was a revision of the message originally intended by House, on certain other points Brandeis's May 6 interview with the president gave Brandeis no grounds to differ with House's restricted view of the official policy. The Zionists were fully aware of the president's unwillingness, at least for the time being, to make a public statement of his own, and they accepted it once more, explicitly, in framing the cables to be sent to London. Nor could they easily oppose House's request that they bring the French, Italian, and Russian governments as near the attitude of Great Britain and the United States as possible.[111]

On the first point, however, the Zionists were not satisfied simply to reassure Weizmann themselves and let the matter rest, as House proposed. They hoped for a direct assurance by the president to the British approving a Zionist statement but without making the commitment public, for they realized that such support might be crucial in London—as far as they understood Weizmann's needs—in view of the opposition that had developed.[112] The matter was raised by Brandeis with House at the end of September, but apparently without an immediate response. On the second point, Brandeis was in a position to refer to Sokolow's mission to Paris and Rome, and he also supplied House with a set of news clippings indicating Russian approval of Zionist aims—a matter in which House continued to show a special interest in light of his talks with the Russian ambassador about the new Russian doubts concerning Turkish partition.[113]

Throughout the summer of 1917 House continued to be interested in the possibility of a separate peace with Turkey, and the American Zionists had to respect the limits this preoccupation imposed on their ability to apply pressure to the administration. Henry Morgenthau, whose new interest in keeping Turkey-in-Asia intact was becoming more anti-Zionist in tendency, was no longer considered a useful channel for government approaches to the Turks. His successor as ambassador in Constantinople, Abram Elkus, who had returned from the field, was ready to take up the task instead, if House desired. Elkus, like Morgenthau, had been a leading member of Stephen Wise's Free Synagogue, and he told the Zionists that he was ready to make a public avowal of his support. Clearly neither he nor the leading American Zionists considered his Zionist sympathy incompatible with his prospective service in the negotiation of a separate peace with Turkey. Brandeis, however, advised that House be consulted before Elkus's pro-Zionist statement was decided on. House promptly vetoed the idea, and the Zionists were obliged to accept the decision with good grace—though in the end no Elkus mission to the Turks was ever launched.[114]

In England, Weizmann watched the developing situation with growing strain. Not only did the United States still fall short of the support he felt he needed, but the Russian Zionists' response to his pleas was disappointing in spite of the positive reactions he communicated to his British and American contacts. Weizmann's urgent arguments failed to move the Russian leader, Yehiel Tschlenow, to give up the fixed policy of Zionist neutrality in favor of reliance on a single power—England.[115]

On September 24, 1917, Tschlenow wrote to Weizmann and Sokolow that the Russian Zionists would not be prepared to come out, as they had been pressed to do, in favor of a Jewish Palestine under British protection in the absence of clearer and more positive pledges from the British government. Tschlenow also demanded to know whether sufficient thought had been given to the situation that would arise should the war end without the Turks having been expelled from Palestine. He believed that the Zionists could count on the support of the Russian government.[116]

A few months earlier, Weizmann and, to a lesser degree, Sokolow, were reprimanded once again by the Smaller Actions Committee, meeting in Copenhagen at the end of July, for their breach of Zionist neutrality. Arthur Hantke conveyed the dissatisfaction of the executive: "The entire work of Weizmann and his colleagues is undertaken in too partisan an English direction. . . . Weizmann's statement at the conference of the English Zionist Federation [on May 20, 1917], fills the Jewish public with expectations which bear no relation to that which had been accomplished [in England]. Finally, Weizmann and Sokolow have operated much too independently, without consultation with the SAC or the committee in the Hague."[117]

Thus, during the months of August and September 1917, as he looked around him to assess the measure of support he could count on to push the declaration through, Weizmann found little of it in the Zionist world, while his own close circle had also begun to question his judgment on certain key issues. One person who did not question Weizmann's un-mitigated pro-British policy was Aaron Aaronsohn. But a conflict had been brewing between the London leadership and the headstrong Pal-estinian over the disbursement of monies to aid the Yishuv. Mark Sykes's suggestion in spring 1917 that Weizmann appoint Aaronsohn as his rep-resentative in Cairo was not followed up by Weizmann. The latter did not know about Aaronsohn's intelligence work for the British, though by the summer of 1917 Weizmann and his colleagues suspected as much. In any case, they were not entirely comfortable with entrusting large sums of money, which they received from the United States and Russia, to Aaronsohn's sole discretion. Instead, they suggested that the Alex-andria-Palestine Committee, headed by Zeev Gluskin, a Palestinian vint-ner, and the Special Committee for Relief of Jews in Palestine, formed on Aaronsohn's initiative and headed by Jacques Mosseri in Cairo, be unified, to be headed by Mosseri and Gluskin with Aaronsohn as sec-retary and executive officer.[118]

Weizmann and Sokolow had great confidence in Gluskin, whereas the British authorities in Egypt had complete faith in Aaronsohn and there-fore allowed money for Palestine to be handled only by the Special Committee in Cairo.[119] Complicating matters was Aaronsohn's strong dislike of Gluskin, with whom he refused to cooperate on any basis.[120] After a lively exchange of cables between Weizmann and Aaronsohn—facilitated through British channels—Aaronsohn finally wrote Weiz-mann two letters on August 15 and 25, 1917, protesting in the strongest terms against the London Zionist leaders' attempts to force their Alex-andria nominees on the Special Committee in Cairo.[121] Ronald Graham, who saw the letters, referred to them as "violent, not to say hysteri-cal."[122] The British tried for a while, unsuccessfully, to mediate among the Zionists. Exasperated, Sir Ronald wrote to Sir Reginald Wingate, who had been watching these internal squabbles in Egypt at close range, "I wish that on this and other questions the Jewish community was less divided."[123]

Thus, when Aaronsohn arrived in London on October 1, 1917, he was already angry with the London Zionist leadership. For his part, Weiz-mann did his best to smooth Aaronsohn's feelings—not always success-fully. Aaronsohn often felt excluded and insulted and in turn insulted other members of the Political Committee. His relations with Sokolow had not been good even before the war, and the two avoided each other. Aaronsohn's presence in London considerably heightened the tensions that already existed within the group of political activists, though he and Weizmann seem to have settled on a relationship based on cordiality, respect, and wariness.[124] In addition to sharing the belief that England was Zionism's most effective and natural ally, they also both supported Jabotinsky and the Jewish legion. Both, moreover, held a condescending attitude toward the more contemplative Sokolow and Tschlenow while, by contrast, considering themselves decisive men of action.[125]

In England, meanwhile, the Zionist drive for the declaration was encountering resistance both from the Jewish side and from the cautious and skeptical British civil service. Montagu, too, was not content to let matters rest after his partial victory at the war cabinet meeting. In a letter to Robert Cecil on September 14, 1917—and like the former document also distributed to members of the war cabinet—Montagu claimed that the majority of British Jews were anti-Zionist; his evidence was the more or less balanced vote on the issue of Zionism at the Board of Deputies of June 17. Though not a member of the war cabinet, Montagu was well briefed, and he also made reference to President Wilson's noncommittal cable as transmitted by House. He also came back to a common anti-Zionist charge that had been made on occasion by Lucien Wolf, namely that Zionism was a movement of foreign origin, led by foreign Jews: "It was founded by Theodor Herzl, an Austrian, . . . his successor as leader of the Zionist movement was David Wolffsohn of Koeln, who was succeeded by Otto Warburg of Berlin. . . . Jews of foreign birth have played a very large part in the Zionist movement in England. Among its best known leaders in England are Dr. Gaster, a native of Roumania, Dr. Hertz, a native of Austria, and Dr. Chaim Weizmann, who is, I believe, a native of Russia." Montagu concluded by stating that a British declaration "would be felt as a cruel blow by the many English Jews who love England." He suggested a formula stating that Jews who wished to go to Palestine would receive the aid of the British government, which would also consider any suggestions made by Jewish or Zionist organizations.[126]

It is not clear whether the Zionists actually read Montagu's official documents, but they had heard enough from their various good contacts in the Foreign Office and war cabinet secretariat—transmitted chiefly via Weizmann—to know the gist of his arguments. In a letter to Louis Brandeis, Ahad Ha'Am commented: "Unfortunately . . . we must admit that there are still too many in our midst whose hearts, like those of Pharaoh, are hardened and whose eyes are blind to the 'signs' of the time. . . . We here are faced by the shameful spectacle of Jews doing their utmost to wreck the ancient hope of Israel for a national resurrection."[127]

Weizmann's rage was channeled into much more sarcastic prose when he wrote to Philip Kerr, the prime minister's trusted adviser:

The "dark forces" in English Jewry have again been at work and this time they have mobilised their great champion who although a great Hindu nationalist now, thought it his duty to combat Jewish Nationalism. It is—I confess—inconceivable to me, how British statesmen still attribute importance to the attitude of a few plutocratic Jews and allow their opinion to weigh against almost a unanimous expression of opinion of Jewish Democracy. Here we are after three years hard work, after having enlisted the sympathies practically of everyone who matters in England, faced again by opposition on the part of a handful of "Englishmen of the Jewish persuasion." . . . [The] declaration . . . is still hung up owing to opposition of a few Jews, whose only claim to Judaism is that they are working for its disappearance.

The fact that the British Government with all its sympathies towards national Judaism does not desire to give a definite expression to it, is doing considerable harm not only to Zionism, but also to the interests of the British Government.[128]

Lloyd George was about to return to London on September 23 when Weizmann asked Kerr to arrange a meeting with the prime minister "for a few minutes it may help to clear it all up."[129] In the meantime, Weizmann met on September 19 with Arthur Balfour, who provided some more details about the September 3 cabinet meeting. Balfour also promised to see Lloyd George on the matter.[130] Yet, two days later Balfour received Lord Rothschild in his office and was more discouraging. Rothschild reported to Weizmann: "Balfour began, before I could open my lips, by saying he had seen you, and that he had told you that in his and the Prime Minister's absence, the Cabinet had discussed the matter and had concluded the moment was not opportune for a declaration." Balfour—who should have known from his staff about Weizmann's contacts with Brandeis—also urged Rothschild to get the American Zionists, Brandeis in particular, to bring pressure on President Wilson to break the impasse.[131] A few days later Balfour minuted on a memorandum Ronald Graham had written to Lord Hardinge urging a declaration that would be at least as strong as the Cambon letter to Sokolow: "Yes. But as this question was (in my absence) decided by the Cabinet against the Zionists, I cannot do anything until the decision is reversed."[132]

Lord Hardinge had a different view on the matter. His minute to the Graham memorandum read: "I think we might and ought to go as far as the French."[133] In a letter to Sir Reginald Wingate of September 21, Graham noted that Lloyd George, Arthur Balfour, and Robert Cecil were "all in strong sympathy with Zionist ideas and aspirations," but owing to Montagu's opposition and Wilson's coolness to the idea of a declaration, "we ought not to move too fast."[134] Mark Sykes, too, gave his views in a paper setting the background for the conflict between Zionists and their opponents and pronouncing Zionism "a positive force." He suggested that either the United States or Great Britain be chosen to govern Palestine, guaranteeing equal rights to all religious groups.[135] Jan Smuts, since June 1917 a member of the war cabinet, met with Weizmann on September 21 for one hour. He assured Weizmann of his sympathy and asked for literature on Zionism.[136] Philip Kerr, too, spoke to Lloyd George, who promised to support the declaration; and on September 28, 1917—the cable from Brandeis assuring Wilson's support already in hand—C. P. Scott contrived a three-minute meeting between Weizmann and the prime minister, who ordered his secretary, in Weizmann's presence, to place the question of the Zionist declaration on the agenda of the next war cabinet meeting.[137] On October 1, Weizmann

managed to get an interview with George Barnes, the Labour party representative to the war cabinet. With the exception of Lord Curzon, he
had thus managed to meet and impress most of the important members
of the cabinet.

Contributing to the perceived urgency of the subject were reports,
conveyed by the Zionists and the British press, that the Germans were
contemplating measures of their own to persuade the Jews that only the
victorious Central Powers would grant the Jewish people a new status
in Palestine.[138] Before the cabinet meeting, not wishing to leave anything to chance, Weizmann sent in a joint statement with Lord Rothschild setting forth the Zionist arguments and objecting strongly to the
"one-sided manner" in which the views of Jewry had been permitted to
be presented through Montagu's participation in the last cabinet session.[139]

When the cabinet met on October 4, 1917, Montagu was again present, but so, too, were Arthur Balfour and Lloyd George, who presided
over the meeting. The cabinet was now presented with a revised draft,
hastily drawn up by Leopold Amery at Lord Milner's request some thirty
minutes before the deliberations commenced. Instructed to take account
of the objections raised in the preceding debates, Amery drew on letters
written by Lord Rothschild and others to the *Times* in answer to Alexander's and Montefiore's open letter, in which claims that Zionism en-
dangered the citizenship of British Jews or the rights of Arabs were denied.[140] The draft Amery composed, in language drawn from these sources
and Milner's earlier draft, read:

> His Majesty's Government views with favour the establishment in Palestine
> of a national home for the Jewish race and will use its best endeavours to
> facilitate the achievement of this object, it being clearly understood that
> nothing shall be done which may prejudice the civil and religious rights of
> existing non-Jewish communities in Palestine, or the rights and political sta-
> tus enjoyed in any other country by such Jews who are fully contented with
> their existing nationality.[141]

Two final words—"and citizenship"— were added at the cabinet meeting.

Balfour opened the debate. In the ten days since he minuted his
equivocating remark on Graham's memorandum, he had become firm
in his resolve to support a pro-Zionist declaration wholeheartedly. His
remarks, as recorded in the minutes, also took account of the opposition
to Zionism:

> This Movement, though opposed by a number of wealthy Jews in this coun-
> try, had behind it the support of a majority of Jews, at all events in Russia
> and America. . . . He saw nothing inconsistent between the establishment
> of a Jewish national focus in Palestine and the complete assimilation and
> absorption of Jews into the nationality of other countries. Just as English
> emigrants to the United States became, either in the first or subsequent

generations, American nationals, so, in future, should a Jewish citizenship be established in Palestine, would Jews become either Englishmen, Americans, Germans, or Palestinians. What was at the back of the Zionist movement was the intense national consciousness held by certain members of the Jewish race. They regarded themselves as one of the great historic races of the world, whose original home was Palestine, and these Jews had a passionate longing to regain once more this ancient national home.[142]

It was Montagu's turn, and once again he forcefully argued his position. What was more disturbing—from the point of view of the Zionists and their supporters—was that Lord Curzon—a former viceroy of India and now lord president of the Council—"urged strong objections upon practical grounds." Curzon, who had visited Palestine before the war, stated that "the country was, for the most part, barren and desolate; . . . a less propitious seat for the future Jewish race could not be imagined." Moreover—and this seems to have been his more urgent worry— "How was it proposed to get rid of the existing majority of Mussulman inhabitants and to introduce the Jews in their place?" In any case, how many Jews would actually wish to come to Palestine, and how will they earn their livelihood? He suggested that granting Jews already in Palestine equal civil and religious rights was quite sufficient; repatriating the Jews on a large scale was "sentimental idealism, which would never be realised and His Majesty's Government should have nothing to do with it."[143]

At one point during the proceedings, possibly after Montagu and Curzon had made their statements, it was suggested that Weizmann be called in to answer the various objections raised. He could not be found, though he was at that very moment close by, in Captain Amery's office.[144] One can only speculate whether the outcome of the meeting would have taken a different turn had Weizmann made a presentation. In the event, the cabinet, instead of coming to a decision on the matter, again proposed to consult President Wilson.

In view of Montagu's strenuous opposition and the promise once made to consult the Conjoint Foreign Committee, reconstituted as the Joint Foreign Committee, it was agreed to solicit instead the opinions of a representative group of non-Zionist and Zionist Jews. The list of non-Zionists to be approached for a statement was provided by Montagu and Sir Lionel Abrahams. They included Sir Stuart Samuel, the new chairman of the Board of Deputies; Leonard J. Cohen, the chairman of the Jewish Board of Guardians; Claude Montefiore, president of the Anglo-Jewish Association; and Sir Philip Magnus, MP. Weizmann suggested Dr. Joseph Hertz, the chief rabbi of England, as well as Lord Rothschild, Sokolow, and himself.[145] The suggestions were accepted and the requests were solicited by the cabinet secretary, Maurice Hankey, on October 6.[146]

Montagu had, in the meantime, shortly after the cabinet meeting of October 4, written directly to Lloyd George. Apparently referring to

Weizmann, Montagu half-threatened (intimating resignation), half-pleaded with the prime minister:

> It is a matter of deep regret to me . . . that you are being . . . misled by a foreigner, a dreamer, an idealist . . . who . . . sweeps aside all practical difficulties with a view to enlisting your sympathy on behalf of his cause. . . .
>
> I don't want to make difficulties. If I were to resign now I believe that after what has happened . . . a match would have been put to the Indian fire. . . .
>
> It seems almost inconceivable that I should have to give it up [his office] for something wholly unconnected with India at all, and yet what am I to do? I believe firmly that if you make a statement about Palestine as the national home for Jews, every anti-Semitic organisation and newspaper will ask what right a Jewish Englishman, with the status at best of a naturalised foreigner, has to take a foremost part in the Government of the British Empire. Palestine is not now British. It belongs to our enemies. At the best it can never be part of the English Empire. The country for which I have worked ever since I left the University—England—the country for which my family have fought, tells me that my national home, if I desire to go there, therefore my natural home, is Palestine. How can I maintain my position?[147]

Montagu did not sit back, waiting for the answer he requested from the prime minister. He expended much effort and time, in the days prior to his departure for India, gathering as much evidence as he could as to the harmful impact a Zionist declaration would have on British interests in India, and he submitted to the cabinet the names of prominent English Jewish anti-Zionists who agreed with his views.[148]

The decision by the cabinet to solicit more opinions brought Weizmann again into a state of alarmed indignation.[149] The Milner-Amery draft itself held some disappointments; it contained neither the reference to the historic title that Zionists claimed ("Palestine . . . *reconstituted* as the national home of the Jewish people") nor the clause implying, if not conferring, a special status for the Zionist organization—both present in earlier drafts. It was acceptable, nevertheless, as the best then obtainable, and the Zionists were prepared to do vigorous battle to secure it. What alarmed them, and made a battle seem necessary, was the provision to poll non-Zionist as well as Zionist opinions.[150] The reference of the matter to the American president also aroused some uncertainty.

The English Zionists at once mounted a campaign of public meetings and mass resolutions that, together with the balance of opinions received by those the government consulted, as per Weizmann's suggestion, left an impression of strong support in British Jewry for the Zionist demands.[151] They also, through Weizmann, appealed at once for similar action as well as for urgent intercession with the U.S. government by Brandeis and the other American Zionist leaders. Weizmann, moreover, sent letters requesting mass demonstrations and written support from Jewish leaders in Russia, Australia, France, and elsewhere.[152] On Octo-

ber 23, he was able to send Ronald Graham a list of some 250 representative Jewish bodies in the United Kingdom that, as a result of the campaign launched by the EZF, had passed resolutions favoring the
"reconstitution of Palestine as the National Home of the Jewish People."[153]

This strong demonstration of support from official Jewish organizations was coupled with a weakening of resolve and commitment to obtain a declaration on the part of some members of the British Palestine
Committee. Some of them were discouraged by what they considered to
be British indecision and insincerity. They continued, moreover, to be
angry at Weizmann's personal support for Jabotinsky, and other personal conflicts continued to linger and came to the fore when it seemed
that the fate of a British declaration was in doubt. As usual, it was Harry
Sacher who sounded the harshest note as he wrote to Leon Simon: "I
agree that this Declaration business is of no very great importance and I
do my best with my own little circle to keep the sense of proportion. It's
not hard, because they take a pretty similar view. I incline to think also
that W[eizmann] has outlived his usefulness as a Zionist leader. He has
got to break with Jab[otinsky] or with us."[154]

Disagreement over the Jewish legion and Weizmann's attempt to draw
Jabotinsky into the Political Committee continued to raise the level of
frustration and discontent, with some members of Weizmann's circle
claiming that "Jab[otinsky] is the tail that wags C[haim] W[eizmann]."[155]
Thus, while Leon Simon responded to Weizmann's overture and agreed
to rejoin the Political Committee,[156] Joseph Cowen threatened to resign
because of the way Jabotinsky had been treated by Sacher.[157] The tensions among his closest advisers must certainly have taken their toll, but
Weizmann continued to maintain the air of a man in full command of
his forces.

By mid-October, Weizmann—together with Ahad Ha'Am and the stylistic assistance of Wickham Steed[158]—had composed his reply to Maurice Hankey's letter asking for his view on the draft declaration. Weizmann could not refrain from starting his letter with yet another attack
on "those Jews who by education and social connections have lost touch
with the real spirit animating the Jewish people." He then made two
suggestions for rewording the declaration: "re-establishment" instead of
"establishment"—a suggestion also made by Sokolow and not accepted—and "Jewish people" instead of "Jewish race," a suggestion
that was accepted in the final draft. Weizmann also suggested rewording a passage that could be interpreted as saying that those Jews who
will not emigrate to Palestine would totally dissociate themselves from
the Jewish national home. This suggestion was also made by Hertz, and
the final part of the last sentence of the Milner-Amery draft was in the
end simply dropped.[159]

Even before receiving the draft declaration from the cabinet secretary,

Weizmann sent a long letter to Brandeis in which he described Montagu's attempts to sabotage the British declaration and asked for the support of American Jewry for the Zionist position.[160] After he received a
copy of the Milner-Amery draft declaration, Weizmann cabled it to Brandeis on October 9.[161] In the meantime, the British government acted expeditiously as well. On this occasion its approach to its American ally
was clearly intended, by the form it took, to elicit a positive, favorable
reply. On October 6, 1917, two days after the cabinet session, Balfour
cabled Colonel House, this time including the text of the declaration
under discussion.[162] A second cable, sent at the same time, called attention to reported German overtures to the Zionists that made action
timely.[163] All these communications—Weizmann's and, of course, the
official British messages—reached House's desk through his regular British intelligence contacts.

On October 13, House went to Washington to confer with President
Wilson.[164] His journal entry for the day mentions, in regard to the Ottoman area, "We spoke of . . . the partition or non-partition of Turkey." At that time House was still actively considering the possibility of
a separate peace with Turkey and had recently spoken with Elkus about
employing his services for the purpose. He also spoke with the Russian
ambassador about the desirability of leaving Turkey "intact" after the
war. The president's reaction, however, hardly encouraged either idea:
"The President suggested the making of another speech in which to say
that our people must not be deceived by Germany's apparent willingness to give up Belgium and Alsace Lorraine, for it would leave her
impregnable in both Austria and Turkey."

House nevertheless was able to get the president's agreement that if
he made such a speech—which House carefully did not recommend—
he should not confine himself to the formula he originally intended: that
"Turkey should become effaced, and . . . the disposition of it should be
left to the peace conference." To this House proposed to add—and the
president agreed—"that Turkey must not be partitioned among the belligerents, but must become autonomous in its several parts according to
racial lines."

House's journal for October 13 does not mention one matter that must
have come up in their discussion—the British request for an opinion on
their proposed pro-Zionist declaration. On October 16, following his return to New York, House received in the morning mail Wilson's note of
October 13, evidently written after their meeting: "I find in my pocket
the memorandum you gave me about the Zionist movement. I am afraid
I did not say to you that I concurred in the formula suggested by the
other side. I do, and would be obliged if you would let them know it."
House then sent through British channels the following message: "Colonel House put formula before President, who approves of it but asks
that no mention of his approval shall be made when His Majesty's Gov-

ernment makes formula public, as he had arranged that American Jews shall then ask him for his approval, which he will give publicly here."

In the meantime, Weizmann's cable to Brandeis with the text of the proposed declaration was received by the justice on October 14. Brandeis sent the text on to Wise and DeHaas in New York and asked them to see Colonel House immediately. They did so on October 16. By then Wilson's note had been received and acted upon. All that remained for House to do was to inform the Zionists that their wishes had been anticipated and that no publicity must be made of the president's cooperation in this matter with the Entente governments. The president, House said, would later express his approval in response to an inquiry by "leading Jews"—which, of course, Wilson did in reply to Wise only much later, many months after the Balfour Declaration was issued.

DeHaas, in reporting the interview to Brandeis, asked what should be the response to Weizmann's request for public pressure by American Jews in support of the British Zionists in their still pending battle for the declaration. Brandeis, perhaps sharing House's view that if the Zionists had the governments on their side they need no longer defend themselves against non-Zionists, decided that the Americans should take no further action.[165] Brandeis's cable to Weizmann of October 17, 1917, simply states, "President has sent London message of approval but believes public declaration by him would be injudicious."[166]

Some American suggestions, however, were introduced into the text, and Wise regretted that Brandeis had not been consulted before the president agreed.[167] The Americans conveyed to Colonel House their objections to the section of the draft declaration that referred to the Jews as a "race" and, by its assurances to "such Jews who are fully contented with their existing nationality," seemed to base Zionist claims on a principle of discontent not shared by these American Zionists with regard to their country.[168] House does not seem to have sent on the American observations. In any case, Weizmann and others who were consulted by the war cabinet had made the same general suggestions for revisions as the Americans themselves desired.[169] It would seem, moreover, that the Americans sent their suggestions to Weizmann and Sokolow much too late to have made an impact.[170]

All seemed set for government approval of a pro-Zionist declaration. Not only were the Zionists anxious for this final step; the Foreign Office, too, was impatient. Once again Ronald Graham reminded Arthur Balfour on October 24—more than three months after Lord Rothschild had first submitted the Zionist draft—that

> further delay will have a deplorable result and may jeopardize the whole Jewish situation. At the present moment uncertainty as regards the attitude of His Majesty's Government on this question is growing into suspicion, and not only are we losing the very valuable co-operation of the Zionist forces in Russia and America, but we may bring them into antagonism with

us and throw the Zionists into the arms of the Germans who would only be too ready to welcome this opportunity. . . . The French have already given an assurance of sympathy to the Zionists on the same lines as is now proposed for His Majesty's Government, though in rather more definite terms. The Italian Government and the Vatican have expressed their sympathy and we know that President Wilson is sympathetic and is prepared to make a declaration at the proper moment.

Graham then went on to discuss the important role attributed to Russian Jewry in determining the political alliance of the Russian government. Their sympathies were currently with the Germans, but an assurance by England might turn them around. He then continued with a promise Weizmann must have made countless times in the offices of government officials: "The moment this assurance is granted the Zionist Jews are prepared to start an active pro-Ally propaganda throughout the world. Dr. Weizmann, who is a most able and energetic propagandist, is prepared to proceed himself to Russia and to take charge of the campaign. Propaganda in America is also most necessary. I earnestly trust that unless there is a very good reason to the contrary the assurance from His Majesty's Government should be given at once."[171]

Balfour no longer needed to be convinced, as is clear from his minute to the prime minister the following day that the Zionists "have reasonable ground for complaint."[172] Weizmann, for one, was increasingly nervous. He had heard rumors that the matter would come up before the war cabinet on October 23; it was actually on the agenda for October 25 but was postponed to give Lord Curzon time to complete a memorandum on the subject.[173] On hearing the news that day, Weizmann felt he was at the end of his tether. "I shall never in my life forget this day," he wrote to Ahad Ha'Am. "I was awaiting the decision in the morning and it ended with a postponement. I went wearily to the Laboratory and found that there had been a fire and that half of it was burnt out. . . . I shall be in touch with you when I have recovered a little."[174] Wickham Steed, head of the Foreign Department of the *Times,* also became alarmed at the delay and called for a British declaration in a leading article that employed terms similar to those used by Graham in internal Foreign Office correspondence.[175]

The same day on which Steed published his article in the *Times*— October 26—Lord Curzon finally distributed his memorandum to his colleagues. Like Herbert Samuel more than two years earlier, Curzon also titled his paper "The Future of Palestine." He focused on two issues. One was the meaning of the phrase "a National Home for the Jewish race in Palestine," and he showed the many contradictions in statements made by supporters of Zionism as to whether a Jewish state was the final aim of the movement. The bulk of his arguments—as was the case in his statements at the cabinet meeting of October 4—related to the question of successful realization for such a British policy. Curzon pointed to the poverty of Palestine, its lack of resources, and the need for prolonged and patient toil of its soil by people who had no agricultural tradition. Then one had to consider what would become of the half million Arabs who "will not be content either to be expropriated for Jewish immigrants, or to act merely as hewers of wood and drawers of water to the latter." How could such a country, then, absorb a large number of Jewish immigrants or be called a national home of the Jewish people?[176]

Mark Sykes, who had shepherded the Zionists ever since his meeting with them on February 7, 1917, was given another chance to rise to their defense. On October 30—possibly after consulation with the much-admired Aaron Aaronsohn, who had arrived in London at the beginning of that month—Sykes submitted a long paper relating almost exclusively to Palestine's capacity to absorb a large immigration. He contradicted Curzon's assertions and pointed to the rich agricultural potential of the country. He cited many examples of the enormous strides that had been made in the cultivation of oranges, vegetables, and grapes. He argued that the population of Palestine could be doubled in seven years, provided the necessary security and infrastructure were supplied.[177]

On October 31, 1917, at the war cabinet meeting, Balfour made it quite clear that he wanted to issue a statement endorsing Zionist aims.[178] The foreign secretary stated that "he understood that there were considerable differences of opinion among experts regarding the possibility of the settlement of any large population in Palestine, but he was informed that if Palestine were scientifically developed, a very much larger population could be sustained than had existed during the period of Turkish misrule." In any case, as he observed in his opening remarks, everyone (including Curzon) seemed to agree that the most important underlying reasons for a declaration were of a diplomatic and political nature. As to the meaning of the words "national home," that "did not necessarily involve the early establishment of an independent Jewish state, which was a matter for gradual development in accordance with the ordinary laws of political evolution." He also felt that Zionism would not hinder the process of Jewish assimilation in Western countries.[179]

Edwin Montagu had sailed for India some two weeks earlier, and it was left to Curzon single-handedly to hold the banner of opposition. He was now much less forceful than at the last cabinet meeting that had discussed the declaration or even than he had been a few days earlier in his memorandum. He admitted the force of diplomatic and political considerations, and he conceded that the majority of the Jews were Zionists. In any case, he did not approve of Montagu's attitude. His objections centered on his—as he saw it—more sober assessment of conditions in Palestine, and he feared Britain was raising unrealistic expectations. The Christian and Muslim Holy Places, moreover, had to be protected, and if this were to be done effectively, how could the Jews build up their own political capital? He agreed to some declaration of sympathy but asked that the language be guarded. With this statement all present deemed that the objections to a pro-Zionist declaration had been removed. The war cabinet then authorized the secretary of state for foreign affairs to take a suitable opportunity of making such a declaration.[180]

On November 2, 1917, Balfour sent to Lord Rothschild the declaration that bears Balfour's name, describing it as a "declaration of sympathy with Jewish Zionist aspirations"—in this way satisfying at least nominally the Zionist interest in being recognized as the accredited agent representing the Jews in negotiating and carrying out the policy foreshadowed in the declaration. In its familiar final form, the Balfour Declaration reads:

> His Majesty's Government view with favour the establishment in Palestine of a national home for the Jewish people, and will use their best endeavours to facilitate the achievement of this object, it being clearly understood that nothing shall be done which may prejudice the civil and religious rights of existing non-Jewish communities in Palestine, or the rights and political status enjoyed by Jews in any other country.[181]

While the war cabinet began its deliberations behind closed doors, at noon on October 31, Weizmann was anxiously waiting a few feet away, no doubt wondering whether this time, too, he would be disappointed. Some two hours later, Sykes came out, exclaiming, as Weizmann recorded in his autobiography: "Dr. Weizmann, it's a boy!" In the hindsight of some thirty years, Weizmann wrote that this was not quite the boy he had expected,[182] but on that momentous day and for a long time to come he felt he had advanced the cause of Zionism a great step forward. On more than one occasion in the past few months he had frankly acknowledged that he had done most of the political work leading to the declaration, often without consultation with others. At one point he even suggested that he manage the Political Committee as a dictator.[183] He knew well that if Zionist efforts failed, the blame would have been his, the Political Committee notwithstanding. He also understood well that a successful outcome would be interpreted as his personal achievement.

Conscious of his historical role, Weizmann had insisted since the summer of 1917 that proper archives be maintained by the Zionist office;[184] he hoped that such an archive would make possible the writing of a well-documented history of the Zionist-British negotiations.[185] Clearly he would have preferred Balfour's letter of November 2 to have been addressed to himself rather than to Lord Rothschild. Had he been in England on July 18—rather than in Paris on the final leg of the Morgenthau mission—he might have been the person submitting the Zionist draft declaration to Balfour and to whom, in turn, the famous declaration was directed. As it was, Lord Rothschild had asked in his letter transmitting the draft declaration that "His Majesty's . . . message" be sent to him. When the government was ready to send the final declaration to the

Zionists, Lord Hardinge pointed out, "The publication will depend upon Lord Rothschild to whom the declaration of the Government will be made in a reply to his original letter."[186] Weizmann had to content himself with a private letter from Ronald Graham, his most reliable ally in the Foreign Office, who on November 1 sent Weizmann his warm congratulations, to which he appended, "for [Weizmann's] private information," the text of the declaration.[187] Thus, ironically, one of Weizmann's best-known political achievements is associated with a member of the Rothschild family who was, until he met Weizmann, far removed from Zionist affairs.

Nothing, however, could have dampened Weizmann's happiness when the news of the declaration was conveyed to him by Sir Mark. He rushed to 175 Piccadilly, where Simon Marks and Shmuel Tolkowsky were waiting to hear the news. They immediately cabled to Manchester, to Baron Edmond de Rothschild, and to others. Marks went to James de Rothschild's residence to convey the news personally, whereas Weizmann and Tolkowsky took a taxi to Ahad Ha'Am's home. Tolkowsky recorded in his diary that on route Weizmann "behaved like a child: he embraced me for a long time, placed his head on my shoulder and pressed my hand, repeating over and over *mazel tov.*"[188] Ahad Ha'Am was just as excited, by the news and by the fact that Weizmann had come personally to bring it to him.[189]

That evening the Weizmanns gave an impromptu dinner party with Tolkowsky, Jabotinsky, and Eliezer Margolin, formerly a Russian-born Jewish pioneer in Palestine, now an officer in the Australian army. Just before they sat down to eat, they were joined by Vera in Weizmann's study and formed a circle to dance a hassidic dance;[190] it provided a welcome release to their pent-up anxieties and worries over the past few months. Later that evening Colonel Patterson also joined them, and the conversation naturally turned to the subject of a Jewish legion.[191] No doubt they must have also been excited by the news that on that very afternoon, after a difficult month-long battle, the British finally captured Beersheba. A few days later, on November 7, the British conquered Gaza, and by mid-November they were in control of Jaffa as well.

It was a period of great joy and hope for the Zionist and Jewish world.[192] The Balfour Declaration, together with the military conquests in Palestine, seemed to promise a great deal. It remained to be seen whether Lord Curzon was right about the declaration's raising expectations too high. Hearing that the declaration had been approved by the war cabinet, Weizmann went to thank Balfour. The foreign secretary responded: "Now we expect you to turn it into a success."[193] This would prove to be the Zionists' greatest challenge.

The Balfour Declaration has for a long time been considered Weizmann's greatest political achievement; even his political enemies had to concede that this feat captured the imagination of most Jews and had a force of its own. Though later historians—mostly those friendly to the cause of Zionism—have in hindsight questioned Weizmann's role in obtaining the declaration, in the immediate aftermath of the cabinet's decision there was little doubt in the minds of those who had observed the entire political process at close range as to who deserved most of the credit. On November 2, 1917, the day Balfour signed his letter to Lord Rothschild, one of Weizmann's longtime opponents, Leopold Greenberg, wrote to Weizmann:

> I am sure I did not say half or even much less of what I felt in regard to your wonderful success when I had the pleasure of seeing you this evening. You have performed miracles, especially having in mind surrounding circumstances and not only have you abundant justification for being proud of your accomplishment, but the Jewish People has manifest reason for being proud of you, one of its truest and best sons. Your victory so far should be an encouragement to you to carry on further for there is much to be done and only the beginning—great and glorious as it is—has been reached.[194]

Greenberg would hardly have gone out of his way to praise a man with whom he had so often in the past had profound ideological differences. The evidence available on Weizmann's political activities must have seemed clear-cut to him. The editor of the *Jewish Chronicle* maintained good contacts in government circles and was no doubt also kept informed by James Malcolm, Sykes's friend, whom he had introduced to Weizmann early in 1917.

Yet few knew as intimately what transpired behind the scenes as the editor of the *Manchester Guardian,* who a few days later wrote in response to a letter from Weizmann: "Heartiest congratulations on the great step forward of your movement. To you personally it will be a tremendous relief. . . . The movement owes almost everything to you."[195] Lord Rothschild, to whom Balfour's letter was addressed, saw the declaration as the joint personal achievement of Weizmann and Sokolow.[196] The American Zionists, however, who had been pressed into action by Weizmann, saw him—not his senior partner Sokolow or anyone else— as the Zionist most responsible for bringing about the declaration.[197] There were, of course, dozens, if not hundreds of letters and telegrams sent to Weizmann in the months that followed, praising his political and diplomatic acumen in the highest terms.[198]

As noted, historians have been divided on this issue. On one end of the spectrum we find a distinguished British historian stating that "Weizmann was the main creator of the National Home [because he secured the Balfour Declaration]. . . . It was in my opinion the greatest act of diplomatic statesmanship of the First World War."[199] Sir Charles Webster was in 1917 a staff officer in the Intelligence Directorate of the British War Office. One of his tasks was to study and appraise Zionism for the general staff, thus placing him in a position to evaluate Weizmann's statesmanship on the basis of close personal observation. In his magisterial work on the Balfour Declaration and in a subsequent lecture,

Leonard Stein, who had also been privileged to watch events at close range, has confirmed, though in somewhat more subdued tones, Sir Charles's evaluation.[200] Subsequent historians of a younger generation who have devoted full-length monographs to the origins of the Balfour Declaration have reached similar conclusions.[201]

On the other end of the spectrum one finds the Israeli scholar Mayir Vereté, whose influential article on the subject has greatly discounted Weizmann's role in the attainment of the Balfour Declaration. His interpretation seems to accord Sokolow's diplomatic efforts in Paris and Rome, culminating with the Cambon letter, greater importance than Weizmann's parallel efforts in England. Herbert Samuel's role as the first person to place the Zionist agenda before the cabinet early in 1915 is similarly highlighted. Vereté's thesis is that Weizmann was simply a convenient tool in the hands of British policymakers. His detailed and sophisticated analysis of the data lead him to conclude that Weizmann's role was incidental in the process that led to the declaration. Vereté clearly demonstrates the long-standing British interest in Palestine[202] and the specific reasons leading the British to make a public statement on behalf of the Zionists. One of these reasons was their desire to eliminate the French from Palestine, a position they were entitled to by virtue of the Sykes-Picot Agreement. Indeed, "had there been no Zionists in those days," asserts Vereté, "the British would have had to invent them."[203]

Vereté does not deny Weizmann's work in sounding out ministers and important British public figures, such as Sykes, Balfour, Lloyd George, Cecil, Smuts, and many other officials of various ranks in the Foreign Office, War Office, and cabinet secretariat. At the same time Vereté is unwilling to concede that Weizmann had a greater share in the work than Sokolow; nor does he think that the Balfour Declaration was the personal triumph of the Zionists, whether Weizmann or Sokolow. The British had their own reasons for granting the declaration; in Vereté's interpretation of the events they could be compared to "the lady who . . . was willing and only wanted to be seduced. Britain likewise willed Palestine, wanted the Zionists and courted them. Weizmann happened to come her way, talked to her to have the Zionists and go with them to Palestine, as only her they desired and to her they would be faithful. Britain was seduced. She was ready to be seduced by any Zionist of stature."[204]

Few historians joined Vereté's strong critique of the "Weizmann myth" until another Israeli historian, David Vital, followed his lead.[205] Though Vital declares that Weizmann "probably did more than anyone, even Sokolow, to persuade the British that the Zionists would, in the final analysis, serve their purposes," he asserts elsewhere that "Weizmann was more the epitome of the momentary alliance that was . . . in the making than its engineer," and that "in its two essentials . . . the British decision to couple Palestine with Zionism . . . was one to which the Zionists themselves had made no direct contribution."[206]

Not many historians have agreed with these conclusions—and for good
reason. The factors leading to the Balfour Declaration are so complex
and intertwined that a decisive, one-sided evaluation at either end of
the spectrum is clearly inaccurate. In the final analysis one can perhaps
be permitted to present a few observations that may lead to a more
nuanced evaluation than has been provided by either Charles Webster
or Mayir Vereté and those who have followed their respective analyses.

There is little doubt in the mind of all of the historians who have
occupied themselves with the origins of the Balfour Declaration that it
was meant, first and foremost, to serve British aims and interests. Sir
Edward Grey's proposal in March 1916, independent of Zionist pressure, clearly demonstrates the case; it shows that British policymakers
of the highest rank judged Zionism to be a potentially serious force worth
support and cultivation. As it turned out, Grey's timing was inauspi-
cious.

Throughout 1915 and 1916 Weizmann had no contact with either the
prime minister or the foreign secretary. He understood that the political
climate in England and abroad was not yet ripe for a pro-Zionist declaration. That moment arrived after Lloyd George assumed office as prime
minister, though not simply because "Lloyd George . . . had always
wanted to acquire Palestine for Britain"[207] or solely because Balfour had
pronounced himself a Zionist or because any number of other ministers
had declared themselves in sympathy with Zionism. Their personal and
deeply felt attachment to Jewish aspirations in the Holy Land would not
have been sufficient to move the British cabinet to issue the Balfour Declaration.

Until the end of October 1917, Balfour equivocated and did not press
for passage. The cabinet approved the issuance of a declaration after
being fully convinced that it was in its own best interests to do so. That
moment came late in the spring of 1917, when Britain's political and
military fortunes were at a low ebb and the myth of Jewish power and
influence in the United States and Russia, and the rumors of an impending German initiative to woo the Zionists, had reached new heights.

Yet, if the only, or even decisive, factor at play was Britain's own
interests, one needs to ask why it took three cabinet meetings to arrive
at a resolution. Nothing prevented the British from legitimizing their
moral hold over Palestine by promises to Arab representatives who had
been in touch with British agents in Egypt and elsewhere. If they wished
control over Palestine, why, then, was Balfour interested in sharing such
power with the United States? Why, moreover, did British policymakers
not jettison the Balfour Declaration after the war, as soon as their needs
had been served. Why did they, instead, strengthen their ties to the
Zionist cause by incorporating the concept of a Jewish national home
into the Mandate for Palestine?

The fact of the matter is that until 1917 the British were indecisive
about the best course to follow in regard to Palestine and tried to keep

all their diplomatic options open. Yet, if the British did not yet have a clear policy for the dismemberment of the Ottoman Empire, Weizmann had one from the very start of the war. The long duration of World War I, ironically, gave Weizmann ample time to prepare the ground for his ideas among British policymakers, much as it moved the government to seek wider support and new allies—with the help of the Zionists. The British ultimately reached the conclusion that a pro-Zionist declaration was in their own best interests, but it was Weizmann who convinced them that Zionist and British interests were not in conflict. As noted earlier, the move from a state of readiness to action needed a catalyst. Weizmann, the congenial insider/outsider, served as the ideal partner in creating the necessary fusion. Neither the Arabs nor the Armenians— the two other groups in Sykes's tripartite configuration for a new Middle East—had someone with similar personal assets and qualifications to press their respective cases.

Weizmann had proposed to Graham on June 11, 1917, that a declaration supporting Zionist aspirations in Palestine be issued. Balfour was even then still skeptical whether the moment for such a declaration had arrived. In his response to Balfour of June 19, Graham cited the Cambon letter as an important precedent. Graham's letter demonstrates the weight Foreign Office officials assigned to Sokolow's great achievement on the Continent, though his role in England was more limited. Sokolow made a singular and ground-breaking contribution by securing the Cambon letter. In content and form it was much more favorable to the Zionists than the watered-down formula of the Balfour Declaration. Yet, once Balfour invited Lord Rothschild and Weizmann to present a draft declaration, Sokolow continued to play a preeminent role only as long as Weizmann was on his mission to Gibraltar. Beginning in July 1917 the Zionists actually worked out the wording of the declaration with the Foreign Office personnel under the more or less watchful eye of Balfour. It was, in fact, a mutual enterprise—not a unilateral act—as befits two partners with mutual interests, each watching out for himself while sensitive to his interlocutor's needs.

There was, of course, a readiness in England to support Zionism. Without the religious, moral, strategic, political, and even capricious sentiments animating Lloyd George,[208] Balfour, Smuts, George Barnes, Milner, Sykes, and others, the process might have taken longer or might possibly have been frustrated altogether. Clearly, there were some factors working in favor of the Zionists that had not been initiated by Weizmann and his colleagues but of which they were aware. And, of course, there were many avenues they did pursue and ideas they did suggest to the British.

But someone had to provide the necessary background for all the British statesmen and civil servants who were unfamiliar with the history of Zionism and Jewish aspirations. Someone had to read and interpret the entire political map and fuse the various disparate human and political elements. Someone constantly had to remind those who counted of the mutuality of interests between the British government and the Zionist movement. Someone had to overcome personal hesitations and even antisemitic arguments. Someone had to supply the correct and convincing arguments that the British were looking for and that made sense to justify to themselves, on moral and humanitarian grounds, actions they were ready to undertake on political grounds. That person was Chaim Weizmann.

Weizmann carefully addressed the entire range of concerns expressed by British statesmen and politicians, be they of a personal, religious, imperial, colonial, or moral nature. He knew which arguments to use with whom, and he was able to keep the political process on track—by appealing directly to the prime minister—when it threatened to be derailed. More than thirty years later Field Marshal Smuts told a London audience that "we were persuaded, but remember that it was Dr. Weizmann who persuaded us."[209] Weizmann, as we have seen, had the talent of turning incidental meetings into fateful encounters. He knew how to seize the moment, the idea, the opportunity that does not recur. This ability did not make him a mere opportunist; he truly believed that British and Zionist ambitions were intertwined to the benefit of both.

In the process of working for the British government and in negotiation with its leading representatives, Weizmann had become an Anglophile, a man totally imbued with his adopted country's values and ideals while promoting his own movement's goals. His partners no doubt sensed this volitional identification and shared ambitions and were therefore more ready to be persuaded by him. Weizmann's method was not that of a petitioner. Rather, he tried to provide the British with arguments buttressing their resolve to control Palestine. Weizmann supplied strategic, historical, religious, and general humanitarian reasons; often he used all arguments simultaneously. His main aim was to give substance and reality to the idea of a British protectorate while reassuring the British that the Jewish people approved of the idea.

One of Weizmann's chief assets, from the British point of view, was that he freed them of responsibility for mobilizing the Jewish support that was deemed so valuable by the Foreign Office. Weizmann—at least in the first two years of the war—served as a one-man ministry of propaganda, foreign affairs, and strategic planning. By the time Sokolow and Tschlenow appeared in England, Weizmann had already crystallized his ideas concerning a British protectorate, had met with Balfour and Samuel, courted the Rothschilds, and won the confidence and invaluable support of Scott. All along he had built around him a loosely defined "think tank" of men and women whose judgment he trusted and on whom he could rely. He translated the ideas that germinated in that group into political action. Within the context of the fragmentary and split Jewish and Zionist world, in England and elsewhere, this group filled a vacuum by its resolve and activist stance. With Ahad Ha'Am as the moral guide and with Sokolow providing official cover, Weizmann and his loyal, if sometimes more radical, group stood out by their determination.

One needs to keep in mind that Weizmann simply elected himself—with authority from no one—as a representative of the Jewish people, even before he had offered the government his scientific discoveries. What one must wonder at is the fact that the British accepted him almost from the start as such a legitimate representative, though they were well aware that he lacked official credentials. But perhaps even more remarkable was Weizmann's ability to build sufficient consensus in the Zionist ranks to back his particular point of view. This was perhaps his most difficult task. Whereas those British statesmen and officials with whom he spoke tended to be favorably inclined toward his cause, there was no unanimity in the Jewish or Zionist world that Britain ought to be the protector of the Jews in Palestine.

Appearing cool and confident to the men of authority in England, whom he assured of worldwide Jewish support, or potential support, for Britain, Weizmann was at the same time engaged in a complicated balancing act. He had to convince his colleagues in Russia and the United States that he had the full backing of the British government while trying to get their agreement to move their own governments to support his point of view. Moreover, his own colleagues in England did not always back him—particularly when prospects of success seemed bleak. Sokolow, Lord Rothschild, Sieff, and Tolkowsky were among the few who supported him throughout.[210] Amazingly, and solely through his powers of persuasion, Weizmann was able to mobilize support from his reluctant, or discouraged, fellow Jews—both abroad and in England—when critical moments demanded it.

Weizmann's relentless and single-minded determination that the only possible course for the Zionists was to have England as the patron won the day in at least a segment of the Zionist world, as his stature in the eyes of the British rose. The source for his authority within the Zionist movement was the esteem he acquired among the British. Thus his rise to power within his own movement was not gradual and organic; it was sudden and effected from the periphery. A man as finely attuned to political nuances as Weizmann was, of course, aware of the source of his power, which, in turn, deepened his attachment to England. Similarly, he understood that if his political course were to fail, the blame would all be his.[211]

Whether Weizmann was the prime begetter of the Balfour Declaration or simply a tool in the hands of British imperialists is a subject that will no doubt be debated for a long time to come. But it is indisputable that Weizmann had an inkling from the start of the war—in fact from October 1914 on—that the fate of Zionism was bound with that of England. He acted on this instinct and became its most eloquent promoter. In the process he discovered that many British statesmen had similar notions.

If one examines the entire record, not just one document, one is left with the impression that both on the British side and on the Zionist side there were men who were not afraid to put the wheels of history in motion to translate their mutual desires into political facts. The British produced activists such as Mark Sykes and Ronald Graham. In the Zionist camp Weizmann first and foremost shaped and carried out the lion's share of the political work, though other activists included Aaron Aaronsohn and Vladimir Jabotinsky. The evidence suggests that if the British "used" the Zionists for their own purposes, the Zionists also "used" Britain. They needed each other, and they benefited from one another, at least in the short term. A long history of mutual affinities between some leading Zionists and some British statesmen who were in control at the crucial moment made the process of securing the Balfour Declaration smoother and personally more gratifying to men like Lloyd George, Balfour, Milner, Smuts, Edward Carson, George Barnes, and, of course, Weizmann. One observer has commented, "The Balfour Declaration had a very British begetting. It was born out of a mingling of self-interest and a moral attitude informed by powerful sentimentality."[212]

From the point of view of the British policymakers, the Balfour Declaration was a last-minute bid to tip the scales of the war in their favor.[213] But as just another arrow in the secondary quiver of the Middle East, it created little interest in the corridors of Whitehall and Westminster. That task was left in the hands of a few ranking civil servants of the Foreign Office and cabinet secretariat. Even on October 31, 1917, when it came up for discussion for the third time, the Balfour Declaration was not the first item on the agenda. It came to be invested with moral and political meaning principally by the Zionists—and later by their enemies who, of course, gave it a different moral and political interpretation.[214] What makes the Balfour Declaration stand out from so many other documents that were issued by the British is the fact that the British did not renege on their promise—at least not at first—suggesting that this particular declaration was issued for reasons that went beyond political expediency. The fact that thirty years following its issuance the British had still not formally renounced this by then distasteful policy[215] can be attributed mostly to Weizmann. That, perhaps, was his greatest political accomplishment.

VII

The Zionist Commission

The Balfour Declaration was made public on November 9, a week after its transmission to Lord Rothschild.[1] It introduced an entirely new situation for Zionist tacticians, one vastly complicated, moreover, by crucial military and political events. Shortly before the war cabinet finally acted on its projected statement of Zionist sympathy, the British attack on Palestine was renewed by General Sir Edmund Allenby. Allenby's campaign drove the Turks from Gaza and, six weeks after the Balfour Declaration, culminated in the capture of Jerusalem on December 9. Two days later Allenby, the first Christian to conquer the city in eight hundred years, entered it through the Jaffa Gate. And there, for almost a year, the advance was stopped. On another political front equally critical changes occurred when, on November 8, the Bolsheviks overthrew the Kerensky regime.

These events, together with the still-developing American mobilization for active participation in the war, forced the Zionist leaders to reconsider their plans for immediate and future activity in Palestine as well as in Russia and the United States. In addition, it became urgent for them to establish closer and smoother relations between the American and British Zionist movements and between their respective leaders, Louis Brandeis and Chaim Weizmann. These leaders needed to reorganize for new tasks, taking into account the specific desires of their host countries and the constituencies upon whose support they relied.

From the British point of view, the most immediate task was to publicize the declaration among Jews in foreign countries, particularly Russia and the United States, and in enemy-occupied areas. The Zionists were able to point with pride, as a testimony to the support they enjoyed, to demonstrations of Jewish enthusiasm for the declaration in all the important countries, even in Germany itself. The British government financed large printings of Zionist leaflets and pamphlets and dropped them from airplanes over enemy territory. In England the declaration was warmly received by the press, but there was no effort to make it widely known, and it was passed over as a minor event.[2] For the Zionists, on the other hand, the Balfour Declaration marked a new high point in their efforts to win international recognition and respectability as a national movement. In fact, from their point of view the declaration was issued in the nick of time, given the competing and negative general news as well as the declining support of British public opinion toward Jews.[3]

Among those Foreign Office officials most responsible for the issuance of the Balfour Declaration there was a strong sense that the British ought to use it for their own political purposes as quickly and effectively as possible. The first to take the initiative was Ronald Graham, who, with Weizmann's agreement and cooperation, arranged for a meeting on November 3, to which he invited Sir Mark Sykes, Nahum Sokolow, Aaron Aaronsohn, and Weizmann.[4] These veterans of the declaration campaign worked closely for many months. The three Zionists at the meeting could be counted on to have a strong commitment to England. Their common commitment might explain why Yehiel Tschlenow, who had arrived in England on October 25, was not invited despite his senior status in the World Zionist Organization. The group decided to dispatch Tschlenow, Sokolow, and Vladimir Jabotinsky to Russia; Aaron Aaronsohn was to proceed to the United States. Weizmann was to travel briefly to Paris to consult with Baron Edmond de Rothschild, though he would have preferred to go to Russia. "We came to the conclusion," wrote Graham in a memorandum which Balfour circulated to the cabinet, "that [Weizmann's] presence at Headquarters was so valuable for the moment that he should remain here. . . . He will superintend the central organisation."[5] Events in Russia canceled the plan to send the three Zionists there for propaganda purposes. Aaronsohn, on the other hand, sailed for the United States on November 17, and Sokolow, rather than Weizmann, went to Paris on January 28, 1918, accompanied by Joseph Cowen and Zalman David Levontin.

Graham noted "the intense gratitude of the Zionists for the declaration."[6] Indeed, the first order of business for the Zionists in England was to express this gratitude in a variety of public meetings and demonstrations, the largest of which, organized by the English Zionist Federation, took place at the London Opera House on December 2, 1917. That impressive gathering filled the Opera House to capacity. On the platform were members of the government and Parliament, representatives of Jewish organizations and synagogues, and Arab and Armenian delegates. Lord Rothschild presided,[7] and the speakers included Lord Robert Cecil, Mark Sykes, Herbert Samuel, William Ormsby-Gore, the Haham Dr. Gaster, Chief Rabbi Dr. Joseph Hertz, James de Rothschild, and Israel Zangwill. Sokolow and Weizmann responded on behalf of the Zionist Organization.[8] Once again Yehiel Tschlenow was notably absent from the platform and the roster of speakers.

Those present at the Opera House on December 2, hearing Weizmann's measured and confident speech, could not doubt that he was the undisputed leader of a growing and united movement. In fact, the situation was quite different. Personal tensions among Weizmann's closest associates and criticism of his policies and conduct, which had been voiced for many months, were not muted by the Zionist diplomatic success. Rather, the Balfour Declaration seemed to exacerbate already existing disagreements, for it created new challenges for Zionist policymaking and action.

On October 31, the very day of the government's decision, Vera noted in her diary: "No end of telegrams of congratulations to Ch. Everybody is most enthusiastic except Dr. Tschlenow, who still advocates the Jewish neutrality policy of sitting on the fence. But at the bottom of the things [sic] there is nothing, but pure jealousy, that it is not he who carried it through. He is so clumsy, that he even cannot hide it. And at every occasion rubs in, that he is [involved in all Zionist affairs] in [his] capacity [as a member] of [the Smaller Actions Committee]."[9]

Tschlenow's arrival in England on October 25 exacerbated the already tense relationships that existed within the Political Committee and between its members and those who were excluded from it, notably Jabotinsky and Aaronsohn. Tschlenow's insistence that Aaronsohn be kept at arm's length from the deliberations of the Political Committee and that Aaronsohn's activities in the United States be carefully circumscribed fueled the latter's sense of being ostracized and intentionally mistreated. On a number of occasions Tschlenow's directives led the volatile and strongheaded Aaronsohn to violent outbursts. He found a ready ally in Jabotinsky, who had similar grievances against Weizmann's circle of confidants.

Having their own personal supporters in the Foreign Office, Aaronsohn and Jabotinsky could seek to redress any actual and imagined injustices on the part of their Zionist colleagues by using government contacts to direct Zionist policy. Despite his ambivalent feelings about Jabotinsky and Aaronsohn, Weizmann managed to remain on relatively good terms with both. To avoid a crisis he saw to it that shortly before Aaronsohn's departure for the United States both he and Jabotinsky were added to the Political Committee.[10] Within the private domain of the Zionist inner circle both were allowed to pour out their long-held grievances, thus averting a public showdown.

Simultaneously, another confrontation between Weizmann and Tschlenow over present and future Zionist policy took place during two meetings of the Political Committee. On November 3, Tschlenow reminded those assembled that during the meeting of the Smaller Actions Committee on July 29–31, 1917, in Copenhagen, the policy of strict Zionist neutrality, declared early in the war, had been confirmed until further notice.[11] The implication of this decision was that the Balfour Declaration ought not to be made public so as to protect the Jewish communities within the Central Powers and in Palestine. Weizmann, whom Tschlenow previously accused of being a British agent, responded, with tears running down his cheeks, that he and his collaborators would disobey the resolution of the SAC and continue to pursue their pro-British policy; he demanded that the Russian do nothing to hamper this work.[12]

The heated discussion continued on November 6. Tschlenow answered that nothing should be done that might endanger the Yishuv and that he could foresee the growth and development of the Jewish community in Palestine even under Turkish suzerainty. Weizmann's threat to continue conducting Zionist policy without regard to the decisions of the SAC and that, should he withdraw from the political work, the doors of the British government would close before the Zionists, led Tschlenow to charge that Weizmann wanted dictatorial powers, something not granted even to Theodor Herzl. Heeding Tolkowsky's advice, Weizmann waited for the end of the debate before settling his score with Tschlenow. Contrary to his performance on November 3, he was now factual, deliberate, and cool. He then reaffirmed Zionism's tie to England as the only choice if the work in Palestine was to succeed: "If Germany will maintain the status quo in the East, Turkey will become its vassal state and Germany will never agree to any arrangement leading to the dismemberment of Turkey. . . . If England will conquer Eretz Israel, then . . . the very fact that European civilization will border on Beirut would be sufficient guaranty for the development of our enterprise."[13]

Weizmann dismissed Tschlenow's idea that a victorious Germany, which humiliated its Jewish citizens, would support the Zionist movement. He took the Russian Zionist leader—and his colleagues—to task for failing to support the political work of the English Zionists during the spring and summer of 1917. The German Zionists, he said, were currently powerless and could not make independent judgments on behalf of the WZO. In fact, intimated Weizmann, it was time for a change. The personnel of the SAC had outlived their usefulness. "Our propaganda must be based on the identity of our interests with England. I therefore suggest that in Russia and America a propaganda campaign be conducted along these lines."[14]

Weizmann's charges throughout the debate on November 3 and 6 were deliberately provocative. Knowing full well that he was speaking from a position of strength, he hinted a number of times at a possible split in the movement if his pro-British policy were to be rejected. Sensing defeat and trying to preserve his own dignity and that of the Russian Zionists as well as that of the SAC, Tschlenow backed away from a decisive vote on the subject. In the end, a compromise was reached, granting the English Zionists the freedom to stay their course and openly to acknowledge all Zionists' gratitude to England by means of public demonstrations while doing their utmost not to anger the Central Powers and Turkey.[15] Though both Tschlenow and Weizmann could claim that their position was maintained intact, Weizmann clearly emerged from the debates with greater stature.

For the first time in his political career Weizmann directly challenged the executive of the WZO. He must have felt special satisfaction that this confrontation was with Tschlenow, the elder statesman of the Russian Zionists who scarcely paid attention to Weizmann before 1914. Weizmann might have recalled that Tschlenow's vacillations in 1903 on the issue of East Africa had caused Weizmann temporarily to choose the wrong side, thus incurring the wrath of his colleagues while the Russian leader escaped unscathed. Now Weizmann was able to assert his preeminence and independence as a leader who, even without high office within the WZO, could no longer be treated lightly. His status as peer of the members of the SAC was symbolically and practically asserted when cables sent out on November 19 to all Zionist federations, requesting contributions to a political fund with a goal of £200,000, were cosigned by Sokolow, Tschlenow, and Weizmann. On December 12 this fund was officially named Zionist Preparation Fund.

Though Weizmann was able to have his way in most internal Zionist controversies, they caused him to become agitated and tense. In mid-December, matters came to a head over an apparently minor incident. During a speech in Manchester on December 9, Weizmann made some disparaging remarks about Jewish financiers. James de Rothschild, who sat on the platform, was incensed and wrote protesting to Weizmann the following day.[16] Apparently the matter was discussed at an executive meeting of the EZF on December 12 or 13, and those present also disapproved of Weizmann's remarks. Weizmann immediately announced his resignation—for the third time—from the presidency of the English Zionist Federation. This time it was Tolkowsky and others close to the EZF who persuaded him to resume his duties.[17]

Even as he attempted to sort out disagreements over Zionist policies and personal rivalries, Weizmann became increasingly attuned to and aware of the Arab question. The issue was certainly not new to him, though prior to 1914 he had no particular reason to be occupied with the subject. This changed once he assumed a larger representative role and was seen, at least in England, as a legitimate spokesman for the Zionists. Thus, in January 1915, while preparing Weizmann for the kinds of issues likely to emerge during his conversations with Lloyd George, C. P. Scott brought up the subject of the relatively large Arab population in Palestine as compared to the Jewish one.[18] Similarly, during his first meeting with the Zionist leaders on February 7, 1917, Mark Sykes stated that one ought to "go carefully with the Arabs."[19] Writing from Cairo in the spring of 1917, Sykes asked the Foreign Office to bring to Weizmann's attention that regardless of the status Jews were to acquire in Palestine, the "actual population [i.e., the Arabs] must have equal recognition."[20] In March 1917 Weizmann told C. P. Scott that he wished to go to the East as soon as possible in order to "enter there into negotiations with the leading Arabs from Palestine."[21] Weizmann and his close collaborators recognized the inherent difficulties of Jewish predominance in a country with an Arab population that outnumbered them. Harry Sacher expressed these worries in a letter to his friend Leon Simon:

> At the back of my mind there is firmly fixed the recognition that even if all our political schemings turn out in the way we desire, the Arabs will remain our most tremendous problem. I don't want us in Palestine to deal with the Arabs as the Poles deal with the Jews and with the lesser excuse that belongs to a numerical minority. That kind of chauvinism might poison the whole of [the] Yishuv. It is our business to fight against it . . . and we must have a big constructive program to oppose the rifles and the machine guns of our jingoes. . . . It is going to to be extraordinarily difficult and it will give us unhappy years, but it has to be done.[22]

The Zionists were encouraged to think and ask not for a Jewish state but for a Jewish commonwealth. The distinction was not clear even to the Zionists, though they seemed agreed that Jews would and should eventually form a majority in Palestine. They never intended to drive the Arabs, or any other group, from Palestine. On the contrary, they assumed that there was sufficient room for both groups to live side by side. Many Zionists discussed the idea of an eventual Jewish state from the outset. But even those contemplating such a state did not seriously expect that it could be implemented in the near future. For the time being, Zionists believed the term "Jewish commonwealth" or something similar would be appropriately neutral and unchallenging to Arab sensibilities. Zionist debates in England immediately after the Balfour Declaration indicate a quest for a peaceful *modus vivendi* with the Arabs though little agreement on the best means to achieve it.

In mid-November 1917, at a meeting of English and Zionist leaders in London, Tschlenow expressed concern over Arab national aspirations and British policy in the Middle East. He was dissatisfied with the wording of the Balfour Declaration, which called for the establishment of a Jewish national home *"in* Palestine" rather than *"of* Palestine." Perhaps, he wondered, the Zionists ought to ask for an independent state, though he realized that a period of transition was necessary before such a demand could be realized. Sokolow, who, at Sykes's initiative, had by then met with a number of Arabs, believed that the British were interested in fostering harmonious relations between Jews and Arabs and wished to mitigate any Arab opposition to Zionism. Sokolow seemed to believe that cooperation with the Arabs was indeed possible. Ahad Ha'Am, who shared Tschlenow's worries, arrived at different conclusions. How inappropriate, he stated, to demand a Jewish state for an absentee nation. One cannot demand Jewish currency or Jewish governors for cities where the majority of the population was Arab. Ahad Ha'Am implied that all this was subject to change in two or three decades following a large Jewish immigration. All present, including Ahad Ha'Am, agreed that eventually they wished to see the founding of a Jewish state.[23]

Weizmann's view came closest to that of Ahad Ha'Am. At a meeting of the Political Committee at the end of November he stated:

We all agree as to the final aim [Tschlenow's demand for a Jewish state], and from now on it is simply a question of tactics as to how to achieve it. We need an evolutionary tactic. For example: we ought not to ask the [British] government if we will enter Palestine as masters or as equals to the Arabs. It all depends on the number of Jews residing in Palestine currently or in the future. The Declaration implies that we have been afforded the opportunity to become the masters of Palestine. As long as we do not have people and money we cannot demand any more than that. . . . There is a British proverb about the camel and the tent: at first the camel sticks one leg into the tent, and eventually it slips into it. This must be our policy.[24]

Weizmann's and his colleagues' efforts not to offend Arab national feelings were shared by most British Foreign Office officials and by the military authorities in Egypt and Palestine. None was more concerned with this issue than Mark Sykes, the architect of the tripartite solution of independent Armenian, Arab, and Jewish entities. He had been in close touch with Sir Reginald Wingate, the high commissioner in Egypt, and Brigadier General Gilbert Clayton, Allenby's chief political officer, who kept him informed of the political mood of the Arabs. Some six weeks prior to the Balfour Declaration, Clayton advised Sykes that for the time being it might be a good idea for the British government to refrain from any pro-Zionist proclamations, since they would clearly increase Arab displeasure.[25] Following the publication of the Balfour Declaration, Sykes cabled Sir Reginald Wingate that the Zionists were prepared "to work wholeheartedly for Arab and Armenian liberation." He suggested that the high commissioner call the Arab Committee into existence once again and impress this fact on its members. For his part, Sykes promised to try to set up a committee in London "composed of Dr. Weizmann for Zionists, Mr. Malcolm for Armenians, Mr. Nejib Hani for Syrian Christians and an Arab Moslem. . . . This committee will act on behalf of the oppressed nationalities in the non-Anatolian provinces of Turkey in Asia."[26] In a letter written to General Clayton but intended for circulation to the Syrian committees in Cairo, Sykes made a forceful case: "The British Government have recognised Zionism. Zionism is the greatest motive force in Jewry—Jewry is scattered throughout the world— if Zionism and Arab nationalism join forces, I am convinced that the liberation of the Arabs is certain. If on the other hand Zionism and Arab nationalism are opposed [to one another] . . . Arab nationalism will subside into its natural elements of desert, town, village, Christian and Moslem, and there will be nothing to pull it together."[27]

But despite Sykes's sincere and untiring efforts, the various Arab national groups in Egypt, Syria, and elsewhere were quick to express opposition to the Balfour Declaration and any plans for Zionist colonization. Captain William Yale, an American intelligence agent resident in

Cairo and an acute observer of political developments, reported in November 1917, "The Palestinians are very bitter over the Balfour Declaration. . . . They are convinced that the Zionist leaders wish and intend
to create a distinctly Jewish community and they believe that if Zionism
proves to be a success, their country will be lost to them even though
their religious and political rights be protected."[28] Yale's observations
were confirmed by Clayton: "Recent announcement of His Majesty's
Government on Jewish question has made profound impression on both
Christians and Moslems who view with little short of dismay prospect
of seeing Palestine and even eventually Syria in hands of Jews whose
superior intelligence and commercial abilities are feared by all alike."[29]

Five days later, while touring in Palestine, Clayton cabled Sir Reginald
Wingate a similar message, which was probably communicated to Sykes
as well: "Dislike of the Jew is very deep-rooted and, in the case of Arabs
in Palestine and Syria is accumulated by fear of Jewish enterprise and
ability, of which an object lesson is given by the existing Jewish colonies."[30]

Still heeding Clayton's warning, Sykes addressed a Zionist meeting in
Manchester on December 9. He warned those assembled "to look through
Arab glasses." He also told his audience that the Arabs feared that Jewish financial corporations would eventually buy out not only Palestine
but Syria and Mesopotamia as well and that the Arabs would become a
proletariat working on the soil for alien masters. The Jewish colonists
must not turn into middlemen and crush the Arabs out of existence.
Rather they ought to win the right to the land by the sweat of their
brow. He also reminded the Zionists that Jerusalem was sacred to Jews,
Muslims, and Christians. It ought to be approached not with the sense
of triumph and ancient wrongs but in the spirit of brotherhood and af-
fection.[31]

In a letter to Georges Picot written a few days after the meeting, Sykes
admitted that he had "adopted the boldest course in Manchester" when
addressing the Zionists.[32] What he failed to report to the Frenchman
was that the retort to his warnings was perhaps even bolder. Clearly
angry at Sykes's condescending speech, Weizmann shunted aside diplomatic niceties and rose to give a forthright and courageous response:

> May I be permitted to state that I was listening to some of these warnings
> with a certain sense of astonishment and humiliation. . . . Why, it is the
> very essence of Zionism not to do those three things against which Sir Mark
> Sykes has warned us. Have not we Zionists, as members of a democratic
> movement, fought constantly against these so-called international Jewish
> financial speculators? . . .
>
> It is a truism to Zionism that as long as the land is bought by Jews and
> not worked by Jews, it is not Jewish land. . . .
>
> For the last ten years of our colonising activity there has been an increas-
> ing tendency to replace systematically . . . Arab labour by Jewish labour,
> and I would ask the Arabs to remember that we do this not because we are

against the Arabs, but because we desire to heed the warning of which Sir Mark Sykes spoke tonight and really make the country Jewish. . . .

Another warning has been given to us tonight—you Jews try and be united. Of course we understand the absolute necessity of unity . . . but may I remind you all that very often Jews are reproached for being too united— the so-called Jewish solidarity has always been a beam in the eyes of our enemies. . . .

We don't desire to be particularly loved and patronised, and don't wish to be an object of hatred. We wish to be taken just as we are, with all our faults and all our qualities, just as we try to take others. Here we are, just Jews and nothing else, a nation among nations; take it or leave it. All these are the essence of Jewish nationalism and Zionism.[33]

Honor satisfied, Weizmann cabled Jacques Mosseri in Cairo urging meetings with Arab leaders to remove any misunderstandings.[34] Such meetings took place but with meager results.[35] Sykes continued to pressure not only the Zionists but the various Arab groups as well. Clayton, for his part, continued to sound a pessimistic note: "Mecca dislikes Jews and Armenians and wishes to have nothing to do with them," he cabled on December 12, "while Arabs of Syria and Palestine fear repetition of story of Jacob and Esau."[36] Clayton judged that Sykes was moving too quickly,[37] forcing the issue at a time when the Arabs were not ready to accept his solutions:

I quite see your arguments regarding an Arab-Jew-Armenian combine. . . . We will try it, but it must be done very cautiously and, honestly, I see no great chance of any real success. It is an attempt to change in a few weeks the traditional sentiment of centuries. The Arab cares nothing whatsoever about the Armenian one way or the other.—As regards the Jew the Bedouin despises him and will never do anything else, while the sedentary Arab hates the Jew, and fears his superior commercial and economic ability.[38]

Clayton met with the Syrian Welfare Committee in Cairo as well as with Mosseri and other Jewish and Zionist leaders from Egypt and Palestine. The general was able to allay some of the Arabs' worst fears once he assured them that issuance of the Balfour Declaration did not mean that the British government was about to establish a Jewish state or a Jewish government in Palestine. The Syrians felt that, given their numerical strength and overwhelming hold on the land, they had all the necessary advantages and would be able to meet the Zionist challenge. Thus, for the moment at least, they were willing to continue their discussions with the Zionists and the Armenians while making no commitments.[39]

The Syrian Welfare Committee and other Arab groups actually seemed better informed about the Balfour Declaration and its possible implications than some of the British officers with whom they came in contact. At the very least, Arab groups took the declaration seriously, whereas for many British officers it was at best of secondary importance, one war declaration among many. On the Palestine front, in the very area where it was to be applied, the declaration was, to all intents and purposes, suppressed. The officers on Allenby's staff remained virtually ignorant of it or assumed they could disregard it in the interests of smooth relations with Arab spokesmen in Egypt, who met it with suspicion and alarm. Even General Clayton, who was in almost daily contact with Sykes, had no idea what this document actually meant in terms of concrete British policy in Palestine.[40] In London, where the Zionists found positive support, their efforts to give the Jewish legion being recruited in the United States and England a more definite nationalist aspect succeeded only at the cost of sustained effort and Zionist pressure.[41] The Thirty-eighth Battalion Royal Fusiliers under the command of Lieutenant Colonel John Henry Patterson finally left England on February 5, 1918, and arrived in Palestine four months later after training in a camp near Cairo. The Thirty-ninth Battalion under the command of Lieutenant Colonel Eliezer Margolin left in April, and the Fortieth Battalion under the command of Lieutenant Colonel Fred Samuel left in late August.[42] In the spring of 1918, the volunteer committee in Palestine, assisted by Weizmann, petitioned Allenby to allow Palestinian Jewish recruitment into the battalions. At first reluctant, Allenby finally gave permission on May 16, 1918, and recruitment was successfully conducted under the supervision of James de Rothschild.[43]

Weizmann, who pressed for action on all these fronts, also urged another line of approach: that an official Zionist Commission, which he would head, be attached to Allenby's advancing army. Such a commission would protect Zionist interests at a time when Arab opposition to Zionism was increasing and the French and Italians were eager to attach symbolic forces and official representatives to the British offensive for their own purposes.[44] In his approach to the British, Weizmann argued that the commission would powerfully enhance the prestige of the Zionists in the Jewish community while improving considerably the propaganda impact of the Balfour Declaration. To Zionists, he pointed out that whatever happened in Palestine under British occupation in the period prior to the peace conference would have decisive effects on the subsequent work in the country.[45] His proposals for terms of reference for the commission reflected faithfully the several aims he intended to achieve.

The idea for a Zionist Commission that would safeguard Jewish interests in Palestine was broached by Weizmann for the first time on November 6 during a meeting of the Political Committee.[46] Six days later, presuming approval of his plan, he wrote to Louis Brandeis asking for nominations of American participants in the commission.[47] Only on November 27, 1917, did the Political Committee accept the proposal to send a "Jewish Commission" to Palestine at the earliest opportune moment, that is, as soon as permission could be obtained from the British government. The committee suggested that the commission be a consultative

Weizmann in 1918.
Courtesy: Weizmann
Archives

body. The members of the commission were to represent the Zionist organization, but no one doubted that Weizmann was to head it.[48]

In mid-December 1917, after prior consultation, Weizmann sent Ronald Graham a concise summary of the Political Committee's lengthy memorandum outlining the status, objects, composition, and specific goals of the proposed commission.[49] After review by Arthur Balfour and his staff, a new draft was prepared by Weizmann and Ronald Graham.[50] After more meetings with Balfour, Sykes, and General George Macdonogh, the director of British military intelligence, in the early part of January 1918, the proposal was referred to the Eastern Committee of the war cabinet.[51] At its meeting of January 19, the Eastern Committee approved the dispatch of the Zionist Commission, headed by Weizmann and accompanied by a British political officer. The Zionist Commission was charged:

1. To help in establishing friendly relations between the Jews on the one hand, and the Arabs and other non-Jewish communities on the other.

2. To form a link between the British authorities and the Jewish population in Palestine.
3. To help with relief work in Palestine and to assist in the repatriation of evacuated persons and refugees, so far as the military situation will allow.
4. To assist in restoring and developing the Jewish colonies, and in reorganising the Jewish population in general.
5. To collect information and report upon the possibilities of future Jewish developments in Palestine in the light of the declaration of his Majesty's Government.[52]

The objectives of the commission, as defined by the Eastern Committee, were not substantially different from those presented by the Zionists, but they were phrased in more moderate language and did not include all that the Political Committee wished to see in its original memorandum. Weizmann's conversations with Ronald Graham, as sympathetic a Foreign Office official as he could hope to deal with, no doubt convinced him not to make excessive requests at this stage. He sensed that the political winds in England were shifting away from the Zionist sails. No doubt he was also mindful of the fact that Lord Curzon of Kedleston, neither a supporter of Zionism nor an admirer of Weizmann, was the chairman of the Eastern Committee, and that some of the other members who were favorably inclined toward Zionism, such as Sykes, Hardinge, and Balfour, would not support maximal requests. Weizmann's political instinct told him that the very creation of the Zionist Commission, even with a moderate charge, was triumph enough in view of the warnings coming from Cairo. He did, on advice from Ronald Graham, write a private letter to Sykes in which he asked for permission to lay the groundwork for the Jewish university, assuming the military authorities approved of the idea. Representatives of the Allied countries were also to participate as members in the commission.[53]

The various drafts, whether composed by the Zionist Political Committee or by Foreign Office officials, assumed that Weizmann was to head the commission. This was a clear public recognition that Weizmann had ascended to a new level of leadership in the Zionist movement, even if he was propelled to this position by the British. If he was not yet the official head of the World Zionist Organization, he was certainly, for the time being, its uncrowned heir apparent. By 1918, no one other than Weizmann could claim to be the foremost elected representative of the movement. Louis Brandeis expressed the high regard those in the front ranks of the WZO had for Weizmann: "We must, to the utmost of our ability, support Weizmann and not permit his heavy task to be increased by any desertion in the ranks. My opinion is, that even if we should at times think some other course wiser than the one from time to time pursued by him—success can be best attained by loyally following his lead, which has proved itself worthy in the work of the last three years. He should be made to feel that he has our unswerving allegiance."[54]

Weizmann took the unswerving allegiance and support, personal and financial, from other Zionists as a matter of course. This was particularly true in his relationships with the English and American Zionists. With the Americans he kept in constant touch, especially through Louis Brandeis and Jacob DeHaas, from the moment the Balfour Declaration was sent to Lord Rothschild. Brief cables and letters took time to reach their destination, creating some confusion in the early stages of communication. Moreover, there were differences in style and management between the Weizmann group and the American organization, leading DeHaas—who had early on adopted a hostile attitude toward Weizmann—to write in exasperation to his chief, "There is something hysterical in these messages. . . . There is lack of clarity . . . a good deal of these requests appear to me as coming out of the darkness."[55]

DeHaas was referring to Weizmann's cables and letters requesting funds without specifying how the money would be managed and what amounts were required for which projects. He constantly complained to Brandeis that "neither Tschlenow, Sokolow nor Weizmann has a business head. . . . We feel responsible here for the accounts that we are creating abroad and . . . [Weizmann's] cables are not too distinct. . . . We must establish a clearing house as between different countries, otherwise we are simply throwing money into a hopper."[56] Even Aaronsohn's explanations did not persuade DeHaas that the Europeans knew how to manage their financial affairs, and he insisted on sending someone to London to do it on their behalf.

By the end of January 1918 the Americans had a better idea of Weizmann's expectations. "It is now clear," wrote DeHaas to Brandeis, "that Weizmann expects $400,000 from us for Commission." Weizmann asked, in addition, for the same amount to place the Anglo-Palestine Company back on its feet.[57] These sums did not daunt the American Zionists, who in December 1917, at a conference in Baltimore, had established the Palestine Restoration Fund.[58] DeHaas tried as a first step to secure $1 million to meet the most pressing needs.[59] On both sides of the Atlantic, the Zionists were ready to undertake far greater financial burdens than they had ever envisaged before—amounting, in the program foreseen at the Baltimore conference, to a global sum of $100 million for a long-term reconstruction program.

Weizmann expected to be the channel through which all Zionist funds invested in Palestine would flow. The American Zionists, who were keeping their promise to raise funds in record time, agreed to Weizmann's request, but they strongly urged that Weizmann establish in turn proper accounting procedures. Specifically, they suggested the creation of a committee that would assume responsibility for correct bookkeeping and that, in Weizmann's absence, would assume the authority to dispose of the funds. In his letter of January 30, 1918, which outlined these financial procedures, DeHaas also added some political advice. He warned Weizmann against collaboration with or even communication with the American Mizrahi or the Poalei Zion, organizations at odds with the PZC. It was a *quid pro quo*, warned DeHaas; the Americans do not interfere in the affairs of the English Zionists and they expected their European colleagues to reciprocate.[60] Weizmann understood the thinly veiled threat. Over the next few months, he and Sokolow communicated with American Zionists solely through the official channels of the PZC.

Under the conditions likely to prevail after the war, American Jews would have to raise the largest sums for the reconstruction of Palestine, which had been ravaged by the Turks.[61] The participation of Americans in the Zionist Commission was therefore considered indispensable both in England and by the American Zionists. From his first letter to Brandeis following the Balfour Declaration, Weizmann took it for granted that there would be American Zionist representation on the commission.[62] For six weeks the American Zionists considered whom to send, the most frequently mentioned candidates being Rabbi Stephen Wise, Judge Julian Mack, and Eliyahu Lewin-Epstein.[63]

The British government wanted substantial participation by American Zionists, hoping thus to draw the American government into approval of, if not some share of the responsibility for, the prospective British protectorate. But this was just the outcome that Colonel House and President Wilson took care to avoid. In a conversation with Wise and DeHaas, House expressed his objections quite bluntly: "In the first place, it is unwise, and in the next place it is not needed. Cable to Weizmann that you are ready to give all the money and counsel that may be needed. But the Government cannot give its sanction to any American participation in the enterprise just now."[64] Against their inclination, the Zionists in Washington and New York were compelled to disappoint Weizmann.[65] He thus went to Palestine without any American member on the commission.

Not until after the armistice did two Americans, Dr. Harry Friedenwald and the young lawyer Robert Szold, officially join the commission. Some American contact was provided in the meantime by Walter Meyer, the brother of the financier Eugene Meyer.[66] Meyer went along at Weizmann's request as a secretary to the commission without official status and sent back reports to the American Zionist leaders. A more important contact for the Americans proved Aaron Aaronsohn, who was also denied membership on the commission.[67] He was still a crucial expert, enjoying the confidence of the British as well as of Weizmann and Brandeis.

Aaronsohn's espionage ring had been exposed at the very beginning of the British invasion of Palestine, bringing death to his sister Sarah and his friends and precipitating a wave of arrests and searches through the Jewish settlements by the vengeful Turks.[68] The local leaders, who had resented the control over American relief funds the Aaronsohn family and espionage ring enjoyed,[69] were terrified and infuriated by these events and tried unsuccessfully to remove Aaronsohn from any connection with the commission.[70] On the other hand, Aaronsohn's demand for full membership, in the face of the existing hostility, did not recommend itself to Weizmann and his associates.[71] In spite of this disappointment, Aaronsohn and Weizmann shared too much—their decidedly pro-British stand, their scientific-professional background—to do other than stand together, in common bonds with the British military and in correspondence with Brandeis.

The commission was to have Russian members; the Russian Zionist Central Committee had nominated Leo Motzkin and Menahem Ussishkin.[72] Weizmann was unhappy with both nominations, but there was little he could do to remove so respected a veteran as Ussishkin. Motzkin was another matter. He had far less support, and Weizmann was no doubt pleased to settle scores with his erstwhile mentor-turned-detractor by dismissing him as "quite useless and cumbersome."[73] Ussishkin, as it turned out, was unable to leave the Ukraine and arrived in England only in early 1919. A French member, Dr. Sylvain Lévi, an orientalist of some note and a member of the Alliance Israélite Universelle, joined the commission at the start at the insistence of Baron Edmond de Rothschild[74] and with the full approval of the French Foreign Ministry. French officials assumed quite correctly that Lévi would be guarding French interests in Palestine,[75] though Sokolow, whom the baron strongly pressed to put Lévi on the commission, could not have known how deep-seated his anti-Zionism was. Indeed, Lévi's appointment was initially welcomed by Weizmann.[76]

Sokolow's sojourn in Paris was successful from every point of view. Within three weeks of his arrival at the end of January 1918, he secured a large loan from Baron Edmond de Rothschild, despite the latter's initial negative reply to Weizmann. Sokolow was received by Stephen Pichon, the French foreign minister, who reaffirmed the French government's full accord with England regarding "the problem of Jewish existence in Palestine."[77] Yet, upon his return to London, Sokolow found Weizmann less than delighted with the good news. That day Sokolow recorded in his diary:

> I found Weizmann in our office and reported on the results of my trip to Paris. I cannot shake off the impression, that he is insincere and that his ambition is consuming him. It seems to me that more and more he suspends any rational and objective thinking and instead operates on the basis of personal motivations which are aroused by his impatience. He is blatantly suspicious, afraid of challengers and does not suffer any opposition. I showed him the French document [from Pichon]. He said that this is a very fine document, but I felt that he sees it as some kind of competition. I told him

that in my view, I must go to Palestine, but he did not react at all. It is absolutely clear that he is against this idea, but that he does not have the courage to express his view.[78]

The following day when Sokolow discussed his grievances about Weizmann's attitude toward him, Weizmann replied that he did not get sufficient recognition for his achievements and was made to look as if he took orders from Sokolow. In the end, Sokolow, who shied away from confrontation, backed down and remained in London to conduct political negotiations with the government and oversee the affairs of the London office.[79]

Toward the end of Weizmann's active leadership of the commission in 1918, the Italians, too, were represented. One of the Italians, Commandante Angelo Levi-Bianchini, whose contribution came to be highly regarded by the Zionists, was a naval intelligence officer plainly detailed to promote Italian interests.[80] In a group so laboriously constructed to balance the Allies against one another, the British nonetheless secured their predominance. The British Zionists and members of the Political Committee—Israel Sieff, Leon Simon, and Joseph Cowen—were joined by David Eder, a London psychiatrist and a representative of the Jewish Territorial Organization. The others traveling with the commission—in addition to Walter Meyer and Aaron Aaronsohn—were Zalman David Levontin of the Anglo-Palestine Company and Jules Rosenheck, an official of the Jewish Colonization Association. With Weizmann at the commission head—a chairman who enjoyed their entire confidence—and with Major William Ormsby-Gore as its political officer[81] and James de Rothschild attached to it,[82] the British were well equipped to control a body that, in any case, came within the jurisdiction of General Allenby's command. Weizmann clearly dominated this odd group, being the only member who was well known in the Zionist and Jewish world,[83] but it was the best group that could be assembled in so short a time given the prevailing political constraints.[84]

Precluded from sharing from the first in the direction of the Zionist Commission, the American Zionists managed to gain a foothold in the work of reconstruction at an early stage by an undertaking of their own, the American Zionist Medical Unit. The American Zionists planned the project even before they realized that they would be unable to join the Zionist Commission.[85] Nursing care in Palestine had been the special project to which the American women's Zionist organization, Hadassah, had devoted itself before the war, and it was eager to take up the task on a broader base in the postwar reconstruction.[86]

General relief activities for the Palestine community had been a primary wartime responsibility of the Provisional Executive Committee for General Zionist Affairs (PZC), shared in an occasionally uneasy relationship with the American Jewish Joint Distribution Committee (JDC). The three now cooperated in the new venture—the JDC and the Zionists sharing in the financial support of the medical unit, in the preliminary tasks of staffing it, and in securing the authorizations needed for its work. Hadassah undertook its contribution to the funding and the current management of the project.[87]

Thus, by mid-1918, the Americans as well as Weizmann had assumed direct responsibility for the practical work of constructing the Jewish national home. Weizmann immersed himself in the entire range of Palestinian problems. Circumstances forced the Americans to confine their immediate efforts—apart from fund-raising for Weizmann's and Sokolow's work—to the operation of the medical unit. This limitation, fortuitous though it was, had its roots in the Americans', and specifically Brandeis's, temperamental and tactical preferences. The medical unit was a limited, manageable project, not a diffuse commitment to meet any and all future contingencies. It had a clear, functional relationship to any future work, being an essential preliminary—a preventive, sanitary clearing of the ground—required for the success of whatever else might be planned; and it was a specifically American project, funded and to be managed by the Americans alone and marked by the special qualities of the American way.[88] Weizmann, on the other hand, not only perceived himself, and was perceived, as identified with the whole Jewish people, even while serving as a British agent. By the position he had assumed, he also exposed himself to all the pressures of the entire world Jewish community and implicitly claimed the support of their general will. This claim had yet to be tested and proved.

Organizing the American Zionist Medical Unit and getting it under way proved to be long and laborious. Negotiations with both the American and the British governments were begun during the first stages of the consideration of the Zionist Commission itself.[89] But the initial contingent of the medical unit did not arrive in Palestine until September 1918, when Weizmann was waiting impatiently for release from his long stay in the field. The Americans managed to establish direct contact with Weizmann through Felix Frankfurter, who was sent to London on American government business in mid-February 1918. Frankfurter arrived on February 17 together with Aaronsohn, who reported to Brandeis that they found Weizmann "nearly on the point of collapse."[90]

These were the final weeks prior to the commission's departure; with Yehiel Tschlenow's death on January 31 and with Sokolow in Paris, all major decisions were left in Weizmann's hands. But Frankfurter's immense and open admiration for Weizmann,[91] and his and Aaronsohn's message from Brandeis that the whole Zionist organization pledged its full support to Weizmann's "undivided leadership," did much to lift Weizmann's spirits,[92] especially after Frankfurter announced at a meeting of the Political Committee—in the presence of Sokolow and Ahad Ha'Am—that the Americans recognized Weizmann as the only leader they could trust and insisted that all funds be controlled by him.[93]

Unlike the suspicious DeHaas, whose letters to Weizmann became increasingly unpleasant, Frankfurter, who had a chance of viewing Weizmann's work at close range, was greatly impressed. He made sure to report his views to DeHaas: "Things in England are in wonderfully good shape. The political work there has been handled with an effectiveness that must challenge the admiration of us all for its persistent skill and far-sighted statesmanship. The success of the work, however, depends upon us to a degree that is hardly realized here. . . . A steady stream of money must flow to Weizman's [sic] credit. . . . There ought to go to him not less than at the rate of $50,000 a week until nearly the million dollars is reached."[94]

Weizmann lacked administrative skills and disliked daily office routine. He ran the organization on instinct and impulse, relying on his devoted staff to handle uninteresting details.[95] But he had to restructure the Zionist office in London and appoint a new executive committee before his departure for Palestine. The complicated issues that were sure to arise had to be dealt with smoothly by a streamlined organization. In January 1918, Samuel Landman, editor of the *Zionist,* was invited to join the Zionist office staff as assistant to Simon Marks; both oversaw eight clerks. Tolkowsky became treasurer, overseen and assisted, as the Americans demanded, by a financial executive committee. Moreover, from May to August 1918, Tolkowsky was assisted in the management of financial affairs by Eliyahu Lewin-Epstein, treasurer of the PZC and, like Tolkowsky, well acquainted with Palestinian affairs. A Palestine administrative subcommittee was likewise established to investigate projects for the future administration of Palestine, as well as a propaganda committee.

The Political Committee, which included Ahad Ha'Am, Herbert Bentwich, Joseph Cowen, Akiva Ettinger, Paul Goodman, Albert Hyamson, Leopold Kessler, Samuel Landman, Simon Marks, Harry Sacher, Israel Sieff, Leon Simon, and Shmuel Tolkowsky, served at the pleasure of the "leaders" (i.e., Weizmann and Sokolow) and continued as a purely consultative and advisory body chaired by Sokolow and Weizmann. The four rooms Simon Marks rented in July 1917 no longer sufficed to accommodate the increased Zionist activity, so in March 1918 an additional six rooms were let at the same address.[96] Weizmann feared that matters would not be handled precisely as he wished, for he did not trust Sokolow to follow his directives from afar. He therefore asked his two most trusted collaborators, Tolkowsky and Vera, to keep an eye on affairs in the London office.[97]

At last Weizmann and the commission were ready to depart on March 4. Two days earlier Weizmann was to have an audience, at Sykes's initiative, with King George V. On the appointed day Weizmann arrived with top hat, but Sir Mark wished to cancel the interview because the previous day he had received a cable from Wingate reporting heightened hostility of Arabs to Zionism.[98] Weizmann, who at first did not fully appreciate the propaganda value for Zionism of such an interview,

Weizmann, his sister Gita, and Israel Sieff in Palestine, 1918. Courtesy: Israel State Archives

now insisted that Balfour decide the issue. The foreign secretary ruled in favor of the interview, which took place on the morning of Weizmann's departure for Palestine. Once again Weizmann had to don his newly bought top hat and make his way to Buckingham Palace. It was a friendly discussion of thirty-five minutes; the king seemed well informed about and sympathetic to Zionism.[99] Lloyd George was unable to fit Weizmann into his schedule,[100] but he did provide him with a letter of introduction to General Allenby, as did Balfour.[101]

On the evening of March 4, 1918, the Zionist Commission set out for Paris, then on to Rome and Taranto, from whence they sailed on the *Canberra* for Alexandria on March 17. The previous few weeks had been so hectic that Weizmann had no time to contemplate the larger meaning of his mission. As on other visits, Rome seemed to move him to philosophical reflections on the history of the Jews and his own part in that history. He wrote to Vera:

My dear child, it's difficult to describe to you everything I feel as I get nearer
to Palestine. This is such a huge task, shall I have enough strength and
wisdom not only to decide about everything, but to set things on the right
course . . . [?]

Remember that this is my military service, service for the good of [our]
native land. You as well as I will endure this separation in the knowledge
that the finest and noblest share has fallen to us. We're both paying a high
price for it. . . . The whole of [our] life was an introduction to the chapter
we're beginning now.

Be strong and of good courage! That was Joshua's cry when he was near-
ing Palestine; with great love I repeat the call to you! My strength is in your
strength![102]

The Zionist Commission began working prior to its embarkation. It
held its first meeting on March 11 in Rome. Weizmann reviewed its
scope of activities, while Ormsby-Gore read excerpts of the directives he
had been given.[103] During the second meeting, which took place aboard
ship on March 14, Ormsby-Gore outlined some of the questions the
commission would need to address in Palestine concerning the Arabs,
land purchase, the Holy Places, and future plans of the Zionists. Summarizing the discussion, Weizmann stated frankly that Zionism had as
its ultimate political objective the creation of a Jewish commonwealth,
but that for the moment it was too early to indicate how this aim would
be achieved. He thought the Arabs might become a political liability to
the British after the war and that the Arab effendis "were a cancer
ruining the country."[104]

The Zionists, nevertheless, were anxious not to cause any unnecessary problems for the British, and one way to avoid such trouble was to
keep off private lands and restrict purchases to waste, crown (British-
owned), and unoccupied lands until the peace conference. The Christian
and Muslim Holy Places obviously needed to be respected, but Weizmann thought the Jews ought to retain the Wailing Wall, place a fence
around it, and mount a Jewish guard on it. The Zionists had no wish to
expropriate the Arabs and would pay fair prices for the land. On the
other hand, they intended to bring as many Jews as possible into Palestine, which was as much the land of the Jews as the land of the Arabs
with plenty of space for both. Finally, turning to Ormsby-Gore, Weizmann asked that as a visible sign of the Balfour Declaration, Hebrew be
used as one of the official languages in the proclamations of the British
authorities and that currency and stamps bear a Hebrew inscription. The
psychological effects of such a manifestation on the Jews of the world
would be far reaching.[105]

So heterogeneous a group, as might be expected, generated personal
and ideological clashes. No sooner did they arrive in Taranto than Weizmann quarreled with Sylvain Lévi and James de Rothschild, neither of
whom had been his choice for the commission. From the outset Lévi
made no secret of his antagonism toward Jewish nationalism and the

idea of a Jewish state. A number of heated discussions ensued on this topic between him and Weizmann. The clash with James de Rothschild was not purely ideological. Rothschild had already taken umbrage at Weizmann's Manchester speech in which Weizmann, among other issues, also lashed out against the rich and assimilated Jewish magnates.[106]

In Taranto, James, possibly influenced by his father's representative on the commission, Sylvain Lévi, suggested that the term "Jewish" be dropped and that the Zionists speak instead about building up a Hebrew nation in Palestine, thus minimizing the offense to Frenchmen and Englishmen of the Jewish persuasion.[107] Weizmann might have let it go at that, but he was becoming increasingly irritated by James de Rothschild's tendency to sulk and keep aloof from the rest.[108] In the presence of Ormsby-Gore, Weizmann took Jimmy to task, as Leon Simon recorded in his diary: "He told J . . . that either the mantle of his father would fall on him, and he would come along with us, or he would be wiped out of existence. O[rmsby-Gore] said afterwards that he thought that the talk had done J. good, and I believe that it has—at any rate for the time being."[109] For some time thereafter Weizmann adopted "a policy of sternness" with Jimmy, vowing that the young Rothschild "would eat dirt before he is restored to favour."[110]

Indeed, Weizmann's reprimand had a short-term good effect on Jimmy, though for a number of months their relationship would continue to be cool, at times even unpleasant. Such open rebuke to the scion of the house of Rothschild was not without its risks, but its public display also served notice that Weizmann was clearly in charge and that he was not going to be cowed by the prestige and wealth of the young heir. It clearly impressed Ormsby-Gore, whose admiration for Weizmann grew steadily over the next few months. Weizmann reciprocated, observing, "Gore is splendid."[111] Leon Simon noted in his diary that "O[rmsby-Gore] is very understanding and sympathetic [toward Zionist aspirations] and will certainly help us all he can. I doubt if we could have a better political officer."[112] Both assessments were correct; Ormsby-Gore turned out to be one of the commission's most valuable assets.

Arriving in Alexandria on March 20, the Zionist Commission was greeted by a large and enthusiastic crowd of local notables led by Edgar Suarès and Baron Felix de Menasce, as well as Palestinian refugees bearing Zionist banners and singing the "Hatikvah." Arriving later by train in Cairo, they enjoyed a similar reception.[113] The only thing that marred their arrival was a news item which appeared in the *Egyptian Gazette* the previous day concerning anti-Zionist activity in London. The reference was to the first general meeting of the League of British Jews, which had been founded on November 14, 1917, to protect the political status of British Jews and objected to defining them as a separate national political entity. At the general meeting of March 14, 1918, those assembled protested against the use of the term "Jewish national home" in the

Balfour Declaration and objected to the founding of a Jewish university.[114] Weizmann, as well as Ormsby-Gore and Reginald Wingate, were
concerned lest the news from London add fuel to Arab anti-Zionist
propaganda.[115] With the assistance of Balfour, Sykes moved even before
receipt of the cables from Cairo to counteract the league's anti-Zionist
propaganda. Its publications were censored after the appropriate order
was issued to Lord Beaverbrook, the minister of information.[116]

On March 22 the Zionist Commission was introduced by Ormsby-Gore
to Sir Reginald Wingate. The high commissioner was cordial and talka-
tive and seemed sincere in his pro-Zionist sympathies, which may have
been strengthened by his recent visit to the Jewish colonies.[117] He reiterated the by now well-known Arab fear of Jewish expropriation, while
Weizmann reassured Sir Reginald and his staff that the Zionists had no
such intentions, that they did not contemplate a Jewish state in the near
future, and that there was complete identity of interests between the
Zionists and the British.[118] After the hour-long meeting with the commission, Wingate, Ormsby-Gore, and Weizmann conferred privately. Both
the British and neutral observers were impressed that Weizmann was
doing his utmost to allay Arab fears by his moderation and conciliatory
stance.[119] For his part, Weizmann encountered for the first time the depth
of ignorance of British officers, even high-ranking officers such as Clayton, about the immediate aims of the Zionists.[120] He realized that they
were either uninformed or misinformed about some basic facts and that
he would have to spend a great deal of time and effort explaining his
position to both the British and the Arabs.[121] Weizmann was, therefore,
eager to accept offers from Wingate, Clayton, and Ormsby-Gore to arrange for meetings with Palestinian and Arab leaders.

Ormsby-Gore arranged for Weizmann to meet Faris Nimr, the editor
of *Al Mokattam,* on March 27, together with Said Shuquayr and Sulay-
man Nasif of the Palestine Committee of Moslems and Christians from
Syria and Palestine, which had recently been founded in Cairo. They
seemed to be satisfied with Weizmann's assurances that the Zionist
Commission would act to prevent land speculation and that the commission did not intend to control the administration or plan to establish
a Jewish state immediately after the war; nor did it wish supervision
over the Holy Places, except those sacred to Jews.[122]

On March 29 members of the Zionist Commission met the members
of the Palestine Committee of Moslems and Christians and some members of the Syrian Welfare Committee. These leaders promised to calm
their followers in Palestine while reasserting their claim to full equality
with the Jews. Weizmann assured them that the Jewish university and
schools would be open to Arabs, a promise that was well received.[123]
On April 1, Weizmann, together with Dr. David Eder, Sylvain Lévi,
Aaronsohn, Sieff, and Ormsby-Gore met with Kamil Abu Kasib, Abd al-
Rahman Shahbandar, the editor of *El Kawkab,* and Said Shuquayr for
further discussions. It was a vague but friendly discussion about histor-

ical developments and national destinies of the two nations.[124] Subsequently the Arab leaders presented Ormsby-Gore with a memorandum containing "the fundamental lines on which should repose the desired policy of mutual understanding, cooperation and alliance between Palestinians and Zionists." Weizmann felt, however, that it was premature to deal with this memorandum since these negotiations ought to take place with the Arab leaders in Palestine.[125] All in all, the meetings with Arab leaders were deemed successful by those concerned, the only discordant note being struck in some of the negotiations by Aaronsohn, who vehemently denied certain accusations put forward by the Arabs.[126]

The ten-day sojourn in Cairo afforded Weizmann the opportunity to visit the Thirty-eighth Battalion Royal Fusiliers, who had arrived shortly before and were training near the city. A young English Jew described how Weizmann addressed them:

> Lolling at a table, with his hands deep in his trouser pockets, he just spoke to them easily and racily and familiarly, in their own and his own native Yiddish, getting his points well away with that idiomatic shrug and gesture which constitute one of the most integral parts of the language.
>
> The audience responded to a man. They were all his, body and soul, ready to leap into his pocket at the first word of command. As he walked across the camp, the men, like rats after the Pied Piper, just followed him, to the long drawn out wistfulness of the *Hatikvah*.[127]

The Zionist Commission was detained in Egypt until the end of Easter-Passover on April 2. General Allenby invited Weizmann to visit the next day at his headquarters at Bir Salem, just south of Ramleh, within viewing distance of Rehovot, Weizmann's future residence. The rest of the members of the commission were to follow Weizmann a day later. Upon his arrival at the train station of Bir Salem on April 3, Weizmann was greeted by Captain James de Rothschild and Major Ormsby-Gore,[128] who briefed him on Allenby and political conditions in Palestine. James de Rothschild's pessimistic account of the military condition, which, he felt, would impede the work of the Zionist Commission, was tempered by news that Lady Crewe and Lady Allenby, whom Weizmann had met in Cairo, had sent favorable reports about Weizmann and Zionism to the commander in chief and some of his senior officers.[129] Though tired from his overnight trip from Cairo, Weizmann had little chance to rest before he was ushered in to meet Allenby. The general, who had been briefed by Ormsby-Gore, expressed sympathy with Zionist aims but also made it clear that he wished to govern the country justly and "hand over Palestine at the end of the War in a good condition." After a brief exposition on Zionism, Weizmann launched into a lengthy description of the power of the Jews in various parts of the world who wished to see a British Palestine. This kind of analysis had had good effect with British officials and statesmen in London in the months leading to the Balfour Declaration. Weizmann also made sure to point out to the general—as he had done with Sir Reginald Wingate—that the Arabs might be an asset to Britain at this stage of the war but could just as easily turn out to be a liability in the future. The Jews, however, were a permanent asset to Great Britain. Weizmann did not seem to have elaborated on this comparison, unless his remarks about the global power of the Jews can explain what he meant by "permanent asset." For his part, Allenby wisely refrained from commenting.[130]

Weizmann was clearly impressed by Allenby. He "is a great man, intelligent, well-read, straightforward and interested in many things," Weizmann reported to Vera. The commander in chief likewise told his senior officers that he was very satisfied and pleased by the interview.[131] That evening, at dinner, Weizmann was wedged in between General Allenby and Major-General Louis Bols, Allenby's chief of staff. It was not an opportune moment for the head of the Zionist Commission to be there. Allenby's advance in Palestine had been checked, and all attention was on the Western front; the two generals were eager to talk about the war, which they did across Weizmann. The discussion did glide to an assessment of the activities of Picot in Palestine, and Weizmann was able to agree wholeheartedly with Allenby's directives restricting the Frenchman's activities there. Whatever he said that day and the following morning, the consensus among Allenby's top officers was that Weizmann was the right man to lead the Zionist Commission. General Clayton summed it up succinctly in a letter to Sykes: "We are all struck with his intelligence and openness and the Commander-in-Chief has evidently formed a high opinion of him. I feel convinced that many of the difficulties which we have encountered owing to the mutual distrust and suspicion between Arabs and Jews will now disappear."[132]

Allenby's high opinion of Weizmann meant that he was willing to listen sympathetically to grievances brought by the head of the Zionist Commission, even if such meetings did not always have immediate concrete results. This relationship was illustrated by the Petach Tikvah incident, which Leon Simon dubbed "a first-rate crisis."[133] For some time, the Jewish residents of Petach Tikvah, which was close to the enemy lines, were suspected by some British officers of passing information to the Turks. Weizmann and the residents of the town had vehemently protested this charge as totally unfounded, but to no avail.[134] On May 17, without the knowledge of Allenby and Clayton, the British military authorities ordered the evacuation of all Jewish civilians. This order smacked of outright discrimination, because the neighboring Arab population was not being evacuated. Two days later Weizmann had an interview with Allenby. The evacuation order was not rescinded, but Weizmann was able to secure a number of concessions from the commander in chief. "We have won all along the line," recorded Simon jubilantly.[135] It was also agreed that Allenby would pay an official visit to Jerusalem. On May 24, in the company of some of his highest-ranking officers, Allenby was received by Weizmann, who presented him with a

Torah scroll.[136] It was a visible demonstration of high regard for Weizmann, though it did not mean that Allenby was willing to deviate from the prescribed *status quo ante.*

One of the officers who was truly "struck" by Weizmann was Colonel Wyndham Deedes, chief intelligence officer of the Egyptian Expeditionary Force and a man deeply moved by religious considerations to support Zionism.[137] At Bir Salem, Deedes had alerted Weizmann to the prevalence of antisemitism among the British troops by showing him extracts of the best-selling fabrication, *The Protocols of the Elders of Zion.* According to Weizmann's autobiography, Deedes had assured him that the book could be found in the haversacks of a great many British officers, who believed it.[138] This latter assertion is rather doubtful, since the first English edition of the *Protocols* was published only in 1920. There was a mystical strain in Deedes's personality that combined practical ability, lofty idealism, and humanitarianism. He had a profound appreciation of the Jewish problem in its spiritual aspects and a deep belief in the blessings that the restoration of the Jews to the Holy Land would bring, not only to the Jews themselves but to the world at large.[139]

Weizmann recognized Deedes's unusual qualities, and the two immediately became friends. Weizmann had a keen eye for those British statesmen and officers whom he could fully trust to help further his cause; in some ways he became more intimate with them than with some fellow Zionists. Deedes was one of those Britons to whom Weizmann revealed, within days of their acquaintanceship, his long-range plans for Palestine.[140] For his part, Deedes was anxious to make a good impression on Weizmann; in order to lighten the Zionist's heavy work load, he assigned to him a member of his own staff, Herbert Samuel's son, Edwin.[141]

Weizmann understood the depth of Arab fears and hostility toward the Zionists and the ignorance of many British officers as to the plans of the Zionist Commission. Within days of his arrival in Palestine he was also to realize how correct Deedes had been in his assessment of the attitudes of British officers toward the Yishuv and the Zionist Commission. Many years later Weizmann recalled the intellectual and emotional shock of the transition from negotiations in London to negotiations in Palestine. In Whitehall he did not have to spell out every Zionist plan; he operated within a framework of common trust. In Palestine he encountered mistrust and resentment, and he had to start all over again before he could gain the confidence of some of the British officers.[142] A letter from Ormsby-Gore to Sykes described some of the difficulties Weizmann faced in his dealings with the British military administration: "[Ronald] Storrs [the military governor of Jerusalem] is doing very well indeed—but though they are all excellent men, the other governors are all Sudan or Gippy Army men whose experience in the Sudan does not make for a ready realisation of the very wide questions of world policy which affect Palestine. One can't help noticing the ineradicable tendency

Members of the Zionist Commission on their way to Jaffa via Lod, April 1918. Standing, from left: Robert Waley-Cohen, unidentified clerk, Zeev Gluskin, Zalman David Levontin, Leon Simon, Sylvain Lévi, Israel Sieff, Joseph Cowen, Weizmann, William Ormsby-Gore. On the train, from left: Private Aloni, David Eder, Walter Meyer, Aaron Aaronsohn, Jules Rosenheck. Courtesy: Central Zionist Archives

of the Englishman who has lived in India or the Sudan to favour quite unconsciously the Moslem both against Christian and Jew."[143]

Though he firmly believed that "the Zionists are the one sound, firmly pro-British, constructive element in the whole show" and that, on the other hand, "the Arabs in Palestine are . . . showing their old tendency to corrupt methods and backsheesh,"[144] Ormsby-Gore, like General Clayton,[145] felt that the Zionists ought to tread carefully lest they offend Arab—and possibly British—sensibilities. He thus advised the Jews of Jaffa–Tel Aviv, who had intended a festive welcome for the Zionist Commission, against carrying out their plans.[146] "Things did not exactly begin well for us in Palestine . . . when we arrived in Tel Aviv," noted Leon Simon in his diary. "It is no exaggeration to say that we (i.e. the whole party except Chaim who came by motor before us) were received rather like refugees than like a Zionist Commission."[147] This was also the impression their arrival made on Mordechai Ben-Hillel Hacohen, a founding father of Tel Aviv and one of its most respected citizens, who welcomed the commission members. Few people came to greet the com-

Reception for General Edmund H. Allenby, Jerusalem, May 24, 1918. Speaking, far right: David Eder. Standing, from left: Dalmeny, Ronald Storrs, Weizmann, Allenby, Rabbi Sonnenfeld, Sephardi chief rabbi, Gilbert Clayton, James de Rothschild, Leon Simon. Courtesy: Weizmann Archives

mission, and, because of poor planning by the military authorities, commission members even had to walk part of the way.[148] The official reception at the town council office had to wait for the following day, while a public meeting to welcome the commission members took place on April 6. Thus, the entry of the Zionist Commission into Palestine was awkward, almost embarrassing. It did not augur well for the future.

In April 1918, as the Zionist Commission was adjusting to its new setting and making plans to meet its many responsibilities, a new set of regulations began to govern the British-occupied area of southern Palestine. An Occupied Enemy Territory Administration was formed, usually referred to as OETA. Major General Arthur Money was appointed at its head with the title of chief administrator and took his orders from Allenby. Clayton retained his post as chief political officer, taking his orders directly from the Foreign Office.[149] OETA was administered strictly in accordance with the laws and usages of war (Hague Convention) as laid down in the *Manual of Military Law*. This code regarded the administration of occupied enemy territory as being purely temporary and decreed the maintenance as far as possible of the *status quo ante bellum*. Thus the Turkish systems of law, taxation, and administration remained as they were, and the most visible change was the replacement of Turkish with British personnel.[150]

The military system imposed on the occupied territories was by definition inhospitable to any attempt to carry out the declared Zionist policy of the British government. As Weizmann noticed from his first conversations with British officers in Cairo and Bir Salem, moreover, there
was a lack of definition on the part of the British and Allied governments in regard to the future political status of Palestine. The Sykes-
Picot Agreement had not yet been formally scrapped, and the specter of
internationalization and division of Palestine into British and French zones
was still in the air, even if the British pretended to ignore this possibility.

At the same time, both the Zionists and the military administration
felt hampered by the lack of decisive political direction. While the Zionists and other segments of the community in Palestine were being
encouraged to carry on propaganda in favor of British Palestine,[151] a
good deal of agitation took place in Egypt by Francophile Syrians and
French agents in favor of a united French Syria and Palestine. This propaganda sought to prove that Palestine was an integral part of Syria and
that the postwar settlement should involve the creation of a French Syria
stretching from the old Egyptian frontier to Alexandretta.[152]

Under these circumstances, the most that the Zionist Commission could
hope to achieve was to ensure, as much as possible, that no changes be
made by the military administration in Palestine which would adversely
affect the Zionist enterprise after the war. At the same time, Weizmann's policy was to create political and economic bases wherever he
could so as to give the Zionists the strongest possible case before the
peace conference. First and foremost he strove to rehabilitate and
strengthen the Palestinian Jewish community from within by attending
to its most immediate as well as long-range economic, social, and political needs.

The terms of reference under which Weizmann launched the Zionist
Commission were sufficiently broad, but under his dynamic leadership
the commission developed an unanticipated depth of involvement in
Palestinian affairs that proved decisive for the future. Clearly, any ambitious leader in charge of a project so broadly defined as the Zionist
Commission would have taken advantage of the existing chaos in Jewish
Palestine to extend its original mandate widely. Given Weizmann's flair
and nervous energy, the commission took off with kangaroo leaps and
bounds.

A number of rooms were prepared for Weizmann's use at the home
of Zalman Levontin, while other members of the commission were similarly taken care of. No sooner had Weizmann settled in than he began
briefing the local leadership of Tel Aviv and Jaffa of the political events
that took place during the war period. For their part they described in
some detail the condition of the Yishuv during the past four years.

The Yishuv, which by 1914 already had an existing base for building
a Jewish homeland, had suffered severely from siege and Turkish

oppression.[153] Cut off from overseas markets and sources of supply, the hapless community was saved from general starvation only by the emergency efforts of Diaspora Jews.[154] Political interventions by the Diaspora spared the Yishuv from suffering the full ferocity of a suspicious and vengeful Turkish military governor, who considered Zionists, no less than Armenians and Arab nationalists, to be enemies of the Ottoman Empire.[155] The Yishuv nonetheless lost one-third or more of its prewar numbers, leaving something less than fifty-seven thousand Jews in the Holy Land toward the close of hostilities.[156]

The wartime loss was not evenly distributed throughout the Yishuv; nor were the Yishuv's component groups equally able to make the necessary adjustments in the face of crisis. The heaviest blow was suffered by those least able to organize to meet it—the Old Yishuv, constituting two-thirds of the prewar Jewish population. The Jews of Jerusalem, Safed, and Hebron were greatly reduced in numbers by hunger and disease, and many emigrated to survive.[157] The plantation colonies, hit by the loss of markets and by Turkish exactions, also lost ground, and Jaffa Jews were among those expelled. But, together with the rest of the New Yishuv, the coastal settlers responded actively to the crisis with emergency measures of cooperative organization.[158] Those in the most favorable position were the new grain-growing settlements and other colonists of the inland and northern regions. Their produce was a major source of food for the urban community during the war.[159]

Among the special targets of Turkish hostility were those most active in the Yishuv's newest leadership. Second Aliyah labor leaders, even though they had increasingly sought to identify with the Ottomans since the Young Turk revolution, were, as Russians, enemy aliens; and, as socialist militants, they were also particularly suspect. The new official Zionists, many of whom, like Arthur Ruppin, were German nationals and hence Turkish allies, were nevertheless held under suspicion as Jewish nationalists. These circles were carefully watched; from time to time arrests were made, and, in the end, many were exiled.[160] Thus in the first few months after the arrival of the Zionist Commission, few of the veteran leaders of the New Yishuv were in Palestine, ready to shoulder new burdens and create new structures. Nevertheless, the news of the Balfour Declaration and the fall of Jerusalem served as a catalyst for those leaders who remained to create an authoritative political structure to represent the Yishuv. An initial meeting in Petach Tikvah on November 18, 1917, was followed in Jaffa on January 2–3, 1918, by the first founding assembly of the Yishuv, which elected the thirty-six-member Provisional Executive Committee of Jews in Eretz Israel in the Occupied Territory (Vaad Zmani).[161]

Like many other Zionists in the front ranks of the movement, Weizmann was well aware of the fate of the Jewish community in Palestine throughout the war. As a member of the GAC and through his many contacts and ever-growing reputation, he was the regular recipient of

detailed reports on the Yishuv from various segments of the movement;[162] on occasion he also served as a channel for news and a conduit
for appeals for aid.[163] Moreover, he was kept informed by Jacob Thon,
Ruppin's successor as director of the Palestine office of the WZO and
soon to become president of the Vaad Zmani in Palestine, of the successful efforts to organize the Yishuv.[164]

Despite his awareness of the Yishuv's efforts to reorganize, Weizmann
intended to manage the work of the Zionist Commission without any
local checks or balances. With the authority of the British conqueror behind him, he set out to reorganize not only the administration of relief
to the Jewish community but all other urgent aspects of its affairs. The
Zionist Commission eventually displaced other, local claimants to represent the community before the government and asserted itself as the
ultimate authority in seeking, with varying success, to regulate local internal issues as well.

The Vaad Zmani attempted to change Weizmann's mind on the subject of representation during their first joint meeting on April 15, 1918,
but to no avail. Weizmann successfully sidestepped the issue by declaring that only the Zionist Organization and the British government could
appoint new members to the commission.[165] A compromise was finally
reached, and regular meetings were set up to maintain a liaison with the
official representation of the Yishuv. In addition, during its meeting of
April 29, 1918, the commission accepted the suggestion of the Palestine
office of the WZO that seven subcommittees be established to deal with
specific tasks.[166] Having satisfied—at least to some extent—the desire of
the local leadership to be involved in the work of rehabilitation and reconstruction, Weizmann avoided a direct confrontation but still made it
clear that he was the final arbiter.

The Zionist Commission steadfastly presented itself as the authorized
channel through which all relief funds and supplies contributed abroad
should flow for distribution. The two contending committees in Egypt,
through which Zionists had sent their support previously, were readily
absorbed,[167] and Joint Distribution Committee direct support was also
channeled, more or less consistently, through the commission.[168] Even
the *halukkah* donations for the upkeep of the institutions and beneficiaries of the older, traditionalist community—already dependent since the
war on Zionist transmission—came under the commission's dispensa-
tion.[169]

With this source of prestige and persuasion at their disposal, Weizmann and his chief helpers on the commission—mainly Dr. David Eder—
attempted bold and far-reaching reforms, especially in Jerusalem, whose
poverty, moral and physical deterioration, and internal dissensions they
viewed with dismay. Weizmann wanted to impose on the *yeshivot*, totally committed to traditional Talmud studies, a new curriculum drawing on the model of a European university and to introduce appropriate
secular studies in the Orthodox lower schools.[170] He also attempted to

unite the disputatious Zionist Vaad Hair[171] and ultra-Orthodox Havaad Haashkenazi subcommunities and divided sects of Jerusalem Jewry into a common communal organization.[172] He failed in both, and his demands for educational reforms provoked an ultra-Orthodox opposition that presaged the anti-Zionist faction of later days among these traditionalists.[173]

Economic and social issues, particularly in Jerusalem, pressed the Zionist Commission to meet immediate contingencies as well as affected its ambitious designs to plan the future reconstruction.[174] Weizmann was able to use the funds assigned to him, flowing from American and Russian sources through the London Zionist office, to bolster the Zionist bank, the Anglo-Palestine Company, by depositing commission funds there and persuading the military authorities to use its facilities. On the other hand, he quashed the attempt of Eliezer Siegfried Hoofien, the acting general manager of the Anglo-Palestine Company and the Joint Distribution Committee representative in Palestine, to receive relief funds directly and control their distribution, and he confined Hoofien's role to recording and accounting.[175] Weizmann's ambitious hope, to have the Anglo-Palestine Company recognized as a bank of issue, was not realized; the British instead used Egyptian currency as the local legal tender.[176]

The demands on his budget for relief and immediate needs—including maintenance of the network of Hilfsverein der deutschen Juden schools formerly owned by the German Jewish philanthropists and now taken over by the Zionists[177]—allowed Weizmann no margin for commercial loans. He had to borrow from the bank to cover the commission's current expenses, with growing arrears owing to the lagging transmissions from abroad. He repeatedly appealed to the Americans to advance part of their fund collections for long-term loans to the plantation colonies to help them reestablish their orchards and vineyards. Since any such operation strained the capacity of the Anglo-Palestine Company, he proposed that an agricultural mortgage bank be established to fill the need in the future.[178]

The main focus of Weizmann's economic planning, and that of other Zionists, was the acquisition and development of new lands. They assumed—and certainly hoped—that Britain's promise to use its "best endeavours," as stated in the Balfour Declaration, to facilitate Zionist settlement would include allowing them to purchase and develop lands, especially crown lands not being fully utilized in Palestine. Brandeis, taking cognizance of this prospect, counseled Weizmann that the commission should make sure that *all* land purchases be held in public ownership and not exploited by private speculators.[179] Weizmann readily, perhaps casually, agreed to this advice, though referring specifically to "crown lands" in his reply, no doubt accepting it as in line with traditional Zionist policy exemplified in the Jewish National Fund.[180] But it soon became clear that land transfers even of those types of lands Weizmann thought would be easiest to acquire—crown lands, unoccupied lands, and waste lands—were more or less ruled out for the time being owing to the military administration's strict adherence to the Hague Convention requiring the maintenance of the *status quo ante* in occupied territories and because the Turks had taken the land registers with them in their retreat.[181] Weizmann therefore had to direct his policy to provisional alternatives.

Weizmann still hoped for approval for some land transfers, especially on options initiated before the war or for special purposes of great symbolic importance. One such case was the land of the Gray-Hill estate on Mount Scopus in Jerusalem, where the Jewish university was to be built. Another was his project to purchase, from the Moroccan religious foundation that owned it, the land adjoining the Wailing Wall—a proposal the British regarded as too risky to handle and advised Weizmann to negotiate directly with the Muslim authorities.[182]

Apart from such exceptions, Weizmann had to face the fact of a strict *status quo ante* policy. He may perhaps have understood that in this way the British were blocking not only Zionist hopes temporarily but also the French pretensions signaled when Georges Picot appeared in Allenby's train with the significant title of "High Commissioner of the French Republic in the Occupied Areas of Palestine and Syria."[183] The Zionist Commission now favored a policy, in line with British ideas, of banning land transactions generally in order to forestall speculative pressures that could increase the cost of land for the Zionists in the future.

One other opportunity for land development was suggested by the current needs of the military administration, and the Zionist Commission believed it might be able to supply expert assistance. Aaron Aaronsohn pointed out that large areas of land along the coast between Jaffa and the Sinai border had been abandoned and lay fallow in the wake of the British advance. He proposed that the Zionists undertake immediately to farm half a million acres by American methods of extensive, mechanized dry farming and thus provide support for the army and the military administration in the coming seasons. He proposed that the army take over untilled private land and lease it, together with crown lands, to be farmed by the commission. There would be the immediate gain for the military administration and a long-range gain for the Zionist enterprise by establishing a claim to the land it would cultivate if that land were found not to be registered as private property.[184] Similar ideas had already been suggested before the arrival of the Zionist Commission by Eliyahu Krause, the director of the Mikveh Israel Agricultural School, and Yitzhak Wilkansky, the director of the Agricultural Department of the Palestine office of the WZO. They now joined Aaronsohn to produce a joint memorandum for the military authorities.[185]

The army was initially inclined to favor the plan and informed Weizmann accordingly on April 23, 1918.[186] But General Money, the military administrator, made it clear that the army was unwilling to implement the plan on its own initiative. Aaronsohn and Wilkansky were authorized to accompany army personnel in surveys of the area that might be used. Indeed, one joint exploratory survey was conducted. The commission corresponded through Weizmann with its American friends concerning the recruitment of engineers and technical experts and supply of necessary machinery and found them, in principle, prepared to participate. But the project required London's approval since Allenby would not depart from the *status quo ante* policy on his own authority. He suggested approaching Balfour, but Balfour delayed indefinitely, bringing the project to an end.[187]

In any case, by mid-July 1918 the army lost interest in the plan. It feared antagonizing the Arabs, and the protracted period of military immobility that was the basis of the plan ended during the summer months. After all the effort and planning connected with this project, Weizmann's disappointment was profound. He continued to cling to the idea that the plan could still be implemented and instructed Aaronsohn, who was once again being sent to the United States in the summer of 1918, to try to obtain the necessary means for implementing this scheme should it be approved by the British authorities.[188]

Even while it seemed that the army was favorably disposed to the idea of the Zionist Commission's land scheme and he himself recognized the potential importance of the areas proposed for cultivation by Jews, Weizmann was uneasy. He understood the heavy financial commitment that would be required of the World Zionist Organization should the scheme be approved, and he wanted to have some independent, reliable information—apart from that given him by Aaronsohn and Wilkansky—as to the value of the territory south of Jaffa. Shortly after the arrival of the commission in Palestine, Rahel Yanait Ben-Zvi, an active member of the Hashomer, a Palestinian Jewish self-defense group, informed him that its members had secret plans to settle in the Negev. Weizmann appreciated the fact that the members of Hashomer knew Arabic and the territory to be investigated and could be relied upon to keep a secret. Upon the recommendation of Yanait, Weizmann authorized three Hashomer members—Mordechai Yigael, Noah Sunin, and Shaul Karbel—to conduct a survey of the Negev and investigate the Bedouin tribes and their lands. The funds for this expedition were provided from a secret account.[189] The three went on their expedition during the last days of April or early May 1918, but their mission was soon aborted. Since they had no official permits, they were arrested by the British army in Ashdod. Weizmann was eventually able to arrange for their release, and the military authorities preferred, on this occasion, to overlook Weizmann's involvement in the affair.[190]

The British were interested in the Zionist Commission mainly as a political instrument. Their hopes for the Balfour Declaration were pinned to the presumed influence of the Zionists with their brethren in the United States and Russia. Their fears centered on the antagonism their pro-Zionist policy might provoke among Arabs and other Muslims. They could guard against this danger by avoiding public notice of the declaration in the Middle East as a temporary measure, but they relied on Weizmann to ease the inevitable, eventual implementation of their Zionist commitment, in however attenuated a shape, by presenting Zionism to the Arabs in a relatively palatable form. The part of the commission guidelines that primarily interested them was its assignment to help forge the Arab-Armenian-Jewish alliance by which men like Sykes hoped to find a graceful escape from the inconvenient arrangements laid down in the Sykes-Picot Agreement.

Weizmann, who held that the cardinal point for the Zionists was to rely on their relationship of mutual confidence with the British, undertook this task in spite of what must have seemed to him its excessive demands. The British themselves, he may have thought, should bear primary responsibility for carrying through their policy *vis-à-vis* their allies the French and their clients the Arabs. He concluded that the British failed to do so because they lacked the understanding of Zionism he had found among Britons in London. To solve this problem London must clearly instruct the officers in the field that British policy was pro-Zionist and that the "non-Jewish communities" in Palestine must understand this. But in the meantime he accepted his responsibility to teach the British officers and Arab leaders about the nature and goals of Zionism, just as he had done as part of his special, personal contribution to securing the Balfour Declaration.

Weizmann addressed himself primarily to the stereotypical, distorted view of Zionist intentions. Zionists did not seek immediately to establish a Jewish government in Palestine. Jews were not about to seize Arab lands by massive coercion and force the Arabs to leave. Jews certainly never intended to destroy Muslim Holy Places in order to build their Temple, and the Jews were not agents of the Bolshevik Revolution.[191] Antisemitic propaganda and outright lies demanded action by the authorities. On the political and economic intentions of Zionism, Weizmann formulated more positive responses. He stressed that Zionism had no immediate (a qualification sometimes omitted) aim to set up a Jewish state or government in Palestine. Zionist economic activities would redound to the benefit of the entire population. The first proposition was well received by the British officers whom he met, and some were inclined to interpret Weizmann's renunciations of a Jewish state as probably final and not simply a deferment of the goal.

Although the political climate in Palestine was considerably less favorable to Zionism than what Weizmann was used to in London, he still had, at least during 1918, considerable room for maneuver in his relations with the military administration. Relations between the army and leaders of the Yishuv had begun to sour even before the arrival of the Zionist Commission,[192] but French ambitions for the same territories dictated a British policy that militated against unnecessarily antagonizing the Zionists. Senior army officers, moreover, were well aware that London had decided to secure a British Palestine at the peace conference. Politically attuned officers like Clayton could foresee problems for Britain were the Zionist Commission, and particularly Weizmann, to become disenchanted with the British government:

> To defer all development of the Zionist policy and to ask the Zionists to rest content that the assurances given to them will be fulfilled at some future date after the war . . . is to present them with a stone in fulfillment of what they regard, with some justice, as a promise of at least a small portion of bread. There is little doubt that such a course would involve the withdrawal of Dr. Weizmann from his position of leader of pro-British Zionism and the departure of the Zionist Commission from Palestine. This would be a severe blow to British diplomacy in the eyes of the whole world. . . . Indeed, the result might well be to throw Zionism into the arms of America or even at worst on to Germany. Thus the death-blow would be dealt to pro-British Zionism, and at the same time to any hope of securing Zionist influence at the Peace Conference in favor of a British Palestine.[193]

Despite the army's attempt to placate the Zionists, and Weizmann's own view, during the early months in Palestine, that the authorities were unenlightened, not anti-Zionist, there were constant daily frictions and often unintended insults between the Zionists and the British. Many of these were in themselves meaningless, but they did produce, through a cumulative effect, festering mutual resentment. The root causes of these tensions were due not only to lack of sufficient information on the part of the British as to Zionist aims. Another fear held by the men in the field, even among those inclined to carry out the British government's promise, was that any strong pro-Zionist demonstration might antagonize the Arabs;[194] the notion that it might not be possible to bridge Arab and Zionist aims and aspirations was slowly taking hold. Indeed, the Arab question and the attitude of the British authorities in Palestine were inextricably intertwined, as Weizmann understood soon after his arrival in Palestine. He confessed to Ormsby-Gore: "The political atmosphere is not so favorable as we could wish. . . . We refer in particular to the attitude of the Arabs and Syrians, and to the way in which that attitude is regarded by the Military Authorities."[195]

The immediate cause for Weizmann's charge against the military authorities was an incident, reported to Weizmann and his colleagues by eyewitnesses, which took place a few days earlier, on April 11, during the commission's first official visit to Jerusalem. It seems that during a theatrical performance staged at a Muslim orphanage, in the presence of Ronald Storrs, the military governor of Jerusalem, anti-Zionist speeches were made to which the governor did not react. In the eyes of the Zionists the incident gained further significance because it took place on the very day on which a large gathering of Jews welcomed the commission on Mount Scopus.[196]

Referring to himself as a "convinced Zionist," Storrs vehemently denied that the incident took place in the manner described by Weizmann.

Leaders of Palestinian Jewry and the Zionist Commission, 1918. Sitting, from left: two unidentified, Menashe Meirovitch, Aaron Eisenberg, Bezalel Jaffe, Sephardi Chief Rabbi Uziel, Jacob Thon, David Eder, Weizmann, Angelo Levi-Bianchini, Zeev Gluskin, others unidentified. Standing, sixth from left: Joseph Sprinzak, Mordechai Ben-Hillel Hacohen, Eliyahu Berlin, Eliezer Volcan, Israel Sieff, two unidentified, Rahel Yanait Ben-Zvi. Courtesy: Central Zionist Archives

Moreover, he did not think it was the duty of the military authorities "to bring home to the Arabs and Syrians the fact that H.M.G. has expressed a definite policy with regard to the future of the Jews in Palestine." Storrs felt it was the duty of the Zionists themselves to explain their case to the Arabs and Syrians in as accurate and conciliatory a manner as possible.[197] He decided to act on his conviction and invited Weizmann and other members of the Zionist Commission to a dinner party at his residence on April 27, 1918, where they were to meet the non-Jewish notables of Jerusalem and make a public statement concerning Zionist aims.

Weizmann had already, in fact, met two of Jerusalem's most important Muslim leaders on April 11, during the commission's visit to the city. Accompanied by Major Ormsby-Gore, he paid a formal visit to the home of Ismail Bey al-Husseini, where they also met his cousin, Kamel Bey al-Husseini, who held the dual title of grand mufti and grand kadi of Jerusalem. Weizmann informed his hosts that it was not his aim to establish a Jewish state or Jewish government at the end of the war. On the contrary, the Zionists preferred to see the establishment of a British

The Zionist Commission in Jerusalem, 1918. Standing, first row, from left: Edwin Samuel, William Ormsby-Gore, Weizmann, James de Rothschild, unidentified. Behind them from left are, among others, Mordechai Ben-Hillel Hacohen, Israel Sieff, David Eder, Sylvain Lévi, Aaron Aaronsohn. Courtesy: Weizmann Archives administration under which Jews and Arabs could work harmoniously for the development of the country. He also assured his hosts that the Zionists intended to respect the Muslim and Christian Holy Places; nor did they wish to expropriate any Arabs from their land. The two Arab notables were obviously relieved to hear these statements and related their favorable impression of Weizmann to Colonel Storrs.[198]

Unlike the more informal meeting at Husseini's house on April 11, the dinner party was carefully orchestrated by Storrs and Clayton in collaboration with Ormsby-Gore.[199] It was an impressive ecumenical gathering: in addition to Weizmann, Sylvain Lévi, James de Rothschild, and Ormsby-Gore were the grand mufti and his cousin whom Weizmann had met on April 11. Also present were Musa Kazem Pasha al-Husseini, the mayor of Jerusalem; Abu Suan of the Latin Patriarchate; Arif Pasha Daudi, a former Ottoman official; Thorgom Kushagian, the acting Armenian patriarch; D. G. Salameh, Orthodox Christian vice-mayor; and Archbishop Porphyrios II of the Orthodox Patriarchate. Storrs's aide, Lieutenant Colonel Lord William Percy, was also present.[200] It was by all accounts a distinguished gathering, representing some of the major religious and ethnic groups whose concerns constantly focused on how best to check each other's political ambitions. No doubt they all worried that the Zionists might unsettle the precarious balance they pretended to preserve. Weizmann could not afford to offend any of them. Thus, the king's health having been drunk, Weizmann read a carefully crafted speech that had previously undergone Clayton's scrutiny. He summarized for those assembled the major points he had been making ever since the Zionist Commission had arrived in Egypt a month earlier:

> I wish to speak of peace, harmony, and cooperation between the communities represented here. . . . We desire . . . to create conditions under which the material and moral development of those of our people who have chosen freely to come here will be rendered possible; and we are convinced that it will . . . be made possible, not to the detriment of any of the great communities already established in this country, but on the contrary to their advantage. There is land enough and room enough in Palestine . . . to sustain a population many times larger than the present one. And all the fears which have been expressed openly and secretly by the Arabs, that they are to be ousted from their present position, are due either to a fundamental misconception of our aims and intentions or to the malicious activities of our common enemies.[201]

Though the speech was received with applause, Storrs judged that, "from an oratorial point of view the speech was not impressive being neither rhetorically nor, as English, accurately pronounced." The grand mufti, on the other hand, "replied with the ease and polish of a practiced speaker" that he had full confidence in Weizmann's declarations and looked forward to loyal cooperation with the Zionists in the future development of Palestine.[202] An almost identical scenario took place nearly two weeks later, when, at the invitation of the military governor of Jaffa, Weizmann met with the local Muslim and Christian leaders.[203]

Weizmann presented his case to the Arab leaders in Palestine in the same way in which he had explained it to the Syrian Arabs in Egypt. The various meetings took place under the sponsorship of British officers who acted as hosts for the two sides. On the whole, the hosts professed their satisfaction with the results. The British officers who were in constant touch with Weizmann were impressed by his statesmanship in dealing with the Arabs. Ormsby-Gore, who was present at most of these meetings, wrote to Sir Maurice Hankey, the secretary to the war cabinet, "Weizmann is doing well. He is very fair and reasonable with the Arabs."[204] General Clayton, who continued to advise caution in implementing the British government declaration,[205] was full of praise for the head of the Zionist Commission: "Weizmann is a very sensible fellow and excellent to work with. . . . I think he sees that undue haste and precipitate action will wreck his own policy as well as embarrass us."[206] Toward the end of Weizmann's sojourn in Palestine, Clayton confided in a secret note: "Dr. Weizmann hopes for a completely Jewish Palestine in fifty years, and a Jewish Palestine, under a British facade, for the moment."[207]

Weizmann's actions encouraged those British officers entrusted with responsibilities for Arab affairs. Major K. Cornwallis, director of the Arab Bureau in Cairo, reported: "The Palestinians had the conviction forced upon them [by Weizmann] that Zionism has come to stay, that it is far more moderate in its aims than they had anticipated, and that by meeting it in a concilliatory spirit they are likely to reap substantial benefits in the future. Suspicion still remains in the minds of some, but it is tempered by the above considerations and there is little doubt that it will gradually disappear if the [Zionist] Commission continues its present attitude of concilliation."[208]

But privately Weizmann remained skeptical; indeed he was undergoing an evolution. He felt that the Syrians, under French influence, were fixed in their demand, anti-Zionist by its very nature, that Palestine be treated as an inseparable part of Syria. As for the Palestinians, he believed they would come to terms with Zionism only if they were convinced that the British were unalterably committed to it; and he let the British know that it was they, and not the Jews, who could, and should, bring this conviction home.[209] He felt that the attempts at conciliation during the early spring of 1918 were only superficially satisfactory. Both he and the Arabs seemed to role-play for the sake of the British.[210] Moreover, he did not trust the Syrian or Palestinian Arabs' polite assurances of cooperation. Weizmann's views were shared by other members of the Zionist Commission, including Leon Simon, who, under the influence of Ahad Ha'Am, had been a strong proponent of accommodation,[211] not to speak of Aaronsohn, whose judgment of the Arabs was much harsher.

In his diary Simon wrote, "The Arabs in Palestine are a blot on the landscape." Perhaps, he reflected, their leaders "can be bought off." [212]

By the end of May, Weizmann had formed a strongly negative view of the Arabs. In his first letter to Balfour from Palestine he judged them to be "superficially clever and quickwitted," respecting "only power and success" and "treacherous [by] nature." He complained that the military administrators failed to understand the qualitative differences between the "somewhat shifty and doubtful sympathies of the Arabs" and "the conscious and considered policy of the majority of the Jewish people, which sees in a British Palestine the realization of its hopes and aspirations." Finally, assuring Balfour that his declaration in Jerusalem about peaceful Zionist intentions toward the Arabs was sincere, he arrived at what he felt was the crux of the Arab question and the solution he proposed:

> The problem of our relations with the Palestinian Arabs is an economic problem, not a political one. From a political point of view the Arab centre of gravity is not Palestine, but the Hedjaz, really the triangle formed by Mecca, Damascus and Baghdad. I am just setting out on a visit to the son of the King of Hedjaz. I propose to tell him that if he wants to build up a strong and prosperous Arab kingdom, it is we Jews who will be able to help him, and we only. We can give him the necessary assistance in money and in organizing power. We shall be his neighbors and we do not represent any danger to him, as we are not and never shall be a great power. We are the natural intermediaries between Great Britain and the Hedjaz. Such relations would protect the Northern Hedjaz against becoming a French sphere of influence, the one thing which the Hedjaz people seem to dread. With him I hope to be able to establish a real political entente. But with the Arabs of Palestine—in whom, so far as I can gather, the Shereef is little interested—only proper economic relations are necessary; and these will develop in the natural course of things, because they will be essential in our interests as well as in those of the Palestinian Arabs. [213]

Weizmann's assessment may have been colored by a little-known meeting that took place sometime in May between him and a number of Palestinian Arabs. [214] The meeting was recorded by the Palestinian historian Aref al-Aref, and there seems to be no other evidence to support it. It was initiated by two of the foremost leaders of Palestinian nationalists, both members of the Husseini family: Musa Kazem, a former governor of the Yemen and later mayor of Jerusalem and president of the Arab executive, and Amin al-Husseini, who in 1921 was appointed mufti of Jerusalem. Until May 1918, Amin had been liaison officer between the Hashemites and the Palestinians, and he was in a good position to observe Feisal's aims at close range. Amin was concerned about the extent of Hashemite commitment to the British. He understood from Colonel T. E. Lawrence that Feisal would never grant the Palestinian Arabs independence and that the Jews were about to come to an agreement with the Hashemites. Amin and his fellow Palestinian nationalist leaders thought that the best policy was to drive a wedge between the Zionists and the British while playing the British against the French and pursuing a course of action independent of the Hashemites. Upon Amin's return to Jerusalem, Musa Kazem decided to contact the Zionist Commission.

With the help of David Yellin of Jerusalem, a secret meeting was arranged between Weizmann, David Eder, Leon Simon, and Israel Sieff on the one side and, on the other, Musa Kazem; Kamel Bey al-Husseini, the mufti of Jerusalem; Abdul Rauf Bitar, the mayor of Jaffa; and Faris Nimr, the editor of the Cairo paper *Al Mokattam*.

Weizmann's speech at the outset of the discussions confirmed Amin's warning about a Hashemite-Zionist collaboration, and the ensuing conversation was little more than play-acting. Musa Kazem produced a copy of *The Protocols of the Elders of Zion*, which had been given him by a British officer, and asked Weizmann if the Zionists had the same program and were connected to the "Elders of Zion." He also suggested that in future no talks between the Zionists and the Hashemites should take place unless representatives of Syrian and Palestinian nationalists were present. According to the Arab record of the talks, Weizmann agreed to this suggestion, though it is difficult to understand why, since his trip to the Hedjaz was already planned and there could be no hope of keeping such a meeting secret for any length of time. Amin al-Husseini was assigned as representative of the Palestinian Arabs to serve as a liaison with the Zionist Commission.

If such a meeting did take place and if the conversation was accurately reported and recorded, it only served to confirm the assessment both sides had of each other's intentions. The Palestinians were convinced more than ever that the Hashemites, Zionists, and the British were collaborating in a grand scheme that would leave the Arabs shorn of their nationalist goals. For Weizmann, the meeting must have confirmed his view that Arab opposition to the Zionists was so deeply ingrained in prejudice and misconceptions that it could probably never be uprooted. The Arabs, moreover, did not seem inclined to compromise and wished nothing less than acceptance of their terms, which would have ensured a minority status for the Jews in Palestine. Clearly, Weizmann had good reason to hope that he would get much better terms from Feisal. It is doubtful that Weizmann's secret meeting with the Palestinian Arab nationalists substantially changed his analysis of the Arab question, but it did provide additional proof to support it. What is not in doubt is that after June 1918, both the British and Weizmann shifted their efforts away from the Palestinian Arabs and more toward the Hashemites.[215]

On May 30, the very day on which he sent his letter to Balfour, Weizmann journeyed from Tel Aviv to meet the Emir Feisal. Having become disillusioned and discouraged by his meetings with the Syrian and Palestinian notables, he tried another approach for which—as can be seen from his letter to Balfour—he had more sanguine hopes.

Weizmann and Feisal, Maan, June 1918. Courtesy: Weizmann Archives

Weizmann had sufficient reasons to feel confident about his forthcoming meeting with the Emir Feisal, the son of the Sharif Hussein. Early in January 1918 the Foreign Office had sent Commander David G. Hogarth to meet Hussein in order to clarify British aims in the Middle East with him. The Foreign Office instructed Hogarth to point out to the king that the friendship of world Jewry toward the Arab cause was equivalent to support in all places where Jews had political influence, that the leaders of the movement were determined to bring about the success of Zionism through friendship and cooperation with the Arabs, and that such an offer was not to be spurned lightly.[216] Following numerous meetings with the king in Jedda, Hogarth reported in the *Arab Bulletin* that "the King had declared himself quite in sympathy with both international control in Palestine, and the encouragement of Jews to settle there."[217]

Weizmann was fully aware of Hogarth's mission.[218] It is not clear whether he was aware of a letter from Mark Sykes to Feisal, which, among other things, exhorted the sharif's son:

I know that the Arabs despise, condemn and hate the Jews, but . . . those who have persecuted or condemned the Jews could tell you the tale. The

Empire of Spain in the old days and the Empire of Russia in our time show the road of ruin that Jewish persecution leads to. . . . Believe me, I speak the truth when I say that this race, despised and weak, is universal, is all powerful, and cannot be put down. . . . In the councils of every state, in every bank, in every business, in every enterprise there are members of this race. . . . And remember these people do not seek to conquer you, do not seek to drive out the Arabs of Palestine. . . .

Look on the Jewish movement as the great key to Arab success, as the one guarantee of strength when the nations come together in council . . . and above all, recognize that the Jews desire to live their national life in Palestine; recognize them as a powerful ally.[219]

By the time the Zionist Commission had reached Palestine, the Emir Feisal was fully prepared to meet with Weizmann.[220] He was well aware, says a scholar of the negotiations, of "French opposition to Arab nationalism and of Syrian objections to French control, but he had not given up hope of gaining, with the help of the British, a favorable compromise."[221] Thus, although he did not initiate the meeting with Weizmann, he was quite open to it once General Gilbert Clayton suggested it.[222] Both Weizmann and Feisal felt that they could gain from such a meeting.[223] Both faced powerful enemies of their respective national aspirations; forging a common political understanding could be a source of support for their respective movements.[224] This background might help explain why Weizmann had struck such an optimistic note in his important letter to Balfour.

Together with Major Ormsby-Gore, Weizmann set out by train to Suez and from there by boat to Akaba, which they reached by June 2.[225] Since Ormsby-Gore had contracted dysentery, Weizmann continued the following day by car in the company of a British officer and an Arab guide. The car broke down on route, and they reached the British camp on foot, where they met Colonel P. C. Joyce, who accompanied Weizmann to Feisal's camp at Wadi Waheida on June 4. After the usual ceremonies prescribed by traditional Arab hospitality and presentation of General Allenby's letter of introduction,[226] Feisal and Weizmann discussed their mutual concerns. The hour-long conversation was translated by Colonel Joyce, since T. E. Lawrence—the natural candidate for such a task—was just then conducting military operations in the northern area of the Transjordanian plateau.[227]

The meeting was cordial. Feisal and Weizmann agreed that the close cooperation of Jews and Arabs was necessary in the interests of the movements they represented, but Feisal declined to make a statement as to the precise political arrangements he contemplated, asserting that his father alone was competent to make such a statement. Weizmann told him that the Jews did not propose to set up a government of their own but wished to work, under British protection, to colonize and develop Palestine without encroaching on any legitimate interests.

Feisal replied that in view of the dangerous use that his enemies could make of any pronouncement by him in favor of an Arab territory being controlled by non-Arabs, he could only state his personal opinion that Weizmann's wish could be realized and that he personally accepted the possibility of future Jewish claims to territory in Palestine. Feisal was pleased by Weizmann's offer to represent Arab interests in the United States during his planned visit. He would also welcome another meeting later on. The interview ended on a note of cordial greetings.[228] Immediately after the meeting, Weizmann returned to Akaba and from there, via Suez and Cairo, proceeded to Alexandria, which he reached on June 8. After briefing Clayton, Wingate, and George Stewart Symes, Weizmann returned to Cairo on June 12 for meetings with T. E. Lawrence and Arab and Jewish notables. He arrived in Allenby's headquarters on June 15.[229]

The meeting with Feisal did not have immediate practical results. Colonel Joyce, who watched the interaction between Feisal and Weizmann at close range, commented in the *Arab Bulletin* that it did serve to establish a personal relationship between "the leader of Entente Zionism and the Arab who is likely to have as much say as anyone in shaping Syrian destinies. . . . Some mutual esteem has resulted."[230] For Weizmann the meeting with Feisal confirmed his view that he did not have to negotiate with the Palestinian Arabs, whom he had found to be suspicious and antagonistic from the start.[231] The meeting also confirmed his view that the Palestinian Arabs represented local, narrow interests, whereas Feisal represented the regional leadership of Arab nationalism that would be realized through the institution of his sovereignty over Damascus. Moreover, negotiating with a leader—any leader who had the power to make decisions—rather than with numerous and splintered groupings was Weizmann's personal preference. Two weeks after the meeting in Wadi Waheida he was still under the spell of Feisal. Weizmann wrote to Vera: "He is the first real Arab nationalist I ever met. He is a leader! He's quite intelligent and a very honest man, handsome as a picture! He is not interested in Palestine, but on the other hand he wants Damascus and the whole of northern Syria. He talked with great animosity against the French, who want to get their hands on Syria. He expects a great deal from collaboration with the Jews! He is contemptuous of the Palestinian Arabs whom he doesn't even regard as Arabs!"[232]

For his part, Feisal was impressed by Weizmann.[233] Their conversation seemed to confirm for him Mark Sykes's remarks about the great international power of the Jews, a notion Weizmann had used so effectively with the British and alluded to during his meeting with the emir on June 4. Some six weeks later, Feisal wrote to Sir Mark that "far away as I am from the world's centre, I have a perfect notion of the importance of the Jews' position, and admiration for their vigour and tenacity and moral ascendancy, often in the midst of hostile surroundings. . . . On general grounds I would welcome any good understanding with the Jews."[234]

During his meetings with the British intelligence officers in Cairo,

Weizmann was frank about his assessment of the Palestinian Arabs "as a demoralized race with whom it was impossible to treat." He also discussed plans for consolidating ties with Feisal through a *quid pro quo* exchange of economic support by the Zionists in return for recognition of Zionist aims in Palestine by the king of the Hedjaz. He went so far as to pledge £10 million, if necessary, to obtain the support of King Hussein. Moreover, the Zionists were prepared, according to Weizmann, to offer political support to the sharif in Europe and the United States.[235]

The idea appealed to the British.[236] No one seemed to question Weizmann's ability to raise the sums of money necessary to buy the favor of the king of the Hedjaz. It was taken for granted that the Jews had the money and that offering it for political purposes was the way things were done in that part of the world. The American intelligence agent in Egypt, William Yale, exclaimed in admiration to his superiors in the State Department after he was informed that Weizmann offered £10 thousand sterling for the restoration and protection of the Arab-owned orange orchards in Jaffa:

> Dr. Weizmann is the outstanding figure on the Zionist Commission, he is a man of large calibre, who has obtained a thorough grasp of the situation and realizes all of its dangers and possibilities. He is enough of an Oriental and an accomplished enough diplomat to be able to meet and deal on their own ground with any of the Oriental leaders. . . .
>
> Dr. Weizmann, though heart and soul devoted to Zionism, is sufficiently great a man and astute enough politician to realize that undue expression of zeal at the present moment would but injure the Zionist cause. . . .
>
> If Dr. Weizmann should be unable to win the confidence of the Palestinians, and it does not seem as if he would be able to do so, he would win a diplomatic victory of some importance if he should gain the support of the Hedjaz group. Their backing would have a certain weight in the Arab and Moslem world, and as the Allies have recognized the King of the Hedjaz to some degree as the leader of the Arab movement, such support would be of value to Dr. Weizmann in an international Peace Conference.[237]

Weizmann had, in effect, already won at least a partial diplomatic victory. Even if no immediate concrete results could be pointed to from his meeting with Feisal, it was nevertheless a dramatic demonstration to the Palestinian Arabs that he could negotiate for Palestine with or without them. Perhaps more significant was the impression his meeting with Feisal made on the British. One of the major charges to the Zionist Commission had been to forge friendly relations between the Jews and the Arabs and other non-Jewish communities. This Weizmann had certainly tried to do from the moment the Zionist Commission had landed in Alexandria, with the Syrian Arabs, the Palestinian Arabs, and the sharifians. In the process he was able to persuade many ranking British officers—Reginald Wingate, Gilbert Clayton, Wyndham Deedes, William Ormsby-Gore, George Stewart Symes, and Richard Meinertzhagen—of two things: that in those instances in which he failed to make headway with the Arabs it was because of the hostility and suspicion with which he was met, and that the Yishuv and the World Zionist Organization were the lynchpin on which a British protectorate in Palestine hinged. In short, those British officers detailed to keep an eye on the Jews and the Arabs viewed Weizmann's meeting with Feisal as a promising beginning, and they reported in this sense to their superiors in the War Office and Foreign Office.[238]

Prodded by the British and his own sense that the Arab question needed to be solved, Weizmann continued to meet with Palestinian and Syrian Arabs after he returned from his meeting with Feisal. But in the order of priorities he had set for himself and for the Zionist Commission the Arabs were, for the time being, not his primary concern. As he saw it, providing a firm economic, cultural, and political foundation for the Yishuv had to be his paramount mission. Within this context he viewed laying the cornerstone for the Hebrew University in Jerusalem as the crowning achievement of his sojourn in Palestine in 1918. It was the fulfillment of a project he had been concerned with personally since 1901 and a concrete symbol of the cultural renaissance of the Jewish community in Palestine. Ormsby-Gore, who strongly supported the founding of a Jewish university, described Weizmann's views in a letter to Felix Frankfurter: "As Weizmann says, the University at Jerusalem is needed if only as a compensation for the loss of Harvard or Oxford to those Jews that come to Palestine. There must be a progressive beacon light of culture to give an objective to Jews in Palestine quite as much as to Jews outside Palestine."[239]

When the university committee, headed by Weizmann, had met in Berlin on January 6, 1914, it decided to buy the estate, including the house, of Sir John Gray-Hill of Liverpool. The site on Mount Scopus in Jerusalem was more than one hundred acres, a quarter of which was to be allocated to the university.[240] Shortly before Arthur Ruppin purchased the land, Sir John died and his nephew, Sir Norman Hill, took over the negotiations. The outbreak of the war had prevented execution of the original deed of sale, and the option of £4,400 at 5 percent interest was extended until the end of 1917. After the British entered Jerusalem, Sir Norman insisted on full and immediate payment. Weizmann turned to Shmuel Tolkowsky, asking him to request the money from his father-in-law, Isaac L. Goldberg, an enthusiastic supporter of the university idea. While Goldberg was making up his mind, Tolkowsky himself advanced almost £5,000. Toward the end of January 1918, Goldberg instructed an immediate payment of £10,000 with registration of the land and house in his name. The contract with Sir Norman Hill was signed on behalf of the Zionist Organization by Tolkowsky on February 7, 1918.[241]

As he set out for Palestine, Weizmann knew that he had Arthur Balfour's support for implementation of the university project, but this support was conditional on approval by the military authorities. No sooner did the Zionist Commission arrive in Palestine than a letter arrived from

General Clayton requesting Weizmann to refrain from any mention in public of the plans to erect a university.[242] General Allenby also objected, since he had received no instructions from Whitehall.[243] It was not until mid-June that approval was finally obtained from the British government.[244]

The date for the stone-laying ceremony was set for July 24, 1918. The British soldiers who camped on the site helped prepare it by providing a tent and benches, and the place where the stones were to be laid was covered by a canopy of carpets and flowers prepared by the Bezalel Art School. The children of all the Jewish schools in Jerusalem were brought to the ceremony. Members of the Jewish legion and the heads of the Egyptian Jewish community were also there. In attendance were the Ashkenazi and Sephardi chief rabbis of Jerusalem, the Anglican bishop, and the grand mufti. Commanders of Italian and French units serving with the Allies were present in their dress uniforms. All in all, six thousand people from all over the country gathered on that hot summer day. At 5:00 p.m., General Allenby, accompanied by Weizmann, took his place.[245] Weizmann laid the first stone, out of thirteen, in the name of the Zionist movement. An awkward situation was created when General Clayton forbade any man in British uniform to participate in the ceremony, including James de Rothschild.[246]

Telegrams from Balfour and the French government were read,[247] but Weizmann was the sole speaker. He had labored for many days over his speech, which had undergone Jabotinsky's scrutiny as well.[248] As the declining sun flooded the hills of Judea and Moab with golden light, Weizmann spoke briefly about his hopes.[249] He promised that the university on Mount Scopus would be open to all, regardless of class, race, or creed.

> It seems at first sight paradoxical that in a land with so sparse a population, in a land where everything still remains to be done . . . we should begin by creating a centre of spiritual and intellectual development. But it is no paradox for those who know the soul of the Jew. It is true that great social and political problems still face us, and will demand their solution. We Jews know that when the mind is given fullest play, that when we have a centre for the development of Jewish consciousness, there will also come the fulfillment of our material needs. . . .
>
> Our Hebrew University, informed by Jewish learning and Jewish energy, will mould itself into an integral part of our national structure which is in [the] process of erection. It will have a centripetal force, attracting all that is noblest in Jewry throughout the world. . . . And inspiration and strength will go forth to revivify the forces latent in our distant communities. Here the wandering soul of Israel shall reach its haven; its strength no longer consumed in restless and vain wanderings. Israel shall at last remain at peace within itself and with the world. There is a Talmudic legend that tells of the Jewish soul, deprived of its body, hovering between heaven and earth. Such is our soul today; tomorrow it shall come to rest, in this our sanctuary. That is our faith.[250]

One development that began to disturb Weizmann shortly before the ceremony on Mount Scopus, and also upset some of the British staff because of its suspected political implications, was the arrival of an American Red Cross relief unit in Palestine in June 1918.[251] Arriving with a staff of sixty and some thirty vehicles, the unit attempted to take over some of the sanitary work in Jerusalem. The project was partly financed by the Jewish bankers of the Joint Distribution Committee[252] whose German ties, in Weizmann's opinion, extended to still-active German sympathies. He saw in it an attempt, through humanitarian activities, to advance the political designs of its sponsors and directors—the combined missionary activists of the American Near East Relief Group and the by now openly anti-Zionist Henry Morgenthau. He viewed with alarm—as did some of his British friends—the connections of the Red Cross personnel with Syrian Arabs, whom the French were coaching to assert the claim that Palestine was an integral part of the Syrian area.[253] His warnings on these points to Brandeis, Wise, and DeHaas in the United States fed their already lively suspicions, and they fully shared his urgent desire for the American Zionist Medical Unit to come and take over some of the activities the Red Cross missionaries were all too eager to preempt. To the British and Americans, the Zionists not only urged their own claims but argued that the Red Cross's missionary associations and Christian symbolism would preclude the full and ready acceptance by local Muslims essential to effective work.

In September 1918, General Allenby reopened his attack on the Turkish lines. By the end of the month he had cleared the area of Palestine and was pursuing the Turkish retreat into Syria, with the end of the Turkish resistance in sight. For the Zionists, a new chapter was opening just as they had come to the close of another. By the autumn of 1918, Weizmann had rounded out the first phase of the work in Palestine and was planning his trip back to England and, he hoped, to the United States, to iron out the difficulties that had emerged and to prepare for the next phase. The Americans, having financed most of the activities directed by Weizmann in Palestine and by Sokolow in England, had initiated through the medical unit—which finally reached Palestine in September 1918—an undertaking not only financed but directed by themselves, and they were chafing to assert themselves in other ways as well. Subtle differences in approach, later to emerge in direct confrontation between Weizmann and Brandeis, were barely beginning to appear on the surface. But there was already a relapse from the warmth and enthusiasm of the exchanges between them, engendered by cooperation and heightened by success in achieving the Balfour Declaration. Weizmann in particular grew steadily more impatient and irritable—between the euphoric stages of his changing moods—as the weight of his endless responsibilities bore down on him, without the relief, under the difficulties of wartime communication, of prompt and considerate responses to his urgent calls for aid from London and Washington–New York.

Throughout his months of service with the Zionist Commission, Weizmann felt increasingly isolated from his Zionist colleagues abroad, at times almost abandoned. He had sufficient evidence of the difficulties of communication in wartime in his personal correspondence with Vera;[254] nevertheless, he could not escape the fear that owing to his long absence, his friends in London and New York were no longer taking him into account. These fears were fed by Vera's letters, which described Sokolow's poor administration of the Zionist office in strong terms.[255] She often complained that while Weizmann was sacrificing his career and health for the cause, his friends were conducting "business as usual." They were "making millions"; "their idealism was all but gone when confronted by harsh reality," and she included in this group Weizmann's friend Julius Simon, who was not hurrying to come to Palestine.[256]

What the Weizmanns did not fully realize was how much Vera's interference in the daily work of the Zionist office, and the private communications to her from Weizmann in matters relating to Zionist affairs, angered Sokolow, Marks, Tolkowsky, and the others. Since they did not dare confront Vera directly, they tried to disclose to her as little information as possible. It was clear to them that Vera was watching their doings and reporting back to her husband. Her personal dislike of Sokolow meant that her reports on his activities were consistently negative.[257] Little wonder, then, that the Zionist office staff was not eager to send frequent reports, which only confirmed Weizmann's assessment that they were shirking their responsibilities while the members of the Zionist Commission were "virtually collapsing from overwork."[258]

When he carried out the groundbreaking ceremony for the Hebrew University at Mount Scopus and no congratulatory message was received from Sokolow, Weizmann took it as an unforgivable, almost a calculated offense.[259] He complained regularly of the insufficient flow of funds and information; and he sent a constant stream of requests for reinforcements and replacement of personnel. He demanded English-speaking, technically and professionally trained young people capable of communicating freely with the British officers, particularly with the middle-echelon ex-Egyptian or Sudanese civil servants whose ignorance of Zionism, if not ill-will, he discovered to be a major problem for the Zionist Commission. He considered that the Russian Jewish leaders in Palestine only aggravated the anti-Jewish bias of such men by their assertive, foreign manner. He insisted, therefore, that some of his younger friends in England and Julius Simon, his old friend in Germany who had served the Zionists in the Hague during the war, be sent immediately to relieve him in Palestine and permit him to return to England and the United States. There he hoped to reorganize the supporting activities he had missed so sorely hitherto, and then to return to Palestine, where he would convene an assembly of world Jewish and local Palestinian leaders authorized to decide pressing issues while also engaging in long-range planning.

As early as January 1918 Weizmann had hoped to proceed to the United States, if possible directly from Palestine.[260] He repeated this desire to Brandeis on more than one occasion.[261] On instructions from Brandeis, Lewin-Epstein finally informed Vera in London that the Americans did not wish Weizmann to come since they did not think he could raise large sums in the United States and failure would only harm his prestige.[262] They suggested instead that Ormsby-Gore come to the United States in time for the first anniversary of the Balfour Declaration, while Weizmann remain in Palestine as long as possible to consolidate the accomplishments of the Zionist Commission.[263]

This disappointment was somewhat ameliorated by the opportunity it gave Weizmann to send Aaronsohn to the United States, thus eliminating a great source of friction and almost daily conflict between Aaronsohn and other members of the Zionist Commission and leaders of the Yishuv.[264] Aaronsohn's departure took care of only one source of aggravation. Weizmann's relations with James de Rothschild continued to be strained, leading later on to problems with his father, Baron Edmond de Rothschild.[265] Much more taxing for Weizmann were the constant demands made on his time and the Zionist Commission's resources.[266] To Ahad Ha'Am he complained, "A Jew always comes to me with a long list of requests before he will do the Jewish people and myself a favour and accept any position below that of a general."[267] Weizmann had to be certain at all times, moreover, that the various forces in the Yishuv and on the Zionist Commission itself pull the Zionist cart in the same direction. "He has a difficult team to drive," commented General Clayton.[268] Weizmann had high expectations of his colleagues, according to Ormsby-Gore. "He wants all Jews to be 100% Zionist and few even here can stand quite so strong a dose." From the start Weizmann managed to assert himself as the dominant force in Palestine. "[He] rules his own people with a big stick. So far the latter don't seem to mind and accept him as an autocrat."[269]

Yet, though Weizmann usually had his way in his dealings with his fellow Zionists and even with the British administration, the cumulative impact of daily strain and stress was growing unbearable. Since his student days he was prone to "attacks of nerves" whenever he was under too much pressure. The negotiations for the Balfour Declaration had been punctuated by occasional outbursts of anger and frustration, culminating in three "resignations" from office. In Palestine, too, Weizmann was increasingly more irritable. In the days prior to and following the groundbreaking ceremony on Mount Scopus, he was given to moods of anger and depression because of disappointments with his fellow Jews.[270] His poor relations with the military administrators were likewise marked by a high level of anxiety that pushed him on occasion to strongly worded public attacks.[271]

More than once during the spring of 1918, Weizmann expressed his wish to return to England. An additional pressing reason was that due to a misunderstanding between him and some of the officials in the Admiralty, his Wandsworth Laboratory was closed as of June 1, his appointment as adviser on acetone production was terminated, and his collaborators, including the faithful Harold Davies, were dismissed.[272] Moreover, the negotiations for the payment of royalties on acetone in England, Canada, and the United States were dragging on, and even Weizmann's legal advisers at Adam and Cooke, with their wide connections in government circles, could not expedite matters.[273]

Vera was running out of money, and Weizmann was worried about his future income. Yet, at least during the spring of 1918, Vera dissuaded him from returning precipitously; she did not think he could advance matters much more in person if he were to come to London, and she was sure it was much more important for him to stay in Palestine until he had won over the military authorities to the Zionist cause, much as he had done in England.[274] In fact, for once reversing roles, Vera was confident that their financial situation would sort itself out in due time. She and the children continued to maintain the lifestyle of the upper bourgeoisie, with the indispensable nanny Miss Usher, the cook, and the few weeks of mandatory vacation during the summer in Hindhead. Vera proudly refused to accept the £200 Weizmann had received from the funds of the Zionist Commission.[275] She maintained, moreover, her social contacts with the ladies of high society, being invited to lunch at Nancy Astor's, having Mrs. Herbert Samuel over for tea, participating in an ecumenical Pageant of Freedom under the direct patronage of the royal couple, and organizing receptions and tours for the American Zionist Medical Unit, which had finally arrived in London, on route to Palestine, in late spring 1918.[276]

But by mid-summer 1918 Vera stopped urging her husband to remain in Palestine. More than four months had passed since the Zionist Commission had left England. This was Chaim's longest separation from his family, and at the end of June she wrote: "My dear and beloved Chaimchik, I am burning with longing for you and I have no idea when you will return and for how long. I am very lonely. Your letters arrive at long intervals. . . . Well Chaimchik, [Zionist] affairs have pushed me and the kids further and further away from you; it seems like it was a different world, when, once upon a time, we lived together."[277] Vera, too, began to be concerned about the lack of progress in Weizmann's financial affairs, and she now felt that only Weizmann could resolve the difficulties.

But her greatest concern had to do with their older son Benjy, who turned eleven on June 2, just as Weizmann was on his way to see Feisal. Benjy was a bright child, mature, articulate, and doing well in school.[278]

But Vera's letters indicate that the fifteen-month-old Michael was her favorite: "He is adorable, marches like a duckling, sings like a bird, laughs, babbles—in brief, fantastic. . . . Benjy is at home, looks very good, learns well and has grown quite a bit."[279] A few weeks later her letter shows the difference in her attitude even more clearly: "God—how I love this baby [Michael]. And Benjy is already grown up. Bright, interesting, but I find it very difficult to get along with him without the authority of his father."[280] It seems that Benjy already understood that his mother favored Michael and he therefore did what he could to attract more attention. Both children missed their father, but especially Benjy, and Vera did not know how to cope with him. Her solution: "Benjy needs very much the authority of a father, and I am seriously considering a boarding school."[281] By the end of July 1918, Vera had had enough. She was exhausted, and she wanted Chaim to come home.[282]

By that time Weizmann did not need to be persuaded to return to England. Announcing his imminent departure for home, he used the occasion to sum up his struggles and his vision:

> I feel from the tone of your letter that you are depressed and lonely. This all makes my heart ache, but I am coming to you soon and we shall be happy and contented together, my Verochka! But what people are like and especially Jews! . . . But they are our people. . . . One must come to terms with it, just as with the climate of Palestine, the rocks of the Judean hills, the Arabs and other difficult obstacles. . . . In these five months I have lived through at least 10 years and have gone noticeably more grey, but I have become spiritually stronger in the struggle, for there is something here that inspires one to great deeds! This something is that sacred tradition, unforgettable, strong, the voices of our prophets and sages telling us that we shall have to create our Palestine with pain and torment. . . . But I haven't wavered for even a second. . . . Indeed, faith is essential, and those without faith had better not come here, they would only be a burden—and there are many such people here; it would be better without them; they are the merchants who should be driven out of the Temple![283]

During the months of hard work in Palestine, Weizmann had come to value David Eder as a delightful and indefatigable worker,[284] and he felt comfortable leaving the Zionist Commission in his charge. Weizmann and Israel Sieff sailed from Port Said on September 16, 1918. They arrived in London on October 6. The period of the Zionist Commission opened a new era in Zionist activity for Weizmann, for his London associates, and for the World Zionist Organization as a whole. The new political reality confronting the Zionists, in Palestine and in England, did not always accord with their expectations and presented them with some difficult and painful dilemmas. Weizmann's uncertainty in late summer and early fall 1918—should he remain in Palestine, return to London, or travel to the United States—was a reflection of that new reality. His mood swings also reflected the difficult process of arriving at a decision that would be appropriate both for him personally and for the movement as a whole.

In anticipation of Weizmann's arrival, his staunch friend Ormsby-Gore, now an enthusiastic and unabashed supporter of Zionism, concluded his report to his superiors at the Foreign Office:

> Dr. Weizmann stood out from among the rest [of the members of the Zionist Commission] as a real leader who succeeded in acquiring authority not only with his own people but with the non-Jewish population of Palestine and with the British military authorities. With the exception of the ultra-Orthodox religious element in Jerusalem he has behind him all the active forces in the country. His strong Jewish national sympathies did not in any way detract from his genuine and thorough loyalty to Great Britain, and I think it would be a good thing if on his return in the course of the next few weeks he were given a suitable British decoration.[285]

The suggestion by Ormsby-Gore was supported by Herbert Samuel and others in government circles.[286] In the event, Weizmann was not to be knighted, but not because he was not held in the highest esteem by the prime minister, who had final say in this matter. It seems that despite Ormsby-Gore's and Samuel's efforts to obtain a knighthood for Weizmann, there was not "a great deal of enthusiasm for it in certain quarters of the Foreign Office."[287] This probably meant that Lord Curzon opposed it. There is no evidence to indicate Weizmann's reaction to the news, which was conveyed to him by Samuel. He must have reflected on the fact that the British were rather stingy when it came to honoring a foreign Jew. After all, did he not deserve the appointment as Fellow of the Royal Society prior to the war? Had he not done yeoman's service for the empire during and after the war? As Ormsby-Gore's report indicates, Weizmann's accomplishments during the mere five months in Palestine were quite extraordinary. They prompted even the usually reserved Vera to exclaim: "I must admit Chaimchik, that I often think about the fact that you with your genius-like talents, your personal charm and the eternal fire burning in your soul, were created differently from all other people."[288] In the months that followed his return to England, he had to cope with organizational and political problems that taxed his talents, his stamina, and his political genius to the utmost.

VIII

The Road to San Remo

Chaim Weizmann returned in October 1918 to London—after brief stops in Rome and Paris—mainly to deal with the difficulties he had encountered in Palestine. He expected to return to Palestine as soon as they had been overcome, but the political scene soon shifted with bewildering speed. Bulgaria, Turkey, and Austria were forced to sue for peace in rapid succession, and on November 11, the armistice with Germany brought an end to the First World War. The mood of uncertainty and stagnation that for so long had been brooding over the British position was dissolved. On the day the armistice was announced, David Lloyd George kept a previously arranged lunch with Weizmann and C. P. Scott. They found the prime minister reading the Psalms and in a melancholy mood. He congratulated Weizmann on the conquest of Palestine and asserted he was convinced more than ever that the country must be in the hands of England.[1] All at once the problems of a peace conference and the unforeseeable postwar situation faced the Zionist leadership, and Weizmann had to give up the idea of returning to head the Zionist Commission until the pressing immediate problems were dealt with.

Zionist postwar planning was seriously complicated by the course of the war in its closing stages. It did not draw smoothly and gradually to an end; nor did it end all at once. Its final years were marked by abrupt shocks on every front, until the German collapse in the West rang down the curtain. With all the doubts about the war's outcome, local Jewries in many countries faced an uncertain future. Once the outcome was decided, there were vast political changes to adjust to. After the German occupation of Russian Poland and the subsequent rise of a democratic Provisional Government in Russia, it was evident that Polish or Ukrainian nationalism, rather than Great Russian imperialism, might be a dominant force. Rather than become mere pawns in conflicts among Central and Eastern European nationalities, Jews turned with renewed interest to their own nationalist movements.[2] In this world of turmoil the British thrust into Palestine, accompanied by the issuance of the Balfour Declaration, had an even more decisive impact.

In German-occupied Poland during 1917, Jewish communal elections held on the basis of an expanded franchise yielded victories for the Zionists and other nationally oriented factions.[3] The All-Russian Zionist Conference in Petrograd on June 6, 1917, reaffirmed the "national-political" Helsingfors Program. A preliminary conference of all Russian Jewish factions, held in the same city from July 31 to August 3, 1917, proposed to convene a Russian Jewish congress to deal with the "national self-determination of the Jews in Russia" and the "civil and national rights" of Jews in independent Poland, Palestine, and Rumania. For a short time in 1918 a full system of "national personal autonomy" was instituted in the Ukraine under the authority of a Jewish national council and a Jewish minister in the Ukrainian government. Even the Salonican Jews set up a Congress Committee in the spring of 1917, adopting the program agreed on in the United States for the anticipated session of the American Jewish Congress.[4]

The local Zionist awakening evident in all these developments was reinforced by the activities of the movement on the international plane. Concerted efforts by the Poalei Zion produced an international socialist declaration in favor of "autonomy of nationalities" adopted by a Dutch-Scandinavian committee in Stockholm on October 10, 1917. The Copenhagen Manifesto issued by Victor Jacobson, head of the World Zionist Organization's liaison office in Denmark on October 28, 1918, shortly before the war ended, called on Zionists everywhere to work for a postwar settlement providing for the following: Palestine as the national home of the Jewish people; full, effective equal rights in all countries; and "national autonomy, cultural, social and political, for the Jewish population of countries largely settled by Jews, as well as all other countries whose Jewish population demands it." The manifesto concluded with a ringing statement that the Jewish people must enter the "League of Free Nations" as an equal member.[5]

European Zionists thus joined vigorously in the campaign for autonomous national minority institutions within the proposed structure of new, free states of a postwar Europe. They expected such democratically constituted Jewish communities and autonomous public institutions to join together in a world Jewish organization that would play a cardinal role, as a fully recognized member nationality, in securing and rebuilding Palestine as the Jewish national home, with the approval and support of the proposed international organization that would become the League of Nations.

The Palestine Jewish community, meeting on December 18, 1918, in Haifa, shortly after the war's end, framed its resolutions in the same spirit, even though it addressed itself to the question of Palestine and not to Diaspora issues. Its formula for recognizing Palestine as the Jewish national home was squarely based on the assumption that the whole dispersed Jewish people, not only the local community, was entitled to self-determination in Palestine. Thus the community demanded a determining voice for the Jewish people as a whole in the affairs of Palestine, as their national home. In this way it implicitly justified further demands that the country be named Eretz Israel and its flag be a Jewish flag. Consequently, the rights proposed for other national and religious groups, and the recognition of Arabic as well as Hebrew as an official language, implied guarantees of national minority rights for non-Jews.[6]

The Zionists in the United States also prepared for their future commitments in response to wartime developments, but under different conditions. The struggle over the American Jewish Congress, like the disputes over the administration of relief, forced them to distinguish sharply between Palestine and the Diaspora as areas of concern. They singled out Palestine-related activities, including wartime relief and postwar political and reconstructive planning, as their special domain. On the other hand, they conceded the primary role in administering extra-Palestinian overseas relief to the American Jewish Joint Distribution Committee. Political and reconstructive planning for the overseas Diaspora was to be handled by the anticipated American Jewish Congress. Here Zionists were to contribute their efforts individually, while organized Zionist facilities, mainly in Europe, would be offered only in support to help the work of the Joint Distribution Committee and American Jewish Congress.

The American Jewish Congress movement had been suspended at President Woodrow Wilson's request following the election of delegates in June 1917 and did not reconvene until December 1918. Although public activity ceased, preparatory studies were done in anticipation of decisions to be taken at the congress. The December 1918 session, presided over by the Zionist leader and close associate of Louis Brandeis, Judge Julian Mack, adopted resolutions on Palestine and on national rights in the postwar European and Ottoman successor states based on earlier compromises between Zionist and non-Zionist views. In these formulations, critical wartime developments like the Balfour Declaration and the national minority rights movement, which influenced the preparatory studies commissioned for the congress, were clearly reflected.

Thus the congress resolved that the peace conference should require the new states to give constitutional guarantees to their minorities concerning equal citizenship and "civil, political, religious and national rights" as well as communal autonomy, minority representation in government, unrestricted use of minority languages, and observance of their Sabbath and holy days. With regard to Palestine, the congress instructed its delegates to the peace conference to cooperate with the World Zionist Organization to achieve recognition of "the aspirations and historic claims of the Jewish people" and the establishment of "such political, administrative and economic conditions . . . as will assure, under the trusteeship of Great Britain acting on behalf of such a League of Nations as may be formed, the development of Palestine into a Jewish Commonwealth."[7]

American Zionists, in the meantime, had adopted more specific proposals regarding their special concern, Palestine, in the Pittsburgh Platform of June 25, 1918, which they expected to advance through the agency of the World Zionist Organization. Without referring to the ultimate goal of a Jewish commonwealth, subsequently specified in the American Jewish Congress resolution, they concentrated on the immediate political, administrative, and economic concerns. They demanded for "all inhabitants" of Palestine "political and civic equality irrespective of race, sex, or faith" and a "system of free public instruction . . . [embracing] all grades and departments of education." In order "to insure in the Jewish National Home . . . equality of opportunity," they proposed a policy favoring (though with "due regard to existing rights") the nationalization of "all natural resources and . . . public utilities"; the leasing of nationally owned (Jewish) land "on such conditions as will insure . . . development and continuity of possession"; and the application of "the cooperative principle . . . so far as feasible in the organization of all agricultural, industrial, commercial, and financial undertakings." A final paragraph stipulated that "Hebrew, the national language of the Jewish people, shall be the medium of public instruction."[8]

The last item alone reflected the influence of the national rights provisions that European Zionists were then stressing and that, like the omitted reference to the "Jewish commonwealth," were introduced later into the resolution of the American Jewish Congress—which, of course, aimed to represent *all* American Jews—under Zionist pressure. There was thus a wall of separation between Diaspora and Palestine policy in the theory of American Zionists. American Zionists reinforced the distinction in practice by organizational reforms initiated at Pittsburgh in June 1918. Indeed, the proposals advanced in the Pittsburgh Platform clearly indicate the difference in milieu and outlook between American and European Zionists. On the whole, the platform reflected American ideas, mainly the kind of social democracy popular among progressives in the United States.

The American Zionists' immediate concern raised by the prospect of the war's end was one of internal reorganization. Now, through the immense prestige of the Brandeis leadership and bolstered by the mass of new members, the time seemed ripe for a new organizational structure. The Federation of American Zionists (FAZ), the main permanent body, was to be rebuilt as the controlling center of American Zionism by bringing the entire loosely attached large new membership into a tightly organized union. Thus the FAZ was converted at the June 1918 Pittsburgh convention into the Zionist Organization of America (ZOA), of which all members of the FAZ affiliates individually became members. Judge Julian Mack was elected president, and Justice Brandeis kept close contact through Jacob DeHaas, who continued as executive secretary, the post he held in the PZC. Louis Lipsky became secretary for the organization. Hadassah and other nonideological bodies with special functions more or less willingly submitted themselves to the ZOA. Mizrahi and Poalei Zion held out, however, for their status as independent parties.[9]

There remained the immediate task of formulating definitely the legal foundations in international law under which the constructive effort could be launched. For this task the eminent group of lawyers around Brandeis—men like Julian Mack, Felix Frankfurter, Bernard Flexner, Benjamin V. Cohen, and Robert Szold—felt themselves to be professionally and personally the best suited among all contenders. This task had to be undertaken in London and Paris, where the negotiations for a postwar world order were taking place, and in Palestine, where the groundwork of the Jewish national home had to be laid, at a time when the shape of the prospective British administration and of the country as a whole remained highly uncertain. The end of the war, then, saw the beginning of a series of American Zionist overseas missions that encountered practical problems not planned for in detail by theoretical, general planning.

While the American and other Zionist organizations around the world were in the process of formulating their postwar policies, Weizmann, too, took similar concrete actions to prepare himself and his close associates for the new political opportunities. He approached the task under conditions different from those facing the Americans, conditions arising from the wartime strategies and postwar policies toward Palestine and the Middle East adopted by the British government. Weizmann and his associates could rely on the correspondence of their aims and anticipations with the declared official policy in London. The prime minister and Foreign Office were firmly committed to the Zionists, and to Weizmann personally, in spite of opposition from such quarters as the India Office, the Arab Bureau in Cairo, and many of the officers in General Edmund H. Allenby's military occupation force in Palestine.

Weizmann and Nahum Sokolow had worked hard to enlist organized British Jewry as a whole behind the Zionist plans immediately upon the issuance of the Balfour Declaration; their efforts had moderate success.[10] The day after Weizmann returned to London, he and Vera were invited to dinner at the home of Herbert Samuel, where they had "hours of Palestinian talk of the most absorbing kind." Samuel, who in public always seemed cool and unemotional, was in private a warm and sensitive man. He was fascinated by what he heard and by the man who told it: "I never see [Weizmann] without being more and more impressed by his breadth of view and sound judgement, and by—a rare combination—his union of those qualities with a passionate fervour and enthusiasm. The Zionist cause is wonderfully fortunate in having such a leader."[11] Samuel was not specific about the nature of their "Palestinian talk," but either that evening or soon thereafter they must have discussed how to enlist non-Zionists in Zionist work.

At the end of October, Weizmann formed the Advisory Committee on

Palestine under the chairmanship of Herbert Samuel and including, in addition to himself, Nahum Sokolow, Joseph Cowen, and Israel Sieff as well as influential non-Zionists like Sir Alfred Mond of Imperial Chemical Industries, Sir Robert Waley-Cohen of Shell Oil, Lord Bryce, Sir Lionel Abrahams (a senior civil servant), and William Ormsby-Gore, who served as a consultant to the group.[12] They met for the first time on November 2, 1918.[13] Even before the first meeting, following interviews with Arthur James Balfour on October 9 and with Lord Robert Cecil on October 31, Weizmann prepared ten proposals regarding the work of the Zionist Commission in Palestine, which he submitted to Cecil on November 1.[14]

The proposals dealt with the status of the Zionist Commission until the end of the military occupation and recommended that the commission "be appointed the advisory body to the Military Authorities in all matters affecting the welfare of the Jewish population." They urged the recognition of Hebrew as the language of the Jews in Palestine, a survey of all available lands and other resources in Palestine, establishment of permanent contacts with the Arabs, and permission to begin preparing the site for the Hebrew University on Mount Scopus.[15] All in all, though couched in terms suggesting only a temporary plan, these were far-reaching proposals. Not surprisingly, they were rejected by Gilbert Clayton, to whom the Foreign Office sent the matter for review. In light of growing Arab unrest, Clayton advised that the *status quo* be maintained: his counsel was independently reiterated by Mark Sykes,[16] and their suggestions were accepted in London.[17]

Weizmann initially expected the Advisory Committee on Palestine to serve the aims he had defined for the future work of the Zionist Commission in Palestine. Members would give expert advice on the plans for future development and possibly manage, as well as secure, capital investments in major development projects the Zionist Commission might undertake. In line with these ideas the committee, under Samuel's guidance, met a number of times during the first two weeks of November and prepared a roster of immediate proposals for advancing the Zionist work in Palestine.[18]

On the basis of these suggestions as well as its own parallel deliberations, the London Zionist Political Committee prepared a document[19] titled "Proposals Relating to the Establishment of a Jewish National Home in Palestine," which Weizmann—with the concurrence of Ahad Ha'Am—submitted to the Foreign Office on November 19, 1918.[20] It included the recognition of "the historic title of the Jewish people to Palestine," which the Political Committee considered the cardinal point, and claimed "the right of the Jews to reconstitute in Palestine their National Home." It stated that the aim of the national home was to develop into a "Jewish Commonwealth" and made some specific proposals for the boundaries of this entity. It also stipulated that, in promoting Jewish immigration and "close settlement on the land," the protecting power, or mandatory, would "accept the co-operation . . . of a Council representative of the Jews of Palestine and of the world" and give the council priority in offering "any concession for public works or for the development of natural resources."[21]

The latter provision in particular embodied Weizmann's idea of the relations that would be appropriate between the Jews and the mandate government. He trusted more to mutual understanding with the British than to binding legal contracts about detailed obligations. But he did not expect the British to do more than give the Jews a fair chance to succeed in building their national home. He expected the British to assume no responsibility for the ultimate success of the project and intended that the Jews themselves would bear the direct burden, and expense, of the enterprise. Not only did he understand that such a division of labor was the condition Britain would insist on for giving the Zionists its support; he considered it a Zionist condition as well that the Zionists, rather than any protecting power, take responsibility for the form and spirit in which the Jewish national home would be built.

On December 4, 1918, Weizmann met with Balfour and reiterated the main points of his proposals. He also described the critical situation facing the Jews of Eastern Europe and emphasized that only Zionism could solve their pressing problems. Though he acknowledged that Zionism could not cope with all the evils befalling the Jewish people, it could, nevertheless, serve as a beacon of hope, particularly if a Jewish community in Palestine, four to five million strong, was allowed to grow. In response to Balfour's question whether such a development was consistent with the declaration bearing his name, which guaranteed the rights of minorities, Weizmann replied by using analogies from English political life[22] to illustrate the fact that there was no inherent denial of rights to a minority just because it found itself within the framework of a dominant majority culture. Balfour, who had listened politely most of the time, nonetheless made no commitments regarding the proposals. He agreed with Weizmann that "the Arab problem cannot be considered as a serious hindrance in the way of the development of a Jewish national home," but he thought Weizmann and Feisal should iron out any disagreements between their respective movements.[23]

Balfour may have been informed all along by members of the Foreign Office about the ongoing discussions between David Eder, the acting chairman of the Zionist Commission, and Feisal's representatives and the latter's request for financial assistance from the Zionists. In a cable he sent to Weizmann at the end of October 1918, Eder indicated that he favored the idea of a loan.[24] After seeking advice and getting encouragement from Herbert Samuel, Commander David G. Hogarth, and Lord Robert Cecil as well as Colonel T. E. Lawrence, Feisal's close adviser, Weizmann came to the conclusion that it was necessary to have a political agreement with Feisal, to be ratified by the British government, before any financial assistance could be contemplated.[25] On the other hand,

Weizmann, much like the military authorities in Palestine and the staff of the Foreign Office, continued to believe that his real partner for discussions concerning the final disposition of Palestine, apart from the British themselves, was Feisal and not the Palestinian Arabs. Balfour seemed to hold the same notion. After all, both the French, under the Treaty of London agreement, and the Arab nationalists in Syria were laying claim to full or part control of Palestine. With the concurrence of his British consultants, Weizmann believed that the contact initiated with Feisal was his most promising opening. Through an agreement with the leader of the broader Arab movement, both the antagonism of local Palestinian interests and the claims of the French might be overcome.

On December 11, 1918, Weizmann met with Feisal—who was in London on route to the peace conference—at the Carlton Hotel, with Lawrence acting as interpreter. The emir had just recently found out about the Sykes-Picot Agreement, and he opened the meeting by expressing his indignation and belief that it was dangerous to both Arabs and Jews. Weizmann, who had long been aware of the agreement and had often protested against it, readily agreed with Feisal. In response to the emir's query, Weizmann outlined the main elements of the Zionist program. Before they parted they were in complete accord about the destructive influence of French colonial designs for their respective movements and the corollary need to have Britain appointed as trustee for "Arabia." Feisal, whose ambitions were by now firmly centered on the newly liberated Syria, was less interested, for the moment at least, in Palestine.[26] He was therefore sincere in telling Weizmann that he did not foresee a potential conflict on the question of land, there being, he felt, sufficient space to accommodate both Jews and Arabs. "Zionism and the Arab movement were fellow movements," he said, "and . . . complete harmony prevailed between them."[27]

Complete harmony did prevail until the first week of January 1919. One of the highlights of that winter was an elaborate dinner given by Lord Rothschild for Feisal on December 21, which was attended by prominent British statesmen.[28] This phase culminated with the well-known agreement between Weizmann and Feisal of January 3, 1919.[29] The document signed by both leaders explicitly juxtaposes in its preamble the "Arabs and the Jewish people" and "the Arab State and Palestine," implying that "Palestine" was to be an independent "Jewish State" equal in status to the "Arab State." The equal status of the two national entities is further underlined in the paragraphs that follow, particularly Article III, which stated that the constitution of Palestine shall "afford the fullest guarantees for carrying into effect the . . . Declaration of the 2nd of November, 1917"; Article IV, which urged that "all necessary measures shall be taken to encourage and stimulate immigration of Jews into Palestine on a large scale" while "the Arab peasant and tenant farmers shall be protected in their rights"; and Article VII, which declared that "The Zionist Organization will use its best efforts to assist the Arab State."

Feisal appended a handwritten proviso in Arabic to the above articles that made them conditional on Britain's punctilious acquiescence to his demands.[30]

The agreement between Weizmann and Feisal was meant to serve the political ends of their respective movements as well as those of Britain, all of which wanted to weaken French influence in the region.[31] Within weeks, however, this momentous agreement seemed useless. Feisal's opposition to a Jewish commonwealth in Palestine was reported in *Le Matin*, and Weizmann pressed for a denial. It came in the form of a letter from Feisal of March 3, 1919, addressed to Felix Frankfurter. In addition to his warm appreciation of Weizmann, Feisal asserted that "Arabs and Jews are cousins . . . and have by happy coincidence been able to take first steps together towards the attainment of their national ideals. We Arabs . . . look on the Zionist movement with deepest sympathy. . . . We will wish Jews a hearty welcome home and we will, so far as we are concerned, do our best to help them through."[32] Clearly, the mutual interest of the Zionists and the Arabs in annulling the Sykes-Picot Agreement was a dominant consideration at the time; and the relations between the two were maintained, for the moment, at a level of harmony that gave their British sponsors cause for satisfaction.

Feisal's agreement with Weizmann and his letter to Frankfurter may have been sincere attempts on his part to reach a *modus vivendi* with the Zionists, but events in Syria and Palestine forced him to jettison any such plan. Since the Arab revolt in 1916, few Palestinian leaders acknowledged the Hashemites as their legitimate representatives. Feisal's dealings with the Zionists were indeed regarded as a betrayal by most of them, and some Palestinian leaders accused Feisal of trading Palestine for a secure, internationally recognized Arab monarchy in Syria.[33] By July 1919 Feisal succumbed to the pressure of extremists in his camp. The First Syrian Congress, which met in Damascus that month, flatly rejected the claims of the Zionists for the establishment of a Jewish commonwealth "in that part of Southern Syria which is known as Palestine" and opposed Jewish immigration into any part of the country.[34]

Shortly afterward, Colonel John French, a British intelligence officer in Egypt temporarily replacing Gilbert Clayton, wrote Lord Curzon that "Dr. Weizmann's agreement with Emir Feisal is not worth the paper it is written on or the energy wasted in the conversation to make it."[35] Some of Weizmann's closest collaborators called the agreement a "blunder," since it did not realize all the Zionist objectives, and they accused Weizmann of naïveté.[36] Yet, despite the fact that later developments bore out French's analysis, Feisal's statements encouraged many Zionists to hope that the national aspirations of Jews and Arabs would prove compatible. Given the lack of interest on the part of any respectable Palestinian leader in negotiating with the Zionists, moreover, and the fact that the British themselves urged Weizmann to deal directly with the emir, Weizmann had little choice but to make the best of it. That this course of events also suited his own inclinations and that the emir seemed a congenial partner made the task more palatable. Consummating the negotiations with an agreement that clearly conceded to the Zionists some of their major aims was considered by most observers of the time another personal achievement by Weizmann and, at the very least, a timely boost for the Zionist claims at the peace conference.[37]

At the end of November 1918, the Zionists opened a bureau in Paris, headed by Sokolow, to disseminate information to the delegates at the peace conference and to coordinate Zionist efforts on the Continent.[38] Weizmann was pleased to have Sokolow out of the way, but, on the other hand, he did not trust his diplomatic maneuvers. By contrast, he trusted Aaron Aaronsohn, who had just returned from the United States and gone to Paris at Weizmann's request. Weizmann valued Aaronsohn's connections with President Woodrow Wilson's circle and with the top leadership of the American Zionists. He relied on Aaronsohn's sound judgment and counted on him to keep an eye on Sokolow and his aides and to report back directly.[39] These arrangements were typical of the way Weizmann functioned. He often lacked full confidence in the formally elected Zionist leadership—in Palestine, Paris, London, and the United States—and therefore used personally loyal informants to keep him abreast of events and advise him informally on the political action to be taken.

The Zionists were not the only group presenting Jewish demands at the peace conference. Parallel with their endeavors, energetic efforts were made to secure the rights of the Jewish national minorities in those states created as a result of the postwar peace treaties. Jewish representatives from Eastern and Western Europe, joined by delegates of the American Jewish Committee and the American Jewish Congress, had this matter under their charge. All these delegates joined in March 1919 to form the Comité des Délégations Juives auprès de la Conférence de la Paix, whose purpose was to protect the rights of Jewish minorities. Leo Motzkin, dedicated equally to Diaspora autonomy and to Zionism, was the initiator and secretary of the Comité.[40]

The question of minority rights became acute as news arrived of pogroms in Poland and the Ukraine. With the disintegration of the Austro-Hungarian Empire in Eastern Galicia, fighting broke out between Poles and Ukrainians in October 1918. On October 24, representatives of Eastern Galician Jewry declared their neutrality in the conflict. Nevertheless, throughout the winter and spring of 1918–19 the Poles carried out pogroms against the Jews of Poland on the pretext that local Jews supported the Ukrainians.[41] Weizmann expressed deep concern about this situation.[42] He worked to save the Galician refugees from being expelled from Bohemia, to which they had fled.[43] He appealed to governments throughout Europe to intercede on their behalf. The persistent news of pogroms provoked the British government into issuing a warning against further outrage. Nevertheless, serious attacks against the Jews in Galicia continued. The leaders of the Zionist Organization in London thereupon resolved to send a special commissioner to investigate the situation, and on December 6, 1918, Israel Cohen departed for Poland.

In other ways, too, the Zionist Organization was actively involved in Jewish minority rights. As pointed out earlier, on October 28, 1918, the Copenhagen Zionist Bureau issued the Copenhagen Manifesto, which set forth the demands of the Jewish people before the impending peace conference. Despite this public appeal and despite Weizmann's concern for the fate of Eastern European Jewry, he was not involved personally in this issue. Contrary to the view of Sokolow, Judge Julian Mack, Victor Jacobson, and Menahem Ussishkin, Weizmann feared that demands for Jewish rights in the Diaspora might detract from the Zionist effort in Palestine. He did not consider the struggle for such rights an integral part of the aims of the Zionist Organization because he was convinced that only in Palestine would Eastern European Jewry find relief, though he did not believe that it would be easy to integrate Russian Jewry into the Yishuv. Ever since his early days in the West, Weizmann had adopted and retained a measure of contempt, even hostility, toward a certain segment of Russian Jewry, particularly those involved in revolutionary activities. In November 1919 he acknowledged to Herbert Samuel:

> The young Russian Jew who comes from the revolutionary atmosphere of disordered Russia is singularly unfit to do pioneer work and we are up here against the most difficult problem in the whole system of our work. The hills and valleys of Judea, however rocky and desolate, can be terraced, watered and covered with trees and transformed into smiling landscapes, but how are we to transform these *farouches* embittered souls into productive human beings I don't quite see yet. The difficulties of the labor problem are not so much economic as psychological. A very powerful process of regeneration will be needed in order to render all this human material fit for the great task of reconstruction in front of us, and a very considerable dilution of those Jews with the Jews of America, Germany, Austria and perhaps Canada will be required, at least in the first periods of work.[44]

Nevertheless, Weizmann concentrated all his efforts on convincing the British statesmen of the necessity of a Jewish national home that, under a British trusteeship, would have the capacity of absorbing a large Jewish immigration. Yet, even as he achieved a measure of success in London and Paris, Weizmann was well aware that these gains were constantly eroded by events in Palestine. There, the Zionist Organization and the Yishuv faced a hostile British military administration and a hostile Arab population. Throughout 1918–20, until the civil administration was installed in Palestine, Weizmann exercised considerable diplomatic skill in Europe and Palestine to reach an agreement with them both. His efforts were complicated by the interdependence of British and Arab attitudes in Palestine and by the contradiction between the policies of the British military administration in Palestine and the cabinet in London. Accordingly, Weizmann was continually frustrated by the fact that diplomatic achievements in London did not bear fruit in Palestine.

As noted, the Occupied Enemy Territory Administration (OETA) was in the hands of the military, under General Allenby, commander in chief of the Egyptian Expeditionary Force and high commissioner of Egypt from 1919 until 1925. Under his command a succession of generals served as chief administrators for Palestine: Major General Arthur Wigram Money (March 1918–July 1919); Major General H. D. Watson (August–December 1919), and Major General Louis Bols (January–June 1920). In addition to the chief administrator directly responsible to Allenby, Brigadier General Gilbert Clayton served as chief political officer (CPO) until July 1919. In July 1919, Colonel John French became acting CPO, to be replaced in September by Colonel Richard Meinertzhagen, who remained in his post until April 1920. Subsequently General Bols assumed responsibility both as chief administrator and CPO until June 1920. The top echelon of city governors comprised senior British officers with experience in Egypt, the Sudan, or India. The lower cadres were composed of Palestinian Arabs, Syrians, and a few Jews.[45]

Relations between the military on the one hand and the Yishuv and the Zionist Commission on the other, strained from their inception, deteriorated further after Weizmann left Palestine in the fall of 1918.[46] Most British officers continued to be ignorant of Zionist aspirations, and a number of those in key positions were outright hostile.[47] As an example of the British attitude, Mordechai Ben-Hillel Hacohen, a moderate and respected leader of the Yishuv, cited the refusal of officials of the OETA to include Hebrew with Arabic and English as an official language on railway tickets, tax forms, and other documents.[48] This refusal was viewed by the official representation of the Yishuv as an act of outright discrimination.[49] While theoretically adhering to the *status quo ante*, the military administration still developed policies that imposed legal and political inferiority on the Zionists. Thus it forbade immigration while giving key governmental positions to Arabs hostile to the Yishuv and attempted to reverse the pro-Zionist stance of Whitehall.

In November 1918 the British military administration prohibited dispositions of immovable property such as land transfers, *waqf* endowments, and enforced payments on mortgages due. Since much of the land registry documentation had been removed from Palestine by the retreating Turkish armies, local land registry offices were unable to function. The commercial classes in Palestine who wished to collect debt payments were thereby prevented from foreclosing mortgages. Benefiting from these circumstances, however, were agriculturists, who had suffered considerable economic dislocation during the war but could not be evicted. In 1918 and 1919 the Zionist Commission favored keeping the registries closed. It wished to obviate land speculation in anticipation of major Jewish land purchases, to prevent occupants from acquiring official title deeds that rightfully belonged to landowners, and to prevent the conversion of Arab-owned land into religious domains *(waqf)* that would exclude it from potential purchase.[50]

The British delegation in Paris in July 1919 did not oppose reopening the registers if Zionists received preferential considerations. Nevertheless the registries remained closed until much of the documentation was restored. After several revisions, Herbert Samuel—by then the high commissioner for Palestine—signed the Land Transfer Ordinance in October 1920. To prevent land speculation, the ordinance fixed limits to the value and the location of transferable land. The small owners and tenants were protected by retaining an undefined subsistence area if the land they tilled was sold. Palestinian Arab landowners, however, feared that the ordinance was a legal ruse whereby the Zionists would acquire large areas of land. The Arabs' protest to the high commissioner led to the Land Transfer Amendment Ordinance in December 1921, which removed the area and value limitations and opened the door to speculation. As a consequence of the amendment, Arab landowners received high prices for their land, while Jewish purchasers were not compelled to provide compensation in land; the British looked on quietly at this self-feeding conflict.[51] The Land Transfer Ordinance had clearly benefited the Zionists who did not have sufficient funds to buy large tracts of land at that time. But its main purpose was to protect the large mass of impoverished Arab tenants from becoming landless as well. On the whole, however, it was difficult to find any British regulations that would favor Jews, even accidentally.

The attitude of the British military authorities was portrayed in a series of reports by Vladimir Jabotinsky, who became the political officer of the Zionist Commission after Weizmann's departure from Palestine. In a trenchant letter to Weizmann, revealing an attempt to understand the British without condoning their actions, Jabotinsky described the situation as follows:

When they [the military administrators] come here they find, on the one side, Arabs whose position is simple and clear, who are just the same old "natives" whom the Englishman has ruled and led for centuries, nothing new, no problems; on the other side, the Zionist who is a problem from top to toe, a problem bristling with difficulties in every way—small in numbers yet somehow strong and influential, ignorant of English yet imbued with European culture, claiming complicated claims. . . . The kindest of Englishmen hates problems and riddles. . . . Whatever may be in store for us in the future, at present we are not as a rule governed by sympathizers.

My dear friend, it will grieve you, but I must say that the whole official attitude here is one of apologizing to Arabs for Mr. Balfour's *lapsus linguae*, of endeavours to atone for it by putting Jews always in the background.[52]

Jabotinsky's assessment was confirmed and detailed by the acting chairman of the Zionist Commission, David Eder.[53] It was further supported by high-ranking British officers, even those who had developed sympathy for the Zionist cause. In a minute circulated among members of the Foreign Office, William Ormsby-Gore accused two high-ranking British officers in Palestine—Colonel Vivian Gabriel, financial adviser to the chief administrator, and Colonel Hubbard, the governor of Jaffa, of outright antisemitism.[54] Colonel Stirling, a member of Clayton's staff, made similar charges in a conversation with Colonel Richard Meinertzhagen,[55] who in May 1919 noted in his diary that "we should inform the Palestine Administration in no uncertain voice that anti-Jew sentiments must not be tolerated in official circles in Palestine."[56] A report written by an unidentified British official, which was certainly more balanced in its attitudes toward Zionists and Arabs, also urged that the military authorities in Palestine exhibit "a spirit of understanding and appreciation of the Jewish problem in Palestine."[57]

Weizmann at first seemed to exhibit a spirit of understanding toward the British and to dismiss the gloomy reports from Palestine concerning the hostility of the military authorities. This, at least, was his public posture within the Zionist camp, possibly so as not to create undue pessimism. He assured his colleagues that the Zionists "shall be able to come to an understanding with the British regarding all the details."[58] Weizmann's meetings in January 1919 with General Clayton, who was on vacation in London, with Sir Henry Wilson, chief of the military staff, and, to a lesser extent with General Money, were somewhat reassuring.[59] But by the end of January 1919 he adopted almost word for word Jabotinsky's earlier assessment of the motives and attitudes of the military authorities.[60] This analysis was reinforced by his own visit to Palestine in the fall of 1919. He realized that the polite and friendly attitude exhibited toward him personally did not reflect the real situation. "The relations between the Jewish population and the British authorities have certainly been unsatisfactory, in many cases very bad," he summarized. Echoing Meinertzhagen's memorandum of February 1919, Weizmann attributed the causes to lack of a definite policy on the part of the British and their general prejudice against Jews.[61]

A report probably written in February 1919 by a British official linked attitudes of British military authorities to those of the Arabs:

> The evil of the situation does not only lie in the misunderstandings which do so much harm to the relations between the Jews and the authorities, but also in the somewhat aggressive and difficult attitude adopted by the Arabs. The Jewish population is constantly being presented with acts and utterances by the British officials utterly at variance with the spirit of Mr. Balfour's declaration. It is only natural therefore that the Arabs should feel that the British authorities have no definite policy *vis-à-vis* the Jews, and this indefiniteness, which is wrongly interpreted by the Arabs as weakness, stimulates the Arabs both inside and outside Palestine to carry on openly an anti-Jewish propaganda.[62]

Since his first days in Egypt and Palestine, Weizmann had been well aware of difficulties the Arabs might create for the Zionists. His meetings with Syrian and Palestinian Arab leaders in Cairo and Palestine in 1918 and his contacts with Feisal were intended to ease apprehensions that the Zionists intended to dispossess the Arabs. Thus, from the start of these negotiations and until the spring of 1920, Weizmann considered Arab-Zionist relations in economic and social, rather than political, terms. "I quite realize that the Arabs are becoming restive," he wrote to David Eder in late November 1918, "but does it amount to much? We know that it is not serious." [63] He was convinced, he wrote General Clayton, that "the Arab peasant will fare better under a new, just administration than he has under the Turk or would even under a retrogressive feudal Arab regime. . . . The Jewish Commonwealth is bound to be a democratic organization. . . . Under such a system the small man, whether a Jew or Gentile, would be amply protected." [64] In a letter to his colleagues, Weizmann wrote a year later from Palestine that "the poor ignorant fellah does not worry about politics, but when he is told repeatedly by people in whom he has confidence that his livelihood is in danger of being taken away from him by us, he becomes our mortal enemy." [65] To Herbert Samuel, Weizmann argued that the Arabs in Palestine were

> broken up in factions, each led by one or two agitators who give vent to their feelings in abusing us grossly, threatening us and insulting us sometimes very vulgarly, but all that is not deep enough. It is a movement which develops simply *par ricochet* from Egypt and Damascus. I had numerous proofs that the Fellah is friendly to us. Whenever I go into an Arab village I am received very well. . . . The Fellah is peaceful and hates politics; the effendis in town are the villains of the piece and will settle down to a *fait accompli!* . . . The fellaheen groan under their heel and those villages would rather have us than their present taskmaster. [66]

Weizmann dismissed what he called "Arab agitation." It was, in his estimate, "not serious or deep, it is still there," he wrote to a friend, "as are the mosquitoes." [67] In September 1919, just before a visit to Palestine, Weizmann presented some of his thoughts on the Palestinian Arabs in an address before the English Zionist Federation:

> The Arabs need us with our knowledge, and our experience and our money. If they do not have us they will fall into the hands of others, they will fall among sharks. They must be convinced that we want to deal with them honestly. We must stick to them. . . . We need them and they need us, and with good will on both sides we can get an arrangement with the Arabs. . . .
>
> They are a very difficult people to get on with, even more difficult than the Jews to get on with. . . . The Arab is primitive. He believes what he is told [about the Zionists coming to take his land]. He reads speeches that certain Zionists make. He says that what I say is nothing; what Zangwill says [about driving the Arabs from Palestine] is the right thing. . . . I have never hidden anything. I do not say, nor do I wish to say that we are going to drive out 700,000 Arabs from the country. I do not think it is needed, I think it is unjust, I know it would be impolitic. [68]

These assessments, which Weizmann maintained until the spring of 1920, failed to fully recognize the increasing strength of Arab nationalist sentiments after the war. The Zionist Commission's celebrations in Palestine on November 2, 1918, marking the first anniversary of the Balfour Declaration, provoked the Arab population to send a delegation to Ronald Storrs protesting the founding of a Jewish national home.[69] On the same occasion the Arab delegation announced the establishment of the Moslem-Christian Association, a Palestinian nationalist group encouraged from its inception by anti-Zionist British officers. In January 1919 leaflets were distributed in Jerusalem and Jaffa urging Arabs to resist the Zionists.[70] Together with other Arab nationalist groups, the Moslem-Christian Association convened during the first week of February 1919 the First Arab Congress in Jerusalem. Its deliberations led to a resolution to abolish the name "Palestine," to henceforth call the area "Southern Syria," and to immediately annex Southern Syria into the Arab Kingdom.[71]

Though events in Palestine were strongly influenced by the center of the Arab nationalist movement in Damascus, they were far from developing simply *"par ricochet,"* as Weizmann had contended. In the summer of 1919 Palestinian Arabs at the First Syrian Congress rejected both the Sykes-Picot Agreement and the Balfour Declaration and proclaimed the Arabs' desire to form a united Syria, including Palestine and Lebanon. The Palestinian Arabs were further encouraged in their nationalist aims by the Anglo-French Declaration of November 7, 1918, which affirmed the Allies' support of Arab independence.[72] In March 1919, President Woodrow Wilson, confronted with the conflict of interest between France and Great Britain concerning the territories of the Middle East and subjected to the pressures from anti-Zionist groups, including Christian missionaries, suggested that an inter-Allied commission study the wishes of the peoples of the Middle East regarding their political future and needs. Since Britain and France opposed such a mission, Wilson assigned the task to two Americans, Henry C. King and Charles R. Crane, who arrived in the Middle East in June 1919 and issued an anti-Zionist report.[73] It was at this time that *Filastin biladna* (Palestine is our country) became the slogan of the Palestinian Arabs. In another slogan they demonstrated awareness of the British authorities' encouraging, or at least nonobstructing, attitude: *Ad daula ma'na* (The government is with us).

General Clayton reported in November 1918 that Arab opposition stemmed from their fear of the "danger of Zionist predominance."[74] During the following months he warned repeatedly that public Zionist declarations had created excitement and restlessness among the Arabs, and he counseled the Zionists to be less provocative and demanding.[75] With few exceptions, officials of the military administration in Palestine supported the Palestinian Arabs' rejection of Zionism. These anti-Zionists included the three chief administrators. On May 2, 1919, Clayton telegraphed to London the text of a memorandum by General Money advising the British government to, in effect, rescind the Balfour Declaration and substitute it with a declaration supporting the wishes of the Arab majority in Palestine,[76] while General H. D. Watson wrote on August 16 to the Foreign Office that "the great fear of the people is that once Zionist wealth is passed into the land all territorial and mineral concessions will fall into the hands of the Jews whose intensely clannish instincts prohibit them from dealing with any but those of their own religion, to the detriment of Moslems and Christians." The letter concluded with the suggestion that Zionist aims in Palestine be curtailed.[77] Balfour himself felt constrained to ask Weizmann to curb incautious actions and pronouncements by Zionists in Palestine.[78]

Members of the Zionist Commission and friends in the Foreign Office kept Weizmann informed of developments in Palestine. Weizmann at first trusted the military administration and preached conciliation and patience.[79] His initial sympathy for the British administrators was coupled with his criticism of the Palestinian Jews' aggressive attitude toward the administration and the exaggerated pronouncements of Zionists in Palestine and Europe concerning a future Jewish state. Such statements, he agreed, aggravated tensions in Palestine. In response to Balfour's gentle rebuke, he expressed his regret for these sources of irritation, though he also blamed the British administrators in Palestine.[80] His report from Palestine in November 1919 to his colleagues in London did acknowledge, however, that full blame did not rest with the British. "You must bear in mind," he wrote, "that the Jewish population has not been free from blame all this time. Much could have been avoided if the Jews would have shown more tact, more tolerance and more *savoir faire* in their dealings with the British authorities."[81]

To a certain degree Weizmann's gains in the London political arena did serve to counteract the hostility of British officials in Palestine. His efforts[82] were largely responsible for the appointment in September 1919 of Colonel Richard Meinertzhagen, a fervent pro-Zionist,[83] as chief political officer in Palestine, succeeding General Clayton. In addition, on August 4, 1919, the British Foreign Office sent instructions to the military administration, clearly stating that the government intended to accept the mandate for Palestine and that the document constituting the mandate would include the Balfour Declaration. The instructions required that the Arabs be impressed with the fact that this commitment be accepted as a *chose jugée*.[84] Finally, on February 27, 1920, General Bols was ordered to proclaim officially and publicly that Britain intended to carry out the Balfour Declaration.

Weizmann was less successful with other political and economic proposals. He understood the significance of visible achievements in Palestine in preparation for the civil administration. The inflexible policy of the military administration, however, resisted constructive Jewish projects. In a letter to a leading member of the British delegation in Paris,

Louis Mallet, Weizmann suggested practical steps the Zionists in Palestine could undertake, such as the acquisition of certain properties and land, the establishment of a shipping line, and the development of public utilities.[85] Mallet responded evasively.[86]

As a countermeasure to British obstructionism, Weizmann repeatedly attempted to forestall those economic and political measures proposed by the British in Palestine that discriminated against the Jews and favored the Arabs. He continued to propose plans for the future development of the country. In a lengthy memorandum to Curzon, who in October 1919 replaced Balfour as foreign secretary, he outlined Zionist aims in Palestine.[87] This outline became a blueprint for Zionist work under a civilian administration; for the time being, though, under Curzon's highly unsympathetic gaze, the Foreign Office remained noncommittal. Curzon's attitude to the Zionist enterprise was summarized in one short sentence three months earlier: upon reading a report of a meeting between Ronald Graham and Weizmann in which the latter complained about British discrimination, Curzon minuted: "To a large extent the Zionists are reaping the harvest which they themselves sowed."[88]

Given the political uncertainty about the future of Palestine, the Zionists were interested in the continued presence in the country of the wartime Jewish legion.[89] Most Zionists hoped that the legion would become the militia force of the mandatory power and thus enhance the political strength of the Jewish national home; Jabotinsky, on the other hand, favored a scheme by which the Judeans would be established as a permanent unit of the British Army.[90] On January 1, 1919, David Eder telegraphed Weizmann in London with the news of the initial demobilization of the legion.[91] On February 4, Weizmann wrote to Sir Henry Wilson, chief of the Imperial General Staff, suggesting the retention of the five-thousand-man Jewish legion as a Jewish militia in Palestine.[92] Sir Henry responded positively, as did General George Macdonogh, director of British military intelligence. But on April 21, Allenby wrote from Palestine opposing the scheme. In addition, Curzon's skepticism influenced the Foreign Office, whose assent to the plan was required.[93] Sir Ronald Graham, acting permanent undersecretary in the Foreign Office, and Sir Eric Forbes Adam, responsible for Middle Eastern affairs at the Foreign Office, refused to act prior to a decision on the mandate.

Resentment in the battalions led to occurrences of mutiny—especially among the American volunteers—and court martials.[94] In August 1919 Jabotinsky was discharged. The Zionists also demanded that volunteers wishing to do so be allowed to settle as landworkers in Palestine. Weizmann was able to postpone the disbandment of the legion until March 31, 1921, with the direct intervention of Winston Churchill and the help of Herbert Samuel. In the interim, the legion's morale sagged to the point of voluntary demobilization. On July 31, 1920, most of the remaining group of four hundred soldiers of the first battalion of the Judeans

(Thirty-eighth Battalion Royal Fusiliers) went home, thus marking for all practical purposes the end of the Jewish legion. On March 31 of the following year, when complete demobilization was to take place, there were still thirty-four men under the command of Colonel Eliezer Margolin. Weizmann again urged that they be retained to form a nucleus for a Jewish force under the mandate. During the riots in Tel Aviv in May 1921, however, Margolin and his men acted without authorization to defend Jewish neighborhoods against Arab attack. As a result, Margolin was forced to resign, and his men were discharged.[95]

Throughout this period Weizmann was the authoritative figure in Europe best suited to negotiate with the British statesmen and officers in London and Palestine. By 1919 he knew all the major players. Even those who did not support his Zionist policies did not fail to take account of his ideas. Others often heeded his advice and were as attuned to him as he was to them. On the other hand, the great unknown for Weizmann and other veteran European Zionists was the American group that had emerged during the war and their eminent and formidable leader, Justice Louis D. Brandeis. With the peace conference at hand, the long-delayed activation of the force Brandeis had patiently assembled had to be put into effect. The American Zionists' tactic of coordinating their moves with those of President Wilson, like the British Zionists' parallel relationship with the British government, now demanded the enunciation by both of clear policies and the deployment of their forces to realize them. It became necessary for the British and American Zionists to reach a working understanding.

In the latter part of 1918, the American Zionists were finally able to move beyond the limits the American government had imposed on their activity in Palestine. That spring the American Zionist Medical Unit, as we have seen, was finally cleared, over State Department objections, to go to Palestine, where it resumed Hadassah's interrupted services on a much-expanded basis. In August, Rabbi Stephen Wise, vice-president of the Zionist Organization of America, aroused by rumors of Henry Morgenthau's anti-Zionist campaign, appealed to President Wilson for the long-awaited public endorsement of Zionism and the Balfour Declaration. In his response on August 31, 1918, Wilson bracketed his paraphrase of the Balfour Declaration with an avowal of "deep and sincere interest [in] the reconstructive work which the Weizmann Commission has done in Palestine."[96]

By the end of 1918 the moment had come for the American Zionists, no less than for the Wilson administration, to put to the test the policies and procedures for which they had been patiently preparing themselves all through the war. As the opening of the peace conference approached, Weizmann communicated frequently with Brandeis, urging him to send a strong American delegation.[97] On November 25, 1918, the national executive of the Zionist Organization of America approved the composition of its official delegation to the peace conference: Rabbi Stephen Wise, leader of the delegation and Brandeis's personal representative,[98] as well as Shmarya Levin, Mary Fels, and Louis Robison. Bernard Flexner was legal adviser.[99] The delegation—except for Levin, who came a month later—arrived in London on December 12, 1918.[100] Felix Frankfurter came in February 1919, followed by the delegation of the American Jewish Congress headed by Julian Mack, president of the ZOA. Mack was accompanied by his secretary, Ben Cohen, who remained in Europe until early 1921. The young and unassuming Cohen was to play a crucial role in drafting the Mandate for Palestine and other important legal documents.

The close and sustained contacts of American delegations with the complexities of the Zionist situation and Zionist politics in Palestine and Europe considerably sharpened the issues that the Brandeis leadership had to face. The consequences were as complex as they were fateful. The net result of American cooperation with the London leadership in negotiations during the peace conference and the drafting of the Mandate for Palestine was to align them with Weizmann's policy, leading them to give him invaluable support in the initial postwar reorganization of the World Zionist Organization. But the direct experience with Zionist work in Palestine led to a growing cleavage and, eventually, to an alliance of the Brandeis leadership with other opponents in an open break with Weizmann.

The final break was, of course, many months away, but some of the seeds of disharmony can be traced to the spring of 1918, when the Zionist Commission was set up by the Allied governments, each of which nominated its own Jewish representative to share in the proposed cooperation with the British military authorities. Weizmann, the *homme de confiance* of the British, resigned his post at Manchester University at once to go to Palestine as the head of the commission. The American leaders were unable to participate as fully, since the American government, in view of its neutrality in the war with Turkey, disapproved of an official American Zionist representation.

Even if that obstacle had not existed, not only Brandeis but lesser lights like Mack and Wise were not willing to give up their professional positions, as Weizmann did. The United States did, of course, have its unofficial and lower-level contacts from the start, first through an observer named to the commission and above all through the active presence of Dr. Isaac Rubinow, who led the American Zionist Medical Unit, and leaders like Alice Seligsberg and, soon, Henrietta Szold. In 1919 able Americans took over leading positions on the Zionist Commission, but it was clear that they did not conceive their participation as involving permanent resettlement. Unlike veteran European Zionists on the commission, such as Menahem Ussishkin, the Americans served for a limited period. The few Americans who did permanently move to Palestine, however, contributed significantly to the structure of Palestine Jewry. The land purchases of Simon Goldman's Achooza movement, upon which

Poriah was growing up, were succeeded by the efforts of the American Zion Commonwealth, which founded Balfouria and helped settle Jewish legion veterans in Herzliyah. Eliezer Jaffe, father of the Moshav movement, a prewar settler, was joined by other Americans destined to provide Israel with one prime minister (Golda Meir) and the father of another (Yitzhak Rabin). The Jewish legion volunteers included men like Gershon Agron (Agronsky) and Dov (Bernard) Joseph. Other Americans, like Henrietta Szold and Judah Magnes, who came after the war to serve temporarily, stayed on and became major figures in the cultural and social welfare institutions as well as in the political life of the Jewish national home and of Palestine generally.

The top leaders of the new ZOA, however, conceived their role not as that of settlers or lower- and middle-echelon civil servants. They undertook, as the war drew to a close, to play a decisive part both in the postwar reorganization of the world Zionist movement and in formulating the legal foundations for the Jewish national home in Palestine. As they arrived in Europe, beginning in December 1918, in groups or individually, they studied those problems that interested them most, expecting to play a major role in their solutions. They encountered complications they had not foreseen and found themselves struggling with what seemed irrelevant issues that sent some, like Stephen Wise and Jacob DeHaas, home with reports of bitter frustration and left others, like Cohen, Flexner, and Frankfurter, to struggle on with dogged, if irritated, goodwill.

The Americans were, generally, not intimately familiar with internal Zionist politics; and those who were more attuned to these disputes, like Stephen Wise and Jacob DeHaas, were predisposed to suspect Weizmann as an old foe of their revered late leader Theodor Herzl. Weizmann, the central man in all British calculations regarding the Zionists and therefore vital to any effective work under the prospective British mandate, was himself without firmly established authority in the World Zionist Organization at the war's end. The old German leadership, as well as Brandeis in the United States, were disposed to support his claim to paramount leadership, especially as Brandeis made himself unavailable for this post. But others, such as Wise and DeHaas, saw in Weizmann's claim only unwarranted self-promotion. As the quarrels grew more strident, the Americans generally came to regard the issues as petty and personal, and increasingly the top American leaders began to lose patience.

The issue of reorganization—in the London office as well as in the leadership of the WZO itself—was far from insignificant for Weizmann. Even while negotiating for the Balfour Declaration and appearing to be in full control, he was theoretically operating under a mandate from Nahum Sokolow and Yehiel Tschlenow and occasionally reflecting the drawbacks of unclear lines of command and communication. During his months in Palestine, often frustrated by his inability to move his colleagues—particularly Sokolow—to take desired actions, Weizmann came to appreciate all the more the necessity of rectifying this state of affairs. Moreover, as chairman of the Zionist Commission, theoretically representing world Jewry, Weizmann was its undisputed leader; yet upon returning to London he was faced with the unpleasant prospect of sharing power with Sokolow. Thus, one of Weizmann's first priorities upon returning to England was the reorganization and expansion of the Zionist Bureau in London. For this task he requested that Julius Simon, a member of the Greater Actions Committee and his friend from the prewar days, improve the operation of the London office. Simon rented the house at 77 Great Russell Street, near the British Museum, which for many years was to be the headquarters of the WZO and its affiliate institutions.[101] By the spring of 1919 the bureau's work had become streamlined: Weizmann and Nahum Sokolow headed the political department, while Simon, Victor Jacobson, Berthold Feiwel, and later Samuel Landman handled administration.

As soon as he reorganized the London Zionist Bureau in October and November 1918, Weizmann was determined to establish his own authority in the Zionist hierarchy more securely. Within two weeks of his return to London, his intimates floated the idea of appointing him head of all political activities, with Sokolow reporting to him,[102] though the notion of his co-optation into the Smaller Actions Committee did not seem to originate with Weizmann. On November 19, 1918, Sokolow and Weizmann invited Victor Jacobson, a member of the Smaller Actions Committee and head of the Copenhagen Zionist Bureau, to join them in London, where Shmarya Levin, another member of the SAC, was soon expected. They asked that Jacobson bring with him a power of attorney from Arthur Hantke and Otto Warburg, the German members of the SAC, which would entitle him to act on their behalf.[103] This, in a sense, meant the transfer of authority from Berlin and Copenhagen to London. Hantke and Warburg readily agreed to this suggestion.[104] They went a step further. Just before Jacobson departed for London, the SAC met in Copenhagen, November 30–December 2. Warburg, Hantke, Jacobson, and Leo Motzkin, a member of the GAC, were present, and they decided to co-opt both Chaim Weizmann and Julius Simon into the SAC. The announcement was to be made from London.[105]

On December 15, 1918, following Jacobson's arrival in London, the reorganization of the Smaller Actions Committee was discussed among the inner circle of the Political Committee as well as with Jacobson and the members of the American delegation, who had arrived a few days earlier. Primarily for the benefit of the Americans, Weizmann began the discussions with a long review of events of the political achievements leading to the Balfour Declaration. Though he gave due credit to Sokolow's "valuable propaganda work amongst Jews and Christians," particularly in France and Italy, Weizmann clearly viewed himself as responsible for the accomplishments in England. Now he wished to be in control.

The journal of the American delegation quoted Weizmann thus: "I say to you quite frankly, gentlemen, I cannot continue any longer under the order of Sokolow. I do not wish to hurt Sokolow . . . but again I say that the difference in temperament between him and myself makes it impossible for me to sit under [him], although I am ready to give up the leadership, my work in England being done, and leave to him the con- duct of future negotiations."[106]

Though they did not believe that Weizmann's offer of resignation was sincere, the Americans agreed that, at this time, with his connections with all branches of the British government and their own support for his pro-British policy, he was irreplaceable and that even a partial with- drawal was unthinkable. Given the tight control Brandeis exercised over the Zionist organization in the United States, they, perhaps naturally, favored a similar presidential arrangement in Europe.[107] Nevertheless, they could not agree to Weizmann's implied demand to become presi- dent of the Smaller Actions Committee and thus the undisputed leader of the WZO without consulting Sokolow, whom they cabled the follow- ing day requesting his immediate arrival in London.[108] In any case, even if Sokolow would have agreed, such action could only be taken by the *Jahreskonferenz* or the Zionist Congress itself.

By the time the cable reached Sokolow in Paris, he had already heard of Weizmann's plans and refused to comply, citing urgent work. In fact, he and his closest adviser in Paris, the veteran Russian Zionist Israel Rosov, were furious at Weizmann's dictatorial pretentions.[109] Others, like Shmuel Tolkowsky, who had witnessed three previous "resignations" by Weizmann, worried that he would do so again, while Aaron Aaron- sohn, who was also in Paris at the time, openly supported the move to co-opt Weizmann into the SAC. Aaronsohn could barely conceal his contempt for Sokolow's personality and had even less regard for him as a diplomat. He was all too happy to report to Weizmann on Sokolow's doings and plans, intelligence Weizmann used to good effect in Lon- don.[110]

Still Sokolow would not budge, and attempts in late December 1918 and early January 1919 by Simon Marks, Stephen Wise, and Victor Ja- cobson failed to change his views. Moreover, even those who supported Weizmann's claims, as well as Weizmann himself, felt they could not force Sokolow's hand in this matter.[111] Weizmann departed for Paris on January 4, 1919, and during the first part of that month he discussed the issue directly with Rosov and Sokolow, but again to no avail.[112] On Jan- uary 9, at a meeting at the Hotel Meurice, Sokolow's headquarters, at- tended by Wise, Joseph Cowen, Angelo Levi-Bianchini, Israel Sieff, Aar- onsohn, Weizmann, Rosov, and Sokolow, the discussions became shrill; they were later described by Wise as "very, very, very painful."[113] Claiming he had had enough of the whole affair, Weizmann blurted that reorganization was no longer necessary, whereupon Rosov turned to Weizmann and quietly, but firmly, said:

You are crazy [*Du bist meshugge*], you are suffering from megalomania. You treat us like a usurer. You know we need you, you come to us and say to us "I am willing to let you have my services at a price" and you think you can name your price. I say to you that you cannot name your price and treat us in this usurious and blackmailing fashion. Remember that what you are, you have become through the organization, you have used the organization, you have been built up by the organization. The organization has made you what you are and the organization is greater than you. If you say that you will not work, unless we accept your terms, very well then, we shall send out word that we have lost Weizmann and it will be a great loss—but Zionism will survive and you will perish.[114]

These harsh and emotional recriminations deeply repelled the Americans. They and others recommended compromises that suggested postponement of a decisive resolution to a later time. Sokolow also resigned himself to "crown Weizmann" a few weeks later. But Weizmann forced the issue and prevailed. He insisted on naming his price and being rewarded right away, and his colleagues had no choice but to succumb to his ultimatum—or blackmail, as some of them saw it—even if it meant engaging in a procedure whose legality, under the rules of the World Zionist Organization, was questionable.

On January 22, 1919, a meeting of the SAC took place in London, attended by Jacobson and Shmarya Levin (who had arrived in London a few days earlier) as well as Weizmann, Israel Rosov, and Leopold Kessler, all members of the GAC. Jacobson presented the "Deed of Power" signed by Warburg and Hantke, and the meeting decided to co-opt Weizmann into the SAC in place of the deceased Tschlenow.[115] Since Jacobson also voted on behalf of Warburg and Hantke, and Rosov declared that he voted in the affirmative on behalf of Sokolow, Weizmann's co-optation could be considered to have received the assent of all members of the SAC. It was confirmed at a meeting of the GAC held in London during February–March 1919.

Sokolow reconciled himself quickly to the inevitable rise of Weizmann to leadership and continued to carve out his own area of political activities on the Continent as a liaison with Christians and Jewish non-Zionists and other dignitaries. These were spheres in which he felt comfortable and was the acknowledged master. For his part, Weizmann could feel satisfied, at least for the moment. True, he had not been recognized as the undisputed leader of the movement but rather co-opted as an equal member of the SAC. Yet he viewed this co-optation as a reward for his past and present political successes. It was a personal achievement of a man who some four years earlier had clearly not been part of the inner circle of the WZO. It was attained, like his previous positions, through sheer hard work and talent, by using his own personal connections and by virtue of recognition by the British. The drawback of his current situation was that it was achieved mainly due to his esteem in British quarters; the movement's democratic machinery was not part of the process.

Thus future severance of his contacts with his British patrons was almost sure to result in his fall from leadership within the Zionist movement. Moreover, the rise of the party system within the WZO, in which Weizmann did not take part, also changed the constellation of power. For the moment, however, he was poised to take on an ever-more-preeminent role within the World Zionist Organization. He was, of course, well aware of the fact that he owed his rise within Zionism to the British. This debt did not, however, present a conflict of interest for him, since he was determined from the outset that Britain become the dominant power in Palestine.

An unfortunate coincidence for Weizmann was the fact that his conflict with Sokolow occurred just as the American delegation arrived in London. Given the letters of praise and support from Felix Frankfurter that preceded their arrival, Weizmann could have expected the Americans to back him in this affair.[116] But the Americans, bearing in mind their own leaders' more patrician distance from petty power struggles, found Weizmann's behavior in the matter distasteful. Their commitment to support Weizmann and work together with him was further strained by a growing divergence of views on major administrative, political, and economic positions, particularly with regard to the proposals to be presented to the peace conference at Versailles. Finally, there were among the Americans those who—like DeHaas and Wise—were still resentful of Weizmann's anti-Herzlian stance before World War I and viewed Brandeis as the most natural leader of the WZO. Their initial negative attitude toward Weizmann was reinforced by the events they witnessed in London.

After his interview with Balfour on December 4, 1918, Weizmann reformulated the Zionist proposals to some degree and, following his meeting on December 11 with the Emir Feisal, planned to present them in printed form to the British delegation to the peace conference. As soon as members of the American Zionist delegation arrived on December 12, Weizmann discussed the proposals with them. Their immediate reaction was that "the proposals were too meagre and completely failed to deal with matters of administration that would be the only safeguard against imperialistic domination." They cabled the proposals for suggestions and emendations by Brandeis, Mack, and DeHaas.[117] Simultaneously, the Palestine Jewish community, without reference to the proposals submitted by Weizmann in November or to later modifications, formulated far-reaching demands during their meeting in Haifa of December 18, 1918.[118] Predictably, the five Palestinian delegates who arrived with these demands in London a few weeks later denounced even the more radical proposals of January 1919 as minimalist.[119] In the meantime, the Samuel-Weizmann draft of November was roundly criticized by Zionists and non-Zionists alike.[120]

Having been kept informed by Brandeis and DeHaas, Weizmann was aware in advance of their coming that the Americans would regard the

Samuel-Weizmann proposals as too "moderate and timid."[121] Indeed, the stamp of the Americans was immediately apparent in a cable sent by Weizmann to Eder on December 17 enumerating the "new proposals" being discussed in London:

1. That the whole of Palestine shall be so formed as to make of Palestine a Jewish Commonwealth under British trusteeship.
2. That Jews shall so participate in the administration as to assure this object.
3. That Hebrew shall be the official language of the Jewish population.
4. That the Jewish population be allowed the widest practicable measure of local self-government.
5. That the Jews shall have extensive rights in regard to the taking over of land, including the right of expropriating the Effendis.
6. The right of preemption of public works.
7. A Jewish Council representing Palestinian and world Jewry to be elected at an all-Jewish Congress in Jerusalem. The functions of Council will include to deal with land settlement and land purchase, promote and organize immigration, supervise and control wherever practicable concessions for public works, etc.
8. Jewish population to have educational and cultural autonomy.
9. Sabbath and Jewish holidays to be legal days of rest.[122]

Some of those involved in formulating these maximalist proposals wanted even stronger language. Victor Jacobson, for example, preferred "Jewish State" to "Jewish Commonwealth," but this wording was vetoed by Weizmann, who advised against "demanding more than it is possible to get."[123] In the meantime the Americans, particularly Stephen Wise, completed their own rounds of interviews with British statesmen. Wise came away from his December 19 interview with Arthur Balfour strengthened in the belief that the British would accede to the Zionist wishes for maximalist demands. He also clearly understood, as did Weizmann before him, that the British government did not wish to appear as an occupying force in Palestine but preferred that the League of Nations impose upon it the mandate for Palestine.[124] The implication was that the Zionists were to engineer such a sequence of events. Following a one and one-half hour interview with Lloyd George on December 20, Weizmann and Herbert Samuel came away confident that the prime minister was fully committed to a British trusteeship over Palestine but wished to have the endorsement of President Wilson for such a scheme.[125] That same day Wise and Weizmann cabled Brandeis, asking him to secure such a communication from the American president.[126]

While Weizmann and Wise presented a united front when speaking to the foreign secretary or the prime minister, the behind-the-scenes hammering out of the proposals was conducted in tense and often heated meetings. The issues at hand were what demands could be made of the British without alienating them, but the discussions took place during a

Weizmann, about 1919. Courtesy: Central Zionist Archives

period when the reorganization of the SAC had not yet been settled, a factor that charged the air. During a meeting on December 23, 1918, with Jacobson, Simon, Cowen, and Wise, Weizmann insisted that he could not ask for more lest he be the person responsible for a break with Great Britain. Weizmann felt that his former experience in negotiating with the British gave him a deeper understanding of what it was possible to demand of them. With an obvious reference to the Americans, Weizmann exclaimed: "The Jewish people evidently wish Palestine handed to them upon a golden platter. . . . The pressure which we are able to exercise with respect to the British Government and the Peace Conference generally will depend upon Zionist support, and that Zionist support is not at hand in the degree it should be." He then threatened to resign unless his line of policy was adhered to and the sum of $250,000 secured within the next six weeks. He insisted that the British government could not be tied down in advance to any written declaration, as some of his colleagues, notably Jacobson and Simon, wished. "The British Government is always empirical in its method of conducting affairs. The British Government will probably temporize with us as long as it

Vera Weizmann in Jerusalem, 1920. Courtesy: Central Zionist Archives

can, and, I urge again, our demands are not to be a matter of a formula of the Peace Conference, but to be insistently and tirelessly pursued from day to day and from month to month."[127]

Though resentful of the way Weizmann treated them, members of the American delegation, which met the following morning, decided nevertheless to express their confidence in his leadership. At the same time they were not willing to grant him the kind of powers they granted Brandeis and insisted that Weizmann consult with them before he made any final treaties with Feisal or anyone else.[128] At the request of the American delegation, Wise met privately with Weizmann and communicated these sentiments to him. Wise then added: "We will not consider your threat of resignation, for it is a childish thing to do. We are not free to accept it and you have no right to offer it. Surely you would be sorry to have it appear on the records that you threatened to retire from the leadership now."[129] For the time being, it seemed that the Americans and Weizmann had resolved some of their personal and stylistic differences, even if they were still far apart on matters of substance.

The American Zionists and Weizmann agreed to let a committee, composed of Harry Sacher, Leon Simon, Victor Jacobson, Bernard Flexner, and Julius Simon, compose a new draft of Zionist demands or proposals that, presumably, took into account the Samuel-Weizmann draft of November, the resolutions of the Palestine Jewish community, and the American recommendations.[130] The forty-one-page pamphlet they produced was titled "Memorandum of the Zionist Organization Relating to the Reconstruction of Palestine as the Jewish National Home." It bore the date January 1919 and was submitted to the Foreign Office on January 19 and to the British delegation in Paris on the following day. As the title of the document indicates, it demanded much more for the Zionists than the previous Samuel-Weizmann draft and was closer in content and spirit to the ideas contained in Weizmann's cable to Eder of mid-December 1918. The memorandum repeated time and again the notion that Palestine must be developed into a Jewish commonwealth under a British trusteeship. In order to reconstruct Palestine as the Jewish national home, the memorandum demanded, among other things, the installation of a Jewish governor, the nationalization of all absentee lands, and a Jewish majority on the executive and legislative councils.[131]

Though he had approved this document, Weizmann was not happy with it, sensing it would not be accepted by the British and would be difficult to defend on its merits.[132] The reaction by the British officials was swift. Balfour was baffled by the fact that Weizmann would be party to such a document. Writing to Lloyd George, he commented, "As far as I know Weizmann has never put forward a claim for the Jewish *Government* of Palestine. Such a claim is in my opinion certainly inadmissible and personally I do not think we should go further than the original declaration which I made to Lord Rothschild."[133] General Arthur Money returned the document to Weizmann with many critical marginal notes and added that the Zionist proposals would cause antagonism and hostility among the majority toward the Jewish minority in Palestine. He thus recommended eliminating many of the demands.[134] The most direct criticism and frank guidelines for redrafting the Zionist demands came from William Ormsby-Gore in a letter to Nahum Sokolow. Having consulted with Sir Louis Mallet, a ranking civil servant of the British delegation to the peace conference, and Sir Eric Drummond, the private secretary to the foreign secretary, Ormsby-Gore made suggestions that read more like instructions:

> Both Sir Louis and Sir Eric wished it to be made quite clear to you that there must be no suggestion that your proposals have been approved by the British Government. There is no objection to you asking for Great Britain as Mandatory provided you do this entirely on your own, and without asking Mr. Balfour or the British Government.
> Sir Louis made it quite clear that in his opinion the British Government would not accept the duties of Mandatory if the constitution proposed in the printed memorandum were insisted upon by you and the Conference.

He and I certainly both think this Memorandum is far too extreme as well as being much too long and detailed for submission to the Peace Conference.

Sir Louis recommends you to submit something briefer and less likely to offend the susceptibilities of the majority of the present inhabitants of Palestine.[135]

Ormsby-Gore was even blunter in a personal letter to Weizmann:

Let me be perfectly frank with you. I do not like such phrases as Jewish Commonwealth and Jewish Palestine. They excite fears and opposition. . . . I do urge you to do what you can as a statesman to resist the tendency . . . to prophesy smoother things. . . . As a politician myself I know how the pressure of constituents urges a political leader . . . to say what will be popular. . . .

The time to talk of Jewish political predominance in Palestine or of a Jewish State or Commonwealth . . . or of a Jewish Palestine is not yet. . . .

I am still uneasy about the proposed Constitution and functions of the Jewish Council for Palestine. I don't like political or extra-Palestinian popular control of such a body.[136]

Though personally the target of most of the criticism leveled by the British,[137] Weizmann did not seem to mind too much, possibly because he had anticipated this response. Indeed, it must have pleased him to show his colleagues, particularly the Americans, that he understood the British "empirical approach" to political issues far better than they could. The reaction of some of the other activists in London was quite different. Harry Sacher complained, "We are left rather worse off than under the Turks. We shall not get access to the land, and we shall be ruled by anti-Semitic public school boys . . . with a pro-Moslem bias. . . . The blunt truth is that we have been done. We have helped to give England Palestine and with that our usefulness is exhausted."[138]

But there was little time for self-pity or reproach. The revised document had to be submitted by February 1. This time Weizmann was determined to be directly involved in the process of revision, and thus he traveled to Paris on January 28. Together with Sokolow, DeHaas, Rosov, Aaronsohn, Bernard Flexner, and Herbert Samuel, Weizmann labored for three consecutive days to produce a new version of the Zionist demands.[139] It was not a totally harmonious collaboration; throughout there was a tug between the more extreme demands of the Americans, particularly DeHaas, and those proposed by Samuel and Weizmann, which the Americans disliked "owing to their vagueness and indefinite character."[140] Toward the end of this process, on January 30 and 31, Weizmann and Samuel met with Ormsby-Gore, Arnold Toynbee, and Robert Cecil, all attached to the British delegation, to make sure they were in basic agreement on the major issues. At the last moment the Zionists received an extension, and thus the document is dated February 3, 1919.[141]

Titled "Statement of the Zionist Organization Regarding Palestine," this new version, beginning with its title, clearly shows Weizmann's influence. Reduced to fourteen pages, it added a section concerning the historic title of the Jews to Palestine.[142] It eliminated many of the paragraphs in the previous memorandum to which the British objected, such as expropriation of land and a Jewish governor. In general, it softened the demands for Jewish governance of Palestine and eliminated the demand for a Jewish majority on the executive and legislative councils. The Jewish council, whose role was highlighted in a subsection, was to have the function of a consultant to the government in matters relating to Jews.[143] A major concession to the American Zionist delegation, as Samuel explained to Mallet, was the retention of the concept of a Jewish commonwealth,[144] though the statement spoke of an "autonomous Commonwealth" instead. Finally, the statement also included a section on the boundaries of Palestine that was written mainly by Aaronsohn.[145]

The Paris Peace Conference began its deliberations on January 18, 1919. Writing to his sister, Bernard Flexner commented that the city was crowded with Americans and others, the cafés were full and gay. "The amount of political gossip," he confided, "rumor, etc. that one gets is amazing."[146] But out of the limelight, a variety of agreements were being made and unmade, both before and following the start of deliberations. David Lloyd George may have been a man without principles, as his friend C. P. Scott accused him of being, and Wilson was "like a rock once his mind was made up and principle is at stake,"[147] but they both moved along political tracks that were highly congenial to the Zionists at that moment in time. Strong evidence suggests, for instance, that during his visit to London at the end of 1918, the French prime minister, Georges Clemenceau, ceded to Lloyd George both Mosul and Palestine, from Dan to Beersheba.[148]

For his part, Weizmann was not idle.[149] On January 14, thanks to Scott, he met with President Woodrow Wilson for some forty minutes. The two leaders found themselves in agreement on a number of topics. "How do you get along with the French?" asked the president. "I speak French fluently," replied Weizmann, "But the French and I speak a different language." Wilson indicated he had the same problem with his allies.[150] There seemed to be a special symbolism in the fact that as the Sykes-Picot Agreement was crumbling through political machinations, one of its authors, Mark Sykes, succumbed to the flu and died on February 16.

On February 15, Weizmann met again with Balfour in Paris. The affable statesman stated unequivocally that he considered the Zionist Statement to be reasonable in its various sections and promised his help in implementing it once the peace conference had approved it. Balfour was especially emphatic in his support of its economic proposals. The boundaries of the country must be sufficient to accommodate millions of inhabitants.[151] Shuttling back and forth between London and Paris, Weizmann also met with Sir Henry Wilson, Generals Money and Clay-

Comité des Délégations Juives auprès de la Conférence de la Paix, 1919. Among those pictured, from left: Julian W. Mack, Leon Levite, Louis Marshall, Nahum Sokolow, Leo Motzkin, Weizmann, Menahem Ussishkin. Courtesy: Weizmann Archives

ton, and Colonel Edward M. House. He was covering as many bases as he could in preparation for the peace conference, and he believed that all the interviews went well.[152] It was not known when the Zionists would appear before the Council of Ten, and Weizmann used the lull in activity in Paris to return to London, where the so-called London Conference, the first international Zionist gathering to be convened since the Zionist Congress of 1913, met from February 23 to March 12. Weizmann, who arrived in London on February 19, barely had time to greet the delegates. Nor did he have adequate time to assuage their displeasure at the fact that Zionist demands to the peace conference had already been presented before they had convened to sanction them.[153] He was back in Paris on February 25.

The Zionist Mission, as it was officially called, was now scheduled to appear before the Council of Ten on February 27, 1919. It was a historic occasion for the Zionists, the first opportunity to present the Zionist argument before an international forum. Assuming that their delegation would be composed of Weizmann, Sokolow, DeHaas, and Ussishkin, they were greatly agitated when on the day prior to their scheduled appearance they were notified by the French Foreign Ministry that their delegation would not include Ussishkin; instead André Spire, a French poet and a Zionist leader, would speak on behalf of French Zionists, and Sylvain Lévi would speak as a representative of French Jewry in general. DeHaas did not arrive in time from London, and the Zionists succeeded in reinstating Ussishkin, but they could not remove Lévi from their delegation.[154]

Clearly, there was a political force stronger than the Zionists who wished to have Lévi appear; it turned out to be the Zionists' old friend and supporter, Baron Edmond de Rothschild.[155] Since the latter part of 1918 the baron had become increasingly irritated with Zionist policies. He viewed Weizmann as responsible for them and bore an additional grudge for the way Weizmann had treated James de Rothschild in Palestine. In January 1919 the baron referred to Weizmann as "un obstiné, un fanatique, même un homme dangereux."[156] The baron used his contacts to ensure that Sylvain Lévi would be included in the deliberations as an antidote to the Zionists. Last-minute Zionist attempts to coordinate their presentations with Lévi failed.[157]

Nevertheless, the day after their presentation, Weizmann could report to his wife that "Yesterday, the 27th February, at 3.30 p.m. at the Quai d'Orsay there took place an historic session." It ended with "a marvellous moment, the most triumphant of my life!"[158] At one point the session threatened to end on a much less triumphant note. Sokolow opened with a description of the importance of Jews among the Entente Powers and in the United States, as citizens who had contributed toward winning the war. At the same time he drew attention to the condition of Eastern European Jewry, whose plight could be remedied only in a Jewish national center. "From where I stood," wrote Weizmann later in his autobiography, "I could see Sokolow's face and without being sentimental, it was as if two thousand years of Jewish suffering rested on his shoulders."[159] Weizmann, who followed, outlined the tragedy of the Jews in Eastern Europe. In Palestine, he claimed, five million Jews could be settled without encroaching on the legitimate interests of the present inhabitants. A million Jews in Eastern Europe were awaiting the signal to move. Ussishkin addressed the council in Hebrew in the name of the National Assembly representing three million Jews of South Russia. André Spire did not claim that all French Jews were Zionists but assured the council that France had nothing to fear from the Zionist movement.[160]

The concluding speaker was Sylvain Lévi, who praised some Zionist achievements, particularly the colonies in Palestine, which had been supported by Baron Rothschild, but severely attacked Zionist aims. He portrayed the Eastern European immigrants as "people who would carry with them into Palestine highly explosive passions conducive to very serious trouble in a country which might be likened to a concentration camp of Jewish refugees."[161] The Zionists were stunned by Lévi's unexpected attack; there was no procedure for a rebuttal. But Robert Lansing, the U.S. secretary of state, turned to Weizmann and asked him to offer a precise definition for the term "Jewish national home." Did it mean an autonomous Jewish government? Weizmann seized the opportunity to negate Lévi's statements. Claiming that he spoke for 96 percent of the Jews of the world who shared his view, he replied that the "Zionist Organization did not want an autonomous Jewish government, but merely to establish in Palestine, under a Mandatory Power, an administration, not necessarily Jewish, which would render it possible to send into Palestine 70,000 to 80,000 Jews annually." It would build up gradually a nationality which would be "as Jewish as the French nation was French and the British nation British." Later on, when the Jews formed the large majority, they would be ready to establish a government in consonance with their own ideals and aspirations.[162]

It was the right speech at a critical moment, and it seemed to have left its mark on those assembled. The general consensus was that Weizmann had scored a victory for the Zionists. Outside the chambers of the council he had another unexpected chance to deal with Lévi, this time in a more direct manner. Lévi himself reported to the executive of the Alliance Israélite Universelle that in the lobby he went up to Weizmann to wish him good-bye. "Weizmann put his hands behind him and said rudely: 'Je ne vous connais plus. Vous êtes un traitre.' "[163] As far as the Zionists were concerned, Lévi was beneath contempt, but he did represent a large segment of French Jewish opinion. Thus, the Alliance executive strongly endorsed Lévi's point of view. But the laurels clearly belonged to Weizmann. Quite apart from his sweet moment of personal revenge, the two hours he spent before the Council of Ten demonstrated once again his ability to respond well to unexpected situations by finding or recalling a pithy and memorable formulation. It became an event that was told and retold—and sometimes embellished—many times over in Zionist publications. Felix Frankfurter summed up the event in his report to Brandeis, within days after the Zionist presentation: "Weizmann made a wise and powerful presentation. . . . It was Weizmann at his best—and Weizmann at his best is a master."[164]

In hindsight one can, of course, claim that the Zionist presentation to the Council of Ten was in itself of little political consequence; indeed, it showed how vulnerable and weak the Zionists were at that time. Nevertheless, its symbolic value was of great significance and served the Zionists well in their campaign to win public support. On the evening of February 27, as the Zionist activists were celebrating their victory in the company of their close British supporters, rumor reached them that a decision had been made by the powers to establish a Palestinian state under a British trusteeship.[165] But, in fact, the peace conference did not produce a treaty with Turkey; nor, indeed, did it formulate any decisions regarding the future of the former Turkish territories. General agreement was reached that Britain should receive the mandate for Palestine while France would be awarded the mandate for Syria and Lebanon. The Syrian-Palestine border remained undecided.[166]

Weizmann could now concentrate on the internal organizational matters facing the Zionist Organization. The first task was to strengthen and broaden the authority of the Zionist Commission in Palestine. The representation of the Yishuv in late 1918 consisted of the Vaad Zmani. Only in October 1920 did the Elected Assembly (Asefat Hanivharim) convene for the first time and elect its representative organ, the National Council

(Vaad Leumi). For all practical purposes, the Zionist Commission represented both the Zionist Organization and the Yishuv *vis-à-vis* the military administration in Palestine. Weizmann recognized the importance of bolstering this body, which in late 1918 included Jacob Thon, Mordechai Ben-Hillel Hacohen, Commander Angelo Levi-Bianchini, Giacomo Artom, Eliyahu Lewin-Epstein, and Vladimir Jabotinsky, with David Eder deputizing for Weizmann as chairman. In mid-February, following discussions in the London Zionist Bureau and resolutions of the Smaller Actions Committee,[167] Weizmann notified Ormsby-Gore that the Smaller Actions Committee had reconstituted the Zionist Commission, whose executive now included Weizmann (chairman), Dr. Harry Friedenwald (acting chairman), Lewin-Epstein, Eder, Levi-Bianchini, and Robert Szold.[168] The major changes in this body were the addition of the Americans, Szold and Friedenwald, and the exclusion of Jabotinsky.[169]

In October 1919, Ussishkin assumed leadership of the Zionist Commission and proceeded to unite the Palestine Zionist Bureau with the Zionist Commission. He transferred each department, except immigration, from Tel Aviv to Jerusalem. By the time he assumed office, the credibility and authority of the Zionist Commission had been seriously weakened by constant shifts in its composition. Between late 1918 and October 1919 the chairmanship had been transferred from Weizmann to Eder, Lewin-Epstein, Friedenwald, Szold, Eder once more, and Ussishkin.

Throughout 1919 and 1920 Weizmann remained in constant touch with the Zionist Commission and was largely responsible for providing it with a continuous flow of funds from the United States and Europe. Early in 1919 the commission was in severe financial difficulties, remittances from London having ceased as of November 1918, while the Joint Distribution Committee sent its last contribution for relief on December 12. The commission had overdrawn its account at the Anglo-Palestine Company by £90,000 at the beginning of March. As the bank refused further credit, operations, particularly in the field of relief, were considerably curtailed. Weizmann urged, successfully in the end, the JDC and other organizations to do their utmost to relieve the severe cash-flow problems facing the institutions of the Yishuv.[170] In July 1919 the Zionist Preparation Fund, which was established in November 1917, was renamed the Eretz Israel Restoration Fund (Keren Hageulah).[171]

During 1918–19 the Zionist Commission received some £983,000 for its activities in Palestine, most of which came from this fund. Weizmann also provided the commission with experts in agriculture, industry, and land surveying. Throughout 1919 he interceded with the Foreign Office to issue permits for these experts to conduct their surveys in Palestine. Their recommendations to the Zionist Organization were intended to create guidelines for future work in Palestine. Weizmann made special efforts on behalf of Arthur Ruppin, who for a long time was denied a permit to return to the country because of his German nationality. He finally arrived in Palestine in March 1920 as director of urban and agricultural settlements.

Another issue related to the work of the Zionist Commission was immigration. At the end of World War I some 56,000 Jews lived in Palestine; by 1920 their numbers had increased to 67,000. At the same time, the limited economic opportunities resulted in a high rate of unemployment and inflation: in May 1919 approximately 1,200 Jews were unemployed, their numbers augmented each month by those returning from the exile imposed on them by the Turks during the war. Health conditions were extremely poor, with epidemics and a shortage of doctors notwithstanding the heroic efforts of the American Zionist Medical Unit. Such conditions were not conducive to mass immigration, but they did not deter Jewish refugees from Eastern Europe as well as the Middle East, who were fleeing pogroms and extreme economic deprivation.

The Third Aliyah (immigration wave to Palestine) began early in 1919 with a small group that arrived via Siberia and Japan; on March 8, 1919, a group of 115 pioneers came from Russia and Rumania; in April, 150 arrived from Poland and Galicia; and in December, 671 refugees from the Ukrainian pogroms came on the *Russlan*, the first ship to arrive in Palestine from postwar Russia. Others arrived from Turkey, Yemen, Morocco, and Iraq. By May 1921 the number of immigrants had swelled to 14,663.[172] In addition, tens of thousands of Jews hastily abandoned their homes and moved westward and southward, awaiting the opportunity to proceed. The Copenhagen Zionist Bureau received dozens of telegrams from refugees demanding urgent action. In response to these demands, the bureau opened a department of immigration in December 1918.[173] Those immigrants who managed to reach Palestine defied the policy of the military administration; nor were they encouraged by the Zionist Organization, whose immigration department, established in London in February 1919, wanted to delay immigration to Palestine until economic conditions improved there.

Though aware of the physical danger and economic deprivations facing Jews in many countries, Weizmann was worried about the impact of large, uncontrolled immigration to Palestine. The month after his return from Palestine he wrote to Wickham Steed, the foreign editor of the *Times:*

> Palestine is not an immediate solution of the trouble in the Diaspora. . . . We must not be told, as the Poles are trying to do—"You have your Palestine, clear out of here!" If so, we shall have all the miserable refugees who will be driven out of Poland, Galicia, Rumania, etc., at the doors of Palestine. We shall be swamped in Palestine and shall never be able to set up a community worth having there. . . . God knows we desire to do all humanly possible to make a beautiful country out of Palestine . . . but we cannot do it with the rope round our necks.[174]

This letter contradicts the spirit, if not the substance, of Weizmann's assurances to Balfour and the Council of Ten that a million Jews in Eastern Europe were awaiting a signal to move to Palestine and that the Zionists were hoping for a mandatory power that would allow them to send 70,000–80,000 Jews annually into the country. Clearly neither Weizmann, nor the SAC, nor the Zionist Commission were ready for a flood of immigrants, certainly not destitute, untrained ones who would have to be supported by Zionist funds. It was a dilemma that was to plague the Zionist movement until 1948: adhering to the principle of *aliyah,* while in practice unable, at times, to absorb it.

On April 4, 1919, the Advisory Committee on Palestine, chaired by Herbert Samuel, discussed the question of immigration and came to the conclusion that it must be regulated. Preference was to be given to those trained in agriculture, and decisions had to be made as to which immigrants proved to be "the most suitable human material."[175] Two weeks later, writing on behalf of the SAC, Julius Simon advised all Zionist federations:

> The time for immigration has not yet come. Immigration cannot begin until systematic plans of colonisation have been worked out in their economic, financial and other aspects, a matter which depends to a great extent on the solution of the political problems affecting Palestine. Until then not a single immigrant should enter Palestine. . . . No one should hasten to liquidate his business and start for Palestine. Premature, unorganized and precipitate immigration is fraught with the greatest danger, both for the immigrants themselves and for the whole Jewish future in Palestine.[176]

Weizmann fully approved of the circular. When Zionist leaders in London met with General Gilbert Clayton, Weizmann assured him that the Zionist Organization could be safely relied upon to "discriminate between desirable and undesirable immigrants."[177] On behalf of the SAC, another, Hebrew-written circular went out to all Zionist federations on July 24, 1919. More detailed than the one signed by Simon on April 18, this one was signed by Weizmann, Ussishkin, and Simon. The circular repeated the stricture against immigration, save for three categories: those returning to Palestine from exile or who had family in the country; representatives of organizations with an economic interest in Palestine; and experts or people with substantial means who could settle immediately without becoming a burden on the public treasury.[178]

The Zionist Commission supported and encouraged the London leadership in its policies "to cut off immigration at the source." David Eder and his colleagues, moreover, turned to the military authorities, asking them to issue warnings to the steamship companies "against embarking Jewish passengers for Palestine who are not provided with proper permits and authority from some responsible Zionist organization."[179] This policy of the WZO executive and the Zionist Commission precipitated a confrontation with workers' leaders in Palestine, who openly called for immigration.[180]

These disagreements between the Zionist leadership and the Yishuv were not the sole internal problem affecting the Zionist Organization. The latter part of 1919 also saw the beginning of a rift between Weizmann and some American Zionist leaders. The first rumblings of American Zionist disenchantment with Weizmann had been voiced by Wise and DeHaas in late 1918 and early 1919. Questions were raised about mismanagement of funds sent from the United States to London and Palestine,[181] Weizmann's "pretensions to a dictatorship in Zionism,"[182] and the nature of the proposals to be presented to the peace conference.[183] Initially the Americans, thinking in Herzlian terms, were inclined to share the view of men like Max Nordau and Israel Zangwill, as well as some of the Eastern European[184] and Palestinian Zionist leaders, that Weizmann was excessively ready to accept compromise formulas in defining the ultimate status of the Jews in Palestine.[185]

Though Wise, DeHaas, Fels, and other members of the American delegation had appended their signatures to the Zionist statement of February 3, 1919, they left London bitterly resentful of Weizmann.[186] In a letter to Mary Fels, shortly after he returned to New York, Stephen Wise described Weizmann as "a dangerous factor in the movement; and hard and regrettable as it may be, it will be necessary to curtail his power almost to the point of elimination."[187] The leaders of the American delegation found Weizmann arrogant, insensitive to the wishes of others, and obsessed by his need to control all Zionist political activities.[188] Upon their return to New York, both Stephen Wise and Jacob DeHaas delivered reports sharply critical of Weizmann to the ZOA executive.[189]

The most important Americans, however, like Brandeis and Frankfurter, soon swung over to Weizmann's assessment of the political situation. Brandeis was strongly influenced by reports he received from Frankfurter in London that completely contradicted those of Wise and DeHaas. Frankfurter's critique of the New York rabbi and the Zionist functionary was scathing:

> I am sorry to say that Wise seems to have lost sight of the object for which he was sent, namely to devote himself to Zionist matters. . . . The result was that he was not taken seriously by Weizmann nor by the other leaders. . . . The picture that he brought back could not be other than distorted. . . .
>
> You know my affection for Weizmann, but that does not blind me to the limitations of temperament and mind of the man . . . but DeHaas does not seem to realize the greatness of the man. He treats Weizmann as the bright young Zionist whom he knew, or knew of, some 20 or 25 years ago. It is essential not only now, but for the future for DeHaas to understand that whether he likes it or not, Weizmann is the commanding figure in Zionism on this side of the water. It is important for DeHaas to understand that

Weizmann is one of the significant figures in English public life. He has a sway over English public men and over English permanent officials who will continue to govern England when Lloyd George and Balfour will be no more—such as no other Jew in England or on the continent has or can easily acquire. . . . All this DeHaas seems to have forgotten and to give too much weight to the defects of egotism. . . . After all some of the greatest statesmen have these limitations. . . . The closest and most cordial relations between you and him are absolutely indispensable and I have not the slightest shadow of doubt that you will work together with the happiest accord.[190]

Brandeis readily agreed with Frankfurter's assessment and often referred to Weizmann as "our leader," giving him powerful backing. For his part, Weizmann had been conditioned for a number of years by friends he trusted to like the American leader and to accord him the greatest respect.[191] The two first met in London on June 21, 1919, and immediately took a liking to each other. In a letter to Vera, Weizmann wrote: "Brandeis makes an excellent impression; it's a pity he's 63 years old already, and only came to us after he had given his strength to others, to strangers."[192] From London, Brandeis traveled to Palestine for three weeks, returning to London concerned and ready for further talks with the Zionist leadership. The tour had convinced him that immigration should be held off until after the grave health hazards of the country were cleared up and appropriate investments had been made to absorb the newcomers in permanent employment. He accepted Weizmann's view, moreover, that the specific commitment to create a Jewish state, or a Jewish commonwealth, was not as immediately pressing as suitable Jewish organization, under adequate British legal provisions, to carry out those constructive activities that alone could turn the promise into reality.

The Eastern European critics of Weizmann's moderation seemed to the Americans particularly unsuited to lead the movement in its constructive era. Their stress on political issues was based on assumptions different from the legalistic cast of mind of the Americans. The Eastern European Zionists conceived of themselves as virtually a government in exile, based not only on the Balfour Declaration—interpreted as equivalent to the charter Herzl had sought—but on the Jewish national councils that they expected to see organized, preferably under public law, in the European successor states. They hoped for a World Jewish Congress, encompassing the World Zionist Organization as its agency for Palestine, and desired to see this parliament of world Jewry directly represented in the Palestine government.

All of this was utterly foreign to the American leadership. The American Zionists therefore supported Weizmann's efforts to discourage such Diaspora nationalist ideas, especially since Zionism expressed in these terms, contemplating an abrupt, far-reaching transfer of authority to Jews in Palestine before their numbers locally could warrant or support it, threatened to excite Arab hostility and alienate the British. The latter problem was one Brandeis addressed himself to at once. After visiting Palestine he made strong representations in London to change the anti-Zionist, if not antisemitic, complexion of the military administration there and achieved, in his opinion, substantial success. He also came back with strong views on the need to retire from service old Russian Jewish party wheelhorses, like Menahem Ussishkin, whom he regarded as totally unsuited to conduct Zionist relations with either the British or the Arabs.

In all these matters, Brandeis sided with Weizmann in 1918 and 1919 against Weizmann's Zionist critics. After the Zionist presentation at the peace conference there followed a long period of close cooperation in which Frankfurter in particular shared with Weizmann and his British friends, Zionists, and government officials the responsibility for drafting the constitutional instrument upon which the Palestine mandate was based. By now the Americans were fully convinced of Weizmann's method to hold a line as strongly pro-Zionist as the British government would accept and as moderate as the Zionist public could be brought to endorse.

The closest cooperation among Weizmann and the Americans developed in the negotiations with the British in 1919 and 1920, and from it emerged the text of the Mandate for Palestine. Frankfurter, Ben Cohen, and Bernard Flexner played leading roles in composing successive drafts, working with Weizmann and his British aides in complete unanimity of purpose on major issues. Brandeis and his American assistants backed Weizmann's position fully on all the cardinal negotiations. They now accepted Weizmann's premise that a general rather than specific commitment to ultimate Zionist goals in the Mandate text would be sufficient, given a good working relationship between the British and a Zionist agency specifically empowered to achieve massive immigration, close settlement, and autonomous organization of Jews in the national home.

In successive drafts constructed by the Zionist team in London, the powers needed for this purpose were spelled out, though not, as the Palestinian and other Zionist critics continued to demand, as dominant positions in the mandate regime. The first Zionist drafts were composed January–March 1919.[193] In the spring of 1919 a draft was prepared by Herbert Samuel, followed by one from Cohen. In June 1920 the British government presented its own draft, overseen by Curzon, recognizing the "historic connection of the Jewish people to Palestine." On December 6, 1920, Balfour submitted the final draft of the Mandate for Palestine to the League of Nations for ratification, and it was published as an official document of the British government. In addition to acknowledging the "historic connection," the British also defined the purpose of the mandate as a means in "the development of a Jewish 'self-governing Commonwealth.' "[194] In all, it was a most favorable document from the

High Commissioner Sir
Herbert Samuel, 1924.
Courtesy: Central Zi-
onist Archives

Zionists' point of view, who hoped to reconstitute the "historic connection" in the form of a Jewish commonwealth in Palestine.

With regard to the problem of the future boundaries of Palestine, the
Zionists submitted to the peace conference broad economic frontiers.
The borders as conceived included a point on the Mediterranean just
south of the port of Sidon, continuing northeast up the slopes of the
Lebanon, including the greater part of the Litani River and the whole of
the Jordan catchment area up to its northernmost source near Rashaya.
From there the frontier was to run along the crest of the Hermon, then,
turning due east, along the northern watershed of the Yarmuk tributar-
ies toward the Hedjaz Railway at a distance of some twenty kilometers
south of Damascus. The eastern border would run parallel to and just
west of the Hedjaz Railway to the Gulf of Akaba. The frontier in the
southwest was to be determined by negotiation with the Egyptian government.[195] The Zionists, however, were unable to have their way on
the issue of borders, a matter that was ultimately decided between the
French and the British.

Although, as noted, in November 1918 French Prime Minister Clemenceau conceded to Lloyd George control over Mosul and Palestine
(from Dan to Beersheba), thus agreeing to alter the Sykes-Picot line, the
Zionists were dissatisfied by the vagueness of the arrangement. In addition, the Lebanese delegation to the peace conference, encouraged by

the French, presented demands that conflicted with those of the Zionists. In a crucial meeting on March 20, 1919, the French Foreign Minister Stephen Pichon endorsed the Lebanese position and rejected a British appeal to revise the Sykes-Picot boundaries, insisting that northern Galilee with its Jewish settlements remain in French hands.

In response to the Zionists' urgent requests, Balfour sent memoranda to Lloyd George on June 26 and August 11, 1919, supporting Zionist claims to the water resources of the Upper Jordan and the Litani and to an eastern border running just west of the Hedjaz Railway. The French, however, were adamant. In September, General Allenby and Lloyd George proposed drawing the northern border of Palestine well south of the water resources requested by the Zionists. Weizmann attempted to intervene by meeting in September 1919 with Lloyd George, General Allenby, and Robert de Caix, the French chief adviser on the question of Syria.[196] Following this meeting, Allenby sent a telegram to the cabinet supporting Zionist territorial demands for security reasons. A fortnight after his talks with Weizmann, however, Allenby met with the French commander of Syria, General Henri E. Gouraud, and agreed instead that British troops would evacuate northern Galilee to the line running from Achzib to Lake Huleh. This agreement left all the water resources and the Jewish colonies of Upper Galilee in French hands. Allenby emphasized, however, that this line had no implications for future political boundaries.

Weizmann protested vehemently, but unsuccessfully, against the Franco-British territorial agreements.[197] Britain had decided to press for the earliest possible settlement in the Middle East and was less concerned about antagonizing the Zionists than appeasing the French. Consequently, at the San Remo Conference in April 1920, the British government agreed to a comprehensive Middle Eastern settlement by which Britain obtained the mandate for Palestine and Mesopotamia, while France obtained the mandate for Syria. On June 21, 1920, the French government proposed that Palestine's northern boundary stretch from Ras en-Naqura, the southern point of the ladder of Tyre, to a point on the Jordan sources just north of Metullah and Banias Dan to the northern shore of Lake Huleh, running from there along the Jordan and the Sea of Galilee to the Yarmuk. Although this proposal retained all existing Jewish colonies within the proposed borders of Palestine, it simultaneously allocated to Syria all the water resources required for Jewish economic development.[198] The demarcation of the borders remained unsettled even when the civil government took office in Palestine. Despite strenuous efforts by Weizmann and his colleagues, the French and the British signed an agreement in late December 1920 that incorporated the French plan of June 1920 without any significant alterations. This was confirmed in March 1923.

While Balfour was still foreign secretary, the British accepted far-reaching suggestions from the Zionists—usually via Weizmann—concerning a

whole range of issues, from the appointment of particular officers for
administrative positions in Palestine to the question of boundaries and
formulation of the Mandate for Palestine. After Curzon succeeded Balfour, and particularly after the Palestine mandate was allotted to Britain
in April 1920 at San Remo, British official attitude cooled, and fresh Zionist efforts were called for. When the San Remo decision was nevertheless followed in June 1920 by the installation of a civil administration
headed by Herbert Samuel, both Weizmann and Brandeis felt that the
political struggle had been won. The time had come to concentrate on
practical reconstruction, now that the crippling *status quo ante* policy of
the unsympathetic military occupation no longer had to be fought.

But for practical reconstruction to be undertaken, preliminary organization had to enlist the aid of potential non-Zionist supporters and
investors. In approaching this task, Brandeis and Weizmann discovered
their sharply divergent approaches, which arose from their distinctly
different personal and institutional situations. The differences came to a
head in the August 1919 meetings of British, American, and other Zionist leaders assembled in London. Like earlier meetings in 1919, this
session had no clear statutory authority under the rules adopted by the
WZO, and it was conducted in the enforced absence of the German and
Austrian elected leaders. The Americans, however, were there in force.
The American team on the Zionist Commission came armed with conclusions that grew out of its work in Palestine, and Justice Brandeis,
who had taken advantage of the summer recess of the Supreme Court,
came fresh from his own intensive exposure to the problems of Palestine.

The Zionist Statement presented to the peace conference on February
3, 1919, had included proposals for a Jewish council for Palestine, reflecting the deliberations of Herbert Samuel's Advisory Committee on
Palestine as well as current Zionist conceptions: "The Mandatory Power
shall inter alia: . . . Accept the co-operation [in promoting Jewish immigration and land settlement] of a Council representative of the Jews
of Palestine and of the world that may be established for the development of the Jewish National Home in Palestine and entrust the organization of Jewish education to such Council." The council was to be
"elected by a Jewish Congress representative of the Jews of Palestine
and of the world," to be convoked in Jerusalem in about a year. Until
then, "A Provisional Jewish Council of representatives of the Zionist
Organization, of the Jewish population in Palestine, and of such other
approved Jewish organizations as are willing to co-operate in the development of a Jewish Palestine" would be created by the Zionists.[199] The
Zionist Statement of February was considered during the March 1919
meetings in London, and, after some revisions upon which Weizmann
and the Americans were united (and which did not alter the provisions
for election of the council or the constitution of the provisional council),
it was endorsed by a phalanx of the top American leaders closest to
Brandeis himself.[200]

In August 1919, and later in June–July 1920, Brandeis presided over meetings under Anglo-American parliamentary rules, running rough-shod over the European Zionists and the traditional procedural rules of Zionist assemblies, for which he developed a strong aversion. He also pushed proposals that clearly indicated an intention to organize world Zionism on the lines American Zionism had adopted. His own partici-pation would not be direct or full time but represent an ultimate, if ab-sentee, authority; and non-Zionists would be recruited to leadership and individual membership without regard for the existing constitution or ideological commitments of the traditional movement. Weizmann, on the other hand, who came late to the August 1919 meeting fresh from consultations in Switzerland with the old Central European leaders, was still trying to regularize his own position under accepted Zionist proce-dures in order to achieve full legitimacy as the movement's leader. The attempted cooperation of leaders with such different personal perspec-tives and requirements was bound to produce a clash.

The conflict began over the formula for constituting the provisional council, which Brandeis insisted on revising radically over Weizmann's vehement objections and in spite of the opposed views of other partici-pants, who abstained from voting in order to avoid a break with the Americans. Brandeis firmly opposed the provisions of the March draft providing for representation of non-Zionist organizations on the provi-sional council and the election of the Jewish council for Palestine by a congress in which Jewish national councils, organized under the na-tional minorities treaties in the postwar European successor states, might be represented. He favored instead a resolution that the Zionist Orga-nization itself carry out the functions of the provisional council and un-dertake to "secure the cooperation of all Jews who are willing to assist in the establishment of the Jewish National Home."

Weizmann tried in vain to amend the formula to read that the coop-eration of "all Jews and *Jewish organizations*" would be secured. Bitter at the unceremonious rejection of his compromise and unwilling to face the implied possibility of American secessionism, his concession of de-feat proved a passionate exposition of the underlying ideological issues. He raised contentions that would recur in emotional but obscure repe-tition throughout the ensuing years of conflict. But in spite of the clear and fundamental cleavage between Weizmann and Brandeis, the divi-sion was neither as wide nor unbridgeable as that between the respec-tive allies of the two leaders. Yet it was the issue between them, an issue of leadership, that provoked and, on the whole, sustained the conflict.

"You have built a Monroe Doctrine around American Zionism," Weiz-mann charged, plunging to the sensitive core of the conflict:

> I consider it my duty to break through this Monroe Doctrine with full force. There is not one Zionism for America, and another for Europe. You will have to adapt yourselves to general Jewish Zionism. . . . If the creation of a general Jewish organization causes you discomfort, you will have to face

the choice of remaining Americans or joining the general Jewish organization. For such a choice may yet become open to you in the coming twenty-
five years. . . . We, ghetto Jews, have nothing but the Jewish home that
we need; and we are therefore ready to give up everything in order to build
it. . . . You have another home. Since the Jewish national home only hov-
ers in the distant horizon of your visions, you are not prepared to imperil
your [present] home. I respect this position, but I cannot give it my assent.
. . . If the question is one of an indispensable condition for you, if you
cannot on any account accept the Council, I shall yield to you, for I do not
want to break the Organization, but I shall look to the day when I shall be
able to work against you with all my power; that is how we brought the
German Zionists into the Zionist Organization. . . . As we fought for fifteen years for the soul of the German Zionists, so I shall endeavor, by force
of facts and persuasion, to build the Council once again.[201]

"In spite of the pathos of this appeal," suggests Ben Halpern, it did
not mean that in practice Weizmann's plans were as far from Brandeis's
as those of some of his supporters. As Weizmann pointed out, he did
not, any more than Brandeis, wish to commit the Zionist movement
itself to the cause of national minority organization in the Diaspora; but
in his single-minded concentration on the task of building the Jewish
national home, he wished to enlist the backing of all organized Jewish
forces, many of which had other concerns, including especially those of
Diaspora nationalism. The difference, Weizmann implied, was that he
felt himself "one of the people that sought to sustain itself as a national
entity in the Diaspora even while building the national home in Palestine," while Brandeis and the other Americans did not. For this reason
Weizmann's intense, Palestine-directed Zionism, like that of Ussishkin
or Jabotinsky, expressed itself in a full-time professional commitment to
Zionist work and to living in Palestine, while the Americans, in spite of
their doctrine of concentrating solely on the work in Palestine in separation from other general Jewish concerns, "were willing to devote no
more than short-term service to the cause and would not reroot themselves in the national home."[202] All these themes, hinted more than stated,
were echoes of the parallel battle that Weizmann's friends in Germany,
Arthur Hantke and Kurt Blumenfeld and others, had fought against similar
positions of the older German Zionist leaders Max Bodenheimer and
Franz Oppenheimer. This effort was crowned in 1912 by the adoption
of a resolution declaring it the duty of each individual Zionist to strive
ultimately to settle in Palestine.[203]

At the conclusion of his speech, Weizmann directly challenged Brandeis and his supporters to respond:

I do not intend to bring my proposal to a vote. But for me this issue represents a moral cleavage. Now I shall call upon the American gentlemen to
give a clear answer to the basic question: if they reject the Council because
of technical problems, let us unite on a common position. But if there are
moral reasons at play here, say it plainly. All of us who take a different

view will abstain from presenting our proposal and you shall know with certainty that in this act, we have opened a great moral breach.[204]

Brandeis had little choice but to respond. While he professed to base his position on technical objections rather than principle, he shed light on both aspects of the brewing conflict. For, as he said, the Americans were firmly opposed to Weizmann's proposal on both grounds: "We should oppose it on technical grounds, if there were no reasons of principle, and we should oppose it on grounds of principle, if there were no technical reason."[205] First, he welcomed cooperation from anyone in the Palestine work, including Jewish organizations; but his rule was that other organizations should cooperate independently, not in a joint body. But he did not see many such organizations, apart from the Jewish Colonization Association, and felt no need to create them. The main instrument was the Zionist Organization, which must change to suit its new functions and should open to include everyone who wished to work for the Jewish national home. If a Jewish congress would help achieve this goal, it should be convened and constituted by the Zionist Organization itself, not by a loose collection of organizations with diverse and extraneous concerns.

What in Brandeis's view spoke in favor of the Zionist Organization, tactically and technically, was clear: "It is necessary for us to unite for the work in Palestine in a single organization. The Zionist Organization must be that organization—and for practical reasons: it exists, it is recognized, *it is disciplined, and it is trusted.*"[206] Thus, what Brandeis had most in mind was the kind of centralized, disciplined organization he himself led in the United States after the creation of the ZOA.

These, then, were Brandeis's technical grounds for rejecting Weizmann's Eastern European conception. But, in good pragmatist style, he indicated that "practical reasons" could give birth to principles, too. His objection in principle to Weizmann's proposal was pragmatic and did not rule out the possibility that, in due time and given appropriate conditions, it, too, might become acceptable: "It is quite possible that a day may come—perhaps in fifty years—when the arguments Weizmann has presented here will become acceptable to more Jews than now. But that is not the case today. It is impossible for the Americans, the Canadians, as well as others, to accept the principle proposed by Weizmann—the principle of Jewish unity in all matters, including non-Palestinian questions. The conditions that created the differences in [our] views are real and present."[207]

By a vote of 5–4—railroaded through by Brandeis without anyone daring to protest—the American position was adopted at the meeting of August 27, 1919. Julius Simon formulated the decision: "The Zionist Organization is to be recognized as the Jewish Agency, but it is to secure the cooperation of all Jews who are willing to assist in the establishment of the Jewish National Home."[208] The proposals submitted to the Foreign Office on September 24, 1919, reflected the American position and for the first time used the phrase "Jewish Agency" rather than "Jewish Council." This formula was embodied verbatim in the Mandate for Palestine; the Zionist Organization was recognized as the Jewish agency until the Jewish agency should be established.

Weizmann expressed his anger over his defeat in a passionate letter to Felix Frankfurter, written the day on which the final formula was decided: "You have 'scored' a vote today and you have obtained a 'majority' on a question which to you appears an irrelevant issue and to me a fundamental question in Zionism. . . . We shall never forget this vote." After lecturing Frankfurter on the basic principles of Zionism, Weizmann mocked the Americans' detached and practical approach: "Brandeis could have been a prophet in Israel. You have the making of a Lasalle. Instead, you are choosing to be only a professor in Harvard and Brandeis only a judge in the Supreme Court." Nevertheless, as he had promised during the debates, Weizmann agreed to abide by the decision, thereby demonstrating that the need for unity among Zionists and among Jews was his paramount concern: "Now we have bowed our heads and bent our stiff necks only because we cannot afford an open breach today."[209]

In retrospect it is clear that the August 1919 confrontation between Brandeis and Weizmann involved a personal competition for leadership and supremacy that was just as important, if not more so, than the fine technical and political distinctions each side brought to the debate. Nevertheless, there were significant differences that guided their debate even if they were not publicly uttered, differences that became clearer only in 1920–21. For Brandeis, Zionism was never first and foremost a political movement, as it was for Weizmann. Thus Brandeis was only too happy to proclaim at San Remo in 1920 that the political phase of Zionism had come to a close and a period of economic reconstruction had begun. This approach was totally incomprehensible for Weizmann. For him, Zionism had never ceased to be a political movement. This was probably the crux of the differences between them.

For the next year, until a second encounter between Weizmann and Brandeis took place in June 1920, "an uneasy balance prevailed in the conduct of Zionist affairs under which the main leaders seemed to have secured their minimum requirements for playing their respective roles."[210] Following the August 1919 meetings, Brandeis returned to the United States, and it was left to Weizmann to deal with more pressing events bearing on the future of the Zionist movement. Until the decisions in San Remo in the spring of 1920, he continued, with unbounded energy, to conduct his shuttle diplomacy, constantly on the move between the European capitals and Palestine.

The fall and winter of 1919–20 were a particularly difficult period for the Zionist leadership: the appointment in October 1919 of Lord Curzon as foreign secretary instead of Balfour led to a cooling of relations with his ministry. Relations with Feisal also cooled considerably following a statement the emir made in an interview on October 3, 1919, that Palestine belonged to the Arabs and was an inseparable part of their contemplated kingdom.[211] Although, after meetings with Herbert Samuel and others, Feisal again qualified his statements, he was no longer held in high esteem by Weizmann.[212] From the perspective of the Zionist leadership, the most serious issue was the continued unsatisfactory relationship between the military authorities and the Zionist Commission and the Yishuv.[213] For many months Weizmann wanted to return to Palestine. The lull in political activities in London and Paris seemed a propitious time for such a visit.

Together with Vera, Weizmann arrived in Palestine in mid-October 1919. This was Vera's first visit to the country, and she was thoroughly disappointed. It had been an unusually dry season, and the weather was unbearably hot. What she saw in Palestine was worlds removed from the large home and manicured garden in Kensington. "Conditions were primitive," she later observed, almost in surprise. Still, with Mrs. Eder and Mrs. Sieff as her guides, she toured the country, appalled every step of the way by the abysmal living conditions and near-starvation diet of the pioneers.[214] One can only imagine that the colonists were just as intrigued by the three English ladies who traveled by car from one settlement to another, expressing shock and dismay at the sight of the women working side by side with their menfolk. No doubt they would have preferred a financial contribution to the flowers Vera sent them in gratitude for their frugal, but cordial hospitality.

While Vera traveled around the country, Weizmann made the rounds of visits to the various British officials in Cairo and Palestine. In early November 1919, he wrote his first report to his colleagues in London. Although the attitudes of the British and the Arabs still gave him concern, he optimistically assessed the impact of the Foreign Office's directives of August 4, even if they had not been made public. Colonel Meinertzhagen, Weizmann's handpicked chief political officer, meanwhile worked hard to stamp out open hostility toward Zionism.[215] Weizmann devoted his energies to planning housing, education, and agriculture and to the Hebrew University to be built on Mount Scopus. He believed that the British military administration would now cooperate with these endeavors.

Indeed, during his brief visit to Palestine, Weizmann clearly was able to make an impact on the chief administrator, General Watson, and on Allenby, who, since the fall of 1918, had considerably distanced himself from Zionism. Even the hostile General Bols seemed to be taken by Weizmann's plans and personality.[216] At Weizmann's suggestion, the British government, with the concurrence of the military administrators, invited Herbert Samuel to Palestine in early 1920 to prepare a report on the country's future administration and economic potential.[217]

As he left Palestine, ten weeks after his arrival, Weizmann felt that it had been a moderately productive visit.[218] He had the impression that both the British authorities and the Arabs in Palestine could be managed by wise and careful Zionist diplomacy. In his appointment book he made some notes concerning the Arabs in Palestine that reflect cautious optimism. Though he still questioned whether they had a serious and "real" national movement, he thought the Zionists must take action to forestall any violent Arab reaction:

> We must try and get into direct friendly touch with the Arab population ourselves and *not* rely on the British Authorities for that purpose. We have quite a number of persons in Palestine who could make extremely useful agents, who know the language and the mentality of the Arabs, who are trusted by them. These persons must be organized and pressed into action as soon as possible and in that way we shall achieve our purpose more directly and with greater rapidity and success. Closely connected with this propaganda is a good Arabic press, personal contact of leading Zionists with Arab leaders etc. *Our policy of land acquisition* must run parallel with our Arab policy.[219]

Yet, almost as soon as he departed from Palestine, Weizmann was informed by Israel Sieff and other friends that conditions in Palestine had worsened again; discrimination against Jews and favoritism toward Arabs were rampant:

> While the Chief Administrator and Heads of Department at O[ccupied] E[nemy] T[erritory] A[dministration] Headquarters promise to assist us in beginning constructive work here . . . they do not seem to have the necessary power to compel the local officials to carry out their wishes. Thus, though you, by your personality, are able to create a satisfactory political situation at Headquarters, we who have to carry out the details through the local officials, are faced with all kinds of unnecessary difficulties and obstacles, and thus your work is nullified.[220]

On February 27, 1920, following General Bols's announcement concerning the implementation of the Balfour Declaration, the first Arab demonstrations took place, in several urban centers, against Zionist intentions.[221] Over the next two weeks, Mayor Musa Kazem al-Husseini led Muslim and Christian Arabs in Jerusalem in vociferous anti-Zionist and anti-Jewish demonstrations.[222] On March 8, violence occurred, and attacks on isolated Jewish settlements in Upper Galilee became frequent.[223] Friction had, in addition, increased between the leaders of the Yishuv and the Zionist Commission. These problems brought Weizmann back to Palestine, with his twelve-year-old son Benjy, in mid-March 1920.

Shortly before Weizmann's arrival, and following the British surrender of Damascus and Upper Galilee to the French, the Jewish settlements of Metullah, Kfar Giladi, Tel Hai, Hamra, and others became vulnerable to Arab and Bedouin marauders who, in the process of rebelling against the French, looted and murdered Jews at will. During the months of

January and February 1920 the Vaad Zmani held heated debates concerning the fate of these northern settlements, arousing the anger and ridicule of Yosef Trumpeldor and his friends, who had been organizing the defense.[224] Vladimir Jabotinsky advised abandoning the indefensible settlements, while David Ben-Gurion, Yitzhak Tabenkin, and Berl Katznelson favored maintaining them at all costs. The latter position prevailed, and a delegation was sent to investigate the needs of the settlements. It was too late. On March 1, 1920, Tel Hai had fallen, with the loss of Yosef Trumpeldor and five other men and women.[225] Two days later the Jews evacuated Kfar Giladi and Metullah.[226]

Weizmann's first report to the Zionist executive in London reflected the gravity of conditions in Palestine. He warned his colleagues that the situation was very serious and bore no relation to what he had left behind some three months earlier: "We shall be severely tried in the next few months."[227] On March 25, Weizmann reported to members of the Zionist Commission his conversations with the British generals in Palestine—Bols, Allenby, and Walter Congreve, commander of the British forces in Egypt and Palestine. Weizmann had a harsh exchange with Allenby, who suggested that the British ought to support Feisal to avoid a guerrilla war with the Arabs.

Weizmann did not object to British support of Feisal in principle, but he felt that in the process the British had completely lost interest in Zionist aims. "We Jews will get Palestine even if you do not help us," he told Allenby, "with or without England, with or without Feisul; naturally you can greatly increase the difficulty of our work; but note one thing: In case we should not be in Palestine, then you will not be there either. I will go further: You will not be in India!" According to Weizmann's report, the all-powerful field marshal, representative of the mighty British Empire, quietly agreed with this assessment.[228] The increase of Arab violence was doubtless inspired by the proclamation of Feisal on March 7, 1920, as king of "Greater Syria," including Palestine, Lebanon, and Transjordan. These areas were to constitute a single sovereign independent state. The tacit support of Feisal's designs by the British military administration contributed to the agitation among Palestinian Arabs.[229] On April 1, a few days before the Jerusalem riots, Hajj Amin al-Husseini, later mufti of Jerusalem, returned to Palestine from Damascus and announced British support of Feisal's sovereignty over Palestine. This assessment of the British position prompted his incitement of the Arab crowd at the Nebi Musa festival.[230]

Riots began on Sunday, April 4, during celebrations that coincided with Passover, and proceeded unrestrained by the army or the police. Six Jews in the Old City of Jerusalem were killed, and more than two hundred were wounded.[231] After organizing a Jewish defense force, Jabotinsky was arrested on April 7, together with other members of the Haganah, for possession of arms, and on April 19 he was sentenced to fifteen years at hard labor. Weizmann was enraged by the failure of the administration to take proper preventive measures. He had just celebrated the Seder with his family in Haifa and arrived at David Eder's home in Jerusalem on April 3. When he was awakened early the next morning with news of the pogroms, he left Benjy behind and was driven to the Austrian Hospice, the military headquarters of OETA. Without any of the officers present daring to stop him, he stormed unannounced into the office of General Bols, who was in the midst of a meeting with his top aides, Colonel Waters Taylor, the chief of staff, and Colonel Bramley, the chief of police, and demanded an immediate stop to the pogroms.[232] A few days later Weizmann cabled Lloyd George charging that the disturbances derived from the attitude of the local British authorities who had permitted Arab rioters to indulge in provocations and demonstrations and then, during the riots, failed to protect Jews.[233] Weizmann demanded an investigation of the causes of the riot and appropriate punishment for the ringleaders. A commission headed by Major General P. C. Palin subsequently conducted an investigation and confirmed Weizmann's accusations.[234]

Weizmann based his accusations both on his own observations and also on evidence collected by an intelligence service, called the Information Bureau. Established by David Eder and Vladimir Jabotinsky in late 1918 and now headed by a former member of the Nili, Levi-Yitzhak Shneerson, the bureau provided solid intelligence. At the end of March 1920, soon after his arrival in Palestine, Weizmann encouraged the bureau to continue to gather information about Arab plans, particularly those of the nationalist clubs; to conclude alliances with various sheiks in Transjordan and the Negev; and to try to draw into the Zionist camp some of the notables of Nablus and other major cities.[235] Based on the information received from this source, Weizmann may have had at least some idea of the intensity of nationalist feelings among the Palestinian Arabs. After the April 1920 riots, in any case, his views of the Arab national movement seem to have changed, as did those of the Zionist Commission. During meetings of the Zionist executive in May 1920, Weizmann conceded for the first time that the Zionists had to take into account the growing strength of a modern nationalist Arab movement in Palestine. He suggested the creation of a special Arab bureau within the framework of the Zionist Commission that would try to bring about ideological and economic rapprochement between Jews and Arabs in Palestine.[236] An attempt to create such a bureau, as well as an advisory committee, was made by the Zionist Commission in June.[237] With the change of administration, which seemed to promise a new era of peace, these activities were abandoned. The Information Bureau was also disbanded at the end of the military administration.[238]

Summoned by cable to the San Remo Conference, which convened on April 18, Weizmann left Palestine in mid-April. He was crushed by the events he had just witnessed, particularly by the callousness of the British—all "wolves and Jackals!" he wrote to Vera, "except Meinertzhagen and Deedes." He felt he had just escaped from hell.[239] On the eve of Weizmann's departure, Richard Meinertzhagen wrote a detailed report that described the Zionist leader's mood: "Dr. Weizmann leaves Egypt an overstrained man. He has witnessed a serious blow aimed at Zionism. He left Palestine . . . after Jewish blood had been spilt on the streets of Jerusalem. It is therefore not surprising that Dr. Weizmann should evince feelings of deep disappointment and intense sadness." Meinertzhagen proceeded to give a scathing analysis of the anti-Zionist attitudes and activities of the military administration from the chief administrator down.[240] This report cost him his position. After Allenby refused to forward the report to London, Meinertzhagen sent it directly to Lord Curzon, whereupon Allenby demanded his removal as chief political officer.[241]

Exhausted, disheveled, and distrustful of British intentions, Weizmann arrived in San Remo on April 20 after a week of travel by boat and train.[242] During the trip he had ample time to ponder the origins and consequences of the Jerusalem riots. When he met with Lloyd George and Balfour on April 22, he emphasized the need to replace the military with a civil administration. Unlike Allenby, to whom Weizmann stressed the same point a few days earlier in Cairo, the prime minister and Balfour readily agreed. Herbert Samuel and Nahum Sokolow had already, on April 18, submitted a memorandum on the Middle East to the British delegation emphasizing that Palestine should be administered by Great Britain under a League mandate that should include provisions satisfactory to the Zionists.

The leaders of the French delegation, Alexandre Millerand and Philippe Berthelot, objected to the Balfour Declaration's being included in the treaty and demanded that supervision of the Christian Holy Places be placed under an inter-Allied commission appointed by the League of Nations. The Italian delegation, headed by Francesco Saverio Nitti, did not support the French. Millerand and Berthelot surrendered the point in the discussion of April 25 following Lord Curzon's statement that "The Jews attached a passionate importance to the terms of [the Balfour] Declaration and they would be . . . deeply incensed if the pledge given in the Declaration were not renewed in the terms of the treaty. The British Foreign Office had been pressed very closely by the Zionists in order to have the terms of that pledge expanded and improved." The conference finally agreed that "the mandatory will be responsible for putting into effect the declaration originally made on the 8th [2d] November, 1917 by the British Government."[243] A few months later, on August 10, 1920, the Treaty of Sèvres was signed. Paragraph 95 stated that the administration of Palestine would be entrusted to a mandatory that would be responsible for putting the Balfour Declaration into effect.

No sooner did the San Remo Conference end than Lloyd George and Curzon asked Herbert Samuel to accept the position of first high commissioner for Palestine and to establish a civilian administration. Samuel

Reception for Herbert Samuel and Weizmann, 1920. Sitting, from left: David Yellin, Menahem Ussishkin, Herbert Samuel, Weizmann, Benjamin Weizmann, Yosef Meyuhas. Standing, first row, from left: unidentified, Eliyahu Berlin, David Eder, De Sola Pool, Avraham Shapira, Siegfried van Vriesland, Rabbi Epstein. Courtesy: Central Zionist Archives

was delighted and immediately offered the position of chief secretary to Wyndham Deedes.[244] This appointment matched Weizmann's immediate wish, much as it distressed the military authorities and the Arabs in Palestine. "It was a bombshell," reported Meinertzhagen—still in Cairo—to Weizmann, relishing this victory.[245] As far as Weizmann was concerned, this was truly the end of an era, an era that began with the Balfour Declaration. But it was also the beginning of a new chapter cogently summarized by Lloyd George's parting words to the Zionist delegation: "Now you have got your start, it all depends upon you."[246] It all seemed like a dream to Weizmann; three weeks earlier he had lived through a pogrom in Jerusalem not unlike the Russian pogroms except that this one took place under a British flag. Now the Zionists had scored another great triumph. His mood of elation lasted well into the end of the spring. To the Twenty-first Annual Conference of the English Zionist Federation, which took place in mid-June 1920, he declared: "We stand before you with a declaration of independence in our hands, the independence of Eretz Israel and the Jewish people."[247]

Most historians tend to link the resolution regarding the British mandate and the transition from military to civil administration. These were, of course, separate decisions, even if both were taken at San Remo. One was an international agreement, the other an internal British policy. The decision to transform the military into a civil administration was far from "natural," perhaps even illegal from the point of view of international law. Since it affected the Zionists, one might ask why the British proceeded as they did. Clearly the action was not done solely to please the Zionists. Possibly it was undertaken to curb independent minds and tendencies prevalent among the Cairo military administration who hoped for British domination over the entire Middle East. That would have required ousting the French. After the San Remo agreements, the British could no longer afford to indulge in such dreams. Thus the abolition of the military administration achieved two political goals: it placated the French as well as the Zionists.

The period between San Remo and Samuel's induction brought new tasks for Weizmann. News arrived from the Zionist Commission that Jabotinsky was agitating in prison against Weizmann for his compromising attitude toward the British, neglect of the Jewish legion, and abandonment of a comrade. Despite Weizmann's efforts to free him, Jabotinsky accused Weizmann of inviting an anti-Zionist policy on the part of the military administration. Rumors reached Weizmann that the soldiers of the Jewish legion planned to free Jabotinsky by forcibly entering Acre prison.[248] Weizmann feared that such an act would jeopardize the entire Zionist enterprise precisely on the eve of Samuel's arrival in Palestine. On June 8, 1920, Weizmann vented his bitterness and frustration toward the Yishuv: "One could have expected that there would be more patience and more self-control at a time like this, but apparently personal ambition and petty vanity are taking the upper hand. They seem to excel in a game of showing cheap heroism and fictitious martyrdom, and candidly I am beginning to sympathize with the British Administration more now than I ever did before."[249]

During the last weeks of the spring, tempers in the Yishuv cooled, as they did among the British administrators and the Palestinian Arabs. An air of wary expectancy seemed to descend on the land prior to the changing of the guard. On June 30, 1920, Herbert Samuel, the first high commissioner, arrived in Palestine to receive from Major General Louis Bols the formal transfer of administration. Bols had prepared for Sir Herbert—who had been knighted shortly before his arrival—a humorous typewritten receipt for "one Palestine taken over in good condition," which Sir Herbert duly signed, adding "E.O.E."—Errors and Omissions Excepted.[250]

IX

Between London and New York

Following his elevation to the Smaller Actions Committee in the January 1919 battle with Nahum Sokolow, Chaim Weizmann had won legitimacy in the traditional World Zionist Organization structure. He was able to work relatively smoothly thereafter with Sokolow, who had conceded power to Weizmann without a challenge. Indeed, Weizmann immediately gained the status of *primus inter pares* among the members of the SAC, symbolized by the fact that all official circulars and memoranda bore his name as the first signatory. Following Louis Brandeis's victory in the August 1919 meeting, Weizmann's continuing effort to enlist non-Zionist supporters was conducted on terms that did not clash sharply with the Americans' conceptions. But the rapidly changing circumstances of the Zionist movement during this period, together with the recovery of old Zionist factions and the emergence of new Zionist forces over which neither rival leader exercised direct influence, put new and greater pressures on both Weizmann and Brandeis. Their divergent responses to these challenges intensified their basic differences. They clashed again and again on specific issues, and thus their conclusive conflict was provoked.[1]

In the postwar period Zionists in both Europe and the United States were radicalized. The local Eastern European Zionist activists, vigorously supported by American labor Zionists such as Yitzhak Ben-Zvi, David Ben-Gurion, Nachman Syrkin, Baruch Zuckerman, and other leaders of the People's Relief Committee, pressed their militant demands on the American Jewish Joint Distribution Committee. They enjoyed the support of Felix Frankfurter, Stephen Wise, and others in urging strong protests against the pogroms and antisemitic mood of nationalist Poland. But their campaign for greater control over the allocation of American Jewish relief funds by local political forces in the Polish Jewish community and for the "constructive" use of such funds for economic and cultural reconstruction rather than "palliative relief" brought them into sharp conflict with the JDC bureaucracy. In this battle, the Zionist Organization of America leaders lent the Zionist radicals little or no sympathy.

On the international scene, the Eastern and Central European Zionists vigorously prosecuted their campaign to insert national rights clauses in the peace treaties and successfully fought efforts by the Alliance Israélite Universelle and other antinationalist Jewish organizations to control Jewish representation at the Paris peace conference in order to preclude such action. The Comité des Délégations Juives, set up by the Eastern Europeans with the judicious aid of Judge Julian Mack and Louis Marshall, a non-Zionist, and the constant support of such old European Zionist leaders as Nahum Sokolow, Leo Motzkin, and Victor Jacobson, became the animating center of a coalition of European national minorities that continued to work together in the corridors of the League of Nations.

While the budget of the World Zionist Organization covered some of the expenses of these activities, neither Weizmann nor Brandeis took any part in them or saw them as a pressing concern of the WZO. Weizmann's lack of interest in such Diaspora nationalist efforts did not mean that like Brandeis—at least in regard to the American situation—he disapproved of them. He considered them necessary but secondary concerns that other Zionists could, might, or even ought, to handle. Above all, and in sharp contrast to Brandeis, he recognized the leadership and organized strength concentrated on these tasks as important, legitimate Zionist forces, with which he would have to work.

The acute difficulties of the Jewish postwar situation amid the civil wars in Europe, together with the changing political circumstances of the former Ottoman territories, brought to Palestine a whole cadre of Jewish pioneers steeled by personal and national adversity and ready to perform any and all tasks to build the Jewish homeland. They demanded immediate political and social action, and their impact on the internal reorganization of Palestine Jewry was soon felt. This pressure sharply challenged the caution and moderation demanded by both Weizmann and Brandeis. Alienated from the Zionist leaders in England and the United States and facing a hostile British military administration in Palestine, the members of the Third Aliyah, supported and encouraged by the soldiers of the Jewish legion in Palestine, created their own social and political institutions as well as defense units.[2]

As the British continued to grope for long-term policies in the Middle East, sharply and frequently altering the political terms, the Zionist leaders also had to design and redesign their policies toward the outer and inner problems that faced them. As long as the military administration continued, the Zionist leaders' efforts were checked at every turn by the passive and active resistance of the military authorities in Palestine to Whitehall's Zionist policy. Weizmann and Brandeis took parallel positions toward the British and the pressures of the impatient Palestine community and other Zionists. Both relied on the advice of Aaron

Aaronsohn, a man who had always maintained a cool and contemptuous distance from the Zionist establishment in prewar Palestine and whose adventurous espionage activities during the war had ended in calamity for the community as well as for his own family.

The labor leaders of prewar Palestinian Jewry, now beginning their swift and steady rise to prominence and power, were regarded by both Weizmann and Brandeis as among the heedless political extremists who did not know how to cooperate with the British or the Arabs and whose importunate demands for more Zionist militancy had to be suppressed. Weizmann, moreover, sometimes shared the low opinion that the Americans speedily arrived at regarding the economic rationality and functional value of the labor collectives that had developed so close a relationship with the prewar Zionist office in Jaffa under Arthur Ruppin's direction.

Yet in September 1919, directly after Weizmann's clash with the Americans, these Palestinian labor leaders, too—as well as the Central European veterans who for the first time were able to come to London— were among the scattered Zionist forces Weizmann had to reassemble into a consolidated, reorganized movement. The Americans and Brandeis personally went ahead with their plans without regard for the new Palestinians or the old European Zionists. They continuously disapproved of the influence these emotional, fiscally irresponsible, and disorganized types had on Zionist policy. Their attitude was one Weizmann could not share, though it served to strengthen the position of the Americans. The split that occurred in July 1920 and widened thereafter was prepared for by a growing divergence between Brandeis's and Weizmann's policies. They differed not only on the method for securing non-Zionist affiliation to the reorganized Zionist movement but also regarding the proper roles and functions of the new Zionist agencies created during 1919–20 in London and Jerusalem.

The need to consolidate the world movement after the war by building a new center in London was obvious to all. Weizmann and Sokolow began at once to assemble a staff in London by getting veteran officers like Julius Simon from the Hague and Victor Jacobson from Copenhagen to join them. Following the initial reorganization in early 1919, Weizmann had available in London an expanded Zionist office, under Simon's direction, to supervise or carry out all his operations—drafting the Mandate for Palestine and planning its future political and economic structure by legal, financial, and other expert committees; supporting the Diaspora nationalist efforts at the peace conference and in the several countries; and rebuilding the old connections of the movement with its remote, loosely attached branches in Central and Eastern Europe and the Western Hemisphere.

The disorder that prevailed in the early postwar years hampered and delayed all these tasks, particularly the last. Not until the *Jahreskonferenz* in July 1920 could the Zionists convene an assembly under the terms prescribed in World Zionist Organization statutes for valid legislative action. By then the necessities of pressing tasks in Palestine and the Diaspora had initiated *ad hoc* arrangements and shifted the conditions of Zionist policymaking onto grounds unexplored in earlier Zionist conceptions.

Upon his return from Palestine in 1919, Weizmann secured from the British the renewal of the Zionist Commission's assignment to cooperate with the Palestine administration. Now, however, it was constituted as a purely Zionist body, and the disturbing involvement of nominees of the Allied governments was phased out. During his months of active leadership in Palestine, Weizmann had transformed the commission into something far more active than the purely advisory body originally projected. The commission became a quasi-government, seeking within the limits of its meager resources to intervene in every foreign and domestic concern of the Jewish community in Palestine.

British and American deputies who served after his departure were left with massive obligations but no greater means and far more limited legal and personal capacity to carry them out. Weizmann's ability to help and supervise in London, even with the assistance Brandeis could extend to his American emissaries from Washington, could not counteract the declining effectiveness of the commission and its loss of authority.

At the September 1919 meetings in London, after Brandeis's departure, an attempt was made to remedy the deficiency in the Zionist Commission's leadership. The veteran Russian leader, Menahem Ussishkin, would be named Weizmann's new deputy chairman. Representatives of the Palestine community, of Mizrahi, and of the labor Zionists were to be added, and the separate activities of the old Zionist office in Jaffa and the Jewish National Fund were to be integrated into the commission's structure. There remained some disagreement between Ussishkin's wish to exercise central control as chairman and the claim to autonomy for members slated to direct the several departments of the commission's activity. But a general consensus, especially among the new forces to be added to its ranks, obtained that the commission must follow a bold activist program in spite of the prevailing political uncertainty.

Extensive meetings and consultations in London prepared the necessary programs and instruments for work in Palestine under more permanent conditions in the future. In April 1919, Julius Simon's London office, under authorization by the February–March 1919 meetings, revived the Advisory Committee on Palestine chaired by Herbert Samuel and provided it with a series of technical reports on the political, financial, and economic development requirements of the Zionists.[3] This committee drew upon British Jewish leaders like James de Rothschild and Alfred Mond, influential figures like Professor Alfred Zimmern, technical experts like the economist John Maynard Keynes, and noted specialists on land use and land reform, irrigation, and money and banking. The projects it considered amounted to central planning for Palestine.[4] The leading London Zionists, together with the Americans Ben Cohen and Bernard Flexner, participated actively; and as there were continual sessions of assembled Zionists, on a greater or smaller scale, throughout the period of the peace conferences in 1919 and 1920, there was an opportunity to study the ambitious programs for agricultural and industrial development that Palestinian and European agronomists, engineers, and potential investors proposed.

The fact that the British had clearly ruled out any direct role for a Jewish agency in governing Palestine did not cause the London group to lower their sights in their technical plans for the future. For one thing, they were subject to great pressures. Other Zionists in Palestine and in Europe by no means accepted the radically reduced role in the government of Palestine that the British assigned to representatives of the Jewish national interest. Jabotinsky carried out an insistent campaign, even more intensively after his arrest following the April 1920 riots in Jerusalem, to have the remaining soldiers of his Jewish legion recognized as an official garrison force in Palestine. The London group was severely criticized by old Herzlian political Zionists like Max Nordau and Jean Fischer for its accommodating attitude toward British demands for moderation in the formulas for the Mandate for Palestine draft.[5] Menahem Ussishkin was present for most of 1919 in London to represent his Palestinian constituency with uncompromising militancy.

Weizmann and his associates, while they defended their moderation against all these attacks, did not consider that moderation entailed reducing the quasi-governmental scale of their plans. On the contrary, both Weizmann and Herbert Samuel agreed on a policy, which Samuel continued to follow after becoming high commissioner, that required Zionist efforts of quasi-governmental magnitude even though Zionists were explicitly to be excluded from a share in the government.[6] Both understood that the British would *not* make the development of the Jewish national home a direct objective of their administrative policy in Palestine; they would only permit the Zionists to achieve this aim, if they could, while the British would, at most, "facilitate" it under appropriate conditions.[7] Weizmann, like Brandeis, interpreted "facilitate" to mean that certain facilities—preference on concessions, access to crown lands for settlement, recognized functions in regard to Jewish immigration—would be granted in the Mandate for Palestine to a Jewish agency to carry out this task. For Weizmann—but not, after late 1919, for Brandeis—this meant a Jewish undertaking to carry out operations on a quasi-governmental scale from the beginning, which required correspondingly ambitious resources and institutions.[8]

To perform the new tasks, the financial instruments inherited from the prewar movement demanded a drastic overhaul. The economic subcommittees of Herbert Samuel's Advisory Committee on Palestine devised some proposals, such as making the Zionist Anglo-Palestine Company the bank of issue for Palestine's monetary system, that were soon discarded as implying a direct Zionist share in the government. The scale and nature of other operations, which were retained in the plans for cooperation with the government, called for substantial expansion and reorganization of the existing Zionist institutions: the Jewish Colonial Trust, the Jewish National Fund, and the Anglo-Palestine Company.

These agencies had been forced to extend their meager resources far beyond their original purposes or capacities simply to achieve earlier goals. The Jewish National Fund, designed to buy land as a perpetual national possession, had had to provide capital for colonization; the Anglo-Palestine Company, designed as a commercial bank, had had to loan funds to cover the current WZO budget. Proposals were made for the transfer of refugee capital from Russia or Poland that involved freezing substantial available liquid funds. The £25 million needed to finance the plans for the near future submitted by Arthur Ruppin to the September 1919 London meetings required investment and current funds far exceeding the meager capital stock of the Jewish Colonial Trust. New fiscal proposals to meet these needs hoped to draw on all sources—free contributions, membership dues, loans, and investments—and new financial institutions and procedures were to be established so that the distinct needs of the enterprise might severally be served by appropriate instruments, adequately funded, and managed each in terms of financial principles appropriate to its particular task. But it was the unquestioned obligation of the World Zionist Organization, in the view of Herbert Samuel and Weizmann as well as Menahem Ussishkin, Arthur Ruppin, and the Palestinian worker representatives, to undertake and somehow provide for the entire range of traditional and projected Zionist functions. Education, sanitation, health care, immigration, land purchase and development, colonization, and political advocacy were required to reconstitute Palestine as a Jewish commonwealth, not to speak of needs for traditional Diaspora nationalist work.[9]

Brandeis and his American associates, by a complex process of shifting attitudes, came to take sharply opposed views focused on certain narrowly defined issues. The associates from whom Brandeis learned his Zionism, men like Jacob DeHaas, Horace Kallen, and Stephen Wise, generally shared the Herzlian political approach of Max Nordau and Jean Fischer, but they did not long persist in criticizing Weizmann's political moderation. The Brandeis group quickly understood the limits imposed by a policy of working with the British, which they solidly favored. Nor did their commitment to nationalization of the land, adopted in the Pittsburgh Platform, cause them to join the Palestinian socialist Zionists in their fierce opposition to rather modest concessions made to private Jewish land purchase in various 1919 London meetings.

Horace Kallen, who left the ZOA and joined the new left-leaning American Zeire-Zion party in protest, was not typical of the Brandeis group, most of whom took a practical, pragmatic view of this issue. In spite of their progressivism, moreover, the Americans were unable to share the broad conceptions of governmental functions and concession powers readily accepted by British Empire Liberals like Samuel. They tended to view more narrowly the proper role of voluntary associations cooperating with the government and took a correspondingly restrictive stand on the proposals for budgets and organizational structures needed by the postwar WZO.

The United States, of course, was expected to provide the bulk of the required funds,[10] but prospects of meeting these demands were not enhanced by developments in the country after the war. The ZOA began to register sharp declines in membership as the wartime emergencies passed. An economic recession caused the American leaders to hesitate to undertake large new burdens even if they had thought them warranted. These circumstances perhaps reinforced the doubts and criticisms that their characteristically American approach in any case engendered *vis-à-vis* the European enthusiasts.

Brandeis's visit to Palestine in June 1919 served to crystallize certain preliminary conclusions regarding the work there, sharply defining the reservations earlier voiced by Americans on the spot, in the Zionist Commission and the American Zionist Medical Unit. Brandeis applied American experience and principles, tinged by his particular view of Zionism, to everything he saw. Given the shortage of funds at a time when the Americans were experiencing an economic pinch, he suggested that the heavy charges for Jewish education assumed by the WZO be reduced by following the example of the early Puritans, who were content to run three-day-a-week schools. Immigrants had come at their own expense to the United States and should do so to Palestine; or if help were absolutely required, this responsibility should be conceded to the Joint Distribution Committee and not be charged to the Zionist budget.[11]

But there were compelling reasons to halt immigration altogether for a time beyond those recognized by the London Zionists and the British administration. The commitment and idealism of the young pioneers who settled in the swamps deeply moved Brandeis, but he was also appalled at what he considered the reckless disregard for suffering shown by the whole Palestine community and its leaders. Malaria, trachoma, and other diseases afflicted the whole land, particularly Jerusalem. Recalling the saga of George Goethals's construction of the Panama Canal and the need to eradicate yellow fever there, as well as his personal experience with the effects of malaria,[12] Brandeis proposed that all constructive work in Palestine be virtually halted until a major sanitation project—the very task to which the American Zionist Medical Unit could best address itself—was completed.[13]

At the August 1919 meetings in London, Brandeis concentrated on public health issues and the already noted revision of the plans for the projected Jewish council according to his American desiderata. In the aftermath of Brandeis's victory and Weizmann's defeat on this issue, the Americans felt that they had made their point effectively. Brandeis's next opportunity to go further with his plans for reorganization came at the conferences in London in June and July 1920. The Americans approached these meetings in a sanguine spirit.

Weizmann's actions during the period between August 1919 and July 1920 looked like good omens to the Americans. True, he had expressed himself in September 1919 as unwilling to act for the movement in negotiating the revisions of the formula for constituting the Jewish council (or Jewish agency), which was adopted over his protest a month earlier and which ultimately appeared in the Mandate for Palestine text. But much of Weizmann's activity in 1919–20 was directed toward attracting non-Zionist notables to undertake Zionist functions, and his approach was not visibly different from that of Brandeis. James de Rothschild, whose volatile relations with Weizmann improved somewhat in 1920,[14] was offered a leading position in the Political Committee of the World Zionist Organization.[15] Alfred Mond, in particular, was wooed as a replacement for Herbert Samuel, who was preparing to take on his new post as high commissioner for Palestine. As first commissioner of works in the British government at the time, Mond felt unable to join the WZO political leadership but was inclined to head a proposed Economic Council.[16] Since he objected to involving this technical agency with the political decisions of a body like the WZO executive, this council was anticipated to operate independently under a small directorate of competent managers. Finally, Robert Waley-Cohen, managing director of Shell Transport and Trading Co., who had split ideologically in 1919, was approached again during the June–July 1920 discussions and eventually agreed to participate as a member of the Economic Council.[17]

Brandeis was favorably impressed by these developments and in a rather arrogant tone wrote from London on June 28, 1920, that "Weizmann has been much chastened by the year's experience and cooperation with him seems much easier than it did last summer."[18] Felix Frankfurter reported the following day to Julian Mack: "You will be glad to know, as will be the others, that the atmosphere is an entirely friendly one. Weizmann in particular shows hard headedness, reasonableness and a driving force for the practical. The estimate of the man has gone up on all hands, outside of some of the old Russian forces."[19]

After the *Jahreskonferenz*'s formal session opened on July 7, 1920, Weizmann and his executive were sharply attacked by critics, including not only the old Herzlian Zionists and Mizrahi but with particular forcefulness by the representatives of the Palestinian workers, especially Berl Katznelson and David Ben-Gurion.[20] Deflecting all the criticisms concerning the Zionist Commission and its attitude toward the Jewish legion, the Asefat Hanivharim, the rate of immigration, and a host of other issues, Weizmann concluded his speech with an ironic-bitter challenge to his critics:

To us it does not appear possible to go so quickly and to have 600,000 Jews [in Palestine] in a short time [Nordau had suggested admitting half a million in order to attain a majority]. Not today! Tomorrow perhaps. If the Jewish people would read into the San Remo decision the same things that they desire the British people to do, then we could talk about a half a million Jews in Palestine. The Jews merely held meetings and waved flags. Did they give their money? We have done this. Jewish people! What have you done?[21]

Weizmann's spirited, if embittered defense made a deep impression on his audience. It was appreciatively observed by Jacob DeHaas, who reported that "W[eizmann] did up the Mizrachi; attacked P[oalei] Z[ion] [the workers' party], punched holes in Nordau and generally amused himself greatly."[22] DeHaas's general estimate of the meeting, however (like that of most participants, though of course each for his own reasons), was decidedly unfavorable. He reserved most of his praise, in his daily reports to New York, for his own leader, Brandeis, who chaired the session. Brandeis, he suggested, made headway in teaching the unruly Europeans the practice of orderly parliamentary procedure:

3.7.1920:
. . . Nothing is ready for discussion. There are no plans. . . .
   As I wrote you last week we had improved the procedure, but now that W[eizmann] is afraid of the Russians we shall [have] to improve again. . . .
7.7.1920:
The session opened this a.m. at 10:30 in a miserable hall. . . . Sok[olow] led off in Hebrew—nothing really good. W. followed with a diluted form of an address with which he impressed us on Monday. He did it poorly today. . . . There was unanimity at the uninspiring character of the proceedings. LDB[randeis] took the chair on schedule time, hall less than half full—and said his little speech. He did it well but when the USA delegates saw the French speaking group (Nordau bloc) wouldn't rise for LDB they boycotted the latter. This was a very minor incident. The first scrap followed on [Max] Bodenheimer and [Leo] Motzkin trying to railroad something thro'. The resolutions had to be translated, there was confusion. Nordau took every advantage of the situation—the plea for democracy. LDB handled the situation splendidly. It was the brightest spot of the day.
9.7.1920:
The third day ended with W. in the ascendant over his critics. Sok. looking rather foolish as a "me too," Nordau stock going down, LDB showing a good grip in the chair. The hall is bad. There is lots of confusion & the Americans are not impressed tho' they admired W.'s forensic. In fact nothing has been accomplished except a schooling of the conference in procedure, & the speeches.[23]

Not all Brandeis's associates could find even so much comfort in the course of recent events. Neither Julian Mack nor Stephen Wise went to London for the conference, and Wise made clear his serious reservations. As he wrote to Richard Gottheil on June 13, he had arranged deliberately "not to be free to go" since "it is impossible for me to get on with Weizmann and Sokolow." He did not wish to be party "to the coronation of Weizmann," for he lacked "confidence in his intellectual and spiritual integrity." The difficulty that concerned Wise stemmed from the restricted commitment Brandeis would agree to undertake: "Unhappily we have no one else to offer the leadership of the Z[ionist] O[rganization]. . . . Brandeis for the present will not take the leadership. He might if it were offered to him in the right way—with unanimity. . . . I am sure that he will not accept and be one of the triumvirate, checked and controlled at every turn by Weizmann and Sokolow."[24]

But it was not simply opposition by others that prevented Brandeis from assuming the sole leadership of world Zionism. From the moment Brandeis's star showed on the horizon of the movement, he was considered by all as a potential successor to Herzl. Weizmann more than once in the years of his own rise to leadership offered to step down in favor of the Americans and the American leader if Brandeis would commit himself fully to the task. Even if this gesture was less than sincere, it was an open offer that could hardly have been withdrawn if Brandeis had wished to take it up. And there were many in Brandeis's entourage, like Wise himself, who gained the impression that their chief might under proper conditions make just this commitment—a belief that may have had much wishful thinking in it but was certainly not baseless.

Brandeis himself made fully and specifically clear, with his own direct accuracy but not his customary economy of expression, the array of motives that prevented his accepting a Zionist "coronation" of his own. At a caucus of the American delegation at the London *Jahreskonferenz* on July 14, 1920, Brandeis was directly appealed to, or challenged, by Louis Lipsky, Morris Rothenberg, and others on this point. He replied:

Now, as I have been frank with you before, I mean to be frank with you again. This question of assuming a very prominent part—what some would no doubt call the leading part—in the conduct of Zionist affairs, is a matter with which . . . I have been confronted for some time—mostly for the last year since I was in Palestine. I have endeavored . . . to differentiate . . . considerations which were Zionistic purely and considerations which were personal, perhaps in some part accidental. . . . I have become more and more convinced that, treated purely as a question of Zionism, it would be a mistake for me to resign from the Bench with a view to taking up definitely and exclusively this work, and, for this reason—in part it is what I indicated this morning as to the importance of the work in the diaspora. . . . It is perhaps in some ways more important in America because we have a larger number of Jews and we are better able to contribute in money than in men, but I felt owing to the accident of my position in America, not only the fact that I was on the Bench—the highest Bench of the world, but the fact that I represented, independently of being on the Bench, in a certain sense the Liberals, Progressives, that hope in American life. I feel and have felt that if I retired from the Bench you would have on the one hand, a convention developed by the overt act of my resignation, that all we have been saying is not true—that a man cannot be a Zionist and a good citizen of his country . . . and it will gradually injure our movement with Jews and with non-

Jews and incidentally it will tend to deprive us in part of the support—at least in lieu of others—of the American government without which we, in Palestine under the Mandate, will not, in my opinion, be safe.

Brandeis then suggested an alternative that would permit him to apply the lessons of his visit to Palestine and his experience with organized Zionism under arrangements similar to his relations with the American movement:

I said to myself, I have been of some service in America perhaps during the last four years; I have had no power in office—I see no conclusive reason why I cannot hold to the International Organization that position—the position of honorary president . . . ; and, during the period of my vacation, I see no reason why I should not, as I have during the last two years, give more than occasional advice in the conduct of our affairs. . . . That is what I thought . . . the utmost limit . . . ; when I came to a consideration of this question my conclusions were confirmed . . . by the evidence which we saw here and reports which we had from Palestine. It seems to me that perhaps I can go one step further . . . in bringing into existence this board which was to conduct the work and in formulating the details of all the plans under which the work is to be done.[25]

Brandeis, then, had come to London in 1920 determined to take a more active role in reorganizing the movement rather than simply backing Weizmann as he had done in the past. He took this course—apart from his own constant sense of responsibility—upon consideration of his own experience, the reports of his associates in Palestine, and his observation of the disorderly, wasteful management of affairs in London, reminiscent of the state of affairs that Downtown Eastern Europeans in the United States had bequeathed to him when he first assumed Zionist leadership. And in spite of American approval of Weizmann's current behavior, Brandeis now evidently had come to share the reservations many of his associates felt about Weizmann. Felix Frankfurter, Weizmann's staunch supporter in the beginning, expressed in strong terms the judgment Americans reached at the stormy August 1919 meeting. Weizmann had argued there for a world Jewish congress to set up the Jewish agency for Palestine on the grounds that the Zionists were a partisan, not a comprehensively representative, organization of the whole Jewish people in whose name historic rights had to be reasserted in Palestine. They therefore had no right to speak for all Jews. Frankfurter rejected this contention with impatience and contempt: "At the Peace Conference Weizmann spoke for the Jewish people. Why be afraid suddenly now? You were bold in the face of England, but in the face of the Jewish people you are cowardly [*feig*]."[26] Frankfurter immediately withdrew this unparliamentary expression, saying that he would not have called Weizmann a coward if he had been speaking English, but it evidently remained the final judgment among the Brandeis group that they could not rely on Weizmann to stand up to his old European colleagues in the way they desired. Thus, amid his praise for Weizmann's aggressive defense against his European and Palestinian critics, DeHaas's notes on the London *Jahreskonferenz* do not fail to remark also that "now . . . W[eizmann] is afraid of the Russians."[27] This was a view Brandeis apparently shared.

By 1920 it had become clear that four major areas of concern, covering many more subtle issues, separated Weizmann and Brandeis. The first had to do with priorities: Brandeis insisted that Palestine had to be made attractive for potential immigrants, while Weizmann argued that money was better spent on schools, administration, and land reclamation. Second, Brandeis argued that the first order of business was the physical upbuilding of Zion, while Weizmann strongly advocated a parallel concentration on Jewish cultural renaissance. The American leader and his followers also insisted on careful, efficient management of the funds they raised, while Weizmann and his fellow workers in the field could not, or would not, account for every dollar they spent. The final issue revolved around personal commitment. While Weizmann and other European Zionists did not hesitate to sacrifice much of their time, and in some cases jeopardize their careers, Brandeis and his top American Zionist advisers were unwilling to do the same; their personal advancement in the world outside the Zionist orbit took first priority.[28] There were clear and deep cultural, political, ideological, and philosophical differences separating the two major figures in the movement, creating a cleavage that was often attributed to the distance between Washington and Pinsk, a distance that highlighted the very different dynamics shaping American and European Zionists.

Brandeis had been a target of the blandishments of Weizmann's non-Zionist antagonists since the end of the war. During the period of estrangement between Weizmann and the Rothschilds in 1918–19, the Zionists' *bête noire*, Sylvain Lévi, had gone to the United States to woo Justice Brandeis on behalf of Baron Edmond de Rothschild. Robert Waley-Cohen tried the same gambit during his own clash with the London Zionists. In both cases, the Americans resisted these approaches and upheld the London Zionist leaders. But at the London *Jahreskonferenz* Brandeis took a different course.

Given the limited commitment Brandeis was personally willing to assume, the discussions regarding a new leadership for the WZO and for the contemplated Economic Council that would undertake operational responsibilities centered on a "triumvirate" or similar combination that would share the direction of Zionist and Palestine affairs.[29] Weizmann had already approached Alfred Mond, James de Rothschild, and Robert Waley-Cohen to serve in various leading capacities on the WZO executive, on its Political Committee, and on the Economic Council, with the possibility of the council's enjoying considerable independence. But after his arrival in London, Brandeis cut through these inconclusive negotiations and, bolting around Weizmann, conferred with Lord Reading, the

British lord chief justice, a non-Zionist who had no previous ties with the Zionist office in London. The plan the two judges drew up for the reorganization of Zionist affairs was then revealed to Weizmann rather than cooperatively developed with him.[30]

The Brandeis-Reading Plan provided for an executive of three men, with power to co-opt additional full members. This body would have broad authority to direct the development of the Jewish national home for a three-year term. A seven-man executive was contemplated: three non-Zionists, depending on the availability of candidates, and four Zionists—Weizmann, Sokolow, and Bernard Flexner, with Brandeis to serve as honorary president, casting a vote in case of deadlocks.[31]

The proposal resembled Weizmann's earlier projects but differed in significant details: Weizmann as well as Sokolow could now count on being totally subordinated. Such a plan, calculated to permit Brandeis to participate in Zionist affairs and the direction of Palestine development on his own terms—whose full implications now became apparent—was bound to outrage all veteran Zionists. The current American talk of requiring mass resignations of old Zionist professionals did nothing to soothe them. It also implicitly suggested that Weizmann must accept in the world movement the position assigned to old Zionists like Wise, De-Haas, or even Louis Lipsky in the American organization. Not only would the three non-Zionists together with Brandeis's man Bernard Flexner give the American leader built-in control, but Brandeis would operate, as in the United States, on a part-time, absentee basis through second-echelon representatives.

On July 14, Brandeis presented his plan to members of the American delegation and then to the *Senioren Konvent* of the *Jahreskonferenz*. There were strong objections voiced in both forums, but neither rejected the plan since Brandeis seemed amenable to some revisions. Not surprisingly, however, Weizmann, without consulting Brandeis, took the first opportunity to attack the proposal. He effectively killed it at a secret meeting late at night on July 15–16 with Alfred Mond and James de Rothschild, two of the non-Zionists slated to be co-opted to the council under the Brandeis-Reading Plan.[32] Weizmann apparently convinced them that there was no basis for the formation of such a council.[33] This was, in Brandeis's view, an act of betrayal from which he concluded that Weizmann's character was morally flawed and the two could not work together.

Felix Frankfurter and other Brandeis aides tried immediately to repair the damage.[34] Weizmann himself was anxious to do so as well. But Brandeis had already appeared before the *Senioren Konvent* on the morning of July 16 and announced that he stood by his plan. Since Weizmann had betrayed him, Brandeis continued, he could no longer cooperate with him. He could also no longer consent to become honorary president of the WZO.[35] Until the *Jahreskonferenz* ground to a halt on July 22, there were feverish behind-the-scenes efforts to constitute a new WZO executive.[36]

The London *Jahreskonferenz* left all its participants disgruntled and unsettled. Weizmann parted ways with the American leadership, choosing to consolidate his position by seeking the support of the rest of the movement. On the last day of the conference Weizmann was elected president of the WZO, while Brandeis only reluctantly accepted an honorary presidency, on the express condition that he would bear no responsibility for the new executive's policy and no other American would serve. The London *Jahreskonferenz* itself elected only one other officer, Sokolow, as chairman of the WZO executive and left the remaining executive posts to be filled through co-optation by the elected officers. With Brandeis remaining aloof, Weizmann and Sokolow then co-opted Menahem Ussishkin, together with two Europeans more congenial to the Americans, Julius Simon and Nehemia de Lieme, a veteran Dutch Zionist.[37] The differences that later arose between them and Weizmann played into the developing Brandeis-Weizmann dispute.

The two sides found themselves arrayed against each other on new issues concerning fiscal policies and institutions that grew out of decisions adopted at the London *Jahreskonferenz*. Weizmann's plan for an Economic Council, a plan ratified by the conference, to be headed by Sir Alfred Mond, did not supplant the Brandeis-Reading Plan. Later the council became the Economic Board for Palestine, an independent British non-Zionist investment corporation parallel to the American Palestine Economic Corporation initiated by the Brandeis group and the American Jewish Committee leaders. The main fiscal institution created at the London *Jahreskonferenz* was the Keren Hayesod (Palestine Foundation Fund), and this became the prime point of contention between the Brandeis and Weizmann camps.

The idea of this new Zionist fund had been hammered out in long discussions during 1919 in which the Americans participated. In the final form adopted on July 22, 1920, the Keren Hayesod was to serve as a general revenue source for a Zionist budget of £25 million for the next five years, derived from the self-taxation (*maaser,* or tithe) of the Jewish people throughout the world. One-fifth of the amount was to go to the Jewish National Fund, now assigned the sole role of national land acquisition, and would make up for the anticipated decline in the fund's independent collections. The remainder was to be allocated in the ratio of two-thirds for "constructive" or capital investment (with various prospects for returns justifying share capital or self-liquidating loan arrangements) and the remaining third for education, social welfare, and similar current needs.[38]

The main advocates of the Keren Hayesod idea were Russian Zionists, in particular Isaac Naiditch and Hillel Zlatopolsky, men with long and successful business experience. The directorate of the new fiscal agency was made up predominately of their close associates and collaborators, and they demanded a high degree of discretionary authority, without close supervision by the WZO executive. Julius Simon strongly opposed this claim. As head of an executive secretariat set up in London by the WZO executive, he insisted on exercising ultimate control of Keren Haye-sod decisions. Simon, representing the WZO executive would, it was decided, control 51 percent of the voting strength in the directorate. Since he shared the Americans' views on fiscal practices of the WZO, he was supported in this position by the Brandeis group. Weizmann found himself caught in the middle in these disputes and gradually swung into an uneasy alliance with the opponents of the Simon faction.[39]

Another focus of conflict was the continuing problem of the Zionist Commission in Palestine, which the London *Jahreskonferenz* determined should be subjected without delay to careful study and basic reorganization.[40] The conference decided to transfer from London to Jerusalem control of functions directly related to the Palestine work. But given past criticism of the Zionist Commission as well as the specific reservations Americans had about Ussishkin, who was the executive member scheduled to move to Jerusalem as the head of the Zionist Commission, the question of reorganization became urgent. A Reorganization Commission went to Palestine in November 1920 to check past actions and thoroughly revise future policies.[41] It possessed plenary powers and was controlled by Julius Simon and Nehemia de Lieme, members of the London executive secretariat and including Brandeis's own man, the young lawyer Robert Szold, together with Abraham Sonne, general secretary of the executive, and Paul Singer, financial secretary of the executive. The Zionist Commission leaders Menahem Ussishkin, Arthur Ruppin, and Weizmann's man David Eder sparked the conflict by approving, shortly before the arrival of the Reorganization Commission, a major land purchase in Emek Jezreel for which the budget available provided no adequate funds.[42]

This purchase was one of several issues that solidified differences of approach, and Weizmann had to make an unwelcome choice between them. Underlying differences that might otherwise have remained quiescent, making effective cooperation possible, were now dramatically formulated.

At bottom, the European and Palestinian Zionists regarded their task as governmental, and they treated movement funds as generally, even flexibly, available for any of the movement's needs. The predetermined budget would be approved by the legislative organs of the movement according to the strength of Zionist parties at each congress or Actions Committee session, while the executive and its subsidiary agencies would adapt actual expenditures to changing conditions. Guided by their past experience in the movement, moreover, these veterans tended to feel that income depended on conveying a sense of urgency and enthusiasm. They believed that revenue would rise or fall in response to demonstrated needs, and they therefore tended to undertake politically important investments in the expectation that, once launched, such projects would generate a sufficient response to meet the needs.

The Brandeis group was fundamentally hostile to the whole idea of a global, popularly controlled entity implied in such controversial decisions as the Emek Jezreel land purchase and the plans for the Keren Hayesod advocated by Naiditch. The Americans resisted involvement in a system that gave no more weight to their position in the United States than to that of Jews in Eastern Europe. However, they could find enough grounds for criticism in terms of the specific issues without raising these underlying differences. The Emek Jezreel purchase could be rejected as fiscal irresponsibility, far beyond any legitimate executive discretion, and Naiditch's demand for independence of the Keren Hayesod directorate from WZO executive control could be rejected on similar grounds.

What the Americans proposed instead revealed their own, very different, basic position. They wanted more than rigid budget controls restricting funds to allocated uses, and they sought to go beyond compelling the executive officers to limit their expenditures to anticipated income and previously authorized activities. They preferred to earmark funds according to the wishes of contributors, Zionists or non-Zionists, rather than allowing popular whims, or even emerging need as defined locally by elected officers in the field, to determine expenditures. Executive discretion was to be exercised, in their design, not by men responsible to political constituencies or responsive to a broad spectrum of movement needs but by bureaucratic experts and technicians, assigned to specific, limited operations that enjoyed the support of particular groups of contributors or investors, who alone would be authorized to make such decisions. This arrangement guaranteed fiscal accountability, rational and efficient management, and even the official probity that the Americans considered sadly wanting in the old practices.[43] Clearly, the "administrative-national" approach of the Americans was buttressed by their political opposition to the European leadership in the wake of the London *Jahreskonferenz*.

The report and recommendations of the Reorganization Commission met a predictable storm of protests from the vast majority of European Zionists and the Yishuv. Weizmann and his colleagues in London made no secret of the fact that the report was not acceptable to them, and in January 1921, de Lieme, Simon, Sonne, and Singer submitted their resignations. Their departure was just another symptom of the underlying controversies that emerged in 1919 and 1920 and continued into the next year. On returning from the London *Jahreskonferenz*, Brandeis drew up a comprehensive formulation of his position even before the immediate specific issues were sharply, if not absolutely, defined in the controversy surrounding the Reorganization Commission. The basic, underlying opposition was thus inevitably brought into the foreground, as Weizmann, increasingly aligned with the other camp, expressly stated when defining the fundamental cleavage.

In a letter to his friend Bella Berligne, some two weeks after the London *Jahreskonferenz*, Weizmann angrily described his feelings:

> The Conference and all that followed was one big unbearable nightmare, and it is not over yet. I wanted to believe that things would improve, but the noose around my neck tightened more and more and did not ease up. I could not write, the pen fell from my hands. It seemed that all I worked for, that we all worked for, was falling apart. The Americans behaved like boors. They came with the intention of wrecking everything and rebuilding it in their own manner, according to their understanding, but for this they had no money, people, or expertise. The fight was sly, underhand, furtive, dishonest; ignoble means were used. My heart bled to see how our good cause was being soiled. Though we did not break with them formally, in actual fact nothing is left of the Americans' "help." They give no money, their advice is unacceptable. And so, at the very time when work could be begun, we find ourselves on the threshold of a severe financial crisis. Immigration is beginning, it is possible to buy land, but there is no money! Only a large deficit.
>
> All this has to be lived through, the bitter cup drained. But now I somewhat feel easier. We have no illusions, no expectations of America, but we do have confidence that our own strength will suffice to lift the heavy burden.[44]

After a month-long rest in Chamonix and Montreux, Weizmann returned to London ready to tackle the political and economic disarray facing the WZO. While confident that he himself could manage the political questions relating to the mandate and future boundaries, he needed much help from the non-Zionist segment of the community to bolster the movement's finances, particularly since the American Zionists seemed determined to adopt, at the very least, a more cautious approach toward the transfer of funds to London. This insight was coupled with Weizmann's conviction, confirmed by the British themselves, that the Jewish national home would become a reality only if the Jews took the initiative. He had been quite clear about this point in his opening speech at the London *Jahreskonferenz:*

> They [the British government] have set up all the necessary political conditions for the making of the Jewish National Home. They regard us as being free henceforth to make of Palestine as Jewish a country as we are capable . . . and, by make of it, I do not mean by words or phrases, but by deeds, the actual constructive, solid work in Palestine. The task is ours and nobody else's. The financial resources, the material resources, and the intellectual resources for the making of a Jewish Palestine must come from the Jewish people and the Jewish people only. Anybody who may harbor the idea of financial assistance for our specifically Jewish work in Palestine, whether in the form of a loan or otherwise, from the British Government or any other

Government, must put that idea out of his head. Ours and ours alone is the task, the responsibility. . . .

On the political side, six years ago we were faced with the need of creating a position, and a well-founded one, out of a mere idea. We are faced today, on the financial side, with a similar problem. We have to bring into being the best financial resources required to reconstitute a Jewish Palestine. The Jewish people possess these resources, and the Jewish people will put them at our disposal if we bring home to them guarantees that the money will be devoted to solid, constructive work.[45]

On the last day of the London *Jahreskonferenz* the delegates approved the creation of an Economic Council "for the purpose of advancing the economic development of Palestine . . . composed of men well known in the financial and business world . . . and also of representatives of the Zionist Organization."[46] The creation of this council was one of Weizmann's major projects in the fall of 1920. He had set the stage for new economic enterprises during his stopover at Paris on route to London. During his sojourn there, September 15–19, he held conversations with officials of the Jewish Colonization Association, who promised their help for constructive work in Palestine, while Baron Edmond de Rothschild promised to support Pinhas Rutenberg's proposal to harness hydroelectric power from the Jordan River.[47] During the first meeting of the Political Committee following his return to London, moreover, Weizmann also brought up the subject of a loan of £2.5 million, which Herbert Samuel wished to raise for constructive work in Palestine with the active aid of the Zionists.[48]

The first meeting of the Economic Council was held on October 21, 1920.[49] Sir Alfred Mond chaired the meeting, attended by Sir Robert Waley-Cohen, Sir Stuart Samuel (Herbert Samuel's brother and president of the Board of Deputies), James de Rothschild, Albert Belisha (Belisha Shaw & Co.), Hugo Hirst (General Electrical Co.), Harry Marks (Kynochs Ltd.), Fred Stern (Stern Brothers), and Herbert Guedalla (Imperial Foreign Corp.). Though Weizmann had managed to bring together an impressive group of financiers and industrialists and others of similar stature had also indicated interest in the scheme, this first meeting almost turned out to be the last. Sir Alfred did not prepare materials for their consideration in advance, and those assembled seemed fearful that the Economic Council would be too closely allied with the WZO to allow it freedom of action.[50]

For his part, Weizmann rejected Waley-Cohen's suggestion that "the Zionists . . . place the whole machinery and man-power at the disposal of the E[conomic] C[ouncil]. The E.C. to assume absolute financial control. It is obvious that such a demand is tantamount to the abdication of the Z[ionist] O[rganization] and the wolf will dwell with the lamb, but the lamb is to be inside the wolf."[51] The question also arose as to what financial arrangements would be made between the Keren Hayesod and the Economic Council. At a meeting on November 24, 1920, Sir Alfred

Weizmann and Vladimir Jabotinsky in Amsterdam for a Keren Hayesod fund-raising event, sponsored by the Netherlands Zionist Organization, January 1921. Front row, from left: Weizmann, Jabotinsky, L. S. Ornstein (president of NZO), A. Asscher (treasurer of Keren Hayesod). Courtesy: Jewish Historical Museum, Amsterdam, and Jack Polak

agreed to become a member of the board of governors of Keren Hayesod on condition that those of its funds allocated for investments be placed at the disposal of the Economic Council.

Mond's agreement and cooperation were obviously a great victory for Weizmann, but for the time being only Lord Rothschild agreed to the same conditions, whereas James de Rothschild and Waley-Cohen declined to give their assent. In mid-1921 the Economic Council was transformed into the Economic Board for Palestine and henceforth operated independently of the November 1920 agreement. Although he tried to present these negotiations as successful,[52] Weizmann's only gain, by no means a negligible one, was drawing Sir Alfred Mond closer into the Zionist orbit.

In January 1921, Weizmann accompanied Sir Alfred and his daughter Mary on their first trip to Palestine. Weizmann sensed that contact with the country would have great impact on the Monds and give Sir Alfred the kind of direct knowledge with which he could persuade others of his class. Weizmann, moreover, wished to reassure the Yishuv and his colleagues that the unrest about the Reorganization Commission was over. He also felt it was time to see what Palestine looked like under a Jewish high commissioner. On route to Marseilles, his port of embarkation, Weizmann visited Holland and despite dire predictions was able to arouse interest and funds for Keren Hayesod.[53] He described it to Vera as a triumphal tour: "I saw them all, talked to everybody, had public and private conferences, tried to give them all the clear, sincere, unadorned truth and I can tell you my Dear, that people came to life under my very touch. . . . Everything could not have gone better. . . . They treated me like a king."[54] The rest of the trip also went well; the passage enjoyed calm, summer weather, and the Monds proved pleasant travel companions.[55]

Weizmann and the Monds arrived in Jerusalem on January 14, 1921. A large crowd came to meet them, including Weizmann's siblings, Fruma and Feivel. They, as well as Weizmann's sister Minna, his brother Chilik, and his mother—and other brothers and sisters in the following years—had now made Palestine their permanent home. So had his old friend from Manchester, Harry Sacher, who arrived in the fall of 1920 to edit the English-language *Palestine Weekly.* Over the weekend Weizmann stayed at the official residence of the Samuels, Government House, then at the Kaiserin Augusta Viktoria Hospice on Mount Scopus.[56] This was probably the most pleasant and warm welcome Weizmann had received to date upon arrival in Palestine. Yet he felt he ought to live in his own apartment in town, where he could better take the political pulse of the Yishuv.

Though not completely happy by what he saw and heard, Weizmann must have sensed a contrast with his last visit, which had been punctuated by the Arab riots during the last months of the military administration. The old administrators had remained in place, but he was very favorably impressed by Wyndham Deedes. He also gave credit to Herbert Samuel, who, for the time being, seemed to uphold the Zionist cause though constantly pressed to undermine it: "The Arab rabble (forgive the expression)," he wrote Vera, "try the whole time to blackmail Samuel, who is afraid of them."[57]

Weizmann took the Monds on a trip to the Galilee, where they watched with admiration the members of the Gdud Haavodah, the labor battalion formed in 1920 by pioneers who undertook hard physical labor, including road building. Though a bit confused by all he saw, Mond was delighted.[58] Weizmann felt the vibrancy of the Third Aliyah: "There's something new there. Palestine has grown, and the 8,000 new youngsters have brought a fresh current, very fresh and very lively. The new immigration is now undoubtedly the most beautiful phenomenon in Jewish life and the most encouraging thing. . . . Fifty thousand more such men in Palestine, and there will hardly be anyone for us to fear."[59] The pioneers were the first answer of the Jewish people to San Remo, and Tel Aviv, too, was growing and looked more attractive.[60] As he left Palestine on February 1, 1921, after a hectic two-week period, Weizmann felt more encouraged than ever about the country's prospects.

No sooner did Weizmann return to London on February 15 than he began to make preparations for his trip to the United States. He had planned to go soon after he had launched the Keren Hayesod in London on October 25, 1920,[61] but the Americans had urged him to postpone his trip until after the ZOA convention in Buffalo in late November of that year.[62] Events before the convention and the resolutions it adopted made it clear that Weizmann would have to go to the United States at the earliest opportunity. Though preoccupied by urgent problems in England and delayed by his reconnaissance trip to Palestine, Weizmann kept watch—through detailed reports from his supporters in the United States—over the activities of the Brandeis-led American group.

Brandeis's actions at the London *Jahreskonferenz* had disillusioned his adherents as well as his opponents. The latter pointed out that for all his (as they admitted) often justified criticism of past WZO policies, Brandeis formulated no new, clear program of action of his own. This reproach was keenly felt by Brandeis's associates, who were especially disappointed when their chief not only failed to assume full, active leadership but in the aftermath of the London *Jahreskonferenz* insisted that other Americans also renounce responsible positions in the world movement. This demand was not well received by the American caucus at London, even though the Americans bowed to Brandeis's will. From Palestine, where she was working with the American Zionist Medical Unit, Henrietta Szold wrote:

> It is difficult, impossible in fact, to make the Palestinians understand. . . . To them . . . the whole American action at London seems arbitrary, self-willed, petulant, even pettish, and a bit purse-proud. . . . They insist that no matter what [their] quarrel with Palestine and its chosen leaders may be . . . the Americans ought to come over and take charge themselves. They would be given a free hand here, they say, but to criticize, stay outside, and then leave Palestine in the lurch. . . .
>
> To find out what is the actual plan was the objective of our cable. . . . The taunt hardest to bear is that we can collect no money in America and we are making a virtue of a necessity. It is not to save our own faces and protect our comfort that we want an official statement from you, it is because we are ourselves at sea.[63]

In drafting the required statement, Brandeis's freedom of action was limited by unavoidable restrictions. He himself was not prepared to give more than partial service. Even if he had been ready for more, it was clear that Britain rather than the United States held the key to Zionist planning in Palestine. President Woodrow Wilson, Brandeis's anchor in American politics, had lost his control of affairs, and the country was in full retreat from foreign involvements. More clearly than ever, the Zionists had to rely on Britain, and this meant that Weizmann would have to be leader of the WZO.

Brandeis responded by outlining a detailed plan of separate action for American Zionists, the so-called Zeeland Memorandum, on his return voyage from London on the SS *Zeeland*. In his last few weeks in London he had already tightened the reins of American generosity and made it clear that the Americans themselves, not the world leadership, would ultimately determine how money they made available was to be used. Only the desperate pleas of Julius Simon, who was close to the Americans, induced them to supply the sums needed to maintain the activities of the WZO executive for the immediate future.[64] Brandeis's Zeeland Memorandum established with clear, lawyerlike precision the limits and restraints he proposed the ZOA observe in funding its Palestine and Zionist activities.

Brandeis began his memorandum with a survey of the current situation and needs of the Jewish colonization project in Palestine now that Samuel's civil administration had provided a satisfactory political base for constructive work. Brandeis classified the functions to be undertaken according to the funding arrangements appropriate to the institutions that would perform them, using the definitions current among Zionists planners: "Investments" included activities of the Palestine government and Zionist banking institutions, to be funded by bonded indebtedness, with fixed interest charges; "Quasi Investments" included Zionist land syndicates like the American Zion Commonwealth, public utility corporations, housing developments, and "certain agricultural undertakings," to be funded by the sale of company shares; and "Gifts" were to be collected for specified purposes and agencies like the American Zionist Medical Unit, applied scientific research institutes, afforestation, "Universities, Libraries, Museums and the like," the Jewish National Fund, and "Current Needs, limited in extent." Immigrants were not to be subsidized until after arrival, unless by the Joint Distribution Committee; and the organizational expenses of the WZO and ZOA were to be covered entirely by membership dues, with no diversion of contributions to administrative expense unless expressly stipulated "in the prospectus in advance of any collection." It must always be remembered, Brandeis warned in closing, "that our plans should be such as to elicit the full cooperation of all Jews, those who do not want to build up the Zionist Organization, but who do want to share with the Zionist Organization in the upbuilding of Palestine."[65]

These proposals had serious implications for the reorganization of both the WZO and the ZOA. Brandeis referred briefly to the former in saying that the Americans should control the use of their own funds unless and until "such an improvement in administration by the World Organization . . . be effected, that such action may not be necessary."[66] The WZO executive was to be kept on a short leash by the ZOA, and the Keren Hayesod in particular, it was made clear, could expect little cooperation from the Americans. This policy was enough to provoke the beginnings of a rebellion in the ZOA. An opposition, largely of veteran Zionists predating Brandeis's leadership, was formed in August 1920. These Zionists immediately contacted Weizmann and proposed that he establish his own Keren Hayesod bureau in New York with their help. Weizmann, declared Louis Robison on behalf of the rebels, must act immediately:

> We are convinced that only with help from your side shall we be able to get compensation for the lack of support of the "American Group," but you should be prepared to come here and to open the [Keren Hayesod] Bureau *under all circumstances*. Your action must be taken promptly. . . .
>
> [Louis] Lipsky, who knows the Organization comprehensively, assures me that the organizers, the workers, the officers of Districts, etc. may be relied upon to resist effectively any attempt to break the internationality of the movement. . . .
>
> The Organization would rather lose the value of the influence of prominent men than to go counter to what they regard as the fundamental principle of Zionist action.[67]

Brandeis's plans for reorganizing the ZOA itself, only hinted at in the Zeeland Memorandum, angered the opposition further. The brief remarks that "we are no longer a propaganda movement" and must seek new members "who do not want to build up the Zionist Organization"[68] were soon fleshed out in proposals to economize by reducing or eliminating the movement's publications (especially in Yiddish) and educational departments. This retrenchment, of course, involved dismissing veteran officers and workers, especially those with Downtown backgrounds. The morale of the staff and the movement at large, already depressed by loss of membership and fund-raising difficulties in the postwar recession, was seriously affected. An embittered opposition to the Brandeis circle began to gather force.[69] Yet for the time being, Weizmann, who was preoccupied with other problems, felt that the rebels probably lacked the strength necessary to win a direct confrontation. He decided to be cautious. He quietly encouraged—even discretely suggested—how to handle the opposition to Brandeis while sidestepping any decision that would irrevocably sever relations with the Brandeis group.[70]

The struggle began in the United States at the first meeting of the ZOA executive after the London *Jahreskonferenz*, on September 29–30, 1920.[71] Four members of the opposition, led by the young Emanuel Neumann and the Hebrew writer Reuben Brainin, tried to force a resolution requiring the ZOA to seek representation in the WZO executive. In the debate, others, notably including Lipsky, severely criticized the Americans' tactics at London and thereafter.[72] But to pass the proposed resolution, in view of Brandeis's earlier warnings, would have meant to invite his public separation from the movement. With Lipsky and others abstaining, the resolution failed. This failure left Lipsky "in a foolish position," as DeHaas reported to Brandeis with satisfaction, but the situation was far from "over," he believed; it was "merely suspended." The leaders would have to "seriously consider the creation of an administration group and no quarter to the opposition."[73]

The opposition, for its part, found some cause for satisfaction in another resolution it had carried through. This, as Robison reported to Weizmann, "made the National Executive Committee go on record that the American Organization is part of the International Organization, and that the American Organization will not start any private undertakings in Palestine as of and by itself." Except for a small, more radical group, members of the opposition had been unwilling to provoke Brandeis's resignation as honorary president of the WZO at the time, but they suggested the possibility, even the desirability, of ousting Brandeis at the November 1920 convention of the ZOA.[74]

In spite of its belligerent tone, the American opposition was not really ready to challenge the Brandeis leadership unless and until Weizmann himself came to the United States to lend the support of his prestige. Throughout the fall and early winter months of 1920–21, Weizmann's American supporters pressured him to make the journey. "There is not going to be any split or any separate undertaking of work in Palestine by the American Organization," wrote Abraham Tulin, "provided the International Organization takes hold and leads. . . . If you organize the Keren Hayesod carefully on a basis which will appeal to the American Jews, they will, I am sure, respond generously to your demands. Your presence here should prove the decisive factor in that regard. . . . It will be a very great pleasure to assist you in what I believe will be a veritable conquest of America."[75] Weizmann received similar strong encouragement from friends on the Continent as well, particularly from the German Zionist Federation.[76]

But other preoccupations delayed Weizmann's projected visit to the United States. During the fall of 1920 he was either in Europe, consulting with Zionists, or in London vainly seeking a basis for cooperation with non-Zionists in economic projects for Palestine. During the first few weeks of 1921 Weizmann was again in Palestine building bridges to the leaders of the postwar immigrant community and appreciating anew the dedication of the young workers. Likewise, he spent much time repairing his relations with the veteran Eastern European Zionists active in Palestine, taking issue with the harsh criticisms of their work by de Lieme, Simon, and Szold of the Reorganization Commission. Weizmann was busy with the organization of the Keren Hayesod office in London and brought in Jabotinsky, who had been released from prison in early summer 1920, to work with him on this project as well as to assist in the WZO executive. In the midst of all these activities, Weizmann also had to deal with the restructuring of the executive after Simon and de Lieme resigned on January 21, 1921. Not least important was the fact that during the last months of 1920 the United States was experiencing

a short-lived, but critical financial depression, prompting some of Weizmann's supporters to advise postponement of his trip to the spring when
economic conditions might assure greater success for Zionist fund-
raising.[77] Finally, Weizmann knew very well that he would not be welcomed by the official leadership of the ZOA at this time. On October 18,
1920, Julian Mack cabled to ask Weizmann to postpone his trip to the
United States until after the ZOA convention at the end of November.[78]
Since he himself was unsure whether the time was ripe "to conquer
America," Weizmann gladly acquiesced,[79] but he realized that Mack's
"request" was merely a delaying tactic and that even after the Buffalo
convention he would not be welcomed with open arms.[80]

During this period the Brandeis leadership in the United States enforced its increasingly stern authority on the local recalcitrants. The ZOA
Annual Convention, meeting in Buffalo at the end of November 1920,
rejected proposals to support the Keren Hayesod and adopted instead
an ironclad division between funds for various income-bearing investment and construction projects based on business principles on the one
hand and, on the other, gift funds for education, health, and immigrant
aid. The Keren Hayesod was to be limited to such eleemosynary functions. The local educational and publications activities of the ZOA itself
were, in addition, to be sharply curtailed.[81] In short, the ZOA was in a
state of disrepair. The defeated opposition nursed its growing anger in
frustration, awaiting action from Weizmann.[82]

Events had a force of their own. Conditions in the United States were
not ripe. On the eve of his trip to Palestine with the Monds, Weizmann
wrote to his wife: "I won't be going to America. I'm utterly tired of
them. They've ruined the Movement."[83] His outburst did not mean,
however, that he was content to let matters rest; he simply needed to
release the anger and frustration that had built up since the London
Jahreskonferenz. In the wake of the Buffalo convention's decisions, Weizmann had concluded that there was no escape but to confront the Brandeis group.

Weizmann often entered ideological battles with a written statement
that mixed personal and institutional considerations, and this decisive
break with the ZOA leadership was initiated in this way. Early in January 1921, as he was about to board ship for Palestine and still feeling
exhilarated from his *tour de force* in Holland, he wrote to the executive
of the Zionist Organization of America. As he had done on other crucial
occasions, including his letter to Theodor Herzl in May 1903, Weizmann
had Berthold Feiwel, his friend and collaborator since their student years
on the Continent, write the first draft. In it Weizmann reviewed events
since the London *Jahreskonferenz*, the deep-seated dissatisfaction that ensued in its wake, and the destructive and uncooperative role played in
all these developments by the American delegation. Weizmann pointed
to the resolutions passed at the Buffalo convention, which clearly assigned the Keren Hayesod an inferior status, as proof of the intention of

the Americans to sever their connections with the WZO. While appreciating the necessity for economic efficiency in the movement, Weizmann could not agree to the suppression of political, social, and cultural aspirations:

Zionism cannot be converted merely into a development company. . . . The orientation of American Zionism has become purely economic. . . . Your complete ignoring of the motive of sacrifice at this momentous period, your belittlement of the Keren Hayesod by turning it into a fund of contributions, diminishing its importance, has killed the divine spark with which the idea was formed. . . . Do you expect the President of the Zionist Organization to act as promoter of private companies? . . . If I were to deliver addresses on general Zionist matters without touching upon the burning questions of the day, it would simply make my visit [to America] appear ridiculous. . . . The personal question has been merged into a general question to such an extent that I only saw one remedy, that of summoning a meeting of the Actions Committee [for mid-February 1921], so that it might find a way out.[84]

The proposed GAC meeting, as it happened, had to be postponed, but while Weizmann labored in Palestine the Americans were weighing a response to his challenge. Julian Mack called Weizmann's letter "astounding," indicating "there is almost no hope for a successful outcome from the proposed conference. It is one long jeremiad against the leaders of the American Organization. . . . We have got to prepare for an out and out fight, not as regards the World Organization, but leadership in America."[85] On February 16, 1921, after receiving the appropriate approval from Louis Brandeis,[86] Mack responded to Weizmann, defending the position of the American organization. He ended his letter with an invitation to Weizmann "to come to us to confer," trusting that Weizmann would "recognize the correctness of the [American] views."[87] Stephen Wise was much more direct as to how Weizmann should be treated upon arrival in the United States: "We must face the issue frankly from beginning to end. Pleasant social relationships must not be suffered to be a substitute for a definite understanding. If Weizmann will mend his ways . . . we can and must support him, but only as long as he makes it possible for us to do so."[88]

To prepare themselves for the encounter with Weizmann,[89] the American leaders wrote a detailed position paper that was presented to the ZOA executive on March 19–20, 1921. Titled "Summary of the Position of the Zionist Organization of America in Conference with Dr. Weizmann and Associates," it outlined their views concerning principles and policies, reorganization, fund-raising, and "economic instrumentalities."[90] In hindsight the document did not have much impact, but it gives a good indication of the state of mind of the Brandeis group. Adopted by less than half of the members of the ZOA executive, the document was charged by its opponents as smacking of secession or at least completely isolating the ZOA from the WZO.[91]

While the position paper was being presented as official ZOA policy, Weizmann was on board the SS *Rotterdam*. With him were Vera, Menahem Ussishkin, Shmarya Levin, Ben-Zion Mossinson, the director of the Herzliyah Gymnasium, and Leonard Stein, who served as secretary of the delegation. With the assistance of Kurt Blumenfeld, the secretary of the German Zionist Federation, Weizmann managed to persuade no less a personage than Albert Einstein (who brought his wife) to join the official delegation.[92] The Americans clearly realized what impact the appearance of the famous scientist would make and tried their best to prevent his coming.[93] As the ship approached New York harbor, Weizmann received cables from the Brandeis group, as well as from their opponents, indicating the mounting struggle between them.[94] For the time being he asked his supporters to refrain from an open conflict.[95] But despite Mack's and Weizmann's efforts to seek a compromise, the gage of battle was thrown down. By the time Weizmann arrived, there were implacable opponents on each side, including Brandeis himself, who were intent on forcing the issue to a conclusion.

Weizmann arrived in New York on Saturday, April 2, 1921, to an extraordinary public welcome:

> We intended, of course, to proceed straight to our hotel, settle down, and begin planning our work. We had reckoned—literally—without our host, which was, or seemed to be, the whole of New York Jewry. Long before the afternoon ended, delegations began to assemble on the quay and even on the docks. Pious Jews in their thousands came on foot all the way from Brooklyn and the Bronx to welcome us. Then the cars arrived, all of them beflagged. . . . By the time we reached the gangway the area about the quays was a pandemonium of people, cars and mounted police. The car which we had thought would transport us quickly and quietly to our hotel fell at the end of an enormous procession which wound its way through the entire Jewish section of New York. We reached the Commodore at about eleven-thirty, tired, hungry, thirsty and completely dazed. The spacious hall of the hotel was packed with another enthusiastic throng; we had to listen to several speeches of welcome, and I remember making some sort of reply. It was long after midnight when we found our rooms.[96]

This was Weizmann's first encounter with the masses of American Jewry and the first time he had ever been received anywhere with the kind of enthusiasm that, in Zionist annals, had been previously accorded only to Herzl. As he entered the negotiations with Julian Mack, Weizmann felt assured of broad-based support, a fact that did not escape his interlocutors.[97] Weizmann had barely two days of rest at the luxurious Commodore, a hotel on Lexington Avenue that became one of his favorites in New York, before his talks with Julian Mack.

A series of formal and informal discussions began on April 4 and ended on April 9. Weizmann was accompanied by Levin, Mossinson, Ussishkin, and Stein. The American group, headed by Mack, included at various times Wise, DeHaas, Frankfurter, and Szold. Mack wished to discuss the position papers, which Weizmann dismissed out of hand, stating that he had come to the United States to set up the Keren Hayesod on the basis of the London *Jahreskonferenz's* resolutions, not of the ZOA's decisions in Buffalo. Beyond this, the two discussed a range of other questions concerning management of funds, Zionist work in the Diaspora *(Gegenwartsarbeit)*, and reorganization of work in Palestine and London.[98] The confrontations were also probing attempts to determine the range of possible compromise. Neither Weizmann nor Mack budged on the cardinal issues, but both seemed determined to find a peaceful resolution.

At the meeting of the ZOA executive on April 9–10, 1921, it was clear that discussions preceding it had left an impact on the American group. Felix Frankfurter offered a compromise. Since the London *Jahreskonferenz* had stipulated that the Keren Hayesod was to be established in the various countries according to local conditions, he suggested, on the basis of the Buffalo resolution, the establishment in the United States of "a Keren Hayesod Donation Fund . . . to be applied exclusively in Palestine by the WZO, through such instrumentalities as may be agreed upon" between the president of the WZO and the president of the ZOA. Despite the objections of the opposition,[99] the ZOA executive passed Frankfurter's proposal by a vote of 23–14. At the same time the executive also agreed to Weizmann's demand to appoint two or more American members to the WZO executive, thus, at least symbolically, indicating the end of American isolation from the parent body.[100] Weizmann and the opposition group rejected Frankfurter's compromise formula and publicly announced their intention to establish the Keren Hayesod in the United States. Attempts by moderates in both groups to bridge the gap, despite intensive negotiations lasting several days, proved unsuccessful.[101] Stiffening Weizmann's resolve were the hard-line approach of Ussishkin and Levin and the continued public adulation and support Weizmann received. On April 12, during a reception for Weizmann and the members of his delegation, some twenty thousand men and women turned the Sixty-ninth Regiment Armory into a near-riot. According to a clearly partisan report: "Shouting, waving Jewish and American flags, and singing the songs of their people, they welcomed Dr. Chaim Weizmann. . . . Outside the Armory, a crowd at least twice as great . . . stormed the police lines. . . . More than eight hundred Jewish organizations, united in this demonstration. . . . It was the first time in New York's Jewish history, that so many organizations had come together for one purpose."[102]

The moderates in Weizmann's camp—Abraham Tulin, Leonard Stein, and Bernard Rosenblatt—were, nevertheless, also effective.[103] On the evening of April 16, Weizmann seems to have agreed to the proposal that the American Keren Hayesod be a "Donation Fund." But the following morning, upon receiving a more detailed draft of the proposal, he informed Julian Mack that he was rejecting it. Weizmann appears to have given in to ultimatums presented to him by those in his room on April 17. Shmarya Levin, Menahem Ussishkin, and Ben-Zion Mossinson threatened to leave on the next available boat. Louis Lipsky and Emanuel Neumann, as well as others in the American opposition group, warned that they would break Weizmann politically in the United States. They were "not against this agreement only but against all agreements." Eventually Weizmann relented. According to the report, Weizmann was presented by the group with a proclamation establishing the Keren Hayesod in the United States and asked to sign it. "He went into the next room and read the manifesto and he signed it."[104]

The manifesto[105] was immediately circulated and rejected the same day in a public statement by Julian Mack, who blamed the president of the WZO for abruptly breaking the talks.[106] The following day Weizmann went to Washington to confer with Brandeis. The justice met him with icy coldness, making it a particularly humiliating experience for Weizmann. Brandeis rejected Weizmann's attempts to discuss the break in negotiations by rudely turning to a discussion of the weather. Later Brandeis reported the encounter with obvious glee.[107] Brandeis and Weizmann did not meet again until 1927.

The conflict became an increasingly bitter public debate in which the Yiddish newspapers took a prominent part.[108] For the next six weeks Weizmann was engaged in a whirlwind tour of the United States and Canada. He tried to mobilize Zionists in the various districts whose vote would count at the decisive clash at the ZOA convention announced for Cleveland on June 5, 1921. Traveling by train, at a grueling pace and over hundreds of miles, Weizmann also attempted to raise significant funds for the projected $75 million Keren Hayesod Fund.[109] The fund was presided over by Samuel Untermyer, the senior member of the law firm of Guggenheimer, Untermyer and [Louis] Marshall.[110] Fund-raising was an emotional as well as physical strain. Some months earlier, while trying to raise money in Paris, Weizmann wrote to Vera that it would be nice if "there would be less need to run after the wealthy Jews. I'm already sick and tired of them. It's difficult to explain, but there's something humiliating about it. Whenever some little Jew decides he's a millionaire, he expects to be flattered, honored—and what he gives in return isn't money but *eytzes* [advice]."[111] During his sojourn in the United States and Canada, Weizmann must have received a good deal of advice, because his fund-raising efforts did not match his expectations.

In the meantime all attempts to compromise only seemed to fuel the already charged atmosphere.[112] Wise wrote in frustration after one such meeting with Weizmann that he found neither "moderation nor reason in [Weizmann], and his colleagues. . . . All of them feel . . . [that] the break is of no importance."[113] For his part, Brandeis had made up his mind that as far as the ZOA's relation to the WZO was concerned, "we must stand as the Rock of Gibraltar." He was no less firm in his view of Weizmann: "It should be borne in mind that any conference in which

W[eizmann] takes part whatever the purpose or the conditions and attending circumstances—is in view of his character dangerous."[114] Though for some time after April 17 Weizmann still considered a rapprochement with the Brandeis group possible, particularly with Julian Mack, the heated debates and insults hurled back and forth pushed him into an increasingly antagonistic and bitter attitude.

During a nine-hour debate with Julian Mack and Felix Frankfurter on May 19, 1921,[115] Weizmann finally challenged the Harvard law professor: "Your Zionism is not my Zionism. Your Jewishness is not my Jewishness. Your education is not my education. Your point of view is not my point of view, but I am prepared to work with everybody. But I shall not be led by you until the time that the [Zionist] Congress has placed you in this terrible responsibility in which it has placed me, and until then I demand from you all credit. That is all."[116] Weizmann pointed to the inability of the American Zionist leadership to raise large sums of money for the Palestine Restoration Fund and to the precipitous drop in membership—from some 150,000 in 1918 to 17,000 in mid-1921[117]—as evidence that the Brandeis group had lost the confidence of the Jewish masses:

B[randeis] is an American first and a Zionist only a few minutes in the day, and therefore has lost touch with Jewry. . . . His criticism is sterile. . . . In their [the Brandeis group's] arguments against the K[eren] H[ayesod] they stated that American money must not go into a country under a British Mandate. Such arguments make an impression on a few Jewish cowards who pose as 110% Yankees, but not on the Jewish people. . . .

The American Zionist leaders are also frightened of [Henry] Ford and his [antisemitic] propaganda and would therefore like to hide their Jewish lights behind a bushel. In short, all those people are at best pro-Palestinians, philo-Zionists, "Zionists for others" but not for themselves. . . . We are winning here on the whole line, although we are fighting a heavy battle. We are fighting for the integrity of the Z[ionist] O[rganization] and for a Jewish policy.[118]

The final clash between the Brandeis-led ZOA leadership and Weizmann and his supporters came at the ZOA Annual Convention in Cleveland, June 5–8, 1921.[119] The debates reflected the high tension of the past two months. Catcalls as well as applause punctuated long speeches reviewing the events that had led to division.[120] In the end Weizmann emerged the clear victor. Julian Mack was defeated, and a Weizmann supporter, Judge Henry J. Dannenbaum of Texas, was elected chairman of the convention by a vote of 139–75. Stephen Wise's resolution of support for the departing administration, moreover, was countered by a resolution proposed by Emanuel Neumann that carried 153–71.[121]

On June 6, 1921, the second day of the convention, following the vote of no-confidence in his administration, Mack announced the resignation of the entire Brandeis-Mack group from all their posts in the ZOA and

WZO.[122] On June 19, 1921, Brandeis handed his resignation as honorary president to the executive of the WZO.[123] Weizmann supporters totally controlled the field and voted Louis Lipsky into a newly created office, general secretary of the ZOA. The Brandeis faction regrouped quickly on June 10 in Pittsburgh, where it established a rival fund called Palestine Development Associates.[124] During the last two days of the Cleveland convention the delegates passed resolutions affirming the continued operation of the American Keren Hayesod along Weizmann's lines. Weizmann's hopes of raising millions of dollars for the fund were disappointed, though the results were far from negligible. Between April 17 and November 30, 1921, contributions totaling $743,015 were raised for the Keren Hayesod in the United States, of which $588,112 were remitted to London.[125] In Canada, Weizmann was able to raise only $55,000.[126]

Weizmann had keenly felt his previous defeat at the hands of Brandeis in August 1919 and subsequent humiliations. The Cleveland victory, then, proved doubly gratifying. "I went there," Weizmann told the delegates at the Twelfth Zionist Congress, "to discover this Jewish community. It was the journey of a Jewish Columbus who had to rediscover Jewish America, for Jewish America had been hidden from us."[127] And, as Abraham Tulin had predicted, Weizmann's journey was a "veritable conquest of America." But Weizmann's leadership was confirmed and his ego gratified at a high price for the ZOA, which was much diminished in stature and prestige, leaving some of the most able American Zionists bitter and disillusioned. As Stephen Wise put it:

In addition to withdrawing from all relationship to the Organization we are to have nothing to do with the World Organization or with the Congress. . . . This is not bitterness or vindictiveness. The administration has been denied a vote of confidence. The others must now accept responsibility. . . . Let Weizmann explain to the Europeans why Brandeis, Mack, Fels, Frankfurter, Wise, deHaas, et al. are not, as they would have been, at the Congress. Our absence will be significant and Weizmann will be called to account. . . .
     The Convention was sad. We were not really beaten because it was not a convention of our own Organization. . . . I was troubled by the moral obtuseness of the delegates. . . . I said to Weizmann that we had not waited two thousand years in order to Pinskerize Palestine. . . . During our [Wise and Frankfurter] addresses, Weizmann sat white with suppressed rage, but he and his gang heard the truth which . . . may ultimately serve their souls.[128]

Weizmann left New York on June 24 and arrived in London on July 4. His ten days on board the SS *Celtic* proved to be his only rest from the exhausting American trip. Four days after he arrived in London he left for Prague to consult with the local Zionist activists on preparations for the Twelfth Zionist Congress, scheduled for Carlsbad in September. When he returned to London on July 14, he was immediately plunged into yet another crisis facing the WZO following events in Palestine in early 1921.

These developments took the Zionists as well as the British by surprise. Within days of his arrival in Palestine in June 1920, Herbert Samuel wrote Weizmann, "The country is so quiet that you could hear a pin drop."[129] A week later, following his first public address, Samuel reported to Lord Curzon, "The Jewish population is very satisfied; while the Moslems, who had expected the declaration of a much more drastic policy, are relieved and reassured. . . . There is every reason to believe that the pronouncement has greatly relaxed the tension which has existed for so long."[130] Indeed, as noted, during the early months of Samuel's administration the Zionists, and Weizmann in particular, were pleased with Samuel's conduct.[131] During his brief sojourn in Palestine in January 1921, Weizmann was confirmed in his position that, from a Zionist point of view, Samuels had been the right choice for high commissioner. On September 1, 1920, Samuel greatly relaxed the rules for immigration, authorizing an immigration schedule of 16,500 for the first year, a figure much higher than Weizmann and other members of the Zionist executive felt they could absorb in Palestine.[132] A month later land transactions could again be officially recorded.[133]

Indeed, with Weizmann's full support and encouragement, the Zionists immediately proceeded to purchase most of the land in the fertile valley of Emek Jezreel, and Weizmann was pushing hard to purchase the Jiftlik lands in the Beisan valley as well as large tracts in the Negev.[134] Sir Herbert initiated a number of beneficial reforms in banking, health, and education. He also strongly supported Pinhas Rutenberg's hydroelectric project and undertook to help secure the kinds of northern border adjustments that would permit Rutenberg use of the Litani and Jordan headwaters.[135] Though Samuel's sympathy for the Arabs was well known, his wish to be evenhanded in treating all segments of the population[136] was seen by all observers as the kind of attitude any fair-minded governor of the country ought to have.[137] All in all, it appeared to the Zionists that this able administrator and self-declared Zionist was working steadily toward the establishment of a Jewish national home in Palestine.

Yet the unsettled regional political situation could not but affect events in Palestine as well, gradually eroding the Zionist-Samuel honeymoon. In August 1920, the Emir Feisal, deposed from his throne by the French on July 27, sought refuge in Palestine and was received by Samuel with all due honors. The French action created a power vacuum in Transjordan, prompting Samuel to ask Curzon if the government would "authorize occupation [of Transjordan] if there is spontaneous formal and public demand from heads of all tribes and districts concerned."[138] Curzon instructed the high commissioner to send just one or two officers to investigate the situation and demonstrate British presence without any commitment or intention to annex Transjordan within the borders of Palestine.[139] But Samuel, in an uncharacteristically bold move, grossly, and quite intentionally, misinterpreted his instructions and on August 20, 1921, appeared with a large retinue at the city of Es Salt, where he delivered an address to a crowd of some six hundred.[140]

Though chastised by Curzon, Samuel had—to a certain extent—accomplished his goal, and for the time being the area remained loosely under his watchful eye. His aim of keeping Transjordan within the framework of the Zionist mandate eluded him in the long run. After the transfer on January 1, 1921, of the Middle East mandated territories (Mesopotamia, Palestine, and Transjordan) from the Foreign Office to the Colonial Office, administered by Winston Churchill, political changes came quickly. At the Cairo Conference of March 1921,[141] with Churchill presiding, it was agreed that Feisal's brother, Abdullah, would become the ruler of Transjordan with the title of emir.[142]

Weizmann first learned of Samuel's speech at Es Salt from reports in the *Times* of August 25, 1921,[143] and was naturally disturbed.[144] Throughout 1920 and the early months of 1921 the Zionists were unable to receive concrete information from the Foreign Office as to what plans had been made for the disposal of this territory. When it became clear that the main purpose of Churchill's visit to the Middle East in March 1921 was to consider the future of Transjordan, Weizmann wrote the colonial secretary a detailed letter setting out the Zionist claims for inclusion of Transjordan within the area of the Jewish national home.[145] Even after the installment of Abdullah as ruler of Transjordan, the Zionists, encouraged by Samuel, hoped that Jewish settlement would not be excluded from this territory.

But in mid-1922 the temporary arrangement made in the spring of 1921 was formalized, and the boundary line was published on September 1, 1922, in the *Official Gazette*.[146] For the moment the Zionists were more concerned with the northern border, which directly affected Jewish settlements and water rights, but the question of the eastern border would return to haunt Zionist politics from the mid-1920s on. At the time, however, the Zionists were encouraged by Churchill's tough declaration to the Arab representatives who came to see him in Jerusalem on March 28, 1921: that British policy in Palestine based on the Balfour Declaration, was "manifestly right."[147]

If the delimitation of the eastern border only reminded the Zionists that the political settlement of the emerging Jewish national home was far from stable, they were much more rudely jolted by events in the spring of 1921. Signs of trouble had already surfaced in the fall, and Harry Sacher, in a generally pessimistic and critical letter, warned Weizmann of a great deal of unrest among the Palestinian Arabs.[148] These signs became manifest when the Third Arab Congress met in Haifa in mid-December 1920. The thirty-seven delegates adopted strong anti-

Reception held by Sir Herbert and Lady Samuel at Government House for Colonial Secretary Winston Churchill, 1921. First row, from left: Lady Samuel, Emir Abdullah, Sir Herbert Samuel, Winston Churchill, Clementine Churchill. Second row, from left: unidentified, Edwin Samuel, James de Rothschild, Ronald Storrs (profile), Nancy Samuel, Geoffrey Samuel. Courtesy: Weizmann Archives

Zionist resolutions, which they forwarded to London and the League of Nations.[149] But on the whole, the Zionists, though fully aware of these events, were not overly concerned. If anything, they were reassured by Samuel's active interest in the Yishuv and Winston Churchill's unequivocal statement in March. Similarly, though critical of Samuel's appointment in March 1921 of Hajj Amin al-Husseini as mufti of Jerusalem, for he was a rabid anti-Zionist and antisemite who had played an active role in the April 1920 riots, few Zionists expected this appointment to have immediate implications for Arab-Jewish relations.

Weizmann was shaken by the nationalist-motivated Arab riots of April 1920 and more attuned afterward to the political demands of the Palestinian Arabs, but he outlined a purely economic and social program in July 1920 that, he thought, would help bridge the chasm between Zionists and Arabs. In his opening statement before the London *Jahreskonferenz* he had stated:

In all our work of colonization in . . . Palestine a guiding principle must be to seek and win the goodwill of the Arabs. . . . We must be on the best terms with the Arabs in Palestine, because that is the condition of a healthy society of our own and of good relations with the Arab world outside Palestine. If the Arabs were to be mere hewers of wood and drawers of water, a kind of inferior element in the country, then the whole of our economic and social organism would run the danger of being poisoned. We must labor to raise them to our own level, and to assist them to progress as we progress. . . . I look to a policy of friendly economic cooperation as the key to harmony and reconciliation [for] Jew and Arab both inside Palestine and outside its frontiers. . . . [We desire] social justice, not vested interests. It is difficult to promise that every Arab without exception will see the groundlessness of his fears with regard to us, but I am convinced that along the lines suggested we can secure the friendship of all Arabs who really desire the welfare of the Arab people.[150]

This lofty, somewhat condescending vision, was cruelly shattered by the Arab riots in the spring of 1921. They began in Jaffa on May 1, 1921, and quickly spread to other parts of Palestine. By the time they ended, on May 7, there were 47 Jews dead and 146 wounded at the hands of Arab rioters, and 48 Arabs dead and 73 wounded, mostly at the hands of the British, who were restoring order.[151] If this were not bad enough, the Zionists were shocked by the British reaction.[152] The Arab marauders brought to trial received light sentences, and Samuel's immediate reaction was to appoint a commission to investigate the riots, headed by Sir Thomas Haycraft, chief justice of Palestine, rather than publicly to condemn them.[153] Worse yet, on May 14, Sir Herbert announced a temporary suspension of Jewish immigration, a declaration that was greeted with approval by the Arab population and with deep dismay by the Zionists.

Weizmann, who was notified of these events while touring Canada, was upset by the riots but at first cautious in reacting to the decrees of the high commissioner.[154] He remained steadfast in his support of Samuel even after the latter's speech on June 3, 1921, at a ceremony to mark the king's birthday, which was no less than an attempt to reinterpret the meaning of the Balfour Declaration.[155] Among other things, Sir Herbert declared that the Balfour Declaration meant

that the Jews, a people who are scattered throughout the world but whose hearts are always turned to Palestine, would be enabled to found here their home, and that some among them, within the limits that are fixed by the numbers and interests of the present population should come to Palestine in order to help by their resources and efforts to develop the country to the advantage of all its inhabitants. If any measures are needed to convince the Moslem and Christian population that these principles will be observed in practice and that their rights are really safe, such measures will be taken. For the British Government, the trustee under the Mandate for the happiness of the people of Palestine, would never impose upon them a policy which that people had reason to think was contrary to their religious, their political and their economic interests.[156]

It is difficult to understand how, following this major public shift in the attitude of the high commissioner toward the Zionist enterprise, Weizmann could have cabled: "Deeply appreciate your position. Please rely on my cooperation. Have restrained sentiment here. Endeavoring to do so [in] Palestine. Shall act similarly [in] London."[157] As early as March 1920, Weizmann heard reports that Samuel was "weak, frightened and trembling" when dealing with the Arabs.[158] Possibly because Weizmann seemed to accept this judgment, he wished to consider the best option for dealing with the high commissioner. For a while he contemplated a move to replace Samuel with General George Macdonogh though it is not clear why he felt he had enough clout to do so. In any case, Weizmann could not give the matter sufficient attention while embroiled in the events surrounding the Cleveland Annual Convention. Only after he returned to London in mid-July 1921 did he tackle the issue directly and forthrightly in a private letter to Herbert Samuel, which he shared with his colleagues as well.

The immediate impetus to Weizmann's letter of July 19, 1921, was one from Samuel dated July 1, in which he urged Weizmann to enter into negotiations with a delegation of Arab nationalists headed by Musa Kazem Pasha al-Husseini, the former mayor of Jerusalem, which traveled to London in July 1921.[159] The Palestine Arab delegation had been elected in late May 1921 in Jerusalem, at the Fourth Arab Congress.[160] Samuel was convinced that the delegates wished to arrive at an understanding with the British government, though they realized that this was possible only on condition that the Balfour Declaration not be abrogated. Samuel also hinted at his suggestion, alluded to in his speech on the king's birthday, of constituting an elected assembly. Weizmann's reply dealt with both matters, which he saw as related to the shifting attitude of the British administration:

> I would only like to remind you of a statement which was made by me during my last visit to Palestine, when I said that the Hill [the high commissioner who resided on Mount Scopus] is benevolently neutral to us but that the Vale [the British administration] has not changed and that the same old machine which existed under Bols [chief administrator of the Occupied Enemy Territory Administration] continued to operate in the same old direction. . . . The causes in my humble opinion lie deeper. There has, it seems to me, been a shifting of political values, due to transient phenomena which momentarily obscure the vision of British statesmen. . . . The fact remains . . . that there is a tendency for the Balfour Declaration and the San Remo decision to be either ignored, or interpreted in a manner which may possibly give a certain amount of temporary satisfaction to the Arabs, but which destroys the political foundation on which we have been building. . . . It seems that everything in Palestinian life is now revolving round one central problem—how to satisfy "and to pacify" the Arabs. Zionism is being grad-

ually, systematically, and relentlessly "reduced"; Jewish public opinion is not reckoned with; we have ceased to exist as a political factor. . . .

You seem to attach very great importance to the conversations which may be arranged here between the Arab Delegation and the Zionist representatives. . . . I am always anxious to negotiate with Arab representatives, but in these forthcoming negotiations we are, at the outset, placed at a very great disadvantage. Why should the Arabs argue with us at all? They feel that they are in a position to enforce their will on the Government by threats of a rising or by a Jewish pogrom, and that they can extract all the "guarantees" they can possibly wish. What chance have we in these discussions?

Weizmann ended his letter with an open threat:

Unless the Palestine Administration and the Government here are prepared to give us the necessary guarantees that we can go on with our work in Palestine, I don't see how I can take upon myself the crushing burden of conducting Zionist affairs, of raising the necessary funds, and of continuing to assume responsibility before the Jewish masses who have trusted me hitherto.

We are all anxious to help you in your difficult task, but we must be given a fair chance.[161]

In a long, firm letter Samuel rejected Weizmann's accusations suggesting a lack of British sympathy for the Zionist cause. He did insist that the Zionists must come to terms with the reality of Arab nationalism. He urged Weizmann to consider the conflict from the Arab perspective and to realize that Palestinian Arabs viewed Zionism as a real and immediate danger to their political and economic welfare. He countered Weizmann's threat with a veiled warning of his own: "The Zionist policy is not based on such stable foundations in Great Britain that it can afford to see those foundations shaken."[162]

Samuel's statement did not seem to square with Weizmann's personal experience, at least not at that moment. Weizmann could still rely on the strong support of key members in the British government. Only a few months earlier Balfour had written to Lloyd George, "Whether Zionism be good or bad (and, as you know, I think it good), we are now committed to it, and failure to make it a success will be a failure for us."[163] On more than one occasion Weizmann turned to Balfour for help in breaking through the layers of government bureaucracy;[164] invariably Balfour obliged and this time was no exception. At Weizmann's request,[165] Arthur Balfour convened a small conference at his house, on July 22, 1921, at which were present, in addition to the host, the prime minister, Lloyd George; the colonial secretary, Winston Churchill; the secretary of the government, Sir Maurice Hankey; and Edward Russell of the Colonial Office.

Weizmann attacked Samuel's speech of June 3 as an abrogation of the Balfour Declaration. In response, both Balfour and Lloyd George stated that "by the Declaration they always meant an eventual Jewish State." Weizmann then spoke of the lack of security of the Jewish population and informed them that the Jews were "gun-running," shipping guns and ammunition illegally into Palestine. He must have been quite astounded to find out that the three ministers present sanctioned this activity, though Churchill asked that Weizmann not speak of it publicly.[166] They then discussed Samuel's proposal for the establishment of a representative government in Palestine. Lloyd George turned to Churchill and told him he must not allow such a thing to happen. Finally, the prime minister advised Weizmann to set aside some money "for the purpose of bribing the Arabs." Weizmann's reply was that "this was neither moral nor rational and the price was very heavy." Weizmann, the probable author of this report, could record with satisfaction "that the British government remained favorable to Zionism and the Balfour Declaration, in spite of Arab opposition" and in spite of Samuel's more cautious approach.[167]

Clearly, few people in England could have brought about a meeting of this sort at which, in the privacy of the home of one of the elder statesmen of the empire, a naturalized citizen criticized the performance of His Majesty's high commissioner. Far from being reprimanded for presumptuousness, Weizmann was met with a chorus of assent and encouragement. Little wonder, then, that two weeks later Weizmann informed Vera that "a new spirit has recently asserted itself in the Colonial Office."[168] It must be appreciated that the meeting in Balfour's house brought to a halt the political process initiated by Herbert Samuel on June 3, 1921. Lord Curzon was not present, which made it easier to outflank Churchill, but still it was a dramatic moment that had its practical consequences at the cabinet resolutions on Palestine in August 1921. Not for a year would Samuel manage to regain the political initiative.

Despite the fact that such stalwart pro-Zionists as Richard Meinertzhagen and Eric Forbes Adam were now key officials in the Colonial Office, making Weizmann's daily business on Palestinian matters more pleasant and efficient, Weizmann was also aware that the "new spirit" was often shifty and increasingly bore anti-Zionist elements.[169] Even if for the time being the Colonial Office observed the official pro-Zionist stance, it could not control or greatly influence British public opinion. Weizmann saw that a growing number of influential British statesmen, financiers, religious personalities, and others, foremost among them such staunch anti-Zionists as Lord Sydenham and Lord Lamington, the owners of the *Morning Post*, began to pay close attention to complaints and demands by the Palestinian Arabs.[170] They welcomed the Palestine Arab delegation that arrived in London in August 1921 with open arms and much fanfare.

Initially Weizmann made light of the Palestine Arab delegation, referring to its members as "political blackmailers."[171] After their arrival, Churchill asked Weizmann to meet with the delegation. "I said," Weizmann reported to Vera, who was already in Carlsbad, "that I didn't know on what to come together or with whom to come together. I shall probably see that trash tomorrow."[172] No doubt Weizmann's contempt was intensified by the delegation's extreme and vocal anti-Zionism—fed by British advisers—and refusal to accept the Balfour Declaration.[173] Despite his brave words, Weizmann did write to Musa Kazem Pasha al-Husseini, the head of the delegation, suggesting that he meet with Nahum Sokolow, since Weizmann had to leave for Carlsbad.[174] The Palestinians did not reply, making it clear that they had come to discuss their political future with the British, not the Zionists.[175]

Discussions between the Colonial Office and the Palestine Arab delegation continued throughout the fall of 1921, but without apparent results. Herbert Samuel suggested to Churchill that one way to break the impasse was for the Zionists to declare that they had no aspirations to create in Palestine "a state in which Jews would enjoy a position of political privilege."[176] Weizmann categorically rejected this suggestion. John Shuckburgh, head of the Middle Eastern Department of the Colonial Office, prepared to create a legislative assembly and to make an official statement of policy that the prospective state would be one in which Jews would not enjoy "a position of political ascendancy, but a commonwealth built upon a democratic foundation and framed in the best interests of all sections of the population."[177] His proposals were politely but coolly received by Weizmann.[178] On November 28, 1921, Weizmann met with Churchill and suggested some modifications in the proposed statement that was to be read on the following day at a joint meeting of representatives of the Arab delegation and the Zionists. The meeting had been arranged by Churchill after much pressure was exerted on the Arabs. Churchill decided at the last moment not to attend, and the statement was not read.[179]

The meeting in the Colonial Office on November 29, 1921, was the first time official delegates of the WZO met with official representatives of the Palestinian Arabs. Shuckburgh was in the chair, flanked by other Colonial Office members, Richard Meinertzhagen, Gerard Leslie Clauson, and Eric Mills, all from the Middle Eastern Department. The Zionists, led by Weizmann, included Berthold Feiwel, Georg Halpern, Leonard Stein, and Moshe Shertok [later Sharett], then a student at the London School of Economics. The Arabs, headed by Musa Kazem Pasha al-Husseini, included Jamal Shibli, Ibrahim Shammas, and other members of the delegation.

Musa Kazem Pasha al-Husseini declared that if Weizmann was willing to interpret the Balfour Declaration in a manner satisfactory to them they would begin to negotiate with the Zionists. Shuckburgh, who was aware that the final draft of the Mandate for Palestine had been presented in August 1921, emphasized that he could hold out no hope that any future interpretation of the Balfour Declaration by the government would differ materially from the draft Mandate for Palestine. Weizmann, on the other hand, declared himself willing to enter into direct talks with the

Palestinians on the subjects of limitation of Jewish immigration and constitutional safeguards against "Jewish political ascendancy." Though his speech was conciliatory and reasonable, some of those present noted that it was delivered with an air of condescension, verging on contempt, as if to indicate that the Arab delegates were not worthy protagonists. For their part, the Arabs refused to budge and stated that they did not recognize the Balfour Declaration as a legitimate document. The meeting failed to produce agreements on any points.[180]

The inflexible stance adopted by the Arabs toward Zionism contrasted sharply with the resolution adopted by the Twelfth Zionist Congress in mid-September 1921. That resolution stated:

> That the hostile stance of part of the Arab population of Palestine, incited by unscrupulous elements, resulting in acts of bloody violence, cannot weaken our resolve to build the Jewish National Home, nor our intention to live a life of mutual consideration and respect with the Arab people and together with them transform the common homeland into a flourishing community which will assure both peoples a tranquil national development. The two great semitic nations, who were bound in the past by ties of common cultural creativity, will once again find the means, in the hour of their national reawakening, to unite for their common goal.
>
> While preserving inviolate the Balfour Declaration, the Twelfth Zionist Congress exhorts the executive to exert itself to the utmost in attempts to forge a true understanding with the Arab nation on the basis of this declaration. The Congress emphasizes that Jewish colonization will not trespass against the rights and needs of the working elements of the Arab nation.[181]

Though supporting this public declaration, Weizmann was no longer content to rely on negotiations to resolve the conflict with the Arabs peacefully. The bloody Arab riots of April 1920 and May 1921, together with the largely passive role of the British administration, propelled him to support initiatives by the Haganah to buy arms for self-defense, though to members of the British administration in London and Palestine he professed ignorance on matters dealing with arms purchases.[182] Secretly, Weizmann authorized the expenditure of Zionist funds for this purpose at Carlsbad, and he continued to support the purchase of weapons and special collections of funds in Europe and the United States for weapons.[183] Moreover, despite his pious protestations to Lloyd George in July that bribery of the Arabs "was neither moral nor rational," Weizmann authorized Chaim Margalit Kalvarisky, a Zionist agent to the Palestinian Arabs, to use Keren Hayesod funds for exactly such a purpose.[184]

The Twelfth Zionist Congress, which met in Carlsbad, Czechoslovakia, September 1–14, 1921, was attended by some 450 delegates representing 780,000 people paying the requisite *shekel*. It was an impressive affair, the first full-fledged Zionist Congress since 1913 and thus signaling a "return to normalcy" for the World Zionist Organization. Weizmann appeared before the congress confident of his achievements since 1914. His opening address, delivered in Hebrew, was brief, touching on some of his accomplishments as well as the problems still facing the WZO. At its conclusion, he received a standing ovation.[185] Throughout the proceedings of the longest congress to date, Weizmann spoke little, reserving some time at the end of the congress for a reply to some of the criticisms voiced mostly by the Palestinian delegates as well as by Jean Fischer, Nehemia de Lieme, and Julius Simon. The Brandeis group boycotted the congress, with the past administration content to send a written statement to the delegates.[186] Weizmann was aware that none of these criticisms seriously challenged his authority; his reply was calm and to the point. The traditional vote of confidence in his administration was overwhelmingly in his favor, 348–58.[187]

Weizmann was confirmed as president of the WZO; Sokolow was named chairman and president of the executive. The Zionist executive itself was divided into a Palestine Zionist executive, to succeed the Zionist Commission with its seat in Jerusalem, and the London Zionist executive, which continued to wield decisive authority. Sokolow, Jabotinsky, Richard Lichtheim, Joseph Cowen, Max Soloveitchik, and—as a special compromise on Weizmann's part—Leo Motzkin were elected to the London executive; Ussishkin, Arthur Ruppin, David Eder, Hermann Pick, Bernard Rosenblatt, and Joseph Sprinzak were elected to the Palestine executive. The London executive was complemented by a financial advisory group, composed of six members, three of whom—Feiwel, Halpern, and Naiditch—were also full-fledged members of the executive. A number of departments were transferred to Jerusalem to be headed by members of the executive: Settlement (Ruppin), Immigration (Pick), and Labor (Sprinzak). The congress passed a budget of £1,506,000 for the following financial year, an expression of faith in the ability of the Keren Hayesod to raise these funds.[188]

The Zionist Congress in Carlsbad was one of the high points in Weizmann's political career. Even Berl Katznelson, who had criticized Weizmann so sharply at the London *Jahreskonferenz*, recognized the special importance of the moment.[189] It is also interesting to point out that Weizmann's just-completed sojourn in the United States created no reverberations in Carlsbad. While it neutralized American Zionism as a factor in the WZO during the 1920s, it had little impact on the international body. The bloody battles fought in the United States and the Weizmann-Brandeis rift seemed almost detached from the concerns of the delegates, creating no ideological or factional ripples.

The months after the Twelfth Zionist Congress were marked mostly by uneasy wait for the final ratification of the Mandate for Palestine by the League of Nations Council. Internally, the Zionist executive had to adjust to the new roles and tasks set for it by the Congress. These included raising the funds necessary to implement the variety of social,

At Plymouth, prior to the Zionist delegation's departure for the United States, 1921. From left: Shlomo Ginzberg, Menahem Ussishkin, Weizmann, Israel Sieff, Vera and Benjamin Weizmann, Leonard Stein (behind Vera and Benjamin), Gershon Agronsky, Ben-Zion Mossinson. Courtesy: Weizmann Archives

economic, and political projects that the delegates had voted into existence. With the withdrawal of the Brandeis group from active participation in the WZO, it became much harder to raise these funds, a condition that would continue to plague the Zionist executive throughout the 1920s. Though in full control of the executive, Weizmann was not spared criticisms either by the European pro-Herzlian veterans such as Jean Fischer, Alexander Marmorek, and Jacobus Kann or by the progressively more powerful Polish Zionists or the Palestinian labor leaders such as Ben-Gurion, Sprinzak, and Katznelson. But on the whole, this period marked a peak in Weizmann's Zionist political career, allowing him the luxury of almost sole decision making.

After the requisite post-Congress month-long recuperation, this time in Sanatorium Stefani in Merano, Italy, Weizmann returned to London in mid-October 1921. Vacationing with Vera, who had also enjoyed a pre-Congress vacation in Carlsbad, and with their two sons in the care of their nurse in London, Weizmann had much time to consider the most urgent matters on the Zionist agenda. One favorite item was the prospective Hebrew University in Jerusalem. Soon after he returned to London, Weizmann wrote to Nathan Ratnoff, a New York obstetrician,

In the United States, April 1921. From left: Menahem Ussishkin, Chaim and
Vera Weizmann, Albert Einstein, Elsa Einstein, Ben-Zion Mossinson. Courtesy:
Weizmann Archives

suggesting the university begin with a medical faculty, however modest,
and encouraging Ratnoff to begin raising funds for the project.[190] In the
meantime, Weizmann received a memorandum from Andor Fodor, a
Hungarian-born professor of biochemistry at Halle, Germany, who sent
unsolicited ideas concerning research institutes at the university. Weizmann, who knew Fodor's work and reputation, immediately asked for
more information, adding, "Would you possibly consider moving to Palestine?"[191] Fodor did not need to be asked twice.[192] At Weizmann's request Fodor went to Palestine in 1923 to investigate the possibilities and
needs of a department of chemistry. Two years later he received the
university's first academic appointment as professor of chemistry, holding the chair for twenty-eight years.

As early as 1919 the WZO engaged the services of a well-known town
planner, Patrick Geddes, to prepare a plan for the university. After a
visit to Jerusalem in 1919, Geddes prepared a plan on such a grand scale
that it proved to be impractical, though elements were retained. As in
1913, there were debates as to how the university would develop and
grow. Weizmann stuck to his original prewar concept of research institutes, among which he naturally favored chemistry. In 1920, under the
guidance of an Advisory Committee headed in England by Lord Rothschild and in Germany by Otto Warburg, a plan was prepared suggesting

Albert Einstein and Weizmann in New York, 1921. Courtesy: Weizmann Archives

that the university commence with three research institutes in physics, chemistry, and microbiology. The humanities were to be inaugurated with a department of Jewish studies, with other departments and schools added over time. This plan was approved by the London *Jahreskonferenz*. The budget called for a one-time expenditure of £100,000, and annual expenses were projected at £50,000.

One of Weizmann's goals for his trip to the United States in the spring of 1921 was to raise money for the university.[193] For this purpose, among others, he had asked Albert Einstein to join him, knowing of the physicist's keen interest in the establishment of a university in Jerusalem. Shlomo Ginzberg (later Ginossar), Ahad Ha'Am's son, had been appointed secretary of the Department for Hebrew University Affairs in 1920 and joined the delegation to the United States as well. This aspect of Weizmann's mission proved less successful, its most tangible result being the establishment of the American Jewish Physicians' Committee headed by Ratnoff. Weizmann was more successful in raising funds during the fall and winter of 1921–22. He received £10,000 from Baron Edmond de Rothschild, £3,000 from Elly Kadoorie of India and Shanghai, and even £1,000 from Herbert Samuel.[194] These were substantial amounts; clearly this was a project Weizmann was intent on implementing as soon as possible, for its intellectual as well as political implications.[195] As meritorious as these factors were, they do not fully explain Weizmann's passion in bringing this and other projects to fruition. His interest in the educational system in Palestine was rooted in his strong belief that Zionism was more than just a political vehicle for the ingathering of the Jewish people within the Jewish national home. Its aim was no less than the transformation of the psychology of the Jewish people. Weizmann explained the adjustments necessary for those Russian Jews who immigrated to Palestine:

> The Jew in Russia is cut off from the great stream of real facts which make up the life of a normal community. The Russian Jew always strives to become a University professor because the career of a chimney sweep is closed to him. That state of existence, combined with the unbroken tradition of learning, has produced in the Russian Jew this semi-sterile intellectuality which is so characteristic of our present generation in Russia. He lives in a world of thoughts and sentiments which revolve around himself. The Jew reproduces himself always, and creates values out of his own inner existence detached from nature surrounding him. He becomes self-centered and learns to consider the world outside as a medium averse to the existence of the Jew. This produces an intellectual type who is as *Weltfremd,* as devoid of a sense of reality, as was the type of the old Jew who lived only within the walls of the moral and material Ghetto which was constructed round him. . . . What follows from this criticism? . . . We need above all a "Palestinian type of teacher," and we need work of development in the country which would supply the necessary background to all life phenomena, would stabilize all our institutions. We need a teachers' institute, we need vacation courses for our teachers, we need museums, libraries, and we need a University which should lead and set the right standard.[196]

The Hebrew University in Jerusalem, at least in the eyes of the person most responsible for its creation, was to be not only a citadel of learning but also an important vehicle in the shaping of a new Palestinian Jewish identity. Weizmann was convinced that this identity could only be formed within the framework of a Jewish commonwealth where the Jews formed a majority. "What else are we striving for? . . . What other meaning is there to the National Home? What are we all working for? . . . If there is not the ideal of building up a Jewish Commonwealth, then our *halutzim* could go at less cost and with more prospects for a material well-being to America, or Australia, or Argentine," he rhetorically asked Wyndham Deedes after the Haycraft Commission Report criticized the Zionists for aiming to establish "Jewish predominance" in Palestine.[197]

The months that followed would show that the authors of the Haycraft Commission Report investigating the Arab riots of May 1921 were more fully in tune with British conceptions about the Jewish national home than were Weizmann's devoted—but increasingly isolated—friends in high office.

X

Lobbying for the Mandate

Early in February 1922, Chaim Weizmann wrote to Wyndham Deedes, chief secretary to the Palestine government, that he intended to call a special congress later that year which, among other things, would also elect a new president of the WZO. "I am tired out. . . . I have had more than my share of politics, which I heartily detest."[1] Written only five months after the Twelfth Zionist Congress in Carlsbad had confirmed his position as president of the World Zionist Organization, this statement by Weizmann might, at first glance, seem like just another momentary expression of fatigue or frustration to which he was often prone. Yet, over the next few weeks Weizmann continued to speak of his impending resignation, of wishing to leave the reins of leadership to someone else.

Weizmann took no steps to implement these threats, but their persistence mirrors his emotional turmoil. Throughout the winter and spring of 1921–22 Weizmann felt as if suspended in midair, unable to act or plan for the future of the Zionist organization. Internal organizational problems, attacks on the movement in England and Palestine, and uncertainties relating to the confirmation of the Mandate for Palestine all contributed to his malaise and discontent. A man of action, expecting, and used to, quick results in response to pressure on the right political levers, Weizmann found that events within and without the movement were taking a turn he had difficulty controlling, leading toward political results detrimental to Zionism. The nine months between Carlsbad and the confirmation of the Mandate for Palestine would tax his energies to the utmost as he tried to prevent further erosion. Again and again he made propaganda sorties from London to major European centers. In mid-February, for example, he traveled to Scotland, delivering some ten speeches in less than a week.[2] The physical toll of such arduous work, combined with the psychological burden of his many other worries, was reflected in his complaints to friends and relatives.[3]

The main organizational and political burden throughout this period rested, for the most part, on Weizmann's shoulders. One of the first items on the agenda was to repair the financial and organizational damage to the Zionist Organization of America and to the WZO in the wake of the Cleveland Annual Convention.[4] Weizmann had won the political battle, but to some extent this was a Pyrrhic victory, as he himself acknowledged. "We lost blood in Cleveland and we have not been able to renew it, and in consequence we are suffering from severe anaemia." The lion's share of the WZO budget was based on funds to be raised in the United States.[5] The sudden withdrawal of the Brandeis group made it difficult to realize these expectations.[6] Emanuel Neumann, Louis Lipsky, and Louis Robison did not command the same respect and authority in the Jewish community at large as did Louis Brandeis, Felix Frankfurter, and Stephen Wise.[7] The shift in leadership had a direct bearing on fund-raising, organizational discipline, and political lobbying. Even those amounts of money pledged to Weizmann during his whirlwind tour of the United States and Canada were only partially honored. The Zionist executive in London therefore decided to send a delegation to the United States, headed by Nahum Sokolow and Vladimir Jabotinsky, to prop up the political stature of the fledgling leadership of the ZOA while raising funds for the economically strapped Palestinian Jewish community.[8] Weizmann was particularly concerned about the high unemployment in the Yishuv and the inability of the Zionist Organization to buy land and build new settlements. He saw these activities as the backbone of Jewish existence in Palestine and urged the American Zionist leaders to do their utmost to help the delegation raise funds for these purposes.[9] The efforts of Sokolow and Jabotinsky to raise money were only partially successful, while their absence was keenly felt in London.

The Zionist organizational structure that had been built since the war at Weizmann's behest by Julius Simon was faltering not only in London and the United States but in Palestine as well, for reasons beyond Weizmann's control. In January 1922, David Eder, his able deputy in Palestine, announced his resignation, though he was persuaded by Weizmann to stay at his post until the Mandate for Palestine was ratified.[10] This left Menahem Ussishkin, a member of the newly created Palestine Zionist executive, as the most authoritative Zionist representative. Given his tactlessness and inflexibility, he was hardly the right person to deal with the British;[11] and in any event he was devoting an increasing portion of his time to the work of the Jewish National Fund and was not expected to handle routine office chores.[12] Former experienced veterans of the WZO leadership such as Shmarya Levin, Victor Jacobson, Otto Warburg, and Arthur Hantke, were no longer members of the executive, while Julius Simon and Nehemia de Lieme, who had joined it in 1920, resigned after internal conflicts a year later. Leo Motzkin and Max Soloveitchik, who had been elected to the executive at Carlsbad, had responsibilities that prevented them from residing in London, while Georg Halpern and Isaac Naiditch spent most of their time on the Continent.

Though Hermann Pick and Josef Sprinzak were new members of the Palestine Zionist executive, Bernard Rosenblatt could not join them and remained in the United States. In any case, neither Sprinzak nor Pick had attained the stature to step into the vacancy created by Eder's departure, and Arthur Ruppin was invaluable to the various settlement projects to which he devoted all his energies.[13] In short, after July 1921, Weizmann found himself with a skeletal and poorly functioning administration.

What made matters worse was the fact that a number of the young and talented men who had joined the London office during the heady months following the Balfour Declaration—Abraham Sonne, Paul Singer, Samuel Landman, and Ben Cohen—resigned their positions in 1921–22 for a variety of reasons. Throughout the latter part of 1921 and 1922, Weizmann needed to persuade Berthold Feiwel, Joseph Cowen, and Richard Lichtheim not to resign from the WZO executive. They were, in fact, the only SAC members with a permanent residence in London. Richard Lichtheim, assisted by the very able Leonard Stein, was as capable a person as Weizmann could hope to find to head the organizational department of the WZO, but neither he, nor Cowen nor Feiwel, could adequately shoulder the heavy burden created by the absence or departure of their colleagues and staff. The constant change in personnel did not allow for a streamlining of the operation. Confusion was further aggravated by Weizmann's absences during most of this period as he traveled on the Continent from one capital to another, lobbying for the Zionist cause. This state of affairs meant that Zionist policy could not be centrally directed, while communications among the Continent, Britain, and Palestine did not always reach their destination. At the end of May 1922, Richard Lichtheim complained that the executive was no longer acting as a collective body with an agreed policy. "I no longer know what to stand for as a member of the leadership," he wrote to Weizmann.[14] In short, the affairs of the organization were in disarray, compounding the political tensions and worries concerning the Mandate for Palestine.

Perhaps most grating for Weizmann were the criticisms from within the movement, which had been publicly aired at Carlsbad but intensified in the months following the Congress. These were voiced by a group of Western European veterans, most of them political Zionists who on those and other grounds had held a grudge against Weizmann since before the war. The leaders of this small but vocal group were Jean Fischer, a diamond merchant and president of the Belgian Zionist Federation; the Dutch banker Jacobus Kann; the physician Alexander Marmorek of Paris; and the recently resigned member of the executive, Nehemia de Lieme of the Netherlands. Their spiritual guide and an occasional active participant was, of course, Max Nordau, who moved back to Paris after the war. They and a few others were, for the most part, political maximalists who opposed Weizmann's more moderate approach to politics. They attacked the Zionist leadership, moreover, for its waste of public funds, its inefficiency, its unwillingness to coopt new people into the WZO administration, and its general lack of direction.[15] This group did not lack financial resources. In January 1922 it published a pamphlet outlining some of these charges and inviting all like-thinking Zionists to a conference at the end of March of that year.[16]

Weizmann had known the leaders of this opposition group since his first days in the movement. Though on the whole without any tangible power, they were elder statesmen of the organization who could not be dismissed out of hand. Perhaps for this reason he felt hurt by their attacks, which prompted at least four threats of resignation in February 1922 alone.[17] Conceding the justice of some of their criticisms, Weizmann challenged his opponents:

It is not difficult to weaken the Z[ionist] O[rganization], but where is the positive aspect of your work? Where are the people who would be ready to shoulder the heavy burden themselves? . . .

It may be that I am mistaken. I did not receive my wisdom on Sinai. If you have been at it for eight years as I have it is possible to suffer from aberrations. As far as I am concerned, and I think I can say the same for many of my friends, we shall be glad to leave you and your friends the responsibility. . . . I cherish the hope that the Mandate will be issued in the spring. A Congress should then be convoked in the summer. . . . Please make ready to offer the candidates. . . . I am tired with all this reviling. . . . The present Executive has been given nothing for the road but an empty sack to go *schnorring*, and a great deal of abuse. I wish the next leadership an easier life.[18]

Even more abusive than the attacks by the political Zionists were those from Pinhas Rutenberg at about the same time. Weizmann had strongly supported Rutenberg's hydroelectric project and had made financial commitments to it, sometimes against the advice of his colleagues on the executive who wanted more control over it.[19] Despite stiff opposition from many quarters, Weizmann had also interceded with the political authorities in London and Palestine to allow the harnessing of the various bodies of water necessary for the project.[20] Moreover, early in January 1922, Weizmann saw to it that the Jewish Colonial Trust participated with £100,000 in the project. But for a variety of political, ideological, and personal reasons, relations between Weizmann and Rutenberg had been deteriorating since the spring of 1921.[21]

During the winter of 1921–22 the tension reached a climax. Rutenberg became incensed by Zionist Organization demands that in exchange for this large financial participation, it be entitled to a commission, 50 percent of company profits, and general control over its affairs. In a six-page letter reviewing the history of the concession since 1919, Rutenberg lashed out against Weizmann's procrastination, dictatorial manner, lack of foresight, and unnecessary and destructive meddling in the financial aspects of the project while taking credit for Rutenberg's fund-raising abilities. In this brutal letter, Rutenberg made short shrift of all of Weizmann's political achievements:

> Sum up candidly the results of your work.
>
> In Palestine—complete failure: economically—starvation and no money in hand, even for charity; politically—pogroms.
>
> San Remo has no value and is in any case the work of Aref-el-Aref [one of the leaders of the pogrom in May 1920] and not yours.
>
> The boundaries you have ruined. . . .
>
> The Mandate you have ruined. And it could have been obtained and with much better conditions than formulated by you. . . .
>
> Now you are attempting to ruin also my work. . . .
>
> You are a gifted, highly gifted man. Life has however placed you in such a position that your head turned. You really imagined yourself a "Jewish king," a great statesman. But in statesmanship you understand very little.
>
> The interests of our unfortunate people became in your mind equivalent to the interests of petty advertising of your ephemeral successes, of your personality. . . . You speculate in fireworks and delude, criminally delude everybody and everything. You often fully recognize yourself that you are cruelly misleading the unhappy Jewish people. . . .
>
> To denounce you publicly would be to shatter the only beautiful illusion which our long suffering nation has preserved. . . .
>
> In your lightheadedness you attempted to annihilate our last weapon. This weapon is my work and is still in my hands and on my responsibility.
>
> I have no right to allow it and I shall not allow it. . . .
>
> If you will make an attempt to carry out the threat made by you, I shall denounce you. It is my duty. You know me. Once I begin, I am used to carry it to the end. I am more powerful than you.[22]

Weizmann had never before received such a personally abusive letter, and he was naturally shaken by it. He cited it as one of the causes for his intention to resign.[23] Of course he did not carry out his threat and eventually dismissed Rutenberg's attacks as stemming from "a confused mind . . . guided by one principle—lust for power."[24] Rutenberg's electrification scheme was discussed at a number of meetings of the executive, and, Rutenberg's threats notwithstanding, the conditions laid down by Weizmann were supported by his colleagues.[25]

Reporting to Nahum Sokolow and Vladimir Jabotinsky, whose sojourn in the United States extended through most of the spring of 1922, Weizmann remarked, "Apart from the attacks which have been levelled at us within the Organization . . . we have had to bear the onslaught of Northcliffe—and naturally this has given the Arab Delegation, which was dying a natural death, a new lease of life."[26] Weizmann was referring to the influential—and by this time quite erratic—Lord Northcliffe, the owner of the *Times* and the *Daily Mail*, who had just returned from a brief visit to Palestine.[27] Despite Weizmann's efforts to expose him to the Yishuv's best achievements,[28] Northcliffe had formed the impression that many of the Jewish settlers were Bolsheviks, this being a contributing factor to the troubles with the Arabs.[29] On his return trip to England, Northcliffe was accompanied by the staunch anti-Zionist Colonel Vivian Gabriel. Harry Sacher warned Weizmann: "You had better see N[orthcliffe] in London as soon as you can. You will find him very difficult. . . . The Arabs here think that they are top dog now. . . . Undoubtedly N. has filled them with a sense of the power and unity of Islam."[30] Indeed, as soon as he returned to London, Northcliffe made his anti-Zionist views known, and these reverberated in the columns of his papers.

Weizmann requested an interview with Northcliffe and was invited to lunch at Carlton Gardens. Also invited was L. J. Maxse, an ardent defender of English interests. It turned out to be a humiliating experience for Weizmann, which he tried to downplay in his autobiography.[31] After lunch the three adjourned to another room. Lord Northcliffe placed Weizmann and Maxse on either side of himself and declared that Maxse was to represent England, Weizmann was to represent the Jews, and he, Northcliffe, was the umpire. "When the two men were seated," reported Northcliffe's aide, "the Chief took out his watch and said: 'Now, gentlemen, you each have five minutes in which to state your case.' " He handed the watch to his aide, who was told to shout "Stop!" at the end of each speaker's five minutes. The report does not indicate whom Northcliffe had judged the winner.[32] In any case, the debate did not change his views on Zionism.[33]

The Northcliffe press, as well as other papers such as the *Morning Post* owned by the anti-Zionist Lord Sydenham and Lord Lamington, gave a new lease on life not only to the Arabs in Palestine but to the Palestine Arab delegation in London as well. Having failed in their initial diplomatic offensive at the Colonial Office, the delegation used the friendly press at its disposal to air the Arab case in public. Guided by Colonel Vivian Gabriel and Ernest Richmond, both with firsthand knowledge of conditions in Palestine, as well as other well-wishers, they expanded their circle of British supporters to include some members of Parliament.[34] Encouraged, the Palestine Arab delegation presented a memorandum to Winston Churchill on February 4, 1922, rejecting the Balfour Declaration and demanding a national government in Palestine.[35] Even friends of Zionism, such as William Ormsby-Gore, concluded that public opinion was slowly turning against the Zionists. He felt that "Dr. Weizmann's dominating personality, by contrast with so inferior a figure as Mr. Jamal [Shibli, secretary of the Palestine Arab delegation], might in some ways be disadvantageous, as confirming the fear that the Arabs would be suppressed by forces with which they were incapable of coping."[36]

Minutes taken during a series of interviews between someone identified only by the initials D. K. and a member of the Palestine Arab delegation identified as A. Sh. (possibly Ibrahim Shammas) reveal Arab attitudes and beliefs. The interviews took place at the Hotel Cecil, the residence of the delegation, between January 5 and March 10, 1922. They indicate—if they are authentic—the all-important role the Palestinians assigned to Weizmann:

> Weizmann wants to be king. As a matter of fact, he publicly promised to the Jewish people to establish for them a Jewish state in Palestine, and he was elected a president only on this understanding. He persists in this policy; all his speeches and all his doings say plainly that they are going to establish a Jewish state. We will not suffer this tendency. . . .
>
> I tell you it is a kingdom they want. Weizmann promised it to them. He is a very clever man, the cleverest we ever met. . . .
>
> Weizmann threatens the [British] Government. They are afraid of him; he is very powerful. . . .
>
> When Weizmann does not like something in Palestine he appears there like a king and he threatens [Herbert] Samuel. . . .
>
> Nothing is done amongst the Zionists without his consent. He does everything. He wants to kill the Arabs and he can do it. He helped the English in the war. He can use a chemical that will kill the Arabs in twenty four hours. He is a very dangerous man.[37]

To what degree the members of the Palestine Arab delegation actually believed such views about Weizmann and to what extent these were embellishments for public consumption is a moot point. In any event, throughout their long sojourn in England the delegates avoided, with one unsatisfactory exception, any face-to-face official encounters with Weizmann and his colleagues.

The behavior of the Palestine Arab delegation in London did not prevent other Arabs, in Europe and the Middle East, from meeting with the Zionists. In November 1921 Weizmann met in London with Riad as-Sulh, a Lebanese who had served as minister in Feisal's short-lived government in Damascus. In 1922 Riad traveled to Egypt, where he succeeded in persuading a number of Syrian exiles, all members of the Syrian Union party who had assembled in Cairo, to attend a semisecret All-Arab Congress and begin negotiations with the Zionists.[38] On March 18–19, Rashid Rida, Kamil al-Qassab, Riad as-Sulh, and Emile Khouri, all of the Syrian Union party, met with Zionist representatives David Eder; Baron Felix de Menasce, a banker and one of the leaders of Alexandrian Jewry; and Asher Saphir, a Palestinian Jewish journalist with excellent ties to the Arabs.[39] Following the meeting, Eder wrote to Weizmann that the talks created an atmosphere conducive to Arab-Jewish rapprochement and asked for Weizmann's authorization to continue the discussions.[40] Weizmann was pleased with the report, which was elaborated upon by Siegfried van Vriesland, who had arrived to meet him in Rome. He did stipulate that Herbert Samuel be fully informed.[41] For his part, the high comissioner felt it was worthwhile continuing the negotiations.[42]

The Cairo meeting concluded that the problems between Jews and Arabs in Palestine stemmed largely from the conflicting promises made by Britain to both national groups. The suggestion was therefore raised that both parties ignore the Balfour Declaration and the Hussein-McMahon correspondence of 1915 and arrive at an independent agreement based on mutual understanding,[43] to be sealed by a formal contract.[44] During further meetings on April 2 and 4, these ideas were more fully discussed, and both sides seemed ready to implement them.[45] These very suggestions were, it seems, sufficient to arouse the opposition of the Colonial Office, though, in letters to Leonard Stein and to Weizmann, Sir John Shuckburgh cited other factors that would militate against making any irreversible commitments.[46] The Colonial Office's opposition dampened the enthusiasm of the Zionist executive, particularly that of Sokolow.[47] Weizmann, on the other hand, was unwilling to break off the negotiations altogether and instead suspended them for a while,[48] much to the chagrin of David Eder.[49] Attempts were made to resume the discussions in the fall of 1922, but the Mandate for Palestine, once ratified, gave the Zionists little incentive to pursue them.[50]

Independent of the Cairo negotiations with representatives of the All-Arab Congress, Weizmann also authorized and encouraged efforts, supervised by the Palestine Zionist executive, to organize Arabs within political structures that would be friendly to the Zionist enterprise. In November 1921, Chaim Kalvarisky was able to establish in Haifa the Moslem National Association through which, it was hoped, the Zionists could weaken the influence of the hostile Moslem-Christian Association and bring about the desired Arab-Jewish entente.[51] Plans were made for similar associations in other cities.[52] These efforts cost a great deal of money, and, potentially, much more was needed in order for them to be effective. "I am sure," wrote Eder to Weizmann in July 1922, "that £15,000 or £20,000 a year can be spent with great advantage in keeping up certain societies, in maintaining certain people, giving douceurs to certain villages and getting favorable notice in the press in Egypt and elsewhere. With £1,000 a year I could have had nearly the whole Syrian Press, but with the tightness of money we could only do what was possible."[53] These activities naturally encouraged both Palestinian and other Arabs to request further sums while raising doubts among the Zionists as to whether this form of bribery was not counterproductive.[54]

In early April 1922, at a meeting in David Eder's home in Jerusalem, the leaders of the Moslem National Association, Hajj Effendi Aldejani and Hajj Khalil Effendi al-Rossas, stressed the necessity of allotting government posts to Arab leaders of the anti-Zionist movement in order to neutralize their influence. They also asked for specific posts for members of their own organization, financial support for the publication of a newspaper, and other favors. The report of the meeting indicates that Eder viewed at least some of their requests as reasonable but made certain to receive Weizmann's backing before making any commitments.[55] Yet even while strongly approving talks with the Palestinian Arabs, representatives of the Syrian Arabs, and emissaries of the Emir Abdullah of Transjordan, Weizmann continued to authorize the purchase of arms, mostly in Vienna, for the Haganah. He was fully aware of the smuggling of these arms to Palestine, quietly assisting with funds and backing the enterprise with his moral authority.[56]

In the course of 1922 it became clear to the Zionists that they could not count on the discussions with the various, often conflicting, Arab groups in London, Geneva, Cairo, and Jerusalem, to produce a firm entente. Colonial Office officials warned that the Arabs wished to use the Zionists to help remove the French mandatory authority in Syria. Continuing such talks, the Colonial Office cautioned, might, in fact, drive a wedge between the Zionists and the British. Throughout 1922 Weizmann maintained a policy toward the Arabs that he summed up in a letter to Chaim Kalvarisky in October:

> We cannot sacrifice (a) the Mandate, (b) immigration, and above all (c), which is very important, we remain loyal to England and France, and nothing can go into our pact with these [Palestinian and Syrian Arab] gentlemen that could be interpreted or considered as a hostile gesture towards England or France. In my opinion these are the fundamental principles to which we should adhere while trying to arrive at a basis of understanding with these gentlemen in the economic domain, collaboration in business, and the intellectual sphere if possible. And it is still necessary to be absolutely certain that the Palestinian Arabs participate in the negotiations. The Arabs of other countries are only of secondary value.[57]

As important as the negotiations with the Arabs were for him, Weizmann's major preoccupation from late fall 1921 until the summer of 1922 was the delay in passage of the Mandate for Palestine. The Paris Peace Conference decided in 1919 that the mandates system, outlined in Article 22 of the Covenant of the League of Nations, should be applied to the non-Turkish portions of the Ottoman Empire. The mandate for Palestine was assigned to the United Kingdom by the Supreme Council of the Allied Powers at San Remo on April 25, 1920. On July 1, the military regime in Palestine was replaced by a civil administration. The northern border of Palestine was determined in accordance with an Anglo-French Declaration of December 23, 1920, and, as noted, the eastern border by virtue of the recognition, in 1923, of an independent government in Transjordan. Even though a draft had been prepared by the British government in June 1920, the Mandate for Palestine itself could not be promulgated immediately because of the long delay in the signing of a conclusive peace treaty between Turkey and the Allied Powers.[58] Only after the political conditions in the Middle East, upset by Mustafa Kemal, had been settled and the difficulties of the French in Syria and the British in Mesopotamia resolved could the legal process move forward. Even so, the concerns of the Catholic powers and delay of approval by the United States continued to stall the process.

Not until July 1922 were the terms of the draft Mandate for Palestine approved by the Council of the League of Nations. This delay threatened, at least in the estimate of Weizmann and his colleagues, its actual ratification; at the very least it opened the way for damaging revisions. Given Herbert Samuel's speech of June 3, 1921, and subsequent pronouncements by him and senior officials of the Colonial Office concerning the limitation of Zionist prerogatives in Palestine, this concern was reasonable. Weizmann therefore spent most of this period lobbying in the capitals on the Continent and in London for a speedy approval of the Mandate for Palestine.

Indeed, even before Samuel's indications of a shift in British policy toward the Jewish national home, long discussions in the Foreign Office and later in the Colonial Office decreased recognition of Zionist claims in successive drafts of the Mandate for Palestine.[59] Weizmann fought particularly hard for a number of points. The first was to include in the preamble the phrase that had appeared in the draft Mandate for Palestine of June 1920: "Recognizing the historical connection of the Jewish people with Palestine and the claim this gives them to reconstitute Palestine as their National Home."[60] In a memorandum intended solely for the use of members of the executive, Leonard Stein summed up the reasons for retaining this clause: "a. It sets forth the fundamental basis of the policy which the Mandate embodies. b. It sets it forth in a form implying international approval and accordingly raises the policy from the plane of expediency to that of principle. c. Its incorporation will have a profound effect on Jewish opinion."[61]

Weizmann also claimed that having this phrase in the preamble would make it easier to raise funds for the upbuilding of Palestine.[62] Lord Curzon and others in the Foreign Office objected on the grounds that this sentence would constitute the foundation on which the Zionists would make claims "for preferential treatment in Palestine, and ultimately for the complete government of the country."[63] The combined efforts of Arthur Balfour and David Lloyd George overruled Curzon, and the clause was reinstated,[64] albeit in a less forceful form. The June 1922 draft no longer spoke of a Zionist "claim . . . to reconstitute Palestine as their National Home," but of "the grounds for reconstituting their national home in that country."[65]

The June 1920 draft Mandate for Palestine included a clause (Article 3) stating that the mandatory "will secure the establishment of the Jewish National Home and the development of a self-governing commonwealth." The October 1920 draft amended this article to read: "the establishment of the Jewish National Home . . . and the development of self-governing institutions." Weizmann struggled to reinstate the deleted reference to commonwealth. His argument was that "the development of self-governing institutions" would mean that representative institutions would be developed in Palestine before the Jews had attained a majority, thus seriously threatening the original intention of the Zionists to create a Jewish state.[66] On this point, however, Weizmann did not have his way. Personal assurances from Balfour and Lloyd George did not translate into formal statements, and the final version of the Mandate for Palestine maintained the phrase "self-governing institutions."[67] As the Zionists foresaw, the mandatory government did attempt to create representative institutions, which failed due principally to Arab opposition.

A third controversial article in the June 1920 draft Mandate for Palestine (Article 5 in that draft; Article 4 in the June 1922 draft), dealt with the status, rights, and obligations of the proposed Jewish agency.

> An appropriate Jewish agency shall be recognized as a public body with power to advise and cooperate with His Britannic Majesty's Government and with the Administration of Palestine in all economic, social, and other matters affecting the establishment of the Jewish National Home. . . . It shall have a preferential right upon fair and equitable terms to construct or operate public works, services and utilities. . . . The Zionist Organization shall be recognized as such agency. It shall take steps . . . to secure the cooperation of all Jews who are willing to assist in the establishment of the Jewish National Home.[68]

This article was attacked for the undue power it gave the Jewish agency to create institutions parallel to those of the mandatory government. The assignment of "preferential right" to such an agency, moreover, was seen as giving the Zionists too much of an advantage over other segments of the Palestinian population. Thus, reference to "preferential right" was deleted in the October 1920 draft, and did not appear in the June 1922 draft. The other clauses of this article remained intact, thanks to Weizmann's watchful eye on both the Colonial Office and the administration in Palestine.

At times Weizmann overreacted. In early December he heard rumors, spread mostly by Colonel Richmond, who was then in London, that Herbert Samuel objected to recognizing the Zionist Organization as the designated Jewish agency. Weizmann immediately dashed off a letter to the high commissioner reminding him "that the elimination of Article 4 would be a death-blow to the Zionist Organization." He warned Samuel that "Any such suggestion would have to be resisted to the last. . . . I earnestly trust . . . that we shall not be lightly plunged into a conflict of which none of us can foresee an end."[69] In his reply Samuel denied the rumors, adding, "I do not think that Article 4 of the Mandate could be altered."[70] Weizmann, who had contemplated extensive demonstrations in England and the United States, discovered that the rumors were false. He immediately canceled the protests, no doubt with a sigh of relief.[71]

On December 18, 1921, Weizmann departed for a meeting of the GAC in Vienna. On route he was received by a very large gathering in Berlin. During his week-long sojourn he met with the German president, Friedrich Ebert, and with the chancellor, Josef Wirth.[72] The German Zionists made the most of his public appearances and treated him with respect and admiration. In the years to come he would find these Zionists to be among his most loyal supporters.[73] During his trip to Berlin and Vienna, the Colonial Office initiated a series of discussions with the Arabs and the Zionists that eventually crystallized in the White Paper of 1922[74] and the final draft of the Mandate for Palestine.

The first concrete step in this direction came in a letter from John Shuckburgh of December 17, 1921, addressed to both the Zionist Organization and the Palestine Arab delegation. Sir John reminded them that at the joint meeting of November 29, 1921, they had agreed that a formula be prepared to serve as a basis for direct discussions between the two parties. The draft formula he enclosed stated that the British government's policy was based on the full text of the Balfour Declaration, including the safeguarding of the civil and religious rights of all inhabitants and the promotion and development of self-governing institutions. There were some doubts, wrote Shuckburgh, as to what was meant by the establishment of a Jewish national home in Palestine. He explained:

> It does not mean the creation of a state in which Jews will be in a position of political ascendancy or enjoy political privileges denied to other inhabitants of the country. It does not mean the unrestricted admission of Jewish immigrants. But it does mean that His Majesty's Government recognize the historical and religious associations that connect the Jewish people with the soil of Palestine. . . . The intention is that immigration of all kinds should be strictly proportioned to the capacity of the country to receive new inhabitants. Stated in other words, the policy is to build up in Palestine a commonwealth, based upon a democratic foundation. . . . Special priority will . . . be given to Jewish over other immigrants. . . .
>
> His Majesty's Government . . . have before them proposals for the early establishment in Palestine of a Legislative Assembly. . . . They are further considering the question of the future regularization of immigration.[75]

Though the document emphasized that immigration would depend on the economic absorptive capacity of Palestine, this was not a proposition that shocked most Zionist leaders. Indeed, several who had watched with great concern the rising unemployment in Palestine had made similar suggestions. On the whole it was a positive document from the Zionist point of view. It may indicate, to some degree, Sir John's own views, perhaps reinforced by the July 1921 meeting in Balfour's house, that, changes in the draft Mandate for Palestine notwithstanding, the government's support of the Balfour Declaration was unshakable. Shuckburgh's deference to Weizmann, moreover, at this point was unusual. It seems to be confirmed by a remarkable discussion the two of them had in early January 1922, shortly after Weizmann's return from the Continent. Sir John discussed many aspects of British policy in Palestine: the composition of the Palestine Zionist executive, the possibility of installing a monarchy in Palestine, the possible replacement of Samuel as high commissioner, and other matters. On all these issues Shuckburgh seems to have accepted Weizmann's views. He was also eager to know Weizmann's personal plans for the future. "Dr. Weizmann said that if he consulted his own inclinations he would withdraw from the Zionist Executive, immediately the Mandate, which he regarded as his life work, was secured."[76]

While Sir John was trying to break the impasse between the Zionists and the Palestine Arab delegation through a political declaration to which both parties could, in the opinion of the Colonial Office, agree, Samuel had embarked on a different track. From the early days of his administration he felt strongly that a legislative body, representing all segments of the population, was a necessary ingredient of a democratic government. He had therefore established in October 1920 an Advisory Council composed of four Muslims, three Jews, and three Christians, as well as members of the administration.[77] The high commissioner's firsthand observations of the strong anti-Zionist mood of the Arabs in Palestine and reports from the Colonial Office on the similar intransigence of the Palestine Arab delegation[78] led him to conclude that the British government must impose a more permanent solution. This conviction was already implied in his speech of June 3, 1921. Samuel's aim was to create a political framework that would honor British commitment to the Balfour Declaration while drawing the Arabs into the political decision-making process in Palestine. He thought that a constitutional form of government might allay the fears of the Arabs who considered the Balfour Declaration a symbol of the British-Zionist alliance intended to shunt aside Arab rights and demands. During the fall of 1921 and the winter of 1922, Samuel corresponded with the Colonial Office on the appropriate democratic form that would satisfy the various competing forces in Palestine.[79]

During the first week of February 1922, the Colonial Office circulated a draft constitution for Palestine that stipulated the creation of a legislative council composed of the high commissioner and twenty-five members, of which the high commissioner and ten members were to be officials of the Palestine government and fifteen were to be nonofficials. Of the latter group, one was to be nominated by the chambers of commerce and two by the high commissioner. The rest of the members were to be elected, with the stipulation that the council would include at least one Christian and one Jew. The term of office of the members was to be three years. It was made clear that the council could not propose laws contrary to the mandate. In general, the high commissioner retained his power as the final arbiter in all legislative matters.[80]

In the months that followed this proposed legislative draft, there ensued a lively correspondence among the Colonial Office, the Palestine Arab delegation, and the Zionists. Despite some of the potential hazards, particularly regarding the process for handling immigration, Weizmann did not seem too concerned. He suggested only a few modifications to limit the powers of the legislative council.[81] Other members of the executive, particularly Jabotinsky, were not as sanguine. "Platonic reaffirmation of the B[alfour] D[eclaration] is totally outweighed by the elected majority prospect," he protested from the United States.[82] The Zionists' positive, if lukewarm, response became irrelevant in view of the Palestine Arab delegation's reaction. It rejected the draft constitution, refusing to enter into a detailed examination of its clauses, while raising a number of fundamental objections concerning British policy in Palestine. The sole point of agreement between the Zionists and the delegation was that their correspondence would be published in due course.[83] Weizmann's continued equanimity on this issue—though based on insufficient knowledge of the colonial secretary's views—was buttressed by Winston Churchill's letter of March 1, 1922, to the Palestine Arab delegation affirming that the Balfour Declaration represented the settled policy of the British government and was not open to discussion.[84] The relationship of trust that Weizmann had carefully nurtured with John Shuckburgh, moreover, paid off. Sir John kept Weizmann privately informed of the Arab reactions and solicited his views on the Colonial Office responses to their demands.[85]

Opposition to the Jewish national home and to the Mandate for Palestine was not confined to the Palestine Arab delegation and its supporters in England. The latter had used the press to good advantage and had made an impact on circles that hitherto had little interest in Palestine. The situation greatly concerned not only Weizmann and his colleagues on the Zionist executive but their loyal friends outside the movement as well, such as William Ormsby-Gore, now an MP:

> The situation had undergone an unfavorable change. There was growing up a body of opinion which was inclined to view Zionism with scepticism, if not with positive dislike. Some of those who had supported the Balfour Declaration when it was issued were tending to change their minds. . . . There was a disposition in some quarters to fear that what was going on was an attempt on the part of a body of powerful and aggressive Jews to tread down a weak and helpless little people. . . . What had given rise to an enormous amount of misunderstanding was the phrase "as Jewish as England is English" [paraphrase of Weizmann's response to U.S. Secretary of State Robert Lansing at the peace conference]. Many people took this to mean that just as the English rule England, so the Jews were to rule Palestine. No doubt what was really meant was merely that one day the Jews might be expected to give Palestine its tone and color. But it was absolutely essential that the misunderstanding which had been alluded to should be dissipated.[86]

Though he advised against "vociferous propaganda," Ormsby-Gore agreed that the Zionists had to defend themselves, if attacked, to clear any misunderstandings. On that score he recommended that "the recent speeches at Oxford should be widely circulated among M.P.s."[87] Ormsby-Gore was referring to speeches made on February 25, 1922, by Sir Alfred Mond and Weizmann in the Town Hall at Oxford under the auspices of the Oxford University Zionist Society. The Zionists heeded Ormsby-

Gore's advice.[88] This pamphlet was only one of the means the Zionists employed in their counterpropaganda campaign, which was carried out mostly by Weizmann. Since January 1922 he had expended considerable energies in battling the various accusations made by forces maligning the World Zionist Organization. These included such diverse groups as the orthodox Agudat Israel, which had met with Lord Northcliffe in Palestine in February 1922 and actively opposed recognition of the Zionist Organization as the "Jewish agency."[89] Likewise, Weizmann parried charges by the Rt. Rev. Rennie MacInnes, the Anglican bishop of Jerusalem, who accused Weizmann of disseminating false views about church attitudes toward Zionism, the Palestine Arab delegation, and the group of anti-Zionist lords and MPs and the papers that supported them.

In England, Weizmann had several options for responding to charges made against Zionism or lobbying for the Mandate for Palestine. He had the advantage of almost instant access to Balfour, now lord president of the council; to the prime minister, Lloyd George; to the colonial secretary, Winston Churchill (usually through John Shuckburgh); to Jan Christiaan Smuts, the prime minister of South Africa; and to Sir Alfred Mond, the minister of health. The good relations Weizmann had nurtured since the war years with a host of senior officials and men of influence, in or out of office, now paid off as well. Even Richard Meinertzhagen, who had close ties with Weizmann, confided to his diary his astonishment at the Zionist's intimate knowledge of most secret telegrams and dispatches to and from the Middle Eastern Department of the Colonial Office; obviously some senior officials were leaking this information.[90]

Weizmann did not hesitate to call for assistance from C. P. Scott,[91] Lord Milner, or Ormsby-Gore, MP. He continued to forge closer ties with the Labour party, with which the Zionists had exchanged ideas and information during the period after the war.[92] In particular Weizmann established a rapport with Josiah Wedgwood, MP, and Ramsay Macdonald, MP.[93] On February 1, 1922, Weizmann, accompanied by the Palestinian labor leader Shlomo Kaplansky, David Eder and his wife, Leonard Stein, and Moshe Shertok, met with members of the International Affairs Committee of the Labour party, which had previously met with the Palestine Arab delegation. Weizmann, the main spokesman, disputed the Arabs' claims on a number of issues and presented the Zionist point of view.[94]

In the case of Bishop MacInnes, Weizmann induced Winston Churchill—via Shuckburgh—to write to the archbishop of Canterbury.[95] The colonial secretary enclosed Weizmann's letter of protest and asked that the bishop show more discretion in public.[96] T. E. Lawrence, then working in the Middle Eastern Department of the Colonial Office, to whom the bishop wrote on December 15, 1921, and again on June 23, 1922, was less polite in his reaction than his chief, the colonial secretary. In response to MacInnes's repeated demands that he deny a statement he had made to Weizmann concerning anti-Zionist attitudes of the Episcopal dioceses that had missionary interests, Lawrence wrote:

> My dear Bishop, I will now answer your letter. You wish me to deny statements which a third person [Horace Kallen] declares I made to Dr. Weizmann. I will do nothing of the sort. I have never in my life denied any published statement attributed to me, and am not tempted to begin in your three-cornered case. Especially as I suspect you want my denials only to assure yourself triumph over Dr. Weizmann, a great man whose boots neither you nor I, my dear Bishop, are fit to black.

In the event, Lawrence did not send this first draft, but composed a second, less insulting but by no means more accommodating, letter.[97] It indicates the high esteem in which Weizmann was held by the top personnel of the Colonial Office. On the other hand, Weizmann was not successful in his attempts to induce Professor Samuel Alexander, his sympathetic former senior colleague at Manchester University, to write on behalf of the Zionist cause to various newspapers. It was left to Weizmann himself to write such letters to protest anti-Zionist statements or to correct misstatements.[98]

With the principal assistance of Leonard Stein, Weizmann also coordinated efforts of lobbying through other groups. Thus he induced public demonstrations in the United States which attracted much attention.[99] Weizmann naturally employed to greatest advantage the one lobbying method he had honed and perfected into a fine art during the war years—the personal, intimate interview. These interviews took place in Downing Street with the prime minister, for example in April and May 1922, or in the offices of the Colonial Office with John Shuckburgh. But more often than not, they were conducted in the drawing rooms, clubs, and restaurants of Britain's governing elite. Weizmann's appointment book for 1922 indicates that he had lunches at the Carlton Grill, the Ritz, and the Cavalry Club with men and women of personal or official influence. Among those with whom he dined are William Ralph Inge, the greatly influential and outspoken dean of St. Paul's; Lionel George Curtis, a prominent public servant who at this time was adviser to the Colonial Office; Earl Winterton; T. E. Lawrence; Colonel Ronald Storrs; Lord Eustace Percy; Colonel Richard Meinertzhagen; General Sir George Macdonogh; Josiah Wedgwood, MP; and Frances Stevenson, the prime minister's secretary, current mistress, and future wife.[100] Weizmann's correspondence with these and others reinforced the impact of their meetings. His unrelenting and concerted efforts persisted until the ratification of the Mandate for Palestine and beyond.

The Zionists also distributed their own independent publications. In February 1922 the London office published Leonard Stein's *The Truth about Palestine,* a direct response to charges made by the Palestine Arab delegation. Weizmann's speech at Oxford at the end of February 1922, published immediately afterward, summarized his responses to the most frequent charges and concerns raised by his interlocutors as well as other critics:

> The average newspaper reader thought that there was a Jewish state in Palestine, meaning by "State" . . . a sort of body which rode roughshod over anybody who did not happen to belong to the ruling authority. This state was maintained (it was said) by British bounty, and was paid by British taxes. . . . The average Jew was also supposed to be a rabid Bolshevist. . . . So instead of explaining what was really happening in Palestine they had to defend themselves against a series of clumsy accusations. It was always an easy matter to malign a Jew. One day it was Bolshevism, another Capitalism. The real facts were that instead of the Jewish State, there was a British Administration. There was a Jewish Community in difficult circumstances in a difficult country at a difficult time, attempting to do a certain amount of work for the reconstruction of Palestine with a view to bringing about the creation of a Jewish National Home in that country.[101]

Weizmann proceeded to deal with the question of immigration, which, since June 3, 1921, had become the focus of attention of the British administration in Palestine and, obviously, one of the sticking points with the Palestine Arab delegation. Palestine could absorb three times the present rate of twelve thousand immigrants a year, claimed Weizmann, assuming the country continued to develop its agricultural and water resources. "Such immigrants could be brought into the country without in the slightest degree infringing the rights of the present population. So far, the Jews had not only not ousted a single Arab from his position, but wherever they had worked they had increased the economic possibilities and the well-being of the Arab population." The Jews came to Palestine to work and did not expect an easy life. Why did they come to do this work? "It was the first time they had found *terra firma* under their feet. They were moved by an ideal. . . . It was not the gentlemen from Park Lane who built up countries, but the sort of people who were often termed 'undesirables.' " The Jews wanted to build the country and had no reason to oust the Arabs. There was plenty of room for both peoples: "On the land which the Jewish people now possessed in Palestine at present they could place about 150,000 immigrants without touching so much as an inch of Arab property or without having to buy an inch of more ground for the next ten years. Further with regard to Bolshevism, the Zionist Movement in its conception, construction, and ideal, was the very antithesis of Bolshevism."[102]

Weizmann also took issue with those who claimed that the Balfour Declaration was a hastily drawn up document and an ill-considered policy, arrived at suddenly in the excitement of the war, which could now be scrapped. On the contrary, he asserted, it was well thought out and timely and reflected the community of interests between the British and the Jews of the world. The goodwill of the Jewish people was a principal factor in this policy. For their part, the Jews did not expect to build up the Jewish national home at the expense of the British taxpayer. They were relying solely on their own resources. Nor should the Jews be responsible for the upkeep of the British army, which was necessary for the general maintenance of order in the region.[103] The cost of the British garrison could be reduced in half if hostile forces would cease meddling and let the Jews and Arabs arrive at a *modus vivendi*. Just as in Switzerland two or three civilizations co-existed peacefully, just as in previous periods in history Jews and Arabs lived and worked together, so it would happen again that Israel and Ishmael would learn to live with one another. Zionism had existed in a variety of forms since the destruction of Jewish political sovereignty by the Romans. It was the destiny of the Jews, through the Zionist movement, to rebuild the land, and no force on earth could deter them from this task.[104]

During his lecture at Oxford, Weizmann warned his audience that "a broken pledge might be more costly than the maintenance of an army in Palestine. The greater the empire the less it could afford to break its pledge." But he hastened to add that he did not think "for one moment that either the British Government or the British people could countenance such an act."[105] Indeed, he did not fear that the Lloyd George government would renege on its promises.[106] But he did worry about the attitude of the Vatican and such Roman Catholic countries as France and Italy. The Zionists were well aware of the fact that on route from Palestine to London the Palestine Arab delegation had been warmly received by Pope Benedict XV,[107] who had, on a number of previous occasions, made anti-Zionist pronouncements. The Vatican was not satisfied with the clauses of the Mandate for Palestine regarding the Holy Places, while Italy and France had their own strategic interests in the Middle East that would move them to support the Vatican's opposition to the Mandate for Palestine in its current formulation. The Vatican, moreover, was able to influence other members of the League of Nations that had no direct national interests in the area but that might be concerned about the proper safeguarding of the Holy Places. In light of these circumstances, the Zionist executive resolved in January 1922 that Weizmann should travel to France and Italy "in order to take whatever steps should be necessary in connection with the Mandate."[108] The linchpin of Catholic opposition to the Mandate for Palestine was, of course, the Vatican. Cardinal Aquilla Ratti ascended the papal throne in February 1922, and Weizmann hoped to meet the new pope.

Weizmann arrived in Rome on March 31, 1922. The preparations for his various interviews were smoothed in advance, to a large extent thanks to the friendly assistance of Sir Ronald Graham, who had recently arrived to serve as the British ambassador to Italy, and Count John Francis Charles de Salis, the British envoy to the Vatican.[109] On April 1, 1922, King Victor Emmanuel III received Weizmann. The almost hour-long audience was cordial.[110] The king remembered appreciatively his meeting with Theodor Herzl, whose photograph stood on his desk. During his first few days in Rome, Weizmann also met with a number of Italian statesmen and public figures, among them Giovanni Antonio Colonna di Cesaro, a leader of the Social Democrats in the Chamber of Deputies; the former prime minister Luigi Luzzatti, the first Jew to occupy this office; Giovanni Amendola, the minister for the colonies; Francesco Saverio Nitti, the immediate past prime minister; Francesco Ruffini, an influential politician and jurist; Gino Scarpa, a politician whose enthusiasm for Zionism Weizmann compared to that of Ormsby-Gore; and Luigi Sturzo, a popular Sicilian priest who led the Partito Popolare party, forerunner of the Christian Democrats. He also conferred with Celestin Charles Auguste Jonnart, the French ambassador to the Vatican.[111]

Characteristically, Weizmann managed to compress a number of interviews into each day, soliciting much information while doing his own lobbying. His initial assessment held that the Italian government was, at least to some degree, under the influence of the Vatican and that Italy, which had not shared in the spoils of World War I, was positioning itself to become a power in the Mediterranean. On the whole, the Foreign Ministry was still friendly, if reserved. On the other hand, and to his great surprise and delight, Weizmann found among Italian Jewry a small band of enthusiastic and dedicated Zionists led by such men as Dante Lattes, the secretary of the Italian Zionist Federation, who was supported in his activities by no less a personality than Angelo Sereni, the president of the Union of Italian Jewish Communities. Under the chairmanship of Duke Cesaro, Weizmann delivered a paper on April 4 at the Collegio Romano to an audience that included large numbers of the Jewish and non-Jewish academic and political elite of Rome.[112] Weizmann's speech was enthusiastically received, a fact that did not prevent the Vatican's paper, the *Osservatore Romano*, from misinterpreting it as evidence of the Zionists' wish to expropriate Palestine from the Arabs.[113]

Despite this gratifying first encounter with Italian Jewry and some of Italy's most prominent political and public personalities, the stumbling block remained the Vatican. On Sunday, April 2, 1922, accompanied by Dante Lattes, Weizmann met with Cardinal Pietro Gasparri, the papal secretary of state.[114] While a long and, on the whole, friendly discussion, it left little doubt in Weizmann's mind that the cardinal had no benevolent views about the Zionists. Gasparri told Weizmann that the Holy See objected to a number of clauses in the Mandate for Palestine: Article 2, which dealt with establishment of the Jewish national home and the religious rights of all inhabitants, and Article 4, recognizing the Zionist Organization as the Jewish agency. In the Vatican's view these articles contradicted the mandatory concept as defined in Article 22 of the League of Nations Covenant, since, as it stood, the Mandate for Palestine seemed designed to lead to "an absolute preponderance of the Jewish element in the economic, administrative and political field to the detriment of other nationalities" in Palestine and would not adequately protect the interests of the indigenous population.[115]

The Vatican also objected to Article 14, which stipulated that the mandatory "undertakes to appoint as soon as possible a special Commission to study and regulate all questions and claims relating to the different religious communities. In the composition of this Commission the religious interests concerned will be taken into account."[116] The Vatican insisted that only Catholics ought to have voting power in all matters relating to the Catholic Holy Places.[117] Weizmann, who had excellent contacts with the Colonial Office and the British ambassadors in Rome, was surprised at Gasparri's announcement that a memorandum outlining these objections had already been dispatched to the League of Nations. He immediately instructed his colleagues in London to find out what the memorandum contained.[118] In fact, the Vatican had merely sent a letter to the British Foreign Office on April 6, 1922, voicing the same concerns expressed by Gasparri to Weizmann.[119] Only on May 15, 1922, did the Vatican send a formal letter along these lines to the League.[120]

On April 3, 1922, Weizmann received an invitation from Gasparri, transmitted via de Salis, to continue the discussion after Easter. Weizmann accepted, while still pressing the ambassador to arrange for him an audience with the pope, a request denied by the Holy See.[121] In the meantime, while the country was celebrating the holiday, Weizmann vacationed on Capri, returning to Rome on April 16. On April 20, again accompanied by Lattes, Weizmann had his second meeting with Gasparri. Weizmann began by complaining about *Osservatore Romano*'s willful misinterpretation of his lecture on April 4; the cardinal lightly dismissed the charge as a "misunderstanding," and the topic was allowed to drop. As to the alleged privileged position of the Jews in Palestine, Weizmann declared that the Jews would occupy positions in the land to the extent that they earned them by their hard labor. A way should be found for Jews and Catholics to live peacefully together. The cardinal indicated his agreement with both statements.[122] It became apparent that the cardinal had no objection to the colonization work of the Zionists in Palestine, but at some point he turned to Weizmann and exclaimed, "C'est votre université que je crains" (It is your university that I fear).[123] The Catholic church, which had many educational institutions in Palestine, objected to changes in the curriculum and structure of the educational system that had been introduced by Herbert Samuel. The Hebrew University would clearly be an added intellectual challenge in the theological war the Catholics had to fight.[124]

The discussion was throughout civil and less formal than during their first meeting, reflecting the fact that both were experienced statesmen who could discuss controversial matters in a friendly atmosphere. Nothing was changed, however, by the Weizmann-Gasparri meetings, as the continuous and even increased hostility of the Vatican's official organ demonstrated.[125] The Latin patriarch of Jerusalem, Monsignor Louis Barlassina, a sworn enemy of the Zionists, added fuel to the anti-Zionist mood of the Vatican. He arrived in Rome in April 1922, shortly after

Weizmann, preaching everywhere a crusade against the Zionists. His visit coincided with the publication of the first issue of *La Palestine*, which he edited; it was characterized by Weizmann as "a venomous paper full of untruths."[126] On May 13, 1922, Barlassina was quoted as having stated that "Palestine is under an oppressive domination a thousand times more violent than Turkish rule. . . . The whole Zionist movement, directed by a few fanatics, is waging war against both the Catholic and Arab elements."[127] Though the Vatican disavowed direct responsibility for the actions of the Latin patriarch, the fact that he continued in his position for another twenty-five years is sufficient proof that he had the full support not only of Pius XI and Cardinal Gasparri but of their successors as well.[128]

Weizmann returned to England on May 2. During his month-long sojourn in Italy, he had been able to strengthen ties with the Jewish community and the non-Jewish supporters of Zionism. But he had essentially failed to move the Zionists' most implacable enemies in Vatican circles. To some degree his visit, and particularly his speech at the Collegio Romano, were counterproductive, since they became grist for the mills of the *Osservatore Romano* and other hostile elements. Weeks after the event, Cardinal Gasparri's acknowledgment of the mistake of Vatican journalists notwithstanding, the Holy See still used Weizmann's speech as evidence of the malevolent intentions of the Zionists in Palestine.[129]

The one diplomatic victory of the Zionists during Weizmann's sojourn in Italy was scored not on the Continent but in the United States, thanks to the intensive lobbying of Nahum Sokolow and Vladimir Jabotinsky in collaboration with Louis Lipsky. On April 12, 1922, Senator Henry Cabot Lodge, ironically a leader of American isolationism, introduced a resolution in the Senate Foreign Relations Committee affirming support for the establishment of the Jewish national home in Palestine.[130] On May 3, the committee recommended adoption of the resolution.[131]

This momentary diplomatic encouragement from overseas soon evaporated in the face of further disappointments that awaited Weizmann as he left again for the Continent on May 8. The eighteenth session of the Council of the League of Nations was scheduled to take place in Geneva on May 11–17, 1922, and Weizmann hoped to witness the passage of the Mandate for Palestine. Arthur Balfour, with whom he met twice on the eve of the proceedings, was also confident of the passage and did not foresee any special difficulties despite the possible opposition of Brazil, a Catholic member of the League.[132] But two days into the sessions it became clear that the Mandate for Palestine would not pass at this session "for purely technical reasons," as Weizmann reported to Vera. "England should have presented this matter several weeks in advance, and not at the last moment."[133]

But a few days of close observation of the behind-the-scenes machinations led Weizmann and Balfour to conclude that the delay had little to do with "technical reasons"; it was due to the influence the Vatican exerted on Catholic members of the League's Council, including Belgium, Brazil, France, Italy, and Spain.[134] "The Vatican is working full blast and is influencing all the Catholics," reported Weizmann from Geneva. "The Italians and the French are both working under the stick of the Roman priests, and it's never difficult to work against Jews. . . .We shall have to suffer for a few more weeks."[135] The Council decided to postpone discussion of the Mandate for Palestine to its next meeting, which was to commence on July 15, 1922. This further delay was a severe disappointment for Weizmann, mitigated only by Balfour's proclamation to the Council that the Balfour Declaration was not subject to modification. The British had not prepared sufficiently for the meeting in May; they would be much better prepared, thought Weizmann, for the next round. As he returned to London on May 20 he had no inkling of the even greater setbacks in store for the Zionist cause in the next two months.

The first setback came in the form of the White Paper of 1922. Its principal author was Herbert Samuel, who arrived in London during the first week of May after an absence of almost two years. The postponement of the Mandate for Palestine afforded Samuel the opportunity to prepare a new statement of policy. This one was to be based on ideas he had articulated in his speech of June 3, 1921, but had, in fact, held since early in the war and consolidated after he first visited in Palestine in the spring of 1920.[136] These ideas were rejected during the meeting at Balfour's house in July 1921. Now that the Zionists were caught in a moment of political weakness, Sir Herbert had a second chance to force them to accept his vision for the governance of Palestine.[137]

The fact that the discussions of the Colonial Office with the Palestine Arab delegation had come to a halt provided further impetus for a new political initiative. In collaboration with Shuckburgh of the Colonial Office, Samuel prepared a memorandum signed by Winston Churchill on May 27, 1922, three days after he had received it. Usually referred to as the "Churchill Memorandum," it seems that the colonial secretary, who was then preoccupied with Irish problems, paid scant attention to it.[138] Weizmann received a copy of the memorandum immediately after Churchill approved it, so that he could discuss it with his colleagues before its official release on June 3.

In the meantime, on May 30, the Zionist executive hosted a dinner for Sir Herbert at the Royal Palace Hotel, which had been arranged some weeks earlier.[139] Samuel was also invited to attend a meeting of the executive on June 1. On both occasions Weizmann and his colleagues tried to persuade the high commissioner to change certain aspects of the memorandum, but to no avail. At the end of his meeting with the Zionist executive, Sir Herbert urged the Zionists to do "everything to facilitate his task. . . . Although things had been quiet for a year, he did not place any great faith in that tranquility. . . . It therefore behooved the Z[ionist] O[rganization] as well as the Government to do everything they could to diminish friction and to remove misconceptions. They should not put the Zionist flag too high, as too much flag-waving aroused resentment. . . . A great many Arabs were afraid of what they thought the Zionists would do, and many influential people in England had sympathy with them because they thought the Jews would overwhelm them."[140]

Samuel's remarks clearly indicate that the memorandum was written to appease the Arabs and their British supporters. Gone was the era of polite and almost deferential consultations with Weizmann. Though stated in civil terms, the high commissioner clearly implied that it would be better for the Zionists to accept British policy without much fuss. The new tone of authority and the implied threat are even clearer in the June letter from John Shuckburgh that was attached to the memorandum. It left little room for disagreement: "Mr. Churchill . . . would . . . be glad to receive from you a formal assurance that your Organization accepts the policy as set out in the enclosed statement and is prepared to conduct its own activities in conformity therewith."[141] The attached memorandum—officially submitted exactly one year after Samuel's June 3, 1921, speech—established nine principles, or statements of clarifications, providing new guidelines for British policy toward Zionist aspirations in Palestine.

1. Referring to Weizmann's statement in February 1919, before the Council of Ten at the peace conference, the memorandum stated that

> Unauthorized statements have been made to the effect that the purpose in view is to create a wholly Jewish Palestine. Phrases have been used such as that Palestine is to become "as Jewish as England is English." His Majesty's Government regard any such expectation as impracticable and have no such aim in view.
> 2. . . . The terms of the [Balfour] Declaration . . . do not contemplate that Palestine as a whole should be converted into a Jewish National Home, but that such a Home should be founded *in Palestine*.

3. His Majesty's Government reaffirmed its commitment to the Balfour Declaration.

> When it is asked what is meant by the development of the Jewish National Home in Palestine, it may be answered . . . the further development of the existing Jewish community. . . .
> 4. . . . It is essential that [the Jewish people] know that it is in Palestine as of right and not on sufferance.
> 5. . . . [Jewish] immigration cannot be so great in volume as to exceed whatever may be the economic capacity of the country at the time to absorb new arrivals. . . .
> 6. . . . A special committee should be established in Palestine, consisting entirely of members of the new Legislative Council elected by the people, to confer with the Administration upon matters relating to the regulation of immigration. . . .

7. . . . It is not the case, as has been represented by the Arab Delegation, that during the war His Majesty's Government gave an undertaking that an independent national government should be at once established in Palestine. . . . The whole of Palestine west of the Jordan was . . . excluded from Sir McMahon's pledge.

8. Nevertheless, it is the intention of His Majesty's Government to foster the establishment of a full measure of self-government in Palestine. . . . This should be accomplished by gradual stages. . . . It is now proposed [to establish] . . . a Legislative Council. . . .

9. Unstated, but underlying the main planks of the Churchill Memorandum was the principle of dual obligation toward Jews and Arabs as the basis for British administration in Palestine.[142] This dual obligation formed the core of Herbert Samuel's philosophy and political theory: that with goodwill on everyone's part, and assuming that both sides are treated with equal fairness, Jews and Arabs could co-exist and cooperate in Palestine.

Before presentation of the memorandum to the Arabs and the Zionists, Shuckburgh remarked in an internal Colonial Office memorandum:

> There can be little doubt, I think, that the Zionists will accept the statement. It contains certain passages that will not be at all to their liking. But they are beginning to realize clearly that they must modify their ambitions; that the patience of His Majesty's Government is not inexhaustible; and that by claiming too much they run serious risk of losing everything. The Arabs doubtless will not be satisfied, but they may be glad of the opportunity that will be given them of returning to Palestine not entirely empty-handed.[143]

Sir John was wrong in his assessment of the Arab reaction to the Churchill Memorandum. On June 17, 1922, Musa Kazem Pasha al-Husseini and Jamal Shibli rejected it point by point. In their concluding paragraphs they blamed much of the tension in Palestine on the fact that Jewish immigrants were "dumped upon the country from different parts of the world." They asserted that "Nature does not allow the creation of a spirit of co-operation between two peoples so different, and it is not to be expected that the Arabs would bow to such a great injustice, or that the Zionists would so easily succeed in realizing their dreams."[144]

The Zionists' response was quite different. Weizmann's first reaction was tame, almost relieved: "It is perhaps not exactly what we want but considering the great difficulties of the situation it is a satisfactory document. It might depress some of our exalted friends but on the whole it will be accepted loyally."[145] He realized full well from his recent conversations with Shuckburgh and Samuel that the Zionists had no choice but to accept the document, and he preferred, as Shuckburgh noted, to "take his basin of gruel with good grace."[146]

Weizmann realized that though the document reaffirmed the British commitment to the Balfour Declaration and stated that the Zionists were in Palestine as of right, it also contained many clauses potentially damaging to the Zionist enterprise. It limited and hemmed Zionist political

and economic aspirations in language that could be variously interpreted, depending on the degree of hostility of future British adminis-
trations. A man as politically sensitive as Weizmann understood both
the explicit restrictions as well as the nuances of meaning implied in the
document's clauses relating to the Jewish agency, immigration, and "dual
obligation," not to speak of the explicit statement that Britain had no
intention of allowing the creation of a Jewish commonwealth.[147] Indeed,
the memorandum, which became the core of the White Paper of 1922,
was to guide British policy in Palestine at least until 1939, even beyond, and was cited as precedent in the White Papers of 1930 and
1939.

Weizmann also knew when to retreat, cutting his losses. "The great
difficulties of the situation" he spoke of in his letter of June 4 to Alfred
Mond referred to the reexamination of the Zionist case in Parliament,
the general public discussion of the great expense to the British taxpayer
in maintaining a presence in the Middle East, and the not-so-subtle threat
delivered by the Colonial Office that if the Zionists did not accept the
Churchill Memorandum, the Mandate for Palestine might not be forwarded to the League of Nations for ratification—at least not in its present form. All parties understood the importance of the Mandate for
Palestine as an international legal document that, Weizmann hoped, would
outweigh any other policy statements. Thus, if he had to get the Mandate for Palestine at the price of the White Paper, he was willing to take
the risk. At the same time he clearly understood what such an assent
meant: "The High Commissioner drafted a Statement of Policy which
will no doubt be interpreted by the Jewish World as a whittling down
of the Balfour Declaration."[148]

The discussions at two Zionist executive meetings, on June 9 and June
18, 1922, the date on which the government demanded an answer, show
that the other Zionist leaders also understood that a positive response
to the British government, however distasteful its policy statement, was
inevitable.[149] Even J.botinsky, who had arrived from the United States
the day before, gave his assent at the expanded Zionist executive meeting of June 18.[150] Weizmann had been nervous about Jabotinsky's reaction, but Jabotinsky had raised no objection, "merely remarking that the
White Paper, if carried out honestly and conscientiously, would still afford [the Zionists] a framework for building up a Jewish majority in
Palestine, and for the eventual emergence of a Jewish State."[151] Following the meeting of the executive, Weizmann wrote to the Colonial Office
that "the activities of the Zionist Organization will be conducted in conformity with the policy . . . set forth" in the British statement of June
3, 1922."[152] On July 1, 1922, the government presented its policy statement to Parliament in the form of a White Paper that, in addition to its
centerpiece, the Churchill Memorandum of June 3, also included the
government's correspondence with the Palestine Arab delegation and
the Zionist Organization.[153]

The political pressures affecting the Zionists' decisions in June and July are clearly indicated by the prevailing atmosphere in Parliament. On June 21, 1922, Lord Islington, chairman of the National Savings Committee, introduced a motion in the House of Lords that the "Mandate for Palestine in its present form is inacceptable to this House because it directly violates the pledges made by His Majesty's Government to the people of Palestine in its Declaration of October 1915 and again in its Declaration of November 1918, and is, as at present framed, opposed to the sentiments and wishes of the great majority of the people of Palestine."[154] The motion then called for postponement and modification of the Mandate for Palestine. Despite Balfour's opposition on behalf of the government, the motion carried by a vote of 60–29.[155] Though the vote of the House of Lords did not bind the government, it was a tremendous moral blow for the Zionists.[156] Its repercussions were immediately felt in those countries that had a part to play in the ratification of the Mandate for Palestine as well as in Palestine. Writing from Palestine, David Eder noted, "The result of the debate in the House of Lords has, of course, elated the Arabs who now state that it will be impossible to carry through the Mandate."[157]

Once again, good news from the United States somewhat mitigated the setback to the Zionists in England. On June 30, 1922, the House of Representatives passed a pro-Zionist resolution, proposed by Representative Hamilton Fish, which was similar to that proposed earlier by Senator Henry Cabot Lodge.[158] But the American vote did not have much of an impact on the political atmosphere in England.

On the day after the vote in the House of Lords, Hubert Young, Shuckburgh's assistant in the Middle Eastern Department of the Colonial Office, warned Churchill in a departmental minute that unless the Lords' vote could be "signally overruled" by the House of Commons, there would be more trouble once the Palestine Arab delegation returned to Palestine.[159] The Colonial Office debate in the House of Commons took place on the evening of July 4 and centered on Palestine. William Joynson-Hicks led the attack against Zionist activity in Palestine by deploring the fact that the Rutenberg concession contracts had never been submitted to Parliament. He claimed that the Balfour Declaration was inconsistent with the promises made to the Arabs and attacked Herbert Samuel who, as a declared Zionist, was unsuitable as high commissioner. Joynson-Hicks concluded with the demand that the Mandate for Palestine not be forwarded to the Council of the League of Nations in its present form.

The colonial secretary responded for the government. Churchill delivered a brilliant speech during which the House of Commons repeatedly rocked with laughter. He defended the Balfour Declaration as well as the Rutenberg concessions, often quoting statements of those opposing the Zionists to show how, earlier, they had supported Zionism in almost lyrical terms. At the end of his speech Churchill declared that the vote of the House of Commons would be regarded as a vote of confidence. He appealed to the members to reverse the vote of the House of Lords, which they did with an overwhelming majority of 292 in favor of the government and only 35 against.[160] This vote was viewed by everyone as a clear triumph for the Zionists. The next day Churchill telegraphed to Sir Wyndham Deedes that as a result of the vote in the Commons "every effort will be made to get terms of mandate approved by Council of League of Nations at forthcoming session and policy will be vigorously pursued."[161]

The two weeks prior to the opening of the session of the Council of the League of Nations culminated six nerve-racking months. As his patience wore thin and his level of frustration rose, Weizmann was given to outbursts, sometimes self-pitying, sometimes self-righteous, but always angry at the multitude of enemies who never seemed tired of blocking the road toward the creation of the Jewish national home. In June he wrote to Albert Einstein, "All the shady characters of the world are at work, against us. Rich servile Jews, dark fanatic Jewish obscurantists, in combination with the Vatican, with Arab assassins, English imperialist anti-Semitic reactionaries—in short, all the dogs are howling. Never in my life have I felt so alone—and yet so certain and confident."[162]

A month later, with only a week remaining before the Council meetings, Weizmann wrote to his family in Haifa:

> Even in a long letter it's difficult to describe the sorrows and aggravations I have had to endure from all sides in the course of the last six months; at times it looked as if all the hard work of so many sorrowful years was in very grave danger and, God forbid, almost near collapse; days of distress, sleepless nights and endless travelling without a single moment's peace. So, difficult and bitter weeks and months flew by; the last month was perhaps the worst of them all; enemies rose against us from all sides, Jew-baiters crept out of the dark corners and tried to destroy us; they waged their war against us with the help of slander, denunciations, distortion and lies—and we had to stand firm against all this without losing our heads, hoping and trusting that justice and truth would triumph in the end.[163]

On the eve of the Council meetings in London, Weizmann wrote to Julius Simon that he had done everything "which was humanly possible" to prepare for a smooth ratification of the Mandate for Palestine. At his request Lionel de Rothschild, whose bank carried great influence abroad, cabled the president of Brazil, urging that his country not cave in to Vatican pressure but approve the Mandate for Palestine.[164] Weizmann received the sympathetic and active support of Arturo Allessandri, the president of Chile, as well as that of the prime minister of Uruguay.[165] Since January 1922 he had traveled a number of times to France to lobby with French politicians. In mid-June 1922, in the midst of the hectic activities surrounding the impending White Paper and the debate in the House of Lords, he managed to go on a week-long visit to Paris.

He did not wish to leave any loose ends untied, and as he had done in April in Italy, he met with politicians and officials representing the major political forces: Georges Clinchant, permanent secretary of the Eastern Department at the Quai d'Orsay; Senator Anatole de Monzie; Leon Blum, leading socialist member of the Chamber of Deputies and future premier; Marius Moutet, also a member of the Chamber of Deputies and an expert on colonial affairs; and Raymond Poincaré, the French premier. He received satisfactory assurances from all of them,[166] as he had earlier in March from both the former French premier Aristide Briand and the president, Alexandre Millerand.[167] Until the day before the vote of the Council, Weizmann arranged for sympathizers in Spain to appeal to their government, while he himself lobbied with the Spanish representative on the Council.[168] Throughout this period he kept in close touch with Sokolow and Jabotinsky, advising and sometimes directing their efforts at increasing the visibility of Zionism in the United States. These propaganda efforts were far more successful than their fund-raising.

Apart from these public, and often publicized, diplomatic efforts, Weizmann also encouraged lobbying efforts that he tried to keep out of the public eye, such as the formation of committees to influence public opinion in favor of the Mandate for Palestine. In mid-May 1922, David Eder informed the Zionist executive in London that Pere Don Salvatore Bandak, a Catholic priest who opposed the anti-Zionist views of the Latin patriarch of Jerusalem, Louis Barlassina, was willing to travel to London and Rome to support the Zionist cause. Eder provided the priest with the initial funding for his trip and promised that Weizmann would provide the rest. Bandak did arrive in London and probably met Weizmann. For reasons of secrecy and security, they communicated with each other in writing. Bandak proceeded to Rome, where he was aided by Dante Lattes and other Zionists. Bandak met with a number of high church officials, including with Gasparri and the pope himself and apparently attempted to weaken Barlassina's position. It is not clear to what degree his efforts aided the Zionists and to what degree he simply used them in the cause of the local intrachurch rivalries in Palestine.[169] The episode does indicate Weizmann's willingness to employ a variety of lobbying techniques to soften the Vatican's stand on Zionism.

On July 24, 1922, the Council of the League of Nations, meeting at St. James's Palace in London, unanimously ratified the Mandate for Palestine as submitted by Britain.[170] The Zionists were overjoyed. On the other hand, the Fifth Arab Congress, which met in Nablus during the last week of August 1922, rejected both the Mandate for Palestine and the White Paper. Herbert Samuel's subsequent attempt to implement the constitutional plans he so carefully worked out in London were also rejected.[171] The Arab nationalists organized a well-managed and effective boycott of elections to the Legislative Council in February 1923. Even Samuel's attempts to revive the defunct Advisory Committee on Palestine failed completely.[172] The Zionists, on the other hand, who had re-

luctantly assented to the White Paper, felt obliged to also accept its off-
spring, the Legislative Council. Weizmann and his colleagues, who feared
that the White Paper would place the Palestinian Arabs in a position to
veto Jewish immigration,[173] were naturally pleased by the Arabs' absolute rejection of Samuel's attempts to draw them closer into the government's orbit.

The ratification of the Mandate for Palestine came during the final
months of Lloyd George's pro-Zionist government. Lloyd George resigned from office in October 1922, and a new, Conservative government, much less friendly to the Zionists, assumed power. Approved in
the nick of time, the Mandate for Palestine was one of Weizmann's
crowning political achievements to date, the first international recognition of the World Zionist Organization as the legitimate representative
of the Jewish people.[174] By specifically referring to the Balfour Declaration in its preamble, the Mandate for Palestine gave immediate practical
and political meaning to what in 1917 was no more than a letter of intent. Weizmann's cherished dream since the fall of 1914, that "Palestine
fall within the sphere of British influence and [that] Britain encourage a
Jewish settlement there,"[175] finally came true. Weizmann considered this
moment the end of the first chapter of the Zionist political struggle.[176]

In a widely distributed circular to "the Jewish People," Weizmann
declared, "By virtue of this act of international law, significant alike both
for the Jewish people and the comity of nations, the political aim formulated in the Basle Programme—the securing of the [Jewish National]
Home by public law—has been fulfilled."[177] This seemed to have been
the consensus—at least in the immediate aftermath of the ratification—
of the rest of the Jewish world, and an avalanche of congratulatory messages reached him.[178] Even Jabotinsky, who later disavowed the Mandate for Palestine, wrote to Weizmann in August 1922 in almost lyrical
terms:

> a colossal document and absolutely ineffaceable. Its failings you yourself
> know, but on the other hand there is nothing in it, not a single sentence
> which in a severe judicial analysis could exclude our most remote goal—
> even a Jewish State. This Mandate is an almost idealistically elastic recep-
> tacle for our energies. No matter how much we put into it . . . it will not
> burst. When I remember the beginning: Manchester and Justice Walk in
> London [where the two lived together for a while], and how all this was
> built up like children's toy bricks—and *sucked out of the thumb of one man*—I
> must say to you—and I flatter myself that I know a little history—that this
> process is without parallel as a personal performance.[179]

There were, of course, also those who criticized the Mandate for Palestine, including Menahem Ussishkin and Jabotinsky himself, whose
private letter to Weizmann did not square with his public pronouncements. Other critics were mostly members of the older generation of
Herzlian Zionists who felt that it did not quite meet their expectations

of Herzl's envisioned charter. At the *Jahreskonferenz* of the Zionist Organization in Carlsbad, a month after the confirmation of the Mandate for
Palestine, Weizmann defended not only the executive's acceptance of
the Mandate but its consent to the White Paper as well. During the
debate he reiterated his strong belief in the organic growth of the movement and the settlement in Palestine:

> They [the opponents of Weizmann] talk about a legendary Charter which
> nobody has ever seen and nobody has read. They say that this Charter
> contains quite different things than the Mandate. I am quite prepared to
> believe that. But the difference between that Charter and the Mandate is
> that the Charter was never obtained, whereas the Mandate is there. . . .
>
> It is true . . . that the Mandate is different from the way the Jewish peo-
> ple had interpreted the Balfour Declaration in 1917. This fact cannot be al-
> tered; we can only meet it by an imperishable belief that, if only we go on
> working and working in Palestine, the time will come when there will be
> another opportunity of giving the Mandate its true value. . . .
>
> The redemption of Israel cannot be accelerated by resolutions. . . . Of
> course, the Declaration and the Mandate, and our whole life, are nothing
> but stages on the way to this redemption. I believe in the organic growth of
> the Jewish people in spite of all obstacles. That was the fundamental differ-
> ence which has always separated us. The Declaration and the Mandate make
> our way easier; and the value of the Mandate, apart from being a great
> success of Zionism, consists in the recognition of the Jewish people. This is
> of immense value. . . .
>
> When 200,000 Jews will be in Palestine, many a feature of the Mandate
> will change. If only the Zionists do their duty, and do not merely wait for
> the whole of Jewry to do its duty; if the Zionists do not rely on the wisdom
> of their leaders alone, that aim will be attained.[180]

Weizmann hinted broadly, once again, at his resignation, should the
GAC not accept the executive's political judgment. Some of his opponents also threatened resignation, but in the end differences were patched
up, at least for the moment. Most of those assembled agreed that the
Mandate for Palestine was yet another of Weizmann's spectacular
achievements. Weizmann was, of course, not the single most decisive
factor in its final attainment. The political and strategic considerations of
the major powers obviously played the crucial role. But he was doubtless the driving engine and chief coordinator of all the Zionist plans that
helped bring about its ratification.[181] Weizmann's numerous trips across
the Continent, his extensive correspondence with those who had an interest and influence in the matter, and his personal conversations with
statesmen, politicians, and civil servants gave him access to information
that could not otherwise have been obtained. He knew that accurate
intelligence was crucial in the international power play in which he was
involved, and he thus became the nerve center for what was in essence
a battle plan. He employed techniques he had used since his early years
in Geneva when he was the moving spirit and chief strategist behind

the Democratic Faction. Over the years he honed and perfected these techniques. Whereas during World War I he was, more often than not, the general in the field, in this case he was both chief of staff and the officer in charge of daily operations. His formal position as president of the WZO allowed him this time to assume both functions, giving him the advantage of full control and greater efficiency.

Despite the great cost to his health and family life, Weizmann carried out his tasks, as he had from the start of his Zionist career, out of a sense of *noblesse oblige*. As early as 1902 he had written to Vera, then his fiancée, that the burden of fulfilling the Zionist dream was given to a few chosen men and women. The sense that he was one of them continued to be a motivating force of his life. It was a feeling he confided to his closest companions during moments of despair or elation. Just before the Mandate for Palestine was ratified, he wrote to his sister:

> You are right—the Mandate was written for the greater part with my own blood, but who knows, perhaps this is the purpose of my wandering all my life, from Motele to London, in order to accomplish this great task; when I look at the Jewish community here, and in all the Western countries, when I remember the destruction in the East, my heart freezes, and I come to the conclusion that only the Chosen Ones who have acquired all their moral strength from the only true Jewish source—only they are prepared and fit to assume the burden of work for the sake of others. . . . So let us not complain of our destiny: it may be difficult, but it's beautiful![182]

The burden Weizmann was to assume over the next two dozen years would be quite different from anything he had experienced hitherto. It had little of the high drama and personal thrill that were associated with the receipt of the Balfour Declaration or the Mandate for Palestine. It required, nevertheless, every ounce of the statesmanship he had acquired. In the annals of the history of the Jewish national home, these years record achievements by Weizmann, gained through a slow, focused, and determined policy, that were as crucial, and as difficult to attain, as his previous spectacular feats.

XI

Conclusion

Six weeks before the Balfour Declaration was issued, C. P. Scott, whose judgment was respected, if not feared, by the ruling elite of the British government, wrote to Chaim Weizmann: "You are the only statesman among them."[1] Scott, editor of the *Manchester Guardian*, was referring to the Zionist leaders in England. The weight of evidence presented in this volume supports Scott's view that Weizmann had shown wisdom and skill in conducting the public affairs of the Zionist movement. In this conclusion I will attempt to sketch some of the personal features of Weizmann's qualities of statesmanship as well as some of the mechanisms he used in putting them to good effect.

By 1917, Weizmann had been catapulted by events, as well as by his own energy, talent, and ambition, to the position of *primus inter pares* within the World Zionist Organization's leadership on the Continent. Though he was still without official title except for the newly acquired presidency of the marginal English Zionist Federation, few Zionists or outside observers had any doubt as to who was the foremost Zionist leader. Moreover, one could argue that by the spring of 1918 Weizmann had become one of the best-known Jews of his day. He had been received by the king of England, had the blessing of the prime minister and foreign secretary, and had been lionized wherever there was a concentration of Jews for his part in the Balfour Declaration. That a Zionist leader from the provinces, a mere reader at Manchester University and clearly not the man considered heir of Herzl or even Wolffsohn, could appoint himself spokesman for Zionism and succeed so brilliantly is a feat that requires some explanation.

The case of Weizmann inevitably raises the question of the role of the individual in history. To what degree was Weizmann in control of the events that led to the Balfour Declaration, to the diplomatic success in San Remo, or to the ratification of the Mandate for Palestine? Alternately, was he simply a convenient and unsuspecting instrument in the hands of shrewd politicians? Given his unique role as an almost sole representative of the World Zionist Organization during the eight years

covered in this volume, the answers to these questions may shed light
not only on his biography but on larger historical processes as well. It is
wise to state at the outset that the answer may not necessarily be clear-
cut and one-sided. Both interpretations might be true. And no matter
which documentation the historian might present, in the final analysis
the interpretation will be based on the sum total of Weizmann's activities at any given period.

The personal qualities that enabled Weizmann to function as a skilled
diplomat and statesman have been pointed out before: his stamina and
tenacity, grasp of original ideas, clarity of thinking, adaptability to new
political situations, organizational abilities, penchant for synthesizing
difficult and disparate concepts, wit, charm, and perceived authenticity
as a "representative" East-West Jew are but a few. Of great importance
to the period beginning with World War I was his ability to forge and
maintain relationships with non-Jews of all walks of life. All these traits
were in evidence during his years in Manchester from 1904 to 1914,[2] but
in the eight years under consideration they were honed and refined in
the service of his diplomacy. This is not to claim that his less attractive
traits—intense jealousy, inability to share credit, autocratic demeanor,
tendency to impute impure motives to enemies and friends alike, quick-
ness to take offense, impatience—all apparent before 1914, disappeared.
On the contrary, they continued to be a source of great irritation, particularly to those close to him. But, on the whole, the public persona of
the Zionist leader overshadowed the blemishes and warts of the private
man. To politicians and statesmen in Britain and elsewhere, Weizmann
appeared as a dignified spokesman of Jewry.

Weizmann's uncanny ability to consider Zionist proposals as both a
Zionist insider and a British insider was not appreciated at first, not
even by his closest English Zionist collaborators, his unofficial "think-
tank." In 1915, while reviewing a memorandum by Weizmann on Zionist desiderata, Leon Simon could barely contain his criticism:

> I feel it necessary to record my very genuine conviction that you have weak-
> ened the case instead of strengthening it. You are committing *the fatal mis-
> take of Herzl—that of making anti-Semitism the foundation stone of your building.*
> Like him you are approaching the problem from the outside—not essentially
> as a Jew, but from the standpoint of the Goyim. You say with emphasis that
> it is a problem in the solution of which humanity is interested. That is no
> doubt true. But humanity is not interested . . . in a Jewish solution of the
> problem, and we are, or ought to be. . . . Palestine comes into your scheme
> as an accident, not as an essential. To my mind the claim to Palestine of the
> Jew for whom Palestine is an inner necessity—because he approaches the
> problem as the heir of Jewish tradition—is immeasurably stronger than that
> of the Jew who asks the world to get rid of a nuisance for its own sake.
> . . . After all, a generation or two may so change European conditions that
> arguments based on the indigestibility [*sic*] of the Jew, his mobility and so
> forth, may become quite inapplicable. . . .
> It was quite natural that Herzl should take the point of view of the Goyim,
> for he was a Goy. But you, who come from Pinsk—what are you doing in

that gallery? There is only one thought that consoles me: that just as Herzl's work was in fact turned to the service of the real national idea . . . so will yours be. But at this hour of crisis I should so like to see a Jew from Pinsk stand up to the world and say—"I demand the possibility of being a Jew!"[3]

Leon Simon's fear that Weizmann would misrepresent Zionist aspirations in order to curry favor with the British was misplaced, as he himself later realized. Much like Herzl whom he had emulated even as he fought against some of his methods and ideas, Weizmann knew which arguments to present when dealing with his British interlocutors. His timing during such encounters was always exquisite. He knew how to take into account the background, status, motivation, and political outlook of the men and women with whom he discussed Zionism. He never adopted one method or one line of explanation when dealing with British statesmen. He was at his best when unrehearsed, noncollaborative, and unedited. Sir Charles Webster, who in 1917 as a young intelligence officer observed Weizmann's negotiating style at close range, later explained why Weizmann succeeded where his Zionist colleagues had failed:

The significant thing was that these able and active men, some with a lifetime's devotion to the Zionist cause behind them, had often very different views from those of Dr. Weizmann as to how that cause could best be served. Many had little connection with Britain and were not very proficient in the English language. In some cases their very zeal was an embarrassment, and since they knew little of the mysterious processes of British government, they were apt to say and do things which hindered rather than forwarded the cause they had at heart. . . .

   In the critical years 1917 to 1920, all these leaders, with few exceptions, were brought to accept the policy which Dr. Weizmann had advocated from the beginning. Without this measure of unity there could have been no National Home. . . . Would it have taken place without the exercise of Dr. Weizmann's energy, patience, psychological insight, complete knowledge of the various aspects of European Jewry, and, above all, his sense of timing and the courage to take great decisions at the appropriate moment?[4]

Weizmann knew when to advance his case in camera and when to enlist mass support. On a number of occasions, advised by only a few men and women, he coordinated lobbying efforts through other groups including encouraging public demonstrations in the United States that attracted much attention. He employed to greatest advantage the one lobbying method which he had honed and perfected during the war years—the open-ended, intimate interview with a small group, preferably with a key person. These interviews were conducted in official residences, government offices, restaurants, and clubs of Britain's ruling elite. Weizmann became equally skilled in the context of garden parties, teas, and dinner parties. In the midst of small talk and gossip, he was often called upon to explicate, or justify, Britain's support of Zionism. Diaries and letters of the period reveal that without any preparation Weizmann could launch, with or without invitation, into a coherent, synthetic, and satisfying explanation of the present Jewish "condition" and prospects for the future.

Weizmann's approach to the British was quite different from that of his peers. He had no desire to appear as the authentic voice of English Jewry. This may seem surprising, in view of the contention of his local anti-Zionist opponents that the Zionists were a foreign element. They claimed that the true representatives of Anglo-Jewry—themselves—should be those who dealt with the government and should be consulted by the government on matters of Jewish interest. But Weizmann was convinced, as was Herzl in his own way, that by making no claims of kinship with the gentiles whom he approached he made it easier for them to accept him as a negotiating party to whom they could speak frankly. He appeared as the spokesman of world Jewry, not of Anglo-Jewry, and even more specifically as an emigré Russian Jew by origin and a Jewish Palestinian patriot by intent.

With his special interest so clearly stated, and making no claim to rights as an Englishman that were embarrassing to men and women conscious of their prejudice, as so many pro-Zionist British were,[5] Weizmann's Anglophile policy, sometimes questionable in the eyes of other Zionists,[6] was exceptionally persuasive to Englishmen. Successful with politicians in many countries, Weizmann's charm—what he referred to as his "blue voice"—seemed to work best when applied to the British. On the French, Italians, and others it had less impact, and only occasionally did it move his fellow Zionist politicians.

Englishmen often struggled to maintain a certain distance from Zionism but felt drawn to it by Weizmann's personality and the force of his arguments.[7] Two examples—one from a friend of Weizmann, one from a bystander—may suffice to illustrate these conflicting emotions. While serving in Cairo as chief political officer, Richard Meinertzhagen recorded in his diary:

> Zionism under the propelling influence of Weizmann, has been to me what I can best describe as the anomaly of a pleasant infliction. . . .
>
> I am not surprised that people think I must be a Jew, when I stand alone among Christians here as a friend to Zionism. And that is the irony of the whole situation, for I am also imbued with anti-semitic feelings. . . . The idea of fighting for Jews against Christians and my own people is most distasteful to me, but it is what I have had to do out here for the last few months. And I feel that the best in Zionism is an ideal well worth fighting for, an idea which must eventually materialize and win. It was indeed an accursed day that allowed Jews and not Christians to introduce to the world the principles of Zionism, and that allowed Jewish brains and Jewish money to carry it out. . . .
>
> A word about Weizmann, the leader of the Movement. Seldom did I admire a man more. Never did I see such singleness of purpose, such determination, such farsightedness and such a rich intellect, all embodied in one soul. Seldom has a man dealing in such large ideas been so honest and so sincere. So much is this the case, that it annoys me that he should be so far

ahead of Christians in intelligence and general purity of mind, and it annoys me that such a continent of knowledge should be combating Christians for principles which are Christian, and which are as pure and progressive as any principles since the day of Christ.[8]

Ronald Storrs, governor of Jerusalem from 1917 to 1926 and, arguably, one of the most intelligent, able, and controversial administrators during thirty years of British rule, expressed similar views. In his memoirs he sketched a portrait of Weizmann that, though tinged with antisemitism, is nevertheless a fair measure of the Zionist leader during the period of the Zionist Commission:

What European University, diplomatic chancery or legislature assembly, would not be richer by the personality of Dr. Chaim Weizmann. . . . An almost feminine charm combined with a feline deadliness of attack; utter disillusion over both Gentile and Jew, together with burning enthusiasm and prophetic vision of what negotiation may still win from the one for the other. Ruthless and tolerating no rival, yet emotional; contemptuous but . . . a fair dealer. He was a brilliant talker with an unrivalled gift for lucid exposition. . . . As a speaker almost frighteningly convincing, even in English . . . with all that dynamic persuasiveness which Slavs usually devote to love and Jews to business.[9]

Weizmann's affinity with things British[10] was coupled with a detachment from contentious domestic political issues. Partly, this detachment stemmed from the fact that the Britons he favored were upper-class academics and cosmopolitan politicians. Partly, it was calculated to make his dealings with British leaders of all parties easier. Weizmann took care to nourish and preserve his relationship to the gentile milieu even in moments of great frustration. If his judgment was affected by the kind of Britons he met, as Weizmann's detractors charged, it also afforded him special insights as to how to manipulate them to his own advantage.

Weizmann was the sole Zionist representative during World War I who was acceptable as both an insider and an outsider in British government and high society. He could speak to the Britons in tones of intimacy while simultaneously rebuking and protesting with credibility. In turn, they spoke to him frankly about their own colleagues and even confided to him their own prejudices about Jews and Judaism. Those, like Max Nordau, who accused Weizmann of being too cozily cocooned within British policy, misunderstood the advantage such a position gave him. There was virtually no door in Whitehall, no fashionable salon in London, that he could not open, even if he occasionally banged it shut in a calculated burst of emotion. Thus Robert Cecil could describe to his colleagues that Weizmann came to see him "in fine rage" without adding a single critical comment about the Zionist's behavior in his memorandum.

After reading one of Weizmann's memoranda to Arthur Balfour, Ahad

Ha'Am wrote to his disciple, "During the two thousand years of our exile, this is, I believe, the first instance that a Jew writes in such a 'tone' to the Foreign Secretary of a mighty empire about the national interests of the Jews." Ahad Ha'Am attributed Weizmann's ability to conduct himself in such a manner to his personal qualities.[11] This Zionist sage, who always dispensed praise parsimoniously, earlier summarized Weizmann's rise as a symbol of Zionism in a few, short sentences: "You began your work here . . . as a private Zionist. Your personal qualities and favorable conditions brought it about that in a short time you became practically the symbol of Zionism for many men of influence. . . . You were elected by objective conditions and objective conditions will dismiss you when the time comes. . . . But until then you cannot leave your place without evoking attitudes very damaging to the Zionists . . . and no other persons could carry on the work that you began."[12]

The "objective conditions" Ahad Ha'Am referred to were the fortuitous circumstances of the war that made Weizmann the "symbol of Zionism" in the eyes of the British elite. Having filled a vacuum in the leadership of the small and widely scattered World Zionist Organization, he managed to give the impression that he spoke in the name of "world Jewry." For the British, Weizmann was not simply a conduit to other Jews; there were many native-born Jews (Samuel, Mond, Rothschild, Greenberg) and foreign-born, resident or naturalized Jews (Gaster, Sokolow, Jabotinsky, Tschlenow) who might have served this purpose as well as, or better than, Weizmann by virtue of their institutional or personal prestige. But it was Weizmann in whom the British placed their greatest confidence and trust that he spoke for world Jewry. He managed to create the impression, which both sides knew was, at best, grossly exaggerated, that, as Isaiah Berlin puts it, "he himself [was] a world statesman, representing a government in exile, behind which stood a large, coherent, powerful articulate community."[13]

Both partners to the negotiations that led to the Balfour Declaration—to be anchored more firmly by other binding arrangements in the following five years—fully understood that they were using each other for their own political purposes. Though the British treated Weizmann as a statesman representing a sovereign nation, they knew that he was not; it is difficult to attribute their reluctance to acknowledge as much except to Weizmann himself.[14] Given the lack of political and military power at his disposal, one can only marvel at Weizmann's diplomatic brinkmanship in the face of so many major challenges: the Balfour Declaration, the Zionist Commission, the draft Mandate for Palestine, and the Churchill Memorandum, to name just a few. Referring to the large gap between the resources Weizmann commanded and the results he sought, one of his ablest disciples concluded that "Weizmann's achievement was perhaps the last instance in diplomatic history of persuasion without power."[15]

What made it possible for the British as well as for Weizmann to handle their negotiations smoothly, without embarrassment, while maintaining an air of diplomatic propriety and dignity, was their genuine affinity for each other. Weizmann, the most "Jewish Jew"[16] the British elite had encountered until then, understood how to synthesize both sentiment and *Realpolitik* into common interest. That Palestine was a necessary strategic asset for the British is beyond dispute. Standing behind its strategic value were reserves of tradition and religious sentiment for the Holy Land felt even by Britons hostile to Zionism and to Weizmann personally. One cannot underestimate the latent and overt power of biblical images evoked by the geography of Palestine and the Jewish claim on the Holy Land. Weizmann was often able to manipulate these reserves. The depth of these sentiments is evidenced by the fact that they were expressed long after the war utility of the Balfour Declaration had passed. Lord Curzon, who had objected to certain aspects of the Balfour Declaration and was most likely the person who vetoed a knighthood for Weizmann, nevertheless stated in a debate at the House of Lords in June 1920: "Our interest in Palestine had never been and ought not to be, measured in pounds, shillings and pence. It was a historic, traditional, religious and perhaps to some extent a sentimental interest. When we went there early in the War, we did so to prevent the flank of Egypt from being menaced by the Turks."[17]

That Weizmann drew support from a large and varied circle of patrons reflects his adaptability and his ability to coalesce British and Zionist interests. Even before they felt grateful to him as a reliable ally who made significant contributions to their war effort, the British appreciated Weizmann as a shrewd statesman attuned to their ways. For Weizmann was never a leader too vain to accept instruction. In fact he eagerly sought the help of others and was tireless in recruiting talented assistants. He was equally open to the nuances of attitude among those with whom he negotiated and very soon became a sensitive connoisseur of the shades of support and opposition that the Zionist cause encountered among Englishmen. He developed a fine instinct for the different approaches required to activate the sympathy available from various, sometimes mutually opposed, sources of potential friends.

This ability was sharpened as the war wore on. Naturally, Weizmann's scientific successes in the service of Britain, given without strings attached, added to his aura as an honest broker. Perhaps the best evidence for his acceptance is the fact that the British Foreign Office sent Weizmann, a naturalized British subject, a "foreigner," as some Britons and Jews saw it, as its sole representative on a sensitive diplomatic mission to Gibraltar. The men at Whitehall and Downing Street who had placed their faith in Weizmann, the scientist, to solve a problem of national magnitude, were easily persuaded to extend at least an open ear to Weizmann the Zionist statesman. Building on this confidence, Weizmann employed to the fullest his major personal assets: his contacts with the Jewish and British elite, his contacts with the academic community, and his scientific discoveries, which reached their peak in 1915–16. Felix Frankfurter witnessed at close range the impact Weizmann had with the resources at his command:

> Weizmann is the commanding figure in Zionism on this side of the water. . . . Weizmann is one of the significant figures in English public life. He has a sway over English public men and over English permanent officials who will continue to govern England when Lloyd George and Balfour will be no more—such as no other Jew in England or on the continent has or can easily acquire. His service has been a very deep one—not merely the political work arousing the English to an understanding of their own interests, but in educating the English mind to a felt [sic] understanding of what Zionism means.[18]

All along, Weizmann had to worry about forging close relations with British policymakers while keeping a watchful eye on developments in the Jewish and Zionist groups. The semblance of a united "world Jewry" had to be kept up as part of his plan to impress the British. Somewhat in the style of Herzl, Weizmann tried to keep in play the several forces active among Jews so that they would advance a policy he was developing positively in response to the pressures of his non-Jewish contacts. Those issues in which he took little interest he watched with a cautiously passive tolerance. Others, with which he could identify himself, needed to be controlled, lest his friends recklessly indulge in them in a spirit of dangerous "maximalism." Throughout the war years and until the Mandate for Palestine was finally ratified in July 1922, Weizmann focused on the goals he was trying to achieve. In dealing with the various partisan groups within Zionism, he exercised extreme caution to avoid failure in the larger issues.

Despite his high level of energy, Weizmann knew he had to conserve his time carefully. As the war continued, he gave relatively little attention to his responsibilities as leader of the local Zionist organization. His activity shifted radically from his prewar concerns as leader of dissenting student organizations or local head of a provincial branch of the movement. He was no longer primarily concerned with internal Zionist debates. Rather, his new position during the war allowed him to meet the staff and heads of ministries concerned with Zionist aspirations. With such exceptional opportunities for advancing Zionism in the quarters immediately responsible for policy decisions, Weizmann concentrated his personal efforts in this area rather than on the details of administering the affairs of the English Zionist Federation. Indeed, unlike some other Zionist leaders, Weizmann did not personally check the day-to-day performance of the organization he headed. Nor did he take great care to place his own men in charge of operations he wished to supervise at a distance.

On the broader issue of gaining the support of a united English, indeed, international Jewish community, Weizmann grew increasingly detached. Perhaps he accepted Ahad Ha'Am's dictum that the postwar settlement would owe little to Jewish communal power but would be granted by the victors in their own interest. Thus after his initial random efforts, he became cool to the negotiations for a consensus with non-Zionists and attempts to convene a united British Jewry. Simply put, Weizmann tried to keep the various elements in the Jewish community as much as possible out of his way in order to develop his own policy in response to the varied pressures of his non-Jewish contacts.

From the earliest days of the war, Weizmann worked almost as an independent agent to persuade England and his fellow Zionists that a British protectorate over Palestine was the best course of action for the British Empire as well as for the Jewish national cause. More than any other Zionist, Weizmann was certain that the British Empire would continue to be a permanent feature in the international arena and that its imperial interests, particularly in the Middle East, would continue to grow.[19] As soon as he arrived at this conclusion, he devised his diplomatic strategy accordingly, even in the face of stiff opposition from his Zionist peers and senior colleagues.

The support Weizmann received from various quarters in England and abroad waxed and waned. Divisions within English Zionism and the World Zionist Organization as to the political course the Zionists should follow militated against his pursuing his goals within an institutional framework. Despite the hardships such independent work entailed, it was clearly most suited to Weizmann's personality. Beginning in the summer of 1914, he functioned alone, making his own contacts and crucial decisions. When he did consult with others, it was increasingly out of a sense of obligation and collegial respect for his senior colleagues and the coterie of young men and women devoted to him.

After the war, this state of affairs changed little. Weizmann had grown so accustomed to this *modus operandi* that it was inevitable that encounters with strong-minded and independent leaders (Brandeis, Jabotinsky, Rutenberg), unwilling to submit to his will, would result in irreconcilable differences. These conflicts enabled Weizmann to remove competing leaders from his immediate sphere of political activity.

Weizmann's official status as president of the EZF had little effect on his influence on government circles. On the contrary, he may have gained the position because of the acceptance he attained among British political and academic leaders at a time when their interest in Zionism had risen sharply. He remained the chosen instrument of the British for conducting their relations with the Zionists. This position presented special problems for achieving full acceptance for himself and his policies in the constituency he "represented" and was presumed to be able to control. Although a nearly meaningless position, the presidency of the EZF did add a cloak of legitimacy to Weizmann's diplomatic activities. With or without title, it was clear to all who understood the internal dynamics of the Zionist leadership that by 1916 Weizmann had emerged as the paramount leader negotiating with the government.

In good part Weizmann's acceptance was also a direct consequence of the changes in the British government in December 1916. David Lloyd George, who as minister of munitions had been one of the sponsors of Weizmann's acetone project, became prime minister; and Balfour, who as first lord of the admiralty had been Weizmann's other ministerial chief, was named foreign secretary. The change in personnel, so favorable to Zionist prospects, coincided with a new interest in winning Jewish support in the last months of the Asquith government. Given his special status, it was left to Weizmann to lead the Zionist team along the tortuous path to the Balfour Declaration and the Mandate for Palestine.

Much has already been written about Weizmann's part in attaining the Balfour Declaration. Possibly, despite the large body of evidence marshaled by historians and others, some will continue to see Weizmann as a convenient tool in the hands of shrewd British politicians. Yet a careful reading of internal memoranda by these politicians reveals that, if anything, they were manipulated by Weizmann.[20] Others will continue to accord Weizmann credit as a (more or less important) member of a Zionist team that collectively masterminded the steps leading to the Balfour Declaration. Still others, myself included, judge his role to be crucial, if not exclusive. This debate is unlikely to be laid to rest in the near future. Nevertheless, I would suggest that whatever evidence and judgment are produced, one must keep in mind that the process leading to the Balfour Declaration, and operating for some time afterward, took place within the framework of mutual British-Zionist interests, buttressed by genuine and deep-rooted sentiments and affinities dating back to the nineteenth century.

Without reiterating the full story, it might be worthwhile to mention that the men closest to Weizmann had no doubt as to who among them deserved the credit. On November 2, 1917, two days after the final version of the Balfour Declaration had been communicated to the Zionists, Sokolow—the man most often cited by historians as deserving equal or more credit than Weizmann—declared before the fully assembled London Zionist Political Committee that the victory "was attained thanks to the boundless energy and dedication of our dear friend Dr. Weizmann." Sokolow also thanked all those present but did not mention them by name. Those attending then approved unanimously a resolution that began: "After being informed of the content of the Declaration by the British Government, this Committee congratulates the [Zionist] leaders, and particularly Dr. Weizmann, for their great achievement."[21] In the five years that followed Weizmann continued to be the major representative of the Zionists, primarily on account of his political success in 1917, not by virtue of elected office.

Clearly Weizmann was a leader who emerged from the political and organizational "periphery."[22] Of course he was a well-known Zionist who—unlike Brandeis—had strong organic ties to the rank-and-file of the Zionist movement. But politically Weizmann was an outsider—before 1914 kept out by others and after the war staying out by choice. The special circumstances of World War I enabled him to achieve within two to three years what he had been unable to realize in more than a decade of hard work prior to the war. Of course he had to wage a tough political struggle within the Zionist ranks both before and after the Balfour Declaration, but it was obvious by then that he had gained an advantage over his rivals. He was the one Zionist—if we put aside the somewhat different case of Herbert Samuel—who had established close relations with the British government and in whom British leaders had the greatest confidence.[23] Weizmann's stature among the Zionists rested to a large degree on their belief that he was the person who could best present their common cause to the British. The British, on the other hand, were convinced that Weizmann could control his fellow Zionists and large segments of "world Jewry." So certain were they of his standing among the Jews that they simply appointed him head of the Zionist Commission without consulting other Zionists or Jewish bodies. As long as Weizmann could maintain the trust of his constituency and the British, he could be effective in both camps.

With the authority of the British conqueror of Palestine behind him, with his ambition, flair, and nervous energy, Weizmann emerged as a dynamic leader during the period after the Balfour Declaration. At the same time the institutional frameworks of both the Palestinian Jewish community and the World Zionist Organization were in a state of flux. Weizmann took advantage of the chaos and his broad charge to set his own agenda among the Zionists while at the same time extending the original mandate, placing *faits accomplis* before both the British and the leadership of the Yishuv. Throughout he held that the cardinal point for the Zionists was to rely on the British, while to the British he explained that the Zionists were their best allies in the Middle East. As long as the Lloyd George government remained in power, Weizmann continued to maintain the position of the *homme de confiance* of the British. In that capacity he was able to convince them to reinforce their pledge to Zionism through international commitments in 1920 and 1922, while the Zionists finally officially elevated him to the presidency of the World Zionist Organization in 1920.

Some have argued that Weizmann "rose to a position of command in the [Zionist] leadership not by virtue of the Balfour Declaration but in the course of the subsequent political negotiations culminating in the San Remo decisions in 1920."[24] This, as we have seen, is not quite true. One could argue the point with greater force for the period 1921–22 culminating in the ratification of the Mandate for Palestine. In 1920, after all, Brandeis was a commanding figure in the councils of international Zionism. Only a year later, at the Cleveland Annual Convention, he was effectively neutralized by Weizmann. Moreover, Weizmann's co-optation in January 1919 into the Smaller Actions Committee was not a spontaneous act by his colleagues. Weizmann employed utmost skills in maneuvering, cajoling, and threatening, until they relented to partici-pate in a questionable procedure.

Yet, though it is true that the Balfour Declaration did not in itself propel Weizmann to the unchallenged position of leadership within the WZO, the declaration cannot be dismissed quite so lightly as a mere steppingstone in Weizmann's political career. True, it was first and fore-most a political opportunity. As a political and diplomatic achievement, however, it has the marks of genius. After all, Weizmann was the one who sensed in 1917 that, for a very brief moment, the political interests in and the historical sentiment for Palestine and Zionism had converged. He knew just when to give the delicate push. Later, from 1918 on, his achievement consisted of superb political craftsmanship. That crafts-manship would not have been possible without the foundation laid by the Balfour Declaration.

Weizmann's election to the presidency of the World Zionist Organi-zation in 1920 was, of course, important for his Zionist career but also an acknowledgment of a status he attained the moment the British ap-pointed him head of the Zionist Commission. Thus 1918 marks the be-ginning of a new era in Weizmann's leadership. The Zionist Commis-sion was public recognition that Weizmann was the Zionist chief, crowned by the British, with the Zionist rank-and-file following suit. Had he stood in 1918 for election in the World Zionist Organization, it is possible that he would have lost; certainly he would have been challenged. Since he never bothered to form a bureaucratic or institutional base, or to ally himself formally with a political party within the ranks of the World Zionist Organization, Weizmann depended on the actual or perceived backing of his British patrons for his political strength.

Weizmann was not a politician who understood the importance of coalition building or power sharing. He cared little for overseeing a well-oiled bureaucratic apparatus that could be activated on his behalf. Rather, his strength lay in his ability to appear as a statesman and diplomat of the Jewish people in international forums. Such a role accorded well with his elitist inclinations, evident since his student days. They expressed themselves concretely in his proclivity for dealing with notables—be they British, Arab, or Jewish—and for reaching agreements with them that he later presented to his "constituency."

Ironically the man who hailed from the Pale of Settlement did not see the Eastern European masses as important partners in the political decision-making process. Weizmann rarely bothered to travel to the cen-ters of Jewish life in Eastern Europe. Though twenty years earlier he had attacked Herzl for his autocratic manner, he did not arrive at deci-sions through a democratic process or group consensus. In that sense Weizmann was not different from Herzl or Brandeis. Like them, he controlled the flow of intelligence and tried to prevent free discussion on the range of issues whose public airing might be harmful to his negotiations. Like Herzl, and to a lesser degree like Brandeis, he was not immune from criticism, both before and after the Balfour Declaration, but he was able to deflect the opposition by continuing to score one political success after another.

As long as those aligned against him did not coalesce into a united political force, and as long as he was deemed indispensable by his fellow Zionists as well as by his British patrons, Weizmann was secure in his position. When British support for Zionism eroded, however, Weizmann's Zionist position weakened as well. Ironically, Weizmann's temporary forced removal from office in 1931 coincided with some of his most spectacular achievements in Zionism and with Britain as well. These seemingly contradictory processes still need to be explained.

Some of the processes leading to Weizmann's removal from office in 1931 were evident in the period covered here. Between 1914 and 1922 Weizmann solidified positions and principles he had begun to uphold before 1914. These positions, when seen as part of a total *Weltanschauung*, have often been referred to as "Weizmannism." They included a view of Zionism not as one party among many others within Jewry but as *the* force driving and leading the Jewish people as a whole. Weizmann viewed Zionism as a political and moral force that was open, flexible, and powerful enough to encompass and unite all other movements and ideas current in the Jewish world. Zionism was to assume the prime responsibility for the political, social, economic, and cultural fate of all Jews wherever they were.

World War I gave Weizmann the opportunity to attempt to realize this ambitious program by linking Zionism's success with that of Great Britain. His prewar tendencies toward synthetic, really cultural and pragmatic Zionism, were now coupled with a decisive Palestinocentric bent and a lack of interest in *Gegenwartsarbeit*—political and cultural work in the Diaspora. His belief, on the other hand, that there was a community of interests between Great Britain and Zionism that would propel Zionism into the forefront of Jewry was tempered by his conviction that Zionist enterprises of all kinds had to be conducted in a measured and moderate manner.

Weizmann's theoretical and ideological models for political work could be implemented successfully as long as British and Zionist interests were in tandem. After 1921–22, as Britain began to retreat from its wartime commitments, Weizmann's position began to erode—more quickly within the Zionist camp than in the esteem of his British partners. Indeed, the deterioration of his internal status was slowed and retarded by his intermittent political successes. This ten-year process had much to do with his inability to adjust to internal Zionist political changes, particularly the creation of new political parties. He formed no binding ties. The first condition for a successful leadership is a certain measure of consensus.

While there was a degree of consensus in Zionism, it was also—given the many lands, languages, and cultures the movement encompassed—impossible for any Jewish leader to win the confidence and support of a large majority of the Jewish people. Indeed, Weizmann was probably the most representative and prestigious Jew of the first half of the twentieth century. His staying power between World War I and World War II, during some of the most turbulent sociological, political, and economic periods in Jewish history, is adequate testimony to his stature and the reason he was not replaced.

Given these circumstances and his own elitist predilections, Weizmann depended only on the advice of a few trusted individuals. They were directly and personally loyal to him. With their support, Weizmann conducted his own diplomacy without interference—and often without a mandate—from the movement he headed. He was unable to tolerate opposition to his views, and those who worked with him accepted his word and followed his lead without asking too many questions, without offering too much criticism. When Weizmann decided that certain individuals had been disloyal, or that he no longer needed them, he did not hesitate to abandon them. He was never a politician who counted on the backing of others. He was a diplomat and statesman, perhaps even a strategic planner, who relied on his personal charisma and interpersonal skills.

As impatient as he was in some of his personal relations, Weizmann had consummate patience and exquisite timing when engaged in diplomacy. He was fond of comparing himself, politically and personally, to Camillo Cavour[25]—the Italian statesman who was, in his time, the object of constant distrust on the part of Young Italy—rather than to Giuseppe Garibaldi, the popular hero. The reasoned and moderate, if not always brilliant, politics of Cavour were responsible for the unification of Italy, whereas Garibaldi's heroic exploits achieved much less in concrete political terms. Cavour's approach to diplomacy was best suited to Weizmann's temperament and the political context within which he had to negotiate, at least for some time following the Balfour Declaration.

During the twenty years that followed the Balfour Declaration, Weizmann's skills as a statesman and diplomat were demonstrated repeatedly in England, on the Continent, in the Middle East, and in the United States. Since the British Empire continued to be the linchpin controlling the fate of the Jewish national home, most of Weizmann's diplomatic activities were centered in London and Jerusalem. It was mainly in England and Palestine that he continued to wage a rearguard action to retard the process by which Britain retreated from its commitments to facilitate the building of a Jewish national home.

For even while Britain became increasingly cool toward Zionist aspirations, it did not sever its relations with the Yishuv or the World Zionist Organization. Whether in or out of office, Weizmann managed to convince generations of British statesmen and politicians that the Balfour

Declaration—which many of them came to judge a political mistake—meant much more than they had originally bargained for.[26] He also succeeded in driving home the point that the abandonment of support for Zionist aspirations in Palestine would be coupled with a severe loss of prestige and moral stature for the British Empire. To gain some perspective on Weizmann's attempt to hold the British to their commitment to Zionism, one need only keep in mind the fate of Britain's wartime promises to the Armenians, Kurds, and Arabs—though the latter had a powerful spokesman in Lawrence. It seems that many of the concessions Weizmann was able to extract reflected the fact that in the process of negotiation his interlocutors turned pro-Weizmannites,[27] even if they did not become pro-Zionists. Perhaps this constituted his greatest achievement as a Zionist statesman.

Notes

Unless otherwise noted, all translations are by the author and all italics appear in the original.

Preface

1. Georgi Plekhanov, "The Role of the Individual in History," in *Theories of History: Readings from Classical and Contemporary Sources,* ed. Patrick L. Gardiner (New York, 1959), pp. 139–66.
2. Sidney Hook, *The Hero in History: A Study in Limitation and Possibility* (New York, 1950), pp. 153–54.
3. Obviously, I have cited only two views on a subject that has elicited much discussion. See the thoughtful essay by Isaiah Berlin, *Historical Inevitability,* Auguste Comte Memorial Trust Lecture 1, presented to the London School of Economics and Political Science (London, 1954).
4. Ben Halpern, "Weizmann vedoro," in *Haishiyut vedorah* (Jerusalem, 1963), pp. 157–68.
5. Ben Halpern, *A Clash of Heroes: Brandeis, Weizmann, and American Zionism* (New York, 1987).

I War

1. Chaim Weizmann to Yehiel Tschlenow, July 28, 1914, *The Letters and Papers of Chaim Weizmann,* ed. Meyer W. Weisgal et al., English ed., ser. A, vols. 1–3 (London, 1968–72), vols. 4–11 (Jerusalem, 1973–77), 6:426. The letters of Chaim Weizmann, which were published in twenty-three volumes, will hereafter be cited as *WL,* followed by volume and page numbers.
2. Chaim Weizmann, *Trial and Error* (New York, 1949), pp. 146–47.
3. See Egmont Zechlin, *Die deutsche Politik und die Juden im ersten Weltkrieg* (Göttingen, 1969); Isaiah Friedman, *Germany, Turkey and Zionism, 1897–1918* (Oxford, 1977).
4. Concerning the decision to open such offices, see "Protokoll der Sitzung des Grossen Actions-Comités vom 3. bis 6. Dezember 1914," Central Zionist Archives, Jerusalem (hereafter CZA), Z3/450.
5. Otto Warburg to Victor Jacobson, August 29, 1914, CZA, Z3/49.
6. Judah L. Magnes, speech at Aeolian Hall, New York, September 13, 1914,

Weizmann Archives, Rehovot, Israel (hereafter WA). See also Magnes to Weizmann, September 20, 1914, WA.

7. Jehuda Reinharz, "American Zionism on the Eve of the Balfour Declaration," *Studies in Zionism* 9, no. 2 (Autumn 1988): 131–45.

8. Shmarya Levin to Weizmann, October 2, 1914, Louis Dembitz Brandeis Papers, University of Louisville, School of Law, Louisville, Ky., microfilm ed., reel 70, Z/P 3-2.

9. See the two announcements by the Provisional Executive Committee for General Zionist Affairs (PZC): the first signed by Louis Brandeis [August 1914] and titled "To the Zionists of America," and the second, signed by Shmarya Levin and Louis Lipsky, dated September 8, 1914, WA.

10. On Louis Brandeis's road to Zionism, see Allon Gal, *Brandeis of Boston* (Cambridge, Mass., 1980).

11. Concerning the aims of the PZC, see Shmarya Levin to Arthur Hantke, September 10, 1914, WA; Louis Brandeis and Benjamin Perlstein to Chaim Weizmann, October 11, 1914, Brandeis Papers, reel 81, Z/P 22-1.

12. For a general account, financial and organizational, of the English Zionist Federation (EZF), see EZF, "Annual Report," 1915, CZA, L6/304.

13. Joseph Cowen to Weizmann, November 12, 1914, WA.

14. Concerning the membership of the executive, as well as all the provincial and London members of the EZF extended board, see *Jewish Chronicle*, February 20, 1914.

15. Moses Gaster to Weizmann, February 4, 1915, WA.

16. Horace M. Kallen to Alfred E. Zimmern, August 6, 1915, Brandeis Papers, reel 69, Z/P 3-1.

17. For a brief sketch of Israel Zangwill, see David Vital, "Zangwill and Modern Jewish Nationalism," *Modern Judaism* 4, no. 3 (October 1984): 243–53.

18. *Times* (London), August 19, September 9, 28, 1914.

19. See, e.g., *Jewish Chronicle*, January 22, 1915.

20. For a study of Lucien Wolf during World War I, see Mark Levene, *War, Jews, and the New Europe: The Diplomacy of Lucien Wolf, 1914–1919* (Oxford, 1991).

21. Harry Sacher was actually fired from his post at the *Daily News*, whose editors did not like his opposition to the war and toward Sir Edward Grey. See Sacher to Weizmann, June 10, 1915, WA.

22. For a critical evaluation of Simon Marks and Israel Sieff and their careers, see "How Marks Lost Spencer," *Sunday Times Supplement* (London), October 1984. See also Israel Sieff, *Memoirs* (New York, 1970).

23. Concerning Albert Hyamson's views, see his "The Future of Palestine," *New Statesman*, November 21, 1914.

24. For the relationship between Ahad Ha'Am and Weizmann, see Ben Halpern, "The Disciple, Chaim Weizmann," in *At the Crossroads: Essays on Ahad Ha'Am*, ed. Jacques Kornberg (Albany, N.Y., 1983), pp. 156–69.

25. Harry Friedenwald was acquainted with Weizmann's work on behalf of the university in Jerusalem. See Judah Magnes to Harry Friedenwald, May 6, 1914, WA.

26. Also present was another of Ahad Ha'Am's good friends, Zeev Gluskin, who was on a visit from Palestine.

27. Ahad Ha'Am to Mordechai Ben-Hillel Hacohen, September 2, 1914, *Igrot*

Ahad Ha'Am, vol. 5, *1913–1917* (Jerusalem and Berlin, 1924), p. 201; Ahad Ha'Am to Weizmann, September 3, 1914, ibid., p. 202.

28. Chaim Weizmann, speech at public meeting in Paris, March 28, 1914, *The Letters and Papers of Chaim Weizmann*, ed. Barnet Litvinoff, ser. B, vol. 1, *1898–1931* (New Brunswick, N.J., 1983), p. 117.

29. Weizmann to Judah Magnes, September 8, 1914, *WL*, 7:5–6; Weizmann to Shmarya Levin and Magnes, October 4, 1914, *WL*, 7:16–17.

30. Weizmann, *Trial and Error*, pp. 168–69.

31. Weizmann to Ahad Ha'Am, September 28, 1914, *WL*, 7:13.

32. Ahad Ha'Am to Weizmann, December 17, 1914, WA.

33. Weizmann to Ahad Ha'Am, December 18, 1914, *WL*, 7:93.

34. Leopold Greenberg to Weizmann, October 2, 1914, WA.

35. Weizmann to Ahad Ha'Am, September 14, 1914, *WL*, 7:7.

36. Ahad Ha'Am to Weizmann, September 15, 1914, *Igrot Ahad Ha'Am*, 5:201.

37. Weizmann to Ahad Ha'Am, September 16, 1914, *WL*, 7:8.

38. Weizmann to David Jochelman, November 15–16, 1914, *WL*, 7:41.

39. Weizmann to Israel Zangwill, October 4, 1914, *WL*, 7:18–19.

40. Weizmann to Israel Zangwill, October 19, 1914, *WL*, 7:25–28.

41. Ibid., p. 28.

42. Israel Zangwill to Weizmann, October 28, 1914, CZA, A 120/60.

43. Weizmann to Israel Zangwill, November 20, 1914, *WL*, 7:47–48. After circulating this letter to his friends, Weizmann was strongly criticized by Leon Simon for his stance on these two issues. Simon to Weizmann, December 1, 1914, WA.

44. Israel Zangwill to Weizmann, November 23, 1914, WA.

45. Jean Fischer to members of the SAC, December 14, 1914, WA.

46. "Protokoll der Sitzung des Grossen Actions-Comités vom 3. bis 6. Dezember [19]14 im Terminus-Hotel zu Kopenhagen," CZA, L6/37/I.

47. See, e.g., "Protokoll der Sitzung des Actions-Comités vom 23. und 24. März 1916—Haag, Holland," CZA, Z3/453. See also the statement by Shmarya Levin in *Dos Yidishe Volk*, no. 19, May 14, 1915.

48. See, e.g., the letter to Weizmann from his good friend Julius Simon of September 18, 1914, WA: "Es wird dich interessieren, dass die Erfolgen der Deutschen bisher ausserordentlich waren und dass alles von grösster Zuversicht ist." See also Abraham Lubarsky to Ahad Ha'Am, January 16, 1915, Ahad Ha'Am Archive, Jerusalem, concerning Shmarya Levin's pro-German and Austrian attitude.

49. Ahad Ha'Am to Weizmann, November 15, 1914, *Igrot Ahad Ha'Am*, 5:202–3. The translation is adapted, with slight changes, from Halpern, *Clash of Heroes*, p. 127.

50. Herbert H. Asquith, speech, November 9, 1914, *Times* (London), November 10, 1914, pp. 9–10.

51. Weizmann to C. P. Scott, November 12, 1914, *WL*, 7:38.

52. Weizmann to Ahad Ha'Am, November 12, 1914, *WL*, 7:37.

53. Weizmann to Judah Magnes, September 8, 1914, *WL*, 7:5.

54. Dvorah Barzilay, "Shat mashber kishat mifneh: Weizmann bemilhemet haolam harishonah," in *Medinai beitot mashber*, ed. Yosef Gorni and Gdalya Yogev (Tel Aviv, 1977), pp. 35–36.

55. "British Desiderata in Turkey-in-Asia: Report, Proceedings, and Appen-

dices," June 30, 1915, Cabinet Office Papers, Public Record Office, London (hereafter CAB), 27/1. See also Aaron S. Klieman, "Britain's War Aims in the Middle East in 1915," *Journal of Contemporary History* 3 (July 1968): 237–51.

56. Jehuda Reinharz, "Weizmann and the British General Elections of 1906," *Studies in Zionism* 5, no. 2 (Autumn 1984): 210–62.

57. In his reply to Samuel Alexander's request, Arthur James Balfour wrote that he had "the liveliest recollections of my conversation with Dr. Weizmann in 1906 and would be very glad to hear from him." Balfour to Alexander, November 17, 1914, WA.

58. Weizmann to Ahad Ha'Am, December 14–15, 1914, *WL*, 7:81–82.

59. Ahad Ha'Am to Weizmann, December 16, 1914, *Igrot Ahad Ha'Am*, 5:105.

60. Shmarya Levin to Weizmann, cable, September 14, 1914, WA.

61. Louis Brandeis to Weizmann, October 11, 1914, Brandeis Papers, reel 81, Z/P 22-1.

62. Arthur Hantke to Weizmann, October 16, 1914, WA. See also Horace Kallen to Louis Brandeis, October 1, 1915, Brandeis Papers, reel 69, Z/P 3-1.

63. Judah Magnes to Weizmann, cable, December 23, 1914, WA.

64. Judah Magnes to Weizmann, December 24, 1914, WA.

65. Weizmann to Abraham Lubarsky, February 1, 1915, *WL*, 7:132. On this point, see also Yossi Goldstein, "Ahad Ha'Am: A Political Failure?" *Jewish History* 4, no. 2 (Fall 1990): 33–48.

66. Ahad Ha'Am to Weizmann, August 24, 1915, Ahad Ha'Am Papers.

67. See, e.g., Weizmann to Ahad Ha'Am, August 27, 1915, *WL*, 7:234–35.

68. Weizmann, "Report Submitted to the Members of the Executive of the International Zionist Organization," January 7, 1915, *WL*, 7:119.

69. Weizmann to Judah Magnes, January 9, 1915, *WL*, 7:125.

70. Yehiel Tschlenow to Weizmann, February 18, 1915, WA.

71. Weizmann to Shmarya Levin, October 18, 1914, *WL*, 7:22–24. See also Judah Magnes to Weizmann, January 24, 1915, WA: "Shmarya does not write, because, being an Austrian citizen, he does not wish in any way to cause you even the possibility of embarrassment."

72. Moses Gaster to Weizmann, December 20, 1914, CZA, A203/214.

73. Judah Magnes to Weizmann, January 9, 28, 1915, WA.

74. Judah Magnes to Weizmann, January 24, 1915, WA.

75. Weizmann, *Trial and Error*, p. 148.

76. "Summary of a Conversation with Baron James de Rothschild," November 7, 1914, *WL*, 7:55–57.

77. Jehuda Reinharz, *Chaim Weizmann: The Making of a Zionist Leader* (New York, 1985), p. 398.

78. Simon Schama, *Two Rothschilds and the Land of Israel* (New York, 1978), pp. 188–89.

79. Derek Wilson, *Rothschild: The Wealth and Power of a Dynasty* (New York, 1988), p. 335.

80. See, e.g., Dorothy de Rothschild to Weizmann, March 8, 1915, WA.

81. See, e.g., Dorothy de Rothschild to Weizmann, November 19, 1914, WA, in which she informed him that she had seen Lord Crewe and Charles Rothschild, who seemed well disposed toward settlement of Jews in Palestine should it become British. She added, "If I can do anything for you, please let me know as I shall be only too delighted."

82. Richard Davis, *The English Rothschilds* (Chapel Hill, N.C., 1983), p. 245.
83. Dorothy de Rothschild to Weizmann, March 8, 1915, WA.
84. See, e.g., Rozsika Rothschild to Weizmann, June 29, 1915, WA.
85. Rozsika Rothschild to Weizmann, June 9, 1915, WA.
86. Rozsika Rothschild to Weizmann, June 11, 1915, WA.
87. Rozsika Rothschild to Weizmann, May 22, 1915, WA.
88. Miriam Rothschild, *Dear Lord Rothschild* (Philadelphia and London, 1983), pp. 245–46.
89. Harry Sacher to Lucien Wolf, December 1, 1914, Board of Deputies of British Jews Archives, London (hereafter BD), E3/204/1.
90. Harry Sacher to Weizmann, December 3, 1914, WA.
91. Weizmann to Alfred Zimmern, July 4, 1915, *WL*, 7:220.
92. Arnold J. Toynbee, *Acquaintances* (London, 1967), pp. 49–58.
93. Alfred Zimmern, quoted in Horace Kallen to Louis Brandeis, May 27, 1915, Brandeis Papers, reel 69, Z/P 3-1.
94. See, e.g., Alfred Zimmern to Weizmann, April 2, 1915, WA. Zimmern wrote in the fall of 1915: "I hold a watching brief for Zionism." Quoted in Horace Kallen to Louis Brandeis, October 1, 1915, Brandeis Papers, reel 69, Z/P 3-1. Kallen suggested to Brandeis that the PZC keep Zimmern fully informed of all developments in the American Jewish community.
95. Vera Weizmann, *The Impossible Takes Longer* (New York, 1967), pp. 51–52.
96. C. P. Scott did not recognize Weizmann's name even though Weizmann had written the report on the 1907 Zionist Congress for the *Manchester Guardian*. See Scott to J. E. Van der Wielen, July 14, 1907, Guardian Archives, Manchester University, John Rylands Library, Manchester, A/W35/1: "Dr. C. Weitzmann [*sic*] will act as our correspondent at the Zionist congress this year. . . . Mr. H. Sacher . . . will also be present."
97. Weizmann, *Trial and Error*, pp. 148–49.
98. That C. P. Scott knew very little about the Zionist movement prior to this meeting is clear from Scott to Weizmann, December 9, 1914, WA. See also Scott to Weizmann, December 13, 1914, WA.
99. Weizmann to Leopold Greenberg, September 16, 1914, *WL*, 7:9–10.
100. C. P. Scott to Harry Sacher, January 16, 1915, WA.
101. Weizmann to C. P. Scott, November 16, 1914, *WL*, 7:45.
102. Weizmann to C. P. Scott, November 12, 1914, *WL*, 7:38–39.
103. C. P. Scott to Weizmann, November 15, 1914, Victoria University Library, Manchester, A35/26.
104. See, e.g., C. P. Scott to Weizmann, November 22, 1914, WA.
105. See, e.g., Harry Sacher and Leon Simon to Weizmann, [January 1915], WA; Simon to Weizmann, January 5, 1915, WA; Simon and Sacher to Weizmann, February 24, 1915, WA.
106. C. P. Scott to Weizmann, November 29, 1914, WA. Albert Hyamson's article was "The Future of Palestine," *New Statesman*, November 21, 1914.
107. C. P. Scott to Weizmann, December 5, 1914, WA.
108. Weizmann to Harry Sacher, November 30, 1914, *WL*, 7:66.
109. Bernard Wasserstein, "Herbert Samuel and the Palestine Problem," *English Historical Review* 91 (October 1976): 754. See also Herbert Samuel's own testimony to this effect in his *Memoirs* (London, 1945), p. 139.
110. Herbert Samuel, aide-mémoire, November 9, 1914, Herbert Samuel Papers, Israel State Archives, Jerusalem, 100/1.

111. Reinharz, *Weizmann: Making of a Zionist Leader*, p. 338.
112. Weizmann, "Report Submitted to the Members of the Executive of the International Zionist Organization," January 7, 1915, *WL*, 7:111.
113. Ibid., p. 112.
114. See also letter of congratulations from C. P. Scott to Weizmann, December 13, 1914, WA.
115. See, e.g., Harry Sacher and Leon Simon to Weizmann, [January 1915], WA. Sacher and Simon opposed Weizmann's suggestion that he show Samuel a memorandum he was writing to the Zionist executive.
116. "Summary of a Conversation with Baron James de Rothschild," November 27, 1914, *WL*, 7:56.
117. Weizmann, "Report Submitted to the Members of the Executive of the International Zionist Organization," January 7, 1915, *WL*, 7:116.
118. Weizmann to Vera Weizmann, [December 23, 1914], *WL*, 7:97.
119. Weizmann, "Report Submitted to the Members of the Executive of the International Zionist Organization," January 7, 1915, *WL*, 7:118–19.
120. Francis Levenson Bertie, *The Diary of Lord Bertie of Thame*, ed. Lady Algernon Gordon Lennox (London, 1924), 1:105–6.
121. Weizmann to Vera Weizmann, December 29, 1914, *WL*, 7:100.
122. Herbert Samuel to Weizmann, January 11, 1915, WA.
123. C. P. Scott to Weizmann, January 14, 1915, WA.
124. In his autobiography, Weizmann wrote that he had breakfast with David Lloyd George and Herbert Samuel in early December and that C. P. Scott and Josiah Wedgwood were also present. In Weizmann's appointment book—often referred to as his diary (WA)—there is no indication that such a meeting took place. However, an entry in his appointment book for Friday, January 15, 1915, clearly states: "9:15 Ll. G. Breakfast," after which he was going to meet Harry Sacher, the chief rabbi [Joseph H. Hertz?], and Ahad Ha'Am. The fact that this meeting with Lloyd George was marked in his appointment book also shows that it was planned in advance and did not come as a surprise to Weizmann at the last moment, as he suggests in *Trial and Error*, p. 150. All indications are that it went well. See Samuel, *Memoirs*, p. 144. See also Weizmann, *Trial and Error*, p. 152, which recounts Lloyd George's favorable reaction to the meeting as he told it to Dorothy de Rothschild.
125. Herbert Samuel, "The Future of Palestine," memorandum, January 1915, Samuel Papers, 100/1.
126. Louis Brandeis to Julian Mack, September 27, 1933, Stephen Wise Papers, American Jewish Historical Archives, Waltham, Mass., box 106, folder L.D.B. (1928–1933).
127. Herbert Asquith to Venetia Stanley, January 28, 1915, *H. H. Asquith Letters to Venetia Stanley*, ed. Michael Brock and Eleanor Brock (Oxford, 1982), p. 406.
128. Herbert Samuel, notes, February 7, 1915, Samuel Papers, 100/1.
129. Herbert Samuel, "Palestine," memorandum, March 1915, WA.
130. Herbert Asquith to Venetia Stanley, March 13, 1915, *Asquith Letters to Stanley*, pp. 477–78.
131. Samuel, *Memoirs*, pp. 143–44.
132. Edward Grey, minute, March 15, 1916, Foreign Office Papers, Public Rec-

ord Office (hereafter FO), 371/2767/938: "I told Mr. Samuel at the time that a British Protectorate was out of the question."

133. Edwin Montagu to Herbert Asquith, March 16, 1915, David Lloyd George Papers, House of Lords Record Office, London, copy in WA.

134. On British war aims during 1914–16, see David French, *British Strategy and War Aims, 1914–1916* (London, 1986); Paul Guinn, *British Strategy and Politics, 1914 to 1918* (Oxford, 1965).

135. See, e.g., Charles Rothschild to Weizmann, June 9, 1915, WA: "I feel sure that from a psychological point of view . . . the establishment of a Jewish country would help our poor people. . . . I will give you my personal moral support towards Mr. H. Samuel's plan, which I cordially approve of."

136. Such was the case even with anti-Zionists like Leopold Rothschild and Claude Montefiore. See the record of their conversation with Herbert Samuel on February 14, 1915, Samuel Papers, 100/1.

137. "Palestine," February 7, 1915, Samuel Papers, 100/1; Weizmann to Dorothy de Rothschild, February 15, 1915, *WL*, 7:149.

138. Weizmann to Moses Gaster, March 6, 1915, *WL*, 7:165. But in a letter dated March 8, 1915, James Bryce wrote to Herbert Samuel: "I very much agree with your memorandum in principle though there are some minor points I would like to discuss with you. I am extremely glad you have put the matter before the Cabinet." Samuel Papers, 100/1. Thirteen months later Bryce wrote to Edward Grey suggesting that Britain would do well to gain control over sections of Palestine. Bryce to Grey, April 6, 1916, FO, 800/105.

139. Alfred Zimmern, quoted in Horace Kallen to Louis Brandeis, May 27, 1915, Brandeis Papers, reel 69, Z/P 3-1.

140. Halpern, *Clash of Heroes*, p. 134. See also Arthur J. Marder, *From the Dreadnought to Scapa Flow: The Royal Navy in the Fisher Era, 1904–1919*, 5 vols. (Oxford, 1961–70).

141. Halpern, *Clash of Heroes*, p. 134. See also John Terraine, *White Heat: The New Warfare, 1914–1918* (London, 1982), pp. 134–39.

142. Weizmann to Dorothy de Rothschild, February 15, 1915, *WL*, 7:149–50.

143. Weizmann to C. P. Scott, March 23, 1915, *WL*, 7:184.

144. Ibid.

145. Ibid.

146. Weizmann, "Report Submitted to the Members of the Executive of the International Zionist Organization," January 7, 1915, *WL*, 7:119.

147. Weizmann to Harry Sacher and Leon Simon, *WL*, 7:69–70.

148. Robert Cecil [to Theo Russell?], August 18, 1915, FO, 800/95.

149. Judah Magnes to Weizmann, January 9, 24, 29, 1915, WA.

150. Yigal Elam, *Hagdudim haivriim bemilhemet haolam harishonah* (Tel Aviv, 1973), pp. 19–25; Shulamit Laskov, *Trumpeldor: Sippur hayav* (Jerusalem, 1982), pp. 91–95.

151. See Weizmann's protest to Judah Magnes, January 29, 1915, *WL*, 7:127–29.

152. Judah Magnes to Weizmann, January 24, 1915, WA.

153. Judah Magnes to Weizmann, November 23, 1915, WA.

154. Ahad Ha'Am to Shmuel Pevsner, March 8, 1915, *Igrot Ahad Ha'Am*, 5:215–16.

155. See Shmarya Levin to Louis Brandeis, March 3, 1915, Brandeis Papers, reel 69, Z/P 3-1: "Dr. Tschlenow verwährt sich auf's entschiedenste dagegen, dass seine oder Dr. Weizmann's Tätigkeit zur Verschlimmerung der türkischen Beziehungen zur jüdischen Bevölkerung in Palästina beigetragen haben könnte."

156. Concerning the lack of cooperation among the Zionists in England, see Horace Kallen to Alfred Zimmern, August 6, 1915, Brandeis Papers, reel 69, Z/P 3-1.

157. Moses Gaster to Jacob Moser, January 13, 1915, CZA, A203/224.

158. Moses Gaster to Jacob Moser, January 25, 1915, CZA, A203/224.

159. *Jewish Chronicle*, January 29, 1915.

160. Moses Gaster to Weizmann, February 4, 1915, CZA, A203/224.

161. Weizmann to Moses Gaster, February 5, 1915, *WL*, 7:134–35. See also Weizmann to Gaster, February 8, 1915, *WL*, 7:140–42.

162. Moses Gaster to Weizmann, February 7, 1915, CZA, A203/224.

163. Weizmann to Moses Gaster, February 8, 1915, *WL*, 7:142.

164. Yehiel Tschlenow and Nahum Sokolow to EZF, March 10, 1915, CZA, A18/35.

165. See Moses Gaster to Weizmann, February 7, March 11, 1915, CZA, A203/224; Gaster to Jacob Moser, February 16, June 2, 1915, CZA, A203/224. See also Gaster to Nahum Sokolow, July 12, 1915, CZA, A18/41/2/1-4.

166. Weizmann to Ahad Ha'Am, February 9, 1915, *WL*, 7:145.

167. Moses Gaster to Weizmann, March 11, 1915, WA.

168. "Summary of a Conversation with Baron James de Rothschild," November 27, 1914, *WL*, 7:56; Weizmann, "Report Submitted to the Members of the Executive of the International Zionist Organization," January 7, 1915, *WL*, 7:116.

169. Weizmann to Charles Dreyfus, December 6, 1914, *WL*, 7:72.

170. Weizmann to Rozsika Rothschild, June 6, 1915, *WL*, 7:204.

171. *Jewish Chronicle*, February 5, 1915.

172. Weizmann, *Trial and Error*, p. 170.

173. Leon Simon to Weizmann, [January 1915], WA: "The two 'ows . . . have no intention of seeing S[amuel] without you—so don't worry about that."

174. According to Weizmann's appointment book, he saw Samuel on January 15, 1915, for breakfast with Lloyd George as well as on January 30 and February 14.

175. Lucien Wolf, aide-mémoire, November 17, 1914, BD, E3/2041/1.

176. See Lucien Wolf's extensive article on the subject, "The Zionist Peril," *Jewish Quarterly Review* 17 (1905): 1–25. See also Nahum Sokolow, "Eine Unterredung mit Mr. Lucien Wolf über die politische Lage und den Zionismus," June 25, 1912, CZA, Z3/421; Wolf to Nahum Sokolow, June 26, 1912, CZA, Z3/421.

177. Harry Sacher to Weizmann, November 17, 1914, WA. According to Lucien Wolf's record of November 17, 1914, Sacher had assured him that "the last Zionist Congress [1913] had practically eliminated political Zionism from its immediate programme and had resolved to rely on Cultural Zionism and Peaceful Penetration." BD, E3/204/1.

178. See also Lucien Wolf to Israel Zangwill, November 25, 1914, BD, E3/204/1.

179. Harry Sacher to Weizmann, November 17, 1914, WA. The following day, Leon Simon sent Lucien Wolf a number of books and pamphlets concern-

ing Zionist cultural work. See Simon to Wolf, November 18, 1914, BD, E3/204/1.

180. Weizmann to Harry Sacher and Leon Simon, December 4, 1914, *WL*, 7:69.
181. Leon Simon to Weizmann, December 2, 1914, WA.
182. Lucien Wolf to Harry Sacher, November 26, 1914, BD, E3/204/1; Sacher to Weizmann, November 29, 1914, WA. See also Sacher to Wolf, November 27, 1914, BD, E3/204/1.
183. Weizmann to Harry Sacher and Leon Simon, November 28, 1914, *WL*, 7:57–60. Taking his cue from Weizmann, Sacher wrote forcefully to Lucien Wolf: "We approach them [Anglo-Jewry's leaders] as one power in Jewry to another power in Jewry in the hope of securing a union of Jewish forces." Sacher to Wolf, December 1, 1914, BD, E3/204/1. See also Wolf to Sacher, December 2, 1914, BD, E3/204/1.
184. Lucien Wolf to Harry Sacher, November 30, 1914, BD, E3/204/1. See also Wolf to Sacher, December 3, 1914, BD, E3/204/1.
185. Harry Sacher to Weizmann, December 16, 1914, WA. See also Harry Lewis to Weizmann, December 18, 1914, WA.
186. Reported in Lucien Wolf to D. L. Alexander, December 16, BD, E3/204/1. See also Alexander to Wolf, December 18, 1914, BD, E3/204/1.
187. Weizmann to Joseph Cowen, February 16, 1915, *WL*, 7:150–51.
188. Weizmann to Harry Sacher, December 15, 1914, *WL*, 7:86.
189. Harry Sacher to Weizmann, December 16, 1914, WA.
190. Weizmann to Vera Weizmann, December 22, 1914, *WL*, 7:96.
191. Lucien Wolf to William Tyrell, December 18, 1914, quoted in Stuart Cohen, *English Zionists and British Jews: The Communal Politics of Anglo-Jewry, 1895–1920* (Princeton, N.J., 1982), p. 224. See also Wolf to D. L. Alexander, December 23, 1914, BD, E3/204/1, regarding a communication from Tyrell.
192. Leon Simon to Weizmann, January 6, 1915, WA.
193. Lucien Wolf, "Memorandum of an Interview with the Rt. Hon. Herbert Samuel," February 28, 1915, CZA, A77/3/1.
194. Lucien Wolf to Charles Henry, March 30, 1915, CZA, A77/3/1.
195. See report, April 29, 1915, FO, 371/2448/51705/51705, based on Lucien Wolf's report cited in n. 193 above. See also "Strictly Private and Confidential, For the Members of the Conjoint Committee Only," BD, E3/204/2.
196. Conjoint Foreign Committee, written statement, April 27, 1915, CZA, 18/22, also in BD, E3/204/2.
197. "Reply of Zionist Representatives on the Memorandum of the Conjoint Committee dated 27th April, 1915," May 11, 1915, BD, E3/204/2.
198. Lucien Wolf to Nahum Sokolow, June 11, 1915, BD, E3/204/2.
199. Weizmann to Vera Weizmann, December 31, 1914, *WL*, 7:102.

II Acetone

1. Weizmann to Israel Zangwill, October 19, 1914, *WL*, 7:26.
2. Weizmann to Isaac Epstein, December 16, 1914, *WL*, 7:87.
3. For Weizmann's work during this period, as well as his relationship with E. Halford Strange, see Reinharz, *Weizmann: Making of a Zionist Leader*, pp. 352–59.
4. The first detailed, technical overview of the various steps and techniques leading to Weizmann's discovery is contained in Horace B. Speakman, "The

Production of Acetone and Butyl Alcohol by a Bacteriological Process," *Journal of the Society of Chemical Industry* 38, no. 12 (June 30, 1919): 155–61. Speakman was employed during World War I at the British Acetones plant in Toronto, Canada. A less technical overview is provided by Frederick Nathan, "The Manufacture of Acetone," *Journal of the Society of Chemical Industry* 38, no. 14 (July 31, 1919): 271–73. See also Harold Davies, "A Review of the Development of Butyl Alcohol-Acetone Fermentation and Early Work on Synthetic Rubber," in *Papers Collected to Commemorate the 70th Anniversary of Dr. Chaim Weizmann* (Jerusalem, 1944), p. 5, copy in WA. See also Ernst D. Bergmann, "Bergmann on Weizmann," *Rehovot* 8, no. 1 (Spring 1976): 54.

5. I have drawn from five main sources for information on Weizmann's research in chemistry and his connections with William Perkin, Auguste Fernbach, and the company owned by E. Halford Strange. The first source is court proceedings dealing with a suit brought by Weizmann and Commercial Solvents Corporation—a U.S.-based company—against Halford Strange and Synthetic Products Company, Ltd., in 1925. For the court proceedings, see "Reports of Patent, Design and Trade Mark Cases" 43, no. 7 (London, 1926) (hereafter "Reports of Patent"). The second source is the letters and memoranda that were presumably used as evidence during the court proceedings. These are collected in a container labeled "In the High Court of Justice, Chancery Division, Mr. Justice Romer, Commercial Solvents Corporation v. Synthetic Products Company Limited. Correspondence, Agreed Bundle No. 1 from 10th May 1909 to 31st May 1919" and "Correspondence, Agreed Bundle No. 2 from June 1912 [to 1925]. Plaintiff's Solicitors" (hereafter Court of Justice). The entire documentation is housed in the Weizmann Archives. The third source is the *History of the Ministry of Munitions*, vols. 1–12 (London, 1921–22). See also Denys Hay, "The Official History of the Ministry of Munitions, 1915–1919," *Economic History Review* 14, no. 2 (1944): 185–90, which provides the background and an outline of the history of the Ministry of Munitions. The fourth source is a report written by Weizmann on February 2, 1925—obviously in preparation for the legal proceedings about to commence—and titled, "Dr. Weizmann's Technical Statement Dated 2nd February 1925," WA. The last source consists of the detailed, verbatim report under the title "Committee to Suggest a Grant to Dr. Weizmann," June 15, 29, 1917, Treasury Office Papers, Public Record Office (hereafter TI), 12586.

6. "Reports of Patent," pp. 211–12.

7. Document by E. Moore Mumford, an assistant to Weizmann, April 30, 1912, Court of Justice.

8. Halford Strange to William Perkin, March 29, 1912, Court of Justice. Kane also experimented with the isolation of other butyl-producing bacteria and on May 1, 1912, isolated one, which he called "160," from barley. "Reports of Patent," p. 186.

9. Harold Davies, "Development of Butyl Alcohol-Acetone Fermentation," p. 5.

10. The power of producing acetone in the fermentation of carbohydrates was not peculiar to the bacillus FB; it is the property of all butylic ferments of starch.

11. Halford Strange to William Perkin, March 29, 1912, Court of Justice.

12. Bergmann, "Bergmann on Weizmann," p. 54. See also Halford Strange to Auguste Fernbach, May 10, 1912, Court of Justice: "I had a further interview with two of the Nobel Dynamic Trust people yesterday . . . and they admitted that the diminishing supply of acetone and the increasing demand for it by several countries for explosive manufacture is a matter of great concern to the British Government and particularly the Admiralty."

13. "Reports of Patent," p. 214; Weizmann to Ahad Ha'Am, June 25, 1912, WL, 5:311–12. See also Reinharz, *Weizmann: Making of a Zionist Leader*, pp. 356–59.

14. G. N. Burkhardt to Maurice Schofield, November 26, 1974, Manchester University Archives, Manchester University, John Rylands Library, 18/16b. See also floor plans of the Chemistry Department, Manchester University Archives, 18/16f. After 1913, Weizmann occupied the Perkin and Schunk laboratories, with a private office and apparatus room. The Biochemical Laboratories formed a subdepartment of which Weizmann was in charge.

15. "Reports of Patent," p. 216.

16. See December 16, 1913, Court of Justice; Davies, "Development of Butyl Alcohol-Acetone Fermentation," p. 8.

17. Weizmann to [Moses Schoen], November 4, 1913, Court of Justice.

18. Moses Schoen to Weizmann, November 27, 1913, Court of Justice. It seems that in the spring of 1913 Weizmann had also written to Auguste Fernbach with a request for information on the latter's work for Halford Strange. Fernbach refused to disclose any information before Weizmann had concluded negotiations with Strange. See Fernbach to Weizmann, May 17, 1913, Court of Justice.

19. Weizmann to Francis Henley, March 8, 1917, WA; Weizmann to Arthur Desborough, March 10, 1917, WA.

20. Generally, under these conditions, butyric acid or lactic acid bacteria gains the upper hand; these tubes were also discarded.

21. BY, for Bacillus Weizmann.

22. Davies, "Development of Butyl Alcohol-Acetone Fermentation," p. 9.

23. This information is based on an unsigned document in WA, dated 1916, which seems to have been composed by a patent lawyer, perhaps Weizmann's lawyer, Atkinson Adam.

24. "Draft Agreement Relating to Butylic Fermentation dated [early January] 1916 between Dr. C. Weizmann and Jacob Holker. Drawn by Addleshaw Sons and Latham, Manchester," WA.

25. For his part, Weizmann was careful to withhold information about his process. When he had no choice but to share his process with other scientists working for the government, he was careful to have them sign affidavits stating they would not divulge the information about it to others while obliging them to share with him any information about improvement of his patents. See, e.g., the declaration by Professor Gilbert J. Fowler, January 21, 1916, WA.

26. "Summary of Mr. Justice Romer," in "Reports of Patent," p. 217.

27. Maurice Schofield, "Weizmann's Success as a Manchester Biochemist," MS, WA.

28. Fred C. Kelly, *One Thing Leads to Another: The Growth of an Industry* (Boston, 1936), p. 10.

29. "Reports of Patent," p. 217.

30. Halford Strange to Auguste Fernbach, May 10, 1912, Court of Justice.

31. Halford Strange to Weizmann, April 30, 1912, Court of Justice.

32. See, e.g., Halford Strange to Weizmann, August 16, 1912, Court of Justice.

33. Halford Strange to director of army contracts, September 7, 1914, Court of Justice.

34. In 1915, Nobel's Explosives Company agreed to purchase acetone for the explosives trade on behalf of the British government for that year. Competition between British cordite makers was thus eliminated.

35. "Reports of Patent," p. 218.

36. See, e.g., Appleby to Lord Moulton, December 17, 1914, Court of Justice; William Ramsay to Lord Moulton, January 20, 1915, Court of Justice. See also Appleby to F. Hanson, War Office, February 25, 1915, Court of Justice.

37. See, e.g., Halford Strange to R. L. Robinson, Ministry of Munitions, September 24, 1915, Court of Justice: "The large scale experiment tried here with maize was in our ordinary plant in order to determine whether a proportion of maize could be used with potatoes in the plant. It has not proved very successful and we agree with you that its use should be discontinued in the present plant."

38. From June 30, 1915, to March 13, 1916, the average production of acetone at King's Lynn was 8 cwt., 2 qrs., 14 lbs. per week.

39. "Reports of Patent," p. 218.

40. Harold B. Dixon to Weizmann, December 2, 1915, Court of Justice. It may very well be that Weizmann had also filled out a report on his research that he forwarded to the War Office. Weizmann, *Trial and Error*, p. 171. But in view of the fact that the War Office must have received thousands of such reports, Dixon's unequivocal statement *to Weizmann* that "I had suggested it [Weizmann's process] being communicated to Nobel's who brought it before the Admiralty," seems more convincing. See also Weizmann's testimony in "Committee to Suggest a Grant to Dr. Weizmann," June 15, 1917, TI, 12586.

41. Weizmann to Ahad Ha'Am, February 9, 1915, *WL*, 7:145.

42. Weizmann to Frederick Nathan, April 25, 1915, *WL*, 7:193.

43. Weizmann to Harry Sacher, February 22, 1915, *WL*, 7:157; "Reports of Patent," p. 217. See also Weizmann to Dorothy de Rothschild, March 4, 1915, *WL*, 7:162: "The insect behaved very well; now I hope Nobel's will behave."

44. Michael J. Walsh to Meyer W. Weisgal, November 7, 1965, Leonard Stein Papers, Oxford University, Bodleian Library, Oxford, box 66. In August 1915, Walsh was appointed to the research staff of Nobel's Explosives Company.

45. Weizmann filed a provisional specification on March 29, 1915; the complete specification was filed on October 29, 1915. "Reports of Patent," p. 218. See also Patent no. 4845/15, "Reports of Patent," p. 210. William Rintoul introduced Weizmann to a friend of his, Atkinson Adam, a partner in the firm of Marks and Clerk, patent agents in London. Davies, "Development of Butyl Alcohol-Acetone Fermentation," p. 9. Elsewhere in the court proceedings it is stated, incorrectly, that Sir Frederick Nathan had suggested patenting the process. "Reports of Patent," p. 197.

46. The only information on the contract is contained in Weizmann to Ahad

Ha'Am, March 28, 1915, *WL*, 7:189. According to Weizmann, he was offered a £3,000 advance.

47. The Nobel factory at Ardeer was fully operational again by October 1915. Michael Walsh to Meyer Weisgal, November 7, 1965, Stein Papers, box 66.

48. See April 17, 1915, Court of Justice.

49. Ibid.

50. Bergmann, "Bergmann on Weizmann," p. 54. See also Fritz Ullmann, *Enzyklopädie der Technichen Chemie* (Meisenheimer, 1875; Munich, 1951), 16:99.

51. Richard Rhodes, *The Making of the Atomic Bomb* (New York, 1986), p. 89.

52. R. J. Q. Adams, *Arms and the Wizard: Lloyd George and the Ministry of Munitions, 1915–1916* (College Station, Tex., 1978), p. 149.

53. The following description is based on *History of the Ministry of Munitions*, vols. 1–12. See also "Need for Shells," *Times* (London), May 14, 21, 1915. A summary of the situation regarding war materials is contained in a discussion of the War Council on March 3, 1915, CAB, 42/2/3.

54. See L. F. Haber, *The Chemical Industry, 1900–1930* (Oxford, 1971), p. 211.

55. *History of the Ministry of Munitions*, vol. 7, chap. 4, p. 65.

56. The distillation of dried hardwood gives 6.1 percent acetic acid and 2.3 percent of a mixture that is to 65–70 percent methanol, to 10–15 percent methyl acetate, and only 10–15 percent acetone. The actual yield of acetone is only about 0.2 percent. The crude acetic acid can be transformed into acetone by passing it at 400° C over iron containing calcium carbonate, but the amount of wood necessary for making substantial quantities of acetone would be enormous. Ernst D. Bergmann, "Dr. Weizmann's Scientific Work in the Framework of the Industrial and Political Development of His Time," n. 6, MS, WA. This article was published in an altered form without the footnotes and under the title "Bergmann on Weizmann," *Rehovot* 8, no. 1 (Spring 1976): 53–61. A Hebrew version was published in *Mada* 7, no. 3 (August/September 1972): 169–74.

57. This situation was only partially ameliorated by the adoption of a new form of cordite (RDB) manufactured with the solvent ethyl alcohol instead of acetone. *History of the Ministry of Munitions*, vol. 7, chap. 4, pp. 65–66, chap. 2, pp. 98–99.

58. Ibid., chap. 4, p. 68.

59. Bergmann, "Dr. Weizmann's Scientific Work," p. 4.

60. According to Weizmann's appointment book, WA, he went to the Admiralty on April 21, 1915, at 11:00 A.M. and returned for further discussions on April 30 at 4:20 P.M.

61. See Frederick Nathan and others, memorandum and minutes, October 1915, Admiralty Office Papers, Public Record Office (hereafter ADM), 1/8451/65.

62. Ibid. See also "At the Court at Buckingham Palace, 14th day of October 1915" concerning the regulations of the Defense of the Realm (Amendment) Act, 1915 and the Munitions of War Act, 1915, ADM, 1/8451/65. See also Frederick Nathan, memorandum , October 18, 1915, and the minutes of other officials in the Admiralty, ADM, 1/8451/65. On November 1, 1915, Percy Minter wrote to Weizmann on behalf of the director of navy contracts, instructing him as to how to ensure that no publication of particulars of patent no. 4845 took place for the duration of the war. Indeed, later on in the war, Weizmann worried that it was the Ministry of Munitions itself

that did not take sufficient care to guard his patents. See Weizmann to Nathan, December 3, 1917, WA.

63. Weizmann to Frederick Nathan, April 25, 1915, *WL*, 7:194; Weizmann to William Rintoul, May 2, 1915, *WL*, 7:195. See also Nathan to Weizmann, May 25, 1915, Court of Justice. A note in Nathan's handwriting, May 12, 1915, WA, reads: "This is to certify that Dr. Charles Weizmann of Manchester University is engaged on work for the Admiralty."

64. Weizmann, *Trial and Error*, p. 173. This story has been repeated verbatim by other historians as well. See, e.g., Rhodes, *Making of the Atomic Bomb*, p. 89.

65. It was Nehama Chalom who drew my attention to the fact that the story as told by Weizmann in *Trial and Error* is implausible. I thank her for working so hard to convince me. See, e.g., her letter to me of March 4, 1990.

66. After he became the first lord of the admiralty, Arthur James Balfour set up a Department of Invention and Research. Samuel Sambursky, *Balfour's Philosophy of Science* (Rehovot, November 1969), p. 25.

67. Experimental work was first conducted in Bromley under a grant sanctioned by the Treasury Emergency Standing Committee on April 30, 1915. *History of the Ministry of Munitions*, vol. 7, chap. 4, p. 67.

68. Weizmann to Frederick Nathan, February 27, 1916, *WL*, 7:268.

69. Weizmann to C. P. Scott, July 29, 1915, *WL*, 7:229.

70. Ibid. See also report to Ministry of Munitions, October 29, 1915, WA, indicating that Weizmann's sample acetone had been tested and found satisfactory.

71. Weizmann to Ahad Ha'Am, August 23, 1915, *WL*, 7:234.

72. *History of the Ministry of Munitions*, vol. 7, chap. 4, pp. 12–14. See also Trevor Wilson, *The Myriad Faces of War: Britain and the Great War, 1914–1918* (Cambridge, 1986), pp. 234–35; H. Fletcher Moulton, *The Life of Lord Moulton* (London, 1922).

73. Adams, *Arms and the Wizard*, pp. 46–50.

74. Weizmann, *Trial and Error*, p. 150. See also Scott's entry in his diary on November 27, 1914, relating a conversation he had with Lloyd George: "When I mentioned Weizmann [Lloyd George] said he would like to see him and he would ask Samuel too and perhaps I would come." Excerpts of Scott's diaries were edited by Trevor Wilson, *The Political Diaries of C. P. Scott, 1911–1928* (Ithaca, N.Y., 1970). Since that work does not contain all the materials relating to Weizmann and Zionism, I have used a typescript of the complete diary. The original "diary," actually a collection of notes written in Scott's almost illegible hand on stationery and miscellaneous sheets of paper, are housed in the C. P. Scott Papers, British Library, London, vols. 1–7, presented by J. R. Scott and catalogued as 50901–50907, "Memoranda 1911–1928." A typescript of these political memoranda is housed in the Guardian Archives at Manchester University, John Rylands Library, GA 133–134. Unless otherwise indicated, reference to Scott's diaries is based on the typescript in the Guardian Archives. Permission to quote from the typescript was granted by the British Library, which has copyright of the original memoranda; Mr. L. P. Scott; and the *Guardian* (Manchester).

75. On June 3, 1915, C. P. Scott wrote to Weizmann: "I saw Lloyd George this evening. He asks me to ask you to call on Mr. Wolff [Humbert Wolfe, Lloyd George's private secretary at the Ministry of Munitions] at the Mu-

nitions Office on Monday [June 7]. . . . He was interested in what I told him. . . . He has a very clear impression of your personality and spoke very warmly of you." Guardian Archives, A/W35/5. A day before the interview between Weizmann and David Lloyd George, Scott lunched with the minister and talked to him once more about Weizmann. Scott recorded in his diary on June 6, 1915, Guardian Archives, that Lloyd George "seemed interested and took me afterwards to see Dr. [Christopher] Addison [parliamentary secretary to] the Ministry of Munitions."

76. Weizmann to C. P. Scott, June 7, 1915, *WL*, 7:205–6.
77. Weizmann to David Lloyd George, June 9, 1915, *WL*, 7:206–7.
78. Weizmann to C. P. Scott, July 29, 1915, *WL*, 7:229–30. Concerning the scientific committee established by the Admiralty, see ADM, 1/84.
79. Weizmann to Frederick Nathan, February 27, 1916, *WL*, 7:268–69.
80. *History of the Ministry of Munitions*, vol. 7, chap. 4, p. 67.
81. Vera Weizmann, *Impossible Takes Longer*, p. 53.
82. Weizmann to Ahad Ha'Am, August 27, 1915, *WL*, 7:235.
83. Weizmann to Dorothy de Rothschild, September 21, 1915, *WL*, 7:237.
84. From the outset of his work for the government, Weizmann was conscious of the value of his scientific achievements for Zionist work. See, e.g., Weizmann to Dorothy de Rothschild, July 18, 1915, *WL*, 7:227.
85. *History of the Ministry of Munitions*, vol. 7, chap. 4, p. 11.
86. Ibid., p. 13.
87. Weizmann to C. P. Scott, July 7, 1915, *WL*, 7:221.
88. C. P. Scott, diary, October 14–15, 1915, Guardian Archives.
89. C. P. Scott, diary, February 23, 1916, Guardian Archives; Weizmann to Frederick Nathan, February 27, 1916, *WL*, 7:269. See also Weizmann to Nathan, May 12, 1916, WA; Weizmann to David Lloyd George, March 6, 1916, WA.
90. Weizmann to C. P. Scott, March 12, 1917, *WL*, 7:340.
91. Frederick Nathan to Weizmann, October 12, 1917, WA.
92. Weizmann to Arthur Desborough, August 3, 1917, WA.
93. *History of the Ministry of Munitions*, vol. 7, chap. 4, p. 71.
94. See, e.g., Weizmann to C. P. Scott, July 15, 29, 1915, *WL*, 7:224, 229.
95. Weizmann had an interview on November 9, 1915, with the French naval attaché concerning acetone. Weizmann to Dorothy de Rothschild, November 10, 1915, *WL*, 7:243.
96. C. P. Scott, diary, October 1, 1915, Guardian Archives.
97. C. P. Scott, diary, October 1, 14–15, 1915, Guardian Archives.
98. This strategy, too, may have been an idea of Scott's, which he outlined to Weizmann in advance of his interview with Lloyd George. See Scott, diary, October 14–15, 1915, Guardian Archives: "I first brought before him [Lloyd George] the question of chemical munitions on Weizmann's and [on] Sir F[rederick] Nathan's behalf—Weizmann's plan for manufacture of 1) Toluene, for which he has perfected a new method, 2) Benzine of which there is a prospective shortage. . . . G[eorge] admitted vital importance of both. . . . I gathered that he would borrow Sir F. N. from Admiralty and give him and W[eizmann] a free hand. That is W.'s ardent desire."
99. C. P. Scott, diary, November 14, 1915, Guardian Archives.
100. C. P. Scott, diary, November 26, 1915, Guardian Archives.
101. Weizmann to C. P. Scott, December 1, 1915, *WL*, 7:253–54.

102. C. P. Scott to David Lloyd George, December 2, 1915, Lloyd George Papers, D18/15/8.

103. C. P. Scott, diary, December 16, 1915, Guardian Archives.

104. See Weizmann to Herbert Samuel, December 19, 1915, *WL*, 7:256. See also Bertie, *Diary of Lord Bertie of Thame*, 1:105.

105. Weizmann to Joseph Blumenfeld, January 16, 1916, *WL*, 7:261.

106. C. P. Scott, diary, January 25, 1916, Guardian Archives.

107. C. P. Scott, diary, February 23, 1916, Guardian Archives.

108. Weizmann to Harold Davies, January 16, 1916, WA.

109. This decision was communicated to representatives of the distillery trade by the Ministry of Munitions and the president of the Board of Trade on February 16, 1916. *History of the Ministry of Munitions,* vol. 7, chap. 4.

110. Not the least of the difficulties was the opposition of the owners. Weizmann recalled in 1932 that "the adaptation of distilleries to 'the W. process' offered a great many technical difficulties which were, however, overcome after several months of intensive efforts. It was, however, much more difficult to overcome the prejudice which existed among distillers against the process, which differed in many essentials from the ancient art of whisky-distilling. Here was an outsider trying to convert good grain into a mysterious substance about which one thing only was clear—it was certainly not whisky! This was looked upon as something amounting almost to sacrilege, which should certainly not be permitted." It was only through Lloyd George's personal intervention that the opposition of the distillers was removed. Weizmann to Frances Stevenson, memorandum for the use of Lloyd George, December 4, 1932, Lloyd George Papers, G/19/18/6.

111. *History of the Ministry of Munitions,* vol. 7, chap. 4, pp. 67–68.

112. See also undated and unsigned memorandum on the subject, WA, no doubt written by Weizmann in 1916, which estimates the total government savings from acetone and butyl alcohol at £1.8 million.

113. Weizmann to Frederick Nathan, February 27, 1916, *WL*, 7:268–71.

114. See Scott, diary, February 29–March 3, 1916, Guardian Archives.

115. The Department of Explosive Supplies was headed by Sir Sothern Holland.

116. Frederick Nathan to Weizmann, April 5, 1916, WA.

117. Weizmann to C. P. Scott, December 1, 1915, *WL* 7:254. The problems resulting from improper use of his process plagued Weizmann throughout his work for both the Admiralty and the Ministry of Munitions. See Weizmann to Scott, April 5, 1916, *WL*, 7:274–76. See also Weizmann to Frederick Nathan, November 15, 1916, TI, 1/12586.

118. Weizmann to C. P. Scott, April 5, 1916, *WL*, 7:274–76. See also the rather stern letter from the Department of Munitions Finance in the Ministry of Munitions admonishing Weizmann for his excessive traveling expenses, May 23, 1916, WA.

119. Harold Dixon was director of the chemistry laboratories of Manchester University and presumably in a position to follow Weizmann's work closely.

120. Harold Dixon to Weizmann, December 2, 1915, Court of Justice.

121. Weizmann to Harold Dixon, December 3, 1915, Court of Justice.

122. Halford Strange to Weizmann, December 8, 1915, Court of Justice.

123. Halford Strange to Auguste Fernbach, January 9, 1914, Court of Justice.

124. Weizmann to Halford Strange, December 17, 1915, Court of Justice. A further letter to Weizmann, possibly written by Strange's solicitors and imply-

ing that an interview with Strange might avoid "difficulty in the future," remained unanswered. December 20, 1915, Court of Justice.

125. Clapham, Fraser, Cook and Co. to Lord Moulton, March 1, 1916, Court of Justice.

126. Weizmann to Frederick Nathan, April 27, 1916, *WL*, 7:278–79.

127. In their letter, the solicitors used the strongest language: "We feel Prof. Fernbach is justified in seeking this interview. He is a distinguished French professor who has brought his discoveries to England for development and his view is that his process has been improperly communicated to the Government by an ex-assistant . . . [and] that the support of the Government is given entirely to the infringer." Clapham, Fraser, Cook and Co. to Frederick Nathan, May 18, 24, 1916, Court of Justice.

128. Lord Moulton to Weizmann, May 26, 1916, Court of Justice. See also Clapham, Fraser, Cook and Co. to Lord Moulton, May 26, 1916, Court of Justice. From this letter it appears that, during the interview, Moulton had agreed to advise Weizmann to accept arbitration.

129. Weizmann to Lord Moulton, May 30, 1916, *WL*, 7:279–80.

130. Atkinson Adam to Weizmann, June 3, 1916, WA. See also C. P. Scott, diary, June 17, 1916, Guardian Archives: "Reported to [Lloyd] George that W[eizmann] was still being threatened with proceedings—unless he agreed to arbitrate or to compromise— . . . and that this worry was greatly interfering with his work—George at once replied 'I don't care whose process it is; Weizmann has given his invention to the State and the State means to have it.—Tell W. if he has any further trouble from these people simply to refer them to the Minister of Munitions.' Immense relief and gratitude of Weizmann." The reference to threats with proceedings probably refers to the letter written by Strange's solicitors in early June. See Clapham, Fraser, Cook and Co. to Weizmann, June 6, 1916, Court of Justice.

131. Clapham, Fraser, Cook and Co. to Weizmann, June 6, 1916, Court of Justice; Weizmann to Harold Addleshaw, Esq., June 8, 1916, WA; Brestows, Cooke and Carpmael to Clapham, Fraser, Cook and Co., June 8, 1916, Court of Justice; Clapham, Fraser, Cook and Co. to Brestows, Cooke and Carpmael, June 14, August 15, 1916, Court of Justice; C. P. Scott, diary, July 26, 1916, Guardian Archives. See also Scott to Edwin Montagu, minister of munitions, August 21, 1916, Guardian Archives, A/W35/7, in which Scott informed the new minister as to the way Lloyd George had handled the matter. In his letter of August 21, 1916, WA, Scott advised Weizmann if at all possible "to keep out of all litigation, arbitration or anything of the kind. . . . If these people have any claims at all, it is against the Government."

132. Weizmann to Harold Addleshaw, June 8, 1916, WA.

133. See, e.g., [Synthetic Products Co.] to Ministry of Munitions of War, November 22, 1915, Court of Justice.

134. *History of the Ministry of Munitions*, vol. 7, chap. 4, p. 67.

135. Clapham, Fraser, Cook and Co. to Lord Moulton, May 26, 1916, Court of Justice.

136. Weizmann's contract with the Ministry of Munitions terminated on September 30, 1916, but he continued to work for the ministry for some months after that.

137. Atkinson Adam advised Weizmann to see Arthur Balfour and explain "what has occurred, and that you are now asked to take over the Works of the

Synthetic Products Co. You might explain that you cannot take over these Works and work your process there without running some considerable risk of your being prejudiced by information as to your process leaking out through foremen or other workers of the Synthetic Products Co. which information might be used to your detriment—that you feel that the facts as to what the Synthetic Products Co. have done in the past and are able to do, as regards the manufacture of acetone and the materials required for working the process, should be definitely put on record before you take over their works." Adam to Weizmann, June 3, 1916, WA.

138. Weizmann to Lloyd George, June 6, 1916, *WL*, 7:283. See also Weizmann to J. T. Davies, Esq., Ministry of Munitions, June 14, 1916, Court of Justice.

139. Christopher Addison to Weizmann, June 15, 1916, Court of Justice. See also A. Appleyard to Weizmann, June 17, 1916, Court of Justice.

140. See Charles Hose to Weizmann, June 19, 1916, Court of Justice.

141. See Weizmann's long report to Frederick Nathan, November 15, 1916, WA.

142. "Reports of Patent," pp. 218–19.

143. After meeting with Weizmann in early October 1916, C. P. Scott noted in his diary that the "result of work at King's Lynn is that Government got their acetone for nothing and made about £1,000 per week profit." Scott, diary, October 2, 1916, Guardian Archives. Clearly, Scott's entry is colored by his partisan view of the case and by Weizmann's forceful presentation.

144. Scott, diary, July 26, 1916, Guardian Archives. Weizmann himself did not have free access to the reports on results of the production at King's Lynn, even when things did not work out smoothly. See, e.g., Weizmann to Frederick Nathan, July 20, 1916, WA.

145. To mention just one statistic: the productive capacity of the two distilleries in operation in February 1917 was 228 tons monthly, their consumption of maize 4,560 tons. *History of the Ministry of Munitions*, vol. 7, chap. 4, p. 68.

146. Frederick Nathan to Weizmann, April 18, 1917, WA.

147. Davies, "Development of Butyl Alcohol-Acetone Fermentation," p. 9.

148. Frederick Nathan to Weizmann, April 18, 1917, WA; Weizmann to Nathan, April 23, 1917, WA.

149. Frederick Nathan to Weizmann, May 1, 1917, WA; clerk to the Food [War] Committee and to Weizmann, May 1, 1917, WA.

150. See, e.g., Frederick Nathan to Weizmann, September 12, 1917, WA.

151. Weizmann to Frederick Nathan, April 23, 1917, WA; Weizmann to Arthur Desborough, June 20, 1917, WA. See also A. C. Thaysen, "Report on the Value of Horse Chestnuts for the Production of Acetone," WA; Nathan, "Manufacture of Acetone," p. 272.

152. *History of the Ministry of Munitions*, vol. 7, chap. 4, p. 68.

153. The two factories produced 2,563 tons of acetone between January 1917 and November 1918. Ibid., p. 69; Kelly, *One Thing Leads to Another*, p. 13, See also Horace B. Speakman, "Dr. Weizmann's Contribution to Microbiology," in *Chaim Weizmann: Statesman, Scientist, Builder of the Jewish Commonwealth*, ed. Meyer W. Weisgal (New York, 1944), pp. 69–77. In a revised version of this article under the same title, Speakman summarized the production of the factory in Toronto. From April 1916 until the end of the war, the factory produced 5,741,273 lbs. of acetone and 12,660,834 lbs. of butyl alcohol. The yield of acetone was 7.82 percent, i.e., even higher than what had been attained in England. See *Chaim Weizmann: A Tribute on His Sev-*

entieth Birthday, ed. Paul Goodman (London, 1945), p. 135. A factory was also built in Nazik, India, which operated by the Weizmann process, but it was not completed until after 1918.

154. *History of the Ministry of Munitions*, vol. 7, chap. 2, pp. 98–99, chap. 4, pp. 69–70.

155. See Davies, "Development of Butyl Alcohol-Acetone Fermentation," p. 10; Kelly, *One Thing Leads to Another*, pp. 15–52. Nothing came of the original research (the idea to produce isoprene through fermentation) that had initiated Weizmann's association with Strange or of the many attempts made by Weizmann and his collaborators to find new synthetic methods for its production from easily obtainable starting materials. The rubber crisis passed, and the project was abandoned until it surfaced again during World War II.

156. Weizmann to Graham Greene, September 15, 1916, *WL*, 7:295–96; Weizmann to Victor Grignard, September 27, 1916, *WL*, 7:300–301. See also C. P. Scott, diary, October 2–3, 1916, Guardian Archives: "Met Weizmann. . . . He'd been asked to establish acetone manufacture for French and Italian Governments—He'd been offered 25% royalty which even on small French requirement of 5 or 6 hundred tons alone would bring him in about £200 a week, Italian demand probably much larger."

157. See letter to the director of the Chemical War Materials Department, December 27, 1915, Court of Justice. See also draft of contract between Weizmann and E. T. Pearson, [spring 1916], WA. Pearson was Weizmann's representative in his negotiations with Allenet, the French manufacturer.

158. Weizmann to Joseph Blumenfeld, December 25, 1916, *WL*, 7:319–21.

159. Weizmann to Nahum Sokolow, October 4, 1916, *WL*, 7:302.

160. Weizmann to Dorothy de Rothschild, November 12, 1916, *WL*, 7:313.

161. See copy of unsigned letter to Weizmann from the Admiralty, August 9, 1916, TI, 12586/22853.

162. C. P. Scott, diary, March 23, 1916, Guardian Archives.

163. Weizmann to Ahad Ha'Am, April 4, 1916, *WL*, 7:273.

164. C. P. Scott, diary, April 13–20, 1916, Guardian Archives. See also Scott to Weizmann, April 22, 1916, WA; Weizmann to Vera Weizmann, April 14, 1916, *WL*, 7:277.

165. C. P. Scott, diary, May 8–11, 1916, Guardian Archives.

166. C. P. Scott, diary, May 22–26, 1916, Guardian Archives.

167. Weizmann to Atkinson Adam, June 4, 1916, *WL*, 7:282. Eventually the remuneration was given for acetone, not for butyl alcohol.

168. C. P. Scott, diary, February 26–March 1, 1917, Guardian Archives. See also Vera Weizmann to Scott, draft, April 20, 1917, WA; Scott to Vera Weizmann, April 24, 1917, WA.

169. C. P. Scott to Weizmann, March 9, 1917, WA.

170. Weizmann to C. P. Scott, March 12, 1917, *WL*, 7:338–41. The offer to Weizmann was apparently made by the Distilleria Italiana of Milan. See draft contract, TI, 12586/22853.

171. Weizmann to [Graham Greene], extract, March 21, 1917, TI, 12586/22853.

172. Ibid.

173. The question of Weizmann's scientific achievements and the process of granting him an award for them have been described by Zaid, "Chaim Weizmann's Scientific Work, 1915–1918," *Islamic Quarterly* 18, nos. 1–2

(January–July 1974): 226–37. The article is replete with mistakes and gives only a partial and inaccurate description of Weizmann's work. In a subsequent "note," the author listed further sources of which he had been initially unaware, but they did not seem to change his derogatory view of Weizmann's accomplishments. This, even though one of the sources cited—*History of the Ministry of Munitions*—praises Weizmann's work. See Zaid, "Supplementary Notes," *Islamic Quarterly* 20–22, nos. 1–2 (January–June 1978): 29. I owe these references to Professor Meir J. Kister of Jerusalem.

174. Graham Greene to Bradbury, April 20, 1917, TI, 12586/22853.

175. Weizmann to Graham Greene, extract, March 21, 1917, TI, 12586/22853.

176. Graham Greene to Bradbury, April 20, 1917, TI, 12586/22853.

177. Graham Greene to Robert Chalmers, April 28, 1917, TI, 12586/22853.

178. R. C[halmers] to Graham Greene, May 3, 1917, TI, 12586/22853.

179. See Graham Greene to Bradbury, April 20, 1917, TI, 12586/22853; Robert Chalmers to Greene, May 3, 1917, TI, 12586/22853.

180. "Committee to Suggest a Grant to Dr. Weizmann," June 15, 1917, TI, 12586. See also Cobb to Clauson, October 8, 1917, ADM, 1/8508/284.

181. Weizmann to C. P. Scott, June 20, 1917, *WL*, 7:446. Weizmann felt that the whole procedure was "extremely fair and friendly."

182. "Committee to Suggest a Grant to Dr. Weizmann," June 15, 1917, p. 13, TI, 12586.

183. "Extract from Report on Fermentation at King's Lynn for Week Ending July 29, 1916," reproduced in ibid., p. 24, TI, 12586.

184. "Committee to Suggest a Grant to Dr. Weizmann," June 29, 1917, pp. 1–2, 4–6, TI, 12586.

185. Ibid., findings, TI, 12586.

186. Scott, diary, August 9, 1917, Guardian Archives.

187. Robert Chalmers to secretary of the admiralty, September 4, 1917, TI, 12586.

188. Weizmann to secretary of the admiralty, December 1, 1917, WA.

189. Weizmann to C. P. Scott, September 20, 1917, *WL*, 7:517.

190. "Committee to Suggest a Grant to Dr. Weizmann," findings, TI, 12586: "Dr. Weizmann has expressed his readiness to accept the decision of the Committee."

191. See unsigned and undated memorandum, TI, 12586/22853.

192. Weizmann to secretary of the admiralty, December 1, 1917, WA. On November 20, 1918, WA, Graham Greene wrote to Atkinson Adam, Weizmann's patent agent, that before the committee could make any awards in respect to production in Canada it wished to have in advance Weizmann's acceptance of its judgment.

193. Atkinson Adam to Ministry of Munitions, January 1919, TI, 12586/22853. Weizmann did hold a number of joint patents with David Alliston Legg concerning hydrocarbons and secondary butyl alcohol. Apparently Weizmann settled the case with Legg amicably—though the terms are unknown—because his list of patents shows that they continued to work together and took out a joint patent as late as August 1920. See Anthony R. Michaelis, *Weizmann Centenary* (London, 1974), pp. 58–59. See also Graham Greene to Atkinson Adam, November 20, 1918, WA, referring specifically to Legg as a co-patentee for a process used in the factory in Canada.

194. McKenna Committee, second report, March 1919, TI, 12586/22853. The abstention was by Sir Hardman Lever, who had apparently been added to

the committee during the second stage of its deliberations. The minutes do not indicate why he abstained.

195. Graham Greene to secretary of the treasury, January 12, 1920, TI, 12586/22853. Why the quantity of acetone was calculated until the end of October 1918, rather than December 1918, is not explained.

196. Graham Greene to secretary of the treasury, May 20, 1920, TI, 12586/22853.

197. Hardman Lever to undersecretary of state, India Office, June 3, 1920, TI, 12586/22853.

198. Graham Greene to G. Barstow, June 6, 1920, TI, 12586/22853.

199. Reginald McKenna to Warren Fisher, June 4, 1920, TI, 12586/22853.

200. Warren Fisher to Reginald McKenna, June 5, 1920, TI, 12586/22853.

201. Warren Fisher to Reginald McKenna, June 15, 1920, TI, 12586/22853; McKenna to Fisher, June 17, 1920, TI, 12586/22853.

202. Weizmann, *Trial and Error*, p. 174.

203. Lewis Namier wrote in a memoir that Winston Churchill once told him that had Weizmann asked the British government for £250,000 for his discovery, he would have received it. For Namier's memoir, see Norman Rose, *Lewis Namier and Zionism* (Oxford, 1980), p. 161. Churchill was, characteristically, exaggerating, though the story indicates how important Weizmann's discovery was in the eyes of the British.

204. Weizmann to C. P. Scott, March 1, 1917, WL, 7:336–37; Maurice Schofield, "The Impossible Takes Longer," *Chemistry in Britain*, November 11, 1974, p. 433.

205. During World War II, many important synthetic rubber industries utilized the starting materials projected by Weizmann. The introduction of the acetone-butanol fermentation was the forerunner of all modern industrial fermentations such as those of antibiotics and vitamins. It was the desired step in the transformation of micro-organisms into humanly controlled industrial agents. Since ancient times, people had used yeast and bacteria for the production of alcohol and vinegar. But despite the classic discoveries of Robert Koch, Louis Pasteur, and others, no one in industrial practice made use of the wealth of newer bacteriological knowledge. Weizmann paved the way for the utilization of chemical microbiology. See Aharon Katchalsky, "Symbol of New Scientific Approach to Living," *Jerusalem Post*, Chaim Weizmann Memorial Supplement, October 30, 1953, p. 5.

206. David Lloyd George, *War Memoirs of David Lloyd George, 1915–1916* (Boston, 1933), 1:50. See also Lloyd George, foreword to *Chaim Weizmann*, ed. Goodman, p. 9.

207. See, e.g., Moshe Smilansky, "Our Leader," in *Chaim Weizmann*, ed. Goodman, p. 61; Alfred Moritz, Baron Melchett, "Chaim Weizmann," in *Twelve Jews*, ed. Hector Bolitho (London, 1934), p. 280; Yaakov Yaari-Poleskin, *Holmim velohamim* (Petah Tikvah, 1922), 3d ed. (Tel Aviv, 1964), p. 183; John Lawrence Hammond, *C. P. Scott of the Manchester Guardian* (New York, 1934), p. 197; Kelly, *One Thing Leads to Another*, pp. 13–14; Haim Shorer, "Weizmann," *Davar*, November 2, 1962, p. 3; Haber, *Chemical Industry*, p. 212; Bernard Dixon, "Bug Bang That Built Israel," *Observer Weekly*, November 2, 1987.

208. Weizmann, *Trial and Error*, p. 150.

209. Weizmann to Frances Stevenson, memorandum for the use of Lloyd George, December 4, 1932, Lloyd George Papers, G19/18/6.

210. I thank Nehama Chalom for drawing my attention to this play, a copy of which is in WA. See Jehuda Reinharz, "Weizmann, Acetone and the Balfour Declaration," *Rehovot* 10, no. 4 (1988–89): 3–7. See also *New Leader*, November 29, 1936.

211. Michael Walsh to Meyer Weisgal, November 7, 1965, Stein Papers, box 66.

212. "Manufacture of Acetone by the Weizmann Process: Statement Showing Supplies of Acetone Received, 1915–1918, and Processes by Which Obtained, Ministry of Munitions of War," Department of Explosives Finance, November 1918, TI, 12586.

213. Leonard Stein, *The Balfour Declaration* (New York, 1961), p. 120, n. 15. Vera Weizmann seems to have confirmed the story, as told by Lloyd George in his memoirs, despite her husband's ironic denial.

214. Weizmann to Dorothy de Rothschild, July 18, 1915, *WL*, 7:227. She concurred. In a letter to Weizmann of August 27, 1915, WA, she wrote that scientific success "will give you a standing which I feel will be more than helpful on the occasion of future negotiations!"

215. In a letter to Louis Brandeis, July 9, 1915, Horace Kallen (who was not too fond of Weizmann) quoted from a letter written to him by Alfred Zimmern. According to Kallen, Zimmern "speaks of the high importance of Weizmann in British circles." Brandeis Papers, reel 70. The dating of Kallen's letter is significant because it was written *before* Weizmann conducted his first large trials with acetone in Bromley-by-Bow.

216. Dvorah Barzilay-Yegar, "Crisis as Turning Point: Chaim Weizmann in World War I," *Studies in Zionism* 6 (Autumn 1982): 241–42.

217. On Weizmann's Zionist *Weltanschauung*, see Jehuda Reinharz, "Chaim Weizmann: The Shaping of a Zionist Leader before the First World War," *Journal of Contemporary History* 18, no. 2 (April 1983): 205–31.

III Generating Support for Zionism

1. Weizmann to Dorothy de Rothschild, *WL*, 7:314.

2. Dorothy de Rothschild to Vera Weizmann, December 14, 1916, WA.

3. Dorothy de Rothschild to Vera Weizmann, December 29, 1916, WA.

4. Isaac Leon Kandel to Horace Kallen, November 19, 1915, Brandeis Papers, reel 69, Z/P 3-1.

5. Eustace Percy to Brandeis, June 2, 1916, WA. Lord Percy was the son of Earl Percy, who had met Weizmann in 1904.

6. Louis Brandeis to Eustace Percy, June 26, 1916, WA.

7. See Judah Magnes to Louis Brandeis, June 30, 1915, WA. See also Magnes to Brandeis, September 2, 1915, CZA, Z3/759; Brandeis to Smaller Actions Committee, September 15, 1915, CZA, Z3/759; Arthur A. Goren, ed., introd. to *Dissenter in Zion: From the Writings of Judah L. Magnes* (Cambridge, Mass., 1982), pp. 21–22.

8. Benjamin Perlstein and Horace Kallen to Weizmann, July 29, 1915, WA.

9. Weizmann to Louis Brandeis, November 24, 1915, *WL*, 7:247–48; Weizmann to Horace Kallen, November 24, 1915, *WL*, 7:248–50.

10. Horace Kallen to Weizmann, December 16, 1915, WA.

11. See Ahad Ha'Am to Victor Jacobson, May 14, 1916, *Igrot Ahad Ha'Am*, 5:22.

12. Harry Sacher to Weizmann, [August 1915], WA.

13. See, e.g., Rozsika Rothschild to Weizmann, December 13, 1915, WA, telling

of a conversation concerning Zionism between Baron Edmond de Rothschild and Lady Crewe, who was impressed by the baron. Rozsika was also
trying to enlist the support of Edwin Montagu! See Nahum Sokolow to
[members of the SAC], December 14, 1915, CZA, Z3/399.

14. On Weizmann's social contacts during this period, see Vera Weizmann's
diary, which she kept from March 1916 to November 1917, WA.

15. There is some evidence that the idea of a Zionist political coalition came
from Vladimir Jabotinsky, who at the time was sharing an apartment with
Weizmann. See Jabotinsky to J. K. Goldbloom, December 30, 1915, January
6, 1916, CZA, A61/22/2. See also Nahum Sokolow to [members of the SAC],
December 18, 1915, CZA, Z3/399.

16. "Committee Appointed at a Meeting Convened at the Instance of Mr. Cowen
and Dr. Weizmann to Consider the Zionist Situation and Held at the Hotel
Great Central on the 23rd January 1916," WA.

17. Moses Gaster to Weizmann, January 18, 1916, CZA, A203/219.

18. See CZA, K11/6.

19. See, e.g., Political Committee, minutes, January 29, 1916, CZA, K11/6.

20. Paul Goodman, ed., *The Jewish National Home* (London, 1949), pp. 17–18.

21. Joshua Bukhmil, an active Russian Zionist who had been a member of the
Democratic Faction, was assigned the task of raising money among Russian
Jewry for the Political Committee. See Joshua Bukhmil, "Zikhronot, 1916–
1924," *Katzir* (Tel Aviv) 2 (1972): 330–32.

22. See, e.g., Weizmann to Isaac Epstein, December 16, 1914, WL, 7:87; Weizmann to Abraham Lubarsky, February 1, 1915, WL, 7:131, n. 2.

23. See, e.g., the return address Weizmann gives in his letter to Neil Primrose,
[March 15, 1915], WL, 7:178.

24. See, e.g., Weizmann to Dorothy de Rothschild, March 13, 1915, WL, 7:176.
See also Weizmann to Ahad Ha'Am, January 21, 1917, WL, 7:322.

25. See, e.g., Weizmann to Harry Sacher, February 7, 1915, WL, 7:139.

26. Weizmann to Vera Weizmann, April 14, 1916, WL, 7:277.

27. Weizmann to Ahad Ha'Am, February 2, 1916, WL, 7:265.

28. Weizmann to Dorothy de Rothschild, September 21, 1915, WL, 7:237.

29. See Elam, *Hagdudim haivriim*, p. 100. Vladimir Jabotinsky continued to live
in the apartment until the beginning of 1917, staying there alone after the
Weizmanns moved to their larger lodgings in January 1916.

30. Vera Weizmann, *Impossible Takes Longer*, p. 58.

31. See Moses Gaster to Weizmann, January 18, 1916, CZA, A203/219, welcom-
ing Vera and Benjy to London.

32. See the return address on Weizmann's letter to Nahum Sokolow, October
12, 1916, WL, 7:302.

33. I would like to thank the present owners, Mr. and Mrs. Henry M. Strage
and their son David, who tolerated my roaming through the house and
garden in August 1988 and my endless questions.

34. Weizmann to Moses Gaster, November 18, 1916, WL, 7:317; Gaster to Weizmann, November 20, 1916, WA.

35. Vera Weizmann, *Impossible Takes Longer*, p. 54.

36. Ibid.

37. Rozsika Rothschild to Vera Weizmann, [July–August 1916], WA.

38. Rozsika Rothschild to Vera Weizmann, August 14, [1916], WA.

39. Dorothy de Rothschild to Vera Weizmann, December 29, 1916, WA.

40. See, e.g., Rozsika Rothschild to Weizmann, December 31, 1916, WA, offering help with the manufacture of acetone through Charles Rothschild's contacts. The letter also suggests that the various Rothschild family members consulted one another as to how to help Weizmann in his financial affairs.

41. Weizmann to the marchioness of Crewe, June 19, 1915, *WL*, 7:213–14.

42. Vera Weizmann, diary, March 20, 1916, WA.

43. Vera Weizmann, diary, March 15, 1916, WA.

44. Nancy Astor to Weizmann, August 3, 1916, WA. After the war, Nancy Astor's support for Zionism diminished considerably.

45. Vera Weizmann, diary, March 25, 1916, WA.

46. See, e.g., Vera Weizmann, diary, March 15, 16, 20, 25, 1916, WA.

47. On the Zionists' debate over a Jewish legion, see David Yisraeli, "The Struggle for Zionist Military Involvement in the First World War (1914–1917)," in *Bar Ilan Studies in History*, ed. Pinhas Artzi (Ramat Gan, 1978), pp. 197–213.

48. Vladimir Jabotinsky, *The Story of the Jewish Legion*, trans. Samuel Katz (New York, 1945), pp. 41–42.

49. Concerning the formation of the Zion Mule Corps, see Laskov, *Trumpeldor*, pp. 91–96.

50. Joseph Trumpeldor, *Tagebücher und Briefe: Autorische Übertragung aus dem Russischen* (Berlin, 1925), pp. 109–344.

51. Ian Hamilton to Vladimir Jabotinsky, November 17, 1915, FO, 371/2835.

52. Matityahu Mintz, "Yozmat Pinhas Rutenberg lehakamat gdudim ivriim im protz milhemet haolam harishonah," *Hazionut* 8 (1983): 181–94.

53. See Copenhagen Zionist Bureau, memorandum, October 20, 1915, CZA, L6/243, which declared in part: "Diese Ausführungen richten sich im besonderen gegen die Ihnen bekannten Bestrebungen des Herrn Jabotinsky zur Gründung einer jüdischen Legion. Dieses Projekt wird von allen verantwortlichen Instanzen und Persönlichkeiten unserer Organisation, auch von denen, die in Opposition zu der jetzigen Leitung stehen, auf das Entschiedenste abgelehnt."

54. Leon Simon, quoted in Horace Kallen to Louis Brandeis, October 1, 1915, Brandeis Papers, reel 70, Z/P 3-1.

55. See Moses Gaster, diary, April 16, 1916, WA.

56. Elam, *Hagdudim haivriim*, p. 91.

57. Shmarya Levin to Victor Jacobson, February 16, 1916, Shmaryahu Levin, *Igrot Shmaryahu Levin* (Tel Aviv, 1966), p. 345.

58. Victor Jacobson to Simon Bernstein, July 21, 1915, CZA, L6/88.

59. Matityahu Mintz, *Zmanim hadashim, zmirot hadashot* (Tel Aviv, 1986), pp. 269–82.

60. Jabotinsky, *Story of the Jewish Legion*, pp. 59–60.

61. Weizmann enlisted C. P. Scott's help in the matter of the Jewish legion as well. See C. P. Scott, diary, July 28, 1916, Guardian Archives: "My only other business was to get the [War Office] to consider Weizmann's plan [*sic*] for forming a special brigade for the Russian Jews."

62. C. P. Scott to Robert Cecil, December 11, 1915, FO, 371/2835.

63. Russian ambassador, Alexander Benckendorff, October 12, 1915, FO, 371/2835.

64. Ian Hamilton to Vladimir Jabotinsky, November 17, 1915, FO, 371/2835.

65. John Henry Patterson to Vladimir Jabotinsky, November 10, 1915, FO, 371/ 2835.

66. Leopold Amery to Robert Cecil, January 11, 1916, FO, 371/2835.

67. Charles Masterman to Lord Newton, March 27, 1916, FO, 371/2816.

68. Vladimir Jabotinsky to Charles Masterman, memorandum, January 31, 1916, FO, 371/2835, concerning the propaganda value of a Jewish fighting force.

69. H. J. Greedy to G. Locock, January 17, 1916, FO, 371/2835. See also Robert Cecil to Vladimir Jabotinsky, February 10, 1916, FO, 371/2835.

70. Robert Cecil to Vladimir Jabotinsky, February 10, 1916, FO, 371/2835.

71. Earlier in the war there were instances in which recruiting stations refused to accept foreign-born Jews. See *Jewish Chronicle,* October 9, 1914, p. 17. See also Elkan D. Levy, "Antisemitism in England at War, 1914–1916," *Patterns of Prejudice* 4, no. 5 (September/October 1970): 27–30.

72. See Vivian David Lipman, *Social History of the Jews in England, 1850–1950* (London, 1954), p. 160. See also David Saunders, "Aliens in Britain and the Empire during the First World War," *Immigrants and Minorities* 4, no. 1 (March 1985): 9.

73. These figures are culled from Susan Tananbaum, "The Anglicization of Russian-Jewish Immigrant Women in London, 1880–1939" (Ph.D. diss., Brandeis University, 1991), chap. 2.

74. House of Commons, Great Britain Parliament, *House of Commons Official Report* (hereafter HCOR), July 27, 1916, col. 991, October 25, 1916, col. 113. The precise number of those eligible for conscription is not known, and the figures given in the House of Lords are an estimate. See also notice sent to David Lloyd George on April 9, 1917, indicating that there were 31,000 Russian Jews "of serviceable age in this country." Lloyd George Papers, F14/4/34.

75. See Jabotinsky's description of these feelings by the immigrants in *Story of the Jewish Legion,* pp. 60–63.

76. Vladimir Jabotinsky, letter to the *Times* (London), July 15, 1916, p. 7.

77. *HCOR,* June 29, 1916, cols. 1082–84.

78. The Russian immigrants were assisted by Israel Zangwill and a few other English Jewish notables. See "Lord Sheffield and the Right of Asylum," *Jewish Chronicle,* March 30, 1917, p. 22.

79. See the *Jewish Chronicle,* July 14, 1916, for a letter from Joseph Cowen and an article by Leopold Greenberg.

80. *HCOR,* July 24, 1916, cols. 1422–25.

81. Weizmann, appointment book, July 19, 1916, WA. See also Weizmann to Ahad Ha'Am, July 24, 1916, *WL,* 7:285–86.

82. *Jewish World,* September 6, 1916.

83. See the circular signed by Leopold de Rothschild, October 4, 1916, WA.

84. See the full description concerning the formation of the committee in Lucien Wolf to Herbert Samuel, "Russian Jews and Military Service," memorandum, August 15, 1916, WA.

85. Lucien Wolf to Herbert Samuel, August 21, 1916, HO, 45/10819/318095. Information concerning the work of the committee was communicated to Wolf by Weizmann.

86. Arthur Henderson to Gregory Benenson, September 7, 1916, Home Office Papers, Public Record Office (hereafter HO), 45/10819/318095.

87. Superintendent J. Best, report, September 16, 1916, HO, 45/10819/318095.

88. Gregory Benenson to Arthur Henderson, September 15, 1916, HO, 45/10819/318095; Henderson, memorandum, September 15, 1916, HO, 45/10819/318095.

89. See also Weizmann to Herbert Samuel, September 29, 1916, HO, 45/10819/318095; Henderson to Colonel White, September 30, 1916, HO, 45/10819/318095; White to Henderson, October 2, 1916, HO, 45/10819/318095; Samuel to Weizmann, October 3, 1916, HO, 45/10819/318095.

90. Arthur Henderson, memorandum, September 19, 1916, HO, 45/10819/318095. See also circular signed by Leopold de Rothschild, October 4, 1916, WA, admonishing his brethren to enlist voluntarily.

91. Weizmann to [military authorities], August 31, 1916, *WL*, 7:289–90.

92. Arthur Henderson, memorandum, September 19, 1916, HO, 45/10819/318095.

93. Laskov, *Trumpeldor*, p. 140.

94. Vladimir Jabotinsky to Herbert Samuel, September 16, 1916, HO, 45/10819/318095.

95. "On Military Service" (in Yiddish), HO, 45/10819/318095.

96. Flora Solomon, *A Woman's Way* (New York, 1984), p. 80.

97. Special Branch, report 8758, October 22, 1916, HO, 45/10819/318095.

98. Vladimir Jabotinsky to Herbert Samuel, October 26, 1916, HO, 45/10819/318095.

99. The appeals to minorities issued by Russia and the Central Powers early in World War I are summarized by Zbynek A. B. Zeman, *The Break-Up of the Habsburg Empire, 1914–1918: A Study in National and Social Revolution* (London, 1961), pp. 52–54.

100. In 1914 the Central Powers distributed leaflets among the Jews of Galicia and dropped leaflets from the air on Poland's Jews. See Friedman, *Germany, Turkey and Zionism*, p. 232. On German attention to Jewish opinion, including that in the United States, see Stein, *Balfour Declaration*, pp. 207–16.

101. Weizmann, *Trial and Error*, p. 157.

102. Elie Kedourie, *The Chatham House Version and Other Middle Eastern Studies* (London, 1970), p. 17.

103. Philip Magnus, *Kitchener: Portrait of an Imperialist* (London, 1958), pp. 364–65.

104. "Evidence of Lieutenant-Colonel Sir Mark Sykes, Bart., M.P., on the Arab Question, War Committee, Meeting Held at 10 Downing Street, on Thursday, December 16, 1915," CAB, 42/6/10; marquess of Crewe to Lord Francis Bertie, December 17, 1915, marked "confidential," CAB, 42/6/11.

105. For a brief sketch, see Henry H. Cumming, *Franco-British Rivalry in the Post-War Near East: The Decline of French Influence* (Westport, Conn., 1938), pp. 1–50.

106. See the report of the de Bunsen Committee, "British Desiderata in Turkey-in-Asia: Report, Proceedings, and Appendices," June 30, 1915, CAB, 27/1.

107. Archibald P. Wavell, *The Palestine Campaigns*, 3d ed. (London, 1931), pp. 26–33.

108. [David Hogarth], "The Arab Question," [1916], FO, 882/2.

109. Concerning the Gallipoli campaign, see Wolfram W. Gottlieb, *Studies in Secret Diplomacy during the First World War* (London, 1957), pp. 119–31.

110. George Antonius, *The Arab Awakening: The Story of the Arab National Movement* (New York, 1955), pp. 433–34.

111. The best-documented discussion on the whole episode known as "the

McMahon-Hussein Correspondence" can be found in Isaiah Friedman, *The Question of Palestine* (London, 1973), pp. 65–96.

112. Antonius, *Arab Awakening*, pp. 157–59.
113. [David Hogarth], "Arab Question," [1916], FO, 882/2.
114. See Henry McMahon to Edward Grey, November 20, 1915, Israel State Archives, 100/2.
115. Kedourie, *Chatham House Version*, pp. 16–18.
116. Sharif Hussein to Henry McMahon, January 1, 1916, in *Diplomacy in the Near and Middle East: A Documentary Record, 1914–1956*, ed. Jacob Coleman Hurewitz (Princeton, N.J., 1956), 2:16.
117. Wavell, *Palestine Campaigns*, pp. 40–42.
118. Concerning the Arab revolt and British policy toward the Arabs, see the evidence of Mark Sykes presented to the War Committee, July 6, 1916, CAB, 24/2.
119. Antonius, *Arab Awakening*, pp. 192–200.
120. Friedman, *Question of Palestine*, pp. 77–78.
121. Wavell, *Palestine Campaigns*, pp. 45–56.
122. Antonius, *Arab Awakening*, p. 262.
123. "The Constantinople Agreement, March 4–April 10, 1915," in *Diplomacy in the Near and Middle East*, ed. Hurwitz, pp. 7–11.
124. Ibid., p. 11.
125. Ibid., pp. 11–12. See also Jukka Nevakivi, *Britain, France and the Middle East, 1914–1920* (London, 1969); Elie Kedourie, *In the Anglo-Arab Labyrinth: The McMahon-Hussein Correspondence and Its Interpretations, 1914–1939* (Cambridge, 1976).
126. Antonius, *Arab Awakening*, pp. 331–35.
127. For the detailed description of the evolution of these negotiations, see Stein, *Balfour Declaration*, pp. 240–69; Friedman, *Question of Palestine*, pp. 97–118.
128. Edward Grey to Jules Cambon, May 16, 1916, CZA, K11/207/12.
129. "Arrangement of May 1916, Commonly Known as the Sykes-Picot Agreement," CZA, K11/207/12.
130. Friedman, *Question of Palestine*, pp. 210, 218–26.
131. Shane Leslie, *Mark Sykes: His Life and Letters* (New York, 1923), pp. 288–89, 269–70.
132. Elie Kedourie, *England and the Middle East: The Destruction of the Ottoman Empire, 1914–1921* (London, 1956), pp. 67–87; Stein, *Balfour Declaration*, pp. 271–84.
133. See Weizmann, *Trial and Error*, pp. 176–81. Concerning British attitudes toward Jews, the Holy Land, and Zionism, see Albert M. Hyamson, "British Projects for the Restoration of the Jews to Palestine," *Proceedings of the American Jewish Historical Society* 26 (1918): 127–64; Franz Kobler, *The Vision Was There: A History of the British Movement for the Restoration of the Jews to Palestine* (London, 1956); Barbara W. Tuchman, *Bible and Sword* (New York, 1968); Mayir Vereté, "The Restoration of the Jews in English Protestant Thought, 1790–1840," *Middle Eastern Studies* 8, no. 1 (1972): 3–50.
134. Bernard Lewis, *The Emergence of Modern Turkey* (Oxford, 1961), pp. 207–9.
135. A senior member of the Foreign Office, Hugh O'Beirne, claimed in a note of February 28, 1916, that if the Jews withdrew their support for the Young Turk government it would fall. FO, 371/2671/35433.
136. Cecil Spring-Rice to Robert Cecil, January 29, 1916, FO, 371/2835.

137. See, e.g., Vladimir Jabotinsky to [Robert Cecil?], January 26, 1916, FO, 371/2835.

138. Sidney Pollard, *The Development of the British Economy, 1914–1980*, 3d ed. (London, 1983), pp. 40–42.

139. See Friedman, *Germany, Turkey and Zionism*, pp. 191–346.

140. See, e.g., Richard Gottheil to Lucien Wolf, March 11, 1916, FO, 371/2835.

141. Halpern, *Clash of Heroes*, pp. 153–55.

142. Mordecai Altshuler, "Russia and Her Jews: The Impact of the 1914 War," *Wiener Library Bulletin*, n.s. 27, nos. 30–31 (1973–74): 12–16.

143. Isaac Leon Kandel to Horace Kallen, November 26, [1915], Brandeis Papers, reel 70, Z/P 3-1.

144. See Zosa Szajkowski, "The Komitee für den Osten and Zionism," *Herzl Year Book* 7 (New York, 1971): 199–240. See also CZA, A15/VII/1, A15/VII/10, A8/37/2.

145. Concerning Isaac Straus's membership in the Komitee für den Osten, see CZA, L6/45.

146. Stein, *Balfour Declaration*, pp. 214–16.

147. Naoum Slousch, memorandum, May 3, 1916, Archives of the French Ministry for Foreign Affairs, Guerre 1914–1918, Sionisme, vol. 2, no. 2; Slousch letter of August 15, 1916, Sionisme, vol. 2, nos. 41, 42, 43, 44.

148. Victor Guillaume Basch to Weizmann and Nahum Sokolow, cable, October 3, 1915, CZA, A18/40/5.

149. See the summary of confidential reports addressed to the French government by Victor Basch, attached to Lucien Wolf to Robert Cecil, February 27, 1916, FO, 371/2835.

150. Wavell, *Palestine Campaigns*, pp. 41–42.

151. Horace Kallen to Alfred Zimmern, [November 1915], FO, 371/2579. See also Horace Kallen to Alfred Zimmern, February 17, 1916, FO, 371/2835.

152. Lucien Wolf, "Suggestions for a Pro-Allies Propaganda among the Jews of the United States," December 16, 1915, in Wolf to Robert Cecil, FO, 371/2579.

153. Lucien Wolf to Robert Cecil, letter and memorandum, February 18, 1916, FO, 371/2835. See also Cecil to Wolf, February 24, 1916, FO, 371/2835.

154. Lucien Wolf to Lancelot Oliphant, enclosing "Suggested Palestine Formula," March 3, 1916, FO, 371/2835. See also Oliphant to Wolf, March 9, 1916, FO, 371/2817.

155. Stein, *Balfour Declaration*, pp. 225–32.

156. On British dealings with Syrian émigrés in Cairo, see Antonius, *Arab Awakening*, pp. 159–61.

157. Concerning French activities in this regard, see Archives of the French Ministry for Foreign Affairs, Guerre 1914–1918, Turquie 17 (Syrie-Palestine), vol. 4.

158. See Eliezer Livneh, ed., *Nili: Toldoteha shel heaza medinit* (Jerusalem, 1961).

159. Henry McMahon to Edward Grey, February 11, 1916, with the attached memorandum entitled "Palestine," dated January 27, 1916, FO, 371/2671/138708.

160. "Palestine," January 27, 1916, FO, 371/2671/138708.

161. Arthur Nicolson, minute, February 28, 1916, FO, 371/2671/138708.

162. Hugh O'Beirne, minute, February 28, 1916, FO, 371/2671/138708.

163. Robert Cecil, minute, March 3, 1916, FO, 371/2671/138708.

164. Edward Grey, quoted in Friedman, *Question of Palestine,* pp. 55–56.

165. Draft of cabled instructions signed by Lord Crewe, March 11, 1916, FO, 371/2817/137936.

166. George Buchanan to Foreign Office, March 15, 1916, FO, 371/2817/42608.

167. Francis Bertie to Foreign Office, cable, March 22, 1916, FO, 371/2817/42608. See also the full explanation for French resistance to the British proposal in a document dated March 21, 1916, which Bertie forwarded to the Foreign Office with his note. Archives of the French Ministry for Foreign Affairs, Guerre 1914–1918, Turquie 17 (Syrie-Palestine), vol. 6, nos. 40–41 [hand-written]. Bertie himself, no great supporter of Zionist aspirations, was less than happy with the Foreign Office's initiative. See his draft letter to Edward Grey, March 13, 1916, FO, 800/176.

168. "Conjoint Jewish Association: Formula Regarding Palestine," June 27, 1916, FO, 371/2817/42608.

169. Maurice de Bunsen to Lucien Wolf, July 4, 1916, FO, 371/2817/42608.

170. Concerning Lucien Wolf and his relations with the Zionists, see Eugene C. Black, *The Social Politics of Anglo-Jewry, 1880–1920* (Oxford, 1988), pp. 356–88.

171. Edmond de Rothschild to James de Rothschild, [July 1916], WA. See also Lucien Wolf to James de Rothschild, May 1, 1917, WA, referring to the meeting with Weizmann in August 1916. Wolf reminded James that the talks "were proposed and urged upon you and me by your father. . . . I entered upon them with reluctance and doubt, and only in order to endeavour to give satisfaction to your father's wishes."

172. Cohen, *English Zionists,* p. 230.

173. Chaim Weizmann, "Zionism and the Jewish Problem," in *Zionism and the Jewish Future,* ed. Harry Sacher (New York, 1916), pp. 5–7.

174. Lucien Wolf, memorandum, August 17, 1916, FO, 371/2817/137936.

175. James de Rothschild to Lucien Wolf, August 31, 1916, WA; Weizmann to Wolf, September 3, 1916, *WL,* 7:291–92. See also Wolf to Weizmann, September 4, 1916, WA.

176. Lucien Wolf to James de Rothschild, August 31, 1916, FO, 371/2817/137936; "Memorandum on Mr. Lucien Wolf's Letter to Mr. James de Rothschild of the 31st of August 1916," FO, 371/2817/137936, also in University College, Mocatta Library, London, AJ/204/3.

177. Lucien Wolf to James de Rothschild, August 31, 1916, FO, 371/2817/137936.

178. Ibid.

179. *Jewish Chronicle,* October 27, 1916.

180. Leopold Greenberg to Lucien Wolf, October 29, 1916, WA, asking Wolf to deny or confirm the rumor that the formula had been submitted to the government. There is no record of Wolf's reply, if indeed he did reply.

181. *Jewish World,* November 1, 1916.

182. Weizmann to James de Rothschild, October 30, 1916, *WL,* 7:309.

183. "Memorandum on Mr. Lucien Wolf's Letter to Mr. James de Rothschild of the 31st of August 1916," FO, 371/2817/137936, also in University College, Mocatta Library, AJ/204/3.

184. Lucien Wolf, "Notes on the Zionist Memorandum of October 11, 1916," November 20, 1916, FO, 371/2817/137936.

185. See, e.g., Moses Gaster to Lucien Wolf, November 3, 1916, CZA, A203/239; Weizmann to James de Rothschild, November 5, 1916, *WL*, 7:310–12; "Notes on Dr. Weizmann's Letter of November 5th 1916," WA.

186. Edmond de Rothschild to Weizmann, November 10, 1916, WA. The baron ended his letter with the exhortation: "Il faut l'entente avec le Conjoint Comité, c'est indispensable, et faire pour obtenir son concours toutes les concessions possibles. Il ne peut vous le refuser, il me semble, si vous vous posez sûr le terrain economique pur."

187. Friedman, *Question of Palestine*, p. 230.

188. Weizmann to James de Rothschild, October 15, 1916, *WL*, 7:305.

189. Weizmann to Israel Sieff, October 17, 1916, *WL*, 7:305–6.

190. Weizmann to Dorothy de Rothschild, October 14, 1915, *WL*, 7:240–41.

191. Weizmann to James de Rothschild, October 15, 1916, *WL*, 7:304–5.

192. Weizmann to Nahum Sokolow, November 14, 1916, *WL*, 7:315.

193. Weizmann to Nahum Sokolow, November 29, 1916, *WL*, 7:318–19.

194. Levene, *War, Jews, and the New Europe*, p. 120.

195. Lucien Wolf to Lancelot Oliphant, December 1, 1916, FO, 371/2817/137936.

196. Lancelot Oliphant, minute, December 10, 1916, FO, 371/2817/137936.

197. Lucien Wolf, memorandum of conversation with Balfour on January 30, 1917, dated January 31, 1917, CZA, A77/3/1.

198. Moses Gaster, diary, November 4, 1916, WA: "Dr. Weizmann . . . said he had seen Baron James de R. who seems now inclined to join openly the Movement."

199. Harry Sacher to Weizmann, November 17, 1914, WA.

200. Political Committee, minutes, March 14, 1916, CZA, K11/6.

201. See minutes of the meetings of the executive of the EZF, October 9, 16, 22, 1916, CZA, K11/6.

202. "The Demands" is reprinted in *WL*, 7:543–44.

203. Nahum Sokolow to Louis Brandeis, April 7, 1917, WA.

204. Weizmann to Harry Sacher and Leon Simon, December 4, 1914, *WL*, 7:69.

205. Copies of the memorandum and of various drafts of "The Demands" are in WA.

206. "The British Palestine Committee," CZA, L6/90/I. The document was probably written in October 1916 and is likely the "somewhat more detailed statement" enclosed with British Palestine Committee to Mark Sykes, October 11, 1916, WA.

207. See, e.g., Israel Sieff to Weizmann, December 1, 4, 1916, WA.

208. See Israel Sieff to Weizmann, December 11, 1916, WA.

209. Herbert Sidebotham, Harry Sacher, Israel Sieff, and Simon Marks to Mark Sykes, October 11, 1916, WA.

210. Mark Sykes to [BPC], October 14, 1916, WA.

211. Roger Adelson, *Mark Sykes: Portrait of an Amateur* (London, 1975), pp. 207–8.

212. Elie Kedourie, "Sir Mark Sykes and Palestine, 1915–1916," *Middle Eastern Studies* 6, no. 3 (October 1970): 340–45. Sir Mark had certainly not hidden his dislike of Jews in the past, nor of "Eastern" (Levantine) Christians. See his *Through Five Turkish Provinces* (London, 1900), p. 80.

213. Concerning Aaron Aaronsohn's motivations for working against the Turks, see Aaronsohn to Julian W. Mack, October 9, 1916, Ben-Gurion Archives, Sde Boker, Israel.

214. See Aaron Aaronsohn, *Yoman Aaron Aaronsohn, 1916–1919*, ed. Yoram Efrati, trans. Uri Kesari (Tel Aviv, 1970), pp. 118–34.

215. For some of the details of this espionage ring, see *Avshalom: Ktavim u-mikhtavim*, ed. Aharon Amir (Haifa, 1971).

216. Norman Bentwich, *My 77 Years: An Account of My Life and Times, 1883–1960* (Philadelphia, 1961), pp. 42–43.

217. Adelson, *Mark Sykes*, pp. 207–8. See also Mark Sykes to Moses Gaster, July 5, 1916, January 4, 1917, CZA, A203/241.

218. See Moses Gaster, diary, May 2 through mid-November 1916, WA. See also Gaster to Mark Sykes, July 4, November 3, 1916, WA. Sykes and Gaster seem to have been acquainted with one another prior to the war.

219. Aaronsohn, *Yoman Aaron Aaronsohn*, p. 251.

220. Weizmann, *Trial and Error*, p. 181.

221. Moses Gaster, diary, July 24, 1916, WA.

222. Moses Gaster, diary, September 20, 1916, WA.

223. Moses Gaster, diary, January 28, 1917, WA.

224. James A. Malcolm, "Origins of the Balfour Declaration: Dr. Weizmann's Contribution," Zionist Archives and Library, New York.

225. This assertion is confirmed by Weizmann in a letter to James A. Malcolm, March 5, 1941, *WL*, 20:122.

226. Malcolm, "Origins of the Balfour Declaration."

227. Moses Gaster, diary, January 30, 1917, WA.

228. Weizmann to Harris J. Morgenstern, February 1, 1917, *WL*, 7: 323–24.

229. Weizmann to Harris J. Morgenstern, February 4, 1917, *WL*, 7:327.

230. *Jewish Chronicle*, February 16, 1917.

231. Shmuel Tolkowsky, *Yoman zioni medini: London, 1915–1919*, ed. Dvorah Barzilay–Yegar (Jerusalem, 1981), p. 29.

232. A change in Israel Zangwill's attitude is indicative of the esteem Weizmann had attained. In 1914 Zangwill had been haughty when Weizmann approached him, but at the end of 1916 he presided at a lecture Weizmann delivered and referred in glowing terms to Weizmann's contributions to the British war effort. *Jewish Chronicle*, February 16, 1917.

233. Political Committee, minutes, January 21, 1917, CZA, K11/6.

234. Moses Gaster, diary, January 28, 1917, WA.

235. Leon Simon to Weizmann, January 31, 1917, WA.

236. Weizmann to Ahad Ha'Am, January 23, 1917, *WL*, 7:323.

237. Alfred Zimmern to Weizmann, January 28, 1917, WA.

238. Moses Gaster to Mark Sykes, January 31, 1917, Mark Sykes Papers, St. Antony's College, Middle East Centre, Oxford.

239. Ibid.

240. Moses Gaster, diary, July 7, 1916, WA.

241. See James Malcolm to Mark Sykes, February 5, 1917, Sykes Papers.

242. Harry Sacher to Weizmann, [February 1, 1917], WA.

243. Israel Sieff to Weizmann, February 2, 1917, WA.

244. David Ayerst, *The Manchester Guardian: Biography of a Newspaper* (Ithaca, N.Y., 1971), p. 386.

245. C. P. Scott to Weizmann, February 3, 1917, WA; Scott to David Lloyd George, February 5, 1917, Lloyd George Papers, F/45/2/4. In the event, the interview with Lloyd George did not take place before the meeting of February 7.

246. Weizmann to Israel Sieff, February 3, 1917, *WL*, 7:324–26. See also Sieff to Weizmann, February 4, 1917, WA.
247. Weizmann to Israel Sieff, February 3, 1917, *WL*, 7:326.
248. Moses Gaster, diary, February 1, 1917, WA.
249. Moses Gaster, diary, February 6, 1917, WA.
250. Moses Gaster, diary, February 1, 1917, WA.
251. See Mark Sykes to James Malcolm, February 3, 5, 1917, Sykes Papers.
252. Moses Gaster, diary, February 7, 1917, WA.
253. Israel Sieff to Weizmann, February 4, 1917, WA.

IV   Toward a British Declaration

1. *Jewish Chronicle*, February 16, 1917.
2. By contrast, Louis Brandeis supervised the work of the Federation of American Zionists very closely. Melvin I. Urofsky, *American Zionism from Herzl to the Holocaust* (Garden City, N.Y., 1975), pp. 156–63.
3. Ahad Ha'Am to Weizmann, November 15, 1914, *Igrot Ahad Ha'Am*, 5:202–3.
4. Cohen, *English Zionists and British Jews*, pp. 254–58.
5. Aaronsohn, *Yoman Aaron Aaronsohn*, pp. 158–86.
6. Aaron Aaronsohn to Julian Mack, October 9, 1916, WA.
7. Livneh, ed., *Nili*, pp. 193–99.
8. Shaul Avigur et al., eds., *Toldot hahaganah* (Tel Aviv, 1980), 1:460–61.
9. Jabotinsky, *Story of the Jewish Legion*, pp. 78–79. See also Vladimir Jabotinsky, "Proposed Jewish Corps for Service in Egypt and Palestine," January 24, 1917, submitted to David Lloyd George, CAB, 24/9.
10. Vladimir Jabotinsky to Weizmann, February 11, 1917, WA; Mark Sykes to Weizmann, February 14, 1917, WA.
11. Throughout this period Vladimir Jabotinsky kept Weizmann informed of his plans and sought his advice and help on numerous occasions. See, e.g., Jabotinsky to Mark Sykes, February 11, 1917, WA. See also Jabotinsky to Weizmann, March 15, 25, April 5, August 21, 1917, Jabotinsky Archives, Tel Aviv.
12. "Memorandum of a Conference Held on the 7th February 1917 at 193 Maida Vale," CZA, A226/30/1.
13. In a letter to James de Rothschild dated February 9, 1917, WA, Moses Gaster said that on the day before the conference took place in his house, Weizmann had suggested that Sokolow be nominated to conduct the negotiations, a suggestion that Gaster "hotly resented." See also James de Rothschild to Gaster, February 7, 1917, CZA, A203/5.
14. Moses Gaster to James de Rothschild, February 9, 1917, CZA, A203/241.
15. See, e.g., Moses Gaster to Jacob DeHaas, [March 1917], WA; Gaster to Weizmann, May 10, 1917, WA.
16. See, e.g., Moses Gaster to Jacob Moser, June 1, 1917, CZA, A203/241, which reflects the depth of Gaster's animus toward Weizmann: "You know my confidence in Dr. W. has never been great. I felt him to be a time-server, playing a peculiar game of his own, believed to be very diplomatic, but only diplomatic in as far as it meant trickery and underhand game." See also Gaster to Moser, March 3, 1917, CZA, A203/241, expressing similar sentiments.
17. Moses Gaster, diary, February 7, 1917, WA.

18. Weizmann to Vladimir Jabotinsky, February 8, 1917, *WL*, 7:328–29.
19. Ahad Ha'Am to Shmuel Pevsner, February 24, 1917, *Igrot Ahad Ha'Am*, 5:60–61.
20. "Notes on a Meeting Held on Thursday February 8th 1917 at the Residence of Sir Mark Sykes, 9 Buckingham Gate," CZA, Z4/728.
21. "Memorandum of Interview between M. Picot and Mr. N. Sokolow, Friday 9th February 1917, at the French Embassy in London," WA.
22. "Notes of Meeting Held on Saturday February 10th 1917 at 9 Buckingham Gate," CZA, L6/90/I.
23. "Our Military Interest in Palestine," *Palestine*, February 1, 1917, p. 1.
24. Tolkowsky, *Yoman zioni medini*, pp. 27–32.
25. "The Boundaries of Palestine," *Palestine*, February 15, 1917.
26. Weizmann probably wrote to Israel Sieff on February 17, 1917; the letter has not been found. See also Weizmann to Nahum Sokolow, February 18, 1917, *WL*, 7:330–31.
27. Israel Sieff to Weizmann, February 19, [1917], WA.
28. Israel Sieff to Weizmann, [spring 1917], WA.
29. Simon Marks to Weizmann, March 3, 1917, WA.
30. Weizmann to Israel Sieff, February 20, 1917, *WL*, 7:332–33; Sieff to Weizmann, February 20, 1917, WA, declaring, "I understand the importance of discipline and unity."
31. See, e.g., Israel Sieff to Weizmann, March 19, 1917, WA; Harry Sacher to Leon Simon, [April] 1917, WA.
32. See, e.g., [Shmuel Tolkowsky] to Israel Sieff, May 7, 1917, WA; Harry Sacher to Leon Simon, [May 5], 1917, WA.
33. Leon Simon to Harry Sacher, May 9, 1917, WA.
34. Harry Sacher to Weizmann, May 9, 1917, WA.
35. Harry Sacher to Weizmann, May 11, 1917, WA.
36. Israel Sieff to Weizmann, May 4, 1917, WA.
37. Israel Sieff to Weizmann, May 14, 1917, WA.
38. Harry Sacher to Leon Simon, May 11, 1917, WA.
39. Weizmann to C. P. Scott, March 20, 1917, *WL*, 7:343–45.
40. C. P. Scott, diary, March 1, 1917, Guardian Archives.
41. The meeting took place on March 7, 1917. Tolkowsky, *Yoman zioni medini*, pp. 33–34. For Herbert Sidebotham's record of the conversation, see "Memorandum," March 9, 1917, WA.
42. Nahum Sokolow to Weizmann, April 4, 1917, WA.
43. Wavell, *Palestine Campaigns*, pp. 73–88.
44. Stein, *Balfour Declaration*, p. 332.
45. See the detailed secret report to the war cabinet by William Ormsby-Gore, "Zionism and the Suggested Jewish Battalions for Egyptian Expeditionary Force," CAB, 24/10.
46. See, e.g., Jules Cambon to the premier, memorandum, March 11, 1917, Archives of the French Ministry for Foreign Affairs, Guerre 1914–1918, Sionisme, vol. 2, no. 117.
47. The letter from Georges Picot to Alexandre Ribot is dated May 5, 1917, i.e., about a month after Nahum Sokolow's meetings with the French officials in Paris, but it indicates that throughout Picot kept close records of conversations he had with the Zionists and Mark Sykes and surely communicated those to Paris. In the letter under discussion, he detailed his discussions

with Moses Gaster ("le Grand Rabbin de Londres"), the February meeting of British and Zionist leaders, and his own meetings with Sokolow on February 8, 1917. See Archives of the French Ministry for Foreign Affairs, Guerre 1914–1918, Sionisme, vol. 3, no. 2, May–December 1917.

48. See Jules Cambon to Georges Picot, cable, March 30, 1917, Archives of the French Ministry for Foreign Affairs, Guerre 1914–1918, Sionisme, vol. 2, no. 185.

49. Vera Weizmann, diary, April 24, 1917, WA.

50. C. P. Scott, quoted in Israel Sieff to Weizmann, April 28, 1917, WA.

51. Nahum Sokolow, "Precise Report of the Special Mission of Mr. N. Sokolow and Mr. J. A. Malcolm to Paris re Zionist Demands for a Jewish Home in Palestine," April 19, 1917, CZA, Z4/798.

52. Nahum Sokolow to Weizmann, April 4, 1917, WA.

53. Mark Sykes to Ronald Graham, cable, April 6, 1917, FO, 371/3045; Sykes to Maurice Hankey, private letter, April 7, 1917, CAB, 21/96.

54. Mark Sykes to Arthur Balfour, April 8, 1917, WA.

55. Nahum Sokolow, "Precise Report of the Special Mission of Mr. N. Sokolow and Mr. J. A. Malcolm to Paris re Zionist Demands for a Jewish Home in Palestine," April 19, 1917, CZA, Z4/798.

56. The text of Nahum Sokolow's cables to Louis Brandeis and Yehiel Tschlenow is included in Mark Sykes to Ronald Graham, cable, April 9, 1917, FO, 371/3045.

57. Mark Sykes to Arthur Balfour, April 9, 1917, Lloyd George Papers, F/51/4/18, no. 7, folder 29, box 71.

58. Count de Salis to Eric Drummond, April 17, 1917, CZA, KH/207/11, reporting on Mark Sykes's activities in Rome.

59. Mark Sykes to Nahum Sokolow, April 14, 1917, WA.

60. This was the assessment of the French officials. See Pierre de Margerie, chef de cabinet at the Quai d'Orsay, "Palestine et les Juifs," May 22, 1917, Archives of the French Ministry for Foreign Affairs, Guerre 1914–1918, Sionisme, vol. 3, nos. 33–34, May–December 1917. See also the assessment of Sergio Minerbi, who is a bit more cautious. *Havatikan, eretz hakodesh vehazionut, 1895–1925* (Jerusalem, 1985), pp. 128–41.

61. Nahum Sokolow to Weizmann, May 12, 1917, WA.

62. Nahum Sokolow wrote an aide-mémoire of the May 4 meeting, trying to record as accurately as possible the actual conversation. CZA, A18/26.

63. Nahum Sokolow to Weizmann, cable, May 7, 1917, FO, 371/3053/92646/84173.

64. Stein, *Balfour Declaration,* pp. 414–15. Concerning Italy's interest in Palestine, see Frank Manuel, "Habeaya haeretz-israelit badiplomatya haitalkit bishnot 1916–1920," in *Shivat Zion,* vol. 4, ed. Ben Zion Dinur and Israel Heilprin (Jerusalem, 1956), pp. 210–39.

65. Nahum Sokolow to Weizmann, May 26, 1917, CZA, Z4/728, reporting on his various meetings upon returning to Paris.

66. Nahum Sokolow to Jules Cambon, June 2, 1917, Archives of the French Ministry for Foreign Affairs, Guerre 1914–1918, Turquie, vol. 22, no. 163.

67. Jules Cambon to Nahum Sokolow, June 4, 1917, FO, 371/3083/143082/143082.

68. This primacy is also indicated in Nahum Sokolow's letter of thanks to Jules Cambon, June 11, 1917, Archives of the French Ministry for Foreign Affairs, Guerre 1914–1918, Turquie, vol. 3, no. 52.

69. Nahum Sokolow to Weizmann, April 19, 1917, WA; Weizmann to Harry Sacher, April 22, 1917, *WL*, 7:368.

70. Nahum Sokolow's report on that meeting was written fully ten days after it took place.

71. Harry Sacher to Leon Simon, April 13, 1917, WA.

72. Harry Sacher to Weizmann, April 14, 1917, WA.

73. Weizmann to Nahum Sokolow, cable, April 27, 1917, *WL*, 7:384.

74. Weizmann to Nahum Sokolow, May 1, 1917, *WL*, 7:390–93.

75. Nahum Sokolow to Weizmann, April 4, 1917, FO, 371/3053/84173/91882. See also Sokolow to Weizmann, May 5, 1917, WA.

76. Nahum Sokolow to Weizmann, May 12, 1917, WA.

77. Weizmann to Nahum Sokolow, May 9, 1917, *WL*, 7:405.

78. Weizmann to Nahum Sokolow, May 20, 1917, *WL*, 7:414.

79. See Ronald Graham, minute, FO, 371/2996/811/94865.

80. Tolkowsky, *Yoman zioni medini*, p. 76.

81. Nahum Sokolow to Weizmann, May 16, 1917, FO, 371/3053/84173/99608.

82. Harry Sacher to Weizmann, June 14, 1917, WA.

83. Lucien Wolf, "Zionism," *Fortnightly Review*, November 1, 1916. See also Cohen, *English Zionists and British Jews*, p. 234.

84. Leon Simon, *The Case of the Anti-Zionists: A Reply* (London, 1917); Harry Sacher, *Jewish Emancipation: The Contract Myth* (London, 1917).

85. Lucien Wolf to Nahum Sokolow, March 8, 1917, CZA, L6/90/I; Sokolow to Wolf, March 15, 1917, CZA, L6/90/I.

86. Lucien Wolf to Nahum Sokolow, March 26, 1917, CZA, L6/90/I.

87. Nahum Sokolow to Louis Brandeis, April 7, 1917, CZA, L6/90/I.

88. Walter Rothschild to Weizmann, April 10, 1917, WA.

89. See Jacques Bigart to Lucien Wolf, April 16, 1917, WA, attaching Nahum Sokolow's statements made to some members of the Alliance Israélite Universelle on April 14, 1917.

90. Claude Montefiore, memorandum, May 17, 1917, CZA, K11/46.

91. Claude Montefiore to Alfred Milner, May 17, 1917, CZA, A77/3/1.

92. Mark Sykes to Ronald Graham, April 28, 1917, FO, 371/3053.

93. "Agenda of the Conjoint Committee for May 17, 1917" and "Statement on the Palestine Question," CZA, A77/3/1.

94. Weizmann's speech was attached to a letter he sent to Ronald Graham, May 23, 1917, FO, 371/3054.

95. D. L. Alexander and Claude Montefiore, "The Future of the Jews—Palestine and Zionism: Views of Anglo-Jewry," *Times* (London), May 24, 1917.

96. "The Future of the Jews: Zionist Projects, Ideals in Palestine," *Times* (London), May 28, 1917.

97. Harry Lewis to Weizmann, May 30, 1917, WA.

98. Weizmann to Harry Lewis, June 1, 1917, *WL*, 7:422–24. See also Lewis to Weizmann, June 3, 1917, WA.

99. *Jewish Chronicle*, June 22, 1917. See also Walter Rothschild to Weizmann, June 17, 1917, WA.

100. Ronald Graham to Charles Hardinge, June 18, 1917, WA.

101. Stuart Cohen has clearly demonstrated that the vote at the Board of Deputies could not be attributed to Zionist strength but resulted from the coalescing of internal issues. The Conjoint's statement in the *Times* of May 24

simply provided a chance to implement an action contemplated for some time. Cohen, *English Zionists and British Jews,* pp. 243–76. This situation, of course, did not prevent the Zionists from claiming the vote of June 17, 1917, as the result of their newfound power.

102. Harry Sacher to Leon Simon, June 20, 1917, WA.

103. Stuart Cohen, "The Conquest of a Community? The Zionists and the Board of Deputies in 1917," *Jewish Journal of Sociology* 19, no. 2 (December 1977): 157–84.

104. *Jewish Chronicle,* June 29, 1917.

105. Chaim Weizmann, "Notes and Comments," *Zionist Review* 1, no. 1 (May 1917).

106. Barzilay, "Shat mashber kishat mifneh," pp. 37–38.

107. Moses Gaster, diary, June 6, [1917], WA.

108. Weizmann to C. P. Scott, March 20, 1917, *WL,* 7:344.

109. Mark Sykes, memorandum, April 29, 1917, Sykes Papers.

110. Weizmann to C. P. Scott, March 23, 1917, *WL,* 7:346.

111. I have in my possession only a fragment of the minutes, which are identified as MSS EUR F112/134, Curzon Papers, India Office Library and Records, London. The assumption that Arthur Balfour's statement was made on March 21 is based on a letter from Leopold Amery to Balfour, March 29, 1917, FO, 800/204, which refers to Balfour's favorable view of Zionism.

112. Weizmann to C. P. Scott, March 23, 1917, *WL,* 7:346–47.

113. See Francis Bertie to Charles Hardinge, April 22, 1917, FO, 800/176, stating that David Lloyd George seemed to believe that the British would be in Palestine by conquest and that the French would therefore have no choice but to accept a protectorate.

114. Vera Weizmann, diary, March 13, 1917, WA.

115. David Lloyd George, quoted in Dvorah Barzilay, "Letoldot hatzharat Balfour," *Zion* 33, nos. 3–4 (1968): 196.

116. C. P. Scott, diary, April 3, 1917, Guardian Archives.

117. Weizmann to Nahum Sokolow, April 4, 1917, *WL,* 7:350–51.

118. "Notes of a Conference Held at 10 Downing Street, at 3:30 P.M. on April 3, 1917 to Consider the Instructions to Lieutenant Colonel Sir Mark Sykes, the Head of the Political Mission to the General Officer Commanding-in-Chief, Egyptian Expeditionary Force," CAB, 24/9.

119. C. P. Scott, diary, April 4, 1917, Guardian Archives.

120. Mark Sykes to Ronald Graham, May 5, 1917, FO, 371/3053.

121. Ronald Graham to Weizmann, May 1, 1917, WA. See also Mark Sykes to Graham, cable, April 28, 1917, FO, 371/3055/87895/87895.

122. For the most comprehensive contemporaneous description of the events leading to the expulsion and its impact on Jews of Jaffa–Tel Aviv, indeed on the entire Palestinian Jewish community, see Mordechai Ben-Hillel Hacohen, *Milhemet haamim,* ed. Shimon Rubinstein (Jerusalem, 1981–85), 2:527–663. See also Friedman, *Germany, Turkey and Zionism,* pp. 347–73; Mordechai Eliav, "Meorvutam shel nezigei Germanya ve-Austria beeruei 1917 be-Eretz Israel," *Cathedra* 48 (June 1988): 90–124.

123. See the inaccurate report by Aaron Aaronsohn, transmitted to Weizmann and Nahum Skolow via Reginald Wingate and the Foreign Office, April 28, 1917, FO, 371/3055/87895.

124. William Ormsby-Gore to Mark Sykes, May 8, 1917, Sykes Papers.

125. See Weizmann to Jacobus Kann, May 2, 5, 1917, *WL*, 7:394, 397–99; Nahum Sokolow to Weizmann, May 14, 1917, CZA, A/18, enumerating the steps he was taking to help the evacuees. See also Jacob DeHaas to members of the PZC, May 7, 1917, WA; draft circular by Weizmann appealing for relief of war victims in Palestine, May 1917, in *Letters and Papers of Weizmann*, ser. B, ed. Litvinoff, 1:160.

126. Moses Gaster to Jacques Mosseri, May 15, 1917, CZA, A203/241.

127. See FO, 382/1639/399/98384.

128. "Minutes of the Third Meeting of the Sub-Committee of the Imperial War Cabinet on Territorial Desiderata in the Terms of Peace, Held at 2 Whitehall Gardens on April 19, 1917," CAB, 21/77.

129. David Lloyd George, afterword to the lecture by Philip Guedalla, *Napoleon and Palestine* (London, 1925), p. 51.

130. Ronald Graham to Francis Bertie, April 16, 1917, FO, 800/176.

131. Ronald Graham to Charles Hardinge, April 21, 1917, FO, 371/3052/78234/82982.

132. Harry Sacher to Weizmann, April 14, 1917, WA.

133. C. P. Scott to Weizmann, April 16, 1917, WA.

134. Vera Weizmann, diary, April 24, 1917, WA. See also C. P. Scott to Weizmann, April 24, 1917, WA, reporting Alfred Milner as saying that "unfortunate commitments had been made a year ago." Scott gathered that these commitments were made to the French. The high level of secrecy maintained by the British is impressive. The fact that so informed a person as Scott was kept in the dark speaks for itself.

135. C. P. Scott to Weizmann, April 16, 1917, WA.

136. Weizmann to C. P. Scott, April 26, 1917, *WL*, 7:379. See also Tolkowsky, *Yoman zioni medini*, p. 45.

137. See Tolkowsky, diary, April 23, 1917, *Yoman zioni medini*, p. 45.

138. Weizmann to C. P. Scott, April 26, 1917, *WL*, 7:379.

139. See, e.g., C. P. Scott to Weizmann, February 11, 1917, WA.

140. See, e.g., C. P. Scott to Weizmann, April 16, 1917, WA.

141. C. P. Scott to Weizmann, April 24, 1917, WA.

142. C. P. Scott to Weizmann, April 25, 1917, WA. On April 28, 1917, WA, Israel Sieff reported to Weizmann that Scott had said "that you would be merely wasting your time, were you to go to Egypt."

143. Walter Rothschild to Weizmann, May 4, 1917, WA.

144. Weizmann to C. P. Scott, April 26, 1917, *WL*, 7:379–80.

145. William Ormsby-Gore to Mark Sykes, May 8, 1917, Sykes Papers.

146. See Robert Cecil, memorandum, April 25, 1917, FO, 371/3053/84173/87062.

147. Foreign Office to Reginald Wingate, April 28, 1917, FO, 371/3052.

148. Mark Sykes to Foreign Office, April 29, 1917, Sykes Papers.

149. Mark Sykes to Weizmann, cable, February 14, 1917, WA.

150. C. P. Scott, diary, April 30, 1917, Guardian Archives.

151. Mark Sykes to Foreign Office, cable, May 19, 1917, FO, 371/3052.

152. Aaronsohn, *Yoman Aaron Aaronsohn*, pp. 247–57, 268–72, and passim.

153. Robert Cecil, memorandum, April 25, 1917, FO, 371/3053/84173/87062.

154. "Note of Interview with Lord Robert Cecil at the Foreign Office, 25 Apr. 1917," *WL*, 7:378.

155. Mark Sykes to Reginald Wingate, June 5, 1917, Reginald Wingate Papers, Durham University, School of Oriental Studies, Durham.

156. Stein, *Balfour Declaration*, p. 429. See also Friedman, *Question of Palestine*, pp. 179–81.
157. Leopold Greenberg, "Russian Jews and the Revolution," April 16, 1917, FO, 371/3052/8324.
158. Robert Cecil to George Buchanan, cable, April 24, 1917, FO, 371/3053/78324.
159. George Buchanan to Foreign Office, April 27, 1917, FO, 371/3053/78324.
160. George Buchanan to Foreign Office, May 10, 1917, FO, 371/2996/811/94865.
161. See Ronald Graham, minute, May 11, 1917, FO, 371/2996/811/94865.
162. Mark Sykes to Ronald Graham, cable, April 28, 1917, FO, 371/3053/87897.
163. Weizmann to Nahum Sokolow, cable, May 14, 1917, *WL*, 7:408–9.
164. Nahum Sokolow to Weizmann, May 16, 1917, FO, 371/3053/84173/99608.
165. Mark Sykes to Ronald Graham, April 28, 1917, FO, 371/3053/87897.
166. Weizmann to Yehiel Tschlenow, cable, April 27, 1917, *WL*, 7:383–84.
167. Weizmann to Yehiel Tschlenow, April 29, 1917, *WL*, 7:388.
168. Weizmann to Israel Rosov, cable, May 16, 1917, *WL*, 7:412.
169. Stein, *Balfour Declaration*, p. 435.
170. Weizmann to Israel Rosov and Yehiel Tschlenow, June 2, 1917, *WL*, 7:426.
171. Weizmann to Yehiel Tschlenow and Israel Rosov, cable, June 4, 1917, *WL*, 7:429–30.
172. Weizmann to Nahum Sokolow, cable, June 4, 1917, *WL*, 7:430.
173. Nahum Sokolow to Israel Rosov, June 6, 1917, FO, 371/3053/84173.
174. Yitzhak Gruenbaum, *Hatnuah hazionit behitpathutah* (Jerusalem, 1954), pp. 98–108.
175. See Yitzhak Maor, *Hatnuah hazionit be-Russyah* (Jerusalem, 1973), pp. 446–50.
176. Israel Rosov to Weizmann, cable, June 20, 1917, FO, 371/3053/138708.
177. Ronald Graham, minute, on ibid.
178. See Mark Sykes to Reginald Wingate, June 5, 1917, Wingate Papers.
179. For background information on these issues, see Naomi W. Cohen, *American Jews and the Zionist Idea* (New York, 1975), pp. 14–24.
180. See Urofsky, *American Zionism*, pp. 109–52.
181. Jehuda Reinharz, "Zionism in the United States on the Eve of the Balfour Declaration," *Studies in Zionism* 9, no. 2 (Autumn 1988): 131–45.
182. Halpern, *Clash of Heroes*, p. 153.
183. On these issues, see Mintz, *Zmanim hadashim, zmirot hadashot*, pp. 253–302.
184. Philippa Strum, *Louis D. Brandeis: Justice for the People* (Cambridge, Mass., 1984), pp. 196–223.
185. Stephen Wise, *Challenging Years: The Autobiography of Stephen Wise* (New York, 1949), pp. 161–81.
186. Kendrick A. Clements, *Woodrow Wilson: World Statesman* (Boston, 1987), pp. 151–71.
187. Frederick S. Calhoun, *Power and Principle: Armed Intervention in Wilsonian Foreign Policy* (Kent, Ohio, 1986), pp. 27–34.
188. Lloyd C. Gardner, *Safe for Democracy: The Anglo-American Response to Revolution, 1913–1923* (New York, 1984), pp. 97–123; Robert H. Ferrell, *Woodrow Wilson and World War I, 1917–1921* (New York, 1985), pp. 1–12.
189. Halpern, *Clash of Heroes*, pp. 154–56.
190. The Blackstone petition and American Protestant interest in Zionism and the Holy Land are issues Ben Halpern has analyzed in a number of publications, particularly in "Brandeis and the Origins of the Balfour Declara-

tion," *Studies in Zionism* 7 (Spring 1983): 71–100. I accept his analysis and conclusions but have expanded on some of the points he raises in his article.

191. For the history and content of the Blackstone petition, see CZA, L6/12/XIV.
192. Stephen Wise to Louis Brandeis, June 30, 1917, Jacob DeHaas Papers, Zionist Archives and Library, reel 2/37.
193. Halpern, "Brandeis and the Origins of the Balfour Declaration," p. 81.
194. Joseph L. Grabill, *Protestant Diplomacy and the Near East: Missionary Influence on American Policy, 1810–1927* (Minneapolis, 1971); John A. DeNovo, *American Interests and Policies in the Middle East, 1900–1939* (Minneapolis, 1963).
195. Naomi W. Cohen, *A Dual Heritage: The Public Career of Oscar S. Straus* (Philadelphia, 1969).
196. DeNovo, *American Interests and Policies in the Middle East*, pp. 91–105.
197. Blanche E. C. Dugdale, *Arthur James Balfour, 1907–1930* (London, 1936), p. 231. See also Louis Brandeis to James de Rothschild, cable, May 15, 1917, DeHaas Papers, reel 2/37.
198. Moses Gaster communicated with the Americans via Jacob DeHaas. See, e.g., his letter of March [date illegible], 1917, giving his own version of Zionist developments, DeHaas Papers, reel 2/37.
199. Nahum Sokolow to Louis Brandeis, March 7, 1917, WA.
200. Nahum Sokolow to Louis Brandeis, April 7, 1917, CZA, L6/90/I.
201. Louis Brandeis to Nahum Sokolow, April 2, 1917, DeHaas Papers, reel 2/37.
202. Weizmann to Louis Brandeis, April 8, 1917, *WL*, 7:357–60.
203. Ronald Graham to Mark Sykes, April 19, 1917, Sykes Papers.
204. Weizmann and James de Rothschild to Louis Brandeis, April 21, 1917, Sir William Wiseman Papers, Yale University, Sterling Library, New Haven, Conn., drawer 91, file 130.
205. Weizmann to Louis Brandeis, April 23, 1917, *WL*, 7:371–73.
206. James de Rothschild, Weizmann, and Joseph Cowen to Louis Brandeis, April 27, 1917, *WL*, 7:383.
207. Weizmann to Louis Brandeis, April 28, 1917, *WL*, 7:386.
208. Jacob DeHaas to Weizmann, May 1, 1917, DeHaas Papers, reel 2/37.
209. Boris Goldberg to PZC, April 28, 1917, WA.
210. See Halpern, "Brandeis and the Origins of the Balfour Declaration," p. 84.
211. See, e.g., Louis Brandeis to James de Rothschild, May 16, 1917, DeHaas Papers, reel 3/474.
212. See May 7, 1917, note in Brandeis's handwriting, recording aspects of his conversation with Balfour the day before, DeHaas Papers, reel 3/337.
213. See draft of letter from Louis Brandeis (prepared by Jacob DeHaas) to James de Rothschild, May 16, 1917, DeHaas Papers, reel 3/473. As can be seen from DeHaas to Brandeis, May 23, 1917, the letter to Rothschild was probably not sent until the end of May 1917. DeHaas Papers, reel 3/473.
214. Louis Brandeis to Jacob DeHaas and Felix Frankfurter, May 6, 1917, and recorded by DeHaas on May 9, 1917, DeHaas Papers, reel 3/437.
215. Frank E. Manuel, *The Realities of American-Palestine Relations* (Washington, D.C., 1949), pp. 165–66.
216. See Louis Brandeis's various statements in "Stenographic Draft PC Meeting, May 20, 1917," DeHaas Papers, reel 2/770.
217. Gustav von Dobeler, *Der Reichsbote*, May 2, 1917; Weizmann to Ronald Gra-

ham, June 6, 1917, *WL,* 7:431, and n. 1. See also Zechlin, *Die deutsche Politik und die Juden im Ersten Weltkrieg,* pp. 367–68.

218. Friedman, *Germany, Turkey and Zionism,* pp. 326–28.
219. Weizmann to Ronald Graham, June 13, 1917, *WL,* 7:438–42.
220. Ronald Graham to Charles Hardinge, June 13, 1917, FO, 371/3058/123458/ 123458.
221. Arthur Balfour, minute, n.d., on ibid.
222. On April 27, 1917, Graham promised in a letter to Lucien Wolf that the Conjoint Foreign Committee would be consulted before any government policy concerning the Jews would be announced. FO, 371/3092/4637/83962.
223. Ronald Graham to Arthur Balfour, June 19, 1917, FO, 371/3058/123458/123458.
224. Cecil, minute on ibid.
225. It was Walter Rothschild who asked for the interview with Arthur Balfour, immediately after the vote of the Board of Deputies that ended the existence of the Conjoint Foreign Committee. See Walter Rothschild to Weizmann, June 17, 1917, WA.
226. Weizmann to Harry Sacher, June 20, 1917, *WL,* 7:445.
227. Arthur Balfour, minute on Ronald Graham to Balfour, June 19, 1917, FO, 371/3058/123458/123458.
228. "I shall be able to prove to him that the majority of Jews are in favour of Zionism," wrote Rothschild to Weizmann two days prior to their meeting with Arthur Balfour. Walter Rothschild to Weizmann, June 17, 1917, WA.

V Gibraltar

1. Weizmann to C. P. Scott, June 20, 1917, *WL,* 7:446.
2. See, e.g., Naomi W. Cohen, "The Abrogation of the Russo-American Treaty of 1832," *Jewish Social Studies* 25 (1963): 3–41.
3. The following discussion regarding Protestant interests in international affairs is based, in large part, on Halpern's account in *Clash of Heroes,* pp. 156–58.
4. "[Stephen] Wise told me that Morgenthau was very keen to get on our band wagon in some way or the other," wrote Jacob DeHaas to Louis Brandeis on May 7, 1917, Brandeis Papers, reel Z/P 81, 22-1. Clearly, Henry Morgenthau felt that it was reasonable to expect Zionist support.
5. Friedman, *Germany, Turkey and Zionism,* pp. 194–95, 275–76, 284–85.
6. See the extensive correspondence and newspaper reports concerning Henry Morgenthau's assertion that he could buy Palestine from its Ottoman rulers. Brandeis Papers, reel 82, Z/P 22-3.
7. The story is recorded in Robert Lansing's confidential diary, 1917, vol. 2, in the Robert Lansing Papers, Library of Congress, Washington, D.C., copy in WA.
8. Ibid.
9. F. W. Brecher, "Revisiting Ambassador Morgenthau's Turkish Peace Mission of 1917," *Middle Eastern Studies* 24, no. 3 (July 1988): 357.
10. Edward M. House to Henry Morgenthau, June 20, 1917, William Yale Papers, Boston University, Mugar Memorial Library, Boston, Mass., box 23, folder 2.
11. Arthur Balfour to Foreign Office, cable, May 23, 1917, FO, 371/3057.
12. Lancelot Oliphant and Robert Cecil, minutes on ibid.

13. Robert Lansing, diary, June 10, 1917, Lansing Papers.

14. This is, in fact, the way the mission was described in the *New York Times*, June 20, 1917.

15. Robert Lansing, diary, June 10, 1917, Lansing Papers.

16. In his sardonic and derogatory description of Morgenthau and his mission, Felix Frankfurter claimed that he was reluctant to go along and did so only at Woodrow Wilson's request. Felix Frankfurter, *Felix Frankfurter Reminisces: Recorded in Talks with Harlan B. Phillips* (New York, 1960), pp. 145–46. Yet in a telegram to Louis Brandeis probably sent on June 14, 1917, Lansing Papers, Frankfurter said, "I'm off with eagerness."

17. *New York Times*, June 17, 1917.

18. Colville-Barclay, British chargé d'affaires in Washington, to Foreign Office, cable, May 30, 1917, FO, 371/3057.

19. Robert Lansing to Louis Brandeis, June 4, 1917, Lansing Papers, inviting him to come to his office the following day. See also Lansing's report of developments in this scheme, June 10, 1917, Lansing Papers.

20. Stephen Wise to Louis Brandeis, June 4, 1917, DeHaas Papers.

21. Jacob DeHaas to Louis Brandeis, June 5, 1917, Lansing Papers.

22. No doubt Henry Morgenthau explained his reasons for selecting Felix Frankfurter to Louis Brandeis when he saw him during the first week of June. See Morgenthau to Brandeis, cable, June 5, 1917, Lansing Papers.

23. Halpern, "Brandeis and the Origins of the Balfour Declaration," p. 89.

24. Robert Lansing, diary, June 10, 1917, Lansing Papers.

25. Louis Brandeis, quoted in Weizmann, *Trial and Error*, p. 195.

26. Ronald Sanders, *The High Walls of Jerusalem* (New York, 1983), p. 553.

27. Tolkowsky, *Yoman zioni medini*, pp. 103–4.

28. Mark Sykes to Gilbert Clayton, July 22, 1917, Sykes Papers.

29. Ronald Graham's minutes are appended to a memorandum of June 9, 1917, circulated to the king and war cabinet, FO, 371/3057.

30. William Ormsby-Gore to Mark Sykes, June 10, 1917, Sykes Papers.

31. Ronald Graham, minute, June 12, 1917, FO, 371/3057.

32. Weizmann to Ronald Graham, June 13, 1917, WL, 7:438–42.

33. Weizmann to Harry Sacher, June 11, 1917, WL, 7:438.

34. Cecil Spring-Rice to Foreign Office, June 12, 1917, FO, 371/3057.

35. Robert Lansing to Walter Page, June 25, 1917, Lansing Papers.

36. Arthur Balfour, minute on Cecil Spring-Rice to Foreign Office, cable, June 15, 1917, FO, 371/3057.

37. Ronald Graham, minute on Cecil Spring-Rice to Foreign Office, cable, June 19, 1917, FO, 371/3057.

38. See, e.g., Barclay, minute on memorandum, May 30, 1917: "Mr. Morgenthau's ideas seem fantastic." FO, 371/3057.

39. Cecil Spring-Rice to Foreign Office, June 19, 1917, FO, 371/3057.

40. Weizmann to Harry Sacher, June 11, 1917, WL, 7:437. There is a confirmation of this assertion by Weizmann in Ronald Graham, minute, June 12, 1917, FO, 371/3057.

41. Weizmann to C. P. Scott, June 26, 1917, WL, 7:453.

42. Tolkowsky, *Yoman zioni medini*, pp. 125–26.

43. Weizmann, *Trial and Error*, p. 196. There is no official record extant of this meeting, but it is possible that a last-minute meeting was arranged. This might explain why it is not recorded in Weizmann's appointment book.

See also William Yale, "Ambassador Henry Morgenthau's Special Mission of 1917," *World Politics* 1, no. 3 (April 1949): 308–20. Yale, who met Weizmann in 1920, relates the same story told by Weizmann.

44. Arthur Balfour to Arthur Hardinge, June 28, 1917, FO, 371/3057. If, indeed, Weizmann *did* meet Balfour on June 28, it stands to reason that the letter was given him on the occasion.

45. Arthur Balfour to Cecil Spring-Rice, cable, June 27, 1917, FO, 371/3057. See also Balfour to Spring-Rice, cable, July 4, 1917, WA, asking him to explain to the State Department the potentially embarrassing impact Morgenthau's mission might have on British affairs in Egypt.

46. Edward House to Henry Morgenthau, June 13, 1917, Yale Papers, box 23, folder 2.

47. Weizmann to Vera Weizmann, June 29, 1917, *WL*, 7:455.

48. Weizmann, *Trial and Error*, p. 196.

49. Weizmann to Vera Weizmann, July 2, 1917, *WL*, 7:457.

50. Arthur Hardinge to Weizmann, cable, July 4, 1917, FO, 371/3057. Abraham S. Yahuda wrote a small pamphlet in which he vehemently refuted Weizmann's account of his day in Madrid. See *Dr. Weizmann's Errors on Trial: A Refutation of His Statements in "Trial and Error" Concerning My Activity for Zionism during My Professorship at Madrid University* (New York, 1952).

51. This meeting is confirmed by Abraham Yahuda, who had close ties with Max Nordau. *Dr. Weizmann's Errors on Trial*, p. 13.

52. Frankfurter, *Felix Frankfurter Reminisces*, p. 149; Vera Weizmann, diary, July 19, 1917, WA.

53. Weizmann to Ronald Graham, July 6, 1917, *WL*, 7:460.

54. Frankfurter, *Felix Frankfurter Reminisces*, p. 149.

55. Weizmann, *Trial and Error*, p. 198.

56. Weizmann to Ronald Graham, July 6, 1917, *WL*, 7:461–62.

57. Ibid.

58. Ibid., pp. 462–63.

59. Henry Morgenthau and Felix Frankfurter to secretary of state, cable, July 8, 1917, Yale Papers, box 23, folder 2.

60. Ibid.

61. Weizmann, *Trial and Error*, p. 198.

62. Chaim Weizman.., Weyl, Henry Morgenthau, and Felix Frankfurter, report on the Gibraltar conference, July 6, 1917, *WL*, 7:465–67.

63. George Clerk, minute, July 13, 1917, FO, 371/3057.

64. Robert Lansing, diary, June 10, 1917, Lansing Papers; "Notes of Interview between President Wilson and Sir W[illiam] Wiseman," July 13, 1917, WA. William Wiseman reported: "The President asked me to assure Mr. Balfour that Morgenthau was not authorised to express his views to anyone, or to approach any Turkish leaders officially." See also Frank Polk, acting secretary of state, to Henry Morgenthau, cable, July 14, 1917, Yale Papers; Edward House, entry for July 13, 1917, Yale Papers, box 23, folder 2, recording his conversation with Wilson, who asked him to clear "the misunderstanding regarding Morgenthau." On July 14, 1917, House recorded that Abram Elkus, Morgenthau's successor, came for a visit. "We had a good laugh over Morgenthau's peace project," he remarked disingenuously. Yale Papers, box 23, folder 2.

65. Frank Polk, memorandum, July 14, 1917, Yale Papers, box 23, folder 2.

66. This opinion was confirmed by his succesor Abram Elkus in his report, August 3, 1917, Yale Papers, box 23, folder 2.

67. Frankfurter, *Felix Frankfurter Reminisces*, p. 147.

68. Weizmann to Vera Weizmann, July 8, 1917, *WL*, 7:469.

69. Henry Morgenthau and Felix Frankfurter to Robert Lansing, July 8, 1917, Yale Papers, box 23, folder 2.

70. Frank Jewett, "Why We Did Not Declare War on Turkey," Yale Papers, box 23, folder 2; Yale, "Ambassador Henry Morgenthau's Special Mission of 1917"; Avigdor Levy, "Shlihut Morgenthau: Parashah miyemei milhemet haolam harishonah," *Hamizrah Hehadash* 16, no. 1 (1966): 58–63; Brecher, "Revisiting Ambassador Morgenthau's Turkish Peace Mission of 1917."

71. Henry Morgenthau, *All in a Life-Time* (Garden City, N.Y., 1922), p. 255.

72. Yahuda, *Dr. Weizmann's Errors on Trial*, p. 16.

73. Yale, "Ambassador Henry Morgenthau's Special Mission of 1917," p. 320. See the more sympathetic account of Henry Morgenthau's granddaughter, Barbara W. Tuchman, "The Assimilationist Dilemma: Ambassador Morgenthau's Story," in Tuchman, *Practicing History: Selected Essays* (New York, 1981), p. 216.

74. Henry Morgenthau, *Ambassador Morgenthau's Story* (New York, 1918), which indicates how—justly—proud he was of his efforts to intercede on behalf of Palestinian Jewry during his tenure as ambassador to Turkey.

75. After the discussions in Gibraltar, Felix Frankfurter cabled to [Louis Brandeis?] from Madrid that Weizmann suggested it would be much more important for the American mission to go to Russia than to Egypt. "Paraphrase of Telegram Sent through American Embassy at Madrid and Signed by Frankfurter," Brandeis Papers, reel 82, 22-2.

76. State Department to Henry Morgenthau, cable, July 12, 1917, Yale Papers, box 23, folder 2. See also Cecil Spring-Rice to Foreign Office, July 18, 1917, FO, 371/3057.

77. Ronald Graham and Arthur Balfour, minutes, July 13, 1917, FO, 371/3057.

78. Mark Sykes to Gilbert Clayton, July 22, 1917, Sykes Papers.

79. Ronald Graham to Charles Hardinge, July 23, 1917, FO, 371/3057.

80. Louis Brandeis to Weizmann, cable, August 10, 1917, WA.

81. Ronald Graham to George Clerk, July 23, 1917, FO, 371/3053/84173/146570.

82. Weizmann to C. P. Scott, July 30, 1917, *WL*, 7:475–76.

83. See Elam, *Hagdudim haivriim*, pp. 127–40.

84. Scott, diary, April 3, 1917, Guardian Archives.

85. Vladimir Jabotinsky to Weizmann, March 25, 1917, Jabotinsky Archives.

86. Harry Sacher to [Leon Simon], May 30, 1917, WA.

87. Lord Derby, memorandum, War Office Papers, Public Record Office (hereafter WO), 32/1537, GT 353.

88. Philip Kerr to Ronald Graham, May 5, 1917, FO, 371/3101/54325.

89. Ibid.

90. Vladimir Jabotinsky to David Lloyd George, April 29, 1917, WO, 32/1539.

91. Lancelot Oliphant, note in the margins of ibid.

92. Lord Derby, "Proposed Formation of a Jewish Corps: Memorandum by the Secretary of State for War," May 23, 1917, CAB, 24/14.

93. [Philip Kerr], "Zionist Movement," May 23, 1917, Scottish Record Office, Edinburgh.

94. *Jewish Chronicle*, July 27, 1917.

95. *Jewish Chronicle*, August 10, 1917. See also John Henry Patterson, *With the Judaeans in the Palestine Campaign* (London, 1922), pp. 18–29.
96. Patterson, *With the Judaeans*, p. 23.
97. C. P. Scott to Weizmann, June 6, 1917, WA.
98. Weizmann to Felix Frankfurter, August 14, 1917, WL, 7:486, and notes. See also Tolkowsky, *Yoman zioni medini*, p. 138.
99. Weizmann to Louis Brandeis, cable, September [12?], 1917, WL, 7:506–7, and notes.
100. Shabtai Tevet, *Kinat David: Hayye David Ben-Gurion* (Tel Aviv, 1976–80), 1:374–400.
101. Quoted in Halpern, "Brandeis and the Origins of the Balfour Declaration," p. 87.
102. Morris Frommer, "The American Jewish Congress: A History, 1914–1950" (Ph.D. diss., Ohio State University, 1978), 1:51–107.
103. Ibid., pp. 106–7.

VI   The Balfour Declaration

1. Harry Sacher, "Perek zikhronot," *Haaretz*, November 2, 1927.
2. Harry Sacher to Leon Simon, July 2, [1917], WA.
3. See conversation with Shmuel Tolkowsky, *Dvar Hashavua*, no. 44, November 2, 1962, Getzel Kressel Collection, Oxford Centre for Postgraduate Hebrew Studies, Yarnton.
4. Ibid.
5. Shmuel Tolkowsky, Leon Simon, Israel Sieff, Harry Sacher, Simon Marks, Samuel Landman, and Albert Hyamson to Nahum Sokolow, February 8, 1917, Ben-Gurion Archives.
6. Israel Sieff to Weizmann, February 14, 1917, WA.
7. Israel Sieff to Weizmann, April 28, 1917, WA.
8. Weizmann to Harry Sacher, June 1, 1917, WL, 7:424–25.
9. See, e.g., Harry Sacher to Weizmann, May 1, June 13, 1917, WA.
10. Harry Sacher to Weizmann, June 25, [1917], WA.
11. Weizmann to George Macdonogh, May 29, 1917, WL, 7:420–21.
12. Weizmann, *Trial and Error*, p. 183.
13. Tolkowsky, *Yoman zioni medini*, p. 129.
14. Ibid., p. 130.
15. Ibid., p. 138.
16. Janet Lieberman Ellison, interview with author, Kfar Shmaryahu, August 20, 1987.
17. Harry Sacher to Leon Simon, July 2, [1917], WA.
18. Tolkowsky, *Yoman zioni medini*, p. 152.
19. Ibid., pp. 115–17.
20. Harry Sacher to Leon Simon, July 2, [1917], WA.
21. Tolkowsky, *Yoman zioni medini*, pp. 118–22.
22. Ibid., p. 122.
23. Ibid., pp. 116–18.
24. Ibid., pp. 124–25.
25. Weizmann to Ahad Ha'Am, [late] July 1917, WL, 7:477.
26. Tolkowsky, *Yoman zioni medini*, p. 139.

27. Ahad Ha'Am's recollection on this subject is not quite accurate. See Ahad Ha'Am's memoir, in Yiddish: "Die Balfour Deklarazie," *Zionistishe Bletter* (Warsaw) 2, no. 7 (1927): 201–3.

28. Weizmann to Harry Sacher, June 20, 1917, *WL*, 7:445.

29. Harry Sacher to Weizmann, June [22], 1917, WA. See also a copy of Sacher's draft, which is attached, with other proposals, to Nahum Sokolow to Leon Simon, July 5, 1917, WA.

30. Harry Sacher to Leon Simon, July 2, [1917], WA.

31. Nahum Sokolow to Harry Sacher, July 10, 1917, CZA, Z4/120.

32. Harry Sacher to Nahum Sokolow, July 10, 1917, CZA, Z4/120.

33. The text of both drafts is in WA. See also Harry Sacher's cover letter to Nahum Sokolow, July 11, 1917, CZA, Z4/120.

34. Ahad Ha'Am's formula is attached to Nahum Sokolow to Leon Simon, July 5, 1917, WA.

35. Ahad Ha'Am to Nahum Sokolow, July 11, 1917, *Igrot Ahad Ha'Am*, 5:303–4.

36. Nahum Sokolow to Joseph Cowen, July 9, 1917, CZA, Z4/120.

37. Ahad Ha'Am to Nahum Sokolow, July 11, 1917, *Igrot Ahad Ha'Am*, 5:304.

38. Quoted in Tolkowsky, *Yoman zioni medini*, pp. 131–32.

39. Nahum Sokolow to Leon Simon, July 13, 1917, WA, mentioning he had sent a copy of the formula to Lord Rothschild.

40. Quoted in Tolkowsky, *Yoman zioni medini*, pp. 133–34.

41. Walter Rothschild to Arthur Balfour, July 18, 1917, FO, 371/3083/143082/143082.

42. Arthur Balfour to Walter Rothschild, August [2], 1917, FO, 371/3083/143082/143082. The date has been determined by a "Note" in this document, prepared by the Foreign Office, of major events leading to the Balfour Declaration.

43. Weizmann to Ronald Graham, August 1, 1917, *WL*, 7:479–80.

44. Weizmann to Harry Sacher, August 1, 1917, *WL*, 7:481.

45. Harold Nicolson to Longhurst, August 17, 1917, CAB, 21/58.

46. Longhurst to Harold Nicolson, August 20, 1917, CAB, 21/58.

47. Lord Milner's proposed draft, quoted in Stein, *Balfour Declaration*, p. 664.

48. Friedman, *Question of Palestine*, p. 257.

49. Walter Rothschild to Weizmann, September 18, 1917, WA.

50. Some fifty years after his death, the Arab League Office gathered Montagu's anti-Zionist views as expressed during his battle against a pro-Zionist declaration and published them in a pamphlet, *Edwin Montagu and the Balfour Declaration* (London, [1972?]).

51. David Vital, *Zionism: The Crucial Phase* (Oxford, 1987), pp. 170–71.

52. Edwin Montagu, "The Anti-Semitism of the Present Government," August 23, 1917, FO, 371/3083.

53. Ronald MacNeill, "Note on the Secretary of State for India's Paper on Anti-Semitism of the Government," [late August 1917], FO, 371/3083.

54. *Times* (London), July 28, 1917.

55. See, e.g., C. P. Scott to Weizmann, [August] 31, 1917, Jabotinsky Archives, 6/1: "I saw Lord Derby yesterday, and he was going to see a big deputation of Jews—Lord Reading, etc.—today who are hotly opposed to the formation of any distinctly Jewish Regiment."

56. Montagu, "Anti-Semitism of the Present Government," FO, 371/3083.

57. War cabinet, minutes, September 3, 1917, CAB, 23/4.

58. *Times* (London), September 13, 1917. See also, FO, 371/3101/65760/171478/ 177692.

59. Colonel John Henry Patterson to [Weizmann], November 26, 1917, WA.

60. Patterson, *With the Judaeans*, p. 25.

61. Ibid., pp. 26–27.

62. On the fear of Turkish reprisals, see the very strong words used by Walter Rothschild in announcing the formation of a Jewish regiment: "This will lead to the Turks massacring the remaining Jews in Palestine." Walter Rothschild to Weizmann, September 2, 1917, WA.

63. Jabotinsky, *Story of the Jewish Legion*, p. 91.

64. Tolkowsky, *Yoman zioni medini*, p. 137.

65. Ibid., pp. 129, 137.

66. Harry Sacher to Weizmann, August 3, 1917, WA. Sacher, as usual, was the one to take Weizmann to task in the most direct manner.

67. Tolkowsky, *Yoman zioni medini*, pp. 139–40, 144.

68. After the legion was finally created, Vera, together with Mrs. Patterson and a number of wives of Zionist leaders, established the Jewish Regiment Care and Comforts Committee. Jabotinsky, *Story of the Jewish Legion*, p. 101.

69. Harry Sacher to Leon Simon, August 11, 1917, WA. See also Simon to Nahum Sokolow, August 30, 1917, WA.

70. Tolkowsky, *Yoman zioni medini*, p. 140.

71. Harry Sacher to Leon Simon, August 5, 1917, WA.

72. Leon Simon to Nahum Sokolow, August 30, 1917, WA.

73. Samuel J. Cohen to Weizmann, August 16, 1917, WA.

74. Tolkowsky, *Yoman zioni medini*, pp. 152–53.

75. Ibid., p. 153.

76. Weizmann to Nahum Sokolow, August 17, 1917, *WL*, 7:490.

77. Nahum Sokolow to Weizmann, August 17, 1917, WA.

78. See letters from Israel Sieff, Becky Sieff, and Leon Simon to Weizmann, August 17, 1917, WA. See also Shmuel Tolkowsky to Weizmann, August 18, 1917, WA.

79. Harry Sacher to Leon Simon and Nelly Simon, August 21, 1917, WA.

80. Tolkowsky, *Yoman zioni medini*, p. 158.

81. Stein, *Balfour Declaration*, p. 475; Tolkowsky, *Yoman zioni medini*, p. 158.

82. Tolkowsky, *Yoman zioni medini*, p. 153. Harry Sacher made the same assumption in a number of his letters to Leon Simon. Sacher credited the British Palestine Committee as having had a hand in the British Labour party's pro-Zionist statement.

83. Leon Simon wrote to Weizmann on September 5, 1917, WA.

84. Harry Sacher to Leon Simon, September 2, 1917, WA.

85. Tolkowsky, *Yoman zioni medini*, pp. 169–72.

86. Ahad Ha'Am to Weizmann, September 4, 1917, *Igrot Ahad Ha'Am*, 5:313–14.

87. Weizmann to Nahum Sokolow, September 5, 1917, *WL*, 7:499.

88. Weizmann to Ahad Ha'Am, September 5, 1917, *WL*, 7:499–500.

89. Ahad Ha'Am to Weizmann, September 5, 1917, *Igrot Ahad Ha'Am*, 5:315–16. The translation into English has been adopted, with certain modifications, from Halpern, *Clash of Heroes*, p. 165.

90. Albert Hyamson to Weizmann, September 5, 1917, WA.

91. Tolkowsky, *Yoman zioni medini*, p. 173.

92. C. P. Scott to Weizmann, September 12, 1917, WA.
93. Weizmann to C. P. Scott, September 13, 1917, *WL*, 7:510.
94. C. P. Scott to Weizmann, September [14], 1917, WA.
95. Tolkowsky, *Yoman zioni medini*, p. 173.
96. Shmuel Tolkowsky, "Hamisha yamim shel drama," *Hashavua*, November 2, 1962, copy in Kressel Collection.
97. Harry Sacher to Weizmann, September 16, 1917, WA.
98. Weizmann to Harry Sacher, September 18, 1917, *WL*, 7:513–14.
99. Political Committee, minutes, August 28, 1917, WA.
100. C. P. Scott, diary, October 19, 1917, Guardian Archives. See also Wickham Steed to Lord Northcliffe, October 14, 1917, Private Papers Collection, St. Antony's College, Middle East Centre, file Papers Concerning Balfour Declaration.
101. War cabinet, minutes, September 3, 1917, CAB, 23/4.
102. Ibid.
103. Robert Cecil to Edward House, cable, September 4, 1917, CAB, 24/27.
104. Edward M. House, memorandum, *The Intimate Papers of Colonel House*, vol. 3, *Into the World War: April 1917–June 1918*, ed. Charles Seymour (Boston, 1928), p. 175.
105. Edward House to Robert Cecil, cable, September 11, 1917, CAB, 24/26.
106. Weizmann to George Clerk, September 9, 1917, *WL*, 7:504.
107. Tolkowsky, *Yoman zioni medini*, p. 174.
108. Weizmann to Louis Brandeis, September 11, 1917, *WL*, 7:505–6.
109. The following account concerning Brandeis's intercession with House and Wilson relies, with minor alterations, on Halpern, "Brandeis and the Origins of the Balfour Declaration," pp. 93–100. See also Richard Ned Lebow, "Woodrow Wilson and the Balfour Declaration," *Journal of Modern History* 40, no. 4, (1968): 501–23.
110. The texts of Brandeis's telegrams are reproduced in CAB, 24/27.
111. Ibid.
112. Jacob DeHaas to Louis Brandeis, September 24, 1917, DeHaas Papers.
113. Halpern, "Brandeis and the Origins of the Balfour Declaration," pp. 94–95.
114. Ibid., pp. 95–96.
115. Weizmann to Yehiel Tschlenow, September 1, 1917, *WL*, 7:495–98.
116. Yehiel Tschlenow to Nahum Sokolow and Weizmann, September 24, 1917, CZA, A18/41/2/8.
117. Arthur Hantke, "Protokoll der Sitzung des Engeren Actions-Komitees am 29. bis 31. Juli 1917 im Zionistischen Bureau in Kopenhagen," CZA, L6/64/I.
118. Weizmann to Cairo, July 18, 1917, FO, 371/3055/132608/87895.
119. Ronald Graham to Reginald Wingate, July 18, 1917, FO, 371/3055. See also Zeev Gluskin to Weizmann, August 13, 1917, WA.
120. Zeev Gluskin to Weizmann and Nahum Sokolow, September 28, 1917, WA. See also Eliezer Livneh, *Aaron Aaronsohn: Haish uzmano* (Jerusalem, 1969), pp. 274–76.
121. Aaron Aaronsohn to Weizmann, August 15, 25, 1917, in Aaronsohn, *Yoman Aaron Aaronsohn*, pp. 331–33, 337.
122. Ronald Graham, minute, FO, 371/3053/174977/84173.
123. Ronald Graham to Reginald Wingate, September 21, 1917, WA.
124. Tolkowsky, diary entries for October 1917, *Yoman zioni medini*, pp. 178–90.

125. See, e.g., Aaronsohn's view of Nahum Sokolow and Yehiel Tschlenow in Aaronsohn, *Yoman Aaron Aaronsohn*, p. 353.
126. Edwin Montagu to Robert Cecil, September 14, 1917, CAB, 21/58.
127. Ahad Ha'Am to Louis Brandeis, October 3, 1917, DeHaas Papers.
128. Weizmann to Philip Kerr, September 16, 1917, *WL*, 7:511–12.
129. Ibid.
130. Weizmann to Philip Kerr, September 19, 1917, *WL*, 7:516.
131. Walter Rothschild to Weizmann, September 21, 1917, WA.
132. Balfour, minute on Ronald Graham to Charles Hardinge, September 24, 1917, FO, 371/3083.
133. Charles Hardinge, minute on ibid.
134. Ronald Graham to Reginald Wingate, September 21, 1917, Wingate Papers.
135. Mark Sykes, "Note on Palestine," WA. The paper was sent to Weizmann for comments, which were made in the margins. Weizmann returned the paper to Sykes on September 22, 1917.
136. Tolkowsky, *Yoman zioni medini*, p. 176. See also Harry Sacher to Weizmann, September 25, 1917, WA.
137. Tolkowsky, *Yoman zioni medini*, p. 178; Weizmann to Nahum Sokolow, September 30, 1917, *WL*, 7:520.
138. See e.g., Heron Goodhart to Arthur Balfour, with attached memorandum, October 2, 1917, CAB, 21/58.
139. Weizmann and Walter Rothschild to Arthur Balfour, October 3, 1917, *WL*, 7:521–22.
140. Leopold S. Amery, *My Political Life* (London, 1953), 2:116. The open letter from D. L. Alexander and Claude Montefiore, "The Future of the Jews— Palestine and Zionism: Views of Anglo-Jewry," was published in the *Times* (London), May 24, 1917; responses appeared in the May 28, 1917, issue.
141. Quoted in Stein, *Balfour Declaration*, p. 664.
142. War cabinet, minutes, October 4, 1917, CAB, 21/58.
143. Ibid.
144. Tolkowsky, *Yoman zioni medini*, p. 179.
145. William Ormsby-Gore to Maurice Hankey, October 5, 1917, CAB, 21/58.
146. Maurice Hankey, form letter, October 6, 1917, CAB, 21/58.
147. Edwin Montagu to David Lloyd George, October 4, 1917, Lloyd George Papers, F/39/3/30.
148. Edwin Montagu, "Zionism," October 9, 1917, FO, 371/3083. This paper, too, was distributed to the cabinet.
149. See, e.g., Weizmann to Philip Kerr, October 7, 1917, *WL*, 7:526–28.
150. The replies of all those contacted by Maurice Hankey are contained in a document titled "The Zionist Movement," October 17, 1917, FO, 371/3083.
151. Stein, *Balfour Declaration*, pp. 519–20.
152. These letters are reproduced in *WL*, 7:523–37.
153. Weizmann to Ronald Graham, October 23, 1917, *WL*, 7:539. The list is in WA.
154. Harry Sacher to Leon Simon, October 7, 1917, WA.
155. Harry Sacher to Leon Simon, October 4, 1917, WA.
156. Leon Simon to Weizmann, October 10, 1917, WA.
157. Harry Sacher had vetoed a decision by the Political Committee that Vladimir Jabotinsky contribute an article on "Zionism and the Entente Powers" to *Palestine*. Joseph Cowen to Weizmann, October 10, 1917, WA.

158. Tolkowsky, *Yoman zioni medini*, p. 181.

159. Weizmann to Maurice Hankey, October 15, 1917, *WL*, 7:533–34, also in FO, 371/3083.

160. Weizmann to Louis Brandeis, October 7, 1917, *WL*, 7:523–26.

161. Weizmann to Louis Brandeis, October 9, 1917, *WL*, 7:530–31. Brandeis's reply states, "Your cable of tenth received." Brandeis to Weizmann [October 17, 1917], Wiseman Papers, drawer 91, file 130.

162. Arthur Balfour to Edward House [via Wiseman], October 6, 1917, FO, 371/3083.

163. Arthur Balfour to Edward House, October 6, 1917, FO, 371/3083.

164. The discussion concerning the steps leading to Wilson's approval of the British draft declaration relies, with some minor deviations, on Halpern, "Brandeis and the Origins of the Balfour Declaration," pp. 96–100.

165. See Jacob DeHaas's report to Louis Brandeis, October 16, 1917, and Brandeis's reply on that same memorandum, DeHaas Papers. See also DeHaas to Brandeis, October 17, 1917, DeHaas Papers.

166. Brandeis to Weizmann, cable October [17], 1917, Wiseman Papers, drawer 91, file 130.

167. Stephen Wise to Louis Brandeis, October 17, 1917, DeHaas Papers.

168. Stephen Wise to Louis Brandeis, October 15, 1917, DeHaas Papers. See also American Zionists to Weizmann and Nahum Sokolow, October 26, 1917, DeHaas Papers.

169. Jacob DeHaas assured the members of the PZC that the changes made in the third part of the draft declaration were due to suggestions made by the American Political Committee. See DeHaas to PZC, November 12, 1917, DeHaas Papers. Stephen Wise, too, believed, until his last days, that it was he and Brandeis who were responsible for the change in the wording of the Balfour Declaration. Stephen Wise to Meyer W. Weisgal, October 8, 1948, WA.

170. PZC to Weizmann and Nahum Sokolow, [October 29, 1917], WA.

171. Ronald Graham to Arthur Balfour, October 25, 1917, Lloyd George Papers, F/3/2/34.

172. Arthur Balfour to Lloyd George, minute, October 25, 1917, CZA, KH/207/1, outlining the most significant dates in the evolution of the declaration, beginning with Walter Rothschild's letter of July 18, 1917. Balfour appended Graham's memorandum to his note to the prime minister. It seems that Graham's memorandum was written on October 24; however, it may have been retyped in the secretary of state's office before it was forwarded to Lloyd George.

173. War cabinet, internal memorandum, October 25, 1917, CAB, 23/4.

174. Weizmann to Ahad Ha'Am, October 25, 1917, *WL*, 7:540.

175. Wickham Steed, "The Jews and Palestine," *Times* (London), October 26, 1917.

176. C[urzon] of K[edleston], "The Future of Palestine," October 26, 1917, CAB, 21/58.

177. Mark Sykes's paper [October 30, 1917] is undated and without a heading. FO, 371/3083.

178. Blanche E. C. Dugdale, *The Balfour Declaration: Origins and Background* (London, 1940), p. 29.

179. War cabinet, minutes, October 31, 1917, CAB, 23/4.

180. Ibid.
181. Arthur Balfour to Walter Rothschild, November 2, 1917, FO, 371/3083.
182. Weizmann, *Trial and Error*, p. 208.
183. Tolkowsky, *Yoman zioni medini*, p. 183.
184. Ibid., p. 163.
185. Weizmann to Simon Marks, [October] 8, 1917, *WL*, 7:528–29.
186. Charles Hardinge, minute, November 1, 1917, FO, 371/3083.
187. Ronald Graham to Weizmann, November 1, 1917, WA.
188. Tolkowsky, *Yoman zioni medini*, p. 190.
189. See Ahad Ha'Am, *Pirkei zikronot veigrot* (Tel Aviv, 1931), p. 60.
190. Vera Weizmann, *Impossible Takes Longer*, p. 78.
191. The information concerning the afternoon and evening of October 31, 1917, is contained in Vera Weizmann, diary, WA, and Tolkowsky, *Yoman zioni medini*, pp. 189–90.
192. See, e.g., "The Reception of the Declaration," *Palestine* 2, no. 16 (November 24, 1917): 145–52.
193. Arthur Balfour, quoted in Tolkowsky, *Yoman zioni medini*, p. 189.
194. Leopold Greenberg to Weizmann, November 2, 1917, WA.
195. C. P. Scott to Weizmann, November 9, 1917, WA.
196. Walter Rothschild to Weizmann, November 1, 1917, WA.
197. Jacob DeHaas to Weizmann, November 20, 1917, DeHaas Papers.
198. See, e.g., the letter signed by the EZF executive, November 6, 1917, WA. The Weizmann Archives contain letters and declarations of praise for Weizmann in a number of containers.
199. Charles Kingsley Webster, *The Founder of the National Home*, Chaim Weizmann Memorial Lecture (Rehovot, 1955), p. 14. Even if we take into account that this statement was made in Rehovot, in a lecture honoring Weizmann, it cannot be dismissed as mere hyperbole.
200. Stein, *Balfour Declaration*; Leonard Stein, *Weizmann and the Balfour Declaration*, Sixth Chaim Weizmann Memorial Lecture (Rehovot, 1961).
201. See Friedman, *Question of Palestine*, p. 283. In Sanders, *High Walls of Jerusalem*, Weizmann also emerges as the central hero. See also Norman Rose, *Chaim Weizmann* (New York, 1986), p. 187. One could add to this category of historians the late Richard H. Crossman, before his untimely death the official biographer of Weizmann. See in particular his article "Weizmann," *Encounter* 14, no. 6 (June 1960): 50–51.
202. On this issue, see also D. Z. Gillon, "The Antecedents of the Balfour Declaration," *Middle Eastern Studies* 5, no. 2 (May 1969): 131–50.
203. Mayir Vereté, "The Balfour Declaration and Its Makers," *Middle Eastern Studies* 6, no. 1 (January 1970): 50.
204. Ibid., p. 67.
205. Vital's high regard for Vereté is expressed in the annotated bibliography to *Zionism*, p. 383. He expressed similar admiration in a lecture he gave in Jerusalem at a symposium commemorating the seventieth anniversary of the Balfour Declaration in November 1987. For a highly critical review of Vital's book, see Evyatar Friesel, "David Vital's Work on Zionism," *Studies in Zionism* 9, no. 2 (Autumn 1988): 209–25. See also Isaiah Friedman's review of the book: "Zionist History Reconsidered," *Studies in Contemporary Jewry* 6 (1990): 309–14.
206. Vital, *Zionism*, pp. 161, 223, 236.

207. David Fromkin, *A Peace to End All Peace: Creating the Modern Middle East, 1914–1922* (New York, 1989), p. 267.
208. See, e.g., Philipp Aronstein, ed., *Speeches of British Statesmen on Judaism and Zionism* (Berlin, 1936), p. 34.
209. Jan Smuts, quoted in Stein, *Weizmann and the Balfour Declaration*, p. 15.
210. Even an outsider like Mark Sykes could discern those Weizmann could trust. He cabled the Foreign Office in the spring of 1917: "Please tell Weizmann from me that it would be best to keep all negotiations strictly to himself and Sokolow. James R[othschild] is enthusiastic and rash." Sykes to Foreign Office, May 1, 1917, FO, 371/3053/88954/84173.
211. In a letter to Weizmann of April 28, 1917, WA, Israel Sieff pointed out to Weizmann that he would be the first blamed if Turkey, e.g., were to sign a separate peace treaty with England.
212. Patrick O'Donovan, "The Balfour Declaration," *Rehovoth* (Winter 1967–68): 31. See also Conor Cruise O'Brien, "Israel in Embryo," review of *High Walls of Jerusalem*, by Ronald Sanders, *New York Review of Books* 31, no. 4 (March 15, 1984): 37–38.
213. There were, of course, other pro-Zionist declarations that followed the Balfour Declaration, each given for a variety of reasons: a Serbian declaration on December 27, 1917; a French declaration on February 14, 1918; and an Italian declaration on May 9, 1918, to mention but a few. See Israel Klausner, "Hadeklerazyah haserbit," *Haolam*, November 4, 1937. Perhaps one of the most remarkable declarations was that issued by the Japanese government in January 1919, in response to Weizmann's request: "The Japanese Government gladly take note of the Zionist aspirations to establish in Palestine a national home for the Jewish people and they look forward with a sympathetic interest to the realization of such desire upon the basis proposed." T. Chinda to Weizmann, January 6, 1919, CZA, Z4/2039.
214. See, e.g., the comments of Elizabeth Monroe, St. Antony's College, Middle East Centre, file Balfour Declaration.
215. Elizabeth Monroe, *Britain's Moment in the Middle East, 1914–1971*, rev. ed. (Baltimore, 1981).

VII The Zionist Commission

1. It seems that Weizmann, at the request of Leopold Greenberg, editor of the *Jewish Chronicle*, agreed to postpone publication of the Balfour Declaration until November 9, the next date of publication of the paper. Lord Rothschild then formally requested this publication date. See Walter Rothschild to Arthur Balfour, November 5, 1917, FO, 371/3083. See also Stein, *Balfour Declaration*, p. 560, n. 3.
2. Stein, *Balfour Declaration*, pp. 559–604.
3. See Shmuel Almog, "Hitpathuta shel hasheelah hayehudit be-Angliyah betom milhemet haolam harishonah," in *Zion: Sefer Hayovel*, ed. Shmuel Ettinger, Haim Beinart, and Menahem Stern (Jerusalem, 1986), pp. 397–431.
4. Ronald Graham to Charles Hardinge, November 1, 1917, FO, 371/3083.
5. Ronald Graham to Charles Hardinge, memorandum, November 3, 1917, FO, 371/3083.
6. Ibid.
7. Lord Rothschild had informed Weizmann that, due to the recent death of

two of his relatives, Evelyn Rothschild and Neil Primrose, he could not take the chair. He asked for a postponement of the meeting. Walter Rothschild to Weizmann, November 19, 1917, WA. Due to misunderstanding, it was announced that Rothschild would be presiding, and Rothschild wrote an angry letter to Weizmann, November 23, 1917, WA. See also Vera Weizmann, diary, November 23, 1917, WA. After Weizmann apologized, and with the helpful intercession of Rozsika Rothschild, the matter was finally settled. Rozsika Rothschild to Weizmann, cable, November 24, 1917, WA. See also Rozsika Rothschild to Weizmann, December 23, 1917, WA.

8. *Jewish Chronicle,* December 7, 1917.
9. Vera Weizmann, diary, October 31, 1917, WA.
10. For the unfolding of these developments during the first two weeks of November 1917, see Vera Weizmann, diary, November 5, 16, 1917, WA; Tolkowsky, *Yoman zioni medini,* pp. 191–92, 196, 211–13; Aaronsohn, *Yoman Aaron Aaronsohn,* pp. 355–56.
11. Tolkowsky, *Yoman zioni medini,* p. 197.
12. Ibid., pp. 197–98.
13. Weizmann, quoted in ibid., p. 205.
14. Ibid., pp. 206–9.
15. Ibid., pp. 209–10.
16. James de Rothschild to Weizmann, December 10, 1917, WA. See also Roszika Rothschild to Weizmann, December 23, 1917, WA.
17. Shmuel Tolkowsky to Weizmann, December 14, 1917, WA. See also Sol Cohen to Weizmann, December 14, 1917, WA; Cohen to Weizmann, cable, December 17, 1917, WA.
18. C. P. Scott to Weizmann, January 14, 1915, WA.
19. Minutes of meeting with Mark Sykes, February 7, 1917, WA.
20. Mark Sykes to Foreign Office, April 29, 1917, Sykes Papers.
21. Weizmann to C. P. Scott, March 20, 1917, *WL,* 7:344–45.
22. Harry Sacher to Leon Simon, June 14, 1917, WA.
23. Tolkowsky, *Yoman zioni medini,* pp. 216–21.
24. Weizmann, quoted in ibid., p. 238.
25. Gilbert Clayton to Mark Sykes, August 20, 1917, Sykes Papers.
26. Mark Sykes to Reginald Wingate, November 14, 1917, FO, 371/3083. See also Sykes to Gilbert Clayton, November 16, 1917, Sykes Papers.
27. Mark Sykes to Syrian Committees [via Gilbert Clayton], November 16, 1917, Yale Papers, box 23, folder 2.
28. William Yale, report 4, November 19, 1917, Yale Papers, box 10, folder 9.
29. Gilbert Clayton to Mark Sykes, November 28, 1917, Sykes Papers.
30. Gilbert Clayton to Reginald Wingate, December 3, 1917, FO, 371/3083.
31. Mark Sykes, speech, December 9, 1917, *Manchester Guardian,* December 10, 1917.
32. Mark Sykes to Georges Picot, December 12, 1917, FO, 371/3054.
33. Chaim Weizmann, speech, December 9, 1917, typescript, WA.
34. Weizmann to Jacques Mosseri, cable, December 11, 1917, *WL,* 8:20.
35. Gilbert Clayton to Foreign Office, December 19, 1917, FO, 371/3054.
36. Gilbert Clayton to Mark Sykes, cable, December 12, 1917, Sykes Papers.
37. This was also the view of the high commissioner. Reginald Wingate to Wyndham Deedes, January 3, 1918, Wingate Papers.

38. Gilbert Clayton to Mark Sykes, December 15, 1917, Sykes Papers.

39. Gilbert Clayton to Foreign Office, December 19, 1917, FO, 371/3054; William Yale, report 9, December 24, 1917, Yale Papers, box 10, folder 9; Syrian Welfare Committee to Mark Sykes, January 17, 1918, FO, 371/3308.

40. William Yale, report 9, box 10, folder 9. See also Gilbert Clayton to Gertrude Bell, June 17, 1918, WA, admitting ignorance as to the true aims of Zionism.

41. See cables and letters from the United States, February 1918, CZA, Z4/2086, Z4/305/1. See also WO, 32/1539; Elam, *Hagdudim haivriim*, pp. 178–205.

42. Patterson, *With the Judeans*, pp. 29–93.

43. See exchange of cables between Edmund Allenby and the War Office in March and May 1918, WO, 32/1539. See also the detailed description in Elam, *Hagdudim haivriim*, pp. 206–28.

44. On French attempts, see, e.g., Gilbert Clayton to Mark Sykes, December 15, 1917, Sykes Papers. See also Clayton to Foreign Office, March 14, 1918, FO, 371/3391. On Italian attempts to make political inroads in Palestine, see Manuel, "Habeayah ha-Eretz Israelit badiplomatyah haitalkit bishnot 1916–1920," pp. 210–26. See also Clayton to Foreign Office, January 14, 1918, FO, 371/3391.

45. See, e.g.,Weizmann to Louis Brandeis, January 14, 1918, WL, 8:50.

46. Tolkowsky, *Yoman zioni medini*, p. 210.

47. Weizmann to Louis Brandeis, November 12, 1917, WL, 8:4.

48. Political Committee, minutes, November 27, 1917, WA.

49. Weizmann to Ronald Graham, December 17, 1917, WL, 8:28–29. See also the short memorandum, probably attached, December 14, 1917, WA.

50. Ronald Graham to Weizmann, December 26, 1917, WA.

51. Weizmann, appointment book, January 6–16, 1918, WA.

52. Eastern Committee, minutes, January 19, 1918, CAB, 27/23.

53. Weizmann to Mark Sykes, January 16, 1918, WL, 8:62–63.

54. Louis Brandeis to Julius Simon, December 26, 1917, Brandeis Papers, reel 82, Z/P 22-2.

55. Jacob DeHaas to Brandeis, December 5, 1917, Brandeis Papers, reel 82, Z/P 22-2.

56. Jacob DeHaas to Brandeis, January 25, 1918, DeHaas Papers.

57. Jacob DeHaas to Louis Brandeis, January 26, 1918, Brandeis Papers, reel 83, 24–1.

58. Jacob DeHaas to Weizmann, December 25, 1917, CZA, Z4/2986.

59. Jacob DeHaas to Weizmann, December 20, 1917, FO, 371/3019.

60. Jacob DeHaas to Weizmann, January 30, 1918, Brandeis Papers, reel 83, 24-1.

61. Weizmann tried to raise funds in England as well, turning to some of his wealthy friends for assistance. Rozsika Rothschild to Weizmann, January 1, 1918, WA.

62. Weizmann to Louis Brandeis, November 12, 1917, WL, 8:4. Throughout the winter of 1917–18 Weizmann continued to urge Brandeis to send Americans to Palestine as members of the commission. Weizmann to Brandeis, January 10, 1918, WL, 8:40; Weizmann to William Ormsby-Gore, January 30, 1918, WL, 8:74–75.

63. Jacob DeHaas to British consul in New York, December 5, 1917, Wiseman

Papers, box 11, folder 279; DeHaas to Weizmann, December 13, 1917, Brandeis Papers, reel 82, 22-3.

64. Stephen Wise to Louis Brandeis, January 11, 1918, Benjamin Rabalsky Papers, American Jewish Historical Archives, box 107, folder 7.

65. Louis Brandeis to Weizmann, January 13, 1918, Brandeis Papers, reel 82, 24-1. See also Brandeis to Weizmann, January 25, 1918, cable, Wiseman Papers, box 11, folder 279.

66. According to Leon Simon, Walter Meyer was chosen by Weizmann precisely because of his business connections. Simon, diary, March 14, 1918, WA.

67. For the reasons denying such a role to Aaronsohn, see British Embassy to Louis Brandeis, January 24, 1918, Brandeis Papers, reel 83, 25-2.

68. Shmuel Aaronsohn to Weizmann, December 18, 1917, cable, CZA, Z4/16016.

69. Norman Bentwich to Harry Sacher, January 1918, WA.

70. See, e.g., Mordechai Ben-Hillel Hacohen, diary, June 11, 1917, *Milhemet haamim*, ed. Shimon Rubinstein (Jerusalem, 1985), 2:735, 873.

71. Aaronsohn, *Yoman Aaron Aaronsohn*, pp. 367, 379, 396, 408.

72. Israel Rosov to Weizmann, January 2, 1918, cable, CZA, Z4/929.

73. Weizmann to Aaron Aaronsohn, January 16, 1918, *WL*, 8:56.

74. Nahum Sokolow, diary, February 14, 17, 1918. The diary was translated from Polish and French into Hebrew by Yoram Mayork in December 1985 and is deposited at the Central Zionist Archives, Jerusalem. I am grateful to him for permission to use the diary and to quote from it.

75. A. Defrance to Stephen Pichon, April 3, 1918, Archives of the French Ministry for Foreign Affairs, Guerre 1914–1918, vol. 5, VI, 85. The letter indicates that Sylvain Lévi reported on his conversations with Weizmann and presumably on other activities of the commission as well.

76. Nahum Sokolow, diary, February 20, 1918, CZA.

77. Nahum Sokolow, diary, February 14, 1918, CZA. See also Archives of the French Ministry for Foreign Affairs, Guerre 1914–1918, Sionisme, vol. 4, V, 124, dated February 1, 1918; Sokolow to Jean Gout, February 9, 1918, Sionisme, vol. 4, V, 145; Sokolow to Gout, February 11, 1918, Sionisme, vol. 4, V, 154.

78. Nahum Sokolow, diary, February 20, 1918, CZA. Aaronsohn also dismissed Sokolow's achievements in Paris as insignificant. Aaron Aaronsohn to Louis Brandeis, February 24, 1918, Nili Archive, Zikhron Yaakov, Israel.

79. Nahum Sokolow, diary, February 21, 22, 1918, CZA.

80. Manuel, "Habeayah ha-Eretz Israelit," pp. 228–30.

81. See instructions to William Ormsby-Gore from the chief of the Imperial General Staff, January 28, 1918, Ben-Gurion Archives.

82. It was James de Rothschild's own idea to be attached to the Zionist Commission. William Ormsby-Gore to Weizmann, February 16, 1918, CZA, Z4/16014.

83. Aaron Aaronsohn to Louis Brandeis, February 24, 1918, Nili Archive.

84. Harry Sacher, e.g., wanted very much to go with the commission but was not released from his duties at the *Manchester Guardian* by Scott. Sacher to Weizmann, February 12, 1918, CZA, Z4/120. Shmuel Tolkowsky, whom Weizmann wanted to include on the commission, could not go because of business considerations. Leon Simon, who did join, was released from his

duties at the postal office for only three months. Simon to Weizmann, February 12, 1918, WA.

85. Jacob DeHaas to Weizmann, December 13, 1917, Brandeis Papers, reel 82, 22-3.

86. Jacob DeHaas to Weizmann, March 22, 1918, WA.

87. Concerning the early history of the American Zionist Medical Unit, see Zionist Organization of America, *American Zionist Medical Unit for Palestine* (New York, 1919), copy in CZA, Z4/763.

88. Jacob DeHaas put it thus: "If you understand something of the whole temper of American life, you would realize that the sending of such a medical mission is, from the American view, a matter of vast political and social consequence." DeHaas to Weizmann, December 13, 1917, Brandeis Papers, reel 82, 22-3.

89. As to some of the difficulties created in the United States by Christian missionary circles, see Jacob DeHaas to Louis Brandeis, March 6, 1918, Brandeis Papers, reel 83, 25-2. The Red Cross also raised objections to the work of the American Zionist Medical Unit. DeHaas to Weizmann, January 30, 1918, Brandeis Papers, reel 83, 24-1.

90. Aaron Aaronsohn to Louis Brandeis, February 24, 1918, Nili Archive.

91. C. P. Scott, diary, March 4, 1918, Guardian Archives.

92. Aaron Aaronsohn to Louis Brandeis, February 24, 1918, Nili Archive.

93. Tolkowsky, diary, February 20, 22, 1918, *Yoman zioni medini*, pp. 276–80. It is, of course, quite possible that Aaron Aaronsohn, who did not trust Sokolow, helped maneuver the Americans to recognize Weizmann as the only Zionist leader in whom they had absolute trust.

94. Felix Frankfurter to Jacob DeHaas, April 1, 1918, DeHaas Papers.

95. Frankfurter, *Felix Frankfurter Reminisces*, p. 185.

96. "The London Bureau: Its Origin and Work," [April 1918], WA. See also Political Committee, minutes, February 26, 1918, WA.

97. Tolkowsky, *Yoman zioni medini*, p. 286; Weizmann to Vera Weizmann, March 17, 1917, *WL*, 8:103.

98. Reginald Wingate to Foreign Office, March 1, 1918, FO, 371/3380.

99. Weizmann, *Trial and Error*, pp. 213–14; Tolkowsky, *Yoman zioni medini*, p. 286. The king's entry in his diary, recording the interview, is factual and one sentence long. Copy in WA.

100. David Lloyd George to Weizmann, March 1, 1918, CZA, A264/26.

101. Both letters of introduction, dated March 1, 1918, are in CZA, Z4/16014.

102. Weizmann to Vera Weizmann, March 10, 1918, *WL*, 8:99.

103. Zionist Commission, minutes, March 11, 1918, WA.

104. Weizmann, quoted in Israel Sieff, diary, March 14, 1918, WA.

105. Zionist Commission, minutes, March 14, 1918, marked as app. 2, CZA, L3/285.

106. James de Rothschild to Weizmann, December 10, 1917, WA.

107. Leon Simon, diary, March 15, 1918, WA.

108. Weizmann to Vera Weizmann, March 15, 1918, *WL*, 8:102. See also Tolkowsky, *Yoman zioni medini*, p. 243: "Jimmy is a spoiled and ill-mannered child."

109. Leon Simon, diary, March 15, 1918, WA.

110. Weizmann, quoted in Leon Simon, diary, March 22, 1918, WA.

111. Weizmann to Vera Weizmann, March 15, 1918, *WL*, 8:102.

112. Leon Simon, diary, March 14, 1918, WA.

113. William Ormsby-Gore to Mark Sykes, cable, March 22, 1918, WA.

114. *Jewish Chronicle*, March 22, 1918. See also *WL*, 8:104, n. 4.

115. Weizmann to Louis Brandeis, cable, March 22, 1918, *WL*, 8:104–5; William Ormsby-Gore to Mark Sykes, cable, March 22, 1918, WA; Reginald Wingate to Foreign Office, March 22, 1928, FO, 371/3394.

116. Tolkowsky, *Yoman zioni medini*, p. 295.

117. Reginald Wingate to Foreign Office, March 18, 1918, FO, 371/3383.

118. Leon Simon, diary, March 22, 1918, WA.

119. William Ormsby-Gore to Mark Sykes, March 22, 1918, WA; William Yale, report 20, March 25, 1918, Yale Papers, box 10, folder 10.

120. Leon Simon, diary, March 27, 1918, WA.

121. Weizmann to Vera Weizmann, March 24–26, 1918, *WL*, 8:106–8.

122. Conference at Shepherd's Hotel, Cairo, minutes, March 27, 1918, marked as app. 10, CZA, L3/285.

123. See William Ormsby-Gore to Arthur Balfour, report 1, April 7, 1918, FO, 371/3394/11053.

124. Meeting of Zionist Commission with Palestine Committee of Moslems and Christians and members of the Syrian Welfare Committee, minutes, April 1, 1918, CZA, Z4/538.

125. Memorandum, with comments by Weizmann and Israel Sieff, CZA, L4/392/I.

126. William Yale, report 22, April 8, 1918, Yale Papers, box 10, folder 10.

127. Horace B. Samuel, *Unholy Memories of the Holy Land* (London, 1930), pp. 15–16.

128. Just prior to his departure for Palestine, William Ormsby-Gore was given the staff rank of major, which would befit his role as political officer.

129. Weizmann to Vera Weizmann, April 6, 1918, *WL*, 8:118; "Report on Dr. Weizmann's Visit to General Allenby at General Headquarters," April 3, 1918, WA.

130. "Report on Dr. Weizmann's Visit to General Allenby at General Headquarters," April 3, 1918, WA.

131. Weizmann to Vera Weizmann, April 6, 1918, *WL*, 8:118.

132. Gilbert Clayton to Mark Sykes, April 4, 1918, WA. In a private conversation with Weizmann, Clayton seemed to indicate that the Arabs would not oppose a Jewish presence west of the Jordan. Leon Simon, diary, March 27, 1918, WA.

133. Leon Simon, diary, May 17, 1918, WA.

134. Weizmann to William Ormsby-Gore, April 19, 1918, *WL*, 8:146–48.

135. The entire episode is recorded in Leon Simon, diary, May 17, 20, 1918, WA. See also Hacohen, diary, May 19, 1918, *Milhemet haamim*, 2:908–13.

136. Israel Sieff to Nahum Sokolow, June 10, 1918, WA.

137. Norman Bentwich, *Sir Wyndham Deedes: A Christian Zionist* (Jerusalem, 1954); Bernard Wasserstein, *Wyndham Deedes in Palestine* (London, 1973).

138. Weizmann, *Trial and Error*, pp. 217–18. The early English editions were called *Protocols of the Wise Men of Zion*. See Robert Singerman, ed., *Antisemitic Propaganda: An Annotated Bibliography and Research Guide* (New York, 1982), p. 31, item 0-107.

139. See the two-page manuscript titled "Sir Wyndham Deedes," January 11, 1926, WA.

140. Wyndham Deedes to his mother, Rose Deedes, April 12, 1918, Wyndham Deedes Papers, St. Antony's College, Middle East Centre.
141. Wyndham Deedes to Rose Deedes, [April 1918], WA.
142. Jon Kimche, *The Unromantics: The Great Powers and the Balfour Declaration* (London, 1968), p. 57.
143. William Ormsby-Gore to Mark Sykes, April 9, 1918, Sykes Papers.
144. Ibid.
145. Gilbert Clayton to Reginald Wingate, March 23, 1918, WA.
146. "Report on Dr. Weizmann's Visit to General Allenby at General Headquarters," April 3, 1918, WA.
147. Leon Simon, diary, April 5, 1918, WA.
148. See Hacohen, diary, April 4, 1918, *Milhemet haamim*, 2:871.
149. Bernard Wasserstein, *The British in Palestine* (London, 1978), p. 18.
150. William Ormsby-Gore, report, August 1918, in "Correspondence Respecting Eastern Affairs," FO, 406/40.
151. War cabinet, "Resolutions on Palestine," January 1, 1918, CAB, 24/72.
152. Some of the most detailed contemporary accounts of these trends can be found in William Yale's reports to the State Department. See also Philip S. Khoury, *Syria and the French Mandate: The Politics of Arab Nationalism, 1920–1945* (Princeton, N.J., 1987), pp. 27–70.
153. See, e.g., "Die Leiden der jüdischen Bevölkerung in Palästina während des Weltkrieges. Bericht Nr. 1," undated and unsigned, but apparently written early in the war as part of a larger memorandum, CZA, L6/5. See also Mordechai Ben-Hillel Hacohen to Ahad Ha'Am, February 12, 1915, WA.
154. See, e.g., Judah Magnes to Arthur Ruppin, September 4, 1914, Brandeis Papers, reel 81, Z/P 22-1, in response to Ruppin's letter of August 12 asking for economic assistance. See also Shmarya Levin and Louis Brandeis to Arthur Hantke, March 28, 1915, WA.
155. Friedman, *Germany, Turkey and Zionism*.
156. Nachum Gross, "Hayishuv bizman milhemet haolam harishonah," in *Bankai leumah behithadshutah*, ed. Nachum Gross (Ramat Gan, 1977), p. 60.
157. Yehoshua Ben-Aryeh and Israel Bartal, eds., *Hahistoryah shel Eretz Israel*, vol. 8, *Shilhei hatkufah haotmanit, 1799–1917* (Jerusalem, 1983), 8:316–18.
158. "Report on Judean Colonies," unsigned, Ben Cohen Papers, Brandeis University Archives and Library, Waltham, Mass., reel 66-2.
159. M. Eliash, "The General Economic Situation," October 14, 1919, CZA, Z3/1648.
160. For a general survey, see *Sefer toldot hahaganah* (Tel Aviv, 1965), 1:315–31.
161. Yitzhak Gil-Har, "Hitargenut vehanhagah atzmit shel hayishuv be-Eretz Israel mireshit hashilton habriti ad leishur hamandat (1917–1922)" (Ph.D. diss., Hebrew University of Jerusalem, 1972), pp. 85–104.
162. See, e.g., Leo Motzkin to Weizmann, April 8, 1915, WA; Communique XIII, May 3, 1915, WA; Cyrus Adler to Weizmann, July 30, 1915, WA; Otto Warburg to Weizmann, general report, February 25, 1916, WA.
163. See report, in German, quoting information received from Weizmann, May 6, 1917, CZA, L6/5.
164. Jacob Thon to Weizmann, December 24, 1917, CZA, L2/565; Thon to Weizmann, March 27, 1918, CZA, L2/186/III.
165. Meeting of Zionist Commission and Vaad Zmani, April 15, 1918, CZA, Z4/538.

166. Zionist Commission, minutes, April 29, 1918, CZA, L2/186.
167. Weizmann to Edgar Šuarès, April 9, 1918, *WL*, 8:125–26.
168. Hagit Lavsky, *Yesodot hatakziv lamifal hazioni: Vaad hazirim, 1918–1921* (Jerusalem, 1980), pp. 46–57.
169. Israel Sieff, report, n.d., WA.
170. "Meeting between the Jerusalem Rabbinate and the Zionist Commission: Report of Dr. Weizmann," app. 34, Ben Cohen Papers, reel 66-2.
171. Shimon Rubinstein and Shmuel Even Or, "Hakamat vaad hair liyehudei Yerushalayim be-1918 vehaishim hamerkaziyim shebo," *Kivunim*, no. 35 (May 1987): 53–66.
172. Zionist Commission, minutes, May 15, 1918, WA. See also Zionist Commission, app. 68, [April 1918], CZA, Z4/16018.
173. Menahem Friedman, *Hevrah vedat: Haortodoxyah halo-zionit be-Eretz Israel, 1918–1936* (Jerusalem, 1977), pp. 50–73.
174. See, e.g., "Report Made to the English Zionist Federation by Dr. Weizmann and Mr. Leon Simon," [1919], Wise Papers, box 129.
175. Weizmann to Jacob DeHaas, April 26, May 19, 1918, *WL*, 8:168, 186.
176. Arthur Money to William Ormsby-Gore, April 20, 1918, CZA, Z4/483.
177. [Israel Sieff], "Report on the Work of the Zionist Commission to Palestine," 1918, WA. See also Zionist Commission, app. 35 [May 1918], CZA, Z4/16018. Expenses related to education accounted for about one-third of the entire budget of the Zionist Commission during the first phase of its operations in Palestine. Lavsky, *Yesodot hatakziv lamifal hazioni*, p. 118.
178. "Jewish Expenditure in Palestine, April 1918 to December 1922," April 26, 1923, WA.
179. Louis Brandeis to Weizmann, March 13, 1918, WA.
180. See Zionist Commission, minutes, April 7, 1918, WA.
181. The most extensive and thorough treatment of this subject can be found in the unpublished manuscript of Shimon Rubinstein, "Al miftanah shel tkufah hadashah," pt. 2, "Hamediniyut hakarkait shel 'vaad hazirim' be-1918" (Jerusalem, 1985). I am grateful to Mr. Rubinstein for allowing me to use his work, upon which I rely in the following discussion.
182. Weizmann to William Ormsby-Gore, May 1, 1918, *WL*, 8:176–77, and n. 3.
183. Foreign Office to Edmund H. Allenby, November 26, 1917, giving instruction as to how Georges Picot should be treated. See also Ronald Storrs to Foreign Office, report, January 15, 1918, WA; guidelines written by Mark Sykes as to how to handle the French commissioner, January 31, 1918, Archives of the French Ministry for Foreign Affairs, Guerre 1914–1918, Turquie, vol. 27, nos. 295–96.
184. Zionist Commission, minutes, April 23, 1918, CZA, Z4/483.
185. Zionist Commission, minutes, April 13, 1918, CZA, Z4/483.
186. Rubinstein, "Al miftanah shel tkufah hadashah," p. 69.
187. Weizmann to Arthur Balfour, May 30, 1918, *WL*, 8:204–5; Balfour to Weizmann, July 26, 1918, CZA, Z4/16018.
188. See *WL*, 8:227, n. 3.
189. It is not clear where this money came from. Aaronsohn, *Yoman Aaron Aaronsohn*, pp. 402–3. Most likely it was provided by the American Zionists.
190. Rubinstein, "Al miftanah shel tkufah hadashah," pp. 69–70.
191. Leon Simon, diary, April 7, 1918, WA.

192. Evyatar Friesel, *Hamediniyut hazionit leahar hatzharat Balfour, 1917–1922* (Tel Aviv, 1977), p. 53.

193. Gilbert Clayton to chief administrator and commander in chief, April 19, 1918, CZA, Z4/16018.

194. Zionist Commission, "The Military Administration of Palestine and the Jews," memorandum, July 19, 1919, WA.

195. Weizmann to William Ormsby-Gore, April 16, 1918, *WL*, 8:128.

196. Israel Sieff to Nahum Sokolow, cable, April 14, 1918, CZA, Z4/305/1.

197. Ronald Storrs to Foreign Office and General Headquarters, April 22, 1918, FO, 371/3398.

198. William Ormsby-Gore, report 2, April 19, 1918, transmitted by Gilbert Clayton to Arthur Balfour, FO, 371/3395.

199. Zionist Commission, minutes, April 23, 1918, WA.

200. Ronald Storrs, "Note by the Military Governor of Jerusalem," April 30, 1918, FO, 371/3395. See also Ronald Storrs, *Orientations* (London, 1945), p. 341.

201. Weizmann, speech, April 27, 1918, CZA, L3/285.

202. Ronald Storrs, "Note by the Military Governor of Jerusalem," April 30, 1918, FO, 371/3395.

203. "Future of Palestine," May 8, 1918, FO, 371/3395.

204. William Ormsby-Gore to Maurice Hankey, April 19, 1918, CAB, 21/58.

205. Gilbert Clayton to Mark Sykes, April 18, 1918, FO, 800/221.

206. Gilbert Clayton to General [Reginald Wingate], April 21, 1918, FO, 800/221.

207. Gilbert Clayton, note, [August or September 1918], WA.

208. Major K. Cornwallis to Lieutenant Colonel George Stewart Symes, April 20, 1918, CZA, L3/285.

209. See, e.g., Weizmann to William Ormsby-Gore, April 16, 1918, *WL*, 8:128; Weizmann to Arthur Balfour, May 30, 1918, *WL*, 8:197–206; Zionist Commission, minutes, April 13, 1918, WA.

210. Weizmann to Vera Weizmann, April 30–May 2, 1918, *WL*, 8:171.

211. Leon Simon, diary, April–May 1918, WA.

212. Leon Simon, diary, April 7, 1918, WA.

213. Weizmann to Arthur Balfour, May 30, 1918, *WL*, 8:197–205.

214. The entire episode is described by Jon Kimche, *The Second Arab Awakening* (London, 1970), pp. 179–83. It seems strange that Weizmann would not have mentioned such a meeting either in letters or noted it in his appointment book, but on the chance that it did occur, it is hereby recorded, albeit with due caution.

215. Ibid., p. 182.

216. Foreign Office to David Hogarth [via Reginald Wingate], January 4, 1918, Wingate Papers.

217. David Hogarth, "Mission to King Hussein," *Arab Bulletin*, no. 77 (January 27, 1918): 21.

218. This is evident from Weizmann's letter to Louis Brandeis, January 16, 1918, *WL*, 8:60.

219. [Mark Sykes] to Feisal, March 3, 1918, FO, 882/3. The document used here seems to be a draft, but it is clear that a revised version of it was, in fact, sent. See Feisal's reply to Sykes, July 18, 1918, FO, 800/221.

220. See William Yale, report 7: "Notes on Syrian Affairs for the Week Ending December 10th," Yale Papers, box 10, folder 9.

221. Aaron S. Klieman, "The Weizmann-Feisal Negotiations of 1918–1919," *Chicago Jewish Forum* 24, no. 4 (Summer 1966): 297–303.
222. Gilbert Clayton to Mark Sykes, February 4, 1918, FO, 371/3398; Clayton to Sykes, June 13, 1918, Wingate Papers.
223. For detailed background information on Hussein and Feisal, their political aspirations and military strength, see William Yale, report 20, March 25, 1918, Yale Papers, box 10, folder 10; Yale to Loland Harrison, April 1, 1918, Sir H. Young Papers, St. Antony's College, Middle East Centre.
224. Neil Caplan, "Faisal Ibn Hussein and the Zionists: A Re-examination with Documents," *International History Review* 5, no. 4 (November 1983): 564.
225. Weizmann, *Trial and Error*, pp. 232–33; Weizmann, appointment book, June 16, 1918, WA. This is one of the rare instances in which Weizmann's appointment book gives detailed information on the trip to Feisal's camp and the ten days following.
226. Edmund H. Allenby to Emir Feisal, [June 1918], WA.
227. Weizmann's description in his memoirs of the events leading to the talk with Feisal and some of the background information are inaccurate. He seems to have merged a number of events and conversations that took place over a number of months into this one visit. *Trial and Error*, pp. 232–35.
228. The description of the meeting between Feisal and Weizmann is based on two accounts: "Interview between Dr. Weizmann and Sherif Faisal on 4th June 1918 at Wahaida," WA; P. C. Joyce, "Feisal and Weizmann," *Arab Bulletin*, June 18, 1918, p. 208.
229. Weizmann, appointment book, June 16, 1918, WA.
230. Joyce, "Feisal and Weizmann," p. 208.
231. William Yale to Loland Harrison, July 8, 1918, Yale Papers, box 2, folder 37.
232. Weizmann to Vera Weizmann, June 17, 1918, *WL*, 8:210. Weizmann described Feisal in even more glowing terms to Rahel Yanait. Rahel Yanait Ben-Zvi, "Pgishah rishonah im Weizmann," *Davar*, November 23, 1918.
233. See, e.g., Feisal to Weizmann [via Gilbert Clayton], July 29, 1918, CZA, L3/87. See also Feisal to Clayton, [August 2, 1918], WA.
234. Feisal to Mark Sykes, July 18, 1918, FO, 800/221.
235. George Stewart Symes, report, June 13, 1918, FO, 800/221.
236. Gilbert Clayton to Arthur Balfour, July 1, 1918, WA. A copy of this letter was sent to the high commissioner, Sir Reginald Wingate.
237. William Yale to Loland Harrison, July 8, 1918, Yale Papers, box 2, folder 37.
238. See, e.g., Gilbert Clayton to Arthur Balfour, September 21, 1918, CZA, Z4/16135.
239. William Ormsby-Gore to Felix Frankfurter, April 24, 1918, CZA, A246/26.
240. Arthur Ruppin to SAC, March 13, 1914, CZA, Z3/1611. For the events leading to the sale, see Jehuda Reinharz, "Laying the Foundations for a University in Jerusalem: Chaim Weizmann's Role, 1913–1914," *Modern Judaism* 4, no. 1 (February 1984): 1–38.
241. Shmuel Tolkowsky to Julian L. Meltzer, January 11, 1964, WA. See also Tolkowsky, *Yoman zioni medini*, pp. 245–66.
242. Gilbert Clayton to Weizmann, April 9, 1918, WA. See also Zionist Commission, minutes, April 13, 1918, WA.

243. William Ormsby-Gore to Weizmann, April 11, 1918, CZA, L3/87.

244. Gilbert Clayton to William Ormsby-Gore, June 20, 1918, CZA, Z4/16019.

245. *Yom hagenu: Pirtei hahagigah shel hanahat even hapinah lebinyan hauniversitah haivrit* (Jerusalem, [July 24, 1918]), pp. 9–10, copy in WA.

246. Hacohen, diary, July 25, 1918, *Milhemet haamim*, 2:952–53.

247. A cable also arrived from Feisal. Feisal to Weizmann [via Gilbert Clayton], July 29, 1918, CZA, L3/87. It is possible that Feisal's cable arrived only after the ceremony. Cables from Balfour and the French government are reproduced in Hebrew in *Yom hagenu*, p. 20.

248. Hacohen, diary, July 19, 1918, *Milhemet haamim*, 2:949.

249. Weizmann, *Trial and Error*, p. 237.

250. Weizmann, speech at stone-laying ceremony, Hebrew University, July 24, 1918, CZA, L6/142, also in Chaim Weizmann, *American Addresses of Dr. Chaim Weizmann* (New York, 1923), pp. 57–64.

251. Weizmann to Vera Weizmann, July 11, 1918, *WL*, 8:223. See also Hacohen, diary, July 29, 1918, *Milhemet haamim*, 2:955–56.

252. Stephen Wise to Louis Brandeis, January 11, 1918, DeHaas Papers.

253. Weizmann to Vera Weizmann, July 11, 1918, *WL*, 8:223.

254. See Vera Weizmann's constant complaints about lack of letters from her husband. Vera Weizmann to Weizmann, April 23, May 2, June 9, 20, July 10, 1918, WA.

255. See, e.g., Vera Weizmann to Weizmann, July 2, 1918, WA.

256. See, e.g., Vera Weizmann to Weizmann, July 23, 1918, WA.

257. Tolkowsky, *Yoman zioni medini*, pp. 303, 313–14.

258. See Weizmann to Vera Weizmann, July 11, 1918, *WL*, 8:222–24.

259. In fact there was a misunderstanding about the date of the ceremony, and Sokolow did send a cable as soon as he found out from the press that it had taken place. Nahum Sokolow to Weizmann, cable, July 29, 1918, CZA, L4/58/I. See also Ahad Ha'Am to Weizmann, August 12, 1918, Dewey Stone Collection, American Jewish Historical Archives, congratulating Weizmann with great praise.

260. Weizmann to Louis Brandeis, January 14, 1918, *WL*, 8:53.

261. See, e.g., Weizmann to Louis Brandeis, April 25, 1918, *WL*, 8:167.

262. Vera Weizmann to Weizmann, May 23, 1918, WA.

263. Nahum Sokolow to Weizmann, June 12, 1918, CZA, L3/370; Aaron Aaronsohn to Weizmann, September 24, 1918, Wiseman Papers, box 11, folder 282; Felix Frankfurter to William Wiseman, September 26, 1918, Wiseman Papers, box 11, folder 282.

264. Concerning Aaronsohn's constant outbursts of anger during meetings of the Zionist Commission, see Leon Simon, diary, March–May 1918, WA.

265. Israel Sieff to David Eder, report, October 23, 1918, CZA, L3/370.

266. Concerning the financial demands made on the Zionist Commission and its available resources, see Lavsky, *Yesodot hatakziv lamifal hazioni*, pp. 130–44.

267. Weizmann to Ahad Ha'Am, August 3, 1918, *WL*, 8:248. See also Weizmann to Vera Weizmann, August 9, 1918, *WL*, 8:252.

268. Gilbert Clayton to Reginald Wingate, April 21, 1918, Wingate Papers.

269. William Ormsby-Gore to Maurice Hankey, April 19, 1918, CAB, 21/58.

270. See, e.g., Hacohen, diary, July 19–25, 1918, *Milhemet haamim*, 2:949–54. See also Berl Katznelson to Weizmann, July 27, 1918, Rahel Shazar Collection,

Gnazim Archive, Tel Aviv. I am grateful to Shimon Rubinstein, who provided me with a copy of the Katznelson letter.

271. Ronald Storrs to Mark Sykes, July 17, 1918, WA.
272. Vera Weizmann to Weizmann, May 7, [15], 1918, WA. See also Gilbert Clayton to Weizmann, June 11, 1918, WA. Two months later, Weizmann was advised by William Ormsby-Gore that the Ministry of Munitions and the Admiralty were anxious for him to return to England to advise them "re chemical work." Ormsby-Gore to Weizmann, [August 9], 1918, WA.
273. Vera Weizmann to Weizmann, June 2, 1918, WA.
274. Vera Weizmann to Weizmann, May 23, 28, 1918, WA.
275. Vera Weizmann to Weizmann, July 23, 1918, WA.
276. See, e.g., Vera Weizmann to Weizmann, April 23, June 30, 1918, WA.
277. Vera Weizmann to Weizmann, June 30, 1918, WA.
278. See, e.g., Vera Weizmann to Weizmann, May 8, 1918, WA.
279. Vera Weizmann to Weizmann, June 2, 1918, WA.
280. Vera Weizmann to Weizmann, July 23, 1918, WA.
281. Vera Weizmann to Weizmann, June 9, 1918, WA.
282. Vera Weizmann to Weizmann, July 23, 1918, WA.
283. Weizmann to Vera Weizmann, August 24, 1918, *WL*, 8:263.
284. Ibid.
285. William Ormsby-Gore, "Report on the Existing Political Situation in Palestine and Contiguous Areas by the Political Officer in Charge of the Zionists' Commission," August 22, 1918, FO, 406/40.
286. Vera Weizmann, *Impossible Takes Longer*, p. 90.
287. Philip Kerr to Herbert Samuel, January 4, 1921, WA.
288. Vera Weizmann to Weizmann, July 23, 1918, WA.

VIII   The Road to San Remo

1. Tolkowsky, *Yoman zioni medini*, pp. 381–82; Weizmann, *Trial and Error*, pp. 238–39.
2. For a general survey, see Ezra Mendelsohn, *The Jews of East Central Europe between the World Wars* (Bloomington, Ind., 1983).
3. Ezra Mendelsohn, *Hatnuah hazionit be-Polin: Shnot hahithavut, 1915–1926* (Jerusalem, 1986), pp. 49–79.
4. See Jonathan Frankel, *Prophecy and Politics: Socialism, Nationalism, and the Russian Jews, 1862–1917* (Cambridge, 1981), pp. 509–51; Oscar I. Janowsky, *The Jews and Minority Rights, 1898–1919* (New York, 1933), pp. 161–90.
5. Copenhagen Manifesto, October 28, 1918, CZA, Z4/124/10.
6. Palestine Jewish community, resolutions, December 18, 1918, in *Hamandat vehabayit haleumi, 1917–1947*, ed. Yehoshua Porat and Yaakov Shavit, vol. 9 of *Hahistoryah shel Eretz Israel* (Jerusalem, 1982), p. 174.
7. American Jewish Congress, resolutions, December 1918, quoted in Jonathan Frankel, "The Jewish Socialists and the American Jewish Congress Movement," *YIVO Annual of Jewish Social Science* 16 (New York, 1976): 318–23.
8. Pittsburgh Platform, June 25, 1918, quoted in Cohen, *American Jews and the Zionist Idea*, p. 23.
9. Jehuda Reinharz, "Zionism in the United States, 1897–1972," *Encyclopaedia Judaica* 16 (Jerusalem, 1973), pp. 1141–49.

10. See Cohen, *English Zionists and British Jews*, pp. 277–313. For a somewhat different perspective, see Black, *Social Politics of Anglo-Jewry*, pp. 337–55, 366–69.

11. Herbert Samuel to Edwin Samuel, October 8, 1918, Israel State Archives, 100/44.

12. Herbert Samuel played an active role in enlisting the non-Zionists for the Advisory Committee on Palestine. See, e.g., Samuel to Robert Waley-Cohen, November 2, 1918, WA; Waley-Cohen to Samuel, November 2, 1918, CZA, Z4/540.

13. "The First Meeting of the Advisory Committee on Palestine," November 2, 1918, CZA, A18/21/1.

14. Weizmann to Lord Robert Cecil, November 1, 1918, *WL*, 9:8.

15. "Proposals Submitted [by] the Zionist Organization to the Secretary of State for Foreign Affairs Regarding Matters Affecting the Jewish Population of Palestine during the Military Occupation of That Country," FO, 371/3395.

16. Mark Sykes to William Ormsby-Gore, November 17, 1918, CZA, Z4/16135.

17. Gilbert Clayton to Foreign Office, November 19, 1918, CZA, Z4/16135.

18. "Meetings of the Advisory Committee of November 2nd, November 6th, November 8th and November 10th, 1918," CZA, A18/21/1.

19. See, e.g., Leon Simon to Weizmann, November 7, 1918, WA.

20. Weizmann to William Ormsby-Gore, November 19, 1918, *WL*, 9:29.

21. "Proposals Relating to the Establishment of a Jewish National Home in Palestine," FO, 371/3385.

22. These analogies were stated in Leon Simon to Weizmann, November 7, 1918, WA.

23. "Note on the Interview with Mr. Balfour," December 4, 1918, WA.

24. See David Eder to Weizmann, cable [via Gilbert Clayton], October 27, 1918, CZA, Z4/537.

25. Weizmann to Gilbert Clayton, November 5, 1918, *WL*, 9:12–13; Weizmann to David Eder, November 5, 1918, *WL*, 9:15.

26. Kedourie, *England and the Middle East*, pp. 177–222.

27. "Dr. Weizmann's Interview with Emir Feisal at the Carlton Hotel," December 11, 1918, FO, 371/3420. See also *Times* (London), December 12, 1918.

28. Bernard Flexner to his sister Nim, December 23, 1918, Louis Brandeis Archive, Brandeis University Archives and Library, reel 12, p. 180.

29. As to whether the agreement was signed on January 3 or 4, 1919, see Antonius, *Arab Awakening*, p. 284.

30. "Agreement between Emir Feisal and Dr. Weizmann," January 3, 1919. The text of the agreement and the amendment by Feisal, as well as its English translation by T. E. Lawrence, are in WA.

31. See, e.g., Reginald Wingate to Foreign Office, October 17, 1918, WA.

32. Feisal to Felix Frankfurter, March 3, 1919, CZA, L3/27.

33. Philip S. Khoury, *Syria and the French Mandate: The Politics of Arab Nationalism, 1920–1945* (Princeton, N.J., 1987), p. 222.

34. Antonius, *Arab Awakening*, p. 441.

35. John French, quoted in Howard M. Sachar, *The Emergence of the Middle East, 1914–1924* (New York, 1969), p. 387.

36. See, e.g., Harry Sacher to Leon Simon, January 29, 1919, WA.

37. Even if, as Mayir Vereté points out, the British "neutralized" a more comprehensive Arab-Jewish agreement, the public perception was that Weiz-

mann had gained another diplomatic victory. A comprehensive discussion of the negotiations between the Zionists and the Arabs, particularly with Feisal, can be found in Mayir Vereté, "Hamasa vehamatan hazioni-aravi beaviv 1919 vehamediniyut haanglit," *Zion* 32, nos. 1–2 (1977): 76–115. See also Moshe Perlmann, "Chapters of Arab-Jewish Diplomacy, 1918–1922," *Jewish Social Studies* 6, no. 2 (April 1944): 123–54; Nakdimon Rogel, "Haish shel Weizmann bedamesek," *Hazionut* 8 (1983): 279–353.

38. Tolkowsky, *Yoman zioni medini*, p. 385. See also Florian Sokolow, "Nahum Sokolow's Paris Diary," *Zion* 3 (November 1952): 42–50.

39. Weizmann to Aaron Aaronsohn, December 12, 1918, *WL*, 9:62–63.

40. Comité des Délégations Juives auprès de la Conférence de la Paix, "A leurs Excellences: Monsieur le President et Messieurs les Délégués de la Conférence de la Paix," CZA, Z3/103; "Minutes of the Meeting of the Executive Committee of May 20, 1919: Judge Mack on the Question of the National Rights," CZA, Z4/302/1. See also Janowsky, *Jews and Minority Rights*, pp. 264–319.

41. World Zionist Organization, "The Jewish Situation in Poland," June 9, 1919, CZA, L6/59.

42. Weizmann to Mordechai Ben-Hillel Hacohen, November 29, 1918, *WL*, 9:48.

43. World Zionist Organization, "Economic Oppression of the Jews in Czecho-Slovakia," June 2, 1919, CZA, L6/59. See also Nahum Sokolow to Tomás Masaryk, December 14, 1918, CZA, L8/361.

44. Weizmann to Herbert Samuel, November 22–23, 1919, *WL*, 9:258–59.

45. Rachela Makover, *Shilton uminhal be-Eretz Israel, 1917–1925* (Jerusalem, 1988), pp. 70–75.

46. David Eder to Weizmann, October 21, 1918, CZA, Z4/305/1.

47. See Storrs, *Orientations*, chap. 15.

48. Mordechai Ben-Hillel Hacohen, "Eretz Israel tahat shilton hazavah habriti," *Hashiloah* 42 (1924): 241–46.

49. Vaad Hazmani to Zionist Commission, October 23, 1918, WA.

50. See, e.g., David Eder to Weizmann, October 21, 1918, CZA, Z4/305/1.

51. Kenneth W. Stein, *The Land Question in Palestine, 1917–1939* (Chapel Hill, N.C., 1984), pp. 39–52.

52. Vladimir Jabotinsky to Weizmann, November 12, 1918, WA. See also Jabotinsky to Weizmann, November 28, 1918, January 21, 1919, WA.

53. David Eder to Weizmann, November 28, 1918, CZA, Z4/16135.

54. William Ormsby-Gore, minute, February 15, 1919, FO, 608/99, responding to Weizmann's complaints.

55. Richard Meinertzhagen, "Political State of Palestine," memorandum, [February 1919], WA.

56. Richard Meinertzhagen, diary, May 30, 1919, *Middle East Diary, 1917–1956* (New York, 1960), p. 20.

57. "Statement on the Internal Jewish Situation in Palestine," February 8, 1919, WA.

58. Weizmann to Mordechai Ben-Hillel Hacohen, January 21, 1919, *WL*, 9:99.

59. Israel Sieff to Eliyahu Lewin-Epstein, January 22, 1919, WA.

60. Weizmann to Arthur Money, January 26, 1919, *WL*, 9:105–6.

61. Weizmann to London Zionist Bureau, November 7–9, 1919, *WL*, 9:236–37.

62. "Statement on the Internal Jewish Situation in Palestine," February 8, 1919, WA.

63. Weizmann to David Eder, November 26, 1918, *WL*, 9:39.

64. Weizmann to Gilbert Clayton, [November 27, 1918], *WL*, 9:42.

65. Weizmann to London Zionist Bureau, November 7–9, 1919, *WL*, 9:239–40.

66. Weizmann to Herbert Samuel, November 22–23, 1919, *WL*, 9:256.

67. Weizmann to Bella Berligne, November 8, 1919, *WL*, 9:251–52.

68. Chaim Weizmann, "Zionist Policy: An Address," September 21, 1919, pp. 19–20, WA.

69. Gilbert Clayton, report, November 8, 1918, FO, 371/3385.

70. Yehoshua Porat, *Zmihat hatnuah haleumit haaravit-hapalestinait, 1918–1929* (Jerusalem, 1971), pp. 24–25.

71. Zionist Commission, "The First Arab Congress in Jerusalem," report, [February 5, 1919], WA.

72. Anglo-French Declaration, February 7, 1918, in *Diplomacy in the Near and Middle East*, ed. Hurewitz, 2:30. See also CZA, Z4/16043.

73. Harry N. Howard, *The King-Crane Commission: An American Inquiry in the Middle East* (Beirut, 1963), pp. 32–34, 57–58. See also "Report of the Zionist Commission to the Zionist Executive in London," June 18, 1919, CZA, Z4/16045.

74. Gilbert Clayton to Foreign Office, November 15, 1918, Gilbert Clayton Papers, Durham University, School of Oriental Studies.

75. See, e.g., Gilbert Clayton to Arthur Balfour, December 5, 1918, FO, 371/3386. See also Clayton to Foreign Office, February 28, March 26, 1919, FO, 371/4179, 371/4153.

76. Gilbert Clayton to Foreign Office, May 2, 1919, quoted in Stein, *Balfour Declaration*, p. 645.

77. H. D. Watson to Foreign Office, August 16, 1919, FO, 371/4171.

78. Arthur Balfour to Weizmann, April 3, 1919, WA.

79. Weizmann to Mordechai Ben-Hillel Hacohen, January 21, 1919, *WL*, 9:98–99.

80. Weizmann to Arthur Balfour, April 9, 1919, *WL*, 9:128–30.

81. Weizmann to London Zionist Bureau, report, November 7–9, 1919, *WL*, 9:241–42.

82. See, e.g., Weizmann to Arthur Balfour, July 23, 1919, *WL*, 9:188.

83. See, e.g., Richard Meinertzhagen to Lord Curzon, September 26, 1919, in *Documents on British Foreign Policy, 1919–1939*, ed. E. L. Woodward and Rohan Butler (London, 1952), ser. 1, 4:425–29.

84. Earl Curzon to John French, cable, August 4, 1919, in ibid., p. 329.

85. Weizmann to Louis Mallet, June 18, 1919, *WL*, 9:162–63.

86. Louis Mallet to Weizmann, July 1, 1919, WA.

87. Weizmann to Lord Curzon, February 2, 1920, *WL*, 9:296–311.

88. Lord Curzon, minute on Ronald Graham, note, July 2, 1919, WA.

89. "Report of the Zionist Commission: From the Departure of Dr. Weizmann to That of Dr. Eder (IIIrd Period)," WA.

90. Vladimir Jabotinsky to Weizmann, December 18, 1919, CZA, Z4/16043.

91. David Eder to Weizmann, cable, January 1, 1919, WA.

92. Weizmann to Henry Wilson, February 4, 1919, *WL*, 9:111.

93. See Edmund Allenby to Lord Curzon, April 21, 1919, and other correspondence in FO, 371/4182.

94. See, e.g., "To His Majesty the King: Petition for Mercy on Behalf of 54 Soldiers of the 38th and 39th Jewish Battalions, Royal Fusiliers, Sentenced

by Court Martial . . . for Mutiny," signed by Vladimir Jabotinsky and fellow soldiers, October 1919, FO, 371/4238.

95. Yigal Elam, *Hagdudim haivriim*, pp. 300–31.

96. Woodrow Wilson to Stephen Wise, August 31, 1918, in Zionist Organization of America, *The American War Congress and Zionism: Statements by Members of the American War Congress on the Jewish National Movement* (New York, 1919), p. 9.

97. See, e.g., Weizmann to Louis Brandeis, November 11, 1918, *WL*, 9:22.

98. Louis Brandeis to Weizmann, November 26, 1918, WA.

99. Jacob DeHaas to Weizmann, December 4, 1918, CZA, A264/51.

100. American Zionist Delegation, journal, December 12, 1918, WA.

101. Julius Simon, *Certain Days: Zionist Memoirs and Selected Papers*, ed. Evyatar Friesel (Jerusalem, 1971), p. 82.

102. Tolkowsky, *Yoman zioni medini*, p. 380.

103. Weizmann and Sokolow to Copenhagen Zionist Bureau, November [19], 1918, *WL*, 9:30.

104. "Deed of Power," signed by Otto Warburg and Arthur Hantke, December 1, 1918, CZA, L6/725.

105. "Protokoll der Sitzung des E.A.C. vom 30. November, 1. u. 2. Dezember 1918, in Kopenhagen," CZA, L6/725.

106. Zionist Organization of New York, report, [December 20, 1918], WA.

107. Halpern, *Clash of Heroes*, p. 185.

108. Zionist Organization of New York to Nahum Sokolow, cable, [December 20, 1918], WA.

109. Tolkowsky, *Yoman zioni medini*, pp. 399–400.

110. Aaronsohn, *Yoman Aaron Aaronsohn*, pp. 443–61. See also "Conference on Tuesday Afternoon, January 7th at Hotel Plaza," Paris, January 9, 1919, DeHaas Papers.

111. "Memorandum of Matters Considered on January 2nd, 1919," DeHaas Papers.

112. "Conference on Tuesday Afternoon, January 7th at Hotel Plaza," Paris, January 9, 1919, DeHaas Papers. See also Weizmann to Vera Weizmann, January 8, 1919, *WL*, 9:93–94.

113. "Report by Dr. Wise, National Executive Committee Meeting," February 9, 1919, DeHaas Papers.

114. "Report of Conference of Dr. Weizmann with Mr. Cowen, Bianchini, Sieff, Aaronsohn and Dr. Wise on Thursday, January 9, 1919," DeHaas Papers.

115. "A Meeting of the Following Members of the IAC . . . January 22nd, 1919 at Empire House," CZA, Z4/302/1.

116. See, e.g., Felix Frankfurter to Weizmann, November 2, 1918, WA.

117. American Zionist Delegation, journal, December 12–13, 1918, WA.

118. Palestine Jewish community, resolutions, December 18, 1918, in *Hamandat vehabayit haleumi*, ed. Porat and Shavit, p. 174. See also David Eder to Weizmann, December 23, 1918, CZA, Z4/16135.

119. Moshe Burstein, *Self-Government of the Jews in Palestine since 1900* (Tel Aviv, 1934), pp. 92–94.

120. See Victor Jacobson to Copenhagen Zionist Bureau, December 16, 1918, CZA, L6/29/XXVI; Israel Zangwill to Weizmann, November 29, 1918, CZA, A77/3/8. See also Zangwill to Lucien Wolf, December 5, 1918, WA; Leopold

Greenberg to Stephen Wise, December 17, 1918, Wise Papers, box 79, folder 9.

121. Weizmann to David Eder, cable, November 28, 1918, CZA, Z4/16135. The cable was read by British intelligence. See Gilbert Clayton's angry reaction to its content, December 5, 1918, CZA, Z4/16135.
122. Weizmann to David Eder, cable, December 17, 1918, *WL*, 9:72.
123. Victor Jacobson to Copenhagen Zionist Bureau, December 16, 1918, CZA, L6/29/XXVI, also quoting Weizmann.
124. "Interview of Dr. Wise with Mr. Balfour, December 19, 1918 at the British Foreign Office," DeHaas Papers. See also American Zionist Delegation, journal, December 19, 1918, WA.
125. Weizmann to Aaron Aaronsohn, December 22, 1918, *WL*, 9:78–79.
126. Weizmann and Stephen Wise to Louis Brandeis, cable, December 20, 1918, *WL*, 9:78.
127. Stephen Wise, "Meeting with Dr. Weizmann, Dr. Jacobson, Julius Simon and Joseph Cowen," December 23, 1918, DeHaas Papers.
128. "American Zionist Delegation of New York, Meeting of December 24, 1918," DeHaas Papers.
129. "Memorandum of Recent Matters Dictated by S. S. W[ise]," December 30, 1918, DeHaas Papers.
130. "Summary of Conference between Julius Simon and Bernard Flexner of January 1, 1919," DeHaas Papers.
131. "Memorandum of the Zionist Organization Relating to Reconstruction of Palestine as the Jewish National Home," January [19], 1919, WA.
132. Weizmann to Mordechai Ben-Hillel Hacohen, January 21, 1919, *WL*, 9:101–2.
133. Arthur Balfour to David Lloyd George, January 20, 1919, CZA, KH11/207/2.
134. Arthur Money to Weizmann, January 22, 1919, WA.
135. William Ormsby-Gore to Nahum Sokolow, January 24, 1919, CZA, Z4/16009.
136. William Ormsby-Gore to Weizmann, February 20, 1919, DeHaas Papers.
137. Friesel, *Hamediniyut hazionit leahar hatzharat Balfour*, p. 77. See also "Minutes by Members of the British Delegation Made January 22–27, 1919," FO, 608/98.
138. Harry Sacher to Leon Simon, January 31, 1919, WA.
139. Leon Simon to Harry Sacher, February 4, 1919, WA.
140. Jacob DeHaas to Louis Brandeis, January 30, 1919, Wise Papers, box 105.
141. Tolkowsky, *Yoman zioni medini*, p. 407. In fact, the "Statement of the Zionist Organization Regarding Palestine" was received at the peace conference only on February 8, 1919.
142. The Proclamation of the State of Israel includes sections that seem to echo this part of the Zionist Statement.
143. "Statement of the Zionist Organization Regarding Palestine," February 3, 1919, WA.
144. Tolkowsky, *Yoman zioni medini*, p. 406, n. 4.
145. Aaronsohn, *Yoman Aaron Aaronsohn*, pp. 500–501; Aaron Aaronsohn to Weizmann, February 16, 1919, WA; Tolkowsky, *Yoman zioni medini*, p. 407, wherein Tolkowsky maintains that Aaronsohn's draft was based more or less on his own, except for the exclusion of Sidon. See also Avraham P.

Alsberg, "Delimitation of the Eastern Border of Palestine," *Zionism* 3 (Spring 1981): 87–98.

146. Bernard Flexner to his sister Nim, February 5, 1919, Louis Brandeis Archive, Brandeis University Archives and Library, reel 12, p. 198.

147. C. P. Scott to Weizmann, November 19, 1918, Guardian Archives, 335/56.

148. Stein, *Balfour Declaration*, p. 614.

149. "Summary of Conference between Julius Simon and Bernard Flexner," January 1, 1919, DeHaas Papers.

150. The interview is quoted in Aaronsohn, *Yoman Aaron Aaronsohn*, p. 478.

151. Memorandum, February 15, 1919, CZA, Z4/16008.

152. Israel Sieff to Eliyahu Lewin-Epstein, January 22, 1919, WA.

153. "Meeting at Hotel Royal Palace," February 23–24, 1919, in *Haprotokolim shel havaad hapoel hazioni, 1919–1929*, ed. Yehoshua Freundlich and Gdalya Yogev (Tel Aviv, 1975–84), 1:1–20.

154. Weizmann to Vera Weizmann, February 28, 1919, *WL*, 9:116–17.

155. The most comprehensive description on the background to this incident is Evyatar Friesel, "Habaron Edmond de Rothschild vehazionim bashanim 1918–1919," *Zion* 38, nos. 1–4 (1973): 116–36.

156. Quoted in Lucien Wolf, Paris diary, January 17, 1919, Central Archives for the History of the Jewish People, Jerusalem, Inv/525.5.

157. Tolkowsky, *Yoman zioni medini*, pp. 426–27.

158. Weizmann to Vera Weizmann, February 28, 1919, *WL*, 9:116.

159. Weizmann, *Trial and Error*, p. 243.

160. David Hunter Miller, *My Diary at the Conference of Paris, With Documentation by David Hunter Miller* (New York, 1925), 15:104–17. There are, of course, many accounts of the appearance of the Zionists before the Council of Ten; the one by Miller was chosen because he seems to be an impartial observer.

161. Quoted in ibid., p. 102.

162. Quoted in ibid., pp. 103–4. There seems to be some uncertainty about the exact numbers Weizmann used and some other inconsistencies among the American, British, and French protocols. Nathan Feinberg, "Letoldot hamunah bayit leumi yehudi," *Zion* 37 (1972): 111–16. In general, there are many reports on Weizmann's speech before the Council of Ten, which have appeared in a number of languages. See, e.g., "Shlihei hazionim beveidat hashalom," *Kuntres* 14 (April 1919): 3–9. See also Weizmann, "The Inner Allied Zionist Conference," report to the London conference, March 6, 1919, CZA, L6/45.

163. Quoted in Lucien Wolf, Paris diary, March 1, 1919, Central Archives for the History of the Jewish People, INV/525.5.

164. Felix Frankfurter to Louis Brandeis, March 3, 1919, DeHaas Papers.

165. Tolkowsky, *Yoman zioni medini*, p. 428.

166. See the documents in Doreen Ingrams, ed., *Palestine Papers, 1917–1922: Seeds of Conflict* (London, 1972), pp. 75–78.

167. Leon Simon to Weizmann, February 7, 1919, WA; Smaller Actions Committee, resolutions, February 9, 1919, CZA, Z4/16015.

168. Weizmann to William Ormsby-Gore, February 12, 1919, *WL*, 9:115.

169. In his letter to Weizmann of February 7, 1919, WA, Leon Simon does not explain why Jabotinsky had been dropped from the commission except to say that Weizmann would well understand why this had been done. Pre-

sumably Jabotinsky was seen as being too undisciplined and aggressive in his attitude toward the authorities.

170. See Weizmann's cables and the response to them in CZA, L4/58/I, L4/58/II.

171. Zionist Organization, "The Erez Israel Restoration Fund," leaflet, signed by Weizmann and Nahum Sokolow, July 1919, WA.

172. *Hamandat vehabayit haleumi*, ed. Porat and Shavit, pp. 162–63.

173. See CZA, Z4/540.

174. Weizmann to Wickham Steed, November 30, 1918, *WL*, 9:50.

175. Advisory Committee on Palestine, minutes, April 4, 1919, CZA, Z4/16034.

176. Julius Simon to all Zionist federations, April 18, 1919, CZA, L6/50.

177. "Minutes of Meeting with General Clayton . . . at Great Russell Street," July 9, 1919, FO, 608/100.

178. Chaim Weizmann, Menahem Ussishkin, and Julius Simon, "El kol hafederaziot haziyoniyot," [July 24, 1919], WA.

179. David Eder to SAC, London, September 17, 1919, CZA, Z4/1147. See also Weizmann to Ronald Graham, July 11, 1919, *WL*, 9:170–72.

180. Mordechai Shalev, "Am Israel Ayeka?" *Haaretz*, January 27, 1984; Yaakov Shavit, "Am Israel Ayeka? Haolim vehamashabim," *Haaretz*, February 10, 1984.

181. See, e.g., Jacob DeHaas to Louis Brandeis, March 3, 1919, DeHaas Papers; Bernard Flexner to Louis Brandeis, March 17, 1919, DeHaas Papers.

182. This is what Stephen Wise had said, according to the Baron Edmond de Rothschild, who related it to Lucien Wolf. Lucien Wolf, Paris diary, January 20, 1919, Central Archives for the History of the Jewish People, INV/525.5.

183. See, e.g., Jacob DeHaas to Weizmann, November 1, 1918, DeHaas Papers; DeHaas to Louis Brandeis, January 22, 1919, DeHaas Papers.

184. See, e.g., "Bericht des Herrn Rechtsanwalt Dr. S. Rosenbaum," March 25, 1919, CZA, L6/610.

185. See, e.g., Israel Zangwill to Weizmann, November 29, 1918, CZA, A77/3/8; Zangwill to Lucien Wolf, December 5, 1918, CZA, A77/3/III; Jacob DeHaas to Stephen Wise, December 29, 1918, Wise Papers, box 107, folder Jacob DeHaas.

186. See Jacob DeHaas to ZOA executive, cable, January 26, 1919, DeHaas Papers.

187. Stephen Wise to Mary Fels, February 17, 1919, Wise Papers, box 108, folder 13.

188. See, e.g., Jacob DeHaas to Julian Mack, January 22, 1919, DeHaas Papers; DeHaas to Louis Brandeis, February 21, 1919, DeHaas Papers.

189. "Report by Dr. Wise, National Executive Committee Meeting," February 9, 1919, DeHaas Papers; "Report of Mr. DeHaas to National Executive Committee," March 30, April 27, 1919, DeHaas Papers.

190. Felix Frankfurter to Louis Brandeis, March 3, 1919, Brandeis Papers, reel 84, 26-2.

191. See, e.g., Felix Frankfurter to Weizmann, March 8, 1918, WA. Concerning the importance of American Zionism in general, see Shmarya Levin to Weizmann, January 30, 1919, in Levin, *Igrot Shmaryahu Levin*, pp. 354–55.

192. Weizmann to Vera Weizmann, June 22, 1919, *WL*, 9:164.

193. See Miller, *My Diary*, 8:369–74, for the full text of the drafts of January–March 1919.

194. For details on all stages of the Mandate for Palestine drafts, see Esco Foundation for Palestine, *Palestine: A Study of Jewish, Arab, and British Policies* (New Haven, 1947), 1:164–77. For an analysis of these processes, see Friesel, *Hamediniyut hazionit leahar hatzharat Balfour*, pp. 120–25, 186–91.

195. Uri Raanan [Heinz Felix Frischwasser-Raanan], *The Frontiers of a Nation: A Re-examination of the Forces Which Created the Palestine Mandate and Determined Its Territorial Shape* (Westport, Conn., 1976), pp. 107–8.

196. Ben Cohen to Louis Brandeis, September 29, 1919, CZA, Z4/16008.

197. Weizmann to Lloyd George, December 29, 1919, *WL*, 9:265–67.

198. Weizmann to Philip Kerr, July 1, 1920, *WL*, 9:383.

199. "Statement of the Zionist Organization Regarding Palestine," February 3, 1919, WA.

200. This discussion is based on the protocols of the SAC and GAC, which are contained in *Haprotokolim shel havaad hapoel hazioni*, ed. Freundlich and Yogev, vol. 1. All quotations in the text are from this source. See also Simon, *Certain Days*.

201. *Haprotokolim shel havaad hapoel hazioni*, ed. Freundlich and Yogev, 1:180–81. Most of the translation of this passage has been adopted from Halpern, *Clash of Heroes*, pp. 203–4.

202. Halpern, *Clash of Heroes*, p. 204.

203. Jehuda Reinharz, *Fatherland or Promised Land? The Dilemma of the German Jew, 1893–1914* (Ann Arbor, 1975).

204. *Haprotokolim shel havaad hapoel hazioni*, ed. Freundlich and Yogev, 1:181.

205. Ibid. p. 181.

206. Ibid. p. 182. Author's emphasis.

207. Ibid. p. 182; Halpern, *Clash of Heroes*, p. 205.

208. Simon, *Certain Days*, pp. 93–96.

209. Weizmann to Felix Frankfurter, August 27, 1919, *WL*, 9:204–5.

210. Halpern, *Clash of Heroes*, p. 205.

211. *Jewish Chronicle*, October 3, 1919, pp. 14–15.

212. "Memorandum of Interview in the Apartment of the Emir Feisal, Carlton Hotel, London," October 15, 1919, Ben Cohen Papers, reel 66/1; Harry Sacher to Weizmann, October 22, 1919, WA; Feisal to Herbert Samuel, December 10, 1919, WA. See also Weizmann to Samuel, November 22–23, 1919, *WL*, 9:256.

213. See the understated and, on the whole, balanced report by Colonel John French to Lord Curzon, August 30, 1919, FO, 406/41.

214. Vera Weizmann, *Impossible Takes Longer*, pp. 91–92.

215. Weizmann to London Zionist Bureau, November 7–9, 1919, *WL*, 9:235–51. Concerning Meinertzhagen's strong pro-Zionism, see Mark Cocker, *Richard Meinertzhagen: Soldier, Scientist and Spy* (London, 1989).

216. See, e.g., Louis Bols to Edmund Allenby, December 21, 1919, CZA, Z4/16043.

217. See correspondence between Weizmann and the military administrators, December 1919–January 1920, FO, 371/4226. See also Herbert Samuel, report, March 23, 1920, CZA, Z4/15445; Samuel to Lord Curzon, April 2, 1920, St. Antony's College, Middle East Centre.

218. "Rede Dr. Weizmanns in der Actionscomitésitzung vom 7. Januar, 1920," CZA, Z4/25/5. See also Weizmann, report on conditions in Palestine, February 8, 1920, WA.

219. Weizmann, appointment book, October 15, 1919, WA.

220. Israel Sieff to Weizmann, January 9, 1920, WA. See also Sieff to Weizmann, January 15, 1920, CZA, Z4/16033.

221. Menahem Ussishkin to Weizmann, February 29, 1920, CZA, Z4/1117; David Eder to Weizmann, March 14, 1920, Brandeis Papers, reel 85/27-2. See also Mordecai Eliash, report for the Zionist Commission, March 10, 1920, CZA, Z4/16078.

222. Menahem Ussishkin to Weizmann, February 29, 1920, WA. Ussishkin was strongly critical of David Eder and Herbert Samuel, who was still in the country, for not taking a stand with Ronald Storrs, the military governor of Jerusalem, against these demonstrations.

223. Zionist Commission Press Bureau, "Last Days in Upper Galilee," March 8, 1920, CZA, Z4/16083. See also Menahem Ussishkin to Emir Feisal, March 10, 1920, CZA, Z4/16083.

224. Laskov, "Havaad hazmani vehaganat hagalil haelyon bishnat 1920," pp. 355–90. See also Yosef Trumpeldor to [Vaad Zmani], February 9, 1920, Lavon Institute for Labor Research, Tel Aviv, 134, IV.

225. For a detailed assessment of the events leading to the fall of Tel Hai, see Nakdimon Rogel, *Tel Hai: Hazit bli oref* (Tel Aviv, 1979). See also Yaakov Goldstein and Yaakov Shavit, "Yosef Trumpeldor kidmut mofet vehavikuah al 'shaikhuto' hatnuatit," *Kivunim*, no. 12 (August 1981): 9–21.

226. *Sefer toldot hahaganah*, 1:575–577.

227. Weizmann to Zionist executive, March 25, 1920, *WL*, 9:325–30.

228. Weizmann, "Meeting of March 25, 1920, Present: Weizmann, Ussishkin, Eder and Jaffe," WA.

229. Zionist Commission Press Bureau, February 25, 1920, CZA, Z4/16078.

230. Philip Mattar, *The Mufti of Jerusalem: Al-Hajj Amin al-Husayni and the Palestine National Movement* (New York, 1988), pp. 15–16.

231. Zionist Commission Press Bureau, April 11, 1920, CZA, Z4/16078.

232. Concerning this incident, see Levi-Yitzhak Shneerson, "Im Dr. Weizmann bi-Yerushalayim bishnat 1920: Reshimah," [April 1920], WA. See also De Sola Pool, report, April 7, 1920, CZA, Z4/16084, confirming the story.

233. Weizmann to David Lloyd George, April 10, 1920, *WL*, 9:333–34. See also "Memorandum Submitted to the War Office in London," in *Book of Documents of the Vaad Leumi in Palestine* (Jerusalem, 1963), pp. 19–29.

234. "Report of Maj. General Palin," FO, 371/5121.

235. "Secret Memorandum to Dr. Eder," May 5, 1920, CZA, Z4/2800/II.

236. Executive committee, minutes, May 1920, CZA, Z4/302/2.

237. David Eder to Weizmann, June 21, 1920, CZA, Z4/16033.

238. *Sefer toldot hahaganah*, 1:664.

239. Weizmann to Vera Weizmann, *WL*, April 19, 21, 1920, 9:336–37.

240. Richard Meinertzhagen to Lord Curzon, April 14, 1920, Ben Cohen Papers, reel 66/2.

241. David Eder to Weizmann, May 5, 1920, CZA, Z4/16033.

242. Weizmann, *Trial and Error*, pp. 259–60.

243. British Supreme Council, minutes, April 24, 25, 1920, in *Documents on British Foreign Policy, 1919–1939*, ed. Woodward and Butler, ser. 1, 8:159–77.

244. Weizmann to Vera Weizmann, April 26, 1920, *WL*, 9:340–41.

245. Richard Meinertzhagen to Weizmann, May 13, 1920, CZA, Z4/305/5. See also cable informing Edmund Allenby of Herbert Samuel's proposed ap-

pointment, April 29, 1920, and Allenby's objections cabled to David Lloyd George, May 6, 1920, CZA, KH/207/21.

246. David Lloyd George, quoted in Weizmann to Vera Weizmann, April 29, 1920, *WL*, 9:343.
247. Weizmann, address to the Twenty-first Annual Conference of the English Zionist Federation, June 15, 1920, FO, 371/5114/61.
248. David Eder to Weizmann, May 14, 1920, CZA, Z4/16033.
249. Weizmann to David Eder, June 8, 1920, *WL*, 9:355.
250. See Israel State Archives, 100/35.

IX   Between London and New York

1. Halpern, *Clash of Heroes*, p. 205. I follow Halpern's analysis.
2. See Anita Shapira, *Hamaavak hanikhzav: Avodah ivrit, 1929–1939* (Tel Aviv, 1977), pp. 15–42.
3. "Haveidah hazionit," in *Haprotokolim shel havaad hapoel hazioni*, ed. Freundlich and Yogev, 1:21–106.
4. See, e.g., John Maynard Keynes to Lionel Abrahams, November 19, 1918, WA.
5. See, e.g., "Yeshivat havaad hapoel," in *Haprotokolim shel havaad hapoel hazioni*, ed. Freundlich and Yogev, 1:269–71.
6. See, e.g., Weizmann, opening address to the London *Jahreskonferenz*, July 7, 1920, CZA, Z4/924/I.
7. See, e.g., Herbert Samuel to Weizmann, June 20, 1920, CZA, Z4/15445; Samuel to Weizmann, September 5, 1920, WA.
8. Allon Gal, "Hashkafato shel Brandeis al ofen binyan haaretz, 1914–1923," *Hazionut* 6 (1981): 97–145.
9. "Yeshivat havaad hapoel," in *Haprotokolim shel havaad hapoel hazioni*, ed. Freundlich and Yogev, 1:202–40.
10. Felix Frankfurter to Julian Mack, June 29, 1920, DeHaas Papers.
11. Simon, *Certain Days*, p. 106.
12. See Strum, *Louis D. Brandeis*, p. 279.
13. "Yeshivat havaad hapoel," in *Haprotokolim shel havaad hapoel hazioni*, ed. Freundlich and Yogev, 1:140–41, 180–81.
14. "A Stenographic Record of a Telephone Conversation between Dr. Weizmann and Mr. James de Rothschild on December 17, 1920 (Reported by Mr. Leo Herrmann)," CZA, Z4/16001.
15. Weizmann's relations with James de Rothschild were further repaired in 1921. See undated and unsigned confidential report, "Relations of Chayim and Jimmie," probably written in February 1921, WA. The report states *inter alia* that James de Rothschild "is favorably disposed to Chayim and regards him as a man of unusual ability, invaluable to the movement. He would not do anything to disturb Chayim in his control of the Organization, would be willing to cooperate, *socially and politically,* if he is treated as his dignity and position require."
16. Alfred Mond to Herbert Samuel, November 18, 1920, FO 371/6388; Samuel to Mond, November 29, 1920, FO 371/6388.
17. Robert Waley-Cohen to Weizmann, December 20, 1920, CZA, Z4/16001.
18. Louis Brandeis to Bernard Flexner, Julian Mack, and Stephen Wise, June 28, 1920, Ben Cohen Papers.

19. Felix Frankfurter to Julian Mack, June 29, 1920, DeHaas Papers.

20. Tevet, *Kinat David*, 2:80–84.

21. Weizmann, speech to the London *Jahreskonferenz*, July 9, 1920, CZA, Z4/241/17.

22. Jacob DeHaas to Julian Mack, notes, July 9, 1920, DeHaas Papers.

23. Jacob DeHaas to Julian Mack, notes, July 3–9, 1920, DeHaas Papers.

24. Stephen Wise to Richard Gottheil, June 13, 1920, Wise Papers, box 106, Zionism/Correspondence.

25. Louis Brandeis, quoted in Simon, *Certain Days*, pp. 345–47.

26. "Yeshivat havaad hapoel," in *Haprotokolim shel havaad hapoel hazioni*, ed. Freundlich and Yogev, 1:177.

27. Jacob DeHaas to Julian Mack, notes, July 3, 1920, DeHaas Papers.

28. Strum, *Louis D. Brandeis*, p. 280.

29. See, e.g., Felix Frankfurter to Julian Mack, June 29, 1920, DeHaas Papers.

30. Yonathan Shapiro, "Hamahloket beyn Chaim Weizmann lebeyn Louis Brandeis, 1919–1921," *Hazionut* 3 (1973): 267–68, mentions a somewhat different cast of characters involved in the plan.

31. "Memo for Executive Council, Prepared by Lord Reading in Conference with LDB," July 14, 1920, DeHaas Papers.

32. David Rudavsky, "Brandeis baveidah hazionit habeynleumit be-London bishnat 1920," in *Hagut ivrit be-America*, ed. Menaham Zohori, Arie Tartakover, and Haim Ormian (Tel Aviv, 1974), pp. 292–308. Rudavsky also mentions Lord Reading as a candidate for co-optation (p. 300), but I have found no supporting evidence for this assertion.

33. For a detailed description of these events, see Evyatar Friesel, "Leil hamashber beyn Weizmann le-Brandeis," *Hazionut* 4 (1975): 146–64.

34. See, e.g., Felix Frankfurter to Weizmann, July 25, 1920, WA.

35. Felix Frankfurter to Julian Mack, August 12, 1920, DeHaas Papers.

36. Some of Weizmann's closest friends felt hurt by their exclusion from all positions of real power in the new constellation of the organization. See, e.g., the impassioned letters from Israel Sieff to Weizmann, July 26, 29, August 10, 1920, CZA, Z4/16032.

37. "Protocol of the Second Week of the *Jahreskonferenz*," July 19–22, 1920, CZA, Z4/241/19.

38. Ibid.

39. Friesel, *Hamediniyut hazionit leahar hatzharat Balfour*, pp. 155–60.

40. Julius Simon to Robert Szold, September 9, 1920, CZA, Z4/4032.

41. See Simon, *Certain Days*, p. 108.

42. Julius Simon to Weizmann, November 9, 1920, CZA, KH1/163/1.

43. Simon, *Certain Days*, pp. 108–11.

44. Weizmann to Bella Berligne, August 7, 1920, WL, 10:6–7.

45. "Protocol of the *Jahreskonferenz*," July 7, 1920, CZA, Z4/924/I.

46. "Protocol of the *Jahreskonferenz*," July 19–22, 1920, CZA, Z4/241/19.

47. Pinhas Rutenberg to Weizmann, August 5, 1920, WA; Political Committee, minutes, September 23, 1920, CZA, Z4/1281/III.

48. Herbert Samuel to Weizmann, July 21, August 25, 1920, CZA, Z4/15445. See also Harry Sacher to Weizmann, October 25, 1920, CZA, Z4/16151.

49. Ben Cohen to Julian Mack, November 1, 1920, Brandeis Papers, reel 85, 27-2, mentions the date of October 17. However, Weizmann to Herbert Samuel, November 8, 1920, WL, 10:83, states that the first meeting took place

on October 21, 1920. No doubt Weizmann is correct in this instance since he returned to London only on October 19.

50. Ben Cohen to Julian Mack, November 1, 1920, Louis Brandeis Papers, reel 85, 27-2.
51. Weizmann to Alfred Mond, November 21, 1920, *WL*, 10:90–91.
52. Weizmann to executive of Zionist Organization of America, January 6, 1921, *WL*, 10:135–36.
53. Weizmann, appointment book, notes from Holland, 1921, WA. See also Ronald Graham to Lord Curzon, January 3, 1921, FO, 371/6386.
54. Weizmann to Vera Weizmann, January 6, 1921, *WL*, 10:124–25.
55. Weizmann to Vera Weizmann, January 12, 1921, *WL*, 10:140.
56. Weizmann to Vera Weizmann, January 14, 1921, *WL*, 10:141–42.
57. Weizmann to Vera Weizmann, February [10], 1921, *WL*, 10:145.
58. Weizmann to Vera Weizmann, January 25, 1921, *WL*, 10:143.
59. Weizmann to Vera Weizmann, February [10], 1921, *WL*, 10:145.
60. Weizmann to Bella Berligne, February 13, 1921, *WL*, 10:147.
61. *Jewish Chronicle*, November 5, 1920.
62. Julian Mack to Weizmann, October 18, 1920, WA.
63. Henrietta Szold to Jacob DeHaas, September 2, 1920, DeHaas Papers.
64. Friesel, *Hamediniyut hazionit leahar hatzharat Balfour*, pp. 152–55.
65. "Plans of Justice Brandeis for Constructive Work in Palestine" [Zeeland Memorandum], August 24, 1920, WA.
66. Ibid. See also Brandeis, speech to meeting of the national executive committee of the ZOA, New York, August 28–29, 1920, WA.
67. Louis Robison to Weizmann, August 27, 1920, WA.
68. "Plans of Justice Brandeis for Constructive Work in Palestine," August 24, 1920, WA.
69. Louis Robison to Weizmann, August 31, 1920, WA; Robison to Bernard Rosenblatt, September 6, 1920, Brandeis Papers, reel 85, 27-2.
70. Weizmann to Bernard Richards, September 24, 1920, *WL*, 10:44.
71. "Memorandum of a Conversation with Justice Brandeis, at Washington, on October 12, 1920, written by Abba Hillel Silver," Brandeis Papers, reel 85, 27-2.
72. Deborah E. Lipstadt, "The Zionist Career of Louis Lipsky, 1900–1921" (Ph.D. diss., Brandeis University, 1976), pp. 287–88.
73. Jacob DeHaas to Louis Brandeis, October 1, 1920, DeHaas Papers.
74. Louis Robison to Weizmann, October 22, 1920, WA.
75. Abraham Tulin to Weizmann, October 6, 1920, CZA, Z4/16047.
76. Julius Berger to Weizmann, December 15, 1920, CZA, Z4/16001.
77. Abraham Tulin to Weizmann, December 21, 1920, CZA, Z4/16047.
78. Julian Mack to Weizmann, cable, October 18, 1920, WA.
79. Weizmann to Felix Frankfurter, October 27, 1920, *WL*, 10:71.
80. Ben Cohen to Julian Mack, November 5, 1920, Brandeis Papers, reel 85, 27-2; Alfred Mond to Louis Brandeis, November 23, 1920, Ben Cohen Papers, reel 66-2.
81. "Document Related to Buffalo Annual Convention," CZA, Z4/820/I, II. See also Jacob DeHaas to Louis Brandeis, November 28, 1920, WA.
82. Joseph Cowen to Vladimir Jabotinsky and Weizmann, December 4, 8, 1920, WA.
83. Weizmann to Vera Weizmann, January 6, 1921, *WL*, 10:126.

84. Weizmann to executive of Zionist Organization of America, January 6, 1921, *WL*, 10:128–37.

85. Julian Mack to Alexander Sachs, February 10, 1921, DeHaas Papers.

86. Louis Brandeis to Julian Mack, Stephen Wise, Bernard Flexner, Jacob DeHaas, and others, February 15, 1921, Wise Papers, 134, box 106; Mack to Brandeis, February 17, 1921, WA, asking for approval of the draft of his letter to Weizmann.

87. Julian Mack to Weizmann, February 16, 1921, WA. Though dated February 16, 1921, Mack's letter must have been sent later since he first gave it to Brandeis for the latter's approval. Mack to Louis Brandeis, February 17, 1921, WA.

88. Stephen Wise to Louis Brandeis, February 8, 1921, Wise Papers, box 106.

89. Jacob DeHaas to Julian Mack and Alexander Sachs, March 14, 1921, Brandeis Papers, reel 85, 28-1.

90. "Summary of the Position of the Zionist Organization of America in Conference with Dr. Weizmann and Associates, Submitted by the President of the ZOA and Adopted by the National Executive Committee at Its Meeting March 19–20, 1921," CZA, Z4/303/13.

91. "A Statement to the Zionists of America, by Ten members of the National Executive Committee Who Declined To Vote on the Summary . . . ," n.d., WA.

92. Kurt Blumenfeld, *Erlebte Judenfrage: Ein Vierteljahrhundert deutscher Zionismus* (Stuttgart, 1962), pp. 129–30. See also Kurt Blumenfeld to Weizmann, February 20, 1921, WA.

93. See Julian Mack, Bernard Flexner, and Felix Frankfurter to Weizmann, cable, March 19, 1921, WA.

94. See cables from Emanuel Neumann and Julian Mack, March 29, 1921, listed in Leonard Stein, "Negotiations between Dr. Weizmann and the Zionist Organization of America," memorandum, May 28, 1921, CZA, Z4/303/9.

95. See, e.g., Weizmann to Shmarya Levin, March 29, 1921, *WL*, 10:175–76.

96. Weizmann, *Trial and Error*, pp. 266–67.

97. Jacob DeHaas to Louis Brandeis, April 5, 1921, Brandeis Papers, reel 85, 28-1. See also Halpern, *Clash of Heroes*, p. 230.

98. "Summary of Conference between Dr. Weizmann and Judge Mack and Their Associates, April 4th–9th, 1921," CZA, Z4/5170; Leonard Stein, "Negotiations between Dr. Weizmann and the Zionist Organization of America," memorandum, May 28, 1921, CZA, Z4/303/9.

99. "Statement of the Minority Group of the National Executive Committee of the Zionist Organization of America [April 10, 1921]," WA.

100. "Minutes of the National Executive Committee held April 9th and April 10th, 1921, Prepared by Reuben Horchow [secretary of the ZOA executive]," CZA, Z4/303/7.

101. Leonard Stein, memorandum, April 1921, CZA, Z4/305/7.

102. "Reception in Honor of Dr. Weizmann and His Associates, Held at 69th Regiment Armory," April 12, 1921, CZA, Z4/303/1.

103. Bernard Rosenblatt to Weizmann, April 15, 1921, CZA, Z4/303/1. See also Bernard Rosenblatt, *Two Generations of Zionism* (New York, 1967), pp. 95–101.

104. "Why Did Weizmann Break with the Zionist Organization of America," April 19, 1921, WA.

105. Chaim Weizmann, "To the Jews of America," *WL*, 10:177–79.

106. "Statement of Judge J. W. Mack," April 17, 1921, WA. See also Julian Mack, "Dr. Weizmann Breaks Negotiation with Zionist Organization of America," *New Palestine* 1, no. 15 (April 22, 1921).

107. Louis Brandeis to Julian Mack and Jacob DeHaas, April 18, 1921, DeHaas Papers.

108. Jewish Press Abstracts, "Digest of News and Comments in the Yiddish Press of Interest to Zionists," April 19, 1921, WA.

109. Weizmann, *Trial and Error*, pp. 271–72.

110. "Keren Hayesod," May 16, 1921, WA.

111. Weizmann to Vera Weizmann, October 14, 1920, *WL*, 10:63.

112. See, e.g., Alice Seligsberg to Weizmann, April 29, 1921, WA; Nathan Straus to Weizmann, May 16, 1921, CZA, Z4/303/10.

113. Stephen Wise to Louis Brandeis, April 29, 1921, Wise Papers, box 106, folder LDB (1920–1928).

114. Louis Brandeis to Julian Mack, Stephen Wise, Bernard Flexner, Jacob DeHaas, and Felix Frankfurter, April 27, 1921, Wise Papers, box 106, folder LDB.

115. Ben Cohen to Louis Brandeis, May 20, 1921, Louis Brandeis Papers, reel 85, 28-1.

116. "Conference of Businessmen," May 19, 1921, CZA, KH1/N2, p. 234.

117. Jacob DeHaas to Felix Frankfurter, May 5, 1921, DeHaas Papers.

118. Weizmann to Alfred Mond, May 18, 1921, *WL*, 10:194.

119. Esther Panitz, "Louis Dembitz Brandeis and the Cleveland Conference," *American Jewish Historical Quarterly* 65, no. 2 (December 1975): 140–62.

120. The proceedings are conveniently gathered in one volume, *Report of the Proceedings of the 24th Annual Convention of the Zionist Organization of America: Held in Cleveland, June 5, 6, 7, 8, 1921* (New York, 1921).

121. Emanuel Neumann, *In the Arena* (New York, 1976), p. 63.

122. *Report of the Proceedings*, pp. 120–22.

123. Louis Brandeis to executive of the World Zionist Organization, June 19, 1921, WA.

124. Louis Lipsky to Louis Brandeis, June 30, 1921, WA.

125. "Verwendung der Keren Hajessod Gelder," CZA, KH4/313/I.

126. Leon Goldman to Weizmann, June 23, 1921, WA.

127. Weizmann, speech to Twelfth Zionist Congress, *Stenographisches Protokoll der Verhandlungen des XII. Zionisten-Kongresses in Karlsbad vom 1. bis 14. September 1921* (Berlin, 1922), p. 283.

128. Stephen Wise to Mary Fels, June 14, 1921, Wise Papers, box 108, folder Mary Fels.

129. Herbert Samuel to Weizmann, July 4, 1920, CZA, Z4/15445.

130. Herbert Samuel to Lord Curzon, July 12, 1920, FO, 406/44.

131. See, e.g., Weizmann to Bella Berligne, August 7, 1920, *WL*, 10:7.

132. To cite one example, "Jewish Immigration into Palestine," marked "strictly confidential," November 22, 1921, WA. In this official Zionist memorandum the Zionist Commission is quoted as having stated that between November 1921 and May 1922, "the number of immigrants who can be received" is six thousand. See also Martin Rosenblueth to Julius Simon, September 16, 1920, CZA, Z4/398.

133. Zionist Commission Press Bureau, "Brief Record of the Zionist Commis-

sion," December 7, 1920, FO, 371/6391. See also Zionist Organization, Jerusalem Office *Bulletin*, June 14–18, 1922, WA.

134. Weizmann to Bernard Rosenblatt, November 26, 1920, *WL*, 10:97; Weizmann to Herbert Samuel, November 30, 1920, *WL*, 10:102.

135. Herbert Samuel to Weizmann, September 5, 1920, CZA, Z4/15445, WA. See also SAC, minutes, March 4, 1921, CZA, Z4/20561.

136. See, e.g., Herbert Samuel to Ronald Storrs, May 30, 1920; Samuel to Weizmann, June 6, 1920, WA; Samuel to Weizmann, July 1, 1920, CZA, Z4/16035.

137. See, e.g., Louis Marshall to Weizmann, June 9, 1921, CZA, Z4/16055.

138. Herbert Samuel to Lord Curzon, quoted in Bernard Wasserstein, *Herbert Samuel: A Political Life* (Oxford, 1992), p. 250.

139. Aaron S. Klieman, *Foundations of British Policy in the Arab World: The Cairo Conference of 1921* (Baltimore, 1970), pp. 71–72.

140. John Bowle, *Viscount Samuel: A Biography* (London, 1957), p. 207.

141. "Extracts from Report on Middle East Conference Held in Cairo and Jerusalem on March 12–30, 1921," WA.

142. See Hebrew translation of Abdullah to Winston Churchill, March 28–29, 1921, WA. See also Abdullah, King of Jordan, *Memoirs of King Abdullah of Trans-Jordan*, ed. Philip P. Graves, trans. G. Khuri (New York, 1950).

143. *Times* (London), August 25, 1921. There are indications, though, that David Eder was aware in early August of some of the events surrounding Transjordan. Eder to Weizmann, August 9, 1921, CZA, Z4/16031. See also Herbert Samuel to Weizmann, August 25, 1920, CZA, Z4/15445.

144. Weizmann to Nahum Sokolow, August 27, 1920, *WL*, 10:37.

145. Weizmann to Winston Churchill, March 1, 1921, *WL*, 10:159–62.

146. Alsberg, "Delimitation of the Eastern Border of Palestine," pp. 94–97.

147. Winston Churchill, quoted in Klieman, *Foundations of British Policy*, pp. 177–79.

148. Harry Sacher to Weizmann, October 25, 1920, CZA, Z4/16151.

149. Porat, *Zmihat hatnuah haleumit haaravit-hapalestinait*, pp. 88–89.

150. Weizmann, opening address to the London *Jahreskonferenz*, July 7, 1920, CZA, Z4/924/I.

151. Untitled document, marked "strictly confidential," sent to Weizmann on May 6, 1921, WA; Political Department of the WZO, "The Jaffa Events," [June 1, 1921], WA; Shmuel Tolkowsky to Herbert Samuel, May 14, 1921, WA.

152. "Report of the Political Department of the Zionist Organization," June 1, 1921, Ben Cohen Papers, reel 66-2.

153. Herbert Samuel, charge to the commission, May 7, 1921, Cmd. 1540, WA.

154. Weizmann to Herbert Samuel, [May] 1921, WA; Weizmann to London Zionist executive, May 13, 1921, *WL*, 10:190.

155. The speech was clearly interpreted in such a manner by some of the high-ranking officers in Palestine. See documentation to this effect in CZA, KH/207/17. See also Evyatar Friesel, "Herbert Samuel's Reassessment of Zionism in 1921," *Studies in Zionism* 5, no. 2 (Autumn 1984): 213–37.

156. "Statement of the High Commissioner for Palestine," June 3, 1921, CZA, Z4/16055.

157. Weizmann to Herbert Samuel, cable, June 12, 1921, *WL*, 10:202–3.

158. Weizmann to Vera Weizmann, March 21, 1920, WL, 9:324.
159. Herbert Samuel to Weizmann, July 1, 1921, WA.
160. Porat, *Zmihat hatnuah haleumit haaravit-hapalestinait*, pp. 111–13.
161. Weizmann to Herbert Samuel, July 19, 1921, WL, 10:218–22.
162. Herbert Samuel to Weizmann, August 10, 1921, WA.
163. Arthur Balfour to David Lloyd George, October 13, 1920, WA.
164. See, e.g., Arthur Balfour to Eric Forbes Adam, September 29, 1920, FO, 371/5245, concerning the matter of frontiers.
165. Weizmann to Arthur Balfour, July 8, 1921, WL, 10:213.
166. "Mr. Churchill's Statement," June 14, 1921, CZA, Z4/16055: "We cannot, after what we have said and done, leave the Jews in Palestine to be mal-treated by the Arabs who have been inflamed against them."
167. [Weizmann?], "Notes of Conversation at Mr. Balfour's on 22/7/21," CZA, Z4/16055.
168. Weizmann to Vera Weizmann, August 4, 1921, WL, 10:243.
169. For an analysis of this new attitude and Winston Churchill's views in par-ticular, see Friesel, *Hamediniyut hazionit leahar hatzharat Balfour*, pp. 270–76.
170. See letter from secretary of the Palestine Arab delegation, Jamal Shibli, to a supporter in the United States, F. J. Shatara, August 24, 1921, WA; "Zionist Aggression in Palestine: Its Objects and Achievements—Speech by Lord Sydenham at a Luncheon given by the Palestine Arab Delegation," Novem-ber 15, 1921, WA.
171. Unsigned memorandum, July 22, 1921, WA.
172. Weizmann to Vera Weizmann, August 14, 1921, WL, 10:251.
173. "A Manifesto from the Arab Delegation," July 29, 1921, WA; Musa Kazem Pasha al-Husseini and Jamal Shibli, "The Future of Palestine," *Times* (Lon-don), December 19, 1929; Porat, *Zmihat hatnuah haleumit haaravit-hapalesti-nait*, pp. 114–16. See also Jamal Shibli, "The Conflict in Palestine," *Eastern Europe* 6, no. 4 (December 1921): 182–96.
174. Weizmann to Musa Kazem Pasha al-Husseini, August 17, 1921, WL, 10:252.
175. Klieman, *Foundations of British Policy*, p. 194.
176. Herbert Samuel to Winston Churchill, October 14, 1921, Colonial Office Papers, Public Record Office, London (hereafter CO), 733/6/632.
177. John Shuckburgh to Winston Churchill, November 7, 1921, CO, 733/15/268.
178. Weizmann to John Shuckburgh, November 2, 1921, WL, 10:280.
179. Richard Lichtheim to Nahum Sokolow, November 30, 1921, CZA, A18/53/2.
180. There seem to have been no official minutes taken at the meeting. There are, however, a number of records written after the fact. See Zionist exec-utive, minutes, November 30, 1921, WA; Weizmann to Colonial Office, De-cember 1, 1921, WL, 10:304–5; John Shuckburgh and Eric Mills, notes, No-vember 29, 30, 1921, CO, 537/855; Klieman, *Foundations of British Policy*, pp. 195–97.
181. *Stenographisches Protokoll*, p. 769.
182. "Memorandum of the Meeting in Balfour's House on July 22, 1921," WA; Weizmann to Wyndham Deedes, July 31, 1921, WL, 10:236.
183. Weizmann to Peter Schweitzer and others, September 8, 1921, WL, 10:255; Weizmann to Zionist Organization of America, October 21, 1921, WL, 10:262.
184. Weizmann to Joseph Cowen, September 24, 1921, WL, 10:256.
185. *Stenographisches Protokoll*, pp. 13–17.

186. "Statement to the Delegates of the Twelfth Zionist Congress on Behalf of the Former Administration of the Zionist Organization of America," July 15, 1921, signed by Julian Mack, Stephen Wise, Harry Friedenwald, Nathan Straus, Felix Frankfurter, Mary Fels, Jacob DeHaas, and Robert Szold, WA.
187. *Stenographisches Protokoll*, p. 328.
188. Ibid., pp. 760–61.
189. Berl Katznelson, *Igrot, 1919–1922*, ed. Yehuda Erez and Abraham Moshe Koller (Tel Aviv, 1970), pp. 119, 306–10.
190. Weizmann to Nathan Ratnoff, October 18, 1921, *WL*, 10:258–60.
191. Weizmann to Andor Fodor, October 24, 1921, *WL*, 10:266–67.
192. Weizmann to Andor Fodor, October 29, 1921, *WL*, 10:272.
193. "The Jerusalem University Project," *Palestine* 10, no. 10 (December 31, 1921): 69–71. See also "The Jerusalem University Library," *Palestine* 10, no. 9 (December 24, 1921): 64–66.
194. Weizmann to David Eder, November 27, 1921, *WL*, 10:296; Weizmann to Gaston Wormser, November 28, 1921, *WL*, 10:299; Weizmann to Wormser, December 5, 1921, *WL*, 10:308–9.
195. Weizmann to Nathan Ratnoff, October 18, 1921, *WL*, 10:259.
196. Weizmann to Abraham Tulin, August 22–31, 1920, *WL*, 10:27–29.
197. Weizmann to Wyndham Deedes, November 12, 1921, *WL*, 10:283.

X Lobbying for the Mandate

1. Weizmann to Wyndham Deedes, February 4, 1922, *WL*, 11:27–28.
2. *Jewish Chronicle*, February 17, 1922.
3. See, e.g., Weizmann to Isaac Naiditch, February 10, 1922, *WL*, 11:37–38.
4. For the division of labor among members of the executive in London prior to the Cleveland Annual Convention, see Zionist executive, minutes, March 2, 1921, CZA, Z4/20561.
5. See, e.g., Weizmann to Emanuel Neumann, January 26, 1922, *WL*, 11:16.
6. George L. Berlin, "The Brandeis-Weizmann Dispute," *American Jewish Historical Quarterly* 60, no. 1 (September 1970): 37–68.
7. See, e.g., David Eder to Leonard Stein, June 23, 1922, WA.
8. For the economic condition of the Jewish colonies, see Wyndham Deedes to Weizmann, March 30, 1922, CZA, Z4/16080.
9. Weizmann to Emanuel Neumann, January 26, 1922, *WL*, 11:17–18.
10. Zionist executive, minutes, January 29, 1922, CZA, Z4/3749.
11. See, e.g., "Note of interview between Dr. Weizmann and Sir J. Shuckburgh, Colonial Office," marked "secret," January 10, 1922, CZA, Z4/16145.
12. See, e.g., Vladimir Jabotinsky to Zionist executive, February 13, 1922, CZA, Z4/16145.
13. I owe much of the information concerning the state of the Zionist executive in London during this period to the discussion in Friesel, *Hamediniyut hazionit leahar hatzharat Balfour*, pp. 280–85.
14. Richard Lichtheim to Weizmann, May 28, 1922, CZA, Z4/16145.
15. See the critique of the WZO executive, signed by the leaders of the group and some two dozen others, *L'Echo Sioniste*, December 23, 1921.
16. *Weakness in the Zionist Organization*, dated January 19, 1922, copy in WA.
17. See, e.g., Zionist executive, minutes, February 9, 1922, CZA, Z4/3749.
18. Weizmann to Jacobus Kann, February 5, 1922, *WL*, 11:30–32.

19. See, e.g., Ben Cohen to Julius Simon, November 3, 1920, Ben Cohen Papers, reel 66-2. Concerning Weizmann's strong support for Rutenberg's project, see Eli Shaltiel, *Pinhas Rutenberg* (Tel Aviv, 1990), 1:43–45.

20. See Pinhas Rutenberg to Weizmann, November 8, 1920, CZA, Z4/1610, urging him to intercede with the British government.

21. Shaltiel, *Pinhas Rutenberg,* pp. 93–127.

22. Pinhas Rutenberg to Weizmann, January 15, 1922, WA.

23. Weizmann to Isaac Naiditch, February 10, 1922, WL, 11:37–38.

24. Weizmann to Nahum Sokolow, May 24, 1922, WL, 11:101.

25. See Zionist executive, minutes, February 7, 9, 1922, CZA, Z4/3749. See also Zionist executive, minutes, May 18, [1922], WA.

26. Weizmann to Nahum Sokolow and Vladimir Jabotinsky, February 22, 1922, WL, 11:60.

27. Concerning the circumstances surrounding Northcliffe's visit, see Leonard Stein to Frederick H. Kisch, March 7, 1922, CZA, Z4/16082.

28. Weizmann to Ittamar Ben-Avi, January 24, 1922, WL, 11:14.

29. *Times* (London), February 8, 1922.

30. Harry Sacher to Weizmann, February 18, 1922, WA.

31. Weizmann, *Trial and Error,* pp. 282–83.

32. Reginald Pound and Geoffrey Harmsworth, *Northcliffe* (New York, 1960), p. 846.

33. Weizmann to Nahum Sokolow and Vladimir Jabotinsky, February 28, 1922, WL, 11:61; Weizmann, *Trial and Error,* pp. 282–83.

34. See, e.g., *Jewish Chronicle,* March 10, 1922.

35. Palestine Arab delegation, memorandum, February 4, 1922, CO, 733/36/7.

36. "Report of Conversation between Leonard Stein and William Ormsby-Gore," March 7, 1922, WA.

37. "Conversations between D. K. and A. Sh. at the Hotel Cecil—on January 5, 1922," marked "strictly confidential," Ben-Gurion Archives.

38. See headnote to letter 75, WL, 11:75.

39. "Note on Conference at Cairo, March 18th, 19th, 1922, received from Dr. Eder," marked "secret," WA.

40. David Eder to Weizmann, March 19, 1922, CZA, Z4/16056.

41. Weizmann to David Eder, March 21, 30, 1922, WL, 11:75.

42. Palestine Zionist executive, minutes, March 26, 1922, WA.

43. "Note on Conference at Cairo, March 18th, 19th, 1922, Received from Dr. Eder," marked "secret," WA.

44. Palestine Zionist executive, minutes, March 26, 1922, WA.

45. David Eder to Weizmann, March 21, 1922, CZA, Z4/16056. See also copy of a confidential memorandum (in French), April 2, 1922, WA; David Eder to Leonard Stein, April 9, 1922, WA.

46. John Shuckburgh to Leonard Stein, April 11, 1922, CZA, Z4/16056; Shuckburgh to Weizmann, April 18, 1922, CZA, Z4/16056. See also Stein to David Eder, April 12, 1922, WA.

47. Nahum Sokolow to Zionist executive, May 2, 1922, WA.

48. Leonard Stein to Nahum Sokolow, May 17, 1922, WA.

49. David Eder to Weizmann, June 21, July 23, 1922, WA.

50. Ascher Saphir, *Unity or Partition!* (Jerusalem, 1937), pp. 25–34.

51. Neil Caplan, *Palestine Jewry and the Arab Question, 1917–1925* (London, 1978),

p. 100. See also Neil Caplan, "Britain, Zionism and the Arabs, 1917–1925," *Wiener Library Bulletin* 31, nos. 45–46 (1978): 10–11.

52. David Eder to Weizmann, March 12, 1922, WA.

53. David Eder to Weizmann, marked "secret-personal," July 17, 1922, WA. There is indication that Sir Herbert Samuel was aware of at least some of the activities that involved the Zionists in payments to Arabs.

54. Caplan, *Palestine Jewry and the Arab Question*, pp. 128–32.

55. "Meeting of the Arabs at the House of Dr. Eder," April 3, 1922, CZA, Z4/16056.

56. *Sefer toldot hahaganah*, 2:128–47. See also Weizmann to Shmuel Tolkowsky, February [13], 1922, *WL*, 11:38–40.

57. Weizmann to Chaim Kalvarisky, October [4], 1922, *WL*, 11:174.

58. *The Political History of Palestine under British Administration*, Memorandum by His Britannic Majesty's Government Presented in July 1947, to the United Nations Special Committee on Palestine (Jerusalem, 1947), p. 1.

59. For an analysis of the political process that led to the Mandate for Palestine, see Ben Halpern, *The Idea of the Jewish State*, 2d ed. (Cambridge, Mass., 1969), pp. 288–343.

60. "Table of Drafts of the Palestine Mandate," *WL*, 10:xxviii–xxix.

61. Leonard Stein, "The Palestine Mandate, marked "for private circulation only," October 21, 1920, CZA, Z4/16011.

62. Weizmann to Lord Curzon, October 30, 1920, *WL*, 10:77.

63. Lord Curzon, quoted in *WL*, 10:77, n. 4.

64. Arthur Balfour to cabinet, November 5, 1920, WA; Balfour to Maurice Hankey, November 20, 1920, WA.

65. "Table of Drafts."

66. Weizmann to Lord Milner, November 23, 1920, *WL*, 10:92. Similar letters were written to Philip Kerr, Winston Churchill, and others.

67. "Table of Drafts."

68. Ibid.

69. Weizmann to Herbert Samuel, December 13, 1921, *WL*, 10:334.

70. Herbert Samuel to Weizmann, January 20, 1922, WA.

71. Weizmann to Nahum Sokolow, December 19, 1921, *WL*, 10:338.

72. *Jüdische Rundschau*, no. 23 (December 30, 1921).

73. Jehuda Reinharz, "Chaim Weizmann and German Jewry," *Leo Baeck Institute Year Book* 35 (1990): 189–218. See also Hagit Lavsky, *Beterem puranut: Darkam veyihudam shel zionei germanyah, 1918–1932* (Jerusalem, 1990).

74. Friesel, *Hamediniyut hazionit leahar hatzharat Balfour*, pp. 299–306.

75. John Shuckburgh to the secretary, Zionist Organization, December 17, 1921, WA.

76. "Note of Interview between Dr. Weizmann and Sir J. Shuckburgh, Colonial Office," marked "secret," January 10, 1922, CZA, Z4/16145.

77. Makover, *Shilton uminhal be-Eretz Israel*, pp. 93–94.

78. See, e.g., "Note of Private Conversation with a Member of the Arab Delegation," marked "secret," January 16, 1922, WA.

79. John Shuckburgh to Weizmann, January 16, 1922, WA.

80. John de Vere Loder Wakehurst, *The Truth about Mesopotamia, Palestine and Syria* (London, 1923), pp. 179–83.

81. Weizmann to James de Rothschild, February 5, 1922, *WL*, 11:33.

82. Vladimir Jabotinsky to Zionist executive, March 16, 1922, CZA, Z4/16102.

83. John Shuckburgh to Weizmann, March 1, 1922, WA.

84. Colonial Office to the Palestine Arab delegation, March 1, 1922, Ben-Gurion Archives.

85. See, e.g., John Shuckburgh to Weizmann, marked "personal," March 1, 1922, WA.

86. William Ormsby-Gore, quoted in Leonard Stein, "Note of Interview with Major, The Hon. W. Ormsby-Gore, M.P. House of Commons," March 7, 1922, WA.

87. Ibid.

88. Alfred Moritz Mond, Lord Melchett, and Chaim Weizmann, *The Jewish National Home and Its Critics: The Oxford Speeches by Sir Alfred Melchett and Chaim Weizmann,* issued by the Zionist Organization (London, 1922).

89. Pound and Harmsworth, *Northcliffe.*

90. Meinertzhagen, *Middle East Diary,* p. 116.

91. See, e.g., C. P. Scott, diary, March 2, 1922, Guardian Archives, recording a conversation with David Lloyd George concerning the Mandate for Palestine. He also arranged for a meeting between the prime minister and Weizmann.

92. See, e.g., "Memorandum on the Arab Population of Palestine, Submitted by the Zionist Organization to the Advisory Committee on International Questions of the Labour Party," August 24, 1920, CZA, Z4/1214A.

93. "Mr. Ramsay MacDonald and the New Palestine," in Speakers' Notes, new ser. 11, May 26, 1922, WA.

94. "Note of Interview with International Affairs Committee of the Labour Party," February 1, 1922, WA.

95. Weizmann to John Shuckburgh, February 2, 1922, *WL,* 11:22–23.

96. Winston Churchill to the archbishop of Canterbury, February 17, 1922, WA; archbishop of Canterbury to Churchill, February 18, 1922, WA.

97. See the correspondence in *The Selected Letters of T. E. Lawrence,* ed. David Garnett (London, 1952), pp. 342–44.

98. See, e.g., Weizmann to the editor, *Westminster Gazette,* February 3, 1922, *WL,* 11:25–26; Weizmann to the editor, *Times* (London), February 17, 1922, *WL,* 11:42–43.

99. Vladimir Jabotinsky to Weizmann, February 25, 1922, WA; Louis Lipsky to Weizmann, March 6, 1922, WA.

100. *WL,* 11:xiii.

101. Weizmann, speech, *Jewish National Home,* p. 9.

102. Ibid., pp. 10–11.

103. In a letter to the editor of the *Times* (London), February 27, 1922, WA (not sent), Weizmann cited British sources which concluded that the cost of the British garrison in Palestine in 1922–23 would not exceed £2 million.

104. Weizmann, speech, *Jewish National Home,* pp. 10–12.

105. Ibid., p. 11.

106. This was also the assessment of William Ormsby-Gore. Leonard Stein, "Note of Interview with Major . . . Ormsby Gore M.P.," March 7, 1922, WA.

107. Porat, *Zmihat hatnuah haleumit haaravit-hapalestinait,* pp. 113–14.

108. Zionist executive, minutes, January 29, 1922, CZA, Z4/3749.

109. See, e.g., John de Salis to Weizmann, March 30, 1922, WA.

110. Weizmann, appointment book, April 1, 1922, WA.
111. Weizmann, *Trial and Error*, p. 286; Weizmann to Zionist executive, April 10, 1922, *WL*, 11:80–83.
112. Weizmann to Zionist executive, April 10, 1922, *WL*, 11:82–83.
113. Weizmann, *Trial and Error*, p. 285.
114. *Times* (London), April 4, 1922.
115. A year earlier, Weizmann reported to the Zionist executive that Professor William Rappard, the director of the Mandates Section of the League of Nations Secretariat from 1920 to 1925, had also objected to the Mandate for Palestine on the ground that it conflicted with Paragraph 22 of the Covenant of the League of Nations in that "it gave undue privileges to the Zionist Organization." Arthur Balfour, with whom Weizmann discussed this issue, seemed troubled by these objections, though the legal advisers to the Foreign Office did not. Zionist executive, minutes, March 21, 1921, WA.
116. "Draft Mandates for Mesopotamia and Palestine: As Submitted for the Approval of the League of Nations," [December 7, 1920] (London, 1921), p. 7, copy in WA.
117. Carnegie to Foreign Office, April 6, 1922, FO, 371/7773.
118. Weizmann to [Joseph Cowen], April 3, 1922, *WL*, 11:76–77.
119. Cardinal Pietro Gasparri to John de Salis, April 6, 1922, CO, 16829/733/30.
120. For the papal protest to the League of Nations, see *Morning Post*, June 11, 1922. See also Leonard Stein to Nahum Sokolow, June 13, 1922, WA.
121. Weizmann to Richard Lichtheim, April 4, 1922, *WL*, 11:78.
122. "Interview between Dr. Weizmann and Cardinal Gasparri, April 27, 1922," *JCB Bulletin*, copy in WA.
123. Weizmann, *Trial and Error*, p. 286.
124. Minerbi, *Havatikan*, p. 204.
125. Ibid., pp. 204–7.
126. Weizmann to Zionist executive, April 10, 1922, *WL*, 11:82.
127. *Times* (London), May 13, 1922.
128. Minerbi, *Havatikan*, p. 211. As noted, two days after Monsignor Louis Barlassina's tirade was published, the Vatican sent a formal letter to the League of Nations raising objections similar to those it had brought up with the British Foreign Office on April 6.
129. See, e.g., Leonard Stein to John Shuckburgh, June 12, 1922, WA.
130. See correspondence between Elihu Stone and Henry Cabot Lodge, February–March 1922, Elihu Stone Papers, 1914–1952, American Jewish Historical Archives, box 6 Senator Henry Cabot Lodge. See also the protest of the Palestine Publicity Committee of the Palestine National League against the Lodge Resolution, published in *Near East*, June 1, 1922, copy in WA.
131. Weizmann to Nahum Sokolow, May 5, 1922, *WL*, 11:91.
132. Weizmann to Vera Weizmann, May 11, 1922, *WL*, 11:92.
133. Weizmann to Vera Weizmann, May 13, 1922, *WL*, 11:93.
134. Arthur Balfour to secretary of the cabinet, May 13, 1922, CO, 733/30/435.
135. Weizmann to Vera Weizmann, May 16, 1922, *WL*, 11:93–94.
136. Harold M. Simansky, "The Churchill Memorandum as a Product of Herbert Samuel's Zionism," typescript, Brandeis University, Waltham, Mass.
137. Evyatar Friesel, "British Policy in Palestine: The 'Churchill Memorandum' of 1922," in *Vision and Conflict in the Holy Land*, ed. Richard I. Cohen (New York, 1985), p. 209.

138. Michael J. Cohen, *Churchill and the Jews* (London, 1985), pp. 142–43.
139. Weizmann to Herbert Samuel, May 5, 1922, *WL*, 11:90.
140. Zionist executive, minutes, June 1, 1922, CZA, Z4/3749.
141. John Shuckburgh to Zionist Organization, June 3, 1922, WA.
142. "Palestine: Correspondence with the Palestine Arab Delegation and the Zionist Organization," June 1922, Cmd. 1700, WA.
143. John Shuckburgh, internal memorandum, quoted in Friesel, "British Policy in Palestine," p. 210.
144. "Palestine: Correspondence with the Palestine Arab Delegation and the Zionist Organization," June 1922, Cmd. 1700, WA.
145. Weizmann to Alfred Mond, June 4, 1922, *WL*, 11:109.
146. John Shuckburgh, quoted in Friesel, "British Policy in Palestine," p. 212.
147. For a general assessment of the Churchill Memorandum and the White Paper, see Evyatar Friesel, *The Balfour Declaration in Historical Perspective*, Kaplan Centre Papers (Rondebosch, South Africa, 1989), pp. 5–18.
148. Weizmann to Wyndham Deedes, June 29, 1922, *WL*, 11:126.
149. Zionist executive, minutes, June 9, 18, 1922, CZA, KH1/306.
150. On the circumstances under which Vladimir Jabotinsky was informed of the White Paper and his later attempt to distance himself from it, see Chaim Orlan, "Hatzharat Balfour, ever hayarden, 'hasefer halavan,' Weizmann, Jabotinsky," *Hadoar* 47 (April 5, 1968): 99–100.
151. Weizmann, *Trial and Error*, p. 291.
152. Weizmann to the under secretary of state, Colonial Office, June 18, 1922, *WL*, 11:117–18.
153. Secretary of state for the colonies to the high commissioner for Palestine, cabie, June 29, 1922, copy in WA.
154. Quoted in headnote to letter 126, *WL*, 11:121, with slight correction.
155. Martin Gilbert, *Winston S. Churchill: The Stricken World*, vol. 4, *1916–1922* (Boston, 1975), pp. 649–50.
156. Weizmann to Alfred Mond, June 26, 1922, *WL*, 11:122.
157. David Eder to secretary, Zionist executive, June 27, 1922, WA. See also Meinertzhagen, *Middle East Diary*, p. 118.
158. Herbert Parzen, "The Lodge-Fish Resolution," *American Jewish Historical Quarterly* 60, nos. 1–4 (September 1970–June 1971): 71–81.
159. On the mood of uncertainty in government circles and Weizmann's own fears concerning the impact of the vote in the House of Lords and the impending vote in the House of Commons, see Stephen Wise to Julian Mack, June 26, 1922, Wise Papers, box 114, folder Julian Mack (1917–1923). See also "Memorandum of Meeting of S[tephen] S. W[ise] with Mr. Forbes Adams," June 26, 1922, Wise Papers, box 104, folder Arthur Balfour (1918–1930).
160. Gilbert, *Winston Churchill*, 4:650–59.
161. Winston Churchill to Wyndham Deedes, cable, July 5, 1922, quoted in ibid., pp. 659–60.
162. Weizmann to Albert Einstein, June 2, 1922, *WL*, 11:104.
163. Weizmann to the Weizmann family, July 8, 1922, *WL*, 11:138.
164. Lionel de Rothschild to Weizmann, July 16, 1922, WA.
165. See, e.g., Weizmann to the president of Chile, June 13, 1922, *WL*, 11:116.
166. Weizmann to John Shuckburgh, June 18, 1922, *WL*, 11:119.
167. Weizmann to Leonard Stein, March 20, 1922, *WL*, 11:73.

168. Weizmann, *Trial and Error*, p. 292.
169. Minerbi, *Havatikan*, pp. 225–31. See also Weizmann to Moshe Beilinson, July 11, 1922, *WL*, 11:140.
170. Jacob Stoyanovsky, *The Mandate for Palestine: A Contribution to the Theory and Practice of International Mandates* (London, 1928), pp. 30–33.
171. "Palestine: The Palestine Order in Council," August 10, 1922, WA.
172. Porat, *Zmihat hatnuah haleumit haaravit-hapalestinait*, pp. 120–28.
173. See, e.g., Weizmann, speech to GAC, Carlsbad, August 25, 1922, in *Letters and Papers of Chaim Weizmann*, vol. 1, ser. B, ed. Litvinoff, p. 356.
174. Leonard Stein, "The Mandate," memorandum, [December 1922], WA.
175. Weizmann to C. P. Scott, November 12, 1914, *WL*, 8:38.
176. See Weizmann, speech to the the Annual Conference of the English Zionist Federation, July 23, 1922, *Jüdische Rundschau*, no. 60 (August 1, 1922).
177. "The Ratification of the Mandate: A Call to the Jewish People," WA. See also Weizmann, speech to the Annual Conference of the EZF, July 23, 1922, *Jüdische Rundschau*, no. 60 (August 1, 1922); Weizmann, opening speech to GAC, Carlsbad, August 25, 1922, *Jüdische Rundschau* (August 29, 1922).
178. See, e.g., David Eder to Weizmann, July 23, 1922, WA; Abraham Tulin to Weizmann, July 28, 1922, CZA, Z4/16131.
179. Vladimir Jabotinsky to Weizmann, August 1922, quoted in Vera Weizmann, *Impossible Takes Longer*, p. 104.
180. Weizmann, speech to GAC, Carlsbad, August 25, 1922, in *Letters and Papers of Chaim Weizmann*, vol. 1, ser. B, ed. Litvinoff, pp. 357–59.
181. Herbert Samuel to Weizmann, July 31, 1922, CZA, Z4/15445.
182. Weizmann to Miriam Lubzhinsky, July 22, 1922, *WL*, 11:157.

XI Conclusion

1. C. P. Scott to Weizmann, September 12, 1917, WA.
2. Reinharz, *Chaim Weizmann: The Making of a Zionist Leader*. The conclusion to this book highlights some of these traits.
3. Leon Simon to Weizmann, May 1, 1915, WA.
4. Webster, *Founder of the National Home*, pp. 18–19.
5. Richard Crossman, "Diplomatic Tour De Force," *Jerusalem Post*, Balfour Declaration Jubilee, November 2, 1967, p. 5.
6. See, e.g., Max Nordau, "Zavaato hazionit shel Max Nordau: Hamilhamah haolamit vehazionut," *Doar Hayom*, February 11, 1930, p. 2.
7. Richard Lichtheim, "Haemunah shepiamah be-Weizmann," *Haaretz*, November 2, 1962; "Hakesem haishi shel Chaim Weizmann," editorial, *Haaretz*, November 11, 1982. See also Robert Weltsch, "Bsorat Chaim Weizmann," *Haaretz*, August 29, 1976.
8. Meinertzhagen, *Middle East Diary*, pp. 66–67.
9. Storrs, *Orientations*, pp. 415–16.
10. David Bergmann, quoting Goethe, described Weizmann's relationship with England as *Wahlverwandtschaft*. See Bergmann's obituary notice about Weizmann in *Journal of the Chemical Society*, August 1953, p. 2840.
11. Ahad Ha'Am to Weizmann, August 15, 1918, WA.
12. Ahad Ha'Am to Weizmann, September 5, 1917, *Igrot Ahad Ha'Am*, 5:316.
13. Isaiah Berlin, *Chaim Weizmann*, Herzl Institute Pamphlet 8 (New York, 1958), p. 59.

14. Abba Eban, *Chaim Weizmann: A Continuing Legacy* (London, 1962), p. 8.

15. Abba Eban, "Chaim Weizmann: The Leader and Today's Vacuum," *Jerusalem Post*, November 3, 1989, p. 6.

16. Richard H. Crossman, *A Nation Reborn: The Israel of Weizmann, Begin and Ben-Gurion* (London, 1960), p. 45.

17. Lord Curzon, speech in the House of Lords, June 29, 1920, WA.

18. Felix Frankfurter to Louis Brandeis, March 3, 1919, Brandeis Papers, reel 85, 63.

19. Leonard Stein, *Weizmann and England* (London, 1964), p. 15.

20. Isaiah Berlin has aptly called Weizmann "an irresistible political seducer." *Chaim Weizmann*, p. 43. He added, though, that Weizmann "did not offer himself except to those whom he truly admired."

21. Tolkowsky, *Yoman zioni medini*, pp. 193–94.

22. Kurt Lewin, "The Problem of Minority Leadership," in *Studies in Leadership: Leadership and Democratic Action*, ed. Alvin Ward Gouldner (New York, 1950), p. 193.

23. Ben Halpern, "Generational Models and Zionist History," *Tmurot bahistoryah hayehudit hahadashah*, ed. Shmuel Almog, Israel Bartal, et al. (Jerusalem, 1987), p. cii.

24. Israel Kolatt, "Chaim Weizmann's Rise to Leadership," in Isaiah Berlin and Israel Kolatt, *Chaim Weizmann as Leader* (Jerusalem, 1970), p. 22.

25. See also Kurt Blumenfeld to Pinchas Rosen, January 31, 1949, in Kurt Blumenfeld, *Im Kampf um den Zionismus: Briefe aus fünf Jahrzehnten*, ed. Miriam Sambursky and Jochanan Ginat (Stuttgart, 1976), p. 229.

26. Kedourie, *Chatham House Version*, p. 70.

27. Vera Weizmann, diary, March 20, 1916, WA.

Bibliography

Archives and Libraries

Ahad Ha'Am Archive, Jerusalem
American Jewish Historical Archives, Waltham, Mass.
    Benjamin Rabalsky Papers
    Dewey Stone Collection
    Elihu Stone Papers
    Stephen Wise Papers
Archives of the French Ministry for Foreign Affairs, Paris
Ben-Gurion Archives, Sde Boker, Israel
Board of Deputies of British Jews Archives, London (BD)
Boston University, Mugar Memorial Library, Boston, Mass.
    William Yale Papers
Brandeis University Archives and Library, Waltham, Mass.
    Louis Brandeis Archive
    Ben Cohen Papers
British Library, London
    C. P. Scott Papers
Martin Buber Archive, Jerusalem
Central Archives for the History of the Jewish People, Jerusalem
Central Zionist Archives, Jerusalem (CZA)
Durham University, School of Oriental Studies, Durham
    Gilbert Clayton Papers
    Reginald Wingate Papers
Ehrenpreis Archive, Jerusalem
Gnazim Archive, Tel Aviv
    Rahel Shazar Collection
Harvard University, Cambridge, Mass.
    Harvard University Archives
    Widener Library
Hebrew Union College, Jewish Institute of Religion, New York
    Klau Library
Hebrew Union College Archives, Cincinnati, Ohio
Hebrew University Archive, Mount Scopus, Jerusalem
House of Lords Record Office, London
    David Lloyd George Papers

India Office Library and Records, London
Israel State Archives, Jerusalem
  Herbert Samuel Papers
Jabotinsky Archives, Tel Aviv
Jewish National and University Library, Jerusalem
Lavon Institute for Labor Research, Tel Aviv
Library of Congress, Washington, D.C.
  Robert Lansing Papers
Manchester Central Library, Manchester
Manchester Polytechnic Archives, Manchester
  Manchester Studies Unit
Manchester University, John Rylands Library, Manchester
  Guardian Archives
  Manchester University Archives
New York Public Library, New York
Nili Archive, Zikhron Yaakov, Israel
Oxford Centre for Postgraduate Hebrew Studies, Yarnton
  Getzel Kressel Collection
Oxford University, Bodleian Library, Oxford
  Oxford University Archives
  Leonard Stein Papers
Public Record Office, London (PRO)
  Admiralty Office Papers (ADM)
  Cabinet Office Papers (CAB)
  Colonial Office Papers (CO)
  Foreign Office Papers (FO)
  Home Office Papers (HO)
  Treasury Office Papers (TI)
  War Office Papers (WO)
Rhodes House Library, Oxford
Scottish Record Office, Edinburgh
St. Antony's College, Middle East Centre, Oxford
  Wyndham Deedes Papers
  Private Papers Collection
  Mark Sykes Papers
  Sir H. Young Papers
University College, Mocatta Library, London
University of Louisville, School of Law, Louisville, Ky.
  Louis Dembitz Brandeis Papers
Victoria University Library, Manchester
Weizmann Archives, Rehovot, Israel (WA)
Yale University, Sterling Library, New Haven, Conn.
  Sir William Wiseman Papers
YIVO Institute Archives, New York
Zionist Archives and Library, New York
  Jacob DeHaas Papers

Newspapers and Selected Reference Works

Arab Bulletin
Bulletin, Zionist Organization, Jerusalem

Davar
Dictionary of National Biography
Dictionary of Scientific Biography
Doar Hayom
L'Echo Sioniste
Encyclopaedia Judaica
Der Fraind
Fortnightly Review
Haaretz
Hadoar
Haenzyklopedia haivrit
Hamelitz
Haolam
Hatzfirah
Haumah
Jerusalem Post
Jewish Chronicle
Jewish World
Journal of the Society of Chemical Industry
Jüdische Rundschau
Das Jüdische Volk
J.C.B. Bulletin
Kuntres
Maccabaean
Manchester Guardian
Morning Post
New Palestine
New Statesman
New York Times
Palestine
Sionisme
Sunday Times Supplement (London)
Times (London)
Der Tog
Westminster Gazette
Dos Yidishe Volk
Zionist Review

Interviews

Janet Lieberman Ellison, August 20, 1987.

Primary Sources

Aaronsohn, Aaron. *Yoman Aaron Aaronsohn, 1916–1919*. Edited by Yoram Efrati, translated by Uri Kesari. Tel Aviv: Karny, 1970.

Abdullah, King of Jordan. *Memoirs of King Abdullah of Trans-Jordan*. Edited by Philip P. Graves, translated by G. Khuri. New York: Philosophical Library, 1950.

Ahad Ha'am. "Die Balfour Deklarazie." *Zionistishe Bletter* (Warsaw) 2, no. 7 (1927): 201–3.

―――. *Igrot Ahad Ha'Am.* Vol. 5, *1913–1917.* Jerusalem and Berlin: Yavneh and Moriah Press, 1924.

―――. *Pirkei zikhronot veigrot.* Tel Aviv: Bet Ahad Ha'Am, 1931.

Amery, Leopold S. *My Political Life.* 3 vols. London: Hutchinson, 1953.

Amir, Aharon, ed. *Avshalom: Ktavim umikhtavim.* Haifa: Shikmonah, 1971.

Arab League Office. *Edwin Montagu and the Balfour Declaration.* London: Arab League Office, [1972?].

Aronstein, Philipp, ed. *Speeches of British Statesmen on Judaism and Zionism.* Berlin: Schocken, 1936.

Ashbee, C. R. *A Palestine Notebook, 1918–1928.* Garden City, N.Y.: Doubleday, Page and Company, 1923.

Asquith, Herbert H. *H. H. Asquith Letters to Venetia Stanley.* Edited by Michael Brock and Eleanor Brock. Oxford: Oxford University Press, 1982.

Ben-Zvi, Rahel Yanait. "Pgishah rishonah im Weizmann." *Davar,* November 23, 1918.

Bentwich, Norman. *My 77 Years: An Account of My Life and Times, 1883–1960.* Philadelphia: Jewish Publication Society of America, 1961.

Bergmann, Ernst D. "Bergmann on Weizmann." *Rehovot* 8, no. 1 (Spring 1976): 52–61.

Bertie, Francis Levenson Bertie, 1st Viscount. *The Diary of Lord Bertie of Thame.* Edited by Lady Algernon Gordon Lennox. 2 vols. London: Hodder and Stoughton, 1924.

Blumenfeld, Kurt. *Erlebte Judenfrage: Ein Vierteljahrhundert deutscher Zionismus.* Stuttgart: Deutsche Verlags-Anstalt 1962.

―――. *Im Kampf um den Zionismus: Briefe aus fünf Jahrzehnten.* Edited by Miriam Sambursky and Jochanan Ginat. Stuttgart: Deutsche Verlags-Anstalt 1976.

Book of Documents of the Vaad Leumi in Palestine. Jerusalem, 1963.

Bukhmil, Joshua. "Zikhronot, 1916–1924." *Katzir* (Tel Aviv) 2 (1972): 330–43.

Djemal Pasha, Ahmad. *Memories of a Turkish Statesman, 1913–1919.* New York: Doran, 1922.

Draft Mandates for Mesopotamia and Palestine, As Submitted for the Approval of the League of Nations. December 7, 1920. London: HMSO, 1921.

Eder, David. *Memoirs of a Modern Pioneer.* Edited by J. B. Hobman. London: Gollancz, 1945.

Frankfurter, Felix. *Felix Frankfurter Reminisces: Recorded in Talks with Dr. Harlan B. Phillips.* New York: Reynal and Company, 1960.

Freundlich, Yehoshua, and Gdalya Yogev, eds. *Haprotokolim shel havaad hapoel hazioni, 1919–1929.* 2 vols. Tel Aviv: Tel Aviv University and Kibbutz Meuhad, 1975–84.

Hacohen, Mordechai Ben-Hillel. "Eretz Israel tahat shilton hazavah habriti." *Hashiloah* 42 (1924): 241–46.

―――. *Milhemet haamim.* Edited by Shimon Rubinstein. 2 vols. Jerusalem: Mitzpeh, 1985.

History of the Ministry of Munitions. 12 vols. London: Ministry of Munitions, 1921–22.

House, Edward M. *The Intimate Papers of Colonel House.* Vol. 3, *Into the World War: April 1917–June 1918.* Edited by Charles Seymour. Boston: Houghton Mifflin, 1928.

House of Commons, Great Britain Parliament. *Official Report.* Volumes for 1916–22.

Hurewitz, Jacob Coleman, ed. *Diplomacy in the Near and Middle East: A Documentary Record, 1914–1956.* 2 vols. Princeton, N.J.: Van Nostrand, 1956.

————, ed. *The Middle East and North Africa in World Politics: A Documentary Record.* 2d ed. New Haven, Conn.: Yale University Press, 1975.

Ingrams, Doreen, ed. *Palestine Papers: Seeds of Conflict, 1917–1922.* London: J. Murray, 1972.

Jabotinsky, Vladimir. *The Story of the Jewish Legion.* Translated by Samuel Katz. New York: Bernard Ackerman, for the American Jewish Legion, 1945.

Katznelson, Berl. *Igrot, 1919–1922.* Edited by Yehuda Erez and Abraham Moshe Koller. Tel Aviv: Am Oved Publishers, 1970.

Lawrence, T. E. *The Selected Letters of T. E. Lawrence.* Edited by David Garnett. London: J. Cape, 1952.

Levin, Shmaryahu. *Igrot Shmaryahu Levin.* Tel Aviv: Dvir Press, 1966.

Lloyd George, David. *Memoirs of the Peace Conference.* New Haven, Conn.: Yale University Press, 1939.

————. *War Memoirs of David Lloyd George, 1915–1916.* 6 vols. Boston: Little, Brown, 1933.

Magnes, Judah L. *Dissenter in Zion: From the Writings of Judah L. Magnes.* Edited by Arthur A. Goren. Cambridge, Mass.: Harvard University Press, 1982.

Malcolm, James A. "Origins of the Balfour Declaration: Dr. Weizmann's Contribution." Zionist Archives and Library, New York.

Meinertzhagen, Richard. *Middle East Diary, 1917–1956.* New York: Yoseloff, 1960.

Melchett, Alfred Moritz Mond, Lord, and Chaim Weizmann. *The Jewish National Home and Its Critics: The Oxford Speeches by Sir Alfred Melchett and Chaim Weizmann—A Reply by the Secretary of State for the Colonies to the Arab Delegation.* London: Zionist Organization, 1922.

Miller, David Hunter. *My Diary at the Conference of Paris, With Documentation by David Hunter Miller.* New York: Appeal Printing Co., 1925.

Morgenthau, Henry. *All in a Life-Time.* Garden City, N.Y.: Doubleday, Page and Company, 1922.

————. *Ambassador Morgenthau's Story.* Garden City, N.Y.: Doubleday, Page and Company, 1918.

Moulton, H. Fletcher. *The Life of Lord Moulton.* London: Nisbet, 1922.

Neumann, Emanuel. *In the Arena: An Autobiographical Memoir.* New York: Herzl Press, 1976.

Patterson, John Henry. *With the Judeans in the Palestine Campaign.* London: Hutchinson and Co., 1922.

————. *With the Zionists in Gallipoli.* London: Hutchinson and Co., 1916.

Report of the Proceedings of the 24th Annual Convention of the Zionist Organization of America: Held in Cleveland, June 5, 6, 7, 8, 1921. Prepared by Maurice Samuel from the Official Stenographic Report of the National Shorthand Reporting Committee. New York: Zionist Organization of America, 1921.

Sachar, Howard M., ed. *The Rise of Israel.* 39 vols. Vol. 6, *1914–1917;* vols. 7, 8, *1917;* vols. 9–11, *1918;* vol. 12, *1920;* vol. 13, *1920–1925;* vol. 14, *1920 and Beyond;* vol. 15, *1920–1939;* vol. 16, *The Jewish Yishuv's Development in the Interwar Period;* vol. 17, *Arab-Jewish Relations, 1921–1937;* vol. 18, *1920–29.* New York and London: Garland Publishers, 1987–88.

Sacher, Harry. *Jewish Emancipation: The Contract Myth.* London: English Zionist Federation, 1917.

————, ed. *Zionism and the Jewish Future.* New York: Macmillan, 1916.

Samuel, Herbert Louis. *Memoirs*. London: Crescent Press, 1945.

Samuel, Horace B. *Unholy Memories of the Holy Land*. London: Privately printed by L. and Virginia Woolf, 1930.

Sanders, Liman von. *Fünf Jahre Türkei*. Annapolis: Williams and Wilkins Company, for the U.S. Naval Institute, 1928.

Scott, Charles Prestwich. *The Political Diaries of C. P. Scott, 1911–1928*. Edited by Trevor Wilson. Ithaca, N.Y.: Cornell University Press, 1970.

Sefer hateudot shel havaad haleumi likneset Israel be-Eretz Israel, 1918–1948. Edited by Moshe Etiash. Jerusalem, 1963.

Sieff, Israel Moshe. *Memoirs*. New York: Weidenfeld and Nicolson, 1970.

Simon, Julius. *Certain Days: Zionist Memoirs and Selected Papers*. Edited by Evyatar Friesel. Jerusalem: Israel Universities Press, 1971.

Simon, Leon. *The Case of the Anti-Zionists: A Reply*. London: Zionist Organization, 1917.

Sokolow, Florian. "Nahum Sokolow's Paris Diary." *Zion* 3 (November 1952): 42–50.

Solomon, Flora. *A Woman's Way*. New York: Simon and Schuster, 1984.

Stenographisches Protokoll der Verhandlungen des XII. Zionisten Kongresses in Karlsbad vom 1. bis 14. September 1921. Berlin: Jüdischer Verlag, 1922.

Storrs, Ronald. *The Memoirs of Sir Ronald Storrs*. New York: G. P. Putnam's Sons, 1937.

———. *Orientations*. London: I. Nicolson and Watson, 1945.

Sykes, Mark. *Through Five Turkish Provinces*. London: Bickers, 1900.

Tolkowsky, Shmuel. *Yoman zioni medini: London, 1919–1925*. Edited by Dvorah Barzilay-Yegar. Jerusalem: Hasifriyah hazionit, 1981.

Toynbee, Arnold J. *Acquaintances*. London: Oxford University Press, 1967.

Trumpeldor, Joseph. *Tagebücher und Briefe: Autorische Übertragung aus dem Russischen*. Berlin: Jüdischer Verlag, 1925.

Weizmann, Chaim. *American Addresses of Chaim Weizmann*. Preface by Samuel Untermeyer. New York: Palestine Foundation Fund, 1923.

———. *The Letters and Papers of Chaim Weizmann*. Edited by Meyer W. Weisgal et al. English ed. Ser. A. Vols. 1–3, London: Oxford University Press and Yad Chaim Weizmann, 1968–72. Vols. 4–11, Jerusalem: Israel Universities Press, 1973–77.

———. *The Letters and Papers of Chaim Weizmann*. Edited by Barnet Litvinoff. Ser. B. Vol. 1, *1898–1931*. New Brunswick, N.J.: Transaction, Rutgers University Press; Jerusalem: Israel Universities Press, 1983.

———. *Trial and Error*. New York: Schocken Books, 1949.

———. "Zionism and the Jewish Problem." In *Zionism and the Jewish Future*, edited by Harry Sacher, pp. 1–11. New York: Macmillan Company, 1916.

Weizmann, Vera. *The Impossible Takes Longer*. New York: Harper and Row, 1967.

Wise, Stephen. *Challenging Years. The Autobiography of Stephen Wise*. New York: Putnam's Sons, 1949.

Wolf, Lucien. "The Zionist Peril." *Jewish Quarterly Review* 17 (1905): 1–25.

Woodward, E. L., and Rohan Butler, eds. *Documents on British Foreign Policy, 1919–1939*. Ser. 1. Vols. 4, 8. London: Her Majesty's Stationery Circle, 1952.

Yahuda, Abraham S. *Dr. Weizmann's Errors on Trial: A Refutation of His Statements in "Trial and Error" Concerning My Activity for Zionism during My Professorship at Madrid University*. New York: Privately printed by Ethel R. Yahuda, 1952.

Yom hagenu: Pirtei hahagigah shel hanahat even hapinah lebinyan hauniversitah haivrit. Jerusalem, [July 24, 1918].

Zionist Organization of America. The American War Congress and Zionism: Statements by Members of the American War Congress on the Jewish National Movement. New York: Zionist Organization of America, 1919.

———. American Zionist Medical Unit for Palestine. New York: Zionist Organization of America, 1919. Copy in Central Zionist Archives, Z4/763.

Secondary Sources

Adams, R.J.Q. Arms and the Wizard: Lloyd George and the Ministry of Munitions, 1915–1916. College Station, Tex.: Texas A & M University Press, 1978.

Adelson, Roger. Mark Sykes: Portrait of an Amateur. London: Cape, 1975.

Almog, Shmuel. "Hitpathuta shel hasheelah hayehudit be-Angliyah betom milhemet haolam harishonah." In Zion: Sefer Hayovel, edited by Shmuel Ettinger, Haim Beinart, and Menahem Stern, pp. 397–431. Jerusalem: Hahevrah hahistorit haisraelit, 1986.

Alsberg, Avraham P. "Delimitation of the Eastern Border of Palestine." Zionism 3 (Spring 1981): 87–98.

Altshuler, Mordecai. "Russia and Her Jews: The Impact of the 1914 War." Wiener Library Bulletin, n.s. 27, nos. 30–31 (1973–74): 12–16.

Amdur, Richard. Chaim Weizmann. New York: Chelsea Publishing House, 1988.

Antonius, George. The Arab Awakening: The Story of the Arab National Movement. New York: Capricorn Books, 1955.

Arab League Office. Edwin Montagu and the Balfour Declaration. London: Arab League Office, 1972.

Avigur, Shaul, et al., eds. Toldot hahaganah. Tel Aviv: Schocken, 1980.

Ayerst, David. The Manchester Guardian: Biography of a Newspaper. Ithaca, N.Y.: Cornell University Press, 1971.

Barzilay, Dvorah. "Letoldot hatzharat Balfour." Zion 33, nos. 3–4 (1968): 190–202.

———. "Shat mashber kishat mifneh: Weizmann bemilhemet haolam harishonah." In Medinai beitot mashber, edited by Yosef Gorni and Gdalya Yogev, pp. 35–41. Tel Aviv: Tel Aviv University, 1977.

Barzilay-Yegar, Dvorah. "Crisis as Turning Point: Chaim Weizmann in World War I." Studies in Zionism 6 (Autumn 1982): 241–54.

Beaverbrook, Max Aitken. Politicians and the War. Hamden, Conn.: Archon Books, 1928–32.

Beloff, Max. Imperial Sunset: Britain's Imperial Empire, 1897–1921. New York: Alfred A. Knopf, 1970.

Ben-Arieh, Yehoshua, and Israel Bartal, eds. Hahistoryah shel Eretz Israel. Vol. 8, Shilhei hatkufah haotmanit, 1799–1917. Jerusalem: Beit Hotzaah Keter, Yad Yitzhak Ben-Zvi, 1983.

Bentwich, Norman. Sir Wyndham Deedes: A Christian Zionist. Jerusalem: Keren Hayesod, United Israel Campaign, 1954.

Bergmann, Ernst D. "Dr. Weizmann's Scientific Work in the Framework of the Industrial and Political Development of His Time." MS, Weizmann Archives.

Berlin, George L. "The Brandeis-Weizmann Dispute." American Jewish Historical Quarterly 60, no. 1 (September 1970): 37–68.

Berlin, Isaiah. *Chaim Weizmann*. Herzl Institute Pamphlet 8. New York: Herzl Press, 1958.

———. *Historical Inevitability*. Auguste Comte Memorial Trust Lecture 1, Presented to the London School of Economics and Political Science, May 12, 1953. London: Oxford University Press, 1954.

———, and Kolatt, Israel. *Chaim Weizmann as Leader*. Jerusalem: Hebrew University, Institute of Contemporary Jewry, 1970.

Black, Eugene C. *The Social Politics of Anglo-Jewry, 1880–1920*. Oxford: B. Blackwell, 1988.

Blau, Moses. *Amuda denehora*. Jerusalem: Hotzaat homot Yerushalayim, 1968.

Bowle, John. *Viscount Samuel: A Biography*. London: Gollancz, 1957.

Brecher, F. W. "Revisiting Ambassador Morgenthau's Turkish Peace Mission of 1917." *Middle Eastern Studies* 24, no. 3 (July 1988): 357–63.

Bullock, David L. *Allenby's War: The Palestine Arabian Campaigns, 1916–1918*. London: Blanford Press, 1968.

Burstein, Moshe. *Self-Government of the Jews in Palestine since 1900*. Tel Aviv: Privately printed, 1934.

Calhoun, Frederick S. *Power and Principle: Armed Intervention in Wilsonian Foreign Policy*. Kent, Ohio: Kent State University Press, 1986.

Caplan, Neil. "Britain, Zionism and the Arabs, 1917–1925." *Wiener Library Bulletin* 31, nos. 45–46 (1978): 4–17.

———. "Faisal Ibn Hussein and the Zionists: A Re-examination with Documents." *International History Review* 5, no. 4 (November 1983): 564.

———. *Palestine Jewry and the Arab Question, 1917–1925*. London: Frank Cass, 1978.

———. "Zionist Visions in the Early 1930s." *Studies in Contemporary Jewry* 4 (1988): 250–63.

Cattan, Henry. *The Palestine Question*. London: Croom Helm, 1988.

Clark, Ronald W. *Einstein: The Life and Times*. New York: World Publishing Company, 1971.

Clements, Kendrick A. *Woodrow Wilson: World Statesman*. Boston: Twayne, 1987.

Cocker, Mark. *Richard Meinertzhagen: Soldier, Scientist and Spy*. London: Secker and Warburg, 1989.

Cohen, Michael J. "Churchill and the Balfour Declaration: The Interpretation, 1920–1922." In *Great Powers in the Middle East*, pp. 91–108. Collected Paper Series, Dayan Center for Middle Eastern and African Studies, Shiloah Institute, Tel Aviv University. New York: Holmes and Meier, 1988.

———. *Churchill and the Jews*. London: Frank Cass, 1985.

———. *Palestine to Israel: From Mandate to Independence*. London: Frank Cass. 1988.

Cohen, Naomi W. "The Abrogation of the Russo-American Treaty of 1832." *Jewish Social Studies* 25 (1963): 3–41.

———. *American Jews and the Zionist Idea*. New York: Ktav Publishing House, 1975.

———. *A Dual Heritage: The Public Career of Oscar S. Straus*. Philadelphia: Jewish Publication Society of America, 1969.

Cohen, Stuart A. "The Conquest of a Community? The Zionists and the Board of Deputies in 1917." *Jewish Journal of Sociology* 19, no. 2 (December 1977): 157–84.

———. *English Zionists and British Jews: The Communal Politics of Anglo-Jewry, 1895–1920*. Princeton, N.J.: Princeton University Press, 1982.

Creasey, John. *The Round Table: The First Twenty Five Years of the Round Table Movement*. London: National Association of Round Tables of Great Britain and Ireland, 1953.

Crossman, Richard H. *A Nation Reborn: The Israel of Weizmann, Begin and Ben-Gurion*. London: Hamilton, 1960.

———. "Weizmann." *Encounter* 14, no. 6 (June 1960): 44–56.

Cumming, Henry H. *Franco-British Rivalry in the Post-War Near East: The Decline of French Influence*. Westport, Conn.: Hyperion Press, 1938.

Davies, Harold. "A Review of the Development of Butyl Alcohol-Acetone Fermentation and Early Work on Synthetic Rubber." In *Papers Collected to Commemorate the 70th Anniversary of Dr. Chaim Weizmann*. Jerusalem: Privately printed, 1944.

Davis, Richard, *The English Rothschilds*. Chapel Hill, N.C.: University of North Carolina Press, 1983.

DeNovo, John A. *American Interests and Policies in the Middle East, 1900–1939*. Minneapolis: University of Minnesota Press, 1963.

Dixon, Bernard. "Bug Bang That Built Israel." *Observer Weekly*, November 2, 1987.

Duff, Douglas Volder. *Sword for Hire: The Saga of a Modern Free Companion*. London: J. Murray, 1937.

Dugdale, Blanche E. C. *Arthur James Balfour, 1907–1930*. London: Hutchinson, 1936.

———. *The Balfour Declaration: Origins and Background*. London: Jewish Agency for Palestine, 1940.

Eban, Abba. *Chaim Weizmann: A Continuing Legacy*. London: Zionist Federation of Great Britain and Ireland, 1962.

Elam, Yigal. *Hagdudim haivriim bemilhemet haolam harishonah*. Tel Aviv: Maarahot, 1973.

———. *Hasochnut hayehudit: Shanim rishonot*. Jerusalem: Hasifriyah hazionit, 1990.

Elboim-Dror, Rachel. *Hahinukh haivri be-Eretz Israel, 1914–1920*. Jerusalem: Yad Yitzhak Ben-Zvi, 1990.

Eliav, Mordechai. "Meorvutam shel nezigei Germanya ve-Austria beeruei 1917 be-Eretz Israel." *Cathedra* 48 (June 1988): 90–124.

Esco Foundation for Palestine. *Palestine: A Study of Jewish, Arab, and British Policies*. Vol. 1. New Haven, Conn.: Yale University Press, 1947.

Feinberg, Nathan. "Letoldot hamunah bayit leumi yehudi." *Zion* 37 (1972): 111–16.

Ferrell, Robert H. *Woodrow Wilson and World War I: 1917–1921*. New York: Harper and Row, 1985.

Frankel, Jonathan. "The Jewish Socialists and the American Jewish Congress Movement." *YIVO Annual of Jewish Social Science* 16 (New York, 1976): 318–23.

———. *Prophecy and Politics: Socialism, Nationalism, and the Russian Jews, 1862–1917*. Cambridge: Cambridge University Press, 1981.

French, David. *British Strategy and War Aims, 1914–1916*. London: Allen and Unwin, 1986.

Friedman, Isaiah. *Germany, Turkey and Zionism, 1897–1918*. Oxford: Clarendon Press, 1972.

———. "The McMahon-Hussein Correspondence: Reply to Arnold Toynbee." *Journal of Contemporary History* 5, no. 2 (October 1970): 83–122.

————. *The Question of Palestine*. London: Routledge and Kegan Paul, 1973.

————. "Zionist History Reconsidered." Review of *Zionism: The Crucial Phase*, by David Vital. *Studies in Contemporary Jewry* 6 (1990): 309–14.

Friedman, Menahem. *Hevrah vedat: Haortodoxyah halo-zionit be-Eretz Israel, 1918–1936*. Jerusalem: Yad Yitzhak Ben-Zvi, 1977.

Friesel, Evyatar. *The Balfour Declaration in Historical Perspective*. Kaplan Centre Papers. Rondebosch, South Africa: University of Cape Town, 1989.

————. "Brandeis' Role in American Zionism Historically Reconsidered." *American Jewish History* 69, no. 1 (September 1979): 34–59.

————. "British Policy in Palestine: The 'Churchill Memorandum' of 1922." In *Vision and Conflict*, edited by Richard I. Cohen, pp. 190–212. New York: St. Martin's Press, 1985.

————. "David Vital's Work on Zionism." *Studies in Zionism* 9, no. 2 (Autumn 1988): 209–25.

————. "Habaron Edmond de Rothschild vehazionim bashanim 1918–1919." *Zion* 38, nos. 1–4 (1973): 116–36.

————. *Hamediniyut hazionit leahar hatzharat Balfour, 1917–1922*. Tel Aviv: Tel Aviv University and Hakibbutz Hameuhad, 1977.

————. "Herbert Samuel's Reassessment of Zionism in 1921." *Studies in Zionism* 5, no. 2 (Autumn 1984): 213–37.

————. "Leil hamashber beyn Weizmann le-Brandeis." *Hazionut* 4 (1975): 146–64.

Fromkin, David. *A Peace to End All Peace: Creating the Modern Middle East, 1914–1922*. New York: H. Holt, 1989.

Frommer, Morris. "The American Jewish Congress: A History, 1914–1950." Ph.D. diss., Ohio State University, 1978.

Gal, Allon. *Brandeis of Boston*. Cambridge, Mass.: Harvard University Press, 1980.

————. "Hashkafato shel Brandeis al ofen binyan haaretz, 1914–1923." *Hazionut* 6 (1981): 97–145.

Gardner, Lloyd C. *Safe for Democracy: The Anglo-American Response to Revolution, 1913–1923*. New York: Oxford University Press, 1984.

Gil-Har, Yitzhak. "Hitargenut vehanhagah atzmit shel hayishuv be-Eretz Israel mireshit hashilton habriti ad leishur hamandat (1917–1922)." Ph.D. diss., Hebrew University of Jerusalem, 1972.

Gilbert, Martin. *Winston S. Churchill: The Stricken World*. Vol. 4, *1916–1922*; vol. 5, *1923–1939*. Boston: Houghton Mifflin, 1966.

Gillon, D. Z. "The Antecedents of the Balfour Declaration." *Middle Eastern Studies* 5, no. 2 (May 1969): 131–50.

Giora, Moshe. "Weizmann, Mussolini, vehazionut." *Haumma* 9 (1972): 279–362.

Goldstein, Yaakov, and Yaakov Shavit. "Yosef Trumpeldor kidmut mofet vehavikuah al 'shaikhuto' hatnuatit." *Kivunim*, no. 12 (August 1981): 9–21.

Goldstein, Yossi. "Ahad Ha'Am: A Political Failure?" *Jewish History* 4, no. 2 (Fall 1990): 33–48.

Goodman, Paul, ed. *Chaim Weizmann: A Tribute on His Seventieth Birthday*. London: Gollancz, 1945.

————, ed. *The Jewish National Home*. London: Victor Gollancz, 1949.

Gottlieb, Wolfram W. *Studies in Secret Diplomacy during the First World War*. London: Allen and Unwin, 1957.

Grabill, Joseph L. *Protestant Diplomacy and the Near East: Missionary Influence on American Policy, 1810–1927*. Minneapolis: University of Minnesota Press, 1971.

Greater London Council. *Survey of London*. Vol. 27. North Kensington: Athlon Press, 1973.

Gross, Nachum. "Hayishuv bizman milhemet haolam harishonah." In *Bankai leumah behithadshutah*, edited by Nachum Gross, pp. 60–63. Ramat Gan: Masadah, 1977.

Gruenbaum, Yitzhak. *Hatnuah hazionit behitpathutah*. Jerusalem: Hamahlakah leinyenei hanoar, hahistadrut hazionit behotzaat R. Mass, 1954.

Guedalla, Philip. *Napoleon and Palestine*. London: G. Allen and Unwin, 1925.

Guinn, Paul. *British Strategy and Politics, 1914 to 1918*. Oxford: Clarendon Press, 1965.

Haber, L. F. *The Chemical Industry, 1900–1930*. Oxford: Clarendon Press, 1971.

Halpern, Ben. "Brandeis and the Origins of the Balfour Declaration." *Studies in Zionism* 7 (Spring 1983): 71–100.

———. *A Clash of Heroes: Brandeis, Weizmann, and American Zionism*. New York: Oxford University Press, 1987.

———. "The Disciple, Chaim Weizmann." In *At the Crossroads: Essays on Ahad Ha'Am*, edited by Jacques Kornberg, pp. 156–69. Albany: State University of New York Press, 1983.

———. "The Drafting of the Balfour Declaration." *Herzl Year Book* 7 (New York, 1971): 255–84.

———. "Generational Models and Zionist History." In *Tmurot bahistoryah hayehudit hahadashah*, edited by Shmuel Almog, Israel Bartal, et al., pp. xcv–cv. Jerusalem: Merkaz Zalman Shazar, Hahevrah hahistorit hayisraelit, 1987.

———. *The Idea of the Jewish State*. 2d ed. Cambridge, Mass.: Harvard University Press, 1969.

———. "Weizmann vedoro." In *Haishiyut vedorah*, pp. 157–68. Jerusalem: Hahevrah hahistorit haisraelit, 1963.

Hammond, John Lawrence. *C. P. Scott of the Manchester Guardian*. New York: Harcourt Brace, 1934.

Hay, Denys. "The Official History of the Ministry of Munitions, 1915–1919." *Economic History Review* 14, no. 2 (1944): 185–90.

Hook, Sidney. *The Hero in History: A Study in Limitation and Possibility*. New York: Humanities Press, 1950.

Howard, Harry N. *The King-Crane Commission: An American Inquiry in the Middle East*. Beirut: Khayat, 1963.

al-Husari, Abu Khaldun Sati'. *The Day of Maysalun: A Page from the Modern History of the Arabs*. Washington, D.C.: Middle East Institute, 1966.

Hyamson, Albert. "British Projects for the Restoration of the Jews to Palestine." *Proceedings of the American Jewish Historical Society* 26 (1918): 127–64.

———. *Palestine under the Mandate, 1920–1948*. Westport, Conn.: Greenwood Press, 1976.

Janowsky, Oscar I. *The Jews and Minority Rights, 1898–1919*. New York: Columbia University Press, 1933.

Jenkins, Roy. *Asquith: Portrait of a Man and an Era*. New York: Chilmark Press, 1964.

Judd, Denis. *Balfour and the British Empire: A Study in Imperial Evolution, 1874–1932*. New York: Macmillan, 1968.

Kantorovitch, Haim. *Geschichte fun der Amerikaner Arbeter Bavegung*. New York: Poalei Zion, 1920.

Kedourie, Elie. *In the Anglo-Arab Labyrinth: The McMahon-Hussein Correspondence and Its Interpretations, 1914–1939*. Cambridge: Cambridge University Press, 1976.

———. *The Chatham House Version and Other Middle Eastern Studies*. London: Weidenfeld and Nicolson, 1970.

———. *England and the Middle East: The Destruction of the Ottoman Empire, 1914–1921*. London: Bowes and Bowes, 1956.

———. "Sir Mark Sykes and Palestine, 1915–1916." *Middle Eastern Studies* 6, no. 3 (October 1970): 340–45.

Kelly, Fred C. *One Thing Leads to Another: The Growth of an Industry*. Boston: Houghton Mifflin, 1936.

Kendle, J. E. "The Round Table Movement and 'Home Rule All Around.' " *Historical Journal* 11, no. 2 (1968): 332–53.

Khoury, Philip S. "Factionalism among Syrian Nationalists during the French Mandate." *International Journal of Middle East Studies* 13 (November 1981): 441–69.

———. *Syria and the French Mandate. The Politics of Arab Nationalism, 1920–1945*. Princeton, N.J.: Princeton University Press, 1987.

Kimche, Jon. *The Second Arab Awakening*. London: Holt, Rinehart and Winston, 1970.

———. *There Could Have Been Peace*. New York: Dial Press, 1973.

———. *The Unromantics: The Great Powers and the Balfour Declaration*. London: Weidenfeld and Nicolson, 1968.

Klausner, Israel. "Hadeklerazyah haserbit." *Haolam*, November 4, 1937.

Klieman, Aaron S. "Britain's War Aims in the Middle East in 1915." *Journal of Contemporary History* 3 (July 1968): 237–51.

———. *Foundations of British Policy in the Arab World: The Cairo Conference of 1921*. Baltimore: Johns Hopkins Press, 1970.

———. "The Weizmann-Feisal Negotiations of 1918–1919." *Chicago Jewish Forum* 24, no. 4 (Summer 1966): 297–303.

Kobler, Franz. *The Vision Was There: A History of the British Movement for the Restoration of the Jews to Palestine*. London: Lincolns-Prager, for the World Jewish Congress, British Section, 1956.

Laqueur, Walter. *A History of Zionism*. New York: Holt, Rinehart and Winston, 1972.

Laskov, Shulamit. "Havaad hazmani vehaganat hagalil haelyon bishnat 1920." *Hazionut* 8 (1983): 355–90.

———. *Trumpeldor: Sippur hayav*. Jerusalem: Keter, 1982.

Lavsky, Hagit. *Beterem puranut: Darkam veyihudam shel zionei germanyah, 1918–1932*. Jerusalem: Magnes Press, Hebrew University, Hasifriyah hazionit, 1990.

———. *Yesodot hatakziv lamifal hazioni: Vaad hazirim, 1918–1921*. Jerusalem: Yad Yitzhak Ben Zvi, 1980.

Lebow, Richard Ned. "Woodrow Wilson and the Balfour Declaration." *Journal of Modern History* 40, no. 4 (1968): 501–23.

Leslie, Shane. *Mark Sykes: His Life and Letters*. New York: Charles Scribner's Sons, 1923.

Levene, Mark. *War, Jews, and the New Europe: The Diplomacy of Lucien Wolf, 1914–1919*. Oxford: Oxford University Press, 1991.

Levy, Avigdor. "Shlihut Morgenthau: Parashah miyemei milhemet haolam harishonah." *Hamizrah Hehadash* 16, no. 1 (1966): 58–63.

Levy, Elkan D. "Antisemitism in England at War, 1914–1916." *Patterns of Prejudice* 4, no. 5 (September/October 1970): 27–30.

Lewin, Kurt. "The Problem of Minority Leadership." In *Studies in Leadership: Leadership and Democratic Action,* edited by Alvin Ward Gouldner. New York: Harper, 1950.

Lewis, Bernard. *The Emergence of Modern Turkey.* Oxford: Oxford University Press, 1961.

Lichtheim, Richard. "Haemunah shepiamah be-Weizmann." *Haaretz,* November 2, 1962.

Lipman, Vivian David. *Social History of the Jews in England, 1850–1950.* London: Watts, 1954.

Lipovetzky, Pesah. *Joseph Trumpeldor: Life and Works.* Jerusalem: World Zionist Organization, Youth and Hechalutz Department, 1953.

Lipstadt, Deborah E. "The Zionist Career of Louis Lipsky, 1900–1921." Ph.D. diss., Brandeis University, 1976.

Livneh, Eliezer. *Aaron Aaronsohn: Haish uzmano.* Jerusalem: Mosad Bialik, 1969.

———. *The Truth about Reparations and War Debts.* Garden City, N.Y.: Doubleday, Doran and Co., 1932.

———, ed. *Nili: Toldoteha shel heaza medinit.* Jerusalem: Shukan, 1961.

Luntz, Yosef. "Hamagaim hadiplomatiim beyn hatnuah hazionit vehatnuah haivrit haleumit im siyum milhemet haolam harishonah." *Hamizrah Hehadash* 12, no. 3 (1962): 212–29.

Mack, John E. *A Prince of Our Disorder: The Life of T. E. Lawrence.* Boston: Little, Brown, 1976.

Magnus, Philip. *Kitchener: Portrait of an Imperialist.* London: J. Murray, 1958.

Mahover, Yonah. "Haumnam 'hudah' Dr. Chaim Weizmann (bacongress ha-17, 1931)?" *Hauma* 6 (1968): 393–96.

Makover, Rachela. *Shilton uminhal be-Eretz Israel, 1917–1925.* Jerusalem: Yad Yitzhak Ben-Zvi, 1988.

Manuel, Frank E. "Habeayah ha-Eretz Israelit badiplomatyah haitalkit bishnot 1916–1920." In *Shivat Zion,* vol. 4, edited by Ben Zion Dinur and Israel Heilprin, pp. 210–39. Jerusalem: Hasifriyah hazionit, 1956.

———. "The Palestine Question in Italian Diplomacy, 1917–1920." *Journal of Modern History* 27, no. 3 (September 1955): 263–80.

———. *The Realities of American-Palestine Relations.* Washington, D.C.: Public Affairs Press, 1949.

Maor, Yitzhak. *Hatnuah hazionit be-Russyah.* Jerusalem: Hasifriyah Hazionit, 1973.

Marder, Arthur J. *From the Dreadnought to Scapa Flow: The Royal Navy in the Fisher Era, 1904–1919.* 5 vols. Oxford: Oxford University Press, 1961–70.

Mattar, Philip. *The Mufti of Jerusalem: Al-Hajj Amin al-Husayni and the Palestinian National Movement.* New York: Columbia University Press, 1988.

McTague, John. *British Policy in Palestine, 1917–1922.* Lanham, Md.: University Press of America, 1973.

Melchett, Alfred Moritz Mond, Lord. "Chaim Weizmann." In *Twelve Jews,* edited by Hector Bolitho, pp. 271–88. London: Rich and Cowan, 1934.

Mendelsohn, Ezra. *Hatnuah hazionit be-Polin: Shnot hahithavut, 1915–1926.* Jerusalem: Hasifriyah hazionit, 1986.

———. *The Jews of East Central Europe between the World Wars.* Bloomington, Ind.: Indiana University Press, 1983.

Michaelis, Anthony R. *Weizmann Centenary*. London: Anglo-Israel Association, 1974.

Minerbi, Sergio. *Havatikan, eretz hakodesh vehazionut, 1895–1925*. Jerusalem: Yad Yitzhak Ben-Zvi, 1985.

Mintz, Matityahu. "Yozmat Pinhas Rutenberg lehakamat gdudim ivriim im protz milhemet haolam harishonah." *Hazionut* 8 (1983): 181–94.

———. *Zmanim hadashim, zmirot hadashot*. Tel Aviv: Hotzaat Am Oved, 1986.

Monroe, Elizabeth. *Britain's Moment in the Middle East, 1914–1971*. Rev. ed. Baltimore: Johns Hopkins Press, 1981.

Nevakivi, Jukka. *Britain, France and the Arab Middle East, 1914–1920*. London: Athlone Press, 1969.

O'Brien, Conor Cruise. "Israel in Embryo." Review of *High Walls of Jerusalem*, by Ronald Sanders. *New York Review of Books* 31, no. 4 (March 15, 1984): 37–38.

O'Donovan, Patrick. "The Balfour Declaration." *Rehovoth* (Winter 1967–68): 31–33.

Orlan, Chaim. "Hatzharat Balfour, ever hayarden, 'hasefer halavan,' Weizmann, Jabotinsky." *Hadoar* 47 (April 5, 1968): 99–100.

Panitz, Esther. "Louis Dembitz Brandeis and the Cleveland Conference." *American Jewish Historical Quarterly* 65, no. 2 (December 1975): 140–62.

Parzen, Herbert. "The Lodge-Fish Resolution." *American Jewish Historical Quarterly* 60, nos. 1–4 (September 1970–June 1971): 71–81.

———. "The Magnes-Weizmann-Einstein Controversy." *Jewish Social Studies* 3 (July 1970): 187–213.

Perlmann, Moshe. "Chapters in Arab-Jewish Diplomacy, 1918–1922." *Jewish Social Studies* 6, no. 2 (April 1944): 123–54.

Perutz, Max F. *Is Science Necessary? Essays on Science and Scientists*. New York: E. P. Dutton, 1989.

Plekhanov, Georgi. "The Role of the Individual in History." In *Theories of History: Readings from Classical and Contemporary Sources*, edited by Patrick L. Gardiner, pp. 139–66. Glencoe, Ill.: Free Press, 1959.

The Political History of Palestine under British Administration. Memorandum by His Britannic Majesty's Government Presented in July 1947, to the United Nations Special Committee on Palestine. Jerusalem, 1947.

Polk, William, et al. *Backdrop to Tragedy: The Struggle for Palestine*. Boston: Beacon Press, 1957.

Pollard, Sidney. *The Development of the British Economy, 1914–1980*. 3d ed. London: E. Arnold, 1983.

Porat, Yehoshua. *Zmihat hatnuah haleumit haaravit-hapalestinait, 1918–1929*. Jerusalem: Hauniversitah haivrit, hamakhon lelimudei Asyah ve-Afrika, 1971.

———, and Yaakov Shavit, eds., *Hahistoryah shel Eretz Israel*. Vol. 9, *Hamandat vehabayit haleumi, 1917–1947*. Jerusalem: Beit Hotzaat Keter, Yad Yitzhak Ben-Zvi, 1982.

Pound, Reginald, and Geoffrey Harmsworth. *Northcliffe*. New York: Praeger, 1960.

Raanan, Uri [Heinz Felix Frischwasser-Raanan]. *The Frontiers of a Nation: A Reexamination of the Forces Which Created the Palestine Mandate and Determined Its Territorial Shape*. Westport, Conn.: Hyperion Press, 1976.

Reinharz, Jehuda. "The Balfour Declaration and Its Maker: A Reassessment." *Journal of Modern History* 64 (September 1992): 455–99.

———. *Chaim Weizmann: The Making of a Zionist Leader*. New York: Oxford University Press, 1985.

————. "Chaim Weizmann: The Shaping of a Zionist Leader before the First World War." *Journal of Contemporary History* 18, no. 2 (April 1983): 205–31.

————. "Chaim Weizmann and German Jewry." *Leo Baeck Institute Year Book* 35 (1990): 189–218.

————. *Fatherland or Promised Land? The Dilemma of the German Jew, 1893–1914.* Ann Arbor, Mich.: University of Michigan Press, 1975.

————. "Laying the Foundations for a University in Jerusalem: Chaim Weizmann's Role, 1913–1914." *Modern Judaism* 4, no. 1 (February 1984): 1–38.

————. "Science in the Service of Politics: The Case of Chaim Weizmann during the First World War." *English Historical Review* 100 (July 1985): 572–603.

————. "Weizmann, Acetone and the Balfour Declaration." *Rehovot* 10, no. 4 (1988–89): 3–7.

————. "Weizmann and the British General Elections of 1906." *Studies in Zionism* 5, no. 2 (Autumn 1984): 210–62.

————. "Zionism in the United States, 1897–1972." In *Encyclopaedia Judaica* 16: 1141–49. Jerusalem: Macmillan, 1973.

————. "Zionism in the United States on the Eve of the Balfour Declaration." *Studies in Zionism* 9, no. 2 (Autumn 1988): 131–45.

Rhodes, Richard. *The Making of the Atomic Bomb.* New York: Simon and Schuster, 1986.

Rogel, Nakdimon. "Haish shel Weizmann bedamesek." *Hazionut* 8 (1983): 279–353.

————. *Tel Hai: Hazit bli oref.* Tel Aviv: Yariv, 1979.

Rose, Norman. *Chaim Weizmann: A Biography.* New York: Viking, 1986.

————. *Lewis Namier and Zionism.* Oxford: Clarendon Press, 1980.

————. "Palestine's Role in Britain's Imperial Defence: An Aspect of Zionist Diplomacy, 1938–1939." *Wiener Library Bulletin* 22, no. 4 (1968): 32–35.

Rosen, Jacob. "Captain Reginald Hall and the Balfour Declaration." *Middle Eastern Studies* 24 (1988): 56–57.

Rosenblatt, Bernard. *Two Generations of Zionism.* New York: Shengold Publishers, 1967.

Rothschild, Miriam. *Dear Lord Rothschild.* Philadelphia: Balaban, 1983.

Rubinstein, Shimon. *Hanegev: Hamehdal hazioni hagadol, 1919–1929.* 4 vols. Jerusalem: By the author, 1988.

————. "Al miftanah shel tkufah hadashah." Pt. 2, "Hamediniyut hakarkait shel 'vaad hazirim' be-1918." Typescript. Jerusalem, 1985.

————, and Shmuel Even Or. "Hakamat vaad hair liyehudei Yerushalayim be-1918 vehaishim hamerkaziyim shebo." *Kivunim,* no. 35 (May 1987): 53–66.

Rudavsky, David. "Brandeis baveidah hazionit habeynleumit be-London bishnat 1920." In *Hagut ivrit be-America,* edited by Menahem Zhori, Arie Tartakower, and Haim Ormian, pp. 292–308. Tel Aviv: Yavneh, 1972.

Sachar, Howard M. *The Emergence of the Middle East, 1914–1924.* New York: Knopf, 1969.

Sakran, Frank. *Palestine Dilemma: Arab Rights versus Zionist Aspirations.* Washington, D.C.: Public Affairs Press, 1948.

Samburski, Samuel. *Balfour's Philosophy of Science.* Rehovot: Weizmann Institute, November 1969.

Sanders, Ronald. *The High Walls of Jerusalem.* New York: Holt, Rinehart and Winston, 1983.

Saphir, Ascher. *Unity or Partition!* Jerusalem: Azriel Press, 1937.

Saunders, David. "Aliens in Britain and the Empire during the First World War." *Immigrants and Minorities* 4, no. 1 (March 1985): 5–27.

Schama, Simon. *Two Rothschilds and the Land of Israel*. New York: Knopf, 1978.

Schofield, Maurice. "The Impossible Takes Longer." *Chemistry in Britain*, November 11, 1974, pp. 433–37.

———. "Weizmann's Success as a Manchester Biochemist." MS, Weizmann Archives.

Sefer toldot hahaganah. 8 vols. Tel Aviv: Am Oved and Hasifriyah Hazionit, 1965.

Shaltiel, Eli. *Pinhas Rutenberg*. Vol. 1. Tel Aviv: Am Oved Publishers, 1990.

Shapira, Anita. *Hamaavak hanikhzav: Avodah ivrit, 1929–1939*. Tel Aviv: Tel Aviv University, 1977.

Shapiro, Yonathan. "Hamahloket beyn Chaim Weizmann lebeyn Louis Brandeis, 1919–1921." *Hazionut* 3 (1981): 258–72.

Sheffer, Gabriel. "Mechanism leshimur otzmah politit shel manhig charismati: Weizmann leahar hadahato minesiut hatnuah hazionit." *Medinah, mimshal, veyakhasim beynleumim* 10 (1977): 36–55.

Shibli, Jamal. "The Conflict in Palestine." *Eastern Europe* 6, no. 4 (December 1921): 182–96.

Shilo, Margalit. *Nisyonot behityashvut: Hamisrad haeretz-Israeli, 1908–1914*. Jerusalem: Yad Yitzhak Ben-Zvi, 1988.

Sidebotham, Herbert. *Great Britain and Palestine*. London: Macmillan, 1937.

Simansky, Harold M. "The Churchill Memorandum as a Product of Herbert Samuel's Zionism." Typescript, 1991. Brandeis University, Waltham, Mass.

Singerman, Robert, ed. *Antisemitic Propaganda: An Annotated Bibliography and Research Guide*. New York: Garland Press, 1982.

Smilansky, Moshe. "Our Leader." In *Chaim Weizmann: A Tribute on His Seventieth Birthday*, edited by Paul Goodman, pp. 61–69. London: Gollancz, 1945.

Smith, George Adam. *The Historical Geography of the Holy Land*. Gloucester, Mass.: Peter Smith, 1894.

Sokolow, Nahum. *History of Zionism, 1600–1918*. London: Longmans, Green and Company, 1919.

Speakman, Horace B. "Dr. Weizmann's Contribution to Microbiology." In *Chaim Weizmann: Statesman, Scientist, Builder of the Jewish Commonwealth*, edited by Meyer W. Weisgal, pp. 69–77. New York: Dial Press, 1944; also in *Chaim Weizmann: A Tribute on His Seventieth Birthday*, edited by Paul Goodman, pp. 130–37. London: Gollancz, 1945.

Stein, Kenneth W. *The Land Question in Palestine, 1917–1939*. Chapel Hill, N.C.: University of North Carolina Press, 1984.

Stein, Leonard. *The Balfour Declaration*. New York: Simon and Schuster, 1961.

———. *Weizmann and the Balfour Declaration*. Sixth Chaim Weizmann Memorial Lecture. Rehovot: Yad Chaim Weizmann, 1961.

———. *Weizmann and England*. Presidential Address to the Jewish Historical Society, London, November 11, 1964. London: W. H. Allen, for the Jewish Historical Society of England, 1964.

Stoyanovsky, Jacob. *The Mandate for Palestine: A Contribution to the Theory and Practice of International Mandates*. New York: Longmans, Green and Company, 1928.

Strum, Philippa. *Louis D. Brandeis: Justice for the People*. Cambridge, Mass.: Harvard University Press, 1984.

Sykes, Christopher. *Two Studies in Virtue*. New York: Alfred A. Knopf, 1953.

Szajkowski, Zosa. "The Komitee für den Osten and Zionism." *Herzl Year Book* 7 (1971): 199–200.

Tananbaum, Susan. "The Anglicization of Russian-Jewish Immigrant Women in London, 1880–1939." Ph.D. diss., Brandeis University, 1991.

Temperley, H.W.V. *A History of the Peace Conference of Paris.* London: Henry Frowde and Hodder and Stoughton, 1924.

Terraine, John. *White Heat: The New Warfare, 1914–1918.* London: Sidgwick and Jackson, 1982.

Tevet, Shabtai. "Charging Israel with Original Sin." *Commentary* 88, no. 3 (September 1989): 24–33.

———. *Kinat David: Hayye David Ben-Gurion.* 2 vols. Jerusalem and Tel Aviv: Schocken, 1976–80.

Toynbee, Arnold. "Comments on Dr. Isaiah Friedman's Article on the McMahon-Hussein Correspondence." *Journal of Contemporary History* 5, no. 4 (December 1970): 185–93.

Tuchman, Barbara W. "The Assimilationist Dilemma: Ambassador Morgenthau's Story." In Barbara Tuchman, *Practicing History: Selected Essays,* pp. 208–17. New York: Knopf, 1981.

———. *Bible and Sword.* New York: Funk and Wagnalls, 1968.

Ullmann, Fritz. *Enzyklopädie der Technischen Chemie.* Meisenheimer, 1875; Munich: Urban and Schwarzenberg, 1951.

Urofsky, Melvin I. *American Zionism from Herzl to the Holocaust.* Garden City, N.Y.: Anchor Press, 1975.

Vereté, Mayir. "The Balfour Declaration and Its Makers." *Middle Eastern Studies* 6, no. 1 (January 1970): 48–76.

———. "Hamasa vehamatan hazioni-aravi beaviv 1919 vehamediniyut haanglit." *Zion* 32, nos. 1–2 (1977): 76–115.

———. "The Restoration of the Jews in English Protestant Thought, 1790–1840." *Middle Eastern Studies* 8, no. 1 (1972): 3–50.

Vital, David. "Zangwill and Modern Jewish Nationalism." *Modern Judaism* 4, no. 3 (October 1984): 243–53.

———. *Zionism: The Crucial Phase.* Oxford: Clarendon Press, 1987.

Wakeford, John. *The Cloistered Elite.* Toronto: Macmillan, 1969.

Wakehurst, John de vere Loder. *The Truth about Mesopotamia: Palestine and Syria.* London: George Allen and Unwin, 1923.

Waley, Sigismund Daley. *Edwin Montagu: A Memoir of His Visits to India.* New York: Asia Publishing House, 1964.

Wasserstein, Bernard. *The British in Palestine.* London: Royal Historical Society, 1978.

———. *Herbert Samuel: A Political Life.* Oxford: Oxford University Press, 1992.

———. "Herbert Samuel and the Palestine Problem." *English Historical Review* 91 (October 1976): 753–75.

———. *Wyndham Deedes in Palestine.* London: Anglo-Israel Association, distributed by Research Publications Services, 1973.

Wavell, Archibald. *Allenby—A Study in Greatness: The Biography of Field-Marshal Viscount Allenby of Megiddo & Felixstowe, G.C.B., G.C.M.G.* New York: Oxford University Press, 1941.

———. *The Palestine Campaigns.* 3d ed. London: Constable, 1931.

Webster, Charles Kingley. *The Founder of the National Home.* Chaim Weizmann Memorial Lecture. Rehovot: Yad Chaim Weizmann, 1955.

Weinberg, Ian. *The English Public School: The Sociology of Elite Education.* New York: Atherton Press, 1967.

Weltsch, Robert. "Bsorat Chaim Weizmann." *Haaretz,* August 29, 1976.

Wilson, Derek. *Rothschild: The Wealth and Power of a Dynasty.* New York: Scribner's, 1988.

Wilson, Trevor. *The Myriad Faces of War: Britain and the Great War, 1914–1918.* Cambridge: Polity Press, 1986.

Wolf, Lucien. *Essays in Jewish History.* London: Jewish Historical Society of England, 1934.

Yaari-Poleskin, Yaakov. *Holmim velohamim.* Petah Tikva: Sh. Z. Gisin, 1922. 3d ed. Tel Aviv: Mizrahi, 1964.

Yale, William. "Ambassador Henry Morgenthau's Special Mission of 1917." *World Politics* 1, no. 3 (April 1949): 308–20.

Yisraeli, David. "The Struggle for Zionist Military Involvement in the First World War (1914–1917)." In *Bar Ilan Studies in History,* edited by Pinhas Artzi, pp. 197–213. Ramat Gan: Bar Ilan University Press, 1978.

Young, Kenneth. *Arthur James Balfour.* London: G. Bell and Sons, 1963.

Zaid. "Chaim Weizmann's Scientific Work, 1915–1918." *Islamic Quarterly* 18, nos. 1–2 (January–July 1974): 226–37.

———. "Supplementary Notes." *Islamic Quarterly* 20–22, nos. 1–2 (January–June 1978): 29.

Zander, Walter. *Israel and the Holy Places of Christendom.* New York: Praeger Publications, 1971.

Zechlin, Egmont. *Die deutsche Politik und die Juden im Ersten Weltkrieg,* with the cooperation of Hans Joachim Bieber. Göttingen: Vandenhoek u. Ruprecht, 1969.

Zeman, Zbynek A. B. *The Break-Up of the Habsburg Empire, 1914–1918: A Study in National and Social Revolution.* London: Oxford University Press, 1961.

Index

c = caption, n = note

517